Critical Reflections on Economy and Politics in India

Studies in
Critical Social Sciences

Series Editor

David Fasenfest (*SOAS University of London*)

Editorial Board

Eduardo Bonilla-Silva (*Duke University*)
Chris Chase-Dunn (*University of California-Riverside*)
William Carroll (*University of Victoria*)
Raewyn Connell (*University of Sydney*)
Kimberle W. Crenshaw (*University of California, LA,*
and *Columbia University*)
Raju Das (*York University*)
Heidi Gottfried (*Wayne State University*)
Karin Gottschall (*University of Bremen*)
Alfredo Saad-Filho (*King's College London*)
Chizuko Ueno (*University of Tokyo*)
Sylvia Walby (*Lancaster University*)

VOLUME 151

The titles published in this series are listed at *brill.com/scss*

Critical Reflections on Economy and Politics in India

A Class Theory Perspective

By

Raju J Das

BRILL

LEIDEN | BOSTON

Cover illustration: Merged image of the following photographs; "Mumbai / India 13 May 2018 Contrast of modern highrise rich buildings and poor slums at Goregaon in Mumbai Maharashtra India" by arun sambhu mishra / Shutterstock.com, and "Communist Party of India (Marxist) or CPI (M) activist holds their party red flag during a mega rally at Brigade ground on February 03, 2019 in Calcutta, India" by Saikat Paul / Shutterstock.com.

Library of Congress Cataloging-in-Publication Data

Names: Das, Raju J., author.
Title: Critical reflections on economy and politics in India : a class
 theory perspective / Raju J. Das.
Description: Boston : Brill, 2020. | Series: Studies in critical social
 sciences, 1573-4234 ; vol.151 | Includes bibliographical references and
 index.
Identifiers: LCCN 2019042413 (print) | LCCN 2019042414 (ebook) | ISBN
 9789004415553 (hardback) | ISBN 9789004415560 (ebook)
Subjects: LCSH: India--Economic conditions--21st century. | India--Economic
 policy--21st century. | India--Politics and government--21st century.
Classification: LCC HC435.4 .D37 2020 (print) | LCC HC435.4 (ebook) | DDC
 330.954--dc23
LC record available at https://lccn.loc.gov/2019042413
LC ebook record available at https://lccn.loc.gov/2019042414

Typeface for the Latin, Greek, and Cyrillic scripts: "Brill". See and download: brill.com/brill-typeface.

ISSN 1573-4234
ISBN 978-90-04-41555-3 (hardback)
ISBN 978-90-04-41556-0 (e-book)

Copyright 2020 by Koninklijke Brill NV, Leiden, The Netherlands.
Koninklijke Brill NV incorporates the imprints Brill, Brill Hes & De Graaf, Brill Nijhoff, Brill Rodopi, Brill Sense, Hotei Publishing, mentis Verlag, Verlag Ferdinand Schöningh and Wilhelm Fink Verlag.
All rights reserved. No part of this publication may be reproduced, translated, stored in a retrieval system, or transmitted in any form or by any means, electronic, mechanical, photocopying, recording or otherwise, without prior written permission from the publisher.
Authorization to photocopy items for internal or personal use is granted by Koninklijke Brill NV provided that the appropriate fees are paid directly to The Copyright Clearance Center, 222 Rosewood Drive, Suite 910, Danvers, MA 01923, USA. Fees are subject to change.

This book is printed on acid-free paper and produced in a sustainable manner.

Contents

Acknowledgements   IX

List of Illustrations   X

1 Introduction   1
- 1   Why Class?   2
- 2   Why Not Class – Why Not a Class-Based Analytical Framework?   4
- 3   Components of a Class-Based Framework for Understanding Contemporary India   5
- 4   The Chapter Outline   16

2 Class in India   21
- 1   Existing Criticisms against Class Analysis of India   21
- 2   Existing Approaches to Class in India   26
- 3   A Critique of Existing Approaches to Class in India   35
- 4   Constructing a Class-Based Framework   44
- 5   Conclusion   61

3 The Capitalist Character of Class Society in Post-colonial India: Moving Beyond the Mode of Production Debate   64
- 1   The Development of Capitalist Relations, and the Barriers to This: A Brief Discussion on the Indian Mode of Production Debate   66
- 2   A Critique of some Influential Ideas in the Indian Mode of Production Debate   72
- 3   Examining India's Capitalist Character on the Basis of Marx's Distinction between Formal and Real Subsumptions of Labor   76
- 4   Class Struggle and the (Slow and Uneven) Transition to Real Subsumption of Labor   86
- 5   Class Struggle and the 'Blocked' Transition to Real Subsumption of Labor   89
- 6   Possibilities of, and Limits to, Real Subsumption of Labor   95
- 7   Jairus Banaji's (and Others') Mistaken Subsumption of Labor Perspective   97
- 8   Conclusion   103

VI   CONTENTS

4 Neoliberal Capitalism with Indian Characteristics   117
  1   Neoliberalism: Its General Traits   117
  2   Neoliberalism in India: The Context   125
  3   Neoliberalism with Indian Characteristics: Eight Theses   129
  4   Concluding Comments: What Is to Be Done?   161

5 Capitalism and Technological Change: Reflections on the Technology – Poverty Relation   168
  1   The Literature on the Green Revolution and Poverty: The Thesis and the Anti-thesis   174
  2   The Literature on the Green Revolution and Poverty: A Critique of Neo-Malthusianism   180
  3   Technology, Population and Poverty: A Contingent Relation   185
  4   The Green Revolution and Poverty in India: An Empirical Analysis   192
  5   Conclusion   197

6 Low-Wage Neoliberal Capitalism, Social-Cultural Difference, and Nature-Dependent Production   202
  1   Shrimp Aquaculture and the Missing Laborer   204
  2   A Labor-Based Approach to Nature-Dependent Commodity Production   207
  3   The Local, National and the Global Contexts   210
  4   Working for Less and in Poor Conditions: 'Capital' Negated   212
  5   Making Sense of Low-Wage Capitalism: From the General to the Locally Specific   217
  6   Conclusion   224

7 Class Relations, Class Struggle, and the State in India   233
  1   Existing Views on the Indian State: A Critical Review   233
  2   The Indian State and Its Class Base   242
  3   A Coalition/Alliance of Proprietary Classes   249
  4   The Indian State, Lower Classes, and Lower-Class Struggle   255
  5   State Form, State Policy, and Class Struggle   263
  6   The Indian State and the Class Contradictions of Economic Development   273
  7   Conclusion   280

CONTENTS VII

8 Class Dynamics of Poverty, State Failure, and Class Struggle 282
  1 Class Dynamics, State Failure and Poverty in Rural India 286
  2 The Naxalite Movement as a Form of Lower-Class Struggle 300
  3 A Marxist Class-Theoretic Critique of the Naxalite
    Movement 304
  4 Conclusion 314

9 State Repression as Class Struggle from Above 316
  1 State Response to 'Social' Movement: A Conceptual
    Discussion 317
  2 The Indian State's Response to the Naxalite Movement 322
  3 Why Does the State Repress the Naxalite Movement? 325
  4 Conclusion 337

**10 Capitalist Development and Liberal Democracy under a Right-Wing
  Regime** 347
  1 BJP Government's Record on Economic Development at the
    National Level 348
  2 The Winners under the BJP Regime: The Capitalist Class (and the
    Richer Elite) 349
  3 The Losers under the BJP Government : The Toiling
    Masses 357
  4 BJP Government's Record on Protection of Democratic
    Rights 360
  5 People's Response to False Promises 365
  6 Conclusion 371

11 Towards a Political Economy of Fascistic Tendencies 376
  1 Fascism and Fascistic Tendencies: Some Conceptual Issues 377
  2 A Short Introduction to the Fascistic Movement in India 386
  3 Political Economy of Fascistic Tendencies, Globally and in
    India 394
  4 Conclusion 417

12 Bourgeois-Political Dynamics of Fascistic Tendencies 420
  1 The Failure of 'Reformist Democracy' to Weaken Fascistic
    Tendencies 420
  2 The BJP, the Fascistic Movement, and (Neoliberal-Peripheral)
    Capitalism 423
  3 Political Techniques of the Fascistic Movement 430

| VIII | CONTENTS |

4   The Contradictory Character of the BJP   450
5   Conclusion   452

13   Forward March of the Right and the Relative Weakness of the Left: What Is to Be Done?   460

1   A General Theory of Left Politics in an Age of Fascistic Threats/Tendencies   461
2   Left Forces in India: Their Strength and Weakness   468
3   The Indian Left and the Two Forms of the Fight against Fascist Tendencies   478
4   Such a Big Compromise?: Return to Vladimir Lenin   492
5   Conclusion   506

14   Conclusions and Reflections   517

1   Class Character of Indian Economy/Society   518
2   Capitalism as Class Relations of Subsumption of Labor   519
3   Capitalist Class Relation in a Neoliberal Form   527
4   Capitalist Class Relation, Technological Change, and Labor   533
5   Export-Oriented Neoliberal Capitalism, Social Oppression, and Dual Metabolic Rift   535
6   Class, Capitalism, and the Capitalist State   540
7   Lower-Class Struggles and the State Response   543
8   Economic Development and Democracy under the Right-Wing Government   550
9   Capitalist Political Economy and Turn to Fascistic Tendencies   553
10   Bourgeois Political System, and the Fascistic Movement   554
11   What Is to Be Done?   559

Appendix 1: Processes Influencing the Balance of Power between Capital and Labor   571
Appendix 2: A Suggested Research Program on Agrarian Neoliberalism   573
Bibliography   575
Index   631

Acknowledgements

I have benefitted from my conversations (online and offline) with many scholars in different parts of the world who take the class perspective seriously. I have discussed with them various issues, including fascistic tendencies and Left politics. They include: Greg Albo, Himani Bannerji, Tom Brass, Patrick Bond, Joseph Choonara, Kevin Cox, Jamie Gough, Kevin Hewison, Sándor John, Robert Latham, David Laibman, Deepak Mishra, Bertell Ollman, Hira Singh, Murray Smith, Mohanakumar S., Steven Tufts, and many others. My current and former graduate students at York University, have been, of course, a permanent source of comradely suggestions, criticisms and encouragement. Yvonne Yim at York University has kindly provided assistance numerous times.

A grant from Canada's Social Sciences and Humanities Research Council in 2006 (*grant* number: 510441) made it possible for me to collect some of the empirical evidence reported in the book to illustrate its theoretical arguments. This is gratefully acknowledged. I am grateful to the men, women and children in various localities in India who have freely shared with me their thoughts about their lives and about their struggles.

I made rough drafts of the diagrams used in the book, but it was Ashley Chen, a former graduate student of mine and now a teacher, who deciphered these drawings and who converted these into their publishable form. I do not know who else can do this. She also produced the graphs based on the statistical data I supplied to her, and she has saved me from many typographical errors as well. I cannot thank her enough.

I imagine this book as a concrete 'application', theoretically and empirically, of the ideas laid out in my *Marxist class theory for a skeptical world* published in 2017. I have wanted to write a book on India from the theoretical perspective of class, but I would not have written that book at this moment, if it was not for the constant encouragement received from Professor David Fasenfest, the editor of Brill's Critical Social Science Book Series. He encouraged me in part because he saw my desire to write such a book. He is incredibly patient, kind and supportive, and like a true comrade, he is never unwilling to offer criticisms when they are due and in my own interest. I am extremely grateful for his unflinching support for unfashionable ideas in my work (and in the writings of many others in the world). I hope that the book meets David's expectation to some extent.

Finally, I am grateful to all those who have kept alive class analysis, both theoretically, and politically.

Illustrations

Figures

2.1 A partial map of what to study in India from a class perspective. Source: Author 63

3.1 Worker Productivity GDP (PPP) per hour ($) worked (2013): Selected rich and poor countries. Source: https://en.wikipedia.org/wiki/List_of_countries_by_GDP_(PPP)_per_hour_worked 65

3.2 Agricultural laborers population (in millions) and as a percentage of the cultivators population. Source: Singh (2002) and http://labourbureau.nic.in/ILYB_2011_2012.pdf 81

3.3 Gross capital formation in agriculture and allied sector (at 1993–94 prices) (in million rupees). Source: Singh (2003) 83

4.1 The evolution of capitalism. Source: Author 118

4.2 Top 0.1% national income share in India, 1922–2015. Source: Chancel and Piketty, 2017 140

5.1 The phases of the Green Revolution. Source: Author 171

7.1 Number of strikes. Source: https://theopendata.com/site/2012/03/strikes-and-lockouts-in-india/; https://www.researchgate.net/figure/Industrial-Disputes-in-India-19952006_tbl1_235622522; https://www.financialexpress.com/economy/fewer-strikes-lockouts-in-last-3-years/1072233/; Labour Bureau. 2015. Shimla: Government of India 259

7.2 Mandays lost (in millions). Source: https://theopendata.com/site/2012/03/strikes-and-lockouts-in-india/; https://www.researchgate.net/figure/Industrial-Disputes-in-India-19952006_tbl1_235622522; https://www.financialexpress.com/economy/fewer-strikes-lockouts-in-last-3-years/1072233/; Labour Bureau. 2015. Shimla: Government of India 260

7.3 Ratio of mandays lost (in millions) versus number of strikes. Source: https://theopendata.com/site/2012/03/strikes-and-lockouts-in-india/; https://www.researchgate.net/figure/Industrial-Disputes-in-India-19952006_tbl1_235622522; https://www.financialexpress.com/economy/fewer-strikes-lockouts-in-last-3-years/1072233/; Labour Bureau. 2015. Shimla: Government of India 261

9.1 Fatalities of Maoists in India (1994–2014). Source: Data from an authoritative source, http://www.satp.org/ 325

9.2 Security personnel fatalities in India (1994–2014). Source: Data from an authoritative source, http://www.satp.org/ 327

10.1 Ease of Doing Business Index 2014–2018. Source: Data from https://en.wikipedia.org/wiki/Ease_of_doing_business_index 351

ILLUSTRATIONS

10.2 Public sector banks' gross NPAs in Rs. Crore, 2014–2017. Source: Data from https://www.firstpost.com/business/bank-npa-trend-in-7-charts-bad-loans-at-state-run-banks-may-be-peaking-select-private-peers-see-rise-4218813.html 352

10.3 Loan write-offs (Rs. Crore) 2014–2017. Source: Data from http://indianexpress.com/article/business/banking-and-finance/psu-banks-write-off-rs-55356-crore-in-six-months-bad-debt-4966594/ 352

10.4 Share of wealth held by Top 1% and 10% in India, 2012–2016. Source: Data from https://www.livemint.com/Money/MML9OZRwaACyEhLzUNImnO/The-richest-1-of-Indians-now-own-584-of-wealth.html 355

10.5 Number of U.S. Dollar billionaires in India, 2014–2017. Source: Data from https://www.statista.com/statistics/324237/india-number-of-billionaires/ 356

10.6 Democracy Index 2014–2017. Source: Data from https://www.sudestada.com.uy/Content/Articles/421a313a-d58f-462e-9b24-2504a37f6b56/Democracy-index-2014.pdf; https://www.yabiladi.com/img/content/EIU-Democracy-Index-2015.pdf; http://felipesahagun.es/wp-content/uploads/2017/01/Democracy-Index-2016.pdf 362

10.7 Press Freedom Index 2014–2018. Source: Data from https://rsf.org/en/ranking/2018; https://timesofindia.indiatimes.com/world/rest-of-world/In-world-press-freedom-index-India-ranks-133rd/articleshow/51941837.cms; https://timesofindia.indiatimes.com/india/press-freedom-is-india-in-decline/articleshow/64009855.cms 363

10.8 Incidences of communal violence, 2014–2017. Source: Data from https://www.firstpost.com/india/india-witnessed-822-communal-incidents-in-2017-says-centre-111-killed-2384-injured-in-violence-4338217.html; https://www.firstpost.com/india/communal-violence-rose-by-28-from-2014-to-2017-but-2008-remains-year-of-highest-instances-of-religious-violence-4342951.html 365

10.9 Hate crime: cow vigilante violence, 2013–2017. Source: Data from http://data.indiaspend.com/ 366

10.10 Voters' perception of the Modi Government's record (in 2018 May). Source: Data from Lokniti survey, 2018 369

10.11 Percent of support for the BJP-led government. Source: Data from Lokniti survey, 2018 369

10.12 Percent of Dalits' supporters for BJP. Source: Data from Lokniti survey, 2018 370

10.13 Percent of farmers' supporters for BJP. Source: Data from Lokniti survey, 2018 370

10.14 Percentage of voters dissatisfied/net-satisfied with the BJP government. Source: Data from Lokniti survey, 2018 372

10.15	Percentage of voters who think Mr. Modi has failed in achieving achhe din (good times). Source: Data from Lokniti survey, 2018 372
11.1	Curve of capitalist politics. Source: Author 383
11.2	Employment growth and GDP growth in India, 1972–2015. Source: Data from The Hindu (2018) 400
11.3	Increasing intensity of strikes in India. Source: Data from AIOE/FICCI (n.d.) 402
11.4	Corporate perception of risk from trikes, closures and unrest. Source: Data from AIOE/FICCI (n.d.) 403
11.5	Structural conditions for fascistic movement produced by capitalism. Source: Author 404
12.1	BJP, Left Party, and Congress Party's vote share, 1977–2014. Source: Author 422
12.2	Income inequality in India, 1980–2015. Source: http://wir2018.wid.world/files/download/wir-presentation.pdf 425
12.3	Congress vote share vs BJP vote share in India's general election, 2014. Source: Author 426
12.4	The fascistic logic of religious-sectarian riots during election season. Source: Author 437
12.5	Incidents involving conflicts between different religious groups in India. Source: Author 449
12.6	Anatomy of the fascistic movement. Source: Author 457
13.1	Relative popularity quotient for lower classes and Dalits (2004 national election). Source: Author 473
13.2	Relative popularity quotient for Muslims (2004 national election). Source: Author 474
13.3	Scale of secularism. Source: Author 484
13.4	Ratio of number of State parties versus number of national parties as listed by ECI, 1951–2009. Source: Author 484
13.5	Congress Party's percentage of vote shares in the 2014 general election in India. Source: Author 488
13.6	Types of temporary revolutionary compromise. Source: Author (based in Lenin's texts) 495

Tables

2.1	Class structure in India (percentage share in population). Source: Basu (2009) 37

ILLUSTRATIONS   XIII

3.1   Share of hired labor in total human labor, and share of purchased inputs in total cost of cultivation, per hectare, 1994–97. Source: Gill and Ghuman (2001)   82

5.1   The Green Revolution and rural poverty, 1970s–1990s. Source: NIRD, 1998; and http://www.sciencedirect.com.ezproxy.library.yorku.ca/science/article/pii/S0016718501000069#TBLFN2   193

5.2   Correlations between the Green Revolution and rural poverty level, 1970s–1990s. Source: CMIE, 1987; and NIRD, 1998   194

5.3   Poverty reduction (1973–1994) with and without the Green Revolution. Source: Data from NIRD, 1998   195

5.4   Poverty, population growth and population pressure on land. Source: NIRD, 1998; and Bansil, 1992   196

5.5   Correlations between the population factor and poverty reduction, 1970s–1990s. Source: NIRD, 1998; and Bansil, 1992   197

5.6   Poverty reduction (1973–1988) with and without GR. Source: Data from various editions of Government of India's Rural Development Statistics   198

8.1   Rural poverty (1999–2000) among most oppressed groups in selected Indian States. Source: Radhakrishnan et al., 2004, in GOI, 2005   300

8.2   Monthly average per capita expenditure of poor people (Rupees) in 1999–2000 in selected States. Source: GOI, 2005   301

9.1   Naxalite development activities. Source: Various newspaper reports and academic sources   328

12.1   Partisan response to the demolition of Babri mosque in 1992 (in %). Source: National election studies, CSDS, Delhi 1996, quoted in Mitra, 2011: 128   443

13.1   Percentage of voters who voted for various parties/alliances (in national elections in 1996 and 2004). Source: Original data from CSDS (Centre for the Study of Developing Societies) and election commission of India, quoted in Mitra, 2011: 118–119   472

13.2   Percentage of voters voting for a parties/alliances (in 1996 and 2004 national elections). Source: Original data from CSDS (Centre for the Study of Developing Societies) and election commission of India, quoted in Mitra, 2011: 118–119   485

Maps

6.1   Four Blocks located in three shrimp districts. Source: Author   212

8.1   Geography of the Maoist Movement. Source: http://www.satp.org/satporgtp/countries/india/database/LWE_conflictmap2015.html   285

11.1 The BJP in power in Indian States, early 2019. Source: https://www.mapsofindia.com/assemblypolls/state-assembly-leading-parties.html 393

Photo

6.1 Women in a shrimp-processing factory. Source: Author 216

CHAPTER 1

Introduction

The Indian society can be characterized by a complex set of inter-connected processes. These include: its relatively low labor productivity, combined with a slow and uneven technological change, its turn to neoliberalism, its emphasis on export-oriented production offering a low-wage platform of global capitalism, and the fact that the majority of its population are in absolute poverty or are very vulnerable to falling in it, while there is a massive on-going concentration of wealth and income in the hands of a tiny minority. These processes also embrace the fact that the post-colonial capitalist state has, more or less, failed to meet the economic needs of the masses irrespective of which political party manages the affairs of the state, while the state has succeeded in maintaining capitalist property relations and creating conducive conditions for capitalist accumulation. India has also been experiencing lower-class struggles led by the Left, and the recent emergence of right-wing/'fascistic' tendencies. Understanding these relatively concrete processes requires a critical theoretical reflection.

This critical reflection must be based on certain principles. For a start, to critically reflect on the concrete political and economic situation in India, one needs relatively general concepts that reflect a set of processes and relations. To understand India, one needs to understand much more than India. Secondly, this set of concepts must be informed by an emphasis on class (more on this below). Thirdly, while it is true that to understand India, one needs general theoretical ideas, a study of India, given its enormous social and geographical complexity, can potentially contribute to the production of general ideas and/ or to the critical scrutiny of existing general ideas. Understanding India – indeed, understanding any country or place – requires a two-way interaction between more general ideas and more specific ideas. One needs general ideas in part because Indian society shares some common traits with many other countries. One needs specific ideas because India has a degree of specificity relative to other countries. The ways in which the *general* attributes of the capitalist economy and the capitalist polity are *combined* elsewhere are different from those in India; also, a given general process (e.g. capitalist exploitation) takes a specific form in India, and this partly explains why what happens in India does not quite happen elsewhere (or does not happen to the same extent and in the same way). To reiterate the features of Indian society mentioned above: India is capitalist, India is neoliberal, India experiences uneven technological changes, India experiences export-oriented production, India has a state that

© KONINKLIJKE BRILL NV, LEIDEN, 2020 | DOI:10.1163/9789004415560_002

fundamentally supports the rich propertied classes vis-à-vis lower classes, India has seen massive and militant lower-class movements, and India faces fascistic tendencies. Many other countries can be said to have experienced all these. But the forms in which these processes are played out in India are different from those elsewhere. India's capitalism is not exactly like that of America's or Canada's, although there are profound similarities. India's neoliberalism shares some common traits with neoliberalism elsewhere, and yet there is something that I will call neoliberalism with Indian characteristics. And so on. So, this is a book on India which is more than about India. And, once again, this book is informed by a class-based general theoretical approach. But one might ask why class?

1 Why Class?

In fact, it is argued that class approach is not that relevant to India because of India's complexity and specificity (its history, its caste relations, etc.). M.N. Srinivas, one of India's well-known sociologists, says that: Indian reality is 'far too complex, regional and sectional differences very real', therefore 'the studies of sociologists seemed to make sense to non-Marxists', and not to Marxists (Srinivas, 2012: 181). Even if some scholars do not reject class analysis, they will not accept the idea that class has a degree of primacy over other social divisions such as caste. The view of Andre Beteille, another well-known sociologist of India, is not atypical of the liberal intelligentsia: Beteille (2007) says that 'Classes are undoubtedly important, but they are not important in the way Marx, or even, Lenin, thought them to be' (p. 9) and that class has no primacy over caste or occupation or income as categories of analysis. This view is shared by even left-leaning scholars.

Subir Sinha (2009) says that Marxist class analysis pays too much importance to the economic and as a result fails to see the worker as embodying many non-economic identities. Herring and Agarwala (2006) lament the decline in class analysis, and yet they say that the sole emphasis in the traditional class theory on the material forms of property deflects attention from cultural capital and the beneficial role of the state for common people. Chakrabarti and Cullenberg (2003) following a postmodernist-Marxist perspective on class say that: contrary to traditional class analysis, class as a social force representing class interests does not exist, and that there is no reason to believe that the working class can have a spark of consciousness.

INTRODUCTION 3

John Harriss (1988) says that: there are 'limitations of existing paradigms and of the various ways in which essentialist constructs (like "peasant economy" or even "capitalism") have been substituted for specific contextual analysis' (p. 55). This criticism of class analysis echoes that of Gidwani, for whom capitalism operates on the basis of what is merely an assemblage of contingent and interrupted logics, without any structural regularities (Gidwani, 2008). Spivak argues that given the erosion of the factory-based stable work, there are no workers in the traditional sense, and that no class consciousness is possible, and therefore, there is no need for class analysis (Spivak, 2000).

Class analysis is also criticized, because its prediction of class polarization and proletarianization has been apparently disproved. This criticism comes not only from liberal scholars but also from many Marxists such as Byres, Harriss, and others. The critics also draw a political conclusion: given incomplete polarization and partial proletarianization, the proletariat is a small section of the population and cannot be assigned the political importance that class analysis has assigned it (Lerche and Shah, 2018: 942). The emphasis on labor *as a class* in class analysis is increasingly replaced by the concept of 'classes of labor' (Bernstein, 2007).

Class analysis, including by Marx himself, is also faulted for ignoring class struggle outside of production (Herring and Agarwala, 2006; also see Chandra and Taghioff, 2016; Omvedt, 1993). Marxist class analysis is also regarded as inadequate because it offers the 'centralized revolutionary party' performing 'vanguard-functions' on behalf of the working class (Sinha, 2009: 157).

While all these criticisms have been mounted, there *are* studies on India's social-economic problems that do not ignore class. Some of the studies are explicitly class-based analysis (see Pattenden, 2016; Sathyamurthy, 1996; see also Desai, 1975). There are studies that pay some attention to class without class being given any special causal significance. For example, scholars such as Amartya Sen (2006) take an intersectionality type approach to class, or an approach in which class is one of several divisions. In fact, for Sen, class is a part of a bigger picture (which concerns inequality), while other scholars subsume it under marginality (Bhattacharyya and Basu, 2018). And, of course, a large number of scholars focus on the dispossession of small-scale producers as a class issue: studies on dispossession have become a cottage industry. There are others who focus on figuring out how many classes there are, while many examine class agency, especially, of precariously employed people.

2   Why Not Class – Why Not a Class-Based Analytical Framework?

It is important to the respond to the criticisms against class analysis of India and to the existing approaches to class analysis, and outline an alternative approach developed in part through a critical and respectful dialogue with those who have problems with class analysis. I begin to do this initially in Chapter 2, and develop the nature of my response and show the relevance of an alternative approach to class analysis, in the remainder of the book.

The book is an attempt to 'apply' to the Indian context, some of the general ideas developed over the years and presented in my *Marxist class theory* (Das, 2017a; also, Das, 2012a). This book is based on the idea that class relations do exist objectively, at a more abstract level and at a more concrete level, and form the context within which non-class relations work and shape class relations. Human beings need 'things' (food, and shelter as well as education, healthcare, software and theatre, etc.) to meet their material and cultural needs. These things need to be produced and shared. Production is a material activity based in a set of *processes*, and can only happen within given social *relations*. These are, above all, the relations and the processes involving those who control the means of production and those who do not (direct producers). These are class relations:[1] these are relations of exploitation, which is why these are also relations of conflict and struggle, whether covert or overt. The class relations have impacts on how classes (e.g. workers, capitalists and small-scale producers), class-fractions and individuals relate to one another, and on the ways in which human beings relate to nature: exploitative class relations of capitalism, based on the unceasing pursuit of profit, adversely impact not only the economic and social lives and the material bodies of members of lower classes, but also the environment. Because class relations prompt conflict of interests between classes, political power is generally mobilized in the economic and political interest of those who control means of production to: (a) persuade the direct producers to accept the arrangements more or less as they are, including by giving some material concessions as well through various methods of deception and illusion, and (b) to suppress their struggle, when necessary. In keeping the direct producers under control, mechanisms of oppression are deployed such that direct producers are not only economically exploited but also socially oppressed on the basis of caste, gender and religion, etc. The matter of social oppression, in the sphere of ideology and material practices, is too important to be left out of concrete class analysis.

---

1   Class relations, and indeed, all relations, are to be seen as relations *and* processes.

INTRODUCTION

These are relatively well-known and very simple ideas in class analysis,[2] and have relevance to India as to any other society. This means that in examining India's economy and polity, one must bear in mind the mutually antagonistic interests of those who control society's productive resources, and the toiling masses (wage-workers and small-scale producers). Economic development processes and political processes are to be seen as ultimately class processes.

It *is* important to talk about individual classes. However, the examination of how many classes exist and how different groups within the working class experience life differently must be a part of a larger consideration in which the emphasis should be given to the fact that there is class as a relationship (with its contradictions), that affects politics, economy and culture and how we relate to nature and one another. It is *that* relationship which form the class-context, and which underlies how classes, class-fractions and individuals of specific classes, as well as state agencies and state elites, function,or do not function, and how they exercise their agency or how they do not.

The class analysis concerns the *entire* society, including the state. The class-perspective on India (and other countries) can prompt theoretically rigorous and empirically-corroborated research on a wide variety of topics. Only a few are covered in this book. These include: nature of India's capitalism as a form of class society; nature of neoliberalism with Indian traits; technological change in relation to direct producers; production for the world market and a dual metabolic rift and their implications for workers of different oppressed categories; the social character of the capitalist state in relation to dominant and subordinate classes; lower-class struggles, and fascistic tendencies as a ruling class response to the capitalist crisis, a response that combines a ruthless pursuit of capitalism as well as oppression of religious minorities, and the potential and actual role of Left politics in social transformation. These themes are slightly elaborated below.

3 Components of a Class-Based Framework for Understanding Contemporary India

3.1 *India's Capitalist Class Relation, and Neoliberal Capitalism*
One must begin by asking what is the nature of capitalist class society of India? Interestingly, the nature of the economic development process in most parts of India, and especially, in the countryside, does not appear to support Marx and Engels's (1848) optimism in *The Communist Manifesto* that the bourgeoisie

---

2   This is not to say that these ideas are widely accepted in India or elsewhere.

(or, the capitalist mode of production led by this class) constantly revolutionizes the mode of production. If capitalism revolutionizes the development of productive forces, and yet if labor productivity per hour is still so low, then could it be that India is not (dominantly) a capitalist country? Conversely, if India *is* a capitalist country, why does it have such a low level of labor productivity? Indeed, the question of whether or not India is a capitalist country proper and the question of what the barriers are to its further development, if capitalism does exist, are not yet settled. It is interesting that there is a lack of a consensus on the meaning of capitalism itself (Wood, 2007). There is a need to conceptualize capitalism as a class relation in the specific context of India.

Like everything else in the world, capitalism comes in multiple forms. The capitalist class relation, in India or elsewhere, exists in different forms: formal and real subsumption of labor, for example. The formal subsumption is the most general form of capitalism, and in this sense India is decidedly capitalist in terms of class relations. The formal subsumption has four traits including, commodification of labor power and of the means of production and subsistence, and exploitation of labor in the workplace, on the basis of the appropriation of absolute surplus value. While overall India is characterized by the dominance of formal subsumption of labor, in specific areas and sectors, there is a transition to real subsumption of labor, a transition that is unevenly shaped, in part by, the changing balance of power between capital and labor. More concretely, India's class structure is characterized by the combination of formal and real subsumptions of labor, coexisting with relations that are not capitalist in terms of *production* relations.

While from one vantage point, India's capitalism can be seen in terms of subsumption of labor (i.e. the way in which labor is integrated into production under capitalist class relation), from another angle (i.e. the way in which and the extent to which the state regulates capitalism), the stages, or the chronological forms, through which capitalism has developed can be expressed, for example, as Keyenesian/developmentalist and neoliberal. The neoliberal form/stage of capitalism in India has rightly attracted much attention but not always in an entirely adequate manner. Indian neoliberal capitalism, with its specific traits and consequences, requires a critical examination.

3.2   *Class Character of Technological Change*

In capitalism, whether it is in its neoliberal form or not, and despite the structural obstacles to technological changes, partly stemming from the formal subsumption of labor, technological changes, whether in mechanical or biochemical, etc. forms, do happen. Technological change happens, even if not in a systemic manner, and is expected to be a means of bringing about

INTRODUCTION

development. For the less developed world, technological change is a means of catching up with advanced countries as well. There is a widespread belief that technological change can solve society's problems, so it is important to examine the social nature of technology. This question can be asked in the context of many different forms of human activity (e.g. agriculture, industry, services). It is useful to ask the question in the context of agriculture which has trans-historical and capitalism-specific importance (production of food and raw materials, and production of surplus value) and which has been going through many technological revolutions in the last 10,000 years or so.

Given that those who depend on agriculture for a living tend to be poor (they cannot satisfy their basic needs), what is the relation between technology and poverty? These issues are discussed in the context of the Green Revolution technology that began to be widely used in the 1960s in India (and elsewhere). The world has seen four agricultural revolutions, all having resulted in a dramatic acceleration of growth (Lipton, 1989: 316). The Green Revolution (GR), which is more than half a century old now, is the last but one of these (the GR is followed by the genetic – biotechnological – revolution). Its speed, scale and spread have 'far exceeded those of any earlier technological change in food farming' (ibid.: 14–15). Indeed, the GR triggered off an extremely important debate in studies on India, including in the form of the celebrated mode of production debate, that focused on the nature and the extent of capitalist development in India.

The relation between the GR and poverty/inequality is among the most widely researched topics. The literature on the GR–poverty relation has been almost polarized between the 'GR enthusiasts' who see favorable impacts of the GR on poverty/inequality and 'GR sceptics' who take almost an opposite view. Separating the poverty issue from the inequality issue, it can be said that there is a near consensus that the GR has caused an increase in inequality.

The GR–poverty relation, the intellectual construction of which has changed over time, is an interesting issue more generally. It can be considered to be a part of the larger literature on the relation between technology and society (Smith, 2010), including the poor people in society. An influential strand is neo-Malthusianism of which Michael Lipton is arguably a representative, and which needs a robust Marxist class-theoretic response. Lipton is one of the most widely cited researchers on the GR and poverty topic. He wrote a book in 1989, *New Seeds and Poor People*. Lipton's work, like much of the massive amount of research on the GR–poverty relation, is firmly within a paradigm which gives much more causal power to technology and to population than they can possibly bear. Lipton's view that the GR has a *necessary* poverty-reducing property, that the poor would be necessarily poorer without the technology, is mistaken. Against Liptonian views, I argue that capitalism as a class relation shapes possibilities for technological change, and it also shapes how technological change benefits the common people or not. Capitalism induces technological change which can increase production, but whether this can benefit the workers is a different matter.

3.3 Capitalist Production for the World Market and a Labor-Environmental Metabolic Rift

To understand such matters as the nature of capitalism as well as prospects of economic development and poverty alleviation, it is important to understand technological change. However, understanding these matters requires a broader perspective, one that is focused on the entire process of capitalist production. Indeed, how capitalist production happens under neoliberalism sheds important light on the social character of production, including the class relation between capital and labor. Capitalism exists in neoliberal forms, and neoliberalism has its specific national traits such as those in India. A specific form of neoliberal capitalism is agrarian neoliberalism.

Crucial to the neoliberal project have been agricultural exports as a source of foreign exchange and fiscal stability. The policy has led to India becoming a member of a group of nations that Harriet Friedman (1993) calls 'New Agricultural Countries' (NACS). Counterposed to the Newly Industrialized Countries (NICS) of recent decades (Brohman, 1996), the emergence of the NACS represents a quintessential strategy of Third World development under neoliberalism, which has occurred, 'paradoxically, with heavy state support'. 'New agriculture' refers to the production, for the world market, of high-value non-traditional crops (e.g. flowers and shrimps), as compared to the traditional crops produced under colonialism and during the immediate post-colonial period (Maitra, 1997). New Agriculture signifies a dialectics of articulation and disarticulation. It *articulates* local social production relations in NACS directly to the world market – and to its price signals – more closely than achieved during the era of the Green Revolution, when national food self-sufficiency was emphasized (Nanda, 1995). New agriculture also *disarticulates* agricultural production from the requirements of local populations and environments (Teubal, 2000): products of new agriculture are not affordable by the ordinary families.

Thus the situation today is that whilst NACS, such as India, are increasingly specializing in luxury and niche-market crops, fish farming, and animal feeds in order to pay back their debts, and are under pressure from evolving World Trade Organization rules, developed countries have specialized in the

INTRODUCTION

intensive export of heavily subsidized basic wage goods. This trend is indicative of an emergence of a new international division of labor in agriculture (McMichael, 2000). This new division of labor signifies, among other things, the relatively deregulated production of commodities for export, based on a low-paid, unorganized working class that is increasingly deprived of government welfare benefits: in other words, neoliberal capitalism in agrarian/rural contexts.

Like many other countries of the South, India is a low-wage platform of global neoliberal capitalism. Such a platform works in industries, services as well as in agriculture, of which aquaculture is an important part. Aquaculture is the fastest growing food-producing sector in the world (World Bank, 2007). Shrimp culture is an important part of aquaculture. Shrimp production is a specific form of new agricultural production. If shrimp-culture is being promoted, we must understand whether the men, women and children who produce shrimps as wage-workers benefit. When explored through a materialist and dialectical class perspective, the issue of shrimp wage laborers reveals the nature of a specific kind of 'metabolic rift' that is generally not talked about in the existing literature. This is a rift that characterizes the relation between wage labor and capital, where capital takes a lot more out of labor than it gives it. This rift co-exists with the ecological metabolic rift (Foster, 2007) where capital takes more out of nature than it gives nature. This approach also shows how place-specific relations of social difference – social oppression mechanisms – along with biophysical conditions of production, influence the more general social relations of capitalism.

3.4   The Class Relations of the Capitalist State

The general social relations of capitalism affect not only economic matters (e.g. technological change, working conditions, etc.) but also political matters. It is in fact a truism that in order to understand the economic issues such as poverty and development that confront India (or any other country, for that matter), one must investigate the nature of the state, for the economic is a deeply political matter and the political is, to borrow a phrase from Lenin, 'concentrated economics'. It is not surprising that the state in a large, under-developed, capitalist country such as India, has been the subject of much discussion. Thus, for example, the Rudolphs look upon the state as a third actor which has seemingly marginalized both capital and labor (Rudolph and Rudolph, 1987). However, their approach substantially underestimates the dominant class bias of the state, a bias that exists structurally and instrumentally (i.e. as a result of the use of state institutions by the capitalist class as an instrument). Bardhan (1998) characterizes the state as an 'above the fray' arbiter between dominant classes, including the landed. Adopting a problematic approach to class (within so-called analytical Marxism), this view does not say much about the actual exploitative class relations and the role of the Indian state in reproducing them. Nor is Chibber's (2003) recent analysis convincing. Chibber (2003) says that the capitalist class accepted, and benefitted from, import-substituting industrialization, which ensured protection from external competition, but it thwarted state initiatives to regulate industrial activity which were thought necessary for rapid industrial transformation. It is not clear to me why the capitalist class would subordinate itself to the state to any significant extent and without complaint, except in exceptional cases. Whether or not the Indian capitalist class refused to be controlled by the Indian state via the latter's planning mechanisms, becomes an important question, not for Marxists, but mainly for those who take – and took – the claim that India has a socialist regime and that was a barrier to economic development. Marxists do not need to be convinced that ultimately it is capital that decides what the state does or does not do. Basically, the state-class relation cannot be understood adequately within any framework including that of Chibber, that abstracts from (a) the *totality* of the relations between all the proprietary classes and the classes they exploit, *including in rural areas*, and (b) the global situation (e.g. imperialism's connection to an economy, both during colonial times and after formal decolonization). It is also important to avoid politicism: explaining state's action in terms of its own capacity (Das, 1999a). Class analysis of the state must prioritize the relation between proprietary classes, and between them and the exploited classes, and see the state and the capitalist class, more or less, as two arms of capital-as-a-class-relation, within which disagreements, including over who should listen to whom and how much, are intra-family matters.

The cultural turn (as exemplified in the work of Stuart Corbridge, Akhil Gupta, Partha Chatterjee, etc.) also fails to appropriately examine the Indian state. Its underlying notion of the state is that it is merely a power relation, but why is there a need for state actors to exercise power relations and in whose interests? Might there be a relation between power relations and the class character of the state? This literature complements the macro, national level structuralist treatment of the state, in which the state appears to be disembodied and working without the involvement of social agents. But it comes at a cost: this literature, influenced by the post-turn (or the cultural or discursive turn) is largely silent on the materiality of the state, on its solidity, its coherence, all of which come mainly from its class logic. It is the latter which one should be able to infer from, and which in turn determines, everyday interaction.

Against the existing views on the Indian state is needed a thoroughgoing historical materialist interpretation, based on class. Just as political-economic

INTRODUCTION   11

processes are class processes and concern class relations, so do the fundamental aspects of the state. What is necessary is an emphatic reassertion of the validity of class analysis, now out of academic fashion, with particular reference to the formation, reproduction and agency of the state. Such an approach says that the state cannot but reflect – and is thus driven by – class interests, albeit in ways that are sometimes contradictory. The material fact of class is the most important social context affecting the conditions under which lower classes (i.e. workers and small-scale producers in urban and rural areas) live and work. Capitalist relations, along with what are taken to be 'pre'/'non'-capitalist relations in rural areas where they exist, define this class context. And the ways in which capitalist and other class relations shape the state are in turn shaped by non-class relations.

The class relation shapes the relation between the rulers and the ruled, and the latter relation shapes the class relation, within a system of relations in which the class relation, ultimately, is fundamental. And the relation between class and the state itself is shaped by various empirically-existing conditions, including mechanisms of social oppression (e.g. caste), external connections such as economic globalization, and so on. Class does not (and cannot) operate in a vacuum: it is accordingly reproduced and impinged on – among other things – both by ideologies and practices of caste, ethnicity, nationality, region and gender and by the political form of the state itself (i.e. democratic form; federal form). Since capitalism is the dominant mode of production in India, the state is predominantly a capitalist apparatus, and as such an agent of capitalist development nationally and locally. For this reason, the state and rural/urban capital are the two arms of what is an overarching capitalist social relationship. The actions of both capital and the capitalist state – class struggle from above – are in turn influenced politically by struggles conducted against them by lower classes.

3.5   *Lower-Class Struggles*

Implicit in the class view of (Indian) society is an interesting dialectical connection. This connection is between the conditions of existence and class struggle. Conditions of existence include what Marx (2000: 425), in *Preface to the Critique of Political Economy*, referred to as 'material productive forces' and 'relations of production' (and the empirical effects, such as various forms of deprivation emerging partly from the contradiction between the two). Because these conditions are exploitative, they *require* (necessitate) class struggle for their alleviation and eventual transcendence, and they *prompt* (make possible) class struggle from below for this purpose. The second aspect of the dialectic is that: these conditions not only prompt lower-class struggle, but also condition, or set limits on, class struggle. The conditions of existence also include ideas of 'people' as well as the actions of the state that seeks to create order in a class society. The state seeks to create an order not only by interventions in support of the dominant classes, but also by *repressing* exploited classes and seeking to elicit their consent to the system's reproduction, including through selective bribes. State policies often take the form of 'development', on the ground and on paper. State policies must be construed partly as a form of class struggle from above, launched on behalf of the propertied, to reproduce the social order.

India's capitalist political system and its capitalist political economy have failed to meet the needs of the masses. Such a failure has prompted not only trade union struggles, which have inflicted a cost on the capitalist economy, about which the capitalist associations complain about. It has also led to the Maoist struggle that has been going on in a quarter of the country's territory for almost half a century. It is also known as the Naxalite struggle because it started in the Naxalbari region of the West Bengal province. The Naxalite movement is a part of the worldwide Maoist movement. It is the longest surviving revolutionary movement in the history of peasant resistance in India. The former Prime Minister of India, Mr. Manmohan Singh, of the centrist Congress Party, called the Naxalites the single biggest national security threat.

The Naxalite movement has mobilized poor people against sections of the propertied class (e.g. landlords, traders; mining companies) for social justice in India. The movement has conferred limited benefits upon the poor in some places. It is not averse to using violence to get these benefits and to stop them from being taken away. The Indian state seeks to violently repress it, killing thousands. Anyone suspected of having any links with the Naxalite movement, and especially, with that faction of it which the state has banned, can be jailed or killed. This raises wider conceptual questions about the relation between 'social movements' (broadly, movements against injustice in a class-society) and the state. Why does a state kill its citizens? The answer lies in the legitimacy threat from the militant Naxalite movement to the state: it does things for the poor that the state has failed to do, and it is not unwilling to defend its gains where necessary by force. Of course, a critique of the Indian state's violent response to the Maoist movement does not *at all* mean an endorsement of how Maoists understand society and seek to change it. The long-term structural changes in society require active participation of politically conscious masses in cities and villages in a process of political mobilization against class exploitation and social oppression. Emphasizing violent methods of destruction as a *strategy* cannot construct the conditions for such mobilization, even though such methods may yield short-term localized results.

INTRODUCTION

3.6   *Fascistic Tendencies as a Form of Class Struggle from Above*

The failure of the bourgeois political economy and of the bourgeois state to meet the needs of the masses, which has been behind lower-class struggle, however uneven and weak, is the context in which a serious threat has emerged to the democratic and social rights of the people, a threat that is posed by right-wing forces in India.

The Bharatiya Janata Party (BJP), a right-wing party, which is supported by fascistic movements and people, won India's 2014 general election partly by promising development or *vikas* for all (and also by stoking hatred against non-Hindus). (The BJP has also won the 2019 election, which will not be covered in this book; on this topic see, Das, 2019b.) Major promises (e.g. a massive creation of jobs, crackdown on black money hidden away in foreign banks) made by the party in power have turned out to be, more or less, false promises but the government keeps repeating them. The government spends millions on publicity to make people believe to be true what is not true, and, in particular, that good days (achhe din) are upon them. As far as the well-being of the masses is concerned, there has been little change, in part because the right-wing government is wedded to pro-business interventions. Yet, many have started understanding the real intentions of the right-wing government, which are both communal (religious-sectarian) and pro-business, and therefore, against the toiling classes. Among those who initially fell for emotionally-charged appeals from the right-wing forces supporting the government, to national and religious pride based on distorted representations of the past (and present), many are now understanding that what is really important is access to decent employment and standard of living, social peace, and so on, and that false pride cannot meet such needs. This is evident in the electoral defeat of the BJP in the by-elections for the Lok Sabha (Lower House of the Parliament) and for provincial legislatures in 2018. (That these disappointments did not produce the BJP's defeat in 2019 is a different matter, on which see Das, 2019b.)

The phenomenon of the right-wing regime in India goes beyond the failure of the government to meet the economic needs of the people. The country is indeed experiencing something like a national emergency. This is in the form of persistent attacks on the basic democratic rights of ordinary citizens, by hyper-nationalist Hindu-supremacist forces, which are supported by, and which support, the right-wing BJP. Religious minorities, especially, Muslims, have become 'near-exact equivalent of the Jew' (Sarkar, 2016: 143). The right-wing forces are bent on creating a Hindu state, where religious minorities will remain subservient to the majority religion, and where Dalits (ex-untouchables) will continue to be oppressed by the higher castes in the Hindu social order. The capitalist class society has always made use of mechanisms of social oppression based on caste, gender and indigeneity; now a new axis of social oppression has been added to the mix: oppression based on religion. Furthermore, the Hindu-nationalist forces are targeting not only religious minorities and *dalits,* but also Leftists as well as rationalists and secularists, who oppose their Hindu-tva (Hindu-ness) ideology and their assault on democratic rights.

The rise of the BJP is a part of the world-wide right-wing bourgeois political trend moving on (or towards) a 'fascistic path'. Contrary to what some believe (e.g. Vanaik, 2017), I argue that there *are* 'fascistic tendencies' – as a form of bourgeois politics or an extreme tendency toward the breakdown of bourgeois politics – in both richer and poorer countries. To the extent that such a danger exists, whether it is in rich countries or in poorer countries such as India, the question is how do we understand the threat as we face it, from the standpoint of removing it?

There *is*, undoubtedly, a fascistic threat in India. This is a threat to India's Left and progressive culture and to the idea of India as a country in which there has traditionally been a large amount of support for secularism and democracy. The fascistic threat has strong material conditions. The development of fascistic tendencies is a class project, more than anything else. The dominance of right-wing forces represents a most extreme form of the latent tendency towards an attack on democracy, the tendency that exists in capitalist societies when there is massive inequality and where the most basic needs of the masses remain unmet while a tiny class basks in obscene amounts of wealth and income, under conditions of capitalist crisis of growth. India, the largest democracy of the world, is home to the largest number of people in absolute poverty. The emergence of fascistic tendencies points to a curious case of ideological and political inversion of sorts whereby the relation of antagonism between the working people and capital, which is their real enemy, is transformed into an antagonistic relation between the working people and their manufactured, or fake, enemies, i.e. minorities, communists, etc. A person can be killed for eating beef or for dealing in beef. Non-human beings (cows) have come to have more value than humans. Could there be a connection between kowtowing to the capitalist market as a holy cow and the extraordinary amount of religious-sectarian reverence for cows?

While the ideology of fascism has been in India at least since the 1920s, the same time when the communist party was also born, its political success has come since the early 1990s. There are at least three political-economic processes behind the rise of the fascistic forces:

1. Like many other countries, India – especially, its bottom 70–80% – faces numerous pressing problems: low wages, un-/under-employment, insecure employment, reduction in government's welfare, forcible loss of

INTRODUCTION 15

access to land or other means of livelihood, crisis of rural economy, ecological degradation, lack of quality health care, education and shelter, etc. These problems are fundamentally caused by the nature of capitalist class relation and exacerbated by its neoliberal form. While the masses have not been doing well, the top 1–10% of the wealth-owning class began doing extremely well, especially, since late 1980s.

2. Ordinary people are engaged in recurrent protests and struggles, which are often organized by the Left, against exploitation, oppression, dispossession and immiserization/inequality. In India, the intensity of strikes (e.g. person-days lost per strike) is actually increasing, and strike is a top risk factor for Indian business associations. So, there is a pressure on the enterprise-owners to reduce not only wage-costs of workers but also the possibility of strikes which inflict an economic cost. To reduce these costs, they need help from political party leaders. This help comes in the form of repression and deception/consent-making. The need for repression is often expressed as admiration for authoritarianism and for a strongman who could solve problems. The deception works in part on the basis of the creation of illusory differences based in religion, etc.

3. Capitalism indeed does not only create the *structural* condition for fascistic tendencies by creating economic problems for the masses, who then blame their conditions on an imaginary enemy (e.g. religious minority; those critical of the system of exploitation and oppression). It also creates the *agencies* through which the fascistic project, including its violence aspect, as a mass movement, is carried out. Here the role of economically frustrated petty bourgeois and lumpenproletarian, and even some proletarian, elements is important as fascistic movement's storm troopers.

Of course, a fuller understanding of fascistic tendencies must take us beyond the sphere of the political-*economic*. We must pay attention to the sphere of politics in a bourgeois society. The political dynamics of the fascistic tendency have been different in different countries. One needs to pay attention to the fascistic tendencies as they are manifested in the *concrete political situation* in India, by remaining mindful of the canvas of the *general* political economic dynamics of the fascistic tendencies.

The Congress Party, and the Communist parties (which are social-democratic *in practice*) constitute the combined forces of the 'Center' and the Left, and can be called, with *some* justification, 'reformist democracy'. There are various failures of 'reformist democracy' – the failures on the economic front and the failures to protect democracy and secularism – which have produced a situation for the right-wing forces to become stronger, electorally and otherwise. In other words, the entire political system – not just the BJP – is responsible for the fascistic tendencies.

3.7   *What Can the Left Do?*

The fascistic forces constitute a very powerful obstacle to, and reflects relative weakness of, the progressive and the Left movement. In several parts of India, communists and their offices are being physically attacked, and communists are being killed or harmed by the fascistic forces. So, the fascistic forces will have to be stopped, and stopped right now. These forces must be the target of an all-out fight, a fight on economic, political and ideological fronts. The question is how, and what role the Left has in this? To answer this, we must begin with the Marxist theory of Left politics, according to which the Marxist Left must mobilize its *basic classes* (skilled and unskilled workers, self-employed small-scale producers, and unemployed people, of all castes and religions) with help from politically progressive ('de-classed') intellectuals, against the fascistic brigade, mainly in the *extra-electoral* sphere, as a part of the struggle to transcend the capitalist class relations that are at the origin of the fascistic tendencies. This should be *the dominant approach* to fighting the fascistic movement. On the basis of their large numbers as well as rallies and general strikes, and local-level people's committees, Marxist forces must take the lead, where possible, in directly countering the fascistic movement and stop it from physically intimidating people.

But how does the power of the Marxist theory of politics relate to India's empirical context? The Indian Left – all the Left parties from the right to the left – must mobilize its forces extra-electorally against the fascistic movement at local, regional and national scales. But to the extent that the electoral arena is also an important area of political struggle in a liberal democracy, the Left must use that sphere as well.

4   The Chapter Outline

The book is divided into 12 main chapters, apart from the introduction and the conclusion. Many of these chapters were written over a number of years in the form of journal articles (as well as progressive electronic online magazines) and have been thoroughly revised.

Chapter 2 is, effectively, a continuation of this Introduction chapter and sets the context for the Chapters 3–13. It begins with the various criticisms raised against class analysis of India and then discusses how class analysis has been

INTRODUCTION   17

conducted in the Indian context. The chapter makes a series of criticisms against (a) the criticisms against class analysis and (b) some aspects of the extant class analysis. It then provides an outline of how class analysis of India should look like.

Chapter 3 is an examination of India's capitalism as a form of class relation. It begins with the famous Indian mode of production debate, critically discussing how certain scholars define capitalism in general and capitalism in the Indian context (including in Indian agriculture), and then presents an alternative approach. In doing so it builds on Marx's discussion in *Capital* volume 1 on subsumptions of labor, a discussion that is often neglected or misinterpreted. It argues that capitalism can exist when formal subsumption prevails and that India is a dominantly capitalist country. It also argues that the transition to real subsumption, with attendant technological change, can be a very long process, and, that *notwithstanding* Marx's view about 'spontaneous' transition to real subsumption, it is anything but spontaneous. That transition is mediated by the changing balance of power of capital and labor, which occurs in a context of a whole host of geographically-specific factors such as capitalist state interventions. I provide some empirical discussion to corroborate my argument about the relation between the balance of power between capital and labor, and the transition from formal subsumption. Thus, I discuss how class struggle can prompt real subsumption though not in any unilinear, straightforward, way, and I show how property owners can respond to class struggle against formal subsumption by way of *reinforcing* formal subsumption and/or introducing hybrid subsumption (exploitation based on mercantile-usury-rental extraction). While there are technical and other reasons for a transition to real subsumption (for example, in the industrial sector), there are limits to such a transition, within the context of peripheral capitalism, operating within the constraints of the imperialist world market.

While Chapter 3 deals with the form of capitalism in India from the vantage point of the subsumption of labor under capital, Chapter 4 deals with the form of capitalism from a different standpoint: neoliberal vs state-directed form of capitalism. It makes some brief conceptual observations on the neoliberal phase of capitalism in general, and examines neoliberal capitalism as it operates, and impacts people's lives, in India.

If Chapter 3 partly deals with the ways in which formal subsumption can be an obstacle to technological change, Chapter 5 asks: when technological change does happen under capitalism (with state-support), how does it benefit the working class? More specifically, Chapter 5 presents a 'slice' of the global intellectual discussion on the social character of technological change in the form of the famous Green Revolution (GR): it discusses Michael Lipton's and others' views on the supposed positive and negative benefits of the GR for the poor. It then critiques this literature for its underlying neo-Malthusianism and for its abstraction from class issues. The chapter goes on to present an alternative statement on the GR and poverty relation putting at the center the nature of the capitalist class relation, a statement that views the relation as contingent and not necessary. It also provides an empirical analysis of the GR–poverty relation in India, which was one of the 'model' GR countries in the mid-1990s. The chapter also very briefly reflects on the genetic (biotechnological) revolution in terms of its proponents' claim about its pro-poor benefits, the claims that are similar to the claims made about the GR's pro-poor effects.

As mentioned, Chapter 4 deals with neoliberalism – neoliberal form of capitalism – with Indian traits at a very general level. A specific form of neoliberal capitalism is agrarian neoliberalism, which, in turn, is expressed in a more concrete form: export-oriented aquaculture. This is the topic of Chapter 6. This Chapter briefly outlines the current state of the analysis of shrimp culture, and offers Marxist criticisms of this analysis, and maps out the contours of a different framework. It then presents the empirical discussion on shrimp farm laborers, including their socio-geographical character, and reflects on the ways in which class relations, social oppression and natural conditions of production are inter-connected.

Chapter 7 deals with the capitalist state in India. It examines the ways in which the Indian state is influenced by its 'base' in the dominant classes, and the coalition character of relations between property-owning classes and between them and the upper bureaucracy which has had a degree of autonomy. It then deals with the relation between the state and lower classes, and the state-form (territorial and liberal-democratic form) and lower-class struggles. Implications of the politically contradictory nature of state intervention in relation to uneven development and neoliberalism are also outlined.

Chapter 8 briefly looks at some of the exploitative and oppressive material conditions in India's rural areas, and also considers the failure of the post-colonial capitalist-landlord state to counter these conditions. The chapter shows how it is the unjust conditions of living that have created a situation 'ripe' for class struggle, one instance of which is the Naxalite movement. The chapter discusses the uneven growth and spread of the movement and presents a theoretical-political critique of the movement.

Chapter 9 is a continuation of Chapter 8 and also builds on Chapter 7. Its focus on the state's repressive response to the Naxalite Movement. It begins by critically discussing the existing conceptual literature on state repression of social movements, and presents a preliminary attempt at an alternative approach to the topic. It then provides some empirical evidence on what the

INTRODUCTION

Naxalite Movement actually does for the poor, and examines the state's ideological-repressive response to the movement. The chapter explains why the state deploys violent means against it. The state is repressive towards the Naxalite movement not just because the movement uses violence. The state is also repressive because the movement seeks to create an alternative landscape of development which potentially poses a crisis of legitimacy.

Chapter 9 is followed by a series of four chapters on the right-wing forces in relation to India's political economy and its Left movement. Using content from media, and data from national and international institutions, Chapter 10 empirically examines India's development under the post-2014 right-wing regime, in terms of its economic and social-political aspects. It discusses the record of the BJP government in promoting economic development and inequality. It shows how the ultra-rich, the class basis of the right-wing government, are benefitting from the government enormously, and how the poorer segments are, more or less, losing under this government. It also shows the government's record of political development, including democracy and social harmony. It discusses how the dismal record of development is slowly getting registered in the minds of people who are getting disillusioned with the government. This disillusionment is an embryonic consciousness against right-wing thinking and policies, but whether it will further develop in a progressive direction and how it will shape electoral and extra-electoral battles against right-wing forces, no one can tell with certainty.

Chapters 11–12 interpret the rise of right-wing forces on the basis of a framework in which the concept of fascism – or, what I call fascistic tendencies – plays a central role. Chapter 11 deals with some definitional/conceptual issues concerning fascism and introduces the topic of the fascistic threat in India and sheds light on its importance to India's Left and progressive culture. It deals with the political economy of fascism and fascistic tendencies, at a general theoretical level, but with an eye towards India, relating the fascistic tendencies to class society, to capitalist class-society and to India's capitalist society. It considers the *economic* as well as *cultural-political* processes, and class *agency* involved in the fascistic movement.

Chapter 12 deals with the failures of 'reformed democracy' (centrist and Left forces) in India to protect democracy and secularism and social-economic rights. This has allowed a political space, within the overall logic of the failure of the capitalist system to meet the needs of the masses, a space within which the BJP and its forces then deploy a battery of political techniques to strengthen fascistic movement and implement right-wing economic policies by capturing power.

Chapter 13 deals with the question of what is to be done about the fascistic threat? It begins with the Marxist theory of Left politics, outlining how the Left anywhere in the world must fight against fascistic tendencies as a part of the fight for socialism. It then discusses the Indian situation in relation to this general theory: it outlines the strengths and weaknesses of the Indian Left movement, and shows how the Left can fight the fascistic tendencies on the basis of extra-electoral mobilization of the toiling masses as well as class-based electoral politics, putting the accent on the first method. Whether the existing Left movement is up to the task is a different matter. I remain skeptical of this possibility (see Das, 2019b).

CHAPTER 2

Class in India

The discussion in this book on India's political economy and politics (of the Right and of the Left) is informed by a class-based theoretical approach. But one might ask: why does one need such an approach? Is Indian society not too complex for the class analysis to be useful? A continuation of the introduction to the book, Chapter 2 deals with this question in a relatively rudimentary manner, on the basis of the general ideas about class proposed in Das (2017a), while the relevance of a class perspective on India will be clearer in the subsequent chapters (Chapters 3–13) on the basis of further development of specific themes.

This Chapter has four sections. In Section 1, I deal with some common criticisms against class analysis (or, Marxist class analysis). In Section 2, I present how class has been treated by various scholars studying India. In Section 3, I critique these views as well as the criticisms against Marxist class analysis. In Section 4, I outline a very broad approach to class analysis of India, anticipating many of the themes discussed in the remainder of the book.

1 Existing Criticisms against Class Analysis of India

1.1 *India Too Complex for Class Analysis*

For some, the Indian society is to be seen in terms of categories defined on the basis of not only caste, which is said to define India's specificity, but also gender, indigeneity, income, occupation, region, religion, community, and so on. If there are so many divisions, one may say: why use the class perspective? In fact, it is often said that Indian society is too complex for class, which is an analytical category from the Western industrial society, to be useful. M.N. Srinivas, one of India's well-known sociologists, says that Indian reality is 'far too complex, regional and sectional differences very real, and the studies of sociologists seemed to make sense to non-Marxists', and not Marxists (Srinivas, 2012: 181).[1]

---

1 Srinivas (2012) says this in a talk delivered at the All India Sociological conference held in 1997: 'the country has been undergoing rapid cultural and social change since the 1940s... Marxism of the more dogmatic variety seemed to help a large number of Indian intellectuals

---

© KONINKLIJKE BRILL NV, LEIDEN, 2020 | DOI:10.1163/9789004415560_003

1.2 Primacy Assigned to Class Mistaken

Even if some scholars think that class analysis has something to contribute to the study of Indian society, the fact that it assigns primacy to class has been a problem for them. Consider the view of Andre Beteille, another well-known sociologist of India. He says that in the 1970s when he began studying India's social structure, he was 'attracted by the Marxian approach' (i.e. by Marxian class analysis), and yet he remained 'sceptical about it' throughout his entire academic life (Beteille, 2007: 1–2). Why? Beteille says that 'Classes are undoubtedly important, but they are not important in the way Marx, or even, Lenin, thought them to be' (p. 9).[2] More specifically, according to him, class analysis (of Marx, Lenin and other Marxists) gives primacy to class over other divisions, so 'for this reason I have been attracted to the more open, flexible, and pluralistic approach of Max Weber' (pp. 7–8).

1.3 Too Much Autonomy to the Economic in Class Analysis

Sinha (2009) criticizes Marxists for treating class as an economic category, autonomous from politics and culture. He says that 'continued and insisted-upon separation of culture and identity from questions of class poses challenges to the Marxist framework in approaching contemporary movements' (Sinha, 2009: 160). Marxist class analysis reduces class to an economic concept.[3] It also fails to 'address the whole set of factors that produce subordination'; in other words, it fails to 'see the worker as embodying a range of identities that are not only not reducible to the economic, but more accurately, which allow us to unravel the cultural underpinnings of the economy' (Sinha, 2009: 171).

From a related standpoint, Herring and Agarwala (2006) say that class analysis has problematically paid much more attention to the material/economic forms of property than it should:

> [The] emphasis [in old or traditional class theory] on the material forms of property alone deflects attention from the importance of cultural capital and the role of the developmental state in distributing life chances. (p. 348)

---

    understand what was happening and where India was heading, but not everyone was satisfied with it' (p. 181).

2 'The work of Marx provided the most important initial stimulus for the analysis of classes. But one has to make a distinction between the historical significance of that work and its contemporary significance' (ibid.: 12).

3 Orthodox Marxists should 'either scale back their notion of "class" so that it is not "economic" in the last instance, or … broaden their concept of the "economic" itself' (p. 171).

CLASS IN INDIA

1.4   *No a priori Existence of Class*

Marxism is also wrong to think of class as an a priori category, and it ignores the fact that the 'constitution' of class occurs on 'the shifting contours of an unstable and fluid socio-cultural terrain' (Sinha, 2009: 168). Sinha seems to think that class is an identity like caste or gender is (p. 163). According to Fernandes (1994), class is a contested category, one that is constituted by conflict and exclusion. As well, class analysis is said to ignore the fact that the making of class politics represents a continual process of reconstruction and conflict rather than a predefined teleology. The author says that the study of working class politics in India suffers from essentialism. Sanchez and Strumpell (2014), in a similar vein, argue for re-centering class analysis, and discuss the historically contingent emergence of Indian working classes through different types of labor, gender and ethnic struggles.

This strand of critique is continued in John Harriss (1988), who himself researches class in his empirical work on India. He appears to support the idea that 'the 'social' is not an autonomous domain but, in important respects, is created by politics' (p. 47). Harriss says: 'Western models of class are applied with great difficulty in South Asia. ... It would help, and assist the elucidation of gender and ethnic relations, to focus on the labour process [read: the struggle for a share of the social product]...rather than starting with particular concepts of class, or modes of production' (p. 51). Harriss also says that: there are 'limitations of existing paradigms and of the various ways in which essentialist constructs (like "peasant economy" or even "capitalism") have been substituted for specific contextual analysis' (p. 55).

This sort of criticism anticipates Henry Bernstein's (2007) implied – and not-so-implied criticism – of classical class theory in the context of the Global South, that informs the view of many scholars working on India:

> [T]here is no "homogeneous proletarian condition" within the "South", other than that essential condition [which is] the need to secure reproduction needs (survival) through the (direct and indirect) sale of labour power. The ways in which this is done defy inherited assumptions of fixed (and uniform) notions of "worker", "peasant", "trader", "urban", "rural", "employed" and "self-employed".

Both Harriss's and Bernstein's views of class analysis are echoed in the thinking of Gidwani, for whom class analysis is too structural and law-given: contrary to the claims of Marxism, he says, capitalism, is not a frame of economic organization based on the consistent operation of laws, but rather an assemblage of contingent and interrupted logics (Gidwani, 2008). This implies that what is interesting about class can be figured out only locally, conjuncturally. One reason for this, one could infer, is that what is interesting about class inheres in the cultural realm which exhibits enormous local variations, and that therefore there can be no general perspective on class.

1.5 *Too Many Changes in the Working Class for Class Analysis to Be Useful*

Subalternists argue that the erosion of the factory-based stable work has meant that there are no workers in the traditional sense, and that no class consciousness is possible, and therefore, there is no need for class analysis (Spivak, 2000).[4] Likewise, Subir Sinha (2009) says, Marxist class analysis has not responded to the fact that the Indian work force is mobile, precarious and informalized, that it is differentiated economically, and that it is also differentiated politically (it has both party-based unions and independent unions).

1.6 *Non-existent Polarization, Contrary to Class Analysis*

While the previous criticism is that society has changed too much for class analysis to be useful, there is another argument according to which the society is not changing as per the premise of class analysis. Class analysis is criticized because its prediction of class polarization and proletarianization has been disproved. A reason for Beteille's skepticism of class analysis is that contrary to the prediction of Marx and Lenin, class polarization is not happening. In fact, the anti-polarization thesis is held by those who claim to be Marxists. They say that there is not polarization but 'partial polarization' (Byres, 1981). This is because small-scale producers can subsist on the basis of self-exploitation, government support, remittance money, etc. (Byres, 1981; Bhaduri, 1986; Harriss-White and Janakarajan, 2004; see also Parthasarathy, 2015). Harriss (2011) says:

> [I]t is clear that Byres' (1981) argument that what was taking place was rather "partial proletarianisation", with small and marginal producers continuing to reproduce themselves, partly by virtue of labouring outside agriculture, was substantially correct.

The partial polarization ideas have even led some to say that class analysis is too determinative in its theoretical expectation. In fact, to them, not only has full-scale proletarianization not happened but also this fact has a political implication which is contrary to class theory: the proletariat is a small section of

---

4   On how subaltern studies is associated with the decline of class analysis, see Chibber (2006). For more recent work on this topic, see Brass (2017): Brass importantly refers to 'the culturalist displacement of class categories in India by the Subaltern Studies project' (p. 24).

the population and cannot be assigned the political importance that class analysis has given it:

> [I]n India, class struggle from below is not being led by the proletariat understood as a class fully reproduced inside a capital – labour relation. The proletariat in India is small, it is not expanding, and the main sections of it are relatively privileged when compared to the majority who are informal workers.
>
> LERCHE and SHAH, 2018: 942

Many scholars working on India take seriously Bernstein's (2007) idea that because polarization has not happened and therefore because direct producers are not wage-earners, there are 'classes of labor', indicating the absence of a 'homogenous proletarian condition'. The term, 'classes of labor', encompasses 'various and complex combinations of employment and self-employment': all those who have to earn their living on the basis of 'insecure and oppressive ... wage employment and/or a range of likewise precarious small-scale and insecure, "informal sector"' (Bernstein, 2007: 6; see also Breman, 2003). If there are not many workers, it is then futile to expect class-based action. In fact, Patnaik (1999: 205–206), like Lerch and Shah (2018), says, as capitalist contradiction in India has not been deep enough, this leads to a situation where the exploited classes (poor peasants and landless agricultural laborers) are not yet a decisive majority in most regions of the country, which weakens potential organization against the exploiting classes.

1.7   *Inadequacy of Class Analysis on Political Grounds*

There are at least three types of argument here. One is that class analysis ignores class struggle outside of production as it pays too much attention to economic capital, or more generally, to economic aspects of class. Class analysis is problematic because it cannot uncover the struggles in civil society:

> Old class analysis was not so interested in these struggles in civil society. Marx himself was convinced that the point of production was decisive as a determinant of class formation and collective action.
>
> HERRING and AGARWALA, 2006: 347–348

The popularity of new social movements, as opposed to class-based movements, is taken to be indicative of the irrelevance of class-based politics and of class analysis (see Chandra and Taghioff, 2016; Omvedt, 1993). Capitalists and workers are divided into many categories, so they – and especially, workers – are not a cohesive group capable of political action.

Marxist class analysis is inadequate politically on an additional ground: Marxist attempts to offer the "centralized revolutionary party" performing 'vanguard-functions' as 'the privileged agent of mediation' are problematic (Sinha, 2009: 157). Sinha rightly says that Marxist-party managers (as in Bengal) have discouraged strike and support the capitalist path that China is following, and from this, he, however, concludes that class analysis itself is wrong (p. 158) rather than subjecting the communist movement to class analysis.

For Chakrabarti and Cullenberg (2003), contrary to class analysis, class as a social force representing class interests does not exist. There is no reason to believe that the working class can have a spark of consciousness. They are against 'any concept of a centered totality of the subject'. They are against concepts of 'false consciousness' and 'vanguard party' (p. 94). They critique the assumption in class theory that the class consciousness of the working class in line with its class interest will be a reality and that it will trickle down to individual members of that class. They say that neither the working class knows, nor the vanguard party knows, what the interests of the working class is. The objective interest cannot be the basis for any knowledge.[5] The working class does not have one subject position but many, so the subjectivity of its members cannot be reduced to a simple class interest. Yet, Chakrabarti and Cullenberg (2003) are deeply critical of the leftist program for small peasantry and labor: their argument is that the Left mistakenly thinks of these classes as being unable to act on their own and as being dependent on it for help. This argument contradicts their idea that the masses cannot correctly know their interests.

Interestingly, while some scholars say that class analysis (and indeed Marxism as such) is problematic because practicing Marxists (communists in power in Indian provinces) have acted in a way that is contrary to Marxism, according to others, class analysis crosses the boundary between analysis and action, so it is not a proper scholarly enterprise: 'Srinivas was inclined to view Marxism and class analysis as motivated by political as against scholarly interests', so he rejected class approach (quoted in Beteille, 2007: p. 3).

2   Existing Approaches to Class in India

Given all these alleged problems with class analysis, different scholars have pursued different analytical paths. Some have (almost) rejected class altogether

---

5   Then why will anyone think that post-modernists know anything about class, even if they have been involved in much academic practice (e.g. reading) and political practice (social democratic action over the redistribution of surplus)?

CLASS IN INDIA

(e.g. Roy, 2005). This strand of thinking includes the work of those, including Srinivas, who talk about all kinds of social divisions and oppressions *but* those that are based in class.[6] There are others who have engaged in class thinking, assigning to it a variable degree of significance. In terms of the latter, there are at least four approaches which can be briefly mentioned below.[7]

2.1 *Class + (or 'Inter-sectionality' Type) Approach*

For some, class is important but it is not *that* important: class is one of several other 'things', and class-based politics is merely one among many different forms of political activity. Class is no more important as an analytical category than any other.

As in the West, often the argument, sometimes implicit and sometimes, explicit, is that: one cannot talk about class unless one talks about non-class categories such as gender or ethnicity. For example, 'There is no point to talk about class without making it clear that it is backward to talk about class without speaking about gender and race' (Yates, 2006, in Gimenez, 2018: 263). And as we have seen, similarly, Sinha (2009: 171) says that one must view the worker, 'as embodying a range of identities' that are not 'reducible to the economic'. A major problem with this sort of views is that it conflates the more abstract level at which the worker exists with the less abstract level, and it misses the point that what exists at more abstract level is real.

Critical of those who emphasize ideas at the expense of interests, Andre Beteille (2007), says that class in terms of property relations is important, but so is caste, and they are mutually irreducible. If property is important, so is education and income as well (p. 11). And he suggests that class theory must be divorced from historical materialist theory of society.

In a chapter entitled 'Class in India' in his influential *Argumentative Indian*, Amartya Sen (2006) usefully emphasizes the importance of class.[8] He thinks about 'class as a source of disparity' or of inequality (or injustice or deprivation; he uses all these terms). He says that 'class is not the only source of inequality' and that 'interest in class as a source of disparity has to be placed within a bigger picture that includes other divisive influences: gender, caste,

---

6 See the recent work on caste, which, more or less, ignores the explanatory framework of class (see: Shah et al., 2006; Sharma, 2002; Judge, 2014; Verma, 2005). On recent work on women's issues, see the collection of articles in Fernandes, 2014 (this is a 350-page book on gender which hardly has any discussion on class issues confronting women; cf. Menon, 1999a).

7 I generally focus on the literature dating from the 1990s.

8 For example, he says that: 'class is not only important on its own, it can also magnify the impact of other contributors to inequality' (Sen, 2006: 206).

region, community and so on' (Sen, 2006: 205). Using a language that is close to the language of intersectionality, Sen says: one should treat different forms of inequality together, making more explicit room for their extensive *interdependencies*' and 'their *complementarity*' (p. 205; italics added). He argues for an '*integrated* understanding of the functioning of class *in alliance* with other causes of injustice' (ibid.; italics added). He talks about: 'interactive presence' of different features of deprivation (e.g. class and gender) (p. 207).

Just as Sen subsumes class to inequality (or injustice or deprivation), other scholars subsume it under marginality: economic deprivation (a proxy for class); dispossession and non-class relations constitute marginalities (Bhattacharyya and Basu, 2018). Or, to elaborate on this point: hunger + forcible land acquisitions + material deprivation of minority groups and tribes + caste discrimination + regional disparities + gendered forms of exclusion, etc. = marginalities.

There is a large amount of literature which treats class, more or less explicitly, in terms of its interaction/intersection with non-class relations: class is seen in the 'multiple matrices of inequality' mode of thinking. For example, Thara (2016) says that as a concept, intersectionality is important to understand how gender is intertwined with experiences that derive from, and shape, caste and class. Focusing on the subjectivities of Dalits across India and on their continued socio-economic and political marginalization, Anandhi and Kapadia (2017) explore what they call the political economy of gender, caste and class in India. Chakrabarti (2001) talks about the inter-connection between the social power wielded by members of the dominant land-owning caste of the capitalist class, and about how class and social power are conditioned by caste. Heller and Fernandes (2006) integrate class analysis with the politics of caste, religion, and language. Lerche and Shah (2018) expand Philippe Bourgois's concept of conjugated oppression 'to express how multiple axes of oppression based on social relations such as race/caste/tribe/ethnicity/ region or gender and sexuality, etc. are co-constitutive of and shape class relations, potentially producing extreme relations of oppression, inseparable from each other in capitalist accumulation' (p. 931).[9] Similarly, in the context of informal workers, Agarwala (2019) talks about the 'intersectional nature of class, caste, and gender identities' (p. 410).

Fernandes (1994) says that the structural and ideological/cultural components of class are constructed through the politics of gender and community. Chatterjee (2012) points to the existence of an assemblage in an Indian city,

---

9   They add that: 'For India we argue that the spread of capitalism has been marked by class relations that are mutually constituted with caste, tribe, gender and region-based oppression' (p. 951).

CLASS IN INDIA

where gender, class, caste and ethnicity intersect in myriad ways creating possibilities for resistance (see also Clarke, 2017; Kapadia, 1997; Velaskar, 2016). All the discussion on so-called 'caste-class dominance', more or less, speaks to the intersectionality mode of thinking without necessarily assigning any primacy to class (Frankel, 1994; Harriss, 2013).

2.2 *The Post-modern-Marxist Approach to Class*

While there is much in this approach that one can agree with (e.g. the emphasis on the surplus value appropriation in the conceptualization of capitalist class relation), there is a lot that is simply troublesome. Influenced by Stephen Resnick and Richard Wolff, as well as Barry Hirst and Ernst Laclau, Chakrabarti and Cullenberg (2003), commenting on the Indian mode of production, argue against the property-relations-focused definition of class. They say that class must be seen solely in terms of the appropriation of surplus labor. The capitalist class, like the working class, is disaggregated in terms of process of performance, appropriation, distribution, and receipts of surplus value. Those (e.g. toy manufacturers) receive surplus value and are productive capitalists. Money-lenders, merchants or landlord capitalists receive a part of this surplus value and are called unproductive capitalists. An individual can be both exploiter and exploited.

2.3 *A Weaker, Agency-Based, Approach to Class*

Those who subscribe to what I advisedly call a weaker, agency-based theory of class emphasize the importance of class, but they make important criticisms of classical class theory of Marx, and argue for a less ambitious class analysis.

Critical of Marxism's focus on economic aspects capital, there is an attempt to add to 'economic capital', social and cultural capitals, on the basis of Bourdieu's theory (Upadhya, 1997; see also Jeffrey et al., 2005).

Herring and Agarwala (2006) do emphasize the significance of class very well:

> Class analysis always takes the material world seriously.... [Class] is never simply a construction or an imaginary. Class structures relations among people; these relations are critical for understanding not only life chances, but also political behavior. (p. 324)

They go on to add that:

> Class structure defines positions for individuals, based on their relationship to economic assets; these class positions in turn differentiate

objective material interests: landlords and tenants, workers and owners. Under certain conditions, these interests may be recognized, mobilized, and acted upon – thus ultimately explaining collective action in which people attempt to improve their life chances through politics and policy: land reform, minimum wages, welfare transfers, income redistribution. (p. 331)

But there is a need to do class analysis differently, according to the two authors. This means that: 'Uncovering mechanisms takes priority, and the uncovering must be an *empirical process*. How do things actually work?' (p. 347; italics added). The mechanisms in question are, however, not the causal mechanisms that lie in social relations, as causal mechanisms, ultimately, should: they are not structural mechanisms. Rather: 'Mechanisms focus attention on *agency* of historical actors' (e.g. informal workers), and this would allow 'recovering in the process human agency' (Herring and Agarwala, 2006: 347; italics added). But the agency is not a macro-scale agency. It operates at the local scale: 'At the micro level, where all of us live, are the day-to-day practices through which classes define and reproduce themselves' (ibid.). So, the implication is that: classes are how classes define themselves and not given a priori, i.e. prior to how individuals think and behave empirically.[10]

Given that most of the workers in India work in the informal sector without government benefits, it is important to notice the ways in which they engage in struggles:

> The informal economy illustrates the necessity of original class analysis and possibilities for *rethinking theory*. It is not that informal-sector workers fail to organize for class interests, but rather that new structures of production alter their strategies.
>
> HERRING and AGARWALA, 2006: 346; see also ROY CHOWDHURY, 2015; italics added

And the struggle of the classes happens in the sphere of civil society, locally, in communities and local institutions, and they have important material effects. Informally employed workers are not permanently employed in a place, so they struggle for government benefits rather than for higher wages and better working conditions from their employers. The old class theory has ignored

---

10   This appears to contradict their own view that 'Class structure defines positions for individuals, based on their relationship to economic assets' (ibid.).

CLASS IN INDIA

these struggles over benefits outside of production, the struggles where class interests intersect with non-class identities:

> In pursuing these ends [in civil society], individuals are strategic, and objects of larger strategies; struggles often take highly euphemized forms, as in struggles over caste, identity, and culture, that are then often interpreted as Indian exceptionalism.
> HERRING and AGARWALA, 2006: 348

Given all this, there is said to be a need to *rethink* class theory:

> In recovering class, we find a useful rethinking of the deductivist and macro-historical logic of dominant versions of European class analytics.
>
> [...] We find that complexities of class structures, and their interpretations from specific class positions, necessitate a less determinative intellectual architecture than The Communist Manifesto. (p. 347)

And, rethinking the old class theory leads to the conclusion that: the gap between the Marxist relational approach and Weber's gradational approach is less than it is thought to be:

> Class analytics itself can and does evoke theological permutations among pure theorists, but the essential perspective is both straightforward and commonsensical. Though much has been made of distinguishing Marxian from Weberian class analysis, for example, both emphasize the primacy of economic assets as differentiating people across classes.
> HERRING and AGARWALA, 2006: 324

So, in the weaker version of class theory, several inter-related claims are made. (1) Marxism does not have the specificity vis-à-vis Weberianism. This is a conclusion that the late Erik Wright, a well-known class theorist, reaches (see Wright, 2015: Chapter 1). (2) Class theory must give up on its greater analytical ambition (be 'less determinative'), as 'bold claims to a universalist framework making strong predictions rendered class theory uniquely vulnerable' (Herring and Agarwala, 2006: 351). This is also a conclusion that Wright reaches (see Wright, 2015).[11] (3) Class analysis must be less theoretical (more 'commonsensical'), according to Herring and Agarwala and similar other authors such as

---

11   See Chapter 2 in Das (2017a) for a detailed presentation of Wright's class theory, and Chapter 4 for a comprehensive critique.

Beteille for whom class analysis must be divorced from the wider historical-materialist theory of society. (4) Correspondingly, class analysis must be more oriented towards the local scale and the everyday life, and it must be more agency-focused. Marxism is also obsessed with the nation as the stage of politics (p. 163) apparently ignoring the local scale struggles. (5) Much more attention needs to be paid to workers who are not stably employed (who are informally employed) and to their struggles, *outside* of production/workplace, over state-benefits.

2.4 *A Multi-class Approach to Class*

In this approach, there are many different classes (and not just many different fractions of a class), beyond the two-class model of class analysis, and they have different life experiences and opportunities and levels of living, etc. So class (as an analytical category, as a thought-object) matters because class*es* matter in the real world. The obverse of the stress on the multiplicity of classes is the idea that class polarization does not happen as quickly as class theory has predicted.

Thorner (1973) talks about the rural society in terms of: malik (big landowners), mazdoor (workers), kisan (peasants). In part influenced by Lenin and Mao, there is a lot of empirical work that has revealed how in different areas a multiplicity of classes exists. Utsa Patnaik, a prominent Indian political economist, uses what she calls labor exploitation index to produce an analytical map of many different classes that the rural society is divided into.[12] This can be, and has been, useful to understand how different classes have different kinds of economic experience (including opportunities for accessing credit).

To the extent that class position can be determined at the family level, a family's class position is a function of the following apart from its ownership of

---

12   The index measures the extent of the use of outside labor or conversely the extent of working for others, relative to the extent of self-employment. The index for a household is defined as:

$E = [(HI–HO) + (LO–LI)]/F$, where,

E = exploitation index;

HI = Labor days hired on property including leased-in property. (Labor is defined as manual labor);

HO = Family labor days hired out to others;

LO = Family and hired labor days used on leased-out property;

LI = Labor days similarly worked on leased-in property;

F = Labor days worked by the household on its property, including leased-in property, is an indicator of self-employment. The index is a ratio which can be positive or negative depending on whether the household is a net employer of outside labor or is itself on balance working for others.

property: available quantity of family labor deployed in production; quantity of work the family does for other members of society for a wage (which could vary between zero and a positive number); and the quantity of work other members of society perform for the family (Patnaik, 1999, 1987). Given these conditions, there can be, as Patnaik shows: a multiplicity of classes. Landlords perform no manual labor in self-employment and they employ others. Rich peasants are involved in as large an employment of others as self-employment. Middle peasant are involved in smaller employment of others' labor than self-employment. Small peasants do not employ others and they either do not work for others, or they work for others to a smaller extent than self-employment. Poor peasants work for others to a greater extent than self-employment. Landless laborers are not self-employed and they work entirely for others (Patnaik, 1999: 236). Landlords and rich peasants are primarily exploiting others. Middle and small peasants are neither exploited nor do they exploit: they are mainly self-employed. Poor peasants and landless laborers are primarily exploited by others.

Bhaduri's (1983) class map has fewer classes than Patnaik's: agricultural capitalist class; money-lending and merchant class; small peasantry (including those who work as part-time wage-earners); and farm labor. For Rudra (1988), a class refers to a group of people defined in terms of their common relation to the means of production, who have a non-antagonistic relation among themselves, and who have an antagonistic relation with members of other classes. There may be conflict of interest within a class, but that is less important than inter-class conflict in interest. In the rural context, on the one hand, there are big landlords (including rich peasants, capitalist farmers and feudal landowners) who constitute the ruling class, and whose power comes from the ownership of productive resources, and on the other, there are laborers (including those who may own small amounts of land) who are the subordinate class. While the latter class exists in an objective sense, they lack class consciousness, because of the geographical isolation of the members of this class from one another.

Similarly, Rudolph and Rudolph (1987: 341) talk about bullock capitalists: they are the self-employed commercial owner-cultivators, with land holdings large enough to support a pair of bullocks (in the 1970s). They are neither capitalists nor workers. They are neither exploiters nor the exploited. They hold more land than any other 'land-holding class' in rural areas. Mention may be made of the view of a liberal political scientist, Ashutosh Varshney. Varshney (1994) talks about class (e.g. farmers as a class), but his view of class is primarily based on the exchange relations as opposed to the production/property relations. *Exploitation* of labor is not a part of Varshney's class mapping. Production for *market* is (see Das, 2001a).

Inspired by Patnaik and Bernstein, Pattenden (2006) divides the rural society in India into two main groups in terms of class: net buyers of labor power, who include the dominant (capitalist) class, and net-sellers of labor power (or 'classes of labor').[13]

While much of class analysis has been about rural areas, Pranab Bardhan (1999) talks about the India's class system at the national scale. On his class map are three proprietary classes (urban bourgeoisie; large-scale landowners; and state elites appropriating scarce rent from their education).

Recently, there has been much talk about the middle class or middle classes (Fernandes, 2016). Their consumption and income potential are stressed, in part thanks to economic growth in new sectors of the post-1991 economy (e.g. Information Technology; financial services). It is said that while a Brahmin will remain a Brahmin, a poor person can join the middle class (Jodhka et al., 2017).

2.5 Dispossession Studies Approach to Class

A large amount of literature which looks like class analysis and/or which has something to do with class, has become a study of dispossession. Dispossession, more or less, refers to, the coercive processes in which small-scale producers and those engaged in natural economy are losing access to their means of production (mainly, land); it can also refer to the privatization of state-owned companies.[14] Dispossession happens because businesses need the land held by the small-scale producers, individually or in common, for both production of goods and services, mining, and real estate (including, speculation), or because big dams, often constructed in the agrarian and urban capitalist class interests, inundate the land, forcing the inhabitants to leave. Dispossession, much of which happens in areas of indigenous communities, is seen by some as internal colonization of the poor (Walker, 2008; see Das, 2019c). In so far as dispossession has come to be associated with neoliberalism, Chakrabarti (2009) says that neoliberalism is a tool to obtain the (post) colonial hegemony

---

13   Net buyers include: the dominant class (a proxy for the capitalist class which has economic and political power) consisting of all those who produce a surplus and who cultivate their land solely or mainly by hired labor. Net buyers also include petty capitalists and petty commodity producers, who produce some surplus; they are primarily self-employed but they also hire some labor. Then there are pure petty commodity producers who produce no surplus, and use only family labor. Finally, the net sellers of labor power include: all those who are mainly self-employed but they also sell labor power; those who sell labor power to a greater extent than they are self-employed, and those who live only by selling their labor power (p. 24).

14   There are simply too many of these studies to cite here (see, for example, Doshi and Ranganathan, 2017; Fernandez, 2018; Levien, 2018; Sugden and Punch, 2014; Whitehead, 2010). Most of the literature is critical, except for a few which argue that the effects are good or can be good (see Ghertner, 2014; Moberg, 2015; Paul and Sarma, 2017).

CLASS IN INDIA

of capital over the small-scale sector. The literature on dispossession has shed light, even if it is very repetitive now, on an important aspect of capitalist class society: the fact of dispossession and struggles against dispossession.

3 A Critique of Existing Approaches to Class in India

3.1 Is Class Just One among Many 'Things'?

It is absolutely important to emphasize oppression based on caste,[15] gender, indigeneity, and other relations. But the idea that class is one that just intersects with these relations of oppression, and that one person may therefore experience all these relations, does not advance analysis much.[16] The question that is not posed is this: what is precisely the logic of interaction/intersection? Why do the class relations, and why do the different non-class relations exist, and why do they (have to) interact?[17] Besides, as Gimenez (2017) says: 'Intersectionality, by stressing identity divisions, unwittingly undermines the possibility of workers uniting across gender, race and other differences, thus strengthening the status quo' (p. 451). At the level of Indian capitalism, capitalists of different castes will all behave as capitalists prioritizing profit-making. Of course, in any given concrete situation the ways in which class relations and class processes affect a person's life are mediated by discrimination and oppression based on caste, gender, religion, etc. and corresponding ideologies and politics. Of course, 'a concrete organization of class is impossible minus historical, cultural, sexual and political relations' (Bannerji, 1995: 31). But all these facts do not mean that class mechanisms do not have any primacy.

It *is absolutely* useful and necessary to highlight that many women, low caste people, Muslims and indigenous groups are not benefitting from

---

15 On atrocities against Dalits, see Teltumbde (2010). He talks about the need for 'trans-caste unity of all the lower-classes of society' (p. 186).

16 This is the case, even if it appears to emphasize an important principle of dialectics: what a process is, it is because of its relation to many other processes.

17 It is not enough to say that X and Y interact; one must say why do X and Y exist in the first place, and why does the reality appear to be divided into X and Y? Why does a Brahmin oppress a Dalit (an ex-untouchable person/group in India's caste hierarchy) or why does a Hindu hate a Muslim? Are there social-material conditions underlying social oppression at the level of *society as a whole*, the logic of which then trickles down to the level of individuals and groups, in order to shape their behavior? And why is it that incidence of certain kinds of oppression (e.g. discrimination against Muslims) increase at a certain point in time (say, early 1990s and especially in the last 5 years or so) and why does the incidence of oppression (against Dalits) tend to be concentrated in specific areas? To what extent might the explanation lie in the historical and geographical character of capitalist class relation?

economic development and social policy and that they are subjected to deplorable levels of discrimination with their democratic rights disrespected routinely. But such an emphasis on social oppression *outside* of class relations fails to seriously consider the following idea: the unequal and oppressive relation between men and women, or between castes and religions, is not the fundamental reason why women, low castes, and religious minorities are experiencing an attack on their lives as workers, although such relationship may explain why some workers (e.g. upper caste male workers) live better than other workers (e.g. female Dalit workers). The fundamental reason why their basic needs remain unfulfilled lies in what the toiling masses of different castes and religions and what both men and women workers have in common: class relations.

Many can agree that class is important, but class is said to be one among many social forces. One can have different entry points in social analysis, so one may start with class, or with caste, or gender, etc. There is no necessary reason for any given entry point, and there is no necessary reason for the primacy of class. However, to refuse to assign primacy to class is to refuse to agree that productive activity is crucial to life, and that productive activity is a social activity that happens in class-structured ways, which means that a tiny minority own and control the use of productive resources, while the majority do not do so, and are, therefore, economically forced to surrender a large part of what they produce to the minority-class supported by the class state. Therefore, it is un-dialectical to reject, or ignore, the following idea: in the lives of a working class person (or of a small-scale producer), class mechanisms relate to non-class mechanisms in a system within which class mechanisms have a degree of causal primacy. It is mistaken to think that class is just one of several categories such as caste, gender, indigeneity, etc. Class is *the* social relation that fundamentally structures the lives of men, women and children, even though it is not the only relationship that counts.

3.2 Is the Two-Class Model, Including the Thesis of Class Polarization, Irrelevant?

It is true that the two-class model of class analysis does not necessarily reflect the concrete empirical reality: there are many more classes than capitalists and workers in India which is experiencing 'belated' capitalist development in a post-colonial context, and this is especially so given that the majority of the population lives in rural areas. Closely associated with the two-class model is the idea of polarization and proletarianization, as indicated earlier.

The two-class model represents class mechanisms at a more abstract level. The model's aim is not to map out – count – what are the different classes on the ground or indeed how quickly a class of commodity producers is being class-differentiated. Its aim is to supply the mechanisms of a class society,

CLASS IN INDIA

including class differentiation among commodity producers, and to show how these mechanisms can be modified by counter-tendencies (as explained later). The tendency towards class polarization and proletarianization can be countered by many processes (e.g. self-exploitation, use of remittance from wage-work in the city, welfare from the capitalist state, etc.). But then all these counter-mechanisms are not unrelated to class (as explained below). So, how is class analysis invalid if polarization is slower than expected in class analysis? Even then, as Basu shows: the relative size of the middle class is shrinking (see Table 2.1), and this implies that, since the size of the ruling class has remained more or less constant, some sections of what is called the middle class are being pushed down into the working class. Arguably, this is consistent with the polarization thesis.

It is true that a person who is an agricultural labor in the village can also be a seasonal migrant in the city. But this fact poses problems for Marxist class analysis and class-based action (Sinha, 2009: 167–168), *only if* the main or sole concern of class analysis, including the two-class model, is to figure out which individual belongs to which class. But such a fact does not pose any problem for class analysis if the latter is about uncovering class processes and relations, which give rise to classes as large groups of people. Neither is class analysis invalidated by the fact that some people who must depend on the sale of their labor power, called middle class people (e.g. professors, journalists, etc.), are much more educated and earn much more than an average worker, and have a degree of control over their conditions of work. After all, they also operate within the logics of commodity economy and profit-seeking capitalism, and they are also being subjected to proletarianization.

In part responding to the inadequacy of the two-class model, some scholars talk about how a given class has a different experience from another class. To examine this matter is useful but it is still inadequate. Once again, to talk about class should be more about class relation giving rise to large groups of people than about figuring out how many of these large groups exist, which individuals belong to which class, and how they behave.

TABLE 2.1   Class structure in India (percentage share in population)

	1993–94	2004–05
Ruling class	11.89	11.71
Middle class	24.26	21.08
Working class	63.85	67.21

SOURCE: BASU (2009)

As we have seen, many say that there is only partial proletarianization. Not only does that criticism ignore the polarization idea as a class-based tendency. It fails to note that proletarianization is a concept that concerns class, and not a concept that concerns sectors or sub-sectors. Just because a person having lost her/his productive assets in market processes does not work in, say, agriculture but works part-time in the city (as a waitress in a restaurant or as a light-boy in Bollywood), that does not mean that she/he is *partially* proletarianized.

Given all this, it is therefore mistaken to say as many do (e.g. Herring and Agarwala, or Beteille, etc.) that classes are important, but not in the way Marx, or even, Lenin, thought them to be. In other words, what they are saying is that class analysis is not that important because polarization is not happening at the pace predicted or that it is not happening in a given sector (e.g. farming). The criticism that class polarization does not (quite) happen is an age-old criticism against class analysis. During Lenin's time, 'the revisionists were systematically painting a rose-colored picture of modern small-scale production' (Lenin, 1908), and this trend of revisionist thinking, including within some version of Marxism, unfortunately, continues. The criticism against class polarization appears to be from the standpoint of small-scale owners in a class society. Lenin (1908) writes about those who critique the class polarization idea:

> From the political point of view, they sinned by the fact that they inevitably, whether they wanted to or not, invited or urged the peasant to adopt the attitude of a small proprietor (i.e., the attitude of the bourgeoisie) instead of urging him to adopt the point of view of the revolutionary proletarian.

To reiterate a point made above, it is true that the two-class model cannot reflect an empirical reality and that in India, there are peasants of different classes, and there are workers, rent-appropriating landowners, and capitalists. It is also true that while the dominant form of exchange involved in surplus-producing activities is based on equal exchange in the market, there are also coercive unequal exchanges. But none of this invalidates class analysis at all because all those things are parts of class analysis.

3.3   *Is Class Mainly about Dispossession?*

As I have said, a large amount of literature which has something to do with class has focused on dispossession. Much of this literature has been influenced by the highly problematic approach of David Harvey to capitalism and dispossession (Das, 2017b for a theoretical critique). Many of the underlying ideas in this literature are simply flawed. One of them is that: the emphasis on the exploitative relation between property owners and the property-less has been, more or less, replaced by the emphasis on the coercive relations between the dispossessor and the dispossessed.[18] And consequently, analysis of class struggle has more or less become one of anti-dispossession struggles. Some even mistakenly claim that Indian workers are not the most important anti-capitalist agent; it is the farmers fighting against dispossession who are (Levien, 2012). For this claim to be true something else must be true: that capital-labor contradiction is not the main contradiction in India. And *that* is not true.

The literature on dispossession (implicitly) recognizes that class is about differential control over property. This is useful. But what is generally forgotten is that there is a world of difference not only between property for personal use and property for accumulation purpose (Subramanian, 2008) but also between property based on family labor and property based on the exploitation of wage-labor. As well, in this literature, it is as if the main class process is one where the capitalist class is forcing the masses to surrender their physical property (e.g. land).

One must ask: if small-scale producers are allowed to keep their property in a society dominated by capitalist market relations, how long will they be able to hold on to their property, given the class-based differentiation? Much class analysis as dispossession analysis also assumes that there is a capitalism that is imperfect and that needs to be perfected through restrictions on dispossession (see Brass, 2011; and Das, 2017b). A focus on primitive accumulation (along with unfree labor) as coercive aspects of capitalism means that: 'what is on the political agenda is a transition not to socialism but – still – to a "fully-functioning" capitalism' (Brass, 2011: 2).

Just like the class analysis that critiques the polarization thesis, the class-analysis-as-dispossession is, objectively speaking, mounted from the standpoint of small-scale property owners, and not the proletariat. To the extent that the literature on dispossession does raise the issue of class, it does this by ignoring crucial issues concerning class: exploitative production relations.

So: as in the West, so in India, class analysis (and attendant political economy) has really become the analysis of dispossession and anti-dispossession

---

18 In a book that seeks to connect caste to capitalism and globalization, Tumbde (2010) says: globalization is 'the intensified extension of the capitalist project' and that it is 'a phase of capitalism seeking to extend capitalist relations across the world economy' (p. 174). And what is capitalism? It is a process of 'accumulation by dispossession' (p. 32). This mistaken claim reduces capitalism as a class relation to a part of what it is about (dispossession) (Das, 2017b).

struggles at the expense of other aspects of class. The dispossession literature really dispossesses the theory of class of some of its analytical power.

3.4   *Is Class Merely about Economic Inequality?*

Amartya Sen (2006) says 'interest in class as a source of disparity has to be placed within a bigger picture that includes other divisive influences: gender, caste, region, community and so on' (p. 205). The question is: how should we *conceptualize*, and what should we *call*, that 'bigger picture'? If it is inequality (or injustice), or some such thing, there is a real danger of stripping class of its explanatory specificity and power. Class is not just an abstract form of inequality or injustice. What *is* the logic explaining why class is only a part of that bigger picture rather than class being *that* bigger picture? What is it that connects the two groups, or many groups, among whom inequality is said to exist? It is also interesting that Amartya Sen, who insists that the capitalist market relation must unavoidably continue to exist,[19] talks about inequality, as if inequality is not the logical outcome of the capitalist market relation and the processes it is associated with?

3.5   *Is Class Analysis Merely about This or That Issue in the Economic Sphere?*

Ignoring class as a context – class character of state and society – leads many scholars to take not only a quantitative approach to class (identifying multiple classes) but also a 'sectoral' approach to class, which explores a class approach to this or that issue, outside of an overall class-theoretical approach to society as such. For example, Amartya Sen's (2006) idea is that public programs can fight against 'class-based inequality' and can even succeed in 'overcoming class divisions in the economic, social and political progress' (p. 218). Sen assumes that it is only society, or economy, that is class-divided but that the class-neutral state can overcome class divisions in society. Therefore, Sen's view effectively amounts to a rejection of two fundamental principles of class

---

19   Sen (2002) asks: 'can those less-well-off groups get a better deal from globalized economic and social relations without dispensing with the market economy itself?' His answer: 'They certainly can'.

The Nobel laureate then goes on to produce more strident defense of capitalism, which he euphemistically calls the market: 'The central question is not whether to use the market economy. That shallow question is easy to answer, because it is hard to achieve economic prosperity without making extensive use of the opportunities of exchange and specialization that market relations offer. Even though the operation of a given market economy can be significantly defective, there is no way of dispensing with the institution of markets in general as a powerful engine of economic progress' (ibid.).

theory: (a) there cannot be *class equality*,[20] (b) that the lack of effective control over state's coercive and powers is an aspect of classness of the toilers, and (c) that the capitalist state cannot overcome class divisions because its own class nature will, more or less, preordain it to maintain the class divisions. Herring and Agarwala (2006) have useful things to say about class and yet they also believe that old class theory's stress on the material forms of property deflects attention from 'the developmental state in distributing life chances' (p. 348). It is not, of course, outside of class analysis to examine welfare schemes. But they need to be seen in terms of their *class* character: the logic of their origin, implementation and effects is all dominantly shaped by the overall logic of capitalist class relations. Heller's (2000) highly optimistic claims (e.g. pp. 115, 140) about the favourable relation between the state/bureaucracy in Kerala and lower-class struggles, often come close to the view that the capitalist state could operate as an instrument of the lower classes. All these claims are far removed from much of the Marxist debate about class and the state, which has shown among other things, how the structure of the capitalist state and bourgeois democracy, in fact, weaken working class struggle (Das, 1996; Das, 2017a: Chapter 9; Clarke, 1991). If the reification of constraints is theoretically and politically unacceptable, an idealist approach to the enabling conditions is no less so.

Class analysis is about the overall context in which all the different classes operate in their mutual political-economic relation. While Sen sees the ability of the state to help the lower classes in significant ways, others talk about the capitalist class constraining the state (Chibber, 2003). This view is also problematic from the standpoint of class theory: even if the capitalist class does not act, there is the court, there is the army, and there are bourgeois ideas, to keep the class order going. To say that the capitalist class constrains the state is to miss the fundamental fact that the capitalist class and the state are two sides of the same coin, two arms of the same body, which is the class context or the class relation. Class analysis is much more than about how two or more classes behave in their economic interests. Class analysis is about the entire class society, including the class state.

---

20 'As long as there is exploitation there cannot be equality' (Lenin, 1919). More specifically, the capitalist or 'the landowner cannot be the equal of the worker, or the hungry man the equal of the full man' (ibid.). Therefore, class inequality, as a term, cannot have an antonym, which would be class equality.

3.6 *Is Class Not about Property?*

Post-modernists (e.g. Chakrabarti and Cullenberg) think about class only in terms of transfer of fruits of surplus labor (including between family members), and for them, ownership of property or anything else does not count. Their concept of exploitation is deeply a-historical as is their tendency to avoid the question of who owns property in the means of production. Underlying their view of class, is a social-democratic consciousness: the emphasis on surplus extraction means that property ownership of the capitalist class should not be a matter of challenge, and that class struggle is about putting pressure on capitalists so they can share the surplus a bit more with workers (i.e. reduce the rate of surplus appropriation) (for detailed discussion and critique of the postmodernist-Marxist theory of class at a general level, and not in an Indian context, see Das, 2017a: Chapters 3–4).

3.7 *Does the State of Class Politics Suggest a Weakness in Class Analysis?*

Some say that class conflict is only one of many different types of conflict (gender-based conflict, caste conflict, etc.) and therefore has no special significance. Others say that class politics is missing or is not very developed (as indicated by the fact that a small percentage of workers is unionized and that communist parties have only a few Members of the Parliament). So class is not a useful category. Some (e.g. post-modernists) say that there can be no such thing as a class actor as a given class can have multiple identities: in other words, there is no a priori class interest as an objective reality and that one cannot expect workers and other classes to act in their class interests. It is also said that the traditional class analysis is too much focused on work-place politics and that Marx himself had this idea (Herring and Agarwala, 2006).

First of all, it is a profound misinterpretation of Marx when Herring and Aggarwal (2016) say this: 'Marx himself was convinced that the point of production was decisive as a determinant of class formation and collective action' (pp. 347–348). Marx – and Marxist class analysis – has always been for class struggle in different spheres. Marx says that while struggle in a given workplace over wages and working day is more economic in character, the struggle for a legislation that forces all capitalists to reduce the working day, is of a political character, and he encouraged this. Similarly, in an article called 'Political indifferentism', Marx (2010) argued against anyone ('apostles of political indifferentism') who would think that workers should not fight for state spending 'to give primary education' to their children on the ground that 'primary education is not complete education' (p. 327). He was always for workers to fight for reforms, but he also argued that there are significant limits to what is possible to achieve within capitalism (Das, 2019). In India, workers have engaged in struggles in the workplace and struggles outside.

CLASS IN INDIA

Secondly, it is mistaken to deny any connection between political activity and class: political activity *is* prompted by class interests and class relations (including trade union struggle) and this always happens. India regularly experiences trade union struggles (see Chapter 7). And in India, a Maoism-influenced movement of small-scale producers and aboriginal peoples is going on for decades (see Chapters 8–9). So, workers and peasants *do* oppose the system, however inadequately. So class analysis does matter from that angle. Class politics is not missing.

Thirdly, to the extent that class politics is not seen more recurrently and more powerfully, it is once again class (class relations and class processes) that explains it. These mechanisms include the influence of bourgeois class and its state on the ideas that circulate in society, and all the coercive and other reactions to lower-class struggle from the capitalists class and its state (explained in the next section). So class analysis matters here as well. When some say that class politics is not happening, they have a narrow view of class and class politics. Indeed, everything that the capitalist class and its state do to respond to lower-class struggle and/or to pre-empt it, is indeed class struggle – it is class struggle from above. Lower classes in India struggle, but they struggle under conditions which they do not always choose.

There is, generally, an inverse relation between the power of lower classes and that of exploiting/dominant classes. When class struggle from below does not seem to happen, it means that the dominant class is winning in the class battle (however, temporarily), in its struggle from above. Class struggle is always in the form of struggle from below and struggle from above. It is important to re-emphasize this: to say that class is not important, because class struggle does not happen much or it does not happen in the way theory 'predicts', is to forget that class is the reason for that!

3.8 *Is Class Analysis Really about the Local Scale and Everyday Life?*
Some say that old class analysis has a deductivist and macro-view. This not only means that class analysis must focus on agency. It is also to prioritize the need to understand how class works at the local and regional level (e.g. Gujarat). It is important that we understand how class mechanisms are played out at the local level. But an emphasis on the local scale can potentially ignore the fact that the regional/national scale is not given, that it is not a class-neutral thing: it is created and reproduced by the capitalist class relation. Capitalism produces uneven development whereby some areas are more developed than others, and it is the context in which multiple scales (national, regional, etc.) exist, and this production of scales and unevenness is a precondition for different class mechanisms operating differently in different ways. So the fact that different mechanisms operate in different areas is not indicative of the

44 CHAPTER 2

autonomy of processes at the local scale vis-à-vis the capitalist class relation. So uncovering how class mechanisms work at the local/regional scale presupposes uncovering how that scale is produced via tendencies towards capitalist uneven development.

4 Constructing a Class-Based Framework

In the light of my criticisms against the criticisms of class analysis and my criticisms against certain ways in which class analysis has been conducted, what is attempted below is a very basic outline of what class analysis should be. It, of course, partially, builds on existing ideas about class that are defensible.

4.1 *Class as a Relation/Process Producing Large Groups of People*

In class analysis, it *is* important to talk about individual classes and their mutual differences. I have indicated the existence of much existing research on this topic. I might mention here the excellent work done by Basu (2009). Building on Vakulabharanam et al. (2009), Basu (2009) comes up with the following class-map. Ruling classes are the owners or managers of the formal and informal sector enterprises and the rich farmers. The working class is composed of the unskilled workers in manufacturing and services, the small and marginal peasants and the landless laborers. And finally, what Basu calls the middle class consists of two main segments: '(a) the petty bourgeoisie, who largely own their means of production: middle peasants in agriculture, the merchants, the traders, and the owner-operators of small enterprises, and (b) the professionals: the technical experts, the managers, and the skilled workers in large-scale private enterprises, and the large majority of the employees of the State sector'. Basically, according to Basu, the middle class consists of professionals and skilled workers in manufacturing and services, middle peasants, rural professionals, and moneylenders.[21] Whether one agrees that everyone in

---

21 Conceptually, the 'middle class' is defined by Basu (2014) by the following two characteristics: '(1) this class is the recipient of a part of the economic surplus, i.e., the total compensation earned by the middle-class is higher than the value of its labour power (i.e., the cost of producing and reproducing the labour power); and (2) the middle class is crucial for the reproduction of the existing social relations in India which is what fetches it the extra income', i.e., the income above the value of its labour power, in the form of rent from the ruling classes. There are two main segments of the middle class: (a) the petty bourgeoisie, who largely own their means of production: middle peasants in agriculture, the merchants, the traders, and the owner-operators of small enterprises, and (b) the professionals: the technical experts, the managers, and the skilled workers in large-scale private enterprises, and the large majority of the employees of the State sector.

CLASS IN INDIA

the middle class position receives more than the value of their labor power, one can get at least a rough overview of the class structure of India from Basu's class analysis.

However, the examination of how many classes exist, what their relative size is, how different groups within the working class (or another class) experience life differently, or how workers live in poorer conditions than rich property owners, must be a part of a larger consideration in which the emphasis should be given to the fact that there is class as a relationship and as a complex set of processes operating at multiple levels of society (see below), that affects politics, economy and culture and how we relate to nature and to one another. It is *that* relationship that underlies how classes, class-fractions and individuals of specific classes of different modes of production including capitalism, as well as state agencies and state elites, function or do not function and how they exercise their agency or how they do not or how they seem not to.

To repeat: class *is* a *relationship* and a *process*. Or, it is a structure of – sum total of – relationships among classes, and processes connecting them. What one class is, it is because of its relations to other classes.[22] Class analysis is about the overall context in which all the different classes operate in their mutual relation. It is about:

> *the sum total* of the relations between absolutely all the classes in a given society, and consequently a consideration of the objective stage of development reached by that society and of the relations between it and other societies.
>
> LENIN, 1914; italics added

Class as a relationship and as a process are materialized – expressed in the form of – large groups of men, women and children called classes. As Lenin (1919) famously said:

> Classes are large groups of people differing from each other by the place they occupy in a historically determined system of social production, by their relation (in most cases fixed and formulated in law) to the means of production, by their role in the social organisation of labor, and, consequently, by the dimensions of the share of social wealth of which they dispose and the mode of acquiring it. Classes are groups of people one of

---

22   A given class, and a system of classes, stands for, and is, a relationship, in the same way that not only is capital related to labor, but also is capital a relationship itself. In one meaning of relationship, X and Y are related, and in another meaning of relationship, X itself and Y itself is a relationship (see Ollman, 2003).

which can appropriate the labor of another owing to the different places they occupy in a definite system of social economy.

The relations between classes, as large groups of people, sets up certain mechanisms (e.g. competition, technological change, exploitation, etc.) which produce certain effects (e.g. unemployment, massive accumulation of wealth, etc.) which are experienced by an entire class, its fractions and individuals of given classes.

To say that class has effects is to say, for example, that class relations enable and constrain the condition for economic development and redistribution of the social product, with implications for poverty. As Marx himself maintained, and as many Marxists have argued since, class relations can fetter or further the development of productive forces: class shapes both incentive and ability to accumulate.

4.2 Class Exists at Multiple Levels and Operates in Both Abstract and Concrete Ways

If class is a set of relationships, these relationships are necessary or contingent, and they exist at multiple levels of generality (e.g. all class society vs capitalism), and can have multiple forms. In other words, class – the system of classes – is very *complex*, and its various elements are inter-connected, so we should examine it by employing various methods of abstraction.[23] One method is to abstract necessary from contingent relations, within an overall perspective of internal relation.[24] In understanding how a given class, or a system of classes, functions, certain things/processes are seen as (more or less) necessary and others as (more or less) contingent: it is necessary that a capitalist will hire and exploit a worker but whether that worker is a male or a female or a Dalit or Brahmin is contingent. That means that: hiring a worker is an essential part of what being a capitalist is about, but hiring a Dalit worker or a female worker is not so. It is possible that a worker hired is a Dalit women, but it is not necessary that a capitalist, to be a capitalist, must hire a Dalit woman. This is the case even if hiring Dalit women can make an enormous difference, at a concrete level, to the way a capitalist makes money.

---

23   While concentrating on a particular aspect, we need to abstract from other aspects, making sure that the abstraction is not chaotic (that we do not separate – abstract – X from Y while they cannot be separated, or we do not put together X and Y where there is no necessary reason to).

24   Such an abstraction must indeed happen within the overall perspective of internal relation which says that X is what it is because of its relations to Y, Z, etc. and that therefore one must start with the social totality (e.g. totality of class society) constituted by relationships.

CLASS IN INDIA

Embedded in the distinction between the necessary and the contingent is another distinction: between the abstract and the concrete. Something that is more concrete is a form of development – or a form of existence – of something that is more abstract. As a category, the worker is more abstract relative to the category of male worker or industrial worker.[25] Of course, this does not mean that an abstract thing (e.g. worker) is less real than something that is more concrete (a worker in a capitalist banks), or even that an abstract thing (worker) does not exist relative to an informally employed worker or an indigenous female worker or an industrial worker.[26] It is mistaken to believe that an abstract thing (worker) does not exist but an informally employed worker or an indigenous female worker does.[27] In *theorizing* class, i.e. in saying what the conditions of class are (e.g. how its development is associated with the development productive forces and the accumulation of surplus product), how the class system works (its mechanisms) and what effects it produces, more or less, irrespective of a time or a place, it is the *necessary* relations involving classes that matter. But in understanding a concrete situation in which classes function, in a given time and place, both necessary and contingent relations need to be combined – that is, the concrete situation must be seen in the light of the abstract relations. A fundamental implication for class analysis is this: understanding social oppression based on relations such as caste and gender is crucial to the understanding of how class works concretely, but class is *not* constituted by social oppression.[28] Another implication is that: in what sectors

---

25   The distinctions between the abstract and the concrete, and between the necessary and the contingent are to be understood in a relative sense, and not in an absolute sense (for example, a category is more or less abstract; what is necessary now can be contingent later in part due to changes in human practice).

26   Much misconception in class analysis is based on a mis-construal of the distinctions of the type mentioned above: if workers are not employed in industry (as in advanced countries), then, some think, the worker does not exist, and class analysis is not important, while others think that unless one talks about informally employed workers or female workers, one cannot legitimately talk about class analysis.

27   In the mode of abstraction in which the necessary is abstracted from the concrete, there are two sub-methods. One is more 'theoretical' in nature, which reflects real historical development: abstracting direct producer from the worker as a direct producer. The second one is the more empirical type of abstraction: one abstracts a worker from a female worker, and the latter from a female worker in capitalist mining. Both types of abstraction are necessary (while I consider the first type to be analytically superior), but we need to bear in mind their differences (cf. Cox, 2013). The theoretical sub-method of abstraction connects to the abstraction of the level of generality (see below).

28   One can, of course, make general statements about how class – or, capitalism – is affected by caste and argue that Indian capitalism is casteist capitalism, but then here, one is no longer theorizing capitalism-as-such, but a more concrete form of capitalism. The question of what is *capitalism itself* is different from the question of what is *capitalism as it*

workers work or what kind of use-values workers produce, does not define workers' *class* status.

In another method of abstraction, and as already alluded to, class must be analyzed at multiple levels: history of class society, capitalism-as-class-society, capitalism at a specific stage of capitalist development, and capitalism in India (see Das, 2017a: Chapter 5). At this level, some class processes (e.g. those that are talked about in a two-class model) are more abstract than other class processes (those that are talked about when one arrives at a concrete map of all the classes). We should also examine capitalism (or capitalism in India) in terms of its specific forms: neoliberalism or state-directed; domestic market oriented or export-oriented, agrarian capitalism and capitalism outside of agriculture, urban and rural capitalism (urbanization of capital and ruralization of capital, in the sense of spatial concentration of capital in cities and transplantation of capital in villages, respectively), and so on. Capitalism-as-class (content) and its specific forms need to be combined.

4.3 Capitalism as Class

At the level of capitalism as a level of class analysis, it is important to examine class relation between capital and labor in the two-class model. The two-class model represents class mechanisms at a more abstract level, and it points to the relations that define capitalism (Das, 2017a: Chapter 7). These relations between workers and capitalists are not only the relations of exchange: the capitalist has a lot more command over exchange relations than the working class does, and has the ability to buy labor power which is sold by the working class only when the capitalist class needs it to make money off the labor power. The relations between workers and capitalists are also relations of property (one class controls means of production, and expands their control through on-going dispossession of small-scale producers, and another class does not), and relations of production, value and surplus value, that underlie the exploitation of the people who have no property or very insignificant amounts of property relative to their reproductive needs. These relations create positions in the structure of capitalism-as-class, the positions which are filled by human practices and individuals.[29] Class analysis at this level must

---

works in a concrete situation by deploying relations such as caste, etc. Once again, the more abstract aspects of capitalism are no less real than the more concrete aspects.

29   It is important to emphasize how these positions are filled by practices signified by class relation and class process: a *given person* may mainly rely on performing wage-labor as a *process*, in a *relationship* to the capitalist, but may also engage in the process of small-scale production, in a relationship to large-scale property owners (e.g. bankers; landlords, merchants, etc.), to supplement her income. If class is seen as a relation and a process,

CLASS IN INDIA

figure out how different classes experience benefits of economic development, or respond to fascistic movement, differently. But a prior question to address is: what is the class logic of capitalist economic development, or what is the class logic of the fascistic movement, as such? Focusing on the class relation – the relation between interests of property owners and property-less toilers (workers and small-scale self-employed producers) – makes sure that we remain focused on this fact: wealth in its capitalist form (that we see and read about in newspapers and government documents and watch on TV), is, ultimately, a product of the labor of these toilers. This issue is prior to the issue of how the wealth/income is concentrated in the hands of a few (e.g. monopoly capitalists) and how wealth/income can be distributed more equally through (less neoliberal) government intervention, etc. The capitalist wealth is, fundamentally, the form that appropriation of surplus value from wage-labor takes, and it is also partly the wealth that has been taken away from small-scale producers through coercive and market-based mechanisms and converted into the capitalist form of wealth. Capitalist wealth exists because a tiny minority of people have control over productive resources (i.e. over property based in exploitation of labor), and because of the dispossession of small-scale producers by capitalists and their state. This is the case, more or less.[30] The majority of people lack control over means of production and how they are used; they lack control over the fruits of their labor; they lack effective control over their property based in their family labor, i.e. their own private property, because they can lose it through market-based class differentiation (see below). All these class

---

then the class position of a worker is to be seen as being filled, primarily, by the content of the relation/process that is an essential part of being worker-class, and secondarily by certain individuals. Such a distinction is necessary as long as a part of the labor that workers perform is not wage-labor, and this happens in part because given certain *class* processes – increasing precarity and the on-going tendency for wages to fall below the value of labor power – those with no property or with insignificant amount of property are forced to engage in some form of non-wage-labor; and some of them even may not perform any kind of labor. Once again, figuring out which individual belongs to the class of worker must be seen as only a part of the larger analytical process of determining the nature of the class position defined as a relationship and as a process.

30   I say 'more or less' because a part of the capitalist wealth is because of the contribution of capitalists as workers: many capitalists (e.g. Mukesh Ambani; Narayana Murthy, etc.) are highly educated (in engineering, management, etc.) and they do perform certain useful functions as highly educated people would in any society, but their personal contribution to their wealth seen as imputed wages is an extremely small part of the total amount of wealth each of them possesses. Nearly all of their wealth exists because it is a form of surplus value, and because they have taken away non-capitalist forms of property (peasants' property and the commons).

mechanisms are enforced by the political arm of the capitalist class, the class state, the state of the capitalist class, irrespective of the parties in power.

Whether capitalism is in its lower, and more general form, or in its higher and more developed form (Chapter 3), whether in its neoliberal or state-directed form (Chapter 4), whether it is based on technological change or not (Chapter 5), whether it is export-oriented or not (Chapter 6), and so on, the fundamental aim of capitalism as a class relation (or the fundamental aim of the capitalist class) is to make profit by exploiting ordinary people (and, where necessary, by dispossessing small-scale owners), and not to satisfy the needs of the masses who lack effective control over society's property and how it is used. This is partly why the interests of capital protected by the state and interests of workers who have little effective control over the state, are incompatible. This fact underlies, in however mediated a manner, major political conflicts and struggles.

4.4 The Two-Class Model, the Tendency for the Class Polarization to Happen, and Counter-tendencies in the Capitalist Society

Mapping out the different classes belongs to a different level of abstraction than the two class model. In a society dominated by private property and relations of commodity production and the logic of value, existing independent commodity producers will be over time differentiated into different kinds of classes. There is a tendency for the class polarization to happen: I will call this TCPH. In rural or urban areas, a very small percentage of all commodity producers will have the ability to exploit the labor power of others, and others will have to, more or less, sell their labor power. In a capitalist society, generally speaking, given the need for commodity owners to sell commodities competitively, if one cannot produce at a cost that is more or less the social average, one is liable to go into debt, and in clearing the debt, one may have to sell off some of the assets that one owns. Consider how many millions of farmers in India, most of them are small-scale producers, are leaving cultivation (on their own property or rented property) to join the class of part-time or full-time workers either in farming or outside of farming: 2035 are leaving farming every day since 1991, as they cannot pay their bills. That's 15 million since 1991 (when neoliberalism formally began). *This* is in line with the class theory including TCPH.

One should hear what Lenin (1899) has to say about class differentiation: 'Undoubtedly, the emergence of property inequality is the starting-point of the whole process [of differentiation], but the process is not at all confined to property "differentiation."' (Lenin, 1899: para 5). The class of property owners does not only differentiate; it also gets dissolved; it ceases to exist (ibid.). This class is ousted by absolutely new types of property owners, 'types that are the

CLASS IN INDIA

basis of a society in which commodity economy and capitalist production prevail'. These types are: a class of property owners, with varying amount of property, who employ wage-laborers, and a class of wage-laborers. In the process, a class of proletarians is produced from the 'class' of independent producers (Lenin, 1899).

Perhaps, Lenin was overzealous to attack those (the populists of his time) who were saying that capitalism was not developing in Russia? Consider then these lines from Lenin written in 1908.

> The technical and commercial superiority of large-scale *production* over small-scale production not only in industry, but also in agriculture, is proved by irrefutable facts. ...Small-scale production maintains itself on the ruins of natural economy by constant worsening of diet, by chronic starvation, by lengthening of the working day, by deterioration in the quality and the care of cattle, in a word, by the very methods whereby handicraft production maintained itself against capitalist manufacture. Every advance in science and technology inevitably and relentlessly undermines the foundations of small-scale production in capitalist society; and it is the task of socialist political economy to investigate this process in all its forms, often complicated and intricate, and to demonstrate to the small producer the impossibility of his holding his own under capitalism, the hopelessness of peasant farming under capitalism, and the necessity for the peasant to adopt the standpoint of the proletarian.

Lenin wrote these lines almost 10 years *after* he completed his *Development of Capitalism in Russia*, which means that he continued to take the class polarization/differentiation idea very seriously.

However, like all tendencies such as the tendency of the rate of profit to fall (TRPF), the TCPH can not only be hastened by certain mechanisms (e.g. globalization of capitalism) but also countered by many mechanisms: self-exploitation (not paying oneself the imputed full value of the labor power per hour), use of remittance money from a family member working as a wage-earner in the city, part-time work in the city or the village (as proletarians or semi-proletarians), and welfare benefits from the capitalist state which seeks to, among other things, calm the anger of the lower classes. But then all these counter-mechanisms, including government welfare, are also *class-based* mechanisms as they primarily concern the totality of all class relations. The mechanisms of TCPH are always modified in their working 'by many circumstances, the analysis of which does not concern us here', i.e. theory cannot do justice to these circumstances (Marx, 1977: 798).

There are two implications of the fact of 'incomplete class differentiation'. One is that all members of a subordinate class do not have to be completely property-less for the capitalist class relation to exist: the capitalist class relation needs only a sufficient amount of wage-labor for the production of surplus value. The other implication is political: 'it would be a profound mistake to think that the "complete" proletarianisation of the majority of the population is essential for bringing about ...a [proletarian] revolution' (Lenin, 1977a: 56). This view is in direct contrast to all those (e.g. Utsa Patnaik, Henry Bernstein, etc.) who think that incomplete polarization is a barrier to class politics. The barrier, much rather, lies in the specific strategy that the communist movement and allied left intellectuals deploy, to organize subordinate classes (see Chapter 3).

4.5 Capitalism as a System of Relations of Accumulation by Class Differentiation, Accumulation by Dispossession, and Accumulation by Exploitation

Capitalist class relations are about property relations (monopolization over property by a few) and not just about exploitative relation between capital and labor, so the dispossession of small-scale producers as a class mechanism must be a crucial aspect of class analysis of India. The surplus value appropriated from wage-earners is converted into capitalist wealth that they see but do not enjoy, and that the capitalists and governments brag about as being a product of their hard work and good policies respectively. And, direct producers (e.g. small-scale producers) are coercively separated from means of production and are then converted into the capitalist form of wealth. Besides: when the capitalist state neglects areas where small-scale producers and wage workers live, by not investing in the physical infrastructure because it needs to meet the financial needs of big business, the value of property in those areas declines and income-earning ability of direct producers is also reduced. This contributes to the low price at which small-scale property owners may – and may have to – sell their property.[31] To understand capitalism as a specific form of class in our times is therefore to see capitalism in terms of a dialectical articulation of: 'accumulation by dispossession' (in the specific sense of dispossession of small scale producers and privatization of society's commons including common

---

31 Vijayabaskar and Menon (2018) say, rightly, that land grabs occur less due to coercive action by the state and more due to the state underinvesting in agriculture, resulting in dispossession by neglect of those who are economically vulnerable (people with tiny amount of asset), and this process means that the boundary between the coercive and voluntary land grabs could be fluid in certain cases.

CLASS IN INDIA

land and state-owned wealth), accumulation by class differentiation, and accumulation by class exploitation (which is expressed as multiple forms of subsumption, as discussed in Chapter 3). The last is the predominant form of the triad.

4.6 Classes and Class-Fractions Have Common and Different Interests

A class can have *some* common interests, at a point in time, with another class. For example, both workers and capitalists benefit from anti-feudal struggles and both, generally speaking, and within limits, may benefit more from a high rate of economic development than from a very low rate or from recession, and both benefit from a better environment or from a social atmosphere where there is respect for democratic rights and for civility, than not. But the two classes are more different from one another than they are similar in terms of material interest: their interests are antagonistic much more than they are harmonious. Capitalists appropriate the fruit of labor from workers, and capitalists can abandon their support for democratic rights and even resort to – or support – fascistic tendencies when it is in their economic-political interests *as capitalists*, as they do in India now. This means that not only does class analysis say that workers and capitalists are the two main classes in a society where wealth is in the form of capitalist commodities, and that class is the most important cause of the problems that the toiling masses, the majority-class, experience because their life is subordinated to the exploiting class. Class analysis also says that the interest of the majority-class (the exploited) and the minority class (exploiters) are, ultimately, incompatible, and therefore, class relations must be abolished.

Those whom capital exploits belong to different classes (classes of peasants; workers, etc.). But there are also important intra-class differences. These are not only social-cultural differences as just mentioned (e.g. Dalit worker vs Brahmin worker) but also economic differences in terms of income, job security, working conditions, etc. Recently, many scholars have stressed the difference between workers in the informal sector and those in the formal sector. This *is* a crucial difference to make,[32] but one should see this difference, as all differences, dialectically, i.e. in relation to their common ground. There are

---

32 In fact, the discussion on the difference between formal sector and informal sector workers can be enriched by pointing to the difference in terms of labor freedom, and this is not generally done. Consider the excellent point made by Brass (2000: 134) in his critique of Jan Breman's approach: 'the most common production relation encountered in the informal sector of India must be unfree labour which, when combined with the additional process of formal sector contraction coupled with informal sector expansion, permits only one conclusion: ... work in the formal sector, and with it free labour, is being

differences *and* common grounds between the two types of workers, at the level of (a) relations of property, production and value (they are all, more or less, property-less and are subjected to the appropriation of surplus value in commodity production, although some are exploited more than others, and they engage in production of different kinds of use-values) and (b) relations of exchange (while all workers rely on the sale of labor power, their wages vary). [33]

4.7 *Changes over Time and over Space, in the System of Classes*
The system – the totality – of classes, and the dynamics of each class, are not static. They undergo changes over time:

> all classes ... are regarded, not statistically, but dynamically – i.e., not in a state of immobility – but in motion (whose laws are determined by the economic conditions of existence of each class).
> Ibid.

Some workers who used to be formally employed could be in the informal sector, and this fact should pose no problems for class analysis. A class that began as a mercantile class can become an industrial class. A peasant can become a proletarian. And the effects of class relations also change over space. The rate of exploitation – and indeed, conditions of existence of each class – may vary from one place to another, within limits, in part because of the ways in which the general mechanisms of capitalism as a class society interact with place-specific mechanisms. And the historical and geographical changes may not be linear: a peasant who has gone to the city to work as a laborer may return to the village to cultivate her land. Or a peasant who has lost her land and has become a laborer may gain some of it.[34] Changes in the class system can be gradual: a situation of passivity may change to one where there is some trade union consciousness at least. It can be more drastic: big political movements can happen when there is a widely prevalent consciousness that interests of capitalists and interests of workers are fundamentally incompatible.

---

    replaced with employment in the informal sector, where unfree working relations prevail. In other words, a process of deproletarianization'.

33   The average daily wage in the informal sector is approximately $2 while that in the formal sector is approximately $3.5, so there is a difference, but the wages of both types of workers are poverty-level wages – they fall below the value of labor power. Besides, increasingly, even those who are in the formal sector are subjected to fixed term contracts which we will talk about in a later chapter.

34   She can do this by using her remittance from a relative in the city or from dowry received for her son, or from a government scheme of land redistribution.

4.8 Non-class Relations within Class Relations

At a general level, class is about the relations between classes, and that capital does not worry about whether a worker is a male or a low-caste person. To say that the life of a low-caste female worker in Delhi is shaped more by class relations than by caste and gender relations, does not, however, mean any moral evaluation of non-class identities.[35] Primacy of class does not mean that women's issues are subordinated to issues that concern men, that a man's life and words are more important than a women. *Not at all.* Indeed, class analysis says that a society which does not treat its women (and children), and one should add, all the hitherto-oppressed groups such as Dalits and indigenous groups, with respect, and which does not meet their material needs, is a society with which there is something terribly wrong.

At a more concrete level, the reality is a little different, because here the effects of class relations, and capitalist class relations, deeply impact, and are impacted by relations of caste and gender, and so on.[36] And how a given class actually functions (reproduction of its conditions of existence) in a given time and a place depends on its relation to non-class relations (e.g. caste and gender): a Dalit worker is class-exploited by land owners/capitalists and caste-oppressed by non-Dalit higher castes. A Brahmin worker may live better than a low-caste worker.

At the level of Indian capitalism, low caste, female Muslim capitalists will not generally behave differently, in any fundamental sense, from their upper caste and Hindu and male counterparts, given the logic of capitalism. Capitalists are and will be capitalists. What an individual capitalist or a group of capitalists does, as a part of the class of capitalists and as a part of the totality of capitalist society, reflects the logic of the functioning of that class as a whole, and it must reflect that totality of the capitalist society as a whole, more or less. They have to be capitalists, given the logic of competition and given the law of value, operating at multiple geographical scales, including the global.

---

35 'To assert the priority of a class analysis is not to claim that a worker is more important than a homemaker, or even that the worker primarily thinks of herself as a worker' (Foley, 2018: 273).

36 Mohanty (2004) makes these useful remarks: 'In studying the interface of class, caste and gender we recognize the centrality of class, especially in the context of the modern history of capitalism where *it is the most powerful force* with a worldwide drive shaping human relationships *in all sectors of society.* This, however, does not in any way reduce the centrality of caste and gender *in particular contexts and spheres of action.* ...In my view, capitalism as a class system is such a powerful, all-encompassing process in the contemporary world that all other categories despite their autonomy and specificity are forced to reckon with it.... This is not to say that caste and gender are not autonomous categories' (pp. 24–25).

Caste and gender relations define some individuals and groups belonging to the class of workers as second-class citizens (as oppressed groups). These groups do not enjoy the full democratic rights that, say, upper-caste, male workers ordinarily enjoy. As a result, these oppressed groups of workers can be exploited more than others by the property-owning class: the value of their labor power could be driven below the value of labor power in society as a whole, and/or their wages could fall below the social average, leading to their *super*-exploitation (i.e. above-average magnitude of exploitation). The oppressed groups' control over their family-based property could be much more tenuous than others'.[37] Their power to resist exploitation and curtailment of democratic rights is restricted. And, the ability of the *entire* class of workers to resist exploitation and curtailment of democratic rights is adversely impacted because they are divided on the basis of gender or caste or religion.[38] Indeed, the anger of some workers (or small-scale producers) is channeled along the lines of caste or gender or religion, and when this happens, some people come to believe that the chief cause of their problems is the caste structure or gender or religious difference, so they politically conduct themselves accordingly – i.e. they engage in what is merely politics of recognition (politics of respect and solidarity with some, and politics of hatred against others).[39]

---

37 Consider the fate of residential property and small-scale business-property of Muslims in certain areas (see Mitra and Ray, 2014). The dispossession of property of people from socially oppressed categories (e.g. Muslims) is not un-connected to the property interests of capitalists of non-oppressed groups.

38 One might say that when a Hindu hates a Muslim or when a Brahmin oppresses a Dalit, the former may enjoy some symbolic value from such oppression, by 'othering' the Dalit or the Muslim, by making the latter look inferior, that such oppression brings a sense of cultural and political superiority to the oppressor. But the question is: what social-material conditions have put value on such symbolic value on social oppression and allow one group to be powerful by curtailing the democratic rights of another group, which is what oppression is about? It is important to uncover what people think and how that thinking shapes their cultural and political behavior. But it is also important to explain the social-material mechanisms behind that thinking. Why is oppression necessary and why is it possible is the question?.

39 Habib (2014), one of India's most well-known historians, rightly says: 'while "class" is a category based on the mode of surplus extraction, ...its reality is obscured....by modes of social gradations' of various kinds ....[which originate in pre-capitalist societies and which] could also survive changes in modes of production...'. Habib continues: 'caste [as a kind of social gradation] has to be seen historically, as not only a divisive social force, but also a mechanism of class exploitation that, by denying status and mobility to the lowest elements of society, reduces labour costs, and facilitates and increases extraction of surplus. The main beneficiary of the caste system must then be not so much the Brahmins, as the ruling classes – whatever be their religion and the prevailing mode of surplus extraction' (pp. 205–206).

CLASS IN INDIA

Of course, none of what is said above means the following: if a Brahmin landlord makes a Dalit worker drink cow urine because the latter dared to challenge the landlord or if a Hindu fanatic lynches a Muslim for exercising his choice of eating beef, then the immediate – proximate – material cause is necessarily some material class interest at the site of oppression. The same goes for a non-Dalit worker oppressing a Dalit worker. There is a reason for this. Firstly, the logic of social oppression is rooted in class mechanisms at the societal level, and not at the individual level.[40] Secondly, the *material practice* of the deployment of social oppression by class relations creates certain *ideas* about the socially oppressed in relation to the oppressor. These ideas travel in space and time. While certain ideas about social oppression may be reflective of caste or gender or religious oppression at the time when such oppression began to emerge, these ideas still stay on, even if the exact social-material conditions which gave rise to those ideas do not exist. The ideas about social oppression also travel beyond the site – or even logic – of class exploitation, and appears to be detached from any class basis, in a concrete situation, so such ideas enter into the common-sense of people, both exploited and exploiting. This partly explains why Dalit workers are oppressed by non-Dalit workers.[41]

The existence of women and low-castes, especially, Dalits, as underprivileged sections within the proletariat (and semi-proletarian masses), is a matter of interest to the proletariat as a whole: it can never emancipate itself from exploitation and domination by capital and capitalist state, while parts of it (i.e. the male part, the high-caste part, the majority-religion part) continue to

---

40 This is akin to the fact that: the main logic of exploitation of a worker (Dalit or not) by a capitalist (Brahmin or not) is not rooted in the workplace owned by that capitalist. That logic only works itself out at the workplace in concrete ways. What the capitalist does must be, more or less, within the limits of the law of value: there is a logic according to which all commodity producers must produce at least at the social value. The value of a commodity produced in a given workplace is not determined by the conditions of production in *that* workplace (by the time needed to produce the commodity in that workplace). The value of the commodity from a given workplace is still the social value. But a capitalist can make use of social oppression either to bridge the gap between the overly high individual value and the social value of the commoddities produced, or even to produce her commodity at below the social value, in which case an extra amount of surplus value is made by that person.

41 It is also the case that an illusory notion of belonginess works among the people who are both exploited and oppressed: non-Dalit workers who are exploited by the Brahmin or middle-caste property owners might identify themselves with their exploiters against Dalit workers/peasants, and such a feeling of belonginess could function as an illusory – ideological – compensation – to offset the effect of their own exploitation by high-caste exploiters. The above does not deny the importance of the fact that upper-caste property owners make a concerted attempt to divide the exploited class on the basis of caste.

oppress other parts (i.e. women workers, low-caste workers, minority-religion workers).[42]

4.9   Ideas, Class Politics, and Objective Conditions in Class Society

Within a system of classes, different classes have different kinds of ideas about themselves and about other classes and about the system of classes, and these ideas/concepts interact with objective conditions (e.g. employment, economic development, rate of profit declining/increasing). But ultimately the objective conditions have a primacy over the ideas. Ultimately, ideas of the exploiting propertied classes have more power vis-à-vis the ideas of subordinate classes as long as the former classes control the means of production.

Class is not just an economic but also a political concept. Class relations, as social relations as such, are relations of contradiction. This is expressed in the fact that class relations are relations of exploitation and relations involving differential control over property and production, which is why the reproduction (or dissolution) occurs as a result of class struggle, which may happen covertly or overtly, whose intensity and expression vary over time and space. Class struggle takes multiple forms (as discussed in Chapter 7). Class struggle depends on class formation (formation of collectivity of groups as a class) and class consciousness (consciousness of the fact that different classes have different interests, at the level of exchange relations, and production and property relations). The latter process is in turn enabled/constrained by the structure of class relations, along with the labor process on which the class structure is based. Consider, for example, how changes in class structure or class differentiation – which is partly enabled by state policies – can affect class struggle.[43] Class mechanisms – exploitation and dispossession, etc. – and their effects prompt class struggle. But there are also class mechanisms that can impede class struggle.

It has been shown that class relations influence how well – and how differently – women, men and children from different classes live. However, 'It is much more demanding to expect class – or any notion of social structure – to predict or explain politics that drive policy' as Herring and Agarwala (2006: 331) rightly note. And that is because there is an objective situation on the

---

42   These lines are based on my paraphrase of a few lines from Sathyamurthy (1999: 39) (and on Marx's statement that 'Labor in the white skin can never free itself as long as labor in the black skin is branded').

43   When property-less people receive some means of production through a government program as a product of prior struggle, they can become petty bourgeois and find more in common with the capitalist class than with labor.

CLASS IN INDIA

ground that is demanding (difficult), which explains why, for example, the subordinate classes face various difficulties in their struggle. For a start, while winning over the hearts and minds is important in any struggle, class-based organizations receive little 'media attention relative to the exploding array of "grassroots organizations"' (ibid.: 329). The dominant class strata in India control media and other means of modes of dissemination of ideas, as they control means of material production as well as the state. And there is also ideological coercion (censorship) against the practice of progressive ideas, and especially, against Marxism itself (see Das, 2012b, 2013a), which *is* a body of scholarly work and which seeks to both understand class relations and class consciousness and contribute towards the further development of class consciousness.[44]

Class politics of subordinate classes is hindered because class formation in the face of the fragmentation of workers and small-scale producers is difficult: as noted earlier, the ruling class and its agencies make use of discourses around caste, etc. to fragment class consciousness, so the masses start engaging in caste-based or religious-sectarian conflicts, instead of fighting as a class against class exploitation, dispossession, as well as social oppression of various forms. Besides, resources are lacking to establish and support class-organizations. The business class and the state are not going to support these, given their own class character. As well, when established, many workers' organizations are influenced by the capitalist context in which they operate: ideas reflecting bourgeois politics of workers and various reformist ideas as well as bureaucratic practices of working class leaders influence the effectivity of workers' organizations. One such organization is a party. As Herring (2013) rightly says: whether a worker or a poor peasant votes for a communist party depends on the presence of such a party and how freely it can operate, but if the political system operates in such a way that political mobilization aimed at significant redistribution is not possible, which is increasingly the case under neoliberalism, then common voters vote on the basis of non-class criteria such as caste, religion, region, etc. Besides, class-based mobilization invites the ruling class repression. A communist party seeks to mobilize votes partly on the basis of extra-electoral resistance against property owners and state. But: 'The obstacles to mobilization along class lines involve serious risk of detention and

---

44 In an article originally written in 1981, Beteille (2000), one of the most progressive liberal-minded non-Marxist scholars of India, laments the attacks on Marxism: 'the current attacks are ...an indication of ...a large and as yet unexplored reservoir of intolerance in India of any serious critique of society'. And attacks on Marxism/Marxists have reached unprecedented level in the recent times with the rise of the fascistic movement.

death: under these circumstances it is not surprising that a class project faces daunting odds' (Herring, 2013: 134).

When the capitalist state sends police and paramilitary forces to repress progressive movements or when it implements economic policies on behalf of the ruling class or when it protects private property rights of capital while taking away such rights from small-scale producers in villages and cities, or when it allows the capitalist class to take away much of what the workers produce (appropriation of surplus value), all this *is* class struggle, pure and simple. This is class struggle from above. What the association/institutions of capitalists (e.g. FICCI, CII) do to lobby the governments, including for labor reforms (to allow capitalists to hire and fire at will), or when they threaten not to invest because they wish to see a more favorable business climate,[45] or when they provide election funding to bourgeois parties while doing everything possible to stop workers' unions from operating, that *is* class struggle. When the ruling class and its political agents (right-wing movements and governments) engage in fascistic politics aiming to destroy democratic rights and progressive organizations of workers and peasants, that *is* class struggle from above. Just as mechanisms and counter-mechanisms in the proletarianization thesis (TCPH) are both class mechanisms, the mechanisms that promote class politics and the mechanisms that impede class politics, are both *class* mechanisms.

Class analysis is about the context in which different classes exist, a context in which the state of the dominant class (the main exploiting class) manages the commons affairs of this class. Alienation from state's coercive power is a fundamental attribute of classness of the exploited classes. Whatever else the state is, its primary job is to protect class relations, including capitalist property relations and the right of capitalists to hire and fire and to exploit and to dispossess, at the cost of satisfying the needs of the masses and by crushing their hard-fought democratic rights. If there is so much inequality and if there is so much dispossession, and if the vast majority cannot meet their basic needs, why is it that the state cannot dispossess the small minority (top 0.1–1%, or at best top 10%) and put the resources under the democratic control of the masses who can then use these resources to produce the things that they need in order to satisfy their material and cultural needs? This fundamental question is asked and answered only in the Marxist class analysis.

Class – class relations and processes – explains class politics, in ways that are more or less mediated, whether it is the politics of the right or of the left, and it also explains why politics takes non-class forms (e.g. clientelism,

---

45   On the functioning of business associations in India, see Bandyopadhyay (2000).

CLASS IN INDIA

populism, etc.).[46] Herring correctly notes that class explains why non-class forms of politics happens.[47] Class relations govern, and set limit within which, non-class politics works (see Chapters 8–9 and 10–13).

5 Conclusion

Class analysis identifies classes, their relations, and the implications of the latter for a wide variety of processes (e.g. economic development, political power, etc.). Class analysis is doubly important: not only does it tell us what society is like at a given moment (class as a structure of relations among multiple classes and class-fractions), but it also sheds light on how society is changing (class as a contradictory process).

Scholars have raised various objections to Marxist class analysis of India. For example, they say that class analysis is mistaken to assign primacy to class as a social relation over other relations, and to assume that class polarization leading to proletarianization will happen. I have tried to theoretically counter these objections. In spite of these objections, there is a tradition of class analysis of India. It deals with a set of inter-related themes: it explores how the Indian society is differentiated into not two classes but a multiplicity of classes, how, for example, the informally employed workers engage in struggle outside of production, how the effects of class 'intersect' with the non-class relations of caste and gender, etc. There has been also much discussion on the dispossession of the small-scale producers class. While appreciating the merits of some of the existing literature on class in India, I have also made a series of criticisms of this literature. Class cannot be treated as one of several social relations; it has analytical primacy. But, once again, that does not imply any moral valuation of social groups: i.e. that does not mean that a woman (or a Dalit) is inferior to a worker. I critically consider the skepticism about the two-class model and

---

46   In many areas, the existence of a substantial self-employed peasantry and a mass of small agrarian capitalists makes the ideological gulf separating workers and exploiters less apparent. For this reason, this is potentially a fertile ground for the emergence of populism ('we are basically all the same') which frequently blunts the edges of class struggle (see Brass, 1999: 266).

47   Herring says that 'The effects of class on politics that are not readily observable as proximate causes, but enable and limit conditions for other forms of political behavior, are difficult to access and account for' and these other forms of political behavior include: quiescence, clientelism, populism, a social movement (Herring, 2013: 129). He says that 'class analysis is compatible with forms of theorizing politics that take for granted structural inequalities' (p. 135).

about the class polarization thesis. Class analysis should be much more than about inequality or injustice and about dispossession. Class analysis is not to be seen as merely figuring out how many classes there are and which individual is in which class. Nor is class analysis anything if it is not about the class character of society *as a whole* and of the state's fundamental class-role: examination of class nature of this or that topic must be situated within the overall class context of society and of the state. It is also mistaken to think that class politics is not happening and therefore class analysis is not relevant. If class politics is not happening in the way it should, the reasons lie in class itself. I then go on to briefly outline some of the aspects of class analysis as I see it.

Class should be seen in its material conditions, in terms of relations between classes, and at a concrete level, in terms of the relations between classes and non-class relations such as caste, gender and religion. We need to have a conception of the structure of class relations (system of classes), and of the contradictions between classes and within a given class, and in terms of how the system is changing, sometimes slowly and sometimes not so slowly, on the basis of various forms of class struggle which coexist with non-class struggles.

Class relations, including specific forms of capitalism as a class relation, and a given level of economic development are combined, and this combination has an effect on political (and cultural) matters which in turn shape class relations and economic development. But ultimately, it is class relations with their impact on the development of productive forces, that have the primacy, over, for example, matters concerning the political (e.g. state actions; political struggles, etc.).

Class analysis must be about the overall context in which all the different classes operate, first at the level of capitalism and then at the level of Indian society as a whole, in their mutual relation. It is about *the sum total* of the relations between all the classes. It is at a more concrete level, where class relations and capitalist class relations deeply impact caste and gender, etc. relations which, in turn, impact the effects of how class relations work.

It *is* important to talk about individual classes. However, the examination of how many classes exist and how different groups within the working class experience life differently must be a part of a larger consideration in which the emphasis should be given to the fact that there is class as a relationship (with its contradictions), that affects politics, economic development and culture and how we relate to nature and to one another. It is *that* relationship that underlies how classes and class-fractions and individuals of specific classes, as well as state agencies and state elites, function or do not function, and how they exercise their agency or how they do not. The class analysis concerns the *entire* society, including the state. The class perspective on India (and other

CLASS IN INDIA

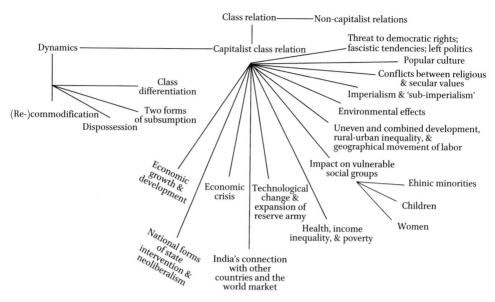

FIGURE 2.1   A partial map of what to study in India from a class perspective
SOURCE: AUTHOR

countries) can prompt theoretically rigorous and empirically-corroborated research on a wide variety of topics. Figure 2.1 is a map of some of these.

Only some of the topics that appear on the map are dealt with in this book: nature of India's capitalism as a form of class society; nature of neoliberalism with Indian traits; technological change in relation to direct producers; production for the world market and a dual metabolic rift and implications for workers of different oppressed categories; the social character the capitalist state in relation to dominant and subordinate classes; lower-class struggles, and fascistic tendencies as a ruling class response to capitalist crisis, in relation to Left politics.

CHAPTER 3

The Capitalist Character of Class Society in Post-colonial India: Moving Beyond the Mode of Production Debate

As in many other countries in the global periphery, overall labor productivity per hour in India remains very low (see Figure 3.1).[1] It was approximately one-tenth of that of the USA in 2015.[2] Both in rural and urban areas, producers/entrepreneurs, generally, work with relatively rudimentary technologies. In rural India, where most people live, millions of people still cultivate land with wooden ploughs or with their improvised versions. The nature of the economic development process in most parts of India, and especially, in the countryside, does not appear to support Marx and Engels's (1848) optimism in *The Communist Manifesto* that the bourgeoisie (or the capitalist mode of production led by this class) constantly revolutionizes the mode of production.[3] Perhaps, his comments were relevant to the place and the time in which they lived, but not to the India (and similar other countries) of today?

If capitalism revolutionizes the development of productive forces, and yet if labor productivity per hour is still so low, then could it be that India is not (dominantly) a capitalist country? Conversely, if India *is* a capitalist country, why does it have such a low level of labor productivity? Indeed, the question of whether or not India is a capitalist country proper and the question of what the barriers are to its further development, if capitalism does exist, are not yet settled. This fact potentially supports Ellen Wood's point that 'there is no general agreement about the meaning of capitalism or its basic dynamics' (Wood, 2007: 145, 159).

The remainder of the chapter, which is a continuation of the previous chapter, is divided into nine sections. Beginning the chapter with the famous Indian

---

1 An earlier version of this chapter appeared as Das (2012c).
2 Labor productivity (GDP per person employed per hour, PPP dollars in 2015) was 6.46 in India and was 59.77 in the USA, according to World Competitiveness Yearbook, 2015 (quoted in GOI, 2015).
3 'The bourgeoisie cannot exist without constantly revolutionising the instruments of production, and thereby the relations of production, and with them the whole relations of society. ...Constant revolutionising of production, uninterrupted disturbance of all social conditions, everlasting uncertainty and agitation distinguish the bourgeois epoch from all earlier ones' (Marx and Engels, 1948).

© KONINKLIJKE BRILL NV, LEIDEN, 2020 | DOI:10.1163/9789004415560_004

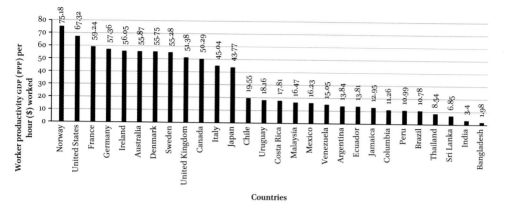

FIGURE 3.1 Worker Productivity GDP (PPP) per hour ($) worked (2013): Selected rich and poor countries
SOURCE: HTTPS://EN.WIKIPEDIA.ORG/WIKI/LIST_OF_COUNTRIES_BY_GDP_(PPP)_PER_HOUR_WORKED

mode of production debate (henceforward, Indian MOP debate), I discuss, in Section 1, how certain scholars working on India define capitalism in general and in the Indian context (including in Indian agriculture). In Section 2, I critique some of the most influential ideas in the debate. In Section 3, I present an alternative framework for understanding capitalism in general and capitalism in the context of the less developed countries such as India. In doing so I build on Marx's discussion in *Capital* volume 1 on formal, hybrid and real subsumptions of labor, a discussion that is often neglected or misinterpreted. I argue that capitalism can exist when formal subsumption prevails. I also argue that the transition to real subsumption, with attendant technological change, can be a very long process, and, that *notwithstanding* Marx's optimistic view about 'spontaneous' transition to real subsumption, it is anything but spontaneous. That transition is mediated by the changing balance of power of capital and labor (class struggle), which occurs in a context of a whole host of geographically-specific factors such as capitalist state interventions. In the next two sections (Sections 4–5), I provide some empirical discussion to corroborate my argument about the relation between class struggle and the transition from formal subsumption. Thus, in Section 4, I discuss how class struggle can prompt real subsumption though not in any unilinear, straightforward, way, and in Section 5, I show how property owners can respond to class struggle against formal subsumption by way of *reinforcing* formal subsumption and/or introducing hybrid subsumption (exploitation based on mercantile-usury-rental extraction). In Section 6, I discuss why there are technical reasons for a transition to real subsumption (for example, in the industrial sector) but why there

66   CHAPTER 3

are limits to such a transition, within the context of peripheral capitalism. In the following section, I critically reflect on Jairus Banaji's (and others') view of subsumption, which was an important part of the mode of production debate, and argue that his views are mistaken. I contrast his views to what I think are Marx's views which I defend and deploy. In the conclusion I summarize the discussion and draw its implications for understanding uneven and combined development, and for political practice.

1   **The Development of Capitalist Relations, and the Barriers to This: A Brief Discussion on the Indian Mode of Production Debate**

In the 1960s and 1970s, the Indian MOP debate took place, which is now known internationally. This debate discussed, among other things, the extent of development of capitalist relations and the barriers to this.[4] I do not want to review this debate in any great detail, as it has been reviewed earlier (see Bidwai, 2015: 353–365; Nadkarni, 1991; Thorner, 1982). Rather, my aim is to develop a critique of some selective parts of this debate, and based on my critique, to address the question of the nature of capitalism in India.[5]

A mode of production is an articulated combination of forces of production (technological development; organization of the labor process) and relations of production (class relations). One mode of production (e.g. capitalism) is different from another (e.g. slavery or feudalism) in terms of the nature of class relations – the actual ways in which surplus labor/product is pumped out of direct producers – and also in terms of the logic and the extent of the development of productive forces based on the deployment of the surplus.

---

4   The Indian debate that mainly took place in the pages of *Economic and Political Weekly* and *Social Scientist,* 'built on' and is a part of, a global debate on the nature of, and the transition to, capitalism. The first of these took place in the 1950s in *Science & Society*; published since 1936 (this is, incidentally, the longest continuously published journal of Marxist scholarship in the world). In this debate stalwarts such as Maurice Dobb, Christopher Hill, Rodney Hilton, Eric Hobsbawm, Paul Sweezy, Kohachiro Takahshi, and others participated. Their work was later reprinted in Hilton (1978). It should be noted that Sweezy (1986) revisited the debate in a *Science & Society* article. The *Science & Society* debate was followed by another debate, known as the Brenner debate, on the issue of the transition. Originally published in 1976 in the influential and progressive British journal, *Past and Present*, the set of articles that constituted the Brenner debate was published in Aston and Philipin (1985). Examining the nature of capitalism – capitalism in general or capitalism in the specific historical-geographical context – constitutes an on-going intellectual task at the international scale, one to which scholars from India as well as those from Europe, North America and other regions of the world continue to contribute. Some of this work will be referenced in this chapter.
5   In this chapter, the term 'development' means development of productive forces (technological change and attendant increase in productivity of land and labor).

CAPITALIST CHARACTER OF CLASS SOCIETY IN POST-COLONIAL INDIA 67

Of several issues discussed in the MOP debate in India, the following were important from the standpoint of this chapter: how to identify the capitalist mode of production, how widespread it was and what were the barriers to the development of capitalist relations. These questions were important not only to the period when the debate took place but also to the current period, and not only for India but also for other parts of the (less developed) world.

While it is widely held that nominally free wage labor is necessary for capitalism to exist, according to Patnaik (1990a: 41), many freely hired laborers in India, however, are not actually free. This is in the sense that the employer of these laborers 'does not appropriate surplus value from free laborers; he [or she] maximizes the returns from exploiting the destitute labor tied to agriculture and with no other employment opportunities' (1972a: 22). And, for her, being tied to agriculture because of lack of alternative employment opportunities is analogous to serfs being tied to feudal lords.[6] This system of exploitation cannot be called feudal, but by default, it cannot be called capitalist either, she says. *Even* if wage laborers are free, she argues, free wage labor by itself, though a necessary, is not a sufficient condition for capitalism, because labor employers must also produce for the market. This is her second criterion for identifying capitalism. Yet, capitalism needs more than this for its existence. She says that 'Production for the market must not ... be confused with capitalist production: the former antedates the latter and though necessary, is not sufficient for its development' (1990a: 44).[7] Thus neither production for the market, nor wage labor, is a sufficient condition for capitalism. She identifies the third necessary criterion of capitalism in India: 'accumulation and reinvestment of surplus value [in modern equipment] in order to generate more surplus value' (1990a: 44). Elsewhere she says 'If the holding [i.e. a landowner] employing

---

6   This is similar to Chandra's (1974) argument that enormous rural unemployment or rural labor surplus is perpetuating the semi-feudal set-up.

7   Patnaik clarifies that: unlike Western Europe: 'India was forced to enter the network of world capitalist exchange relations; its pre-capitalist economy was broken up and a fair section of the peasantry was pauperized into landlessness' (1990c: 93–94). Unlike in Western Europe, this landless labor force was not absorbed in industry as there was none. If the surplus could have been reinvested in Indian industry the latter could have absorbed the rural labor force and provided impetus for capitalist agriculture by expanding markets for agricultural products. But the surplus was transferred to Britain instead. As a result, commodity production 'led to an inordinate development of capital in the sphere of exchange, to a prolonged disintegration of pre-capitalist mode without its reconstitution on a capitalist basis' (ibid.). Exploitation took the forms of rack-renting (leasing out land at very high rents) and usury rather than appropriation of surplus value from wage laborers. This continues till today although to a less extent than before. Because employment of wage labor does not necessarily encourage productive investment in equipment, etc., that has to be added to the definition of capitalism in countries such as India.

wage labor does not reinvest and expand, lower production costs and try to move up on the scale of competitive efficiency, then where is the element of dynamism which marks off this so-called 'capitalist' enterprise ... from other exploitative relations such as the landlord-tenant one?' (ibid.: 91). For Patnaik, because employment of wage labor does not necessarily encourage productive investment in modern equipment, etc. to increase efficiency, as in Western Europe, that has to be added to the definition of capitalism as a separate criterion, in countries such as India. In other words, as Chattopadhyay (1990b) said: she has two different definitions of capitalism for two different geographical contexts. The question is: does she distinguish between capitalism in general and capitalism in its Indian form? It is not clear that she does.

As if to 'echo' Patnaik, Rudra (Rudra et al., 1990) says that: a capitalist has to, among other things, simultaneously: produce things for the *market* for a *profit* by *employing wage labor*, and make wage-payments *in cash*; and invest in *modern equipment*. Unless a property owner satisfies all these criteria, they are not capitalist. Patnaik and Rudra disagree with each other *empirically* on whether and the extent to which capitalism existed in the 1960s,[8] but their *conceptual* views of capitalism are actually more similar than different.[9]

For Bhaduri (1983), capitalism requires free labor in Marx's senses. However, to the extent that labor owns some means of production and that people cannot freely sell their labor power, capitalism does not exist. Banaji does not think that free wage-labor is a defining attribute of capitalism. He (more or less) accepts a definition of capitalism in terms of 'the laws of motion of capitalist production' which include: 'the production and accumulation of surplus-value,

---

8   Patnaik says that capitalism does not appear in a pure form and that it coexists with precapitalist relations and that Rudra was ignoring this.

9   In his study of the Punjab in 1969, Rudra (Rudra et al., 1990) did not find much capitalism there that satisfies his three criteria: 'there was not yet the emergence of any class, how-ever small, of full-fledged capitalist farmers', as he recalled later (Rudra, 1983: 421). Neither did he say that there was feudalism or semi-feudalism. He subscribed to a 'Neither capitalist nor feudal (or semi-feudal) ... position' (ibid.).

In his later (mid-1970s) study of West Bengal, he said this: 'If generation of surplus through the employment of wage labor, appropriation of that surplus by the owners of capital and reinvestment of that surplus for the purpose of expansion of that capital be a characteristic feature of capitalism, then there are indeed increasing manifestations of such capitalist feature in West Bengal agriculture' (Rudra, 1974; also 1978). Describing this research of his, he said: 'my rejection of the emergence of a full-fledged capitalist class was not in any way in contradiction with my later argument that 'there are increasing manifestations of characteristic features of capitalism', which...co-exist with continuing manifestations of characteristic features of pre- capitalist relations' (Rudra, 1983: 421).

the revolutionisation of the labor-process, the production of relative surplus-value on the basis of a capitalistically-constituted labor-process, the compulsion to increase the productivity of labor, etc. The 'relations of capitalist production' are the relations which 'express and realise these laws of motion at different levels of the social process of production' (Banaji, 2013: 60; italics added). Capitalism is whatever form of social relation of production allows these laws of motion to exist, for him. It is sufficient to note that revolutionization of productive forces is a part of the definition of capitalism for Banaji, so his definition is close to Patnaik's and Rudra's, to some extent. We will return to Banaji to see how his views are also different from Patnaik's and Rudra's and are problematic.

We might briefly add here the view of the so-called post-modernist Marxists who have commented on the mode of production debate in more recent times. These scholars reject the concept of mode of production altogether. For them, the question of whether a country is capitalist or not is a wrong question. They say that the criteria of commodity production and wage labor, let alone property relations, do not define capitalism. Capitalism – like any society – has to be defined in terms of relations of exploitation understood as performance, appropriation, distribution and receipt of surplus labor and that 'relations of exploitation [are] ... the constitutive factor in the definition of capitalism' (Chakrabarti and Cullenberg, 2003: 60–61, 65). They also argue that: 'households are sites of surplus generation', that 'most of the household enterprises are noncapitalist' and that 'The characterization of the Indian mode of production as "capitalist" immediately collapses with the inclusion of household class processes' and that Indian mode of production cannot be called semi-feudal either because 'the household class process could be independent or communal' (Chakrabarti and Cullenberg, 2003: 75–76).

Returning to the original debate, if capitalism does not exist – or if it exists in a limited manner, in a few areas – *why* is this the case? Two sets of barriers have been highlighted by scholars. Amit Bhaduri says that the semi-feudal social relations act as a fetter on the development of productive forces under capitalism, and therefore, by implication, on the development of capitalism itself. Semi-feudalism that characterizes Indian social formation has more in common with classic feudalism of the master-serf type than with industrial capitalism (1973: 120; also Prasad, 1990). It has four characteristics in the agrarian context: share-cropping; the perpetual indebtedness of small tenants; existence of two modes of exploitation, namely usury and land-ownership in the hands of the same class (land owners lending money to their tenants at very high interest rates), and lack of accessibility to the market for the poor tenants (the latter 'surrender' their product to the landlord-creditors) (Bhaduri, 1973:

120–121). The last criterion refers to forced commerce as a form of primitive accumulation: because of their poverty, peasants are forced to sell their produce just after harvest when the foodgrain price is lower, and buy back foodgrains at a higher cost at a later time when the foodgrain price is higher. This purchase and sale of products is forced because peasants cannot enter the market when they wish to and cannot freely buy and sell at the market price. This has implication for the development of productive forces. The practice of usury and the appropriation of the surplus product through rent will require that the available balance of paddy with the tenant must always fall short of her family's consumption requirements. So investment in land by landlords might increase the income of tenants, and with increased income, they will not have to borrow from the landlords. As a result, landlords' usury business will be adversely affected. So they have no incentive to invest in land to improve productivity – or more generally, landlords do not have an incentive to cultivate their land by hiring laborers and investing in land to increase productivity.

While for Bhaduri, it is mainly usury – the unequal relation between debtors and creditors – that is the barrier to development of capitalism, for Patnaik (1983; 1972a) and others, it is mainly tenancy or rental extraction – the unequal relation of production between landlords and tenants – that acts as a barrier. Her argument on this topic begins with nature of capitalist rent, which is the rent that represents a surplus of produce (surplus product) *after* all cultivation cost and a normal rate of profit to the cultivator (or the entrepreneur) have been met. We can express her view like this: $R_c = T–C–P$. Where: R_c = capitalist rent, T = total product, C = cost of production, including imputed wage for family labor, and P = profit.

She says that those who lease in property in Indian countryside (tenants) are not paying capitalist ground rent. Instead, they are paying *pre-capitalist* ground rent. This is simply because after paying the high level of rent, tenants do not enjoy the profit part (P) of the total product (P = 0). So: $R_p = T–C$, where R_p is the pre-capitalist ground rent.

The level of this rent (R_p) is very high – 50% of the gross produce for most of the tenants. Tenants can pay such a high level of rent because they can depress consumption per family labor unit for the sake of the minimum secure income ensured by the possession of land through lease (Patnaik, 1972a: 21). In other words, the imputed wage part of the cost of production tends to be extremely low.

Given that the level of rent is very high, tenants do not have any capacity to invest because little is left with them after they pay their rent. In fact, this is a point that Daniel Thorner also made (Thorner, 1969: 332). According to

Thorner,[10] there is a built-in depressor in the form of legal, economic and social relations in a context characterized by unequal landownership, the reliance of the common villagers on usurious loans, landlord domination over direct producers as tenants, and landowners appropriating high profit through trading. All this depresses the tendency towards technological change: landowners can make money through usury, rent and trade so they have little incentive to invest in increasing productivity, and peasants, deprived of any surplus, have little ability to invest either.[11]

Building on Daniel Thorner's work, Patnaik (1986) further explains how the rent-barrier allows only a limited development of capitalist relations. If the members of the property-owning class are to switch to capitalist production from merely buying up assets (e.g. land) and leasing it out, they will have to invest a certain amount of money which already gets them a return any way (in the form of usurious interest, and in the form of rent from the land that someone with money can buy up and lease out). So the person renting out her land to peasants will switch to what Patnaik calls *capitalist* production if the rate of profit becomes at least equal to the sum of: (a) the rate of return from leasing out (i.e. the rental income as a percentage of expenditures in cultivation by the tenant) and (b) the rate of return on money-capital invested in non-agricultural activities (e.g. usury). Such a rate of profit is very high. This is impossible to get unless the investment embodies productivity-raising new techniques, or better ways of organizing production, which raise surplus per unit area by the required quantum. 'A *quantum-jump* is required for the rent barrier to be overcome, so that investible funds are directed into capitalist agriculture' (Patnaik, 1986: 782; stress added). Unlike in the case of peasant capitalism (the American or French path to capitalism), a *small or gradual improvement* in productivity is not sufficient to make landlords invest money to make more money (p. 786; stress added) and become capitalists proper.

Bhaduri and Patnaik thus show that the development of capitalism in India is constrained, at least in the vast rural areas where most people live. Thus it is the social relations of usury or rental extraction from direct producers that fetter the development of productive forces under capitalism. Although from the surface their arguments appear to be different, I will argue, and *pace* Patnaik (1995: 91), that their theories of fetters on productive forces – usury or the rent-barrier – presuppose one common factor, that is, unequal distribution of means of production (land). It is the unequal distribution of land which allows the landowners to (a) engage in usury, because landless and land-poor people

---

10 According to Rudra (1983), the MOP debate was inspired by Thorner's work.
11 On 'the depressor theory', see Harriss (1992, 2013).

need loans (the semi-feudalism thesis of Bhaduri) and (b) rack-rent these people, for they need and compete for land-on-lease (the rent-barrier thesis of Patnaik).[12]

2 A Critique of Some Influential Ideas in the Indian Mode of Production Debate

My critique revolves around the economic and extra-economic coercion in economic transaction, and the nature of the relationship between capitalism and technological change. I accept Patnaik's point that market relations *per se* are not to be conflated with capitalist mode of production – indeed this point has been made in the discussion on the European transition to capitalism by Robert Brenner (1977) and by Ellen Wood (1997). Patnaik goes on to claim, problematically in my view, that the landowner-employer does not appropriate surplus value from free laborers but maximizes the returns from exploiting the destitute labor tied to agriculture. For her, being tied to agriculture owing to the lack of alternative employment opportunities is analogous to serfs being tied to feudal lords. Clearly, Patnaik fails to maintain the distinction between economic and extra-economic (un)freedom of direct producers. If laborers can freely choose their capitalist employers, they are said to have freedom (i.e. there is no extra-economic coercion/unfreedom), although they are not free *not* to choose any employer because they are dispossessed of their own means of production. Laborers are free in 'the double sense that they neither form part of the means of production themselves, as would be the case with slaves, serfs, etc., nor do they own the means of production, as would be the case with self-employed peasant proprietors' (Marx, 1977: 874). It is difficult to accept Patnaik's logic that if people, who are dispossessed of their means of production, cannot find alternative employment outside of a given sector, then these people would never constitute a 'proletariat' in that sector (1995: 82).

I find problematic Patnaik's concept of free labor, a concept (and its opposite, unfree-labor), which has been a subject of much discussion.[13] I will make two arguments briefly. Firstly, the conceptual definition of wage labor concerns her *causal powers* (e.g. she can choose his/her employer) and *causal liabilities* (e.g. she has to depend mainly on wage-work for her subsistence)

---

12 Interestingly, unequal land distribution is considered a given, without it being considered *in relation to* capitalist development in the country, including the penetration of market relations (i.e. Leninist class differentiation).

13 See: Banaji, 2003; Bhandari, 2008; Brass, 1999, 2011, 2012; 2017; Breman, 2010; Lerche 2013; and Rao, 1999. See Das, 2013c for a comradely discussion of Brass's excellent work, that is in fundamental agreement with Brass.

arising out of her structural (= class) conditions (i.e. she has been stripped of the means of production). So, an essential aspect of capitalist production relation is free labor in the sense Marx defines it: it does not have access to any/ sufficient means of production which is why it is economically forced to seek wage-work (so it is freed from means of production),[14] and it is free to sell its labor power to whichever employer it wants to, although it is (generally speaking) not free not to sell labor power at all.

Secondly, and with respect to the second aspect of freedom (being able to freely enter and exit a labor contract), in certain conditions, employers transform what is hitherto free labor into unfree labor, as Brass has been forcefully arguing for decades. Employers employ various strategies (e.g. locking up workers in a place) to stop them from running away. It should be added that while Patnaik fails to distinguish between economic and extra-economic forms of unfree labor, Banaji thinks that the free and unfree labor distinction is fictional: that whether labor is economically free is not an essential aspect of capitalism. Although Marx stipulated free labor as a necessary characteristic of capitalism, as mentioned earlier, the history of actual capitalist societies does indicate that specific capitals do make use of various forms of unfree labor – where labor's right to freely enter and exit the labor market has been taken away by capital, making it difficult for labor to exercise the right to negotiate wages.

Just as Patnaik fails to adequately distinguish between economic and extra-economic forms of labor, Bhaduri fails to distinguish between economic and extra-economic coercion that small-scale direct producers – peasants – experience. He conflates forced commerce with extra-economic coercion: he abstracts from the fact that no extra-economic coercion is imposed on peasants to freely enter and exit the market. What he calls forced commerce is an economic transaction, and any element of coercion is economic in character. It is also not clear why it is that: a property owner leasing their property to a (small-scale) direct producer for a rent is not compatible with capitalism, and more specifically, why it indicates *extra*-economic coercion. How is this different from a property owner leasing in or out a building in the city? (While Patnaik does not view the rental payments by peasants as extra-economic, she sees this as *pre*-capitalist, so for both Patnaik and Bhaduri, the rental payments by peasants are pre-capitalist). As well, Bhaduri fails to explain why property owners

---

14   It is interesting to note what Gerald Cohen (1978) argued: in some cases, unless proletarians own some instruments, (e.g. a spade), they may not be hired, so ownership/possession of some means of production becomes a defining aspect of – a necessary condition for – proletarian-hood. In my view, it is possible that: asking workers to bring their own tools is a way of a) reducing the necessary investment on constant capital and thus the cost of production, and b) recruiting suitable workers (if one has a spade, it is more likely than not that one knows how to use it).

cannot do the following: promote investment in technological change, increase the total net product, and increase the rent, and thus benefit from technological change (Bardhan, 1983).[15]

Let me now deal with the second part of my critique to set the context for my alternative view. This concerns the question of whether generalized commodity production is the necessary and sufficient condition for capitalism or whether an additional criterion of surplus reinvestment *in productivity-raising techniques* has to be specified, which is what Patnaik thinks should be the case.[16]

The idea that technological change in production can raise the rate of profit, attract capital and thus promote capitalism implies that the development of productive forces in itself can result in a change in production relations or class relations. It is as if whether or not capitalism exists is a matter of what individuals are able to choose do (i.e. choose to obtain higher profit in production rather than from another way of making money such as renting out means of production or money lending). Mere opportunities to make money whether by using a new technology or by producing a large volume of a commodity for an external market in itself will not result in a change in class relations to capitalism. The essence of capitalism is not a higher level of development of productive forces. That is generally, but not always or everywhere, a consequence of its essence. Capitalism is fundamentally a class relation.

Chattopadhyay, one of Patnaik's main protagonists, rightly argues that commodity production and wage-labor are necessary and sufficient conditions for capitalism. He correctly says that 'Accumulation and reinvestment of surplus value fall within this definition and need not be stated separately as far as the definition of capitalism is concerned' (1990a: 82). But he mistakenly seems to assume that the *production* of surplus value *necessarily* generates its productive *reinvestment* in technological change: 'The very process of commodity production with the sale of labor power as its ultimate form generates the process of surplus value and its reinvestment...' in technological change (1990a: 82). He argues that the use of sophisticated technical equipment indicates only a higher level of capitalist development, not the capitalist development itself (1990a:

---

15   From an empirical angle, Rudra found no significant differences in the input – output patterns of owner-operated farms and tenant-operated farms, especially when one examines medium and large-sized farms (Chakravarty and Rudra, 1973).

16   For her, if a property owner employing labor does not reinvest profit and expand the enterprise and lower production, then the element of dynamism that characterizes capitalism vis-à-vis pre-capitalism is absent, so there is no capitalism. In other words, she implies that there is nothing in between landlord-tenant relations and relations of a dynamic capitalism. Her view also implies that in the conceptualization of capitalism, productive forces have primacy over production relations or class relations.

82; see also Ram, 1972: 54). This is true, and this is in line with Lenin's point that 'Hired labour is the chief sign and indicator capitalism' (cf. Bukharin, 1933) but the question, not resolved by Chattopadhyay, is this: under what condition will reinvestment of surplus value in technology happen? Why indeed may the surplus value be produced in agriculture under capital-labor relations not necessarily be invested in agriculture to raise productivity of labor? Chattopadhyay's assumption – as Lenin's – appears to be that relations between capital and labor will automatically give rise to technological change. While the Patnaik-Bhaduri type argument seems to deal with the distinction *between* capitalism and its 'other' (pre- or non-capitalism), the Chattopadhyay type argument seems not to bother with any distinction *within* capitalism itself (i.e. between different forms of capitalism itself). On the other hand, post-modernist Marxists think that the very question of whether a country is capitalist or not is a wrong question, a position that is based on a problematic theory of class itself (for a longer critical discussion of their approach, see Das, 2017a: Chapter 4).

A problematic corollary of the conception of capitalism employed by the likes of Patnaik and Bhaduri is this: to the extent that capitalism exists, in whatever sense and to whatever extent, the development of productive forces is retarded mainly/solely by factors (e.g. unequal distribution of land) that are *external* to the logic of capitalism. It is true that the rental extraction combined with usurious 'exploitation' may dominate the labor process in *specific places* within a social formation (and can act as a barrier to capitalist development in the sense that Patnaik and Bhaduri, etc. have discussed). This will not be surprising in the context of a large and geographically diverse country such as India. But the fact of local conditions cannot be used to determine the mode of production and associated *dynamics* (= rules of the game; causal powers and liabilities of property owners and direct producers) at the *national* scale, which is where the concept of mode of production properly belongs, given the connection between class relations and power of the state that is concentrated at the national scale.[17] I will have more to say about the so-called semi-feudal processes later. While the rent and usury barriers may be important at the local scale (in specific localities), it is mistaken to think that these are the main barriers at the national scale. Can the barrier to capitalist development not inhere *capitalist* class relation: can the specific nature of capitalist class relation that exists not be a barrier to the further development of productive forces under

---

17   More adequately, given the tendency of the logic of capitalism to operate at the global scale, the concept of the capitalist mode of production belongs to both the national scale and the international scale but one cannot lose sight of how, in a country that is dominantly capitalist, non-capitalist relations can exist, and articulate with, capitalism at the sub-national scales.

capitalism, in the absence of strong counter-vailing forces (e.g. state policies)? Related to all this is the question of class struggle: what significance does actual/potential struggle of direct producers have for the logic of the capitalist mode of production?

3 Examining India's Capitalist Character on the Basis of Marx's Distinction between Formal and Real Subsumptions of Labor

I suggest that one solution to the problem surrounding characterization of capitalism and the examination of the fetters on the development of productive forces under capitalism, could be achieved by the deployment of Marx's concepts of formal and real subsumption (subordination) of labor under capital, the concepts that signify the importance Marx himself attached to the forms of integration of labor into capitalist production process at the different stages *within* the history of capitalist class relation (Das, 2011, 2017a: Chapter 8).[18] Marx, the historical-materialist, says that capitalist production is differentiated into two forms/stages: the formal subsumption of labor under capital and the real subsumption of labor under capital. Marx also introduces a third form of subsumption as we will see.

Capitalism is based on wage-labor on a large-scale (not sporadically). No wage-labor, no capitalism. In the initial stage of capitalism, wage-labor is only formally subsumed under capital: capital takes over a pre-existing labor process (e.g. a farm/factory existing under pre-capitalist relations) without 'revolutionizing' the labor process (Marx, 1977: 1021). In this stage, capital 'subordinates [subsumes] labor on the basis of the technical conditions within which labor has been carried on up to that point in history' (Marx, 1977: 425). It does not change the socio-technical conditions of production. The necessary part of the working day (necessary labor) – the labor time that the worker expends for producing the equivalent of her own means of subsistence – cannot be generally decreased during the early stage of capitalism, so the only way more surplus value can be produced within a capitalist country is by increasing the other part of the working day (i.e. surplus labor time). This is done by making workers work longer and/or intensifying the pace of labor process (this is also done by depressing wages below the value of labor power, although Marx generally abstracted from the fact that wages fall below the value of labor

---

18   These concepts are present in the middle of *Capital* volume 1 and in the Appendix to it, called 'Results of the Immediate Process of Production' written between 1863 and 1866. This discussion suffered from its delayed publication and relative neglect as a consequence.

CAPITALIST CHARACTER OF CLASS SOCIETY IN POST-COLONIAL INDIA 77

power).[19] During the stage of formal subsumption of labor under capital, absolute surplus value is produced.

Based on Marx's own discussion (1977: 1025–1029), it is possible to identify four main features of formal subsumption of labor in a more systematic way than he did.

1. the absence of extra-economic coercion in the sphere of production: that is, wage-laborers, who do not own (sufficient amount of) means of production and are therefore economically forced to work for a wage, are generally free to choose their employers;

2. no more labor time is consumed in production than is socially necessary (i.e. there is competition to reduce the cost of production of commodities for sale, and this means that the law of value has started operating);

3. the means of production and consumption confront the worker as capital in the sense that they have to be bought in the market;

4. an *economic* relation of supremacy and subordination exists as the worker is supervised and directed by the capitalist.

Formal subsumption of labor is the most general form of capitalism. It need not be associated with pre-modern or non-modern: it 'was no less effective in the old-fashioned bakeries than in the modern cotton factories' (Marx, 1977: 425). Formal subsumption:

> it is at the same time directly a process of the exploitation of the labor of others. [...] It is the general form of any capitalist production process [i.e. production process under the rule of capitalist social relation]; and at the same time, however, it is a *particular* form alongside the *specifically capitalist* mode of production in its developed form [i.e. the real subsumption], because although the latter entails the former, the converse does not necessarily obtain.
>
> MARX, 1977: 1019; parenthesis added

Real subsumption has all the four characteristics of formal subsumption mentioned above. In addition, it involves the reduction of necessary labor time through an increase in labor productivity, through the use of technology, per unit of time and therefore the appropriation of surplus value in its relative form. This happens under what Marx called in his 'Results' the specifically capitalist mode of production. And when this happens, the ratio of constant capital to variable capital tends to increase (Marx, 1977: 762). Of course,

---

19 Marx assumes the wage to cover the means of subsistence. Let's say that the daily wage that covers the cost of maintenance is $10 for 8 hours. If the wage is reduced to $5, this effectively means a working day of 16 hours, other things constant.

technological change has to be such that the time taken to produce workers' means of subsistence is reduced. So, for example, technological change in food production and in the production of means of production of food (e.g. tractors) matters with respect to the production of relative surplus value. Technological change in a systemic manner in various branches of production contributes to technological change that ultimately helps capital appropriate surplus value in its relative form at a societal level.

In addition to the two forms of subsumption, Marx (1977: 645) also mentions in the middle of *Capital* volume 1, what he might call 'hybrid subsumption':

> It will be sufficient if we merely refer to certain *hybrid forms*, in which although surplus-labor is not extorted by direct compulsion from the producer [that is, there is no feudalism or pre-capitalist relation], the producer *has not yet become formally subordinate* to capital. In these forms, capital has not yet acquired a direct control of the labor process. Alongside the independent producers, who carry on their handicrafts or their agriculture in the inherited, traditional way, there steps the usurer or merchant, with his usurer's capital or merchant's capital, which feeds on them like a parasite. (parenthesis added)

Marx adds: 'The predominance of this form of exploitation in a society excludes the capitalist mode of production' which means that *sporadic* existence of these forms does *not* exclude the capitalist mode of production, 'although it may form the transition [to capitalism], as in later Middle Ages'. So, one may treat such things as merchant capital making an advance to petty producers who sell their products to merchants as a transitional process between feudal production relation and capitalist production relation. It should be stressed that hybrid subsumption is *not* the subsumption of wage labor: it is much rather a transitional process between pre-capitalist relations of production and formal subsumption of labor under capital. Banaji is mistaken to conflate hybrid subsumption with subsumption of wage labor (more on this later).

Having developed a historically-inflected (dialectical) view of capitalism, Marx says that real subsumption of labor comes into being spontaneously on the basis of formal subsumption of labor: 'a specifically capitalist mode of production (his code word for technologically dynamic advanced capitalism) ... arises and develops *spontaneously* on the basis of the formal subsumption of labor under capital' (Marx, 1977: 645; italics and parenthesis added).

There are potentially two problems with Marx in my view. *To the extent that* Marx means that the transition to real subsumption is *spontaneous* and thus merely an economic process, not mediated by struggle, this view is mistaken. One cannot assume that the transition to real subsumption is automatic. It was not spontaneous in English capitalism that Marx wrote about in his empirical work. In England, formal subsumption lasted for almost more than two centuries (i.e. until the last third of the 1700s). Here successful working class resistance against appropriation of absolute surplus value (where workers work long hours during the period of formal subsumption of labor under capital) was very much responsible for the introduction of machinery. The transition cannot be spontaneous especially in the global capitalist periphery, given a large reserve army of labor (created partly during colonial times) allowing capital to appropriate absolute surplus value through lower wages and through overwork.[20] The 'spontaneity argument' contradicts Marx's more general view about the proximate role of class struggle in social change – social change both within a mode of production (as in *Capital* – see below) and between one to another (as in the opening lines of the *Manifesto*). In fact, Marx himself said that 'It would be possible to write a whole history of the inventions made since 1830 for the sole purpose of providing capital with weapons against working class revolt' (1977: 563).

It is not just Marx who seems to neglect, or to *under-stress*, class struggle in examining the history of changes in the forms of capitalist class relation. As mentioned earlier, it is surprising that most authors in the Indian mode of production debate talk about class relations as if they can be separated from class struggle. And when class struggle is discussed (see the works of Mencher discussed in Thorner, 1982), the relation between it and capitalist accumulation is not dealt with. They, more or less, ignore this fact: while capitalism is characterized by competing capitalists seeking to cut costs and increase surplus value, it is the case that the rate of surplus (and thus the level of real wages) as well as methods of appropriation of surplus value (e.g. whether labor-displacing technology will be used) depend partly on class struggle (or, on the balance of power between capital and labor).[21] This means that given that capitalists act in pursuit of surplus value and given the logic of competition, whether or not the productivity-improving labor-saving methods are used, and thus the transition

---

20 Both of these processes Marx specifically mentions as products of the existence of a reserve army in Chapter 25 of *Capital*, vol. 1.

21 In this chapter, the changing balance of power between capital and labor (or employers/ owners and direct producers) is used interchangeably with class struggle, which is seen as occurring in covert and overt ways. If, for a variety of reasons, the labor market is tight allowing labor to put pressure on employers to increase wages without having to go on a strike, that is included under the changing balance of power between capital and labor. Of course, there are more overt actions signifying class struggle. And class struggle is seen as happening both from above (employers' strategies to undermine direct producer's power) and from below (struggle and strategies by direct producers).

to real subsumption of labor made, will, to some extent, depend on the changing balance of power between capital and labor, as expressed in the working class struggles *against* capitalism *under* capitalism.

Class struggle is important not just to the transition *to* capitalism (as has been highlighted in the debates on the nature of capitalism and on the transition to capitalism in Europe) but also to the transition *within* capitalism. It is also interesting that in these discussions (Aston and Philipin, 1985; Hilton, 1978), there has been little if any discussion on the forms of subsumption, while the entire stress is on the transition *between* pre-capitalism to capitalism as such.

The second problem with Marx is this. *Whether or not* Marx believed that class struggle intervened in the transition to real subsumption, he *generally* assumed that *given* capital – labor relations, capitalism will develop into a dynamic, developed capitalism (except during the moments of economic crisis) at all times and in all places. Even if Marx could be interpreted as not ignoring the role of class struggle in the transition to real subsumption, there could still be a potential problem: he could be seen as assuming that class struggle against formal subsumption happens but that the transition to real subsumption also happens because of successful class struggle. In other words, given formal subsumption of labor, real subsumption will follow everywhere, class struggle or no class struggle. Generally ignored is the possibility that *within* the global system of capitalism which as a whole is dynamic (labor productivity tends to rise) relative to pre-capitalism and within which the long-term *tendency* is towards the real subsumption of labor but that within a dominantly capitalist nation or a set of nations, there may be strong obstacles to capitalism systemically developing productive forces (in vast sectors and areas). There is a tendency towards the transition to real subsumption, but whether or not the transition occurs in a specific context must be seen as contingent, and specifically in the context of peripheral capitalism. It does not arise spontaneously as Marx had probably assumed.

I will argue that where/when production has the four characteristics of formal subsumption Marx discusses, production is capitalist in terms of social relations of production and exploitation, even if, and *pace* Patnaik (1990a: 49; 1990b: 68–69) reinvestment in machinery does not exist. In such a case, labor is only formally subsumed under capital. In India, the constitution (e.g. Article 23) guarantees the right to choose one's employer, and the laboring class – most of which owns no or little means of production, and whose numbers are increasing relative to those who are considered employers – works for employers for a wage. This is especially true in agriculture (Figure 3.2).

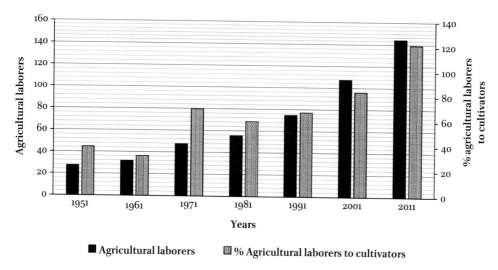

FIGURE 3.2   Agricultural laborers population (in millions) and as a percentage of the cultivators population.
Notes: 2001 numbers include both main workers and marginal workers. Note that cultivators include millions of those who do not hire laborers (they belong to poor and middle peasantry).
SOURCE: DATA IN THE FIRST COLUMNS ARE TAKEN FROM SINGH (2002). THE DATA FOR 2011 ARE FROM: HTTP://LABOURBUREAU.NIC.IN/ILYB_2011_2012.PDF

If we consider, once again the agricultural sector, which contains a near majority of the labor force, a large part of the work is done by hired labor. This is the case, even if, and as expected, the share of hired labor to total human labor varies from province to province. Clearly, a lot of work is still done by family labor (Figure 3.2). As well, in terms of investment in agriculture (as in industry), it is dominantly a *private* affair (Table 3.1), and purchased inputs comprise the majority part of the cost of production in most provinces, meaning that means of production tend to confront labor as capital in agriculture (Table 3.1 and Figure 3.3).

All these methods of exploitation may not increase the surplus value extracted in its relative form but would increase the mass of absolute surplus value appropriated by the capitalist. We cannot expect specifically capitalist production to emerge 'out of the blue'. Given that there is a vast pool of laborers, some of which is historically created under colonialism including through primitive accumulation (and this Patnaik herself recognizes), there is ample scope for the appropriation of absolute surplus value. However, in certain areas (e.g. the Green Revolution areas of the Punjab, and indeed in other parts

TABLE 3.1 Share of hired labor in total human labor, and share of purchased inputs in total cost of cultivation, per hectare, 1994–97

	% Hired labor	% Purchased inputs
Andhra Pradesh	61.6	70.8
Assam	31.1	30.1
Bihar	37.2	60.9
Gujarat	44.4	64.6
Haryana	17.3	52.7
Karnataka	57.2	67.3
Madhya Pradesh	38.4	54.2
Maharashtra	66.4	73.8
Orissa	39.9	54.2
Punjab	57.7	80.5
Rajasthan	13.4	44.5
Tamil Nadu	72.4	78.9
Uttar Pradesh	33.8	53.7
West Bengal	55.4	58.1

Note: Figures are (unweighted) average for the different crops grown in particular provinces. The relatively low figures in some of the advanced provinces such as Haryana may imply that rich peasants use machines to get the work done instead of hiring labor.
SOURCE: GILL AND GHUMAN (2001)

of the Third World) the specifically capitalist mode of production – the process of relative surplus value appropriation – has emerged with the aid of the state that subsidizes the use of the (Green Revolution) technology, which allow capitalists to increase their profits.[22] In advanced countries, capital was confronted with barriers (e.g. barriers in the form of successful class struggle) to absolute surplus value being appropriated through workers working long working days and through intensified labor process. Capital, however, turned worker's struggle to its own use, in a sense: successful struggle against long working days led to the use of new methods of production, to the conscious use of

---

22   That the use of this technology was promoted by imperialism is another matter. As Harry Cleaver (1972) says, the sale of modern farm inputs including tractors by the US in India – as a strategy to counter the crisis of overproduction in the US – was indeed a reason why the US was keen on the introduction of the Green Revolution.

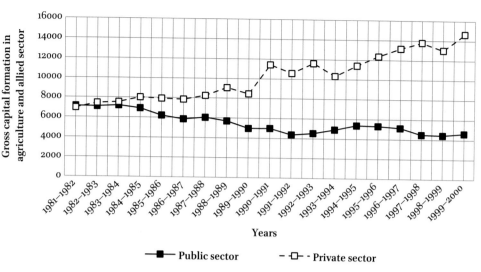

FIGURE 3.3 Gross capital formation in agriculture and allied sector (at 1993–94 prices) (in million rupees)
SOURCE: DATA FROM SINGH (2003)

science and technology, and thus to an increase in the relative surplus value. Such a process countered the loss of surplus value in its absolute form. Class struggle against formal subsumption of labor – along with vast resources flowing from the colonies which, given the presence of capital – labor relations *already*, were turned into capital – contributed to the transition to real subsumption, and in the resultant dynamism we associate capitalism with. But such class struggle against formal subsumption as has been observed in the center of global capitalism is not as easy to conduct in the periphery, and especially given the presence of a vast reserve army. Globally, capitalism is a progressive force – at least in the sense of promoting the development of productive forces. But this does not mean that in every part of the world this will be so always. The 'absence dynamism' is as much a part of it as the presence of dynamism. To say that where capitalism is not playing its 'assigned'/traditional progressive role it must be because of some pre-capitalist relations,[23] or that capitalism as a social relation does not exist, is being blind to capitalism's

---

23 This is not to deny, once again, that there are localities where pre-capitalist relations exist. It is just that these relations do not define the dynamics of the social system, the social formation, although they may affect the specific ways in which the law of value may work and has its actual impacts in specific places.

socio-spatial dialectics (presence and absence of technological backwardness within a single global system of capitalism).

It is important to stress again that: like the transition from pre-capitalism *to* capitalism, the transition *within* capitalism is mediated by class struggle. Class struggle, however, always occurs amidst specific factors, which provide the context for it, and thus makes the transition to real subsumption non-automatic.[24] These include: availability of affordable technology; ecological conditions (for nature-dependent production); concentration of property in the hands of a few; market demand from a given sector; and state interventions (see Appendix 1). The processes within which class struggle happens, including ecological conditions,[25] vary geographically. So the effect of class struggle on the transition from formal subsumption will vary, producing uneven transition to real subsumption of labor and therefore uneven development of productive forces.[26]

In their geographically uneven struggle against capital, laborers can succeed and have succeeded on at least three fronts to varying degrees: increasing real wages, reduction in the working day and in emancipating themselves, to some extent, from unfree labor relations whereby their right to enter into and exit

---

24 Not to acknowledge the existence of the material (= political-economic) context within which labor struggles happen is to fall in the trap of voluntarism [see Anderson's (1980) discussion of E.P. Thompson, in his Chapter 2, and especially, 32–33].

25 'Uneven development is the concrete process and pattern of the production of nature under capitalism' (Smith, 1992: xiv).

26 For capitalist development to happen, it is important that there is a significant amount of concentration of the means of production (e.g. land) in the hands of a few. Now, the degree of inequality in distribution of the means of production (land) is a function of such processes as: market-driven class differentiation referred to in Chapter 2; and demographic change (population growth) and inheritance laws that lead to the break-up of family-owned holdings, and primitive accumulation (which has been an on-going process).

Class struggle against primitive accumulation – which happened during colonial times and continue after 1947 (see Dhanagare, 1991; Gough, 1974; Guha, 1983; Surjeet, 1986, 1992) – can sometimes slow down primitive accumulation to some extent (the recent case of Posco, the South Korean company, not being able to acquire land in Odisha partly due to struggle from below is a case in point). Also, such struggle will be more successful in one place (say West Bengal) than in the Punjab (see Bandopadhyaya, 1989: 59–60; Webster, 1990). And the degree of market penetration underlying agrarian class differentiation will also vary from place to place. Thus both these processes (geography of class struggle and geography of market penetration) will create a differentiated terrain on which not only capitalist relations themselves – and labor struggle against formal subsumption within capitalism – emerge/develop but also as Bharadwaj (1982: 606–607) noted, technologies (e.g. the Green Revolution technology) are introduced.

from a labor contract does not exist because of various forms of bondage. In Andhra Pradesh villages, studied by da Corta and Venkateshwarlu (1999), struggle by laborers led to a decline in traditional/permanent bonded labor relations and to increases in real wages for men and women. Even if no overt collective action exists or if the overt collective action fails, the implicit 'go-slow' by laborers at lower-than-reservation-wage may still lead to many employers having to raise wages, as in several UP villages (Srivastava, 1999). It has been pointed out that non-agricultural wages put pressure on property owners to pay higher wages, either through strike actions or simply to be able to *attract* sufficient laborers, who are free to reject any request from employer for work (Lerche, 1999: 205). In villages in the Uttar Pradesh province also, government program of land redistribution and other pro-poor programs (e.g. employment generation program), however limited they may be, have led to a decline in land- and asset-lessness. This has caused an upward pressure on the supply price of labor power and increased labor's bargaining power to some extent. Further, creation of rural infrastructure has enhanced mobility of rural laborers who are able to access extra-local, alternative (often non-farm) employment, and this has enhanced their bargaining power as well vis-à-vis their local employers.

The question then is: how does capital respond to this sort of successful struggle or even to the very possibility of labor resistance. Capital's response has been many-fold. I will try to address these different responses to class struggle against formal subsumption by using findings from research on rural labor struggle as well as my own on-going work on agrarian transition in the eastern Indian province of Odisha (Orissa). Whether or not the discussion convincingly supports my case – that the transition from formal to real subsumption is not automatic and is impacted by the balance of power between the two basic classes – it at least demonstrates the ways/areas in which more research can be conducted. It is important stress that only some responses from property owners to the changing balance of power between the two basic classes are connected to the transition to real subsumption (employers using labor-saving techniques), especially, in a peripheral-capitalist economy.

When wages rise, working periods shorten and unfree labor relations decline due to class struggle, capitalists may use technology to reduce costs and discipline labor (real subsumption of labor). In the light of my conceptual discussion above, this is to be expected. But employers may also continue to use hired labor but try to reduce costs by various traditional means (deepening formal subsumption), and they may resort to 'hybrid subsumption'-cum-rental extraction. I will discuss the first response (slow and uneven transition to real subsumption) in Section 4, and the other two responses in Section 5. In this section and the next section, then, I will discuss the *different* (and sometimes contradictory) ways in which the balance of power between classes can affect accumulation strategies by capital. The main question is this: when laborers launch struggle – at individual and collective levels, and in formal/overt and informal/covert ways – against capital, how do capitalists who are already formally subsuming labor respond and with what implications for the transition to real subsumption of labor?

4 Class Struggle and the (Slow and Uneven) Transition to Real Subsumption of Labor

Indian employers are sensitive to costs and to market forces. As wages increase due to political action of laborers and other factors, in many villages in Andhra Pradesh in South India and in Uttar Pradesh in North India, and so on, property owners resort to labor-displacing mechanization to reduce the wage bill (da Corta and Venkateshwarlu, 1999: 91). In some places and at given points in time, if the balance of power is effectively in favor of labor, capital's attempt at using technology – and thus the transition to real subsumption of labor – can be resisted/slowed, at least temporarily. I will spend some time to discuss this process in the context of Kerala, located on the south western coast of the country. Kerala is known for the first communist government elected within a bourgeois democratic system anywhere in the world, and here laborers are more strongly organized than in other parts of India. The transition to real subsumption appears to have passed through three stages. First, laborers strike or bargain for higher wages. Second, following their success capital tries to use mechanization to reduce dependence on labor. Laborers then fight against mechanization thus slowing down the transition to real subsumption. Finally, labor's resistance to capital's introduction of technology softens.

In the 1960s and the 1970s, rice fields owned by capitalist farmers were the hotbed of class tension in Kerala.[27] Laborers launched political action demanding higher wages and better working conditions including an eight-hour day, supported by multiple unions, including those organized by communist parties. Capitalists responded by retrenching workers many of whom had worked for them on a long-term basis. They resorted to casualization of employment, and to the use of tractors to reduce dependence on laborers. In many places, workers reacted by forcibly harvesting rice. They were supported

---

27   The Kerala discussion mainly draws from Kannan (1999).

by pro-labor governments in power which would not interfere in labor disputes. In the rice bowl of Kerala, Kuttanad (in Allepey district), some tractors were broken up by laborers – this was reminiscent of the Luddite movement that Marx talks about in *Capital*. Framers gradually lost control over the process of recruiting laborers. Unions themselves would send in a large number of laborers to farms for harvests which would be completed in a few hours.

Because rice cultivation was profitable in the 1970s, farmers persisted in their attempt to introduce tractors, however, in order to increase labor productivity. Unions did not relent either in their protest. Ultimately, landowners agreed to pay wages to the traditional ploughmen for ploughing the fields. In return, the unions agreed to let the farmers use tractors. This meant that farmers would be free to use the tractors for ploughing after they have paid wages to the ploughmen. So the ploughmen would come and plough the field, take their wage and go away. Farmers would then prepare the land with tractors in whatever way they wanted. Over time ploughing by ploughmen became a ritual. Gradually they stopped ploughing, but yet they would come and collect their wages! Writing about one specific district, Oommen says this:

> When the rich farmers in Allepey district introduced tractors, the labor unions of agricultural workers successfully led their struggle against it so that the farmers had to agree that whether or not they used tractors, the land should be ploughed through bullocks/buffaloes at least for two rounds instead of the traditional three rounds in order that the laborers did not face further unemployment or suffer loss of wages.
>
> OOMMEN, 1990: 234

This system was acceptable in the 1970s when rice price was high. But with the decline in rice price afterwards, farmers complained about it, because they were paying more than their counterparts in other parts of the country. They responded by reducing employment in rice cultivation and also through crop substitution (replacing rice with other less labor-intensive crops). This meant the loss of employment for labor. In the late 1980s and afterwards, there developed a new situation – one of labor shortage – in place of labor surplus. There was an expansion of the non-agricultural economy, especially the service sector, due to the flow of remittance money from the Middle East. Younger people preferred to work outside of agriculture. Also, through years of struggle, laborers had earned a high social wage (see Heller, 1989) in the form of poor relief from the government: the social wage was almost equal to the consumption requirement of one adult in a family. This meant that unemployed people could wait for the right employment without starving. Both these factors caused labor shortage and had positive implication for their bargaining power over wages and working conditions. And this prompted landowners to use mechanization as a counter-response. This time unions no longer protested against the use of machines. But they did stick to their earlier strategy of demanding payment of wages to the same number of workers at the prevailing rate when machines were to be introduced. This actually meant the payment of double wages to an operation.[28] This did put a brake on introducing mechanization in post-harvest operations. But eventually, the introduction of tractors and other machines has now been widely accepted.[29]

As Oommen (1990: 234) has said, in Kerala 'mobilization of the agrarian proletariat is moderating, if not halting, capitalist development in Indian agriculture'. This may not happen everywhere. This slowing down of the transition to real subsumption will happen where laborers' organization has reached a sufficiently high level and where there are other favorable factors including a certain degree of support from local state apparatuses to laborers.[30] As the left organization in the industrial sector shows, workers' ability to slow down capitalist mechanization where it occurs is only, can only be, transient, as long as capitalist relations exist.[31]

---

28   When in the 1990s mechanical threshers were sought to be introduced, laborers demanded the same rate of payment 'even when the job is done with the aid of the threshing machine…. The farmers aver that when the machine is introduced, the manual labor involved would be considerably reduced and then there is no justification for paying the labor at the old rates' (Venugopal in Kannan, 1999).

29   More recently, in the harvesting season, farmers brought harvesting machines from the neighbouring Tamil Nadu State on rent and workers resisted it in Kuttanad. However, the Communist Party of India (Marxist) intervened and settled the issue in favour of farmers and allowed them to harvest with the machine. I am grateful to Dr. Mohanakumar, a political economist from Kerala, for this point (personal communication).

30   Kerala has had leftist governments quite frequently which have implemented pro-labor welfare policies better than many other provinces, thus increasing the reservation price of labor power.

31   The West Bengal experience is the most significant example. In this State there had been a Left-Front government in power since 1977 until 2011, and it had shared power for a few years in the 1960s (Mallick, 1994). In the early years of the government, it was supporting workers' strikes enthusiastically, which contributed to capital flight to other States. In consequence, the workers were exhorted by the party leaders to behave in a disciplined manner! Capital is capital, whether it is in agriculture or in industry. As in industry, in agriculture too, workers' ability to even moderate the effects of capitalism on workers (including such effects as technological change) is very transient.

CAPITALIST CHARACTER OF CLASS SOCIETY IN POST-COLONIAL INDIA 89

5 Class Struggle and the 'Blocked' Transition to Real Subsumption of Labor

In less developed countries such as India, the dominant responses of capitalists may be those which are other than real subsumption, resulting in a capitalism that can remain relatively backward (in the sense of per-hour labor productivity) for a long time. The first of these responses is just 'business-as-usual': reinforcement of formal subsumption. The second type of response includes a combination of Marx's 'hybrid subsumption' (mercantile-usury based exploitation) and rental extraction.[32]

5.1 *Reinforcement of Formal Subsumption*

In response to actual/potential struggle from below by men over low wages, long working days and unfree labor relations, capital may intensify/reinforce formal subsumption by increasing the use of women labor. For example, in response to successful male labor struggles against bondage relations and low wages in parts of Andhra Pradesh, capital hired women laborers who accepted relatively unfree labor contracts (more on this below) and lower wages, which their husbands refused, in order to support their families (da Corta and Venkateshwarlu, 1999). Thus capital resorts to a 'gender fix' in response to class struggle: it reinforces formal subsumption of labor through the substitution of male laborers' freedom for the unfreedom for female laborers. It should also be noted that by taking up work refused by men, women enable men to prolong men's strike against capital.[33]

In other areas, when local laborers go on a strike, capital may take advantage of geographical differentiation in wages and in working class organization: capital can use laborers *elsewhere* ready to work with lower wages and less satisfactory working conditions that local laborers are rejecting. Thus capital uses a 'spatial fix' as a response to class struggle. This is exactly what happened in Gujarat on the west coast of India where landowners 'imported' non-local docile aboriginal laborers in order to undermine the bargaining power of local

---

32   Still another response is what I will call political accumulation. Landowners formally subsuming labor use local state apparatuses including police (through bribing, etc.) to beat up laborers on strike, or to have them jailed on false charges or to file court cases. Surplus from agriculture is used to support political parties and to bribe the state bureaucracy which in turn helps capital use state's rural development resources illegally, in a form of primitive accumulation (Wilson, 1999).

33   Studies in future may reveal what the long-term impact of such prolongation of strikes on technological change will be.

laborers who demanded higher wages (Breman, 1985). This is actually a country-wide process. To the extent that property owners can make use of the spatial differentiation in wages and in proletarian solidarity, this differentiation is a barrier to the transition to real subsumption, although the strategy may enhance profits for specific capitalists locally.

A most important response in this category – reinforcement of formal subsumption of labor – is the tied labor use. In response to struggles for higher wages and against permanent bonded relations (permanent laborers work for given landowners almost throughout their lives), landowning capital uses non-permanent attached labor arrangements. Under these arrangements, debtor-laborers are obliged to report to the lender's farm first before other employers and to work off the loan based on a pre-arranged tied wage. Capitalists resort to these arrangements not only to secure labor supply – especially during peak seasons (Bhalla, 1999: 50) – but also to secure it at a lower than the market rate (da Corta and Venkateshwarlu, 1999: 92). The use of attached labor relations must be seen as a mechanism of labor control. This can be seen as a form of class struggle from above (p. 113), which is a response to class struggle from below. More specifically, it segments the labor market by dividing laborers into two fractions: permanent laborers who tend to possess land, and casual or daily laborers who tend to be landless and who belong to the lowest positions in the caste hierarchy (ex-untouchables). The use of attached labor reduces the bargaining power of casual laborers as casual labor days are reduced (Lerche, 1990: 199) which happens as more work is done by attached laborers, and indeed reduces wages of casual workers (Bhalla, 1999: 50). Even in villages in Haryana, a State which is a bastion of capitalism based on the use of the Green Revolution technology, but which is not traditionally known for class struggle from below, many landowners reportedly seek to exercise greater control over labor process by using permanent labor contracts in order to prevent possible struggle.

5.2 *Reversion to Hybrid Subsumption and Rental Extraction*

In many localities as those in Andhra Pradesh, with a rise in real wages, landowners respond partly by moving into commission trading: buying up farm produce at harvest, and reselling them at higher prices to urban merchants. Sometimes merchants advance cash loan to small landholders, and/or lease out some land, and borrowers promise to pay in kind at harvest at a price determined by the lender. This is called tied harvest (da Corta and Venkateshwarlu, 1999: 88). Thus, as wage costs rise, landowners seek to appropriate surpluses indirectly through exchange relations rather than through production relations based on hiring in labor (p. 89). Elsewhere as in many Uttar Pradesh

CAPITALIST CHARACTER OF CLASS SOCIETY IN POST-COLONIAL INDIA 91

villages also, when wages increase, labor-intensive non-mechanized paddy cultivation is leased out for a rent; the lessee does not provide any means of production (Lerche, 1999; Srivastava, 1999).[34]

I will deal with the hybrid subsumption and rental extraction response of landowners in some more detail by using empirical materials based on my on-going field-work in north-eastern Orissa. The main point to note here is this: even if because of successful wage-bargaining (in a condition where government-provided non-farm wage-work puts upward pressure on wages) local employers are forced to pay higher wages, the transition from formal to real subsumption can be counter-acted by locally existing conditions such as the nature of class-(re)composition of direct producers and their consequent lack of solidarity, and degree of land concentration (i.e. the contextual factors mentioned in the last section). This is an area where I first conducted a study in two villages located in Jajpur District (less than 400 kms south of Calcutta) in 1988 and have returned frequently till now. Let me first discuss the situation existing up till the late 1980s. I will then briefly discuss the more recent changes.

The area has fertile soils. But it is completely dependent on the monsoon. Landowners are small owners. The average size of operational holdings (owned land plus land leased in minus land leased out) was less than three acres in the late 1980s.[35] There were half a dozen landowners, among a sample of 70 families, with 10 acres and more land. Instruments of production were (and still are) very rudimentary: bullocks were being used as draught animals; wooden ploughs, wooden yokes and iron sickles were some of the instruments of production. Laborers were mainly of two types. There were those who worked on daily wages. And others were attached laborers on annual contracts, whose wages had two components. They received wages on a monthly basis in cash and/or in kind (paddy). They were also given a piece of land during the annual tenure of the contract by the employer the product of which the laborer kept. The attached laborers did not have any fixed working day: they worked as long as they were needed to by their employer. There was generally no extra-economic coercive relation between laborers and employers. But being an attached labor carried low social status.

Employers in my study-area were and are small capitalists, and they were formally subordinating labor. They did not invest in machines. Rather, the

---

34   It should be noted that rental extraction as a method of exploitation, stressed in the semi-feudal thesis (in the 1960s/1970s), has considerably decreased in importance, nationally, although in certain areas it can be widely prevalent.

35   The all-India figure for the average area operated per holding was 3.31 acres in 1991–92 and 2.62 acres in 2002–03 (Government of India, 2007).

surplus, which was produced on the basis of the methods of formal subsumption of labor (long working day, low wages), found its way into many non-farming avenues including Marx's 'hybrid forms' of subsumption. Usury was very attractive, the annual rate of interest being 36% to as high as 120%. Many landowners did invest in local politics (election campaigning): being a part of local state apparatuses helps one to get government loans (for farming and also for non-farming purposes such as daughter's marriage for which a dowry has to be paid). Also becoming a local politician is a source of earning bribes from the locals in return for official favors. Many invested in children's education: this could fetch money in future in the form of urban remittances and in the form of a dowry for male educated children with good jobs at the time of their marriage. Going into mercantile business also helped many landowner-traders to have some control over the supply of laborers: two biggest landowners in the area were also shopkeepers. Such control is very important because getting farm work done at the right time is crucial to productivity, especially when farming depends entirely on the rainwater. The laborer, who is usually very poor, can get means of subsistence such as flour and rice on credit from the landowner-trader, and this obliges him/her to work for the landowner when he/she wants them and in a relatively 'disciplined' manner. Investing the farm-generated surplus in trading also allows the landowner-trader to sell his/her stock to customers (i.e. laborers whom he/she usually hires) over whose earnings he/she has some control.

It must be stressed here that the landowners in the study area, like landowners elsewhere, are involved in a cycle of expanded reproduction, though this may not show up in investment in productivity-raising techniques *within* the farm sector. This also means that, as Gunder Frank, a participant in the MOP debate, and Brass (1995a: 96; Mies, 2012: 173) have noted, surplus does not have to be reinvested in the individual capitalist enterprise that generates it or even locally, for there to be the capitalist mode of production. More generally, and *pace* Patnaik, the farmers employing legally free wage labor but *not* investing in productivity-raising techniques *in* agriculture *are* capitalists, just as those employing free wage labor and making such investments (as in the Green Revolution areas) are. While in the case of (e.g.) the Green Revolution farmers the tendency for expanded reproduction is expressed in terms of investment in machines enhancing productivity, in the case of other farmers that may not be the case. Expanded reproduction can happen when a property owner can buy a lot of land which she/he cultivates by employing a lot of workers for long hours and low wages.

I notice three stages through which class relations have evolved in the study area. This is an area where strikes for higher wages occurred very frequently between the 1970s and mid-1980s. Nominal wages for farm work increased from Rupees 2.5 in 1974 to Rupees 15 in 1995. In 2008, it was Rupees 50–60 (which would fetch 3.5 kilos of rice now in the local market).[36] Locally, 'real wages' – as measured by the amount of paddy that can be bought at these nominal wages – increased by 200% between the 1970s and the 1990s. The working day has also shrunk by at least two hours relative to the earlier period (i.e. prior to the 1970s). The attached labor arrangement, which was profitable for landowners, has *completely* disappeared as laborers did not like being on call for 24 hours at low wages. Laborers have also become much less 'docile' and 'disciplined' from landowners' standpoint. Landowners complain that unless laborers are supervised directly, the work assigned may not get done, and this is a problem especially for upper caste landowners who will not work on their land themselves. As a result of these changes, however limited they be from laborers' standpoint, landowners who were earlier hiring low-caste laborers to cultivate their land started renting out their lands and often to these same laborers, leading to a process of deproletarianization or re-peasantization. This has been happening in the last 25 years or so.[37] This process – landowners switching from direct cultivation of land with hired labor to the cultivation of land by using tenants – is the second stage in the evolution of relations in the area.[38] The possibility of exploiting these poor peasants (small landholders who rely on wage labor as well as self-employment on their own land or on land leased in) enables the local landowners to shift the negative impact of wage-strikes (e.g. higher wages) on to these laborers who are now poor peasants.[39] If

---

36   In 1999–2000, one rural person needed 19 rupees a day to be able to buy enough food to give her the minimum calories needed (i.e. 2400) (Patnaik, 2007: 141). If the daily wage was 50–60 rupees, one can imagine how far the wage was below the cost of reproduction of a family of five members.

37   It must also be said that with the neoliberal economic policy in force since 1991, the prices of inputs such as fertilizers have been increasing much faster than the price of paddy, the dominant crop in the area, and thus cultivation based on directly hiring wage labor has been unviable for many (smaller) landowners.

38   It can be asked why landowners in the study area, confronted with increasing wage-hikes, did not go in for mechanical innovations, whereas many farmers in Punjab and Haryana would have done so. One important reason is the fact that landowners in the study area are very small owners: less than 10% of them own more than 5 acres, whereas in Punjab and Haryana, 25.3% of owners own more than 5 acres (Sharma, 1992). This means that and as explained earlier, the effect of class struggle on accumulation/development in a place will depend on local contextual factors, including land concentration.

39   It is necessary to consider whether the labor process involved in the leasing of land to poor peasants is to be viewed as (disguised) piece-wage work, and sharecroppers as piece-rated workers, as Srivastava (1999) suggests.

the strikes were organized jointly by poor peasants (i.e. tenants) for lower rents and by laborers for higher wages, landowners would not have been able to rent out land at high rent. This did not happen. For one thing, there was a conflict between their class interests: as more land is leased out to tenants, the availability of wage-work on employers' farm for daily laborers is reduced, and this is what I mean by class-recomposition of direct producers. For another, the local communist organization, many members of which were labor employers, lacked better organizational ability. To the extent that tenants have limited economic resources to invest in land because of high level of rental as well as usurious exploitation, and have less incentive also to make productivity-raising investments (because land does not belong to them), the productivity of land suffered. I have heard many landowners who were hiring labor earlier and have rented out their land now complaining about this.

In more recent times (since 1990s), and this is the beginning of the third stage, some landowners are a bit alarmed at the fact that not far from their villages, poor peasants are getting organized (more informally than formally) to demand a higher crop-share (presently, tenants pay half of the gross produce to landowners who do not contribute anything towards costs of production). In some cases, tenants have stopped cultivating the land they have rented on the basis of a verbal contract, allow the land to remain fallow. It remains to be seen what the response of landowners will be to the growing resistance of tenants to high rent. Development of productive forces will be furthered if in response to increase in both wages and in the crop-share demanded by tenants, landowners individually and/or collectively make productivity-raising investments so that cultivation with hired labor will be profitable. In the last few years, a new development has happened: there has been a sporadic use of tractors and power tillers. Tractors are bought by large owners, many of whom tend to belong to middle castes for whom performing manual labor is not a taboo. They use tractors on their own land cultivated with hired labor, and also lease out tractors to the tenants who have leased in land from higher caste landowners (and in some cases, to the landowners whose land lies fallow because their tenants would not cultivate it). These poor tenants use tractors to plough their own land and land leased-in; note that most of the work is still done by hand, and only ploughing is done by tractors. They do this because there is a pressure on them to cut costs of cultivation as the rental payment they have to make to landowners is high, indeed higher than the legal limit, and this is high because tenants as poor peasants have not been able to be organized to strike against landowners for lower rent. So in this sense the ability of landowners to extract a high level of rent – which reflects their power vis-à-vis poor peasants/laborers-as-tenants, or in other words, class struggle from the top – has started to prompt resorting to tractorization from below, but given the financial situation of poor peasants their turn to mechanization will be limited. And the wage increase to which changing balance of power between workers and property owners in favor of workers has contributed has prompted the (middle caste) landowners to use tractors and power tillers as well. It remains to be seen how far this latter tendency – a form of incipient transition to real subsumption of labor – develops.

6   Possibilities of, and Limits to, Real Subsumption of Labor

Wherever productive activity satisfies the four criteria for formal subsumption of labor, we have capitalism as a class relation. This could be in manufacturing, tourism, mining, etc. And given class struggle against formal subsumption, employers may further reinforce formal subsumption or may resort to real subsumption.

Whether the argument is about agriculture or industry, we need to be mindful of the fact that it is not true that real subsumption is not at all happening. To the extent that it is happening, one can argue that there are islands of real subsumption in an ocean of formal subsumption (and hybrid subsumption in rural areas). Ultimately, the transition to real subsumption is a matter of relative cost: whether an employer will use a machine to make workers process a large amount of raw material and to thus produce more at less cost or they will hire many people for long hours and low wages, depends on what is more profitable. A balance of power between the classes in favour of the direct producers imposes a cost (it can increase wages and reduce the length of the working day, without a corresponding reduction in real wage).

Under certain conditions, real subsumption can indeed happen even if there is no evident class struggle against formal subsumption. One condition is the technical character of labor process. Oil drilling requires machines, and one cannot get the work done by hiring many people for long hours. Nationally operating capitalists are increasingly competing at a global level, so they must cut costs and may be forced to use technology – often borrowed from developed – imperialist – countries – to do so: if machines can lower costs more than the strategy of hiring people for lower wages, the people who can resist low wages in future, real subsumption of labor will be resorted to, even in the absence of class struggle now. Imperialist capital (multinational companies) may sell a given technology as a commodity, which is then used in production. All this means that India – like many other backward countries – does not exactly have to follow the stages that, for example, England followed. As Trotsky (2008) says: 'The privilege of historic backwardness [...] permits, or rather compels, the adoption of whatever is ready in advance of any specified date, skipping a whole series of intermediate stages' (p. 4).

However, there are limits, and obstacles, to the extent to which a late developing country can adopt advanced technology, especially in agriculture and industry, and thus skip the stages of development that already-advanced countries had to travel by having to development the technologies themselves. Some of these obstacles, Trotsky (2008) himself describes:

> The possibility of skipping over intermediate steps is of course by no means absolute. Its degree is determined in the long run by the economic and cultural capacities of the country. The backward nation, moreover, not infrequently debases the achievements borrowed from outside in the process of adapting them to its own more primitive culture. In this the very process of assimilation acquires a self-contradictory character. Thus the introduction of certain elements of Western technique and training... [could lead] to a strengthening of serfdom as the fundamental form of labor organisation. (pp. 4–5)

There are obstacles not only to the transition from pre-capitalist to capitalist development that Trotsky talks about. There are also obstacles to a higher form of development from a lower form of development, within capitalism. Trotsky, unfortunately, abstracts from this.[40] That is, there are obstacles to the transition from one form of capitalist class relation (formal subsumption) to another form (real subsumption). Real subsumption requires investment of capital in machinery and the built environment, but in part owing to the transfer of surplus from peripheral countries such as India to imperialist countries, there is a problem of the relative lack of investible surplus.[41] Then there are opportunities for capitalists to make money outside of production that weaken the pressure to make profit-in-production in a competitive environment. These opportunities include buying up property at cheap prices and speculating on it; getting access to society's resources (commons) at a cheaper-than-market rate; and being able to sell things (e.g. arms) to the state or provide welfare-services to the public on behalf of the state, at the above-the-market rate. Besides, given globalization, the power of unions operating mainly within a sector, within a city or region, is rather weak (in a relative sense), so the struggle against formal subsumption does not succeed (much). This allows the capitalists to continue to exploit workers by making them work long hours for low wages. Capitalism

---

40   One can say that some of the obstacles (e.g. cultural obstacles) that Trotsky talks about are relevant to the transition from formal to real subsumption in India.

41   On the topic of the surplus transfer in the imperialist system, see Ding (2015); and Smith (2016).

is simply not developing productive forces, whether in farming or industry, in a *systemic* way that it was, for example, during Marx's time in England, or indeed, in the US in the 20th century.

To the extent that real subsumption and associated technological change is happening, it is not systemic: there is not a very strong economic compulsion and pressure on those with money to invest in creating and using technology to use labor productivity per hour. To the extent that technology is used, it is often adaptive: borrowed technology being used (sporadically). So Beams's statement about China might apply to India even better:

> The assembly-line system of production, which spread to other major capitalist economies after World War II, lifted the productivity of labor, thereby providing the foundation for capitalist expansion.
>
> Unlike the US, however, Chinese economic expansion has not been associated with a similar development of the productive forces. Its growth has been rooted in an adaptation of assembly line methods, not in the development of the new system of production. While it has provided a boost to profits, this has been obtained not through an increase in the productivity of labour, as was previously accomplished by American capitalism, but through the employment of ultra-cheap labour.
>
> BEAMS, 2012

7 Jairus Banaji's (and Others') Mistaken Subsumption of Labor Perspective

As I have argued, the subsumption perspective is an important one when it comes to understanding the nature of class relations. There is one scholar, Banaji, who was an important participant in the Indian MOP debate and who does talk about subsumption, in his theoretical work and in his historical discussion (of the small-scale producers). My approach to subsumption is different from his and that of some other scholars.

It is true that capital in its usury form can exploit labor (e.g. family labor) without what Marx calls specifically capitalist mode of production (mode of production in the technical sense). But that does not mean that one cannot distinguish between exploitation of wage labor by productive capital and exploitation of labor in the hands anti-diluvean capital (usury).

Banaji sees formal subsumption of labor mainly in terms of 'The subjugation of the *simple commodity form of production* to capital' (2013: 96; stress added). For him: 'The relations of production which tie the enterprise of small commodity producers to capital are already relations of *capitalist* production' (ibid.: 97; italics added). What he calls *capitalist relations of production* are compatible with a variety of forms *of deployment labor*: using share-croppers, bonded labor and labor tenants (who may be given some land by the land-owner to use) are different ways in which '*wage labor* is recruited, exploited and controlled' (2013: 145; italics added). He says: 'The argument is not that *all* share croppers, labor tenants and bonded laborers are wage-workers, but that these 'forms' [of labor] may reflect the subsumption of labor into capital in ways where the 'sale' of labor power for wages is mediated and possibly disguised in more complex arrangements' (ibid.).

Banaji thinks, rightly, that formal subsumption of labor 'presupposes a process of labor that is 'technologically' continuous with earlier modes of labor'. But then he wrongly concludes that: *before* the advent of advanced capitalism (real subsumption), whatever forms of exploitation (e.g. exploitation of small producers selling their products to landlords-usurers) that exist in a commodity producing society, constitute formal subsumption of labor. Banaji says: formal subsumption of labor 'crystalizes when capital confronts the small producer, invades his process of production and 'takes over' without subjecting it to technical transformation' (2013: 280). In formal subsumption of labor, 'the labor process remains *external* to the movement of capital' and it 'is technically fragmented, or decentralised'. There is 'no centralisation of social means of production and labor power', and there is no 'objective social interconnection', among individual capitals.

Banaji argues that: 'Behind the superficial 'surface' sale of products' small-scale producers formally subsumed under capital 'sell their labor power' and not their products, to 'the monied bourgeoisie of moneylenders and merchants through whom the small producer was brought into relation with the market' (2013: 98) by way of the latter receiving advances towards the cost of reproduction and means of production. The 'price' which small-scale producers receive signifies a relation, not of exchange, but of production; it is 'a concealed wage' (ibid.). So they are 'disguised laborers'.[42] Banaji says: 'a monied capitalist

---

42   More broadly: Banaji, who, as mentioned before, rejects the equation of the capitalist mode of production with juridically free wage-labor as a particular form of exploitation, conceptualizes that mode of production, in terms of its laws of motion (i.e. continuous accumulation of capital). Such a mode of production is not about any specific relations of exploitation, and can be based on a variety of forms of exploitation based on free wage-labor, sharecropping, labor tenancy, bonded labor. These forms of exploitation may just be ways in which paid labor is recruited, exploited and controlled by employers. Share-croppers, tenants working on landowners' lands, and bonded laborers are not necessarily wage-workers, but the forms of exploitation these categories represent may reflect the subsumption of labor into capital in ways where the 'sale' of labor power for wages is

CAPITALIST CHARACTER OF CLASS SOCIETY IN POST-COLONIAL INDIA

(for example, a merchant, moneylender) may dominate the small producer on a *capitalist* basis, he may, in other words, extort surplus value from him, without standing out as the 'immediate owner of means of production' (2013: 281–282). Thus 'the labor of small producers... can be seen as formally subsumed under capital'.[43]

'When the process of production of small-peasant household depends from one cycle to the next on the advances of the usurer – i.e. when, without such 'advances', the process of production would come to a halt – then in this case the 'usurer', i.e. the monied capitalist, exerts a definite *command* over the process of production' (2013: 308). And this command over the process of production involves appropriation of surplus value, as happened in the Deccan of the 19th century (p. 308, 329). 'All that is necessary to the constitution of this command is that a relationship of pure economic dependence prevail between the producer and himself, and that on this basis he compels the production of surplus-labour' (2013: 329). When direct producers in villages or towns are unable to engage in production without loans, then the capitalist advances 'them their wages and means of production as 'loans', and recovers his surplus value as 'interest' (Banaji, 2013: 330). This, once again, for him, is formal subsumption of labor. Banaji says: 'forms of bondage [i.e. tying of labor to this or that property owners] are precisely a characteristic of the *formal* subordination of labour to capital' (2013: 328). Associated with Banaji's concept of formal subsumption are his problematic views concerning labor and value, as I show below.[44]

---

mediated and possibly disguised in more complex arrangements. Sharecroppers, etc. are disguised wage-workers (see also Post, 2013; also Srivastava, 1999).

43   In at least one place, Banaji admits that what he describes is in fact 'pre-formal' subsumption. The latter 'would tend *to lead* in the vast majority of cases to the system of formal subordination' (italics added). He says that, for Marx, 'pre-formal' subsumption can be 'assimilated' into formal subsumption, and that is how he (i.e. Banaji) treats the matter (2013: 282).

44   Banaji says that 'free labour, so-called, *cannot* be an essential moment of capital', and it 'is not a precondition for the accumulation of capital or even whole forms of capitalist economy' because 'the self-expansion of value is intrinsically indifferent to the forms in which it dominates labour' (2013: 11, 13) and because free labor is 'the contingent outcome of struggles to shape the law and the social relations behind it' (p. 13). Banaji says, for Marx, free labor means labor without means of production (p. 13). He is against what he calls the vulgar notion of wage-labor in which a wage-laborer is one who is divorced from means of subsistence and means of production and is forced to sell her labor power (p. 53). For him, wage labor does not have to be commodity labor power or free labor: wage-labor is value-creating (p. 55). But what is value for him? He does not define it. In my view, to say that free wage-labor is not the essence – general attribute – of capitalism is to accept the following: when one walks, 'steps may be long or short' and therefore walking cannot be defined (that is, one cannot identify the 'general attribute' of walking) as

Banaji's subsumption perspective is mistaken in many ways. Marx, in fact, clearly distinguishes between formal and hybrid subsumptions, and Banaji does not. Banaji loses sight of the specificity of capitalism as a class relation rooted in the relation of *production*, which is generally based in nominally free wage-labor, although it may make use of unfree labor as a strategy of class struggle from above as mentioned earlier.[45]

Let me return to *Capital* volume 1 again. Formal subsumption is characterized by a relation of *control* between capital and labor.

> The labour process is subsumed under capital (it is capital's *own* process) and the capitalist enters the process *as its director, manager*. For him it also represents the *direct* exploitation of the labour of others. It is this that I refer to as the formal subsumption of labour under capital
>
> MARX, 1977: 1019; italics added

Further:

> A merely formal subsumption of labour under capital suffices for the production of absolute surplus-value. It is enough, for example, that handicraftsmen who previously worked on their own account, or as apprentices of a master, should become wage labourers under the *direct control of a capitalist*.
>
> Ibid.: 645; italics added

This relation of control is manifested in the fact that: 'the capitalist *takes good care* that the labor adheres to normal standards of quality and intensity level of quality and intensity, and he extends its duration as far as possible...' (p. 1020). But Banaji's formally subsumed workers are *not* 'under the direct control of a capitalist' as their director/manager. And it is not important to examine what happens 'within the process of production'.[46]

'a rhythmical motion [of the body] from one place to another' (Dietzgen, 2011: 25). The labor that Marx talks about as being the essence of capitalism is different from the worker in pre-capitalist societies (i.e. the worker as a slave or a serf, etc.) and it is also different from the *sporadically* existing wage-labor in pre-capitalist societies. The worker under capitalism is a unique category and has a unique historical-political role.

45   Besides, it is class struggle, among other things, over formal subsumption of labor, that partly explains the transition to real subsumption, but there is little role of class struggle in Banaji's conception of subsumption.

46   'Before the production process they all [capitalists, and the slaves or peasants turned into wage-laborers] confront each other as commodity owners and their relations involve nothing but *money*; [and] *within* [italics in original] the process of production they meet as its components personified' (Marx, 1977: 1020).

The formal subsumption is characterized by an inversion in the relation between the direct producer and the means of production: 'It is no longer the worker who employs the means of production, but the means of production which employ the worker' (Marx, 1977: 425). Concomitantly, when formal subsumption happens, there is also a deepening of material-economic dependence of one class (direct producer) on another (the exploiting class). 'A man who was formerly an independent peasant now finds himself a factor *in the production process* and *dependent* on *the capitalist directing it* [i.e. the production process]' (p. 1020; italics added). Not only does the way in which the direct producer is integrated into labor process (i.e. the way in which the direct producer as the worker performs the work of production) depend on the capitalist *as the director* of the labor process. It is also the case that 'his [her] own *livelihood* depends on a *contract* which he [she] as *commodity owner* (viz. the owner of labor power) has previously concluded with the capitalist as the *owner of money*' (ibid.; italics added). There is a relation between the market relation between direct producers and capital on the one hand, and the nature of labor process under capitalism on the other. As Marx says: 'The *continuity* of labour increases when producers dependent on individual customers are supplanted by producers who, *bereft of wares to sell*, have a constant paymaster in the shape of the capitalist' (p. 1020). All this simply means that there is a direct, unequal, economically coercive market relation between two commodity owners (laborers and capitalists), a relation which is exploitative. But these considerations, including those about the labor market, are not important for Banaji.

Historically, formal subsumption comes after a stage when capital appeared in a subordinate position. Formal subsumption coincides with the dominance of capital as a relation of production:

> The distinctive character of the *formal* subsumption of labour under capital appears at its sharpest if we compare it [i.e. the formal subsumption] to situations in which capital is to be found in certain specific, subordinate functions, but where it has not emerged as the *immediate owner of the process of production* [italics added], and where in consequence it has not yet succeeded in becoming the dominant force, capable of determining the form of society as a whole.
>
> MARX, 1977: 1023

While Marx contrasts formal subsumption to those situations 'in which capital is to be found in certain specific, subordinate functions', Banaji treats these situations themselves as constituting formal subsumption. Interestingly, Marx gives an example from the India of his time, which is worth considering:

> In India, for example, the capital of the usurer advances raw materials or tools or even both to the immediate producer in the form of money. The exorbitant interest which it extracts ... is just another name for surplus-value.[47] It transforms its money into capital by extorting unpaid labour, surplus labour, from the immediate producer. But it does not intervene in the process of production itself.... *But here we have not yet reached the stage of the formal subsumption of labour under capital.*
>
>> Ibid.; italics added

Marx goes on to add:

> A further example is merchant's capital, which commissions a number of immediate producers, then collects their produce and sells it, perhaps making them advances in the form of raw materials, etc. or even money. *It is this form that provides the soil from which modern capitalism has grown* [and which means that this form is not yet capitalism in the form of formal subsumption] and here and there it still forms the transition to capitalism proper. Here too we find no formal subsumption of labour under capital. The immediate producer still performs the functions of selling his wares and making use of his own labour.
>
>> Ibid.; italics and parenthesis added

It is very clear that Banaji's views on subsumption is different from Marx's use of it, which I defend, deploy and retheorize here. The inadequacy of Banaji's thinking is not necessarily because it differs from Marx's: one's view does not have to coincide with Marx's to be correct or adequate, and one's view can coincide with Marx's and can be incorrect and inadequate. The problem is that Banaji's conceptualization of capitalist production, its historical specificity, is inadequate as he conflates it with forms of commodity production which are not based on nominally free wage-labor. To the extent that the term he uses (formal subsumption) refers to a concept, this concept is a chaotic concept because it includes under it the processes which are not necessarily connected.

It should be added that Banaji is not alone in mis-conceptualizing formal subsumption of labor (in the Indian context). Consider D'Mello (2018: 135), a great scholar, with sympathy for the Maoist view of society, who says the following about formal subsumption in contemporary India:

---

47 Technically speaking, Marx is not accurate in his use of 'surplus value' (what he means is 'surplus labor'), just as he sometimes uses sale of 'labor' when he means sale of 'labor power'. Banaji however makes much of Marx's use of the term 'surplus value'.

there has been mostly a formal subsumption of agricultural labour to capital; the extent of real subsumption of labour to capital, where capital directly takes over the process of cultivation, hires wage labour, reinvests the surplus and adopts new production techniques has been very limited.

Needless to say that D'Mello is wrong on the same ground as Banaji is.[48] In North America, David Harvey also has a mistaken view of subsumption.[49]

8   Conclusion

There are empirical, theoretical and political implications of my argument in this chapter. Using the subsumption perspective on capitalism as a class relation, I have critiqued in this chapter the view of many radicals who doubt that India (especially, rural India), as a place is capitalist. In India, there *are* the necessary conditions for capitalist relations (e.g. a class of legally 'free' laborers; commodity production; investment of money in production and exchange to make more money). Therefore, as capitalists elsewhere, property owners in India hiring these nominally free laborers possess the same sorts of causal powers (e.g. they can earn profits) and suffer from the same sorts of causal liabilities (e.g. they can lose their means of production if they do not produce commodities efficiently, i.e. at the value). They are capitalists whether or not they use, for example, the Green Revolution type technology or biotechnology or any other form of technology.[50] In some areas, property owners may be formally subsuming labor, and in other areas there may exist real subsumption. The ways in which capitalists' powers and liabilities are expressed in actual patterns of investment, and the effects of the exercise of these powers and liabilities on the development of productive forces (i.e. whether the transition from formal to real subsumption of labor under capital happens) are contingent

---

48   Alavi (1981) also sees interaction between capital and peasants as formal subsumption of labor.

49   Harvey (1982: 373) has got the class character of capitalism wrong when he says that: 'Monetary relations have penetrated into every nook and cranny of the world and into almost every aspect of social, even private life. This formal subordination of human activity [or labour], exercised through the market, has been increasingly complemented by that real subordination which requires the conversion of labour into the commodity labour power through primitive accumulation'. One can see how different Harvey's conceptualization of formal and real subordination/subsumption is from Marx's.

50   In a later chapter, we will discuss the class character of the use of technology.

on the balance of power, or struggle, between property owners and workers. The forms and outcomes of the struggle – which are affected by the overall capitalist development and developmental activities of the capitalist state at the national and provincial scales – condition the extent to which capitalists who are competing with one another cut costs of production through the use of technology aimed at increasing labor productivity or through the formal subsumption of labor (e.g. the use of highly vulnerable and low-cost labor, including labor that is reproduced outside of capitalism as in indigenous communities) or indeed through a locally and sectorally varying combination of these two methods.[51]

In the light of what has been said above, the mode of production in India is decidedly and near-exclusively capitalist.[52] This is capitalist at least in the sense of formal subsumption of labor under capital. And it is decidedly not semi-feudal.[53] Of course, the semi-feudal thesis continues to be subscribed to by many (implicitly or explicitly).[54] The view of capitalism and capitalist

---

51 Capital also makes use of labor whose reproduction is only partly borne by the capitalist wage system (e.g. laboring households working seasonally for capital as migrant laborers may collect means of subsistence such as fuel, etc. from common property for free, and/or laboring households who may own some land). Capital also relies on the fact that those responsible for reproduction of the laboring households, and they are generally women and girl children, spend many hours of unpaid labor at home and are often denied access to a normal amount of necessaries to consume, and all these processes in the realm of the private sphere of necessary labor (Vogel, 2014) reduces the social value of labor power that is bought and sold.

52 In some specific localities, land and labor may not have attained the status of full commodities, and extra-economic coercion may be exercised in the sphere of production.

53 Banaji (2010) says that categories such as semi-feudalism 'are all slavishly copied from Mao's theorisations for China that will soon be almost a century old!', indicating that for him the category of semi-feudalism is problematic (at least in part) because it is historically old. On that ground many of Marx's categories developed that predate Mao's would be inadequate. In fact, many mainstream scholars critique Marxism because it was 'so 19th century'. My opposition to semi-feudalism is not on the basis of it being an old category but rather on the ground that it does not help us interpret the reality of class society that India is and that its political implication is reformist (as explained later).

54 For example, Sugden (2017) says that the Mithilanchal area spanning the Nepal – Bihar border is semi-feudal as it is dominated by landlordism and usury, even if the area serves as a surplus labor pool for urban areas in India. Sugden says: 'The concept of a "semi-colonial" social formation remains relevant in the post-liberalization context, even if the term is not always used. In spite of the growth of capitalism in India's (and Nepal's) urban centers and rising rural–urban migration, labor is mostly casual, low paid, and unskilled, being dominated by work in low-value industries such as agro-processing where wages and conditions of employment are poor' (p. 134). So, according to Sugden, if employers use casual wage-labor, they are not capitalist employers. This is a mistaken view.
      Similarly, Kar (2018) says that: in a feudal system there are generally big landlords, the serf system, rent collection, and natural economy, while in a semi-feudal economy, due to

(uneven) development offered here is different from that of many (Indian) Marxists. This is the case even if they, with their inadequate *concept* of capitalism might think that there is 'more' capitalism now than there was earlier. For them, the development of productive forces, to the extent that it has taken place, has taken place only due to capitalist reinvestment of surplus in specific areas. Patnaik, like Bhaduri, thinks that only those property owners who invest in technological change are capitalists.

There are other theoretical implications of the subsumption perspective as well. By deploying Marx's notion of subsumption of labor, I have critiqued a restrictive concept of capitalism that many Indian Marxist political economists subscribe to. This is a concept in which the development of capitalist class relations is conflated with the development of productive forces *under* such relations. In the restrictive concept, capitalism as such is equated with advanced capitalism, rather than the latter being seen as a higher *form* of capitalism-as-class. Therefore, in this restrictive concept, where there is a lower level of economic development, capitalism is assumed not to exist or to exist partly.

In advancing a subsumption of labor perspective, I claim, in line with Marx (1977), that formal subsumption of labor, which is based on the appropriation of surplus value in its absolute form, is the most abstract – general – form of capitalism: it 'is at the same time directly a process of the exploitation of the labour of others. ...It is the general form of any capitalist production process' (i.e. production process under the rule of capitalist social relation) (p. 1019). In other words, the formal subsumption, as the more general form of capitalist production, 'can be found in the absence of the specifically capitalist mode of production', which Marx calls the real subsumption of labor (p. 1019). For Marx, real subsumption of labor entails the formal subsumption, but 'the converse does not necessarily obtain' (p. 1019). Contrary to what Marx might (sometimes) have believed, the transition to real subsumption is not automatic, though. I accept that there *is* a long-term tendency towards the real subsumption of labor, associated with a rise in the ratio of constant to variable capital, that follows formal subsumption in which lots of workers are hired to work for long hours on an enormous amount of raw materials with little labor-shedding

---

the penetration of capital and the operation of markets in the context of the international capitalist system, the feudal traits are somewhat weakened, giving the *appearance* that the system is capitalist. In a semi-feudal economy, *essentially* feudal categories remain operational through the functioning of various capitalist traits relating to capital investment, commercialization, wage labor, and market operation. For Kar, the domination of small-scale production based on family labor, along with various noneconomic forms of exploitation, neither corresponds to capitalist development, nor is a transitional phase moving toward capitalism. This is, once again, a very strong variant of semi-feudalism thesis. I return to the political implication of this sort of problematic views below.

technological change used.[55] This long-term tendency, under certain conditions, is countered by the possibilities for a prolonged process of formal subsumption. The transition to real subsumption is mediated by the balance of power between capital and labor, including more overt struggle against formal subsumption of labor.

The formal subsumption may benefit specific capitals in specific places but opportunities for formal subsumption may counter the long-term tendency towards the development of productive forces at the society-wide scale that Marx associates with real subsumption of labor. This shows that social relations of production in the form of formal subsumption of labor, under certain conditions, can fetter the development of productive forces. From the perspective of many participants in the Indian MOP debate, it is the social relations of usury or rental extraction from direct producers – that is, relations other than those of capitalist production – that fetter the development of productive forces under capitalism.[56] Incidentally, this view is the Marxist counter-part of the non-Marxist modernization theory which says that pre-modern ideas/practices are the main cause of lack of development. While the importance of the relations other than those of capitalist production in specific cases cannot be denied (see below), a larger nation-wide obstacle is formal subsumption of labor itself: being able to appropriate surplus value in its absolute form on the basis of formal subsumption alleviates – or to some extent, counters – the pressure to have to resort to real subsumption in a systemic way.

Even if some might think that relations other than those of capitalist production are less of a barrier to the development of productive forces now than before, the barrier to capitalist development is generally not conceived as the totality of capitalism as a class relation: much rather, the barrier is seen as emanating from such things as inadequate policy influenced by monopolies. For Marx (1991: Chapter 47), the *specific economic form in which unpaid surplus*

---

55   But it is also true that ultimately, there is a limit to the mass of surplus value that can be appropriated in its absolute form, given that there are only 24 hours a day and there are bodily limits to how much a person can perform in an hour and in a working day, which is why there is class struggle over formal subsumption. (Note that both of these limits apply to all forms of society, but they acquire a special significance in capitalism because of its tendency of accumulation for accumulation sake, which means almost limitless tendency towards the exploitation of labor). This is not to say that the rate of technological change (as indicated by c/v) will not rise faster than that of exploitation of labor (s/v), over a reasonably long period of time.

56   This is the Marxist counter-part of the non-Marxist modernization theory which says that pre-modern ideas and pre-modern practices are the main cause of the lack of development (see Bordoloi and Das, 2017).

labor is pumped out of direct producers plays a key explanatory role in understanding society. And, in my view, appropriation of surplus labor in the form of absolute surplus value via formal subsumption of labor *is* key, and especially in the vast rural areas as well as in the massive urban informal sector where most workers work (of course, the dominance of the formal subsumption has to be seen in relation to the appropriation of relative surplus value through the real subsumption, as well as class differentiation, dispossession of small-scale producers, and hybrid subsumption). Marx himself would point to the significance of formal subsumption of labor more than he did, if he had a chance to observe the functioning of capitalism outside of advanced capitalism. *Even in* the more developed countries, the formal subsumption of labor – appropriation of absolute surplus value – is increasingly becoming an important fact of life, given increasing precarity of the proletariat allowing capitalists to appropriate surplus value in its absolute form. This could be a potential *counter-tendency* to the tendency of the rate of profit to fall (TRPF) (see Grossman, 1929; Marx, 1991): this is a topic that is definitely worth exploring. In fact, at the level of the world market, the prevalence of the significant extent of the formal subsumption of labor in the South could be seen within the framework of the TRPF as a counter-tendency to the profitability crisis in advanced countries; examining this is also beyond the scope of the chapter and the book.

There are theoretical implications of the subsumption perspective for understanding capitalist uneven development as well. The view that only those property owners who invest in technological change are capitalists and therefore capitalist relation must necessarily involve reinvestment of surplus in technological change mean that: uneven *development of productive forces* is a function of spatially limited amount of *development of capitalist social relations* as represented by technological change. I disagree. Capitalist property owners must cut costs to remain competitive. But in what ways they do so (for example, whether they use labor-saving technology) is, within limits, a different matter. In large countries such as India, there is much geographical unevenness, ecologically and in terms of other factors such as the degree of concentration of means of production, the balance of power between capital and labor. So one will expect that property owners in some areas are unable to rely mainly on the use of labor that works for low wages and for long hours, and are therefore economically compelled to use productivity-raising technological change, thus manifesting capitalism's long-term tendency towards real subsumption. This causes productive forces to be developed in some areas to a greater extent and more systematically than in others, causing uneven development *under* capitalism. In other words, there is a more general tendency under the capitalist mode of production (i.e. the pressure on competing capitalists to make a profit, i.e. the pressure coming from the capitalist class relations) and that this general tendency interacts with locally existing contingent conditions (e.g. government policies) to produce geographically uneven development, the concrete forms of which must be subjected to empirical analysis.[57]

All political economists agree that there is uneven development in India, but many of them think that uneven development exists because 'non-capitalist' relations (e.g. pre-capitalist type relations) exist in some areas, associated with low level of economic development, and capitalist relations exist in other areas, associated with higher level of economic development. My argument, however, is that, uneven development is mainly taking place because of, and in the framework of, social relations that are predominantly *capitalist in terms* of class relations. Uneven development is partly a product of uneven transition to the real subsumption of labor under capital. Uneven development is a *capitalist* matter.

There is a further implication of the class perspective in this chapter. To the extent that uneven development is happening within the framework of varied class relations in a backward country such as India, one where technological change is partly happening under the influence of the world market and with some support from the state, uneven development is uneven and combined development. But what is the combined character of uneven development? As we have seen: according to Trotsky (2008: 4), backward countries can adopt technology from already-advanced countries, and this means that:

> The development of historically backward nations leads necessarily to a peculiar combination of different stages in the historic process. Their development as a whole acquires a planless, complex, combined character.

Trotsky, who is sadly an untouchable among Marxists in India, and who is the original theorist of uneven and combined development, explains:[58]

---

57 This cannot be fully captured through data at the provincial scale but must be investigated at smaller scales (villages, clusters of villages, etc.).

58 There is a growing amount of attention to uneven and combined development: see Ashman, A. (2010); Allinson and Anievas (2009); Bond and Desai (2006); Lowy (2010); O'Brien (2007); and van der Linden (2007). It is interesting that David Harvey, one of the most influential theorists of uneven development (see Das, 2017c for a critical analysis of his work), pays no attention to this important concept in his work. It is entirely possible that Harvey, like many other Marxists, does not wish to have any intellectual connection to Trotsky and his intellectual legacy, suggesting the existence of sectarianism within Marxism.

Unevenness, the most general law of the historic process, reveals itself most sharply and complexly in the destiny of the backward countries. Under the whip of external necessity their backward culture is compelled to make leaps. From the universal law of unevenness thus derives another law which, for the lack of a better name, we may call the law of *combined development* – by which we mean a drawing together of the different stages of the journey, a combining of the separate steps, an amalgam of archaic with more contemporary forms.

> Ibid.: 5

This means that in a less developed country, technologically backward 'peasant land-cultivation' can co-exist with an industry which 'in its technique and capitalist structure' is 'at the level of the advanced countries', and in certain respects it can even surpass industry in advanced countries (ibid.: 8).

For Trotsky, it is not just that capitalist development is *uneven* but also that capitalist relations are *combined* with pre-capitalist relations (e.g. serfdom). This is an advance over the perspective that focusses only on the unevenness of capitalist development. Trotsky's perspective, however, homogenizes the capitalist class relation (by treating its different forms as one). It thus abstracts from the ways in which class struggle intervenes in the transition from one form of capitalist class relation (formal subsumption) to another form (real subsumption) and from the obstacles to the transition within capitalism. His perspective needs to be broadened a little bit in the light of the subsumption theory presented here. In India and similar other backward countries, it is not just that capitalism is combined with remnants of pre-capitalist or non-capitalist relations existing in specific areas. The matter is more complex than that. What is happening is this: capitalist class relations of formal subsumption of labor co-exist not only with, hybrid subsumption, pre-capitalist relations, including relations of commons (as in aboriginal areas), and small-scale commodity production subjected to market-based class differentiation and extra-economically coercive dispossession (primitive accumulation), but also with capitalist class relations of real subsumption, which is, in part, driven by the external influence (the operation of the imperialist world market).

And there is further complexity when we recognize the fact that there are limits to the extent to which India and other similar countries, operating under the impact of the world market can move quickly to the stage of real subsumption of labor in agriculture and industry, exhibiting a systemic tendency towards a rise in productivity of labor per hour. Trotsky (2008: 4–5) himself says:

> The possibility of skipping over intermediate steps is of course by no means absolute. Its degree is determined in the long run by the economic

and cultural capacities of the country. The backward nation, moreover, not infrequently debases the achievements borrowed from outside in the process of adapting them to its own more primitive culture. In this the very process of assimilation acquires a self-contradictory character. Thus the introduction of certain elements of Western technique and training... [could lead] ... to a strengthening of serfdom as the fundamental form of labour organisation.

I would say that the introduction of advanced techniques could strengthen not only the use of forms of extra-economic relations, but also relations of formal subsumption of labor. We may recall that: formal subsumption of labor can exist 'alongside the *specifically capitalist* mode of production in its developed form' i.e. the real subsumption (Marx, 1977: 1019). In other words, enterprises using advanced technology can – and do – resort to a regime of long hours and low wages (just as they can use unfree labor).[59]

The MOP debate and my alternative views presented here shed light on not only uneven (and combined) development of capitalism but also on the related topic of capital switch. Once we assume that there is a class with money (property owners, more generally) intending to make money by investing it in production and exchange, the concept of switching capital comes to be an important one. There are three forms of capital switch within the landscape of uneven and combined development of capitalist social formation: (1) switch of capital within the real subsumption of labour (the advanced form of capitalism); (2) switch of capital from rental and money-lending business ('anti-diluvean' capital) to productive investment; and (3) switch of capital from formal to real subsumption of labor. Let me explain this briefly.

---

59   If a lot of capital has been sunk in machinery, the latter must be in contact with labor for as long as possible in a day. This is because without such contact, no surplus value will be produced. What Marx calls moral depreciation of machinery is also a permanent threat: when new and better machines are introduced, the existing machines face the threat of being replaced even if they are physically functional, and such replacement prior to the full amortization of the value embedded in the existing machinery, is a potential loss of value: 'in addition to the material wear and tear, a machine also undergoes what we might call a moral depreciation. It loses exchange-value, either because machines of the same sort are being produced more cheaply than it was, or because better machines are entering into competition with it. In both cases, however young and full of life the machine may be, its value is no longer determined by the necessary labour time actually objectified in it, but by the labour-time necessary to reproduce either it or the better machine. It has therefore been devalued to a greater or less extent. The shorter the period taken to reproduce its total value, the less is the danger of moral depreciation; and the longer the working-day, the shorter that period in fact is. ... It is therefore in the early days of a machine's life that this special incentive to the prolongation of the working day makes itself felt most acutely' (Marx, 1977: 528).

CAPITALIST CHARACTER OF CLASS SOCIETY IN POST-COLONIAL INDIA   111

Within advanced capitalism, the capitalism which is dominantly characterized by real subsumption of labor, there are at least two forms of capital switch.
When the rate of profit is low in the production sphere, capital switches to
financial, etc. services (Smith, 2010). And, according to Harvey, when there is
what he calls overaccumulation in the sector that produces commodities that
are produced and consumed within a given time period (primary circuit), capital is switched to the sectors that specialize in the built environment for production and for consumption (e.g. durables) and into science and education as well
as social welfare and repressive and consent-generating activities (Harvey, 1978).

Within economically less developed capitalist social formations, capital
switch takes different forms. Firstly, as Patnaik (1986) and others have argued,
when property owners can make more money by investing it in production,
they will switch capital from rental and usurious activities to production. Patnaik says: a person renting out her land to peasants will switch to what Patnaik
calls *capitalist* production if she can make more profit in production than by
leasing out land (i.e. the rental income) and by lending money-capital at a
higher rate of interest (usury). But a rate of profit that can prompt switching
capital to production is very high (because rental income and usurious interest
are very high), and is difficult to obtain, unless there is a quantum jump in productivity caused by technological change. In other words, the obstacle to the
switch to capitalist production comes from *outside* of capitalist production.
Secondly, there is the switch of capital from formal subsumption (or indeed
from hybrid subsumption) to real subsumption, as I have discussed. This switch
is not yet complete. This leads us to the topic of the specificity of capitalism in
India, as the final theoretical implication of the argument in the chapter.

How different is Indian capitalism from that of the European core which is
characterized by capitalism or mature capitalism? What Sinha (2017: 540) calls
capitalism, or mature capitalism, exists with 'capitalists and workers responding to "the dull compulsion of economic force"'. This 'implies the completion of
a transition to something resembling mature capitalism: a condition of generalized commodity production, in which the imperative of accumulation drives
capitalists' behaviour, and where labour [sic] becomes a commodity'. All this is
quite reasonable.

Sinha, however, goes on to say that 'In places like India today not only is this
process [of emergence of capitalism] not 'complete', but as Sanyal (2007) suggests, it is never likely to be' (ibid.). This means that: 'in India the annihilation
of non-capitalist ways of life ... is necessarily incomplete'. From this, Sinha concludes: 'That deferral of completeness of the transition', or the incomplete
character of the transition to capitalism, is what 'is the central point of difference between capitalism in India and in the original trajectories of the European core' (ibid.). And, this incompleteness, the fact that non-capitalist ways

of life have not been annihilated, has a political reason: 'these ways of life are kept alive by development interventions [of the state] to benefit those who are excluded from capitalist relations but have some political power in the form of laws and justice and solidarity discourses that firm up non-capitalist forms of subjectivity and put limits to the violence of the universalization process on extra-economic grounds' (p. 541). So just as non-capitalist or pre-capitalist relations act as a fetter on the development of capitalist class relations in the work of Patnaik and others, so according to Sinha and Sanyal, 'non-capitalist forms of subjectivity ... put limits' on the universalization of capitalism. So, what limits capitalism is not an agent within capitalism (i.e. the working class) but an agent that is outside of capitalism ('non-capitalist forms of subjectivity'). One can clearly see how close this sort of thinking is to some of the discourse that informs class struggle in India (e.g. Naxalism, discussed in Chapters 8–9).

Sinha and Sanyal are right to say that in India, wage-labor co-exists with other forms of labor. But to the extent that this is the case, India's capitalism cannot be credited with any uniqueness relative to advanced countries. In all capitalist countries, wage-labor exists along with other forms of labor, to varying degrees, with wage-labor as the dominant form of labor. Consider Lenin, the best class-analyst after Marx:

> Capitalism would not be capitalism if the proletariat *pur sang* were not surrounded by a large number of exceedingly motley types intermediate between the proletarian and the semi-proletarian (who earns his livelihood in part by the sale of his labour-power), between the semi-proletarian and the small peasant (and petty artisan, handicraft worker and small master in general), between the small peasant and the middle peasant, and so on
>
> LENIN, 1968: 59

But that does not mean that the imperative of *capitalist* accumulation, does not exist where wage-labor as the dominant form of labor coexists with other forms of labor, as in India. Capitalism does not require that *all* labor power become a commodity. As long as a sufficient amount of labor power is in the commodity-form, capitalism's fundamental mechanisms (e.g. competition, appropriation of surplus value, etc.) can be in full force. In fact, the existence of a semi-commodified labor power is no barrier to capital's pursuit of surplus. Capital can benefit at the expense of petty producers in multiple ways.[60]

---

60   Petty producers are adversely impacted by the capitalist class in at least three different but connected ways. 1) They work as wage-laborers for a part of the year, so they are

The *main* difference between India and the European core is *not* what Sinha and Sanyal say (i.e. the co-existence of non-capitalist forms of labor with wage-labor). The main difference is that India (like similar other countries in the Global South) is characterized by the dominance of formal subsumption of wage-labor under capital, which co-exists, or is unevenly combined, with real subsumption of labor under capital (as well as relations of hybrid subsumption and remnants of pre-capitalist exploitation based on extra-economic coercion, and natural economy), in a context of the operation of the world market and imperialist subjugation. In other words, it is the specific form of uneven and combined development and imperialist subjugation, that define the specificity of India (and countries such as India within the global periphery), relative to advanced regions such as Western Europe and its offshoots (North America). Conversely, the processes that could hasten the transition from formal to real subsumption in Western Europe (e.g. massive out-migration of surplus labor reducing the size of the reserve army, and the resources plundered from the subjugated countries that were then converted into capital) are missing in India and other similar countries.[61] There *is, no doubt,* an incompleteness, indicative of combined development. But this is not in the sense of the incomplete transition *to* capitalism, for India is decidedly a capitalist country already. Much rather, the incompleteness exists in the sense that there is an incomplete – on-going – transition to real subsumption of labor, within the landscape of uneven and combined development of *capitalist* social formation.

Whether capitalism exists or not and if it exists, then in what form it does, is not a matter of academic squabbling. Theoretical ideas about capitalism, like all theoretical ideas, have implications for political practice.[62] To say that a social formation in India (or indeed in other country) is decidedly capitalist has a different political implication than the contrary view. This contrary view is that (a) the social formation is not dominantly capitalist or it is capitalist in limited ways, and (b) obstacles to capitalist development are in pre- or non-capitalist relations of production. There are two implications of this view. One

---

exploited as full-time wage-laborers are. 2) They are dispossessed of their property by the capitalist class and its state. 3) They do not receive the full price of the products of their labor from the capitalist class and its state, so they are exploited in the commodity market. Note that apart from being impacted by the capitalist class, the petty producers are also exploited by the landlords (on the basis of appropriation of ground rent) and by the state (on the basis of the payment of indirect taxes).

61   Patnaik (2016) also points to these two processes (plunder and out-migration), but her theoretical interpretation of these processes, as well as the political conclusions that follow, are different from mine.

62   Lerche et al. (2013) draw implications for Left politics of their and others' political-economic analysis of capitalism in rural areas.

is that capitalist class relations are everywhere and all times associated with higher level of the development of productive forces.[63] Another is that: the obstacles to capitalist development are not in capitalism-as a class relation as such[64] and can be removed by forces other than those that seek to abolish capitalism. That is, a government that is more democratic than the current form of bourgeois government but that still operates within the logic of capitalist relations can remove these barriers and promote a nicer form of capitalism, thus creating conditions for socialism in the distant future.[65] More generally, for many, inadequate government policies constitute an obstacle to economic development.

If a country such as India is dominantly semi-feudal or if it is not capitalist enough, then the radical strategy is one that is to be directed against semi-feudal landlords or at the creation of advanced capitalism somehow. This is the strategy pursued by India's communist parties.[66] This strategy licenses a long

---

63   Those who have this view are likely to also believe that capitalism is everywhere and always associated with nominally free labor.

64   Sometimes, it is implied that the monopoly section of capital is the problem. This view is also problematic in that it fails to consider that within capitalist class relation, competitive relations between capitals, all of which control capitalist private property and exploit labor, do lead to monopolies, and that a less monopolistic capitalism presided over by, say, a workers' government, would not necessarily be a better capitalism, over the long run. Monopolies and other companies are deeply inter-connected through sub-contracting and other networks, within the structure of capitalism as a relation of social power anyway. What is seen as problematic by many is the idea that monopoly capital makes use of state power in its own interest. This implies that its political power is the problem, and not the matter of its exploitative relation as such, or, not the fact that monopoly capitalists, like other capitalists, are bearers of capital as a class relation. Therefore, almost out of view is the idea of the totality of capitalist relations being incompatible with the interests of the workers and poor peasants.

65   Recall that for Patnaik and many others, whose views shape and/or influence the mainstream communist movement, the rate of profit that can prompt switching capital to production is very high and is difficult to obtain. Why is it high: because property owners can earn a lot of rental income and usurious interest in a backward society. Only when a quantum jump in productivity caused by technological change occurs can the rate of profit from production can be enhanced, an only this can cause a transition from pre- or non-capitalism to capitalism as they see it. In other words, the obstacle to the switch to capitalist production comes from *outside* of capitalist production. So what need to be transcended are relations that are not of capitalism.

66   According to CPI(M-L) Liberation (2018): 'Agriculture [is] ...weighed down by the preponderance of a semi-feudal small peasant economy and caught in a perennial crisis of capitalist transition via landlord path...'. It further says that: 'Indian society is driven by four main contradictions – the contradiction between imperialism and the Indian people, that between feudal fetters and remnants and the broad masses of the people, between big capital and the Indian people, the working class and the peasantry in particular, and the contradiction among various sections of the ruling classes. ...The antagonism between

CAPITALIST CHARACTER OF CLASS SOCIETY IN POST-COLONIAL INDIA

and indefinite wait for the fight for socialism (= abolition of class relations) to start and requires collaboration with some good (progressive) capitalists.[67] But if what is present is already capitalism, albeit one that is not very progressive,[68] and one that is not going to be very progressive for a long period of time because of all the constraints on the transition to real subsumption of labor within the contemporary imperialist world market which severely constrains economic development in India and other low-income countries, and if there are forces that make the appropriation of absolute surplus value salient, then the nature of class politics must be seen in an entirely different manner: this means that revolution as the highest point of class struggle against capitalism in India must be on the agenda right now.

But does this mean that one cannot fight for reforms within capitalism? Or, more specifically, does this mean that small-scale producers' demand for access to means of production (land and credit) can be ignored?[69] The answer is no: within limits, the fight for land and for other such concessions is a means of po-litical mobilization of the masses, and under the pressure of mass mobilization, *some* land redistribution and some restriction on primitive accumulation might even happen under a bourgeois government. What the anti-semi-feudalism claim made in this Chapter suggests is this: it is only a state under the control

---

this nexus and the broad Indian masses thus constitutes the principal contradiction of present Indian society...These main contradictions determine the stage of our revolution – the stage of people's democratic revolution with agrarian revolution as its axis. ... The main force of the democratic revolution led by the working class is the peasantry'.

One of the major communist parties in India, CPI (Maoist) (2014), says that: 'The contemporary Indian society is semi-colonial and semi-feudal under neo-colonial form of indirect rule, exploitation, and control'.

According to the CPI(M) (2017), India's largest communist party: 'The three main con-tradictions that exist in Indian society are: (i) the contradiction between landlordism and the mass of the peasantry; (ii) the contradiction between imperialism and the Indian people; and (iii) the contradiction between the working class and the bourgeoisie'. It says that 'the contradiction between big landlordism and the mass of the peasantry is the principal contradiction'.

In other words, as one can see, the capital – labor contradiction is not the main con-tradiction, and the labor is not the main revolutionary agent in contemporary times and the socialist movement is a distant goal, for any of these organizations and their organic intellectuals.

67 Basole (2016: 297) says that such a view signifies 'the stagism of historical materialism'. More correctly, to me, such a view characterizes the *Stalinist* version of historical materi-alism, rather than historical materialism *as such.*

68 Progressive (non-monopoly capitalists) capitalists will develop productive forces and re-move pre-capitalist or non-capitalist barriers to capitalist development.

69 It has been argued (for example, by Kar, 2018) from the semi-feudal perspective that: the claim that a country such as India is a dominantly capitalist economy (and not a small peasant economy) means that land redistribution is off the agenda.

of the proletariat, following a *socialist* revolution, that can successfully carry out land redistribution *and* stop the beneficiaries from losing their land through extra-economic dispossession or market-based class differentiation. No government that still respects the rules of the capitalist market, whether or not there are capitalist monopolies, can protect the small-scale producers against the loss of their property that is based on family labor. And it is only a socialist government that can create a situation where small-scale producers will voluntarily opt out of family-based production and join large-scale demo-cratically-organized workers-controlled production units, in part because only such a government can *drastically* expand the remuneration of workers by dis-possessing the capitalist class and by cutting down on wasteful and unproduc-tive expenditures that are the hallmarks of capitalist society.

If India is dominantly capitalist, then the core of the political agenda must be the anti-capitalist struggle of the working class (both proletarian and semi-proletarian elements) against the totality of capitalist class relation, including in its most general form (i.e. formal subsumption of labor). This class must be politically allied with small-scale producers which are adversely impacted, in so many ways, by the capitalist class (and by its class partner, i.e. rent-receiving landlords). The combined and common goal of these two toiling classes must be a socialist state, a state of workers, allied with self-employed small-scale producers. By driving all propertied classes (pre-capitalist or capitalist) from their ruling positions, such a state can create conditions for a higher level of development of productive forces and for a society without exploitation and oppression as a part of a South-Asia-wide and global revolutionary process.

CHAPTER 4

Neoliberal Capitalism with Indian Characteristics

Like everything else in the world, capitalism comes in multiple forms (and many stages) (see Figure 4.1 below).[1] We have seen in the previous chapter that capitalist class relation, in India or elsewhere, exists in different forms: formal and real subsumption of labor, for example. The formal subsumption is the most general form of capitalism. It has four traits including, commodification of labor power and of the means of production and subsistence, and exploitation of labor in the workplace (on the basis of the appropriation of absolute surplus value). From another angle, the stages (or the chronological forms) through which capitalism has developed can be expressed as: laissez faire; monopolistic; Keyenesian/developmentalist; and neoliberal (Fine and Saad-Filho, 2017: 695).[2] The focus of this chapter is on the neoliberal form/stage of capitalism.

The remainder of this chapter is divided into four sections. In the first section, it makes some brief conceptual observations on the neoliberal phase of capitalism in general. In the second section, it sets the context for a discussion on neoliberalism as it is expressed in India. The third section presents nine theses on how neoliberal capitalism operates, and impacts people's lives, in India. The fourth, and the final section summarizes the discussion and then addresses the following question: how should we think about various forms of struggle – struggle around the agrarian question, national question (anti-imperialism), and the democratic question, and the struggle against capitalism – in a *neoliberal*-capitalist world?

1   Neoliberalism: Its General Traits

Neoliberalism is a historical *form* of capitalism *itself.* The neoliberal form of capitalism is a capitalism where the business activity is relatively less 'state-directed' in the interest of national development and welfare of the masses, and where the *nation*-state responds to *global* market forces relative to national-level market forces (Steger and Roy, 2010).

---

1   Sections 3–4 of this chapter draw on: Das (2012d) and Das (2015).
2   Of course, no stage is a pure stage: a given stage will have traits from a preceding stage and the succeeding stage, and yet a given stage will have a trait which distinguishes it from other stages.

© KONINKLIJKE BRILL NV, LEIDEN, 2020 | DOI:10.1163/9789004415560_005

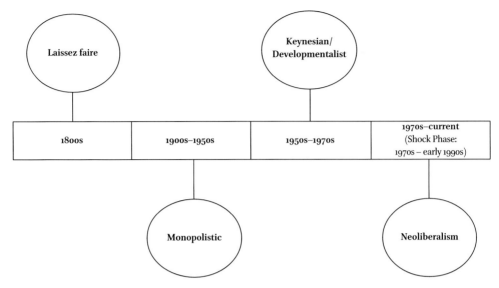

FIGURE 4.1   The evolution of capitalism
SOURCE: AUTHOR (BASED ON FINE AND SAAD-FILHO, 2017)

Neoliberalism is above all 'a theory of political economic practices that proposes that human well-being can best be advanced by liberating individual entrepreneurial freedoms and skills' by reducing governmental regulation and by promoting 'strong private property rights, free markets, and free trade' (Harvey, 2005: 2). The state's role is usually restricted, at least in theory, to the following: money supply, private property rights and the creation and maintenance of the markets, all of which are essential elements of capitalism as such but which cannot be created by individual capitalists.

Neoliberalism is a capitalist class project 'on steroids' as reflected in governmental policy. Marx's (1977) general formula in *Capital 1* to describe capitalism – i.e. to describe capital's circuit – is: M–C (MP + LP) –P–C'–M'.[3] At each of the points in capital's circuit (e.g. supply of credit/money; conditions of profitable production with a relatively pliant labor force; ensuring import and export of new commodities produced), capital wants – 'uses' – the state to help it make money, and quickly, through pro-business policies (this is explained in the next section in the discussion on Indian neoliberalism). The

---

3   This formula says that money (M) is invested to buy commodities (MP = means of production including machines/tools and raw materials; LP = labor power) to use them to produce (P) new commodities (C') which is sold for more money (M') than invested.

capitalist state intervenes at each moment of the circuit, more or less, in all the different phases of capitalism, but the capitalist state in its neoliberal form behaves in a much more pro-capitalist way than before. The turnover-time – including the transition from M' to M and from M to C, and so on – has to be quickened, and any obstacles to that must be annihilated by the state itself, directly or indirectly.

In spite of the state helping capital at each point in the circuit and in spite of relaxation of state control over capital, there has not necessarily been fast economy-wide growth in most countries going neoliberal over a sustained period of time. Harvey (2005) has said that neoliberalism has been less successful in generating growth and more successful in redistributing wealth between and among fractions of the capitalist class. This has led to increasing level of financialization: 'the immediate realization of profits based on the anticipated creation of surplus value' (O'Connor, 2010: 702). In other words, 'This new form of neoliberal appropriation manifests itself in short-term speculative gains, foreign exchange arbitrage, and various forms of financial trading' (ibid.). As the rate of profit has dropped in the actual production of commodities, thanks to the rising organic composition of capital, a section of the capitalist class has been in pursuit of 'financial returns at the expense of production' under neoliberalism.[4] As Fine and Saad-Filho (2016: 691) say, 'The creation and circulation of these financial assets is an intrinsically speculative activity that tends to become unmoored from the constraints of production, even though this autonomy can never be complete'.[5] This is why the long circuit of capital mentioned before is shortened to M–M'. Even while certain parts of the economy (e.g. IT-related industries) have grown,[6] the financial sector under neoliberalism has failed to address the major problems of the world. Neoliberalism has

---

4 'In this sense, a mortgage, for example, remains a simple (transhistoric) credit relation between borrower and lender. However, it becomes embroiled in financialization once that mortgage obligation is sold on as part of some other asset, which becomes routinized only under neoliberalism' (O'Connor, 2010: 691).

5 The fact of 'financial sector control of economic resources and the main sources of capital allows it to drain capital from production; at the same time, neoliberalism systematically, if unevenly, favours large capital at the expense of small capital and the workers, belying its claims to foster competition and 'level the playing field'. As a result, accumulation in neoliberal economies tends to take the form of bubbles which eventually collapse with destructive implications and requiring expensive state-sponsored bailouts. These cycles include the international debt crisis [and regional debt crises]' (p. 698).

6 How the IT industry promoted under neoliberalism has benefitted some and excluded many, see D'Costa (2011).

not produced much employment, while it has produced enormous inequality in income and wealth.[7]

The essential feature of the capitalist society is in the relation between capital and labor, which is based in relations of exchange, property, and value/surplus-value (Das, 2017a: Chapter 7). In capitalist society which is dominated by the commodity-form or value-form (generalized commodity production), workers must sell their commodity (labor power) to capital. They must depend on capital for a given amount of exchange value, with which to buy the commodities they need in order to meet their needs.[8] Capitalism is not only dominated by the value-form or commodity-form (of things and of labor power). It is also dominated by a specific property-form (capitalist form of property). It is 'that kind of property which exploits wage-labour' and which 'is based on the antagonism of capital and wage labour' (Marx and Engels, 1848: Chapter 2). One special characteristic of capitalist property (as opposed to property based in family labor) is that only a tiny minority can possess it and that the vast majority must have none of it or very little of it.[9] Without any property or with a very limited amount of property, labor is not only compelled to rely on capital for living. Because labor has been, more or less, separated from property, a process of separation that must be maintained, capital can also economically force labor – that is, impose market relations on labor whereby, at best, wages cover the average cost of reproduction of the commodity labor power – to surrender to it a large part of the net product that labor produces. The latter – the surrendered/alienated product (which takes the form of surplus value) – is then transformed into fresh capital, which, in turn, controls and exploits labor in an incessant movement. Marx and Engels say in the *Communist Manifesto*: 'To be a capitalist, is to have not only a purely personal, but a social *status* in production. ... Capital is therefore not only personal; it is a social power' (ibid.).[10]

---

7   'So-called global cities of finance and command functions have become spectacular islands of wealth and privilege, with towering skyscrapers and millions upon millions of square feet of office space to house these operations. Within these towers, trading between floors creates a vast amount of fictitious wealth. Speculative urban property markets, furthermore, have become prime engines of capital accumulation. The rapidly evolving skylines of Manhattan, Tokyo, London, Paris, Frankfurt, Hong Kong, and now Shanghai are marvels to behold' (Harvey, 2005: 157).

8   If capital cannot make money out of such an exchange (purchase and sale of labor power), labor will not be able to sell its commodity.

9   The distribution of property is an aspect of class relation. If everyone, or if most men and women, have capitalist property, that property cannot be capitalist property, and there will be no capitalism. The fact that most of the productive resources (property) is in the hands of the capitalists class explains why capital has the social control over labor.

10   Because of the nature of the relations between labor and capital, capital is a *social* power: its power lies in the totality of relations between capital and labor. A capitalist, or a group of capitalists, personifies that social power.

There is a distinction between power and its effects. More specifically, power (social power of capital) is one thing, and effects that are produced when that power is exercised (by capital) are another. Capital has the power to exploit labor, but the actual effects of the exercise of that power can vary a bit. This is the case when the ratio of wages to surplus value can change to some extent, depending on political bargaining by labor, the level/pace of accumulation, etc., or when the reliance of labor on capital to provide wage-work can be a little less strong with the availability of alternative sources of income (e.g. state benefits), or when the amount of exchange value in the hands of the capitalist class is reduced through taxation, and so on.[11] There are indeed times when, as Marx says in *Capital* volume 1, 'the length and weight of the golden chain the wage-labourer has already forged for himself allow it to be loosened somewhat' (1977: 769). But 'the exploitation of the wage-labourer, and his [or her] situation of dependence' on capital remain intact (ibid.). That is because the social power of capital remains intact, whose *effects* are the varying 'length and weight of the golden chain'.

In any fundamental sense, in capitalist societies, there is not a time when the capitalist class does not have its social power to control and exploit labor (and indeed to dispossess small-scale producers). But the effects of the exercise of that power can change, within limits. So the neoliberal phase of capitalism, strictly speaking, cannot represent the *restoration* of class power, as Harvey and others mistakenly think. As long as there is capitalism, there cannot be any question of *restoration* of the power of capital. The capitalist class must have had to lose that power in the past for that power to be restored in the present.[12] Neoliberalism must be seen as enhancing the *effects* of the exercise of power that the capitalist class always has by virtue of it being that class. Under neoliberalism, that power is the power that large owners of business have over the working masses in a situation where markets are less and less regulated by the state in their interests or indeed on behalf of weaker/smaller capitalists. Neoliberalism represents an increase in the *effects* of capitalists' political power over the economy, as a response to the crisis of capitalism itself (crisis of profitability).

---

11   Even then one has to distinguish between different forms of such restriction: restrictions as a purported solution to the problems of capitalism (e.g. socializing some companies in trouble; putting some exchange values in the hands of workers in order to create a market for capitalists) are not the same as restrictions that are fundamentally caused by class struggle from below in the interest of toiling masses.

12   The thesis about the restoration of capitalist power does apply to countries such as Russia where capital's social power was overthrown, but not to the countries which have remained capitalist throughout the 20th century. It is a great mistake to club the two types of social formation in one category of countries that are neoliberal.

Neoliberalism is not a product of certain ideas, any more than capitalism is. But like all class projects, neoliberalism's existence and continuation is supported by certain ideas. As a class project, the neoliberal discourse *must* represent the interests of the capitalist class (including certain hegemonic fractions within it, and especially, those which do business globally), and the interests of all those sections of the 'middle class' (e.g. top officials; editors of journals, etc.) that are allied with, and serve, the capitalist class.[13] That is not enough. Any project of an exploiting class must have a dual ideological/discursive project of universalization and temporalization. The exploiting class, which is always the minority, must represent, through a discourse (a certain set of ideas informing certain practices), the material interests of its own (and a narrow section of the population that serves it) *as the interests of society as a whole*. Such false discursive universalization of parochial-class interest (where, for example, the capitalist class is seen as the wealth- and job-creator, and capitalist growth at any cost is said to be good for the country) is necessary if neoliberalism has to make people (the toiling masses) tolerate its intensely contradictory and adverse consequences. What is also necessary is a false discursive temporalization: to make the majority-class believe that any sacrifices (e.g. cuts in wages and welfare) they are made to experience are only temporary, and that those sacrifices are good for them over the long-term. The reality is that those sacrifices are in the interest of the minority class, and are not in the short-term or long-term interests of the toiling masses. In all phases of capitalism, false universalization and false temporalization are necessary, but their need is stronger under neoliberalism because now the adverse effects of capitalism on the majority are worse.

In the discourse of capitalism, growth/development is a very important idea. Growth/development indicates that total investment (sum of constant and variable capital) rises and that with it rises the income from such investment for the investing class. The stress on growth/development has become much more important under neoliberalism. National governments and international institutions such as the World Bank always talk about this, justifying neoliberalism in the name of growth/development. Neoliberalism is indeed associated with the fetishism of growth: the endless and unmindful pursuit of growth at any cost is everywhere to see. An important indicator of growth is taken to be increase in GDP:

---

13   On the topic of how neoliberalism has benefitted the middle class, see D'Costa (2013); Mukherji (2008); and McCartney (2013). Murphy (2011) discusses how neoliberalism is causing an emergence of transnational middle class values, especially, in the IT-related industries.

> The GDP statistic has become a potent force in the globalization of a particular way of economic thinking that we term neoliberalism. The hegemony and spread of this way of understanding our world and the way forward are powerfully underlain by the GDP and the meanings imputed to its trajectory.
>
> KRISHNA, 2015: 869[14]

Such an obsession with growth (as a rise in GDP) is in spite of the fact that neoliberalism has not been particularly associated with long-term high rate of growth in the majority of countries of the world.

Connected to the idea of growth/development in the neoliberal discourse is the idea of nationalism. There is a reciprocal relation between neoliberalism and nationalism. The neoliberal state works to promote globalization. Yet, 'Forced to operate as a competitive agent in the world market and seeking to establish the best possible business climate, it mobilizes nationalism in its effort to succeed' (Harvey, 2005: 85). Although Harvey does not quite explain this, it is not difficult to see why this is the case: when all capitalist states are competing to attract (the mobile) global capital to the areas under their jurisdictions, they will have to create an idea of national uniqueness. That is: they have to say that what their nation has – in terms of helping global capital make higher profit – is superior to what exists in other nations. This discourse of national uniqueness is a potentially cheap fodder for national*ism*. Nationalism is used by capital and its politicians to implement a neoliberal project including austerity that demands self-sacrifice on the part of the masses. Nationalism can also be a product of neoliberalism. When capital's mobility (and especially that of money-capital) has increased tremendously, all the nations, competing with another, may not succeed in attracting much foreign capital. Some may succeed. Others may not. This can produce pride for some nations and pain for others, and thus antagonism between nations. Harvey correctly says: 'Competition produces ephemeral winners and losers in the global struggle for position, and this in itself can be a source of national pride or of national soul-searching' (Harvey, 2005: 85). Nationalism can also serve as a psychological compensation for the adverse effects of neoliberalism or neoliberal globalization, that threatens a nation's economy, culture and sovereignty. All this is the "inter-state aspect" of the nationalist discourse of neoliberalism.

There is an intra-state aspect as well. Neoliberalism produces massive suffering for the people, thus creating a potential for antagonism towards

---

14   Therefore, 'The fascination with number and the fetishization of a highly misleading index should be evaluated in terms of the illocutionary force of this economic concept' (ibid.). In fact, 'A progressive politics that can think outside the thrall of neoliberal globalization would do well to begin by demystifying the GDP' (ibid.).

it, from the toiling masses (and also from small-scale business-men and business-women). To pre-empt this and to cope with struggle against neoliberalism when it happens, the capitalist state has to mobilize all sections of the people. It does so, in part, on the basis of national unity created by appeal to culture, language, history, etc. The purpose is to produce people's loyalty to the nation and to the state, a state of the nation that, however, fundamentally works for a tiny minority of the nation, the capitalist class.

Appeals to national unity do not have to be based on extra-economic traits (language, history, etc.). Such appeals can indeed be made to the need for growth/development. This is where two sets of ideas within the neoliberal discourse come together: nationalism (a trait of a territorially-bounded people), and growth/development (which is basically an international process – thanks to the global law of value and international character of capitalism – which is manifested differently in different national territories). Socially-created belief in growth/development binds all the people in a nation, and this economic basis for nationalism adds to the extra-economic basis (culture, etc.). Anyone against growth/development runs the risk of being constructed as anti-national. Besides, neoliberalism causes suffering for people – and this is expressed in the form of the absence of development for the masses, including loss of employment, lack of good infrastructure, etc. – and yet they are told that what is necessary is growth/development and that neoliberalism is the way to achieve it. Quietly, development/growth is equated to the (state-promoted) production of the conditions necessary for an increase in profit for the capitalist class, such as roads, so development is not about reduced unemployment or increased income for the common people. What is hidden is that development/growth really means capitalist growth/development. And, national unity – non-antagonism towards the agenda of development/growth and towards the capitalist class driving the neoliberal project – makes the pursuit of that agenda easier.

Belief in the necessity of growth/development as capitalist growth/development has a dual ideological effect: it not only produces consent to capitalist relations (that growth/development can only occur within a capitalist framework unleashing the entrepreneurial spirit, etc.), but also reproduces nationalism (uniting masses with the capitalist class) that serves the capitalist class. Growth and development – i.e. neoliberal capitalist growth and development – are justified in the interest of the nation as a whole, even if it is the case that the discourse of nationalism represents the interests of the capitalist class (domestic and foreign) as the interests of the nation as a whole.[15]

---

15   Of course, as a method of securing citizens' loyalty, nationalism might not work always. This is because, Harvey says, nationalism 'is profoundly antagonistic to the neoliberal agenda', as 'the nationalism required for the state to function effectively as a corporate and competitive entity in the world market gets in the way of market freedoms more

Then there is a series of other neoliberal ideas: the ideas of competition; citizens-as-clients/consumers; naturalization of buying and selling (the idea that to satisfy a need, one must buy and sell things); obsession with market-governed actions; privatization-as-all-good; meritocracy; the idea that government deficits and debts are inherently bad while corporates bloat with unpayable debts; and so on (Monbiot, 2016). Because neoliberalism produces massive suffering and inequalities, it must operate on the basis of myths, false promises and false explanations of what is happening in the world. There are myths about state failure, and myths produce more myths. State failure is explained in terms of the state not freeing the markets enough. So the underlying myth is that the neoliberal state, a state that frees the market and is market-conforming, can hardly fail. Another myth is that inequality produces innovation, and if people's living standards do not rise, that is because of their *personal* failures, and not because of the increased effects of the social power of capital.

It is not enough to have neoliberal ideas. These ideas have to have bearers and propagators. As Harvey (2005: 3) says, its advocates 'occupy positions of considerable influence' not only in the education sector (the universities and many 'think tanks'), and in the media but also 'in corporate boardrooms and financial institutions, in key state institutions' and 'in those international institutions … that regulate global finance and trade'.

It is also not enough that a few powerful people have neoliberal ideas and propagate them. A large number of common people must accept neoliberalism as their common-sense. This seems to have happened. 'Neoliberalism has, in short, become hegemonic as a mode of discourse', says Harvey. Indeed, 'it has become incorporated into the common-sense way many of us interpret, live in, and understand the world' (Harvey, 2005: 3). Once people live under neoliberalism, independently of their will, they – the rich and the poor – begin to accept the ideas that, in turn, support the practice of neoliberalism, a process that also applies to capitalism as such. Given the hegemony of neoliberalism-as-common-sense, people – both within academia and outside – talk more and more of neoliberalism and less and less of capitalism explicitly.

2 Neoliberalism in India: The Context

Neoliberalism is called by different names in different contexts. In India, neoliberalism goes by the name of 'economic reforms' and the New Economic Policy (NEP). The views of proponents of neoliberalism have been widely published in India, including in its influential (and slightly progressive) *Economic*

---

generally' (Harvey, 2005: 79). But as with neoliberalism so with nationalism: when it fails, demand is made for a higher dosage of it.

Political Weekly, and the more radical, *Social Scientist*.[16] Bhagwati (2001: 843), a Columbia University economics professor, and an intellectual proponent of neoliberalism, conceptualizes reforms *qua* neoliberalism as representing 'a reversal of the anti-globalisation, anti-market, pro-public-enterprise attitudes and policies that produced our dismal growth performance [during the pre-1991 period]'. He says that these reforms are the most important factor in reducing poverty by increasing growth. His argument is that growth creates employment: it puts money in the hands of the government, which can provide health and other facilities for the poor, and it also provides incentive to the poor to invest in human capital. It is also said that 'the higher post-reform growth rates are delivering a steeper decline in poverty' (Datt and Ravallion, 2010: 57). By raising living standards in urban areas, economic growth has had a positive effect on rural incomes (ibid.).

A former Finance Minister, Mr. Chidambaram, like many others (e.g. Khatkhate, 2006), thinks that 'growth is the best antidote to poverty'; so, he says, 'what is needed is not less, but more reforms' (quoted in the *Hindu* on November 8, 2006). Such views are held by large segments of the Congress party, the traditional party of the big business, and by the BJP, the other national-party of the big business, which has now overshadowed the Congress party.

The former prime minister of India, who is himself an economist, talks about the need to encourage and revive the 'animal spirit' of the investors,[17] which will, in turn, promote welfare; the NEP is about this. The mantra of the current Prime Minister (Mr. Modi) of the BJP, 'minimum government and maximum governance', is a part of the same neoliberal agenda.

While proponents of neoliberalism – in other words, economic reform – say that it benefits everyone, it is interesting that in one survey, 'three-fourths of respondents who had any opinion on the subject say that the reforms benefit only the rich' (Bardhan, 2005). This chapter seeks to discuss neoliberalism in the Indian context in terms of its multi-dimensionality and its contradictions.

---

16   There is a massive amount of literature on the nature of the NEP (or neoliberalism in India), including about its positive and negative effects. Apart from the authors already referred to in the text, the literature includes: Ahluwalia (2002); Bhattacharya (2013); Byres (1997, 2013); Chandrasekhar and Ghosh (2004); Nayar (2001); Sengupta (2008); Subramanian (2008); Sackley (2015) and Tiwana and Singh (2015). This chapter does not aim to review this literature.

17   The *Hindu* (2012) reports: 'Reverse the climate of pessimism ... revive the animal spirit in the country's economy ... Millions of our countrymen look up to the government to throw open channels for their progress, prosperity and welfare', Dr. [Manmohan] Singh told Finance Ministry officials.

The neoliberal form of capitalism with its several general traits mentioned above (liberalization, privatization, globalization, marketization, selective state withdrawal from welfare provision, etc.) in practice will take different forms, depending on peculiarities of a country, thus producing what Harvey calls the 'uneven geographical development of neoliberalism on the world stage'. In considering neoliberalism in India, one has to examine the ways in which what are regarded as the 'general traits' of neoliberalism (which are deployed to increase the exploitation of workers and dispossess small-scale producers) work in India. India shares certain traits with other countries and the global economy, but it has also its own socio-historical specificities. It is important that our views of neoliberalism are not unduly based on the conditions in advanced capitalism of the US, UK, etc. For example, in the context of advanced capitalism, there may be some truth that 'The main substantive achievement of neoliberalization ... has been to redistribute, rather than to generate, wealth and income' (Harvey, 2005: 159), but in the context of less developed countries such as India or China, neoliberalism is very much about neoliberal accumulation in production on the basis of super-exploitation of workers and small-scale producers. According to some, the neoliberal period followed a period of post-war growth which entered into crisis of overaccumulation, a period which coincided with a capital-labor pact and some redistribution in favor of labor. But this was not quite true about India: in fact, the pre-neoliberal period was called the period of sluggish growth (Hindu rate of growth), although economic inequality was less than in neoliberal times. Harvey (2006: 42), following Dumenil, says that 'It [neoliberalism] has either restored class power to ruling elites (as in the US and to some extent in Britain...) or created conditions for capitalist class formation (as in China, India, Russia, and elsewhere)'. This description only partly fits Indian neoliberalism, because pre-neoliberal India did not represent a golden age for Indian private capital or indeed for the masses which experienced massive level of absolute poverty, nor can one say that neoliberalism 'created conditions for capitalist class formation' in India, for pre-neoliberal India did have a capitalist class, however weak, and however dependent on the state.

There are several specificities of India one might consider.

1. India has maintained a liberal-democratic system, even though it has been under pressure. Over the decades the voter turnout has been rather high (greater than 60% or so),[18] and there are more than 3 million elected representatives. The poor people of the country and rural people

---

18 At the general election held in 2014, 551 million people voted, and the voter turnout was 66.38%.

enthusiastically exercise their democratic right, and thus the electoral system is a big source of legitimacy for the socio-economic system. A part of the democratic system is federalism: the 29 States have a degree of autonomy relative to the central government (especially, in relation to agriculture, public order, health, and some aspects of industrial development), although this autonomy is under attack now.

2. While the democratic system gives a semblance of political equality, there is a massive amount of social inequality and oppression, on the basis of gender, caste, ethnicity, religion, language, etc. as well as inequality on the basis of income and wealth/property ownership (capitalists vs workers and petty producers).

3. There is a history of post-colonial state-led capitalist development since 1950s until late 1980s.[19]

4. India is characterized by massive absolute poverty, comparatively low labor productivity per hour, low per capita income and the numerical dominance of the rural population, most of which is in economic distress. These are all associated with the fundamental character of India's peripheral capitalism (including formal subsumption of labor under capital, which we have discussed in the last chapter) and imperialism (in the form of imperialist institutions such as World Bank, and imperialist governments). As well, colonial-era laws continue to exist, and impacts of colonialism continue to be experienced. While there is massive poverty of people, there is also a massive 'poverty' in the way poverty is measured by bourgeois intellectuals and the pliant bureaucrats, which officially underestimates poverty. Free market economics can produce some growth. As a result a person can earn a little more than the absolutely minimal

---

19   Unequal distribution of assets and income, which India partly inherited from its colonial past, meant limited purchasing power in the hands of the majority and therefore limited market for indigenously produced goods and services. Limited market was/is not conducive to growth of productive investment, employment and income, so the state stepped in: to generate demand for indigenous capital through its own investment, and to make resources (e.g. credit) available to the private sector at a subsidized rate. For all this the state needed resources, which it was short of, given its limited abilities to discipline the propertied class (taxation, etc.), so its debt level increased which forced it to look for loans on the condition that it frees up the market. The state also protected domestic market through tariffs, etc. to generate demand for indigenous capital, but such a policy went against the demand of international capital to have access to the Indian market. Protection of domestic markets also went against the appetite of higher-income groups that wanted foreign consumer goods. All of these contributed to the production of a context in which neoliberalism had an appeal.

cut-off point for the definition of poverty,[20] and this allows the state, international financial institutions, and organic intellectuals of the ruling class to declare that there has been a massive reduction in poverty because of neoliberalism, and thus to manufacture support for neoliberalism. This massiveness in poverty reduction, as a legitimizing device for neoliberalism, is therefore actually a gimmick: it is a product of extremely low cut-off point for the poverty definition (which means that a slight increase in income means moving above the poverty line).

5. India's geopolitical location is useful to the imperialist powers such as the US which seeks to counter the China threat by using India. India is also rich in natural resources and has a large pool of relatively cheap skilled and unskilled labor, which satisfies the pursuit of profit by domestic and imperialist capital.

6. India has a 'strong' presence of a communist movement relative to most other countries, prompting the editor of *International Socialism* to suggest that 'India is by far the most important country in the world where Communism remains a powerful political force' (Callinicos, 2010). Millions of people (20–40 million) vote for the parliamentary communist parties, and in large areas there is a presence of a militant Maoist movement. The communist parties as well as mainstream parties have their own labor unions and peasant associations. It is useful to note that labor strikes and farmers' marches happen regularly.

The combination of the general traits of neoliberalism (deregulation, privatization, liberalization, etc.) with India's specificities produces 'neoliberal capitalism with Indian characteristics'. Neoliberalism with Indian traits is thus located at the intersection between the logics of capitalism itself, in India and those in the world. Keeping this in mind, a number of observations are made on the multiple, internally-related aspects of Indian neoliberalism as a class project. No attempt is made to offer extensive empirical evidence for the statements made, nor are there exhaustive references to the existing literature on the topic.

3 Neoliberalism with Indian Characteristics: Eight Theses

3.1 *Neoliberalism as a Form of Capitalist Class Relation: More Than a Matter of Government Policy*

Neoliberalism in India, as elsewhere, is fundamentally a capitalist accumulation project under changed global and national conditions. It is a mistake to

---

20 The per capita monthly cut-off is Rs. 816 in rural areas and Rs. 1,000 in urban areas. This is as per a 2013 Planning Commission report.

see neoliberalism in India or elsewhere as a mere policy. Begun (semi-stealthily) in the 1980s, and formally introduced in 1991, the New Economic Policy (NEP) is not just a government *policy*. NEP – or Indian neoliberalism – is not merely a way of running India's capitalist economy on the basis of a particular set of policy interventions and associated mind-sets that could change (for example, the economy could delink itself from global economy) with support from sections of the capitalist class. Neoliberalism is, more than anything else, something that is *intrinsic* to the present phase of capitalist development in India, as a part of the global capitalist-economy.

While a greater role for the state was tolerated, and indeed, needed, by the Indian capitalist class immediately after independence when that class was economically weak, after almost three decades of state-assisted capitalism, the class became powerful enough to let go of the crutch that was the state, which was now considered a barrier to a higher rate and mass of profit. Indian neoliberalism is partly a specific response to the contradictions of India's post-colonial state-led capitalist development ('Indian Keynesianism' or Nehruvianism) within the global economy, where a state-regulated redistributionist capitalism ran into problems in the 1970s, much earlier than in India.

NEP is neither entirely *new* nor merely *economic*. It basically represents the demands of the capitalist class, and more specifically, the demands of *hegemonic* fractions of the domestic and foreign-diasporic capitalist class, including those capitalists who did not heavily depend on state-support, at a particular stage in the development of Indian and global capitalism.[21] The neoliberal policy signifies the fact that these economic demands get transformed into specific policies, even if in a manner that is state-mediated.[22] This class now

---

21 One of the demands was to open the foreign market for Indian capitalists, and this was to counter the stagnation in the domestic market (Patnaik et al., 2004: 90). The state intervention occurred in the interest of global capital and its Indian allies (ibid.). That the NEP agenda hurts the weaker sections of the capitalist class is a different matter.

22 Note that the demands for liberalization were made a long time ago. 'The opposition (the first force that openly proposed this idea was the Swatantra Party, created in 1959) offered the opinion that the authorities should undertake destatization in their approaches to economic problems, trust more "the forces of supply and demand", liberate prices from the state's control, and, finally, gradually dismantle the state sector. Such was the extreme point of view concerning means of struggling against inflation, which the upper layer of the private corporate sector feared to declare openly. However, the reality did not confirm the justness of the market alternative to the compromising policy of the Congress. At the parliamentary election of 1971, the Swatantra Party and its closest allies fell into political oblivion' (Volodin, 2018: 102). The Swatantra Party was a right-wing secular party while the BJP established in 1980, like its predecessor, Bharatiya Jana Sangh (1951–1977), is a right-wing communal party. Some sections of the Indian bourgeoisie want to see a variant of the Swatantra Party now.

wants to – and with modern technological changes in transportation and communication, is *able* to – do business in a different manner than in the past. It wants the state to clear the way for this new way of doing things. India's annual national budget now, more or less, represents a wish-list of capitalist fractions represented by chambers of commerce and corporate lobbyists in a way not quite possible earlier.[23] The NEP outlines the specific demands of the capitalist class for the state to create conditions where domestic and foreign capital can invest money to make a lot of money.[24] Their wish-list gets a sympathetic hearing from the pro-market state managers, who are the political CEOs occupying important positions within the state.[25]

Much-needed support is provided by the opinion makers in the media and intellectuals (including its television intellectuals and professors from imperialist countries). No social – material practice can continue to operate without a corresponding discursive practice that justifies it.

The idea of neoliberalism is to make money not only by using natural resources like land, water, forests, and minerals that are made available to capital by the state at a cheap rate, and that India has plenty of, but also by using speculation and other non-productive means and by exploiting cheap skilled and unskilled labor. An important goal is to attract foreign capital and strengthen the position of Indian business in the fight for export markets and to obtain

---

23 'The first policy initiatives taken under the banner of liberalisation, lifting many of the restrictions of the licence-control raj, benefitted industrial capitalists disproportionately.... Removing restrictions was definitely easier as policy than implementing new programmes. The consequence was that industrial capitalists were able to secure huge surpluses from expansion through international trade and from catering to the pent-up demands of a growing domestic middle class' (Gupta and Sivaramakrishnan, 2011: 8). The second phase of liberalisation saw the decision to allow the States [provinces] more freedom to promote their own economic strategies, especially to seek out their own sources of foreign direct investment (FDI). This led to the consolidation of industrial capitalists' power and undermined the dominance of agricultural interests at the State level without displacing them entirely. States favour industries by giving them special economic zones (SEZs), tax holidays and other sops; they appeal to farmers by giving free electricity and subsidised canal water (ibid.: 9).

24 Lockwood (2014: 2) says that NEP did not happen because of demand of the bourgeoisie, but because of autonomous state action.

25 The most enthusiastic of the listeners in the government was Dr. Manmohan Singh, the former prime minister who, incidentally, had declared his respect for Thatcher, the co-architect of global neoliberalism with Reagan. The new Prime Minister, Modi, who, some believe, is India's Reagan, is in the same league as Dr. Singh whom he replaced in 2014, as far as economic policy is concerned, except that he is more strident, vocal and unabashed than the quiet, polite and erudite Dr. Singh.

foreign technology and capital. The NEP model pursues the goal of transforming India into a world power by making it an office (e.g. call centers; software companies), a laboratory (for pharmaceutical and biotech companies, for example), a factory and a raw-material source of agri-produce, for international capital, based on (relatively) cheap labor in a labor market characterized by state-promoted flexibility and precarity.[26]

In the NEP model, existing barriers to money-making, such as government regulations of business or small-scale producers' control over property (e.g. land), should be removed and new facilitative conditions (e.g. pro-business policies) for money-making should be created. Indeed, some of the specific demands of business, as expressed politically by the NEP, include: the deregulation of private businesses; the privatization of government businesses;[27] trade liberalization; the granting of permission to foreign capital to own businesses in India; the enactment of tax cuts and other incentives for businesses; regressive taxation (e.g. GST or similar types); and the reduction or complete withdrawal of government benefits for the poor, with extreme targeting as opposed to universal benefits; and complete freedom for private capital to hire and fire labor. The NEP, therefore, is the neoliberal program of the bourgeois class first, and a government policy second.[28]

The specific demands that the NEP articulates emanate from the ways in which capital seeks to connect to each term in Marx's (1977) general formula in *Capital 1* referred to earlier: M–C–P–C′–M′. This is to be seen as integrated into the world market. Through various policies (e.g. low-interest loans; loan waivers to the business class euphemistically called non-performing assets; various bailout packages), the neoliberal state in India makes liquid investible

---

26   Dasgupta (2017) talks about how capitalist accumulation is happening through a flexible labor regime aimed at making labor as cheap as possible. Such flexibilization is creating a reserve army and repressing the organized voice of workers (ibid.: 57; also Tiwana, 2015).

27   In spite of their capitalist and bureaucratic character in terms of functioning, they had a degree of pro-worker orientation as seen in the fact that these units had provided subsidized housing and other facilities to workers (Subramanian, 2015).

28   This does not mean that the NEP can be *entirely* reduced to capital's interests. These interests are mediated by the state (or by the political sphere of society), so the autonomy of the state (including electoral compulsions in India) must be borne in mind. This is one reason why welfare policies are not entirely off the agenda of the neoliberal state, especially in a liberal-democracy existing in a country of massive absolute poverty, a combination that can be a serious threat to the ruling class. Harriss (2011b) says: 'the neoliberal project in India is tempered by India's constitutional design and state tradition as well as by social movements... and popular democracy' (p. 128). This is true, as I have shown elsewhere (Das, 2007). But the point to emphasize is this: to function as a neoliberal state, it does not have to spend nothing for the poor.

resources (M) available to big business, often at below-market rates. Liberalization of financial markets allows domestic businesses access foreign capital, which a relatively under-developed economy is said to rely on. The state makes commodities available in the form of cheap raw materials and cheap land (C), which have been obtained from people via primitive accumulation, including in areas inhabited by indigenous communities. In a developing society such as India's, the state plays an important role in converting what are non-commodities into commodities. Through the liberalization of trade, the state makes foreign commodities available as intermediate goods.

An important part of the C in the capital circuit is labor power that capital buys. The non-implementation of a living wage by the state – in a context where there is a massive and growing reserve army to which primitive accumulation under neoliberalism contributes – drives wages below the cost of maintenance (i.e. the value of labor power). Further, the state, including the courts, often suppresses the right to strike, including in the name of inviting foreign capital. Factory Acts that seek to ensure workers' safety remain unimplemented, in part because of the nefarious nexus of state officials/politicians and the business world and the overall climate of free market ideology. Capital's despotic rule in the labor process becomes even more despotic than before, a despotic rule that is strengthened by the ease with which capital can hire and fire labor. The existing rules protecting nature and workers from the harmful effects of capitalist production are being gutted. All this makes for a heightened level of accumulation by exploitation.

The capitalist class character of neoliberalism can be gauged partly from the following fact: while neoliberalism has put enormous amount of wealth in the hands of the capitalist class (especially top 0.1% to top 1% of the nation), the share of labor in the national income has fallen from an already low level of 40% in 1991 (when neoliberalism was officially launched) to 35% in 2013. If capitalists have subjected labor to super-exploitation (with the average wage for most workers being \$2 a day), one would 'expect' a 'liberal-democratic' state to spend more for labor. However, government spending to alleviate labor's problems has also declined: for example, the funding for the biggest employment generation program for rural workers has come down from 0.42% of GDP in 2010–2011 to 0.42% in 2017–2018, while tax cuts for the capitalist class have been massive.

Following the production process, the state helps capital access foreign markets (C'). Sometimes, the state creates markets (e.g. state-promoted insurance to farmers, which is sold by the private sector; state-promoted building of physical infrastructure which is actually built by private companies for enormous profits). Privatization of state services (e.g. education and health-care, etc.) also creates and expands markets for production of goods and services in the private sector. And finally, the state makes sure that the business world gets to keep much of the surplus value it appropriates from workers and small-scale producers, and that this happens in the form of tax exemptions, tax reduction, write-off of tax arrears, and so on.[29]

The NEP is certainly new, as its name suggests, but it is not as new as is commonly thought. All major interventions, including major anti-poverty policies since de-colonization, have been more or less about propping up a national capitalist regime (with some support from erstwhile 'socialist' countries), a regime that is a little protected from imperialism and a little free from the fetters of feudal remnants. Even in terms of actual spending, the Indian state *has been* a welfare state of the rich elite. Many of the resources in the hands of the state have been used for the propertied classes (in the form of various subsidies and cheap loans) and for wealthier, higher-income, more educated people.[30] According to the government's own estimates, in the mid-1990s (when the NEP was only a few years old), the central and state governments together gave out more than 10 per cent of the GDP in the form of explicit or implicit budgetary subsidies for 'nonmerit' goods and services (the latter largely accrue to the relatively rich) (Bardhan, 2005).[31] The pre-1991 age, including the so-called Nehruvian age, was not exactly a golden age for the masses, although the degree of economic inequality was much less. Mass poverty and (petty) bureaucratic heavy-handedness were rampant. It is not that there is no absolute difference between the NEP and the pre-1991 regime. But the similarity between the two is not to be un-dialectically under-stressed. The neoliberal Indian state is a *capitalist* state like the pre-neoliberal Indian state.

---

29   To the extent that M–C–P–C'–M' can be shortened to M–M' (meaning money can simply be made from money), the state helps capitalists increase their profit in the form of interest and profit from speculation, etc. in the sphere of financialization.

30   See the early work of Bardhan (1990) as well as Bardhan (2005). While I agree that state resources have been used to benefit the proprietary classes, I do not endorse Bardhan's analytical Marxist sympathies for the market economy, nor his viewing of state actors as a class (see Chapter 7 of this book).

31   Advocates of neoliberalism 'do not dither when it comes to condemning any sign of the government using tax revenues to provide transfers or subsidies to the poor or undertake expenditures that are expressly meant to favour the poor, in the form of livelihood protection, poverty alleviation or free and universal provision of basic health and educational facilities. Their justification for this is twofold: that expenditure to support growth must be favoured over spending to directly improve welfare; and that fiscal prudence must be privileged over all else when deciding the use of the exchequer's resources. So, if spending has to be tailored to correspond to revenues, expenditure on "populist" measures must be limited or abjured' (Chandrasekhar, 2018). 'There is a twist in the arithmetic underlying such reasoning. It assumes that the difference between tax and non-tax revenues on the one hand, and total expenditures on the other can be reduced only by reducing expenditures and not by increasing revenues' (i.e. not by increases in taxes on the rich) (ibid.).

NEOLIBERAL CAPITALISM WITH INDIAN CHARACTERISTICS

That neoliberalism is a capitalist project, that it is a project of capitalists, by capitalists and for capitalists, is very clear from what the following top captains of Indian industry and enterprise themselves say about what is euphemistically called new economic policy or economic reforms (or just reforms).

> Post reforms, businesses are much more in control of their own destiny than before.
>
> MURTHY, 2018: 609

> The 1991 economic liberalization was truly an extraordinary leap of faith that not just swept aside the decades-old legacy of socialism and state control but scripted a new landscape carved around fee market and globalization ... The story of Indian liberalization has truly been the story of Indian entrepreneurship.
>
> MITTAL, 2018: 567–568, 574

> Reliance (Reliance Industries Limited) ambitiously seized the opportunities created by the post-1991 reforms, expanding the competencies of our group. This happened because we realized the strong synergies between wealth generation for the nation and value creation for the company.
>
> AMBANI, 2018: 557–558

These words are echoed by T. Das, a capitalist and a former CEO of a national business association (the Confederation of Indian Industry):

> Government and business need each other to strengthen the national economy and the economic growth process in the country. They are two sides of the same coin. Both need each other. To remember this fact of life...is the real need.
>
> DAS, T., 2018: 235

He is not saying what *should* be the case. He is describing what the state of affairs *is*.

3.2 *Agrarian Neoliberalism*

In poor countries such as India, there is a specific form of neoliberalism known as agrarian neoliberalism.[32] This requires a special treatment, given that the

---

32   Just as it is important to think about neoliberalism in terms of agrarian neoliberalism (see Oya, 2005; Vakulabharanam and Motiram, 2011; Walker, 2008; see also Appendix 2), it is also important to think about neoliberalism in terms of industrialization and what can be

vast majority of the workforce still depends on farming in most parts of the country. Agrarian neoliberalism represents an internally contradictory logic: on the one hand, rural areas are *emphasized* as being attractive venues for big business activities because of rural markets and cheap land and labor in rural and semi-rural areas; on the other hand, from the standpoint of state investment, rural areas are not a priority. Rural areas have indeed an interesting relation to the business class. They have become an arena for new forms of private accumulation: buying peasants' land dirt cheap; agribusiness selling seeds and other inputs to peasants at a high price; and patenting of peasants' knowledge; industrial and financial capital selling consumer goods including cell phones, and insurance, etc. Rural areas have attracted investment from agribusiness which is in search of cheap labor and land and new markets (for seeds, etc.). An important form of capitalist investment in rural areas is on the basis of contract farming.[33] This has at least two aspects from the standpoint of the neoliberal state. On the one hand, operating in a context where the neoliberal state is not guaranteeing a remunerative price in spite of rising input prices, farmers enter into contracts with big business on unequal terms. On the other hand, encouraged by the state, contract farming allows coordination of mercantile, financial and productive forms of capital when domestic and foreign businesses are able to procure agro-raw materials, without experiencing any risk involved in the actual production process (which might involve capital-labor conflict and which also involve the risk that nature might create).[34]

In terms of the relation between the state and rural areas, they have been subjected to neglect: rural development expenditure as a percentage of the net national product has been decreasing. Government subsidies for fertilizers, electricity, and other farm inputs, as well as investment in irrigation, have all been slashed. Access to cheap loans for farmers has been limited. Price supports to farmers have been reduced, and the Public Distribution System has been drastically curtailed. It should be noted that the extent of the cuts has been debated, and some say that such cuts have not happened because of India's democratic system in which the poor have some voice and because

---

called extractive neoliberalism, i.e. neoliberalism in the mining sector. On the latter, see Adduci (2017).

33   On contract farming, see Shrimali (forthcoming) and Vicol (2019).

34   The coordination among three forms of capital refer to the fact that contract farming allows capitalist production (productive capital) of an agro-product (e.g. potato chips) by commercial farmers who receive inputs (mercantile capital) and financial assistance (financial capital) from the big business, including the MNCs.

therefore there is a fear of class war owing to the adverse impacts of neoliberalism itself.[35]

Peasants are losing land to capitalist industrialization and land-speculation. Land ceiling laws are reversed because they are considered to be constraints on capital flows into farming. Peasants are being forced to leave their land because farming is not viable: the costs of cultivation are going up due to shrinking government support. These people are also adversely affected by the import of subsidized foreign farm goods. Highly indebted, many are driven to distress sales.

As Utsa Patnaik (2007) has admirably documented, there is a decline in food production and availability per capita. This is in part because land is converted to non-food crops both by big companies and by smaller owners who do not have many alternative ways of earning money and who are therefore attracted to the prospect of making a little cash. This is a grave threat to food security (Patnaik, 2013). Also, in the areas where high-value farm products are produced (e.g. shrimps, flowers), intense exploitation of labor, land, and water happens in order to make the sector competitive in the global market. Declining investment in rural infrastructure (especially flood and irrigation control) is increasing vulnerability to such natural calamities as drought and floods. The role of the government in buying farm produce at a favorable rate from peasants is less and less important. With trade liberalization, changes in international prices make farmers, especially those with less land and limited investible

---

35 'In the standard narrative of neoliberalism, the emphasis has always been on the slashing of public expenditure by cost-conscious governments and not on increasing public outlays to enable people to meet their basic needs. In India, however, the reverse may appear to be true. One could argue that this is a peculiar outcome of Indian democracy because the participation of poor, subaltern, and rural populations in the electoral process is often higher than that of urban, middle-class people; numerically, poor and rural groups form a preponderant part of the electorate'. Therefore, the state resorts to increased public expenditures to enable people to meet their basic needs. This is what explains, according to the editors, ambitious social programmes such as the National Rural Employment Guarantee Scheme (Gupta and Sivaramakrishnan, 2011: 5). Partha Chatterjee has argued 'the paradoxical growth of state welfare programmes after liberalisation can be explained by the political compulsions of a pattern of growth that is immiserising a vast majority of people in the country'. He emphasises the real fear of class war. 'If the effects of liberalisation on the poor and those displaced from their land and deprived of livelihoods by primary accumulation are not reversed by government policies, they might turn into "dangerous" classes' (Gupta and Sivaramakrishnan, 2011: 6). Of course, 'Inclusive growth has not meant including the poor in growth. What it has meant is taking the higher government revenues obtained from rapid growth in sectors of the economy tied to the global market and redistributing them to indigent sections of the population. Growth of the rural economy has not been a central concern of government policy' (ibid.: 6).

surplus, more vulnerable when prices fall; they become dependent on exploitative private traders (as in the pre-1991 times). Agrarian distress (crisis of income and livelihood of the farm-dependent classes) is creating a huge reserve army, a part of which is forced to migrate to cities (permanently or periodically). This, along with shrinking government support for workers reducing the already-meagre social wage, allows capital to raise the level of exploitation (one person does the work of two, which cuts demand for labor from rural areas, from the latent reserve army). That the NEP is producing increasing numbers of wealthy people, on the one hand, and hundreds of millions of (rural) people whose basic needs (e.g. for food) remain singularly unsatisfied, on the other, speaks to the fact that neoliberalism is *a* class project with severe implications for the rural periphery.

Agrarian neoliberalism is often associated with what I will call New Agricultural Production (NAP), i.e. production of high-value farm products such as shrimps (and flowers) for exports (this is discussed in details in a later chapter) with the support of the state. The 'lean' neoliberal state exists in a selectively hollowed out manner (Jessop, 2002) and institutionalizes within its form the tensions of civil society. It encourages, for example, flori- and shrimp production, but, as mentioned before, withdraws, or reduces, food subsidizes for the poorer laborers and peasants who produce fish and flowers neither of which they can afford to consume. Indeed, the drastic reduction of public investment and public provisions of food can be compared in terms of its effect on people to the enclosures of the commons. This trend exists in other countries producing high-value agri-commodities for export (Newly Agricultural Countries), but India has a certain degree of specificity. On the one hand, and more akin to the countries of the Global North, it is a liberal parliamentary democracy; indeed, the world's largest. On the other hand, unlike in these countries a vast majority of India's population of 1.3 billion depend on farming and other rural activities and are adversely affected by neoliberalism (Dasgupta, 1998). This unique context in which neoliberalism is practiced, and the way rural areas are affected, demands comprehensive investigation. Understanding the relation between neoliberal capitalism and rural areas is very important not least because most people live in rural areas but also because the rural areas suffer from more adverse impacts of neoliberalism than urban areas, which happen to be the major seat of capital, including in its neoliberal form, and of the segments of the population that capital absolutely needs (e.g. highly educated people with technical and managerial skills). A fuller consideration of the relation between neoliberalism and rural areas must include: (1) the shift in agricultural production to new and luxury crops for export; (2) emergence of differential rates of development at multiple scales; (3) intensification of pressures emanating from changing agricultural production upon labor and environmental resources; (4) geographically uneven consolidation and centralization in new agriculture; (5) cultural changes that help legitimize neoliberal reforms in rural areas; (6) the state's political and economic role in securing a neoliberal agrarian-development path (see Appendix 2 for details).

3.3 Unspectacular Economic Growth and Rising Economic Inequality

On its own terms, the NEP is not a big success. It has unleashed some entrepreneurial energy. The rate of growth has increased relative to the preliberalization period but it has not been spectacular over a long period of time. India still accounts for barely 5 per cent of the global economy. Even in the IT sector, India remains a relatively minor player dependent on the technology and markets of the West. There is little sign that the average level of labor productivity per hour in key sectors has improved much relative to that in richer countries. As we have discussed earlier, India's capitalism remains one that is more based on the formal subsumption of labor – a regime of exploitation based on long hours and low wages – than real subsumption of labor, which is based on the systemic tendency towards technological changes and increasing labor productivity. Of course, if labor productivity is not rising, how are the rich making money? One answer is from the recently published Oxfam report:

> the richest in India have made their money through crony capitalism rather than through innovation or the fair rules of the market...Specific policy choices which favoured capital rather than labour, and favoured skilled rather than unskilled labour, are part of the structure of the growth trajectory in India.
>
> as quoted in INDIAN EXPRESS, 2018

Not only in terms of its underlying driving forces, but also in terms of its necessary consequences, the NEP is a class project. Not only is it driven by the capitalist class in terms of why and how it happened: it has also produced an enormous amount of economic inequality. According to Chancel and Piketty (2017), inequality has been intensifying, especially since the introduction of neoliberal policies (Figure 4.2). The growth of income in India's post-independence period (from 1951 to 1980) went overwhelmingly to the toiling masses: while national income grew by 67%, the incomes of the bottom half of the population grew by 87% and that of the middle 40% of the population grew by 74%. But, during these three decades, the income of the top 1% of the population grew only by 5%, and the incomes of the top 0.001% of the population have seen a negative growth rate of –42%. The share of top 1% which was

FIGURE 4.2 Top 0.1% national income share in India, 1922–2015
SOURCE: CHANCEL AND PIKETTY, 2017

as high as 21% of the total national income during the British colonial rule (in 1939), declined to 6% by 1983 (ibid.). The decline in inequalities was reversed. From 1983 onwards, the share of top 1% started increasing. From 6% in 1983, their share increased to 22% in 2014, higher than even the British times.

While the 34 years from 1980 to 2014 saw a much higher growth than did previous three decades (67% vs 187%), this growth mainly went to the rich. The income of the bottom 50% only grew by 89% in these 34 years. Compare this to the growth rate of 87% for this group from 1951 to 1980.[36] The fact that this growth entirely benefited the super-rich is evident, as the incomes of the top 0.001% of the population, among whom we can list the likes of Ambanis and the Adanis, grew by 2726% (Srujana, 2017). The share of top 1% of the

---

36   'In fact, the growth of effective incomes of the bottom 50% would be even lower, considering the gradual withdraw of the welfare state. With privatisation of public transport and withdrawal of various subsidies to the poor including the universal public distribution system – the real cost of living has gone up much more in the post-liberalisation era' (Srujana, 2017).

population in India's income has increased from about 6% in 1983 to 22% in 2014. The share of bottom 50% of the country's income fell from about 24% in 1983 to 15% in 2014 (ibid.). This is in terms of *income*, and not *capital* as such.

Inequalities were reduced sharply in India in the post-independence period from 1951 to 1980, *because* of various progressive economic policies that were adopted by the Indian governments after independence (ibid.) in a context where the bourgeois class power was expressed in relatively less extreme and blatant form.[37]

Consider these two facts: 1983–84 was the year of the lowest income-share for the top 1 per cent, after which this share started rising, and that neoliberalism first made its appearance around that very time. 'The association between growth in inequality and the pursuit of neoliberalism is thus strikingly close' (Patnaik, 2017a; see also Jaydev et al., 2011).

As in many other countries, both rich and poor, so in India, neoliberalism is causally associated with wealth inequality. According to Credit Suisse's data on wealth distribution, the top 1 per cent of households in India currently owns more than half (57 per cent) of the total wealth of all households (up from 17 per cent in 1991), and wealth inequality in India has been rising extremely rapidly, indeed more rapidly than even in the United States.[38] There are several reasons for rising wealth inequality. In a brilliant, though, short article, Prabhat Patnaik (2018), the most well-known Marxist economist from India, explains the mechanisms in his characteristically lucid manner. There are five

---

37 'Indian government nationalised railways in 1951 and air transport in 1953.... Subsequently, in the 1960s and 1970s, almost all of the banking sector and the oil industry were nationalised, along with many others. These reforms have allowed the government to redistribute income into the hands of the working class and the peasantry, that would have otherwise gone into the coffers of the rich industrialists' (Srujana, 2017).

38 'Wealth distribution is invariably more unequal than income distribution, because the working class which has no wealth has nonetheless an income. Two separate reports released this year capture the tragedy of modern India. One says that in 2017, the number of dollar millionaires increased by 20%, as did their wealth. 'Dollar millionaires' are those individuals who own wealth of more than one million dollars. The other report, released earlier this year says that 73% of the wealth generated in 2016–17 went to the richest one percent, while 67 crore Indians making up half of the country's population saw a meagre one percent increase in their wealth' (Varma, 2018a). According to a report from a French firm Capgemini, which calculates the dollar millionaires by prices of equities and real estate owned, 'In 2016, there were 219,000 such millionaires in India which increased to 263,000 in 2017, thanks to a rise in the market value of owned shares and in realty prices. The total wealth owned by these millionaires crossed \$1 trillion in 2017' (ibid.). 'Another report by Credit Suisse, a Swiss investment bank, for 2017 had revealed that about 73% of wealth in India is owned by the richest 10% of the population. Within this bracket, the top 1% of Indians owned a staggering 45% of the country's wealth' (ibid.).

mechanisms: the increase in income inequality; the privatization of essential services like education and healthcare; the intensive process of primitive accumulation of capital; tax concessions and tax breaks to the rich, and the formation of asset price bubbles. These may be explained briefly.

a) There is increasing concentration of income in fewer hands resulting in their savings which are converted to an asset base (Patnaik, 2018):

> The tendency under neo-liberalism is to keep worsening income distribution. This is because the number of jobs created under it falls woefully short of the number of job-seekers, which increases the relative size of the reserve army of labour, so that wages remain tied to a subsistence level even as labour productivity increases. The share of surplus accruing to the rich therefore keeps increasing over time under neo-liberal capitalism, entailing an increase in income, and hence wealth, inequality.

b) Privatization of essential services under neoliberalism leads to many people selling their assets to be able to access the services such as education and health-care.[39] Note also that those who have access to education and health care etc. generally earn more than those who do not.

c) The on-going primitive accumulation puts assets in the hands of big capitalists:

> Through a variety of means, ranging from an outright takeover of petty property, including peasant property, (or its purchase "for a song"); to encroachment on common property; to appropriation of State property (which is built up through taxes imposed on ordinary people); to the sheer filching of bank credit from the public sector banks (what is commonly referred to as a build-up of their "Non-Performing Assets"), the big capitalists increase their share in the total wealth of the economy.
>
> PATNAIK, 2018

> Primitive accumulation increases wealth inequality as wealth is transferred from many to a few. It also causes a vast reserve army of labor, keeping wages low and allows entrepreneurs to make a lot of money: primitive accumulation squeezes peasants and petty producers and forces 'them out of their traditional occupations to migrate to cities where they join the ranks of the job seekers and hence swell the relative size

---

39 On an excellent discussion on marketisation of health and educational facilities characterizing the shift from an interventionist state to a neoliberal state, see Tiwana and Singh (2015).

of the reserve army of labor' (Patnaik, 2018); this reduces wages and increases profit' and thus accentuates income inequality, and with it wealth inequality.

d) Concessions (tax breaks etc.) from the governments promote asset concentration.

There has been a decline in the tax payment by the rich and this means they have more income in their hands which is converted into their savings/wealth: the highest marginal income tax rate got reduced from 98 per cent to 30 per cent. Such concessions increase wealth inequality because the resources that the wealthy should share with society/state remain in their hands, while they continue to use public services whose full cost they do not pay.[40]

In addition since they are balanced by reducing government expenditure on education and healthcare, and thereby directly or indirectly privatising these essential services, they contribute to the impoverishment of large segments of the ordinary people, which as we saw earlier, also increases wealth inequality.

PATNAIK, 2018

e) The formation of asset price bubbles also promotes wealth inequality under neoliberalism.

---

40 'The unwillingness or "inability" of the state to tax the rich reveals that it is not a neutral agency standing above all classes. It is partisan: it represents the interests of a few. But such partisanship also serves the specific interests of the party in government. Resources are needed to fight elections or consolidate a political position, leading to a financial nexus between those wielding political power and those with access to the nation's surpluses' (Chandrasekhar, 2014). One should add that: capitalists also need money for luxury consumption and for the accumulation fund, and they need to pay money to obedient politicians to fight elections who in turn introduce pro-business policies, and they need corruption money (money to be paid to specific politicians and officials in order have a competitive advantage vis-à-vis competitors and be able to avoid certain labor and other regulations).

 'Under neoliberalism, which is based on an anti-statist and pro-market rhetoric, this nexus is strengthened. Since the neoliberal state is openly committed to favouring private capital, handouts to the rich in the form of tax reductions or direct transfers are seen as normal, and higher taxes on surplus incomes as abnormal. In such a system, state functionaries who have a role in deciding the magnitude of such transfers and determining the favoured recipients often see nothing wrong in claiming a share in the spoils. The space for corruption is considerably enlarged. The result is that expenditure reduction has to be focussed even more on curtailing so-called "populist" expenditures favouring the poor, to release the resources needed to finance the handouts provided to the rich and the payouts made to state functionaries' (Chandrasekhar, 2014).

Speculative booms on the stock market or on other asset markets give a boost to the value of assets, because of which the top percentiles which figure prominently among the asset-holders find the absolute value of their wealth, and hence their share in total wealth, increasing quite sharply within a very short period.[41]

> Ibid.

It should be borne in mind that whether or not there is neoliberalism, there will be concentration and centralization of wealth so we should not reduce the fact of wealth inequality to the fact that we have capitalism that is less state-regulated. The fundamental reason for wealth inequality remains irrespective of neoliberalism, and this tends to be under-stressed by Patnaik and others: surplus labor appropriated from workers – including when technological change expands the reserve army and depresses wages and increases profits – is converted into capitalist wealth, or into what Marx calls property based on exploitation of others, as opposed to property based on own labor. Arguably, wealth inequality of the type we see in neoliberal India as elsewhere, is a more extreme form of the 'normal' wealth inequality associated with capitalism as such. In considering wealth inequality it is not adequate to see this only in terms of what the government does or does not do.

India's neoliberalism has indeed led to a small minority of winners and a very large majority of losers. It has vastly benefited the capitalist class, including those fractions that specialize in finances, IT, real estate, and natural resources, producing more than 130 dollar billionaires in 2018. It has placed a colossal amount of wealth – wealth produced by the sweat of the property-less masses – in the hands of a few.[42] A part of this wealth has been hidden away in overseas banks or invested abroad. A not-inconsiderable part is publicly displayed via pretentious lifestyles, which constitute one way in which the elite ideologically reinforces its class position by differentiating it from the majority, and this fact is geographically manifested as two *Indias*: one where the elite lives and one where the 'commoners' do. A wide variety of consumer items is indeed now available for those with money (approximately 200–300 million

---

41   Under 'a neo-liberal regime, governments try to prevent a collapse of the bubble (which would have seriously adverse repercussions on the economy) by sustaining it through various means. These range from fiscal support ... to the commoditisation of elements of nature like water and air (so that new profitable assets are introduced to keep the boom going), to the privatisation of government assets such as "spectrum" (with the same objective)' (Patnaik, 2018).

42   As Patnaik (2010a) says: 'The State under neoliberalism ... actively promotes an increase in the share of surplus value in the hands of domestic and foreign corporates as an essential component of its so-called "development strategy".

people in a country of 1300 million). The NEP has certainly brought with it some foreign technology and cheaper intermediate goods. It has also benefited some educated people employed in IT and related industries, including tech-coolies. Many of these people tend to easily acquiesce to their own exploitation, despite the huge difference in remuneration between India and imperialist countries, and between their own remuneration and the earnings of ordinary souls. In spite of them being exploited by global capital, this stratum does enjoy a certain level of economic success, which has promoted a habit of conspicuous consumption among them and which is mobilized as an ideological prop for neoliberalism and market fetishism.

On the other hand, the NEP has heaped unspeakable miseries on the bottom 800–1000 million people in India, who include urban proletarians and semi-proletarians, a large number of urban small-scale business owners, and peasants. Neoliberalism has produced a massive amount of insecurity, unemployment and under-employment, casualization, informalization, greater labor exploitation, and lax or nonexistent implementation of protective factory acts. It has produced what Utsa Patnaik calls 'a republic of hunger' and what Jean Dreze calls 'a nutritional emergency'. It has produced a graveyard of people in villages who have committed suicide (at a rate of two per hour) (Sainath, 2013), because of their economic insecurity and inability to pay the bills. This is also happening in formerly booming cities like Tirupur in South India.

3.4   *Intensifying Geographical Inequality*

The NEP as a capitalist class agenda has definite geographical effects. It is implemented through accumulation projects that involve massive restructuring of space relations, which produces spatial unevenness at multiple scales. It also involves institutions and actors at multiple scales: international, national, regional, and local.

The restructuring of space relations has two aspects. First of all, a new built environment is being produced in order to accelerate the movement of commodities at a cheaper cost between places in India and between India and the rest of the world, and to increase the pace of elite consumption (see D'Costa, 2005; Jenkins, 2011). And such production of the built environment itself is a means of profit-making.[43] What Harvey says about real-estate development in

---

43   Bear (2018) points to 'a triple predation of the private sector on Indian public infrastructures. Firstly, the private sector would benefit from investing and trading in infrastructure bonds making profits from the ruins generated by fiscal austerity. Secondly, it would benefit from the outsourcing of public work and selling of public assets. Thirdly, companies running or constructing infrastructure would gain guarantees of profits from taxpayers' revenues [just like railways companies did during the British times]. These accumulations from PPPs would be invisible to citizens because contracts were private, concealed from

China applies to real-estate development and other forms of the production of the built environment in India: 'Real-estate development, particularly in and around the large cities and in the export development zones, appears to be another privileged path towards amassing immense wealth in a few hands' (Harvey, 2005: 146). The transformation of space relations is revealed not only in the form of special economic zones (Levien, 2011) and urban shopping malls, but also in the form of new roads, highways, railway lines (including dedicated railway lines), airports, seaports, etc.[44]

The production of the built environment can create some employment.[45] But given its unplanned and profit-driven character, it can have adverse consequences as well. For example, the production of the built environment, to the extent that it is occurring on the basis of debt-financing, has its own risk, especially, given the tendency towards 'over-production' of some elements of the built environment (e.g. houses; shopping malls).

Besides, in order to produce the built environment and set up enterprises (e.g. hotels; manufacturing units) as well as construct housing for sale, low-income working class areas or slums are being cleared, and peasants and aboriginal people are being dispossessed of their land. Their land is required not only for residence but also for its natural resources, which are subjected to intense exploitation. Indeed, 'displacement has been an integral constitutive component of the process of development in India' (Vasudevan, 2008: 41). Between the big bosses' right and the little people's right to be in a given place, between these two equal rights, it is usually force that decides the matter. This force is often the brute force wielded by the legal agents of the state (police, paramilitary forces, courts, etc.). This force is also that of the private coercive personnel hired by big business and the illegally-operating goons, including fascistic elements operating inside and outside legal political parties or outfits.[46]

The production of space facilitates accumulation and money-making in the ways just noted. It should be emphasized again that the production of space is

---

public scrutiny.... This vision is being relentlessly pursued by the current BJP government in India. A full-scale 'reform' of the railways is underway and freight corridors are being constructed' (p. 6; parenthesis added).

44 The class bias in the space transformation (road building, etc.) is evident from the fact that while millions of rupees are spent on high-speed roads, the vast majority of villages with a population of 1000 or less are not connected by a road. Obviously, people in these places do not have enough market power.

45 When new cities develop, some employment is created for people in the surrounding villages. Construction work in rural and urban areas does create some jobs.

46 In India, where increasingly the pursuit of money is above most things in life, murdering anyone who is an obstacle to that pursuit can be delivered on a cheap platter to whoever can afford to spend a little.

also an opportunity *in itself* to make money. This is because space – the economic landscape – is a commodity. What is called infrastructure is big business indeed. The production of space has an ideological/discursive moment to it as well. By constantly asserting that the country needs a large amount of money for infrastructure, the state justifies cuts in welfare expenditure as well as measures to court private capital through various incentives.

While today this State or region and tomorrow that State or region is in trouble, it is also the case that there is always a successful State or a region or a city, where things *are* going right in some sense. Because some regions are always doing well, relative to others, people feel that all is well with the system, and all will be well if all regions do what the successful regions do (Harvey, 2014: 154). And, when specific places have problems, it is said, they have to get it right. Capital gets off scot-free. The blame is often on the greedy unions or on political mismanagement (e.g. corruption) or merely on the crony character of capitalism (i.e. some capitalists with nepotistic nexus with selected and powerful politicians and/or officials). The rural and urban landscapes hide the fact that it is capital that is behind them. These landscapes hide the power of capital to create uneven geographical development. 'The landscape of capitalism [both mansions and deprived areas] exists as a diversionary image of another world closer to some transcendental sense of human longing and desire' (ibid.: 160). As well, given that financialization is an important aspect of neoliberal capitalism, even if banks are under nominal state control,[47] there is much speculative activity which is partly expressed in the form of spectacular production of built environment (skyscrapers and shopping malls in big cities such as Mumbai and Delhi), which give the false view of neoliberalism's dynamism.

The NEP has also resulted in an enormous amount of unevenness between areas. This is because neoliberal investment (including in infrastructure), the main motive of which is profit-making, tends to be geographically concentrated, although the actual patterns of unevenness are not written in stone: a region that is backward today can thrive tomorrow. The fact that investment happens in a few cities or States, producing impressive glass buildings, gorgeous shopping malls, and islands of 'high-tech' firms, does not mean that all places in India can experience this: the process through which some places in the country become developed *includes* the process of most places not developing. Yet geographical differences are being put to ideological purpose – that is, to further the neoliberal agenda: a few places have achieved some economic development through neoliberal policies, and people are being told that *all* places can achieve this *in that way*. Neoliberalism *is* a process of production of spatial

---

47   This effectively means satisfying the collective financial needs of capital, and increasingly, of politically-neglected capitalists.

inequalities and spatial displacements – indeed, of 'uneven and combined development'.[48] A highly important manifestation of this unevenness is between rural and urban areas, with urban areas growing five times faster than rural areas.[49] Agriculture has more or less stagnated as public expenditure has dwindled and public resources are being diverted from it to infrastructure projects in the interest of big business. The socio-geographical face of the villages drained of skilled labor and investible surplus is dismal; this is not to deny the enormous unevenness between areas within cities (e.g. between gated communities and slums).[50] It should be borne in mind that: rural India has on average a lower income than urban India, so if rural areas do not do as well as urban areas which is where capital is invested and where middle class workers on whom capital crucially depends work and live, this fact, other things being equal, can widen overall income inequality. Another pattern of uneven development is within the rural hinterland: i.e. between the rural areas which are closer to the cities and those that are in more remote areas (see Das and Mishra, 2019; Pattenden, 2018; Singh, 2017).

The patterns of uneven development both between cities and between States have interesting political dynamics. With regards to pro-business reforms, regional elites (in States and cities) have some power vis-à-vis the central government. These regionally based elites – comprised of alliances between politicians and local-regional businesses – compete with each other for external loans and domestic as well as foreign capital. Some States and cities get more investment than others.[51] And this process creates a new layer of uneven economic development on top of an already existing layer. When all places are equally neoliberal in their courting of capital, small differences in policy and other factors necessary for profitmaking become metamorphosed into large differences. And competition between States and cities becomes a means

---

48 Consider newly constructed good roads and tall buildings in cities in the minerally-rich areas (e.g. Raipur) that are alongside, and are combined with, the poverty of the Adivasis in the surrounding areas and the archaic social relationships within which they live their lives.

49 On urban development under neoliberalism, see Cowan (2018). On the idea that NEP prioritizes urban areas, see Walker (2008).

50 The cities have experienced neoliberalization in specific ways. As Banerjee-Guha (2009: 105) writes, 'The consequences [of neoliberalization for cities] can be seen in the increasing focus on hyper forms and mega construction activities, increased speculation and expanded investment in land and real estate ..., service sector, signature projects, mega cultural events and a reduced focus on the employment generating production process, affordable housing, and collective sharing of urban space and resources'.

51 Sud (2014: 241): 'states can compete directly with each other and other international subnational regions to attract investment and forge neo-liberal development'. See also Murali, 2017.

of discipline and punish by which neoliberalism is imposed/implemented: if a State/city fails to provide enough concessions (i.e. bribe) to big business, it fails to attract (much) investment. Geography of capitalist development is a geography of bribing capital, or sections of capital.

3.5   Neoliberalism and Imperialism

From one angle, in neoliberalism, the market forces are expected to play a more important role than the state in economic development. From another angle, neoliberalism is about the shifting balance between globalization and nationalism (Nayar, 2001): business activities must respond to price signals in the global market places and not (or, not just) within the national boundaries. It is from the latter angle that one can see neoliberalism implemented in a peripheral country such as India as a part of the imperialist project. After all, imperialism is capitalist accumulation (including profit making, inter-capitalist competition, production process) at the international scale, assisted by the coercive and ideological power of the states of advanced capitalist countries.

Neoliberalism in peripheral countries is a part of global neoliberalism, the history of which is connected to working-class struggle in the West and anti-colonial struggles in the periphery. More specifically, since the 1970s, capitalism has been seeking to withdraw many of the concessions (e.g. welfare benefits) it previously conceded to the working class of the advanced countries due to its struggles. Global big business is also no more willing to concede some autonomy to the peripheral states and the national bourgeoisie of poor countries, the bourgeoisie that it tolerated in the aftermath of anti-colonial struggles. From the perspective of global big business, the natural resources, markets, space (including the space to dump waste), and laboring bodies of these poorer countries cannot be entirely left in the hands of the national bourgeoisie to exploit: international capital must have relatively free (i.e. less constrained) and direct access to them. As it plays itself out in India, the NEP, which is both a medium for, and an outcome of, global neoliberalism, establishes a direct exploitative connection between the bourgeoisie (including its financial segments) of rich countries and India's poor masses to a degree that did not quite exist previously. An important aspect of neoliberalism is indeed 'the new determination to drain the resources of the periphery toward the center' (Duménil and Lévy, 2005: 10) via the activities of international financial capital and other segments of international big business. India's debt payment is 65% of its annual GDP, and India's interest payment is a quarter of its budget spending.[52] India has to simply borrow money to pay the interest due on its old loans. Tax concessions to big business, which constitute an important

---

52   Borrowing at a rate of 1–3%, much lower than India's borrowing rate, the US spends 6%.

neoliberal agenda, worsen the situation with respect to the proportion of government budget that goes towards servicing debts.

Interest payments represent a transfer of resources from the country. This is not the only form of transfer. It also occurs when imperialist capital exploits the workers and peasants of India, a process that the NEP furthers. This imperialist exploitation is abetted by the states of imperialist countries as well as by India's pliant compradore[53] state, an exploitation that is epitomized by 'sultans' (monarchs) of reform like the Manmohan Singhs and the Narendra Modis.[54] Not only this. Some of the Indian States are run under budgetary guidelines formulated by the American 'knowledge' firm McKinsey, and by the IMF, the World Bank, the international development agencies of the governments of advanced countries (the DFID of the UK), and 'compradore' intellectuals and advisors bought off by these institutions. In many ways, and as is widely known, neoliberalism (embodied in privatization, cuts in government spending, etc.) was imposed by international institutions under the name of conditionalities for loans. In particular, the World Bank has been instrumental in pushing for the privatization of water-supply and electricity services, as well as other crucial public services, all in the name of efficiency and development. The same sorts of measures (e.g. austerity measures) have been undertaken in the imperialist countries themselves in the interest of their top '1–10%' and to the detriment of their direct producers, who are the vast majority. Neoliberalism, signifying a new onslaught of capital on the toiling masses, is the thread that links the toiling masses of the world, although the masses in poorer countries are affected a lot more than those in richer countries.[55]

---

53   The word *compradore* here it refers to the state managers and businesses in a peripheral country that enter into an alliance with the state and businesses of imperialist countries, an alliance which may promote the development of productive forces under capitalism in the periphery in an uneven manner; it is an alliance in which these class forces of the periphery are subordinate allies. So 'compradore' is used here in a sense which is somewhat different from the way it is used in the dependency literature or by Mao. For Mao (1926): 'the comprador class' is wholly an appendage 'of the international bourgeoisie, depending upon imperialism for its survival and growth, and hinders economic development'.

54   In fact, the state apparatus is increasingly occupied by pro-market ideologues and neoliberal technocrats and indeed by businesspeople themselves. This signifies the neoliberalization and technocratization of the state apparatus, a distinct colonization of the state by neoliberals. Kohli (2012) says that a distinct marker of the current epoch is the increasing and deepening alliance between state managers and the business class in India, an alliance that is responsible for growth with inequality.

55   I am abstracting from the discussion on the idea that Indian neoliberal capitalism potentially is showing signs of what is called sub-imperialism (see Bond, 2014).

3.6   Neoliberalism and Class Struggle from Below and from Above

No economic process is purely economic. Neoliberalism is not merely economic. It is deeply political. It has been an arena of, and an object of, class struggle, both from below and from above.

Given the NEP's devastating impacts, it is not surprising that broad sections of the toiling class have risen up against it.[56] Since the 1990s, millions of people have gone on numerous strikes over wages, freedom to form new unions independent of the management, contractualization of work, anti-people government policies, and so on. Some of the resistance has been against crony capitalism: atrociously corrupt ways in which the partnership between specific segments of capital and the state has undemocratically milked the resources of the society as a whole. Much of the resistance has been directly against privatization, liberalization, globalization, and reduction in state support for the poor and farmers. Because of the struggle from below (both real and potential),[57] the state has sometimes slowed the pace of reforms slightly. Reforms have been slowed especially when a given reform will adversely affect the weaker members of the bourgeoisie, who cannot compete in the global market. The state has also tried to provide some palliatives as a part of the neoliberal policy to ensure that reforms are not derailed by social unrest in a liberal-democratic set-up. So-called employment guarantee schemes, like loan waivers for farmers and legislation guaranteeing access to food, are one such palliative measure. Relative to the amount of damage caused by neoliberalism, there is too little actual support for the poor.[58]

The bourgeoisie needs 'growth' (that is, a massive increase in the money in its pocket in the shortest possible time). The political parties and the neoliberal state, both at the central and the provincial levels, promise to deliver this growth.[59] This is the limit to how much and in what way the workers and peasants can benefit from the palliatives. The idea that there is such a thing as

---

56   On the trade union and political forms of struggles of the masses against neoliberalism, see Meyer (2016).

57   The on-going struggle from below is partly a struggle between laws, as people seek to defend rights enshrined in earlier laws against new legislation that seeks to diminish these as privileges or deny them altogether and people are also struggling for fresh laws to reflect the democratic aspirations of a post-colonial age (Sundar, 2011).

58   The rural poor, and particularly, Adivasis and Dalits have seen little benefit from the country's economic growth over the last three decades (Roy, 2018).

59   For this service, politicians are compensated by businesses. Politicians use some of the money they get from businesses that benefit from neoliberal policies in order to produce trickery and deception (via, e.g. television air time, and bought news) and for bribery, all of which are necessary for obtaining votes and reproducing the political legitimacy of the neoliberal state.

neoliberalism with a human face – and the fact that neoliberalism has had to be *sold* to people – means that neoliberalism itself is inhumane and does not exist in the interest of the masses. Such an idea is essentially based on this lie: basic interests of capital are compatible with basic interests of toiling masses, in a sustainable manner and on a national scale.

In fact, neoliberalism *itself* is a form of class struggle from the top, the class struggle launched by the ruling class with the help of the state to ensure conditions for accumulation. As a form of class struggle from above, several elements of neoliberalism need to be considered. One is the withdrawal of benefits for the poorer sections, which is an attack on their living standards. Making it difficult for labor to launch trade union struggles is another. A major capitalist association says this:

> Industrial Relations paradigm in India had dramatically changed following the adaptation of free market policy in the early nineties. With the dawn of liberalization, privatization and globalization (LPG), the country is, by and large, able to preserve *a sound and positive industrial relations climate*. This is apparent from the statistical figures of Union Government's Labor Bureau, which exhibits drastic decline of industrial disputes from 3049 in 1979 to 391 (P) in 2009.
>
> AIOE/FICCI, n.d.: 1; italics added

India's labor minister said this in 2015 while appealing to trade unions not to strike: 'We in government do not believe in confrontation…We are in favour of industries and workers working towards mutual benefits' (Nanda, 2015). Such a view, not surprisingly echoes the view of employers' organizations such as FICCI which says: 'Strikes can never be hoped to yield any satisfactory solution to pressing labor problems'. Strikes lead to loss of production and also affects investors' confidence and thus foreign investment on which a poor country depends, it is said (ibid.).

Where the numbing of consciousness through the official and academic–market-oriented propaganda, including the propaganda doled out by finance ministers and other spokespersons of capital, fails, where the intoxication wof the masses by the fetishism of seasonal festivals called 'elections' eases off,[60] where official bribing in the form of limited welfare is ineffective, and where, as a result, the masses *do* rise in revolt, the state has been using repression. This is class struggle from above as well. The state's aim is to clear away the barriers to the twin methods of wealth accumulation, whether in agriculture or industry:

---

60   Note that the majority of the masses think that reforms are pro-rich.

dispossession (of small-scale producers) and exploitation. The dispossession, exploitation, and oppression of aboriginal people, all of which have been exacerbated by neoliberalism, have contributed to Maoist resistance in several hundred districts (Das, 2010), although this resistance goes back to the pre-NEP days. The Maoist threat is elevated to be the biggest threat to the nation. It is then conveniently used as an excuse to suppress any democratically organized protest against neoliberalism, as seen in the recent arrest of 6 activists who are labelled 'urban Naxals'. If the Maoist threat did not exist, a similar other threat would be invented. In fact, under the BJP's version of neoliberalism, apart from the Maoist threat (and indeed the general threat from people in the form of resistance against neoliberal government policies), there is the Muslim threat to the nation. Perceiving resistance and dissent against neoliberal capitalist policies that serve the capitalist interests and their political backers, *as a threat to* the nation as a whole, and falsely constructing religious minorities (especially, Muslims) as a threat to the nation as a whole simply because their religious beliefs are not those of Hindus, constitute a convenient way of diverting the minds of common people, Hindus and non-Hindus, from the failure of neoliberal capitalist policies of the government to meet the needs of the masses.

The capitalist class has also directly engaged in struggle from above by undermining the power of workers who strike against capital. Repression of striking Maruti workers is a case in point. Capital has repressed workers by hiring goons to hurt or kill them, by bribing union leaders, and by locking employees out. A major employers' organization justifies the curtailment of the right to strike on the grounds of neoliberal globalization:

> Today, most of the countries, especially the developing countries like India, are dependent on foreign investment and under these circumstances, it is necessary that countries who seek foreign investment must keep some safeguard in their respective industrial laws so that there will be no misuse of right to strike. In India, right to protest is a fundamental right under Article 19 of the Constitution of India but, right to strike is not a fundamental right rather, a legal right with statutory restriction attached in the Industrial Dispute Act, 1947... [A]dequate arrangement should be done including amending section 16 of the Trade Union Act, 1926 to insulate trade unionism from politics.
>
> AIOE/FICCI, n.d.: p. 9

Between investors' right to not invest, and workers' right to not sell their labor power, between these two equal rights, once again, it is force that decides. And force is used more freely under neoliberalism. Employers, backed by the force of the state and by its pro-business laws, want that trade unionism be insulated from politics (read: the efforts of the left political parties to mobilize the workers). The courts also have ruled against the right to strike. To support the private property rights of big businesses whose accumulation strategies are destroying the livelihoods of millions and to protect the increasing inequality between the consuming-and-possessing class and the rest, the state is turning increasingly authoritarian.[61] It even deploys or threatens to deploy, draconian anti-terror laws against anyone opposing neoliberalism.

3.7 *'Neoliberalization' of the Left*

It is undeniably true that parties on the Left in India have put pressure on governments to implement certain pro-poor measures (e.g. public works to generate employment for the rural poor) and to slow the pace of certain reforms.[62] It is partly because of the pressure from the left that public sector banks were not privatized and therefore they were able to withstand the effects of the 2008 financial crisis. But the *objective* effect of the practice of the Left forces has, overall, been this: they have been converted into a conduit for the implementation of the NEP through ideological and political-administrative means.

The parliamentary Left (as well as much of the 'unorganized Left')[63] has not provided a serious ideological critique of the NEP. Whatever critique the Left has is rather muted. The effect of the Left is limited because, philosophically speaking, it has focused on the two 'upper layers' of the reality of capitalism (i.e. the *effects* of the operation of the capitalist system, and especially, the effects of the form in which capitalism comes to exist, i.e. neoliberal capitalism

---

61   Under neoliberalism, 'Governance by majority rule is seen as a potential threat to individual rights and constitutional liberties. Democracy is viewed as a luxury, only possible under conditions of relative affluence coupled with a strong middle-class presence to guarantee political stability. Neoliberals therefore tend to favour governance by experts and elites. A strong preference exists for government by executive order and by judicial decision rather than democratic and parliamentary decision-making. Neoliberals prefer to insulate key institutions, such as the central bank, from democratic pressures. Given that neoliberal theory centres on the rule of law and a strict interpretation of constitutionality, it follows that conflict and opposition must be mediated through the courts' (Harvey, 2005: 66).

62   It should be noted that a section of the capitalist class which was reliant on the government support, and which was not ready for foreign competition, did not wholeheartedly accept the reforms agenda, and this also partly explains why reforms have not been as fast as they could have been (and as they were, in other countries).

63   This Left – like much of the academic Left – is informed by the spirit of civil society activism and micro-political resistance. The specter of 'post-isms' (e.g. post-Marxism) haunts this Left.

as opposed to 'state-directed' capitalism). By doing this, the Left has, more or less, abstracted from, and done little with regard to, the third, underlying, layer (i.e. the sphere of capitalist class *relations* and the associated *mechanisms* of marketization/commodification, competition, appropriation of surplus value, private control over production and production process, production for profit being more important than production to meet human needs, and so on). More concretely, the effect of the Left is limited because it takes place, more or less, from the standpoint of less economically competitive sections of the so-called progressive national bourgeoisie (and a very small segment of the 'relatively well-paid' salaried working class, mainly unionized public sector workers). Not only that, but the critique is 'regulationist': it suggests that the solutions to the problems with the NEP (or with neoliberalism) lie in greater government regulation by the bourgeois governments (i.e. less neoliberalism). The Left critique has not, generally speaking, looked at the NEP as being essentially a *capitalist* project, a project of and by the capitalist class; the Left sees it as merely a new government policy that can be changed by more 'pro-poor' government. The Left critique has not been conducted from the vantage point of the working class and poor peasants as comprising a bloc of anti-capitalist classes, and from the standpoint of the need to intellectually and politically act on all the three layers of the capitalist reality mentioned above. The Left critique has therefore not been from the vantage point of the *transcendence* of capitalism. In terms of strategy, the Left is at the *pre*-democratic-revolution stage – that is, at *least* two stages removed from posing anti-capitalist, proletarian, revolutionary socialism as the goal. Indeed, it is this political vision that directly influences the Left's view of everything, including neoliberalism. Without revolutionary theory, it lacks revolutionary practice.

Politically, in terms of practice, the Left, which has been suffering from the 'parliamentary diseases',[64] and whose framework of operation has, in effect, little to do with the fight for socialism, has propped up and supported various bourgeois parties (e.g. Janata, which included political characters which now constitute the BJP; Congress) from time to time, the parties that have implemented neoliberalism. The Left has justified its support for certain bourgeois parties on two grounds: anti-imperialism (and anti-feudalism), and to keep the Hindu fundamentalists out of power. For the sake of an argument, its support for more-secular bourgeois neoliberal parties, for the purpose of keeping the communal-right-wing BJP out could be considered somehow un-problematic *if* and only if the Left did this tactically/conjuncturally, i.e. just to win a breathing

---

64   A disproportionate amount of its energy is spent on elections rather than on the extra-electoral mobilization of the masses and on raising the level of their class consciousness.

space so it could launch an ideological and political offensive against the capitalist class and landlords, *in the extra-parliamentary sphere,* which should be its main sphere of action on the basis of which it should engage in electoral politics. But that has *generally* not been the case, and especially, at the national and provincial scales.[65] Besides, such a policy of alignment with bourgeois forces has failed as indicated by the 2014 electoral success of BJP which is promoting a naked form of neoliberal capitalism. In fact, in a sense, Left's support for neoliberal parties that are relatively secular such as Congress *in a context* where the Left has not adequately mobilized its constituents (workers and poor peasants) *independently* of bourgeois forces in the extra-parliamentary sphere and where it is pursuing the project of a more democratic and a more egalitarian capitalism, has objectively meant the following. The relatively-secular parties' neoliberal policies have caused the disenchantment of the masses with them as well as with the Left, and this has led the masses to the lap of communal-Hindu-nationalist-neoliberal BJP which has now captured power and which rules on the basis of populist authoritarianism (more on this below). Absence of independent class-based extra-electoral mobilization by the Left and the attendant absence of a real threat to the capitalist class[66] from the Left mean this: the political-electoral subordination of the masses to the politics of bourgeois parties.

The Left, on whose radar anti-capitalist, proletarian socialism does not yet exist because it is more interested in democratic changes *within* the capitalist class system, has lent a pro-poor cover to various bourgeois governments that it has supported. This has allowed the governments of the day to administer the bitter pill of neoliberalism with a little sweetener – that is to say, to give the NEP a human face – and in a more consensual manner. The objective effect of this is that *in practice, if not in theory,* the Left has effectively turned itself into a radical-nationalist fraction of the political bloc of the bourgeoisie.

At the provincial scale, where the organized parliamentary Left was and is in power, it has itself pursued the NEP and pro-big business measures.[67] One prominent State-level Left politician said to me once that 'we [i.e. the Left

---

65 At the sub-national scales, matters can be a bit different as indicated by various on-the-ground-struggles organized by the Left.

66 The Left has, more or less, sought to limit the struggles of the working class to trade union struggles (i.e. bourgeois consciousness/politics in Lenin's words) and to electoral fights.

67 Sumanta Banerjee (2008b: 12–13) says: 'It was under … [Jyoti Basu's] leadership that the West Bengal Left Front government opened up the state's economy to private investors from outside…Following this, in 1994 the CPI(M)-led Left Front government … adopted a new industrial policy which offered concessions to the magnates of the private sector and multinationals to set up industries in the state. … [in the process of pursuing neoliberal policies], the party ended up … grabbing agricultural land (without paying adequate compensation to the farmers) and subsidising the investor industrialists by huge tax relief and other concessions that eat into the state exchequer'.

when it is in power in the States] need to establish industries at any cost and create a working class and make available consumer items before we think about other things'. Underlying this kind of Left politics is its commitment to the reproduction of capitalist social relations. When the Left was in power in Bengal, it embraced neoliberalism, arguing that it was following the model of 'socialist' China.[68] The Left attacked 'the trade unions, saying that workers must learn discipline and forego strikes if West Bengal is to be able to secure investment' (Wickremasinghe and Jones, 2004). Left-in-power has more or less pursued neoliberalism at the provincial scale while sounding critical of it at the national scale. It has done this in a ruthless fashion, using both its control over trade unions and the misperception that the Left is pro-working class. Revealingly, when asked how his government would respond if a labor dispute arose against a foreign company operating in his State, the last Left Front Chief Minister of West Bengal said this:

> Our involvement in trade unions is an advantage. The majority of work-ers are in support of this government. And we are trying to change their mindset. I tell them, look this is a new situation. We need FDI [foreign direct investments], we need infrastructure.
>
> DIAS, 2005

This, to me, is the twenty-first century version of the Stalinist theory of social-ism, as expressed in one country. The slogan of the Left at the provincial scale should really be: 'neoliberal socialism' in one province. In part because of its neoliberal policies, the Left has also lost some of its traditional legitimacy and electoral support, and this serves the capitalist class as a whole, politically. Apart from Left's own neoliberal policies, there is another reason for its loss of electoral support. The pre-neoliberal state used to be a source of some conces-sions (e.g. pro-poor policies), so the Left could politically organize people for various benefits, including, in the form of workers' benefits from the state-owned sector. With the neoliberal turn, the material basis for this kind of Left politics has been weakened.

Let us turn to the non-parliamentary Left in neoliberal times. This includes the Naxalite Left (which is influenced by versions of Maoism), the emer-gence of which was partly sparked by the weakness of the parliamentary Left and the aborted democratic revolution. It is no less responsible, however, for the current rot of the entire Left. Since their emergence in the late 1960s, the

---

68   On neoliberalization of the Left in Bengal, see Das, Ritanjan (2018); Das and Mahmood (2015); Chakrabarty (2008). See Sreeraj and Vakulabharanam (2016) on the neoliberaliza-tion of the Left in Kerala.

Naxalites have focused their activities on the oppressed peasantry and in more recent decades on the aboriginal people living in the most remote parts of India; they have also won some localized concessions (Das, 2010). This orientation is in keeping with the Maoists' nationalist and Stalinist perspective which declares the peasantry the principal revolutionary force (in contemporary India) and the coming Indian revolution to be a type of 'democratic', and not a socialist, revolution. From this perspective, the system of capitalist relations as such is not the enemy of the Naxalite Left. On occasion the Maoists make ritualistic references to the working class, but in practice they are, hitherto, more or less, disconnected from that class, which is the only class that has the potential to radically challenge neoliberalism and capitalism itself. The Naxalite Left is not necessarily against capitalist accumulation as such; it does not even recognize that India is a dominantly capitalist social formation.[69] Ironically, the politics of the state's fight against Maoism is being used to remove all barriers to capitalist accumulation. And the non-Naxalite Left outside of the fold of the electoral-mainstream Left is as good as non-existent: it is thoroughly fragmented into little groups, busy criticizing one another and criticizing the mainstream Left, and without engaging in constructive theoretical developments or immersion in day-to-day struggles.[70]

3.8   Neoliberalism as the Indian Capitalist Class's Political-Ideological Project, Including Communalism

NEP is a political-ideological project of the capitalist class because it must ensure political and ideological conditions for various accumulation strategies. 'Political conditions' in this case means state repression and judicial coercion (including the suppression of democratic rights, to be discussed later).[71] 'Ideological conditions' here includes the fetishism of economic growth at any

---

69   See Chapter 3 for the argument about how to conceptualize capitalism and why social formations such as India are dominantly capitalist.

70   Outside of India as well, this is the situation of much of the revolutionary Marxist Left, which is outside of the mainstream communist movement.

71   The leaders of workers at Maruti Suzuki factory have been targeted for exemplary punishment because they led a struggle at the Japanese-owned car assembly plant, during which a company manager died a mysterious death that was blamed on workers.

      'Prosecutors and judges involved in legal proceedings concerning the victimized Maruti Suzuki workers have stated repeatedly and bluntly that an example must be made of them so as to reassure investors. In arguing for the 13 to be sentenced to death by hanging at their March 2017 sentence hearing, special prosecutor Anurag Hooda declared, "Our industrial growth has dipped, FDI [Foreign Direct Investment] has dried up. Prime Minister Narendra Modi is calling for 'Make in India', but such incidents are a stain on our image"' (in Jones, 2018).

cost (often conflated with development) and indeed promotion of market fetishism in all spheres of everyday life, including social consciousness, and this began happening in a society where the market relations have *relatively* less impact relative to advanced capitalist countries. Associated with market fetishism is the idea of getting rich quickly by any means.[72] Associated with market fetishism is also the idea that market is the dominant method of helping the poor (hence the popularity of such things as self-help groups and micro-credit in the discourse of development, happily promoted by the state and civil society groups).[73] The concept of animal spirits (entrepreneurialism) and unleashing the sleeping tiger, (perceived) prestige associated with working for MNCS, all these are a part of the neoliberal capitalist culture. Neoliberal culture is especially manifested in a craze for technical education in a relatively backward society like India. India's focus apolitical promotion of engineering disciplines has fed into hegemonic discourses on apolitical good governance and meritocracy, propagated more or less by all political parties with an adverse social and political implication: the educated and professionally-oriented middle classes in India and (other developing countries), unlike their Western counterparts, tend to be socially illiberal and politically authoritarian (Krishnan, 2017: 364).

The dominant neoliberal view is one of market idolatry: the poor should be sacrificed at the altar of the god of the market, the god of reforms, the god of growth. This god has more power than the numerous gods in India's holy land. This god will, in the long run, benefit 'the poor' and less well-off people, the ordinary people. In the short term, while the poor are prostrating themselves before the market god, they get bruised laying on the hard surface, so they need some kind of band-aid.

There has been also a change in the culture of state-society relations broadly in the interest of the business class. A former civil servant of the Indian Administrative Service (IAS), Mr. Harsh Mander (2016), who has been a vocal supporter of pro-poor interventions upon leaving office, writes:

---

72 It is thought that 'because the "nation" needs "development", some people are going to lose land, subsistence livelihoods, [and] living space.... The strategy in class terms is to obscure differential rewards of aggressive capitalist development in favour of universal valents summarized by a growing gross domestic product (GDP)' (Herring, 2013: 131).

73 Interestingly, the obsession with growth is such that a party can engage in sectarian violence of religious and other types (e.g. the BJP in Gujarat), but still be more or less 'condoned' if it promotes economic growth through pro-business policies. Neoliberalism and communalism are not unrelated (see Chapters 11–12).

> I think economic reforms have done many things but one of them is that they have entirely transformed the culture, the functioning, and the moral yardsticks of a good government, in ways that could not have been imagined in 1991.
>
> ...What worries me is our collective indifference to inequality. The middle-class feels that this inequality is not only tolerable but justified and legitimate. So the sense of moral outrage against suffering and injustice around us has sharply declined and that is what worries me even more than the material aspects of inequality.

There is still another way in which NEP is political-ideological. This concerns the connection between NEP and what is called communalism in India (i.e. politics based on religious division or Indian version of fascistic tendencies). In the 1980s, as mentioned before, two things happened: increase in inequality and the introduction of neoliberal economics. Something else joined them: rise of communalism. The fact that these three things happened almost at the same time could not have been coincidental. Neoliberal capitalism that has been immiserizing has hastened capitalism's tendency to promote communalism in part as a deflection from the real problems confronting the masses. The right-wing forces, appearing to be pro-poor in the most demagogic-populist manner, and championing the economic interests of the capitalist class, endorse and implement the most virulent form of neoliberalism. And these right-wing forces propagate ideas (e.g. individual initiative and entrepreneurial-ism; nationalism, etc.) that are the legitimizing ideology of such extreme neoliberalism. *In a context* where the Left has not extra-electorally mobilized its constituents (workers and poor peasants) *independently* of bourgeois forces, its parliamentary support for neoliberal parties such as Congress and its regional offshoots has objectively meant this: these parties have been in power and they have formulated and implemented' neoliberal policies which in turn have led the masses to accept communal-neoliberal BJP's demagogic appeal as their friend. It has, of course, and naturally, become the darling of vast sections of the capitalist class, which has secretively funded it and provided public support in some cases. The communal project has been helped by the national and global business class (including in the diasporic elements) who benefit from a national-level conservative and authoritarian government which makes common people gulp bitter pills (read: labor reforms, further privatization of state-owned companies, and the like). These pills are said to be necessary to cure the illness of declining economic growth in the bourgeois economy.[74]

---

74 On the link between neoliberalism and Hindu nationalism, see Ruparelia (2011; Desai, 2011). This theme is discussed in more details in Chapters 10–13 of this book.

4 Concluding Comments: What Is to Be Done?

Neoliberalism and capitalism do not inhabit different worlds. Neoliberalism, in word or deed, is not a 'substitute' for capitalism. Neoliberalism is a specific form of capitalism, whether in advanced countries or in countries such as India. It is not to be seen primarily as a set of government policies which can be replaced by another. Murray Smith reminds us (2018: 21):

> ...most would-be progressives cling desperately to the notion that 'neoliberal capitalism' is but the ugly mutation of a set of short-sighted policies that the capitalist ruling class may prefer but might also be pressured to abandon in favour of a more humane, just, and equitable species of capitalism. For this reason, the established, 'reform'-oriented left is loath to characterise neoliberalism for what it is: a predictable and inevitable strategic response on the part of capital and the state to a deepening crisis of the capitalist profit system – a crisis that has been unfolding now for several decades.

It is mistaken to belief that neoliberalism is facing a crisis, while capitalism is not. Neoliberalism is a form of crisis-ridden capitalism. Capitalism and neoliberal capitalism are both crisis-ridden.

The neoliberal state experiences internal contradictions, like the capitalist form of the state as such. There is clearly a contradiction 'between the declared public aims of neoliberalism—the well-being of all—and its actual consequences' for the people, which are, more or less, negative (Harvey, 2005: 25). Additionally, 'there lies a whole series of more specific contradictions' as Harvey notes: between need for the state to let markets function freely and the need to intervene in order to deliberately create a business climate; need to enforce market rules in an authoritarian way and the ideas of individual freedom; the integrity of the financial system and its volatile character; between competition and monopolistic tendencies; and between individual market freedom and loss of solidarity, and so on.

As a new stage in the development of capitalism emerging in the wake of the post-war boom, neoliberalism has several general traits (deregulation, privatization, liberalization, financialization, etc.) that are affecting all spheres of life, including culture and everyday life.

This chapter seeks to provide a dialectical conceptualization of India's NEP and neoliberalism, on the basis of some general ideas about neoliberalism as outlined in part 1. Such a conceptualization must be sensitive to both the differences and similarities between the pre-1991 and post-1991 regimes, and to both the economic and the non-economic character of the NEP. Such a conceptualization must also see the governmental or policy aspect of the NEP as rooted in the class character of Indian society.

As in many other countries, so in India, neoliberal capitalism has meant a series of *reduction*:

1. reduction in corporate contributions to society/state (= reduction in taxes);
2. reduction in the power of unions;
3. reduction in state control over pricing of services and over business activities;
4. reduction in restrictions on trade (lowering tariffs) (companies can go to a cheaper location, get things made and export them);
5. reduction in state's support for the less-well off (e.g. farmers);
6. reduction in the sphere of state ownership of productive enterprises and facilities (schools, prisons, etc.) and commons, and so on.

As a result, there has been the opposite of this reduction: an *expansion* of the effect of class power of ruling class and expansion of the misery for the masses. So the neoliberal project is a perfect example of the inter-penetration of opposites.

In any fundamental sense, there was not a time before or since independence when the Indian capitalist class did not have its power to exploit labor and dispossess small-scale producers. So neoliberalism, strictly speaking, is not the restoration of class power, as Harvey and others think. Yet, to the extent that there was *some* restriction on its power within the political sphere (e.g. what it could produce and what it could not), neoliberalism is an *effect* of the changing balance of political power between the capitalist class and the masses. On the basis of its growing economic strength, supported in many ways by the state, between the 1950s and the mid-1980s, and with support from imperialist capital and its institutions, Indian capitalist class was able to impose its economic will in a much more strident manner than before. NEP is a political expression of the capitalist class's need to 'bridge' the gap between its economic power (in terms of its control over property) and its political power. NEP is a policy, but it is not just that. It is the political articulation of the interests of the Indian capitalist class in the context of a globalizing world-capitalism. Neoliberalism is 'capitalism without Leftist illusions' (e.g. illusions that there can be such a thing as humane capitalism on a long-term basis). If this is true of rich countries, it is no less true of poor countries such as India. India's NEP is a policy *on behalf* of capital. It is therefore a policy *of* capital, *tout court*, mediated and implemented by the state, at central and provincial scales.[75] This chapter has shown that India's NEP is more than a governmental

---

75   This error is not too dissimilar to the error of thinking about imperialism merely as a government policy, an error that Lenin pointed out in Kautsky.

policy. It is a program of the bourgeoisie that promotes economic growth and bestows benefits to certain privileged sections of the population, but has devastating impacts on the toiling masses, the majority. Indeed, this is what neoliberal capitalism generally does in the less developed world as a whole (Naruzzaman, 2005).

Neoliberalism in rural areas – agrarian neoliberalism – is particularly ruthless in its impacts. Neoliberalism has also produced enormous spatial unevenness. Neoliberalism in India, like in the periphery as such, is also a part of the imperialist project, being implemented via burgeoning 'new compradore' elements both in the bourgeois class and outside. Given the adverse impacts of neoliberalism, it has inspired massive resistance from below, which has been countered by the state via a combination of meagre concession, heavy repression, and unfathomable deception (i.e. the idea that neoliberal growth is good for all). Interestingly, in spite of offering some opposition, the Left has ended up becoming, more or less, a conduit through which neoliberalism has been delivered, even against its own intention.

To conclude, I will consider neoliberalism in terms of the 'What is to be done' question? The less developed countries such as India are often seen as countries that have less income and more absolute poverty. Instead, they must be fundamentally seen in class terms: as countries that have suffered from aborted – or incomplete – revolutions against the propertied class. They have suffered from: aborted democratic (bourgeois) revolutions, including agrarian revolutions against feudal(-type) relations, aborted national (or anti-imperialist) revolutions, and aborted/untried anti-capitalist revolutions.[76] A dialectical view of neoliberalism and the NEP connects them both to the democratic and agrarian questions, the national question, and the question of socialism itself.

Consider the democratic question. There has been massive resistance to the NEP, as mentioned earlier, to which the state is responding in a most undemocratic (= repressive) manner. The state is also promoting *venal* capitalism; massive corruption in the public offices has been endemic since the 1990s, a time during which markets have been less regulated, thus refuting the argument that de-regulation reduces corruption. Corruption means undemocratic use of public offices for private gains ('private' meaning the nexus of the business world and the state managers).[77] Given that all the parties – including the Left

---

76 Indeed, with respect to the socialist revolution, the fertilization has not even happened in many contexts. On India's bourgeois revolution, see Stern, 2011, and Davey, 1974.

77 State actors (government officials and politicians) use the power of the state to illegitimately satisfy their private interests often at the expense of the lower classes (proletarian and semi-proletarian classes). In so far as corruption adversely affects these classes, it is a class issue. Corruption is also a class issue in terms of its origin. The structure of the capitalist state is such that its day-to-day activities at different geographical scales are

parties – are forced to follow neoliberalism, the room for democratic dissent is shrunk, and this is more so now, with the election of a new government led by a Hindu-fundamentalist party with fascistic tendencies. This has a more specific implication: by making all political parties/groups equal as far as their adherence to neoliberalism is concerned, the NEP has created a situation where casteism and religious fundamentalism are used to divide the poor electorate and to garner votes.[78] This creates conditions for the perpetuation of undemocratic relations based on religious and caste identity.[79] This also creates a condition where capitalists can subject workers – including those who belong to vulnerable social groups – to super-exploitation and weaken any potential resistance by dividing the masses along the lines of religion, caste, gender, etc. Given that various petty-bourgeois or regionalist parties (some of which call themselves, bizarrely, socialist) thriving by playing identity politics, it is not unusual for a party or a coalition of parties in power to buy their support for neoliberal policies by giving some material concession to identity politics (e.g. reservation in promotion for scheduled castes). Identity politics becomes a vehicle of capitalist and landlord class politics, that is to say, politics in the service of neoliberalism. The NEP, under which small-scale producers are subjected by the capitalist class and its state to primitive accumulation, is also creating new aspects of the agrarian question. The agrarian question now is the question about peasants' property and about their miseries caused by national and international agribusiness (*not* feudal or semi-feudal landlords) and by the neoliberal state acting on behalf of agribusiness. So the democratic question broadly understood – including democratic governance, equal rights of

---

generally insulated from the direct lower-class political influence. This structure of the state enables it to reproduce class relations. But it is precisely this structure of the state that allows corruption to happen by enhancing the power of state actors over lower classes. The structure and activities of the state are, however, subject to geographically varying class struggle. Therefore, in those places where politically organized lower classes can democratically influence the (everyday) state, the extent of corruption can be a little less than in other places.

78 How else can a party say 'vote for us and not for them', when both the parties are almost exactly the same in terms of economic policies? Teltumbde (2011) writes: 'The beauty of India's parliamentary system is that there is essential similarity between all ruling class parties on most core policy matters and behaviours, whether it is economic reforms or foreign policy or secularism and communalism. They differ at the most in shade. In class terms it may thus be called political oligopoly'.

79 Of course, why the masses fall for these lies – that caste and religious identities are crucial determinants of their economic miseries – is an interesting question (see Kumar, 2008 for a discussion on this).

NEOLIBERAL CAPITALISM WITH INDIAN CHARACTERISTICS

citizens irrespective of their castes or religious backgrounds, and the agrarian question – becomes important in new ways in neoliberal times. Neoliberalism has created the need for a heightened battle for democracy.

In light of this need, consider the national question. This question is no longer about fighting formal colonialism. It is rather about fighting 'new imperialism', which is predominantly practiced through economic mechanisms and ultimately backed up by the threat of force.[80] It is the imperialism of the powerful governments of the developed world, of MNCs, and of international institutions (IMF, the World Bank, MNCs, and 'aid' agencies). This is an imperialism that is justified and sold to ordinary people through the discourse of development (as growth). It is also sold using chauvinistic ideas about India's 'super-power status', which is only as a regional subordinate of the supreme guardian of global capitalism, the USA.[81] The post-colonial neoliberal state itself, managed by people with the neoliberal mentality ('neoliberality'), has become a new mechanism of imperialism. So, neoliberalism has heightened the need for anti-imperialist struggle and for the sovereignty of oppressed nations such as India. The national question and the democratic question (i.e. the questions of the new imperialist subordination, the state and society becoming more undemocratic, and of peasants losing land) are rooted in the fact that the NEP represents capitalism in its most naked and ruthless form.[82]

If the above assessment is broadly correct, it indicates a very different sort of solution to the national and democratic question and to the specific problems, such as mass impoverishment, spatially uneven development and agrarian crisis, that neoliberalism is creating than what the traditional Left has been

---

80 No peripheral country is a permanent friend of an imperialist power.

81 The USA 'guards' the subordinate guardians (= subordinate states such as India) of the capitalist property rights in different parts of the world (Wood, 2003: 133).

82 Class analysis of neoliberalism in Indian shows that those with little or no productive asset – various classes of self-employed non-exploiting peasants and laborers – will gain from a unified political struggle against imperialism, with the intent to unfetter the use (and also the development) of the productive forces. Such an attack on the institutions of imperialism will, of course, need to be linked to challenges mounted against forces within India, among whom the most obvious are (a) traders looting food-grains in the government stores meant for the working class and for the poor peasantry (neither of which are able to purchase this resource due to IMF subsidy cuts), (b) rural and urban capitalists benefiting from the opening up of Indian agriculture to imperialist exploitation, and (c) high-level state actors and institutions supporting and facilitating this process of imperialist penetration.

offering. The intellectual and political fight against the NEP cannot be merely about changing the dirty clothes of the state (meaning changing its policy and making it regulate the affairs of capitalism, as in 'olden times'). It cannot be about interrupting, deconstructing, and destabilizing narratives about neoliberalism and wider society a bit here and a bit there, although the struggle for the regulation of business is not entirely unnecessary. The idea that there is such a thing as neoliberalism (or capitalism) with a human face is, once again, based on the lie, the deception, that the basic interests of capital are fundamentally compatible with the basic interests of the toiling masses in a sustainable, contradiction-free, manner. Unregulated growth, control of society's resources by big business, the exploitation of labor, income inequality, and ecological devastation cannot be compatible with socially coordinated wealth creation, equality, solidarity, popular democracy, and satisfaction of human needs. If this critique is right, then the intellectual and political project must have the larger goal of theoretically and practically transcending the very conditions that produce the neoliberalism model itself and going beyond the content of whose form neoliberalism is.[83]

Indicative of the hegemony of neoliberalism, in India (as elsewhere), is the fact that scholars talk about neoliberalism more than about capitalism. So a major discursive, or ideological, success of neoliberalism is that it has hidden capitalism under its *choli* (a short-sleeved blouse worn by many Indian women).[84] Scholars explain society's economic, social and ecological problems in terms of neoliberalism (and its twin, globalization) and not capitalism. Form is prioritized over content. When critical ideas about economy are produced, they are often against neoliberalism as such and not against capitalism per se.

What is problematic about neoliberalism, including neoliberal policy, is not *this or that* aspect of it (e.g. the idea that it increases poverty and inequality or the idea that restriction on short-term capital flows or shrinking government intervention is the problem).[85] Rather, the *whole* 'policy' is the problem. So it

---

83 And this requires a massive, democratically organized mobilization of workers and poor peasants against profit-making, at multiple scales within India, in South Asia as a whole, and, globally.

84 Interestingly, the Hindi word to describe neoliberalism is mystifying. In Hindi, neoliberalism is नव-उदारतावाद. नव = new. उदारतावाद means such things as generosity (उदार = generous; उदारता = generosity; वाद = ism). One can see that given the massive adverse economic, social and ecological consequences of neoliberalism, there is nothing generous (उदार) about neoliberalism. In English language as well, the liberalism in neoliberalism means such things as tolerance, individual freedom, democratic form of government, equality, etc., all of which are under attack under neoliberalism.

85 Criticisms are now coming from inside the agencies that have promoted neoliberalism: 'there are aspects of the neoliberal agenda that have not delivered as expected', say Ostry

requires a totalizing dialectical critique, one that situates its limited benefits in relation to its enormous costs and sees it from multiple vantage points.

There is nothing wrong in critiquing neoliberalism, and there is nothing wrong in raising anti-neoliberalism demands. But the scope of this anti-neoliberalism is narrow. In explaining society's problems, one needs to include neoliberalism but one must go beyond it to include the content of capitalism itself. And political action that is merely anti-neoliberalism fails to convert the fight against neoliberalism into a fight against the capitalist class relation. It remains merely a partial demand aimed at fighting for a better capitalism.

Indeed much critical discourse and much progressive politics, in India and outside India, are stuck with a critique of neoliberalism as such, in the hope of a world that is less neoliberal, rather than a world that is not capitalist. As we have seen in the last chapter, a restrictive concept of capitalism a concept in which capitalism exists when there is economically advanced capitalism, has licensed a bourgeois politics of the Left that aims to produce a better (= more democratic) and more advanced capitalism. Similarly, a Left critique of capitalism that more or less equates it to neoliberalism is bound to encourage a bourgeois politics of the Left, one that aims for a capitalism that is a little more state-directed than neoliberalism. And underlying this view is not only a profoundly mistaken view of capitalism but also an equally mistaken view of the capitalist state.

---

et al. (2016: 38). These include two policies: 'removing restrictions on the movement of capital across a country's borders (so-called capital account liberalization); and fiscal consolidation, sometimes called "austerity", which is shorthand for policies to reduce fiscal deficits and debt levels' (ibid.). While 'Some capital inflows, such as foreign direct investment – which may include a transfer of technology or human capital – do seem to boost long-term growth. But the impact of other flows – such as portfolio investment and banking and especially hot, or speculative, debt inflows – seem neither to boost growth nor allow the country to better share risks with its trading partners' (ibid.). 'The benefits in terms of increased growth seem fairly difficult to establish when looking at a broad group of countries. The costs in terms of increased inequality are prominent. ...Increased inequality in turn hurts the level and sustainability of growth. Even if growth is the sole or main purpose of the neoliberal agenda, advocates of that agenda still need to pay attention to the distributional effects' (ibid.). The authors say that 'Curbing the size of the state is another aspect of the neoliberal agenda. ...Austerity policies not only generate substantial welfare costs due to supply-side channels, they also hurt demand – and thus worsen employment and unemployment'. They add that fiscal consolidation can raise investor confidence and boost investment, but 'in practice, episodes of fiscal consolidation have been followed, on average, by drops rather than by expansions in output' (ibid.: 40). The IMF economists conclude that: openness to short-term capital flows and fiscal austerity have resulted in inequality, and that 'There is now strong evidence that inequality can significantly lower both the level and the durability of growth' (p. 41).

CHAPTER 5

Capitalism and Technological Change: Reflections on the Technology – Poverty Relation

Technology is seen as a sign of modernity.[1] Technological change is expected to be a means of bringing about development. For the less developed world, technological change is a means of catching up with advanced countries as well.

Often technology is associated with information technology (IT), so much so that IT-related companies are referred to as technology companies. This is a narrow conception of what technology is. Technology simply means application of scientific ideas to solve practical problems. A technology can be a set of ideas (e.g. software) or a mechanical thing (e.g. an equipment) or a (bio-)chemical thing (e.g. fertilizer or a hybrid/genetically-modified seed).

Given society's obsession with technology, in both rich and poor countries, we should ask what is the social nature of technology and whether technological change itself can solve social problems such as poverty? This question can be asked in the context of many different forms of human activity (e.g. agriculture, industry, services). We will ask the question in the context of agriculture which has been going through many technological revolutions in the last 10,000 years or so. One might ask: why should we examine technological change *in agriculture*?

Firstly, agriculture is the sphere of activity that produces food. Summarizing Marx's intellectual contribution, Engels (1883) said this:

> Just as Darwin discovered the law of development or organic nature, so Marx discovered the law of development of human history: the simple fact, hitherto concealed by an overgrowth of ideology, that mankind must first of all eat, drink, have shelter and clothing, before it can pursue politics, science, art, religion, etc.

The idea that the humankind 'must first of all eat, drink, have shelter and clothing' not only signifies the importance that Marx attached to the philosophy of materialism. At a more concrete level, that idea is indicative of the (trans-historical) importance of agriculture, from which food and drink come,

---

1   An earlier version of this chapter appeared as Das (2002).

© KONINKLIJKE BRILL NV, LEIDEN, 2020 | DOI:10.1163/9789004415560_006

and from which some of the raw materials for shelter and clothing, among other things, also come.

Agriculture is therefore an important area of the humankind's productive activity. The fact that a relatively small percentage of the workforce in richer countries is engaged in agriculture and the fact that the percentage of the workforce in agriculture is slowly decreasing in poorer countries such as India, do not diminish the theoretical and practical importance of agriculture and its social relations. Secondly, agriculture is important because of the *historically-specific form* that its contribution to economic development takes. Agriculture provides raw materials and investible surplus for industrial development in capitalist societies, as agrarian political economy (agrarian transition) literature has highlighted (see Byres, 1996). Importantly, it also produces food, which is an important item consumed by the working class. And when less labor time is needed to produce wage-goods including food, other things constant, more profit can be produced (this is explained later).

If agriculture is an important sector of productive activity as a producer of food (and as a producer of raw materials for industrial development producing means of subsistence), this raises the question of technology that is used in that sector. In particular, how do we understand the class character of technology? There is also a distributional issue, which is connected to the previous question: given that those who depend on agriculture for a living tend to be poor (they cannot satisfy their basic needs), what is the relation between technology and poverty? These issues are discussed in the context of the Green Revolution technology that began to be widely used in the 1960s in India (and elsewhere).

The world has seen four agricultural revolutions, all having resulted in a dramatic acceleration of growth (Lipton, 1989: 316). The Green Revolution (GR), which is more than half a century old now, is the last but one of these (the GR is followed by the genetic – biotechnological – revolution). Its speed, scale and spread have 'far exceeded those of any earlier technical change in food farming' (ibid.: 14–15). It has made possible a 'revolutionary' increase in food production in less developed countries. More than hundred poor countries use the new technology.

There is a large literature on the GR which explores various dimensions of what is clearly a complex topic. There are studies on the GR's impacts on changes in the cropping pattern, on agricultural productivity, economic growth, food self-sufficiency, diversification in investment and employment, and on wages (Alauddin and Tisdell, 1995; Harwood, 2013; Jain, 2010; Jeffrey, 1997; Naher, 1997; Palmerjones, 1993; Rao, 1998). Several authors have highlighted its socially and spatially uneven adoption (Das, 1999b; Patnaik, 1986) while others show that GR is poor-farmer friendly (Eicher, 1995). The GR is said to have influenced, and been influenced by, commoditization, agrarian class differentiation, the structure of class relations, including mercantile and usurious relations, and the investment decisions and productivity of petty commodity producers (Dyer, 1997; Harriss-White and Janakarajan, 1997; Patnaik, 1986; Goldman and Smith, 1995). Indeed, the GR triggered off an extremely important debate in development studies, the celebrated mode of production debate, that focused on the nature and the extent of capitalist development in India, which we have discussed in Chapter 3. There are studies on the politics of the GR which show that: on the one hand, the GR enriches larger, surplus-producing farmers who in turn mobilize themselves and put pressure on the state for better prices and other benefits; and on the other hand, rural laborers (those whose main source of income is wage-work) have been involved in struggle over wages (Breman, 1990, 1989; Gill, 1994; Bentall and Corbridge, 1996; Bhalla, 1999; Oommen, 1971). Studies have also dealt with the impacts of the GR on employment opportunities for women and their freedom, and on the environment (Da Corta and Venkateshwarlu, 1999; Shiva, 1991; Rahul, 1995). A post-structuralist, 'anti-developmentalist' approach to the GR has also emerged arguing that the GR represents a development-induced scarcity (Yapa, 1993).

But the fact that there is an enormous literature on the topic does not mean that our level of knowledge about the GR is necessarily adequate. Jonathan Rigg says, the GR 'suffers from a surfeit of attention which has sometimes obscured the issues being discussed' (Rigg, 1989: 144). Rigg suggests that it is clearly time 'to conduct a reappraisal of the Green Revolution' (p. 149). One area that surely needs this reappraisal is the relation between the GR and poverty/inequality.

The relation between the GR and poverty/inequality is among the most widely researched topics not only in the GR debate but more generally in geography and development studies (Alauddin and Tisdell, 1991, 1995; Beck, 1995; Dasgupta, 1977; Frankel, 1971; Harriss, 1991, 1992; Lipton, 1989; Pearse, 1980; Sharma and Poleman, 1993; Yapa, 1993, 1979). The literature on the GR–poverty relation has been almost polarized between the 'GR enthusiasts' who see favorable impacts of the GR on poverty/inequality and 'GR sceptics' who take almost an opposite view. Separating the poverty issue from the inequality issue, it can be said that there is a near consensus that the GR has caused an increase in inequality (Lipton, 1989). Freebairn (1995) reviews more than 300 studies on the GR which were published between 1970 and 1989. Freebairn's analysis shows that in 80% of these studies the GR is associated with a rise in inequality. But there does not seem to be any agreement on whether the GR has caused an increase or decrease in absolute poverty.

Indeed, the research on the GR–poverty relation has gone through several phases (see Figure 5.1 below). Some of these are discussed in Lipton (1989: 18–19). The GR started in about 1960 in the Third World, generally (and in the mid-1960s in India). The period 1960–1970, and more specifically, 1967–1970, is considered to be the period of GR euphoria. This phase was characterized by the normal neo-Malthusian enthusiasm about the positive impact of the technology on the poor. In the second phase (the early and mid-1970s), there were growing fears that the GR hurt the poor, that the technology was enriching the richer farmers at the expense of the poorer farmers, and landowners at the expense of laborers. In the third phase, the later part of the 1970s, the GR's impacts on poverty were subjected to reassessment. Smaller farmers (i.e. family farmers) were said to be catching up with larger ones even with some delay. Laborers benefited from increased labor use, so employment opportunities rose, although wages did so rarely. The poor as consumers gained because increased food production restrained food prices. In the GR areas, the poor benefitted absolutely but lost relatively. The poor living outside the GR areas got nothing.

In the 1980s, the fourth phase started: this is the period when the extreme neo-Malthusian optimism began again. There was a revival of the early

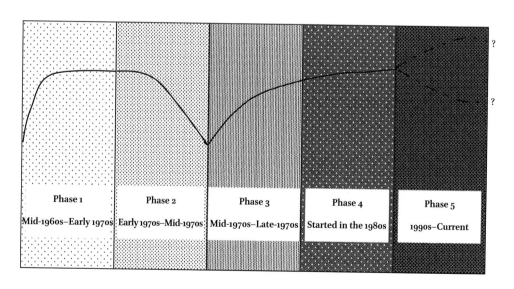

———— The Green Revolution trend from phase 1–phase 4

— - — - Two predictions for the Green Revolution trend for phase 5

FIGURE 5.1 The phases of the Green Revolution
SOURCE: AUTHOR

euphoria. It was argued that smaller farmers sometimes adopted the technology even earlier and more intensively than larger ones and that the GR raised labor's share in rural income. A technically appropriate and profitable technology, if used everywhere, would benefit the poor everywhere.

I would add a fifth phase (1990s–). This would be the most recent phase whose precise direction of development is not clear. There are two possibilities. One is that recent (post-colonial) critiques of science and technology generally and the GR technology more specifically (Ullrich, 1992; Yapa, 1996) and concerns about the ecological impacts of the GR (Shiva, 1991) might resemble the second phase of pessimism (which was based on a critical scrutiny of the GR on more materialist–economic grounds). Alternatively, the 1980s euphoria might continue with the additional support from biotechnology and related research, with the GR technology is increasingly replaced by, or supplemented with, the technology of GM (genetically-modified) crops.

The GR–poverty relation, the intellectual construction of which has changed over time as seen in the above brief description of swings in research on the topic, is an interesting issue more generally. It can be considered to be a part of the larger literature on the relation between technology and society, including the poor people in society.

Michael Lipton is one of the most widely cited researchers on the GR and poverty topic. He wrote a book in 1989, *New Seeds and Poor People*. Lipton says in this book that the GR signifies 'the interplay of institutions with technology and human actions, as causes of social transformation and hence changes in the lot of the poor' (Lipton, 1989: 17). This book synthesises a vast amount of work on the consequences of the GR on poverty in a most comprehensive manner, and at the same time puts forward his own views on the topic. Lipton's work is characterized by his deep and real concern for the poor in the Third World. Unlike many others, Lipton is careful not to reach easy conclusions about the supposed benefits of the GR for the poor. Yet, I find Lipton's causal analysis of the GR–poverty relation faulty. In this chapter I argue that Lipton's work, like much of the massive amount of research on the GR–poverty relation, is firmly within a paradigm which gives much more causal power to technology and to population than they can possibly bear. I hope that my arguments about the GR as a technology will have relevance for the more general issue of the relation between technology and society. Finally, it may be noted that the chapter is a 'negative' statement. This is in that my main aim is *not* to say what the necessary causes of poverty *are* (although I touch on that issue very briefly). It is rather to say what the necessary causes of poverty (or poverty reduction) are *not* ('necessary' as understood in the critical realist philosophy of science) (Sayer, 1992). More specifically, I argue against Lipton's view that the GR has a *necessary* poverty-reducing property. The poor would be poorer without the technology.

Let me clarify some terminological issues pertaining to poverty and the GR. Poverty, even absolute poverty, has many meanings. In this chapter, people are said to be in absolute poverty when they do not enjoy a level of income that is sufficient to secure the *bare essentials* of food, clothing and shelter (Nafziger, 1990: 100; stress added). A person is said to be poor if her/his income falls below the government-determined poverty-line. In the context of rural India, the latter is defined as the mid-point of the monthly per-capita expenditure class having a daily per capita intake of 2400 calories.[2] Similarly, there are several meanings of the term 'Green Revolution' (Dixon, 1990). In this chapter, I have used the term to refer to the use of modern varieties of seeds (MVs) which are also known as high yield varieties of seeds (HYVs). The GR and the use of MVs are taken to be synonymous.[3]

The chapter has five sections. In Section 1, I present a 'slice' of the GR debate – in particular, Lipton's and others' views on the supposed positive and negative benefits of the GR for the poor. In Section 2, I critique this literature for its underlying neo-Malthusianism. In Section 3, I present an alternative statement on the GR and poverty relation, one that sees the relation as a contingent one, rather than necessary. In the light of my criticisms and my

---

2   Lack of income is, however, not the only indicator of poverty. Infant mortality, illiteracy, low life expectancy, and so on are some of the other indicators. Indeed, Dreze and Sen say, poverty lies not merely in the impoverished state in which the person actually lives, but also in the lack of real opportunity to choose other types of living (Dreze and Sen, 1995). In this chapter I am dealing with 'the impoverished state' in which the poor actually live, as indicated by the most popular income-based poverty measure (the head-count ratio), without implying at all that that is the best measure of poverty.

3   I do not include non-irrigation mechanical inputs in the definition. Although I do not accept many of the ideological underpinnings of his work as made clear later, I follow Lipton in considering that mechanical inputs, generally speaking, are not a necessary aspect of the GR. 'The link between capital-linked inputs such as tractors to MVs is usually artificial' (Lipton, 1989: 122, 126–127). Furthermore, many would equate the GR with agrarian capitalism or would consider capitalist property relations as a part of the GR. This, in my view, is erroneous. Agrarian capitalism can exist without the GR, although the introduction of this technology deepened the development of agrarian capitalist relations (Patnaik, 1986). Besides, *non-capitalist* cultivators such as land-poor peasants using the family labor can also use the GR technology; but whether in fact the latter will use the technology is a function not of the technology as such but of the structure of the property relations within which the technology is used (depending on the context, the technology has to be bought or can be provided communally without the mediation of the market). For me, and I am aware that this might be contentious, property relations provide the *context* in which the technology works, but these relations are not a *necessary part* of it.

174   CHAPTER 5

alternative view, I provide in Section 4 a brief empirical analysis of the GR–poverty relation in India, which is one of the 'model' GR countries in the mid-1990s. Section 5 summarizes the discussion and briefly relates it back to the literature. It also very briefly reflects on the genetic (biotechnological) revolution in terms of its proponents' claim about its pro-poor benefits, the claims that are similar to the claims made about the GR's pro-poor effects.

1   The Literature on the Green Revolution and Poverty: The Thesis and the Anti-thesis

Smaller farmers and laborers are the two most important constituents of the poor in India and many other less developed countries. Lipton (and others) argue that the GR can benefit and has benefited these groups. Without MVs, most poor people would be poorer (Lipton, 1989: 160; hence forward, all references to Lipton are those to his 1989 book). As MVs are designed to make better use of nutrients from all sources, including fertilizer and water, than traditional seeds, it has land-augmenting effects that benefit small farmers (Lipton, 1989: Chapter 3; Sharma, 1992).[4]

As Lipton rightly says, world-wide, the poor are increasingly laborers, rather than smaller farmers. Yet, as he points out, the effects on laborers have been relatively neglected until very recently as most of the research has focused on smaller farmers. There are mainly three effects on labor. I will call them employment effects, wage effects, and price effects.[5]

Lipton and others (Bhalla, 1995; Sharma and Poleman, 1993; Vaidyanathan, 1986) argue that the GR has increased employment opportunities for laborers.[6] There are several reasons for this.

(a) Since MVs mature sooner than traditional varieties, they allow multiple cropping.[7] This leads to an increased demand for labor per acre. (b) If MVs are

---

4   This is in the sense that what was being produced on (e.g.) a five-acre land-holding earlier can be produced on less land with the GR technology. So 'the new technology has tended to help the small farms overcome their most restrictive bottleneck, that is, limited land area, to a great extent' (Sharma, 1992: 183).

5   From the standpoint of GR optimists such as Lipton, the effects of the Green Revolution (GR_e) on labor can be represented as thus: $GR_e = (ew) / i$, where e is the employment in person-days and w is the money wage per person-day, and i is the rate of inflation of food price.

6   Labor use per acre could increase by about a fifth at least at the early stage (Barker and Herdt quoted in Lipton).

7   The poorer people are more likely to suffer from seasonal fluctuation in labor demand. Multiple cropping helps them by providing year round employment (Lipton, 1989: 196).

REFLECTIONS ON THE TECHNOLOGY – POVERTY RELATION

to give economically feasible yield, densities of plants in the fields need to be high. This, in turn, requires increased input of sowing and transplantation labor (and, given the gendered division of labor, women often benefit from this). (c) MVs increase returns to fertilizer. This leads to the need for extra labor input required to place the fertilizer. Also, fertilizer-use might lead to seed growth requiring extra labor for weeding. (d) The increased food production, caused by MV-use, leads to increased demand for harvesting and threshing labor and post-harvest labor (e.g. for food processing) (Lipton: 187, 194). (e) MV-use increases larger landowners' income. This rise in income leads to their preference for leisure which then leads to greater use of hired labor by them (Lipton: 179). Further, the increased expenditure of large landowners also causes growth in non-agricultural employment (e.g. employment in trading activities owing to the increased demand for urban goods from the rich farmers) (Sharma and Poleman, 1993; Vaidyanathan, 1986).[8]

The use of MVs not only increases employment opportunities. It is also said to have caused higher wages (Sharma, 1992: 185). Lipton, however, is less sanguine about the wage effect of the MVs, as we shall see later.

Lipton rightly stresses that the poor people are not just small farmers and laborers, and that they are also net buyers of food. He (and others) argue that MV-induced increased food production contributes to lower food prices which benefit the poor food buyers in MV and non-MV areas (Dantawala, 1987; Parthasarathy, 1987; Rao, 1994: 54). Lower food prices benefit especially laborers as they spend the larger part of their income on buying food. No doubt, food prices have increased in many regions. But these prices would have been much higher without MVs (Singh, 1990: 196). This is consistent with Lipton's idea that the poor would have been poorer without the new technology.

Lower food prices affect the poor in another way, according to Lipton. The state in the less-developed countries would not have felt able to undertake the expansion of anti-poverty programs (e.g. food for work) without its large food reserves to back up such schemes, the reserves that were mainly due to MVs (Lipton: 294). Also, cheaper food means less pressure on the state for wage increases in the public sector. This may make it possible for the state to make investments in health, infrastructure, etc., which may benefit the poor (ibid.).

MVs can then lower rural poverty levels in all these ways. This argument is, in fact, a part of the more general idea that there is a negative association between (rural) poverty and (agricultural) development/growth (Ahluwalia,

---

8   This is an argument that Lipton does not make. He does say that the impacts of MVs on non-farm employment have been neglected (p. 205; cf. p. 8; also see Gill, 1994) on lack of non-farm employment in GR areas.

1978; Chadha, 1984; Chadha, 1994; Misra and Hazell, 1996; Parthasarathy, 1995; Tendulkar and Jain, 1995; Dollar and Kraay, 2000).

This is, however, only one side of the debate. This is the thesis, to which there is an anti-thesis. The latter is also shared by Lipton and many others, that the MV technology is socially discriminatory and that it hurts the poor (Byres, 1989, 1983, 1972; Frankel, 1971; Griffin, 1974; Yapa, 1993, 1979). Lipton himself offers several reservations about the positive benefits of the technology. He says that in spite of the possible favorable effects of the *miracle* seeds, the fact that their poverty reduction impact is minimal in many places is a *mystery* (p. 5, 7–8). At a theoretical level, for Lipton, the GR is *necessarily* pro-poor. But this *theoretical* expectation, which is the main subject of my critique, is not materialized empirically. Why is this so?

1) First of all, if the poorer farmers cannot use the technology, it cannot benefit them. Although Lipton believes that the smaller farmers eventually catch up with the larger farmers in adopting the new technology (see also Eicher, 1995; Herath and Jayasuriya, 1996: 1200), he does recognize that poverty delays adoption of the technology by smaller farmers (p. 118). Yapa explains this better. He says that the GR technology 'produces higher yields, but it confers these benefits unequally to different classes' (1992: 260). The GR has a 'material-bias' in that the inputs have to be bought in the market (Yapa, 1979: 373). So one would 'expect the techniques to be adopted chiefly by those who have greater access to credit and capital' (ibid.). Finally, given that the GR depends on the use of heavy doses of water and given that the larger farmers have the resources to use underground water much more than the smaller ones, the level of underground water is reduced. This makes it much more expensive for smaller farmers to use the water, without which MVs will not give high yields on a sustainable basis (Shiva, 1991). Thus, if smaller farmers cannot use the technology, it cannot have the impact that Lipton and others say it will.[9] Besides, given that MVs do better in irrigated areas than in rainfed areas, the benefits from MVs for the poorer farmers will be rather limited in these areas.

---

9 However, while Lipton recognizes that poverty delays adoption of the technology, he nonetheless says that market favors smaller farmers. (a) MVs convert a high proportion of nutrients into grain matter, and (b) using fertilizers and water control is labor intensive, (c) smaller farmers have much family labor to employ, if they can get money/credit to buy the physical inputs. Given (a), (b) and (c), small farmers will use more inputs because they will gain more because they can use more labor per acre; so they can pay more (p. 125). Lipton also says that whether small farmers adopt early or catch up depends on initial inequality and institutional inadequacy or bias. There is no universal law (p. 117).

REFLECTIONS ON THE TECHNOLOGY – POVERTY RELATION

2) Secondly, even if smaller, poorer farmers can get access to the new technology somehow, they may not be able to *continue* using it. This would be the case if they started losing their land in the process of adopting the new technology which caused them to be indebted. Some scholars point out that there are MV-induced mechanisms that cause this. (a) Erstwhile landlords have evicted their tenants, as cultivation with the use of hired labor and the MVs has become more profitable. Lipton indeed agrees that at least at the early stage of MV adoption, MV-induced changes in land distribution occur and that GR enhances proletarianization (p. 187). This is in the sense that, he explains, those farmers who adopt the technology early increase their resources and power and thus are able to push poorer farmers off their land (see also Heble, 1979). (b) Larger landowners lease in land from smaller ones who cannot afford the higher cost of the bio-chemical inputs – this is reverse tenancy (Nadkarni, 1976). (c) Since the inputs are expensive, smaller owners cannot make appropriate investments to increase output and reduce the production cost as larger farmers can. So they incur loss, and go into debts. Then, they try to clear up the debts by selling their land (see Gill, 1988: 2167). This is the classic mechanism of agrarian differentiation from below, as the literature on the agrarian question, inspired by Lenin, has shown (Brass, 2016; Byres, 1991; Lenin, 1899). Thus the GR by causing loss of peasants' access to land (either in terms of the right to use or ownership) is said to have worsened peasants' economic position. Further, the loss of access to land leads to the increased supply of laborers which lowers wages (Lipton: 187). It must be stressed, however, that these mechanisms of GR-induced pauperization and proletarianization, generally, do not occupy an *important* place in Lipton's framework.[10]

---

10   On the one hand, given that the use of MVs does not involve economies of scale, Lipton wonders why should there be eviction or engrossment? Further, large owners cannot buy land as it is too expensive. On the other hand, landlords can capture the extra benefits by raising rents from tenants rather than by dispossessing them (p. 145). And, if landlords rent out from small farmers, the latter should benefit from rents. Besides, even if these problems do occur, Lipton says, these may not have to do with the GR. He says that 'most Marxist commentators on MVs may err by implicitly assuming that there are great and cumulative advantages especially as new techniques increasingly reward (i) the financial capacity to innovate, and (ii) the organizational capacity to engage many workers for large farmers over smaller ones, and for owners over tenants. If such advantages are also operated in adopting, intensifying and getting high incomes from MVs this could indeed play a key role in relative, perhaps absolute, immiserization... Marxists... have not always appreciated that repossession of tenancies, polarization of size of holdings... largely preceded MVs...' (p. 305; cf. Dyer, 1997).

The GR is said to have adverse impacts on the poor *as laborers* as well. There are tendencies toward deceleration in employment opportunities. (a) Increased food output due to MV-use leads to lower food prices. This means that farmers in non-MV areas get lower relative prices for their output and therefore have less incentive to employ labor. (b) MV-associated mechanization – tractors, weedicides, more mechanized irrigation or threshing – has eroded employment opportunities. 'By greatly raising yield, an appropriate MV often renders tractorization and threshers financially feasible' (Lipton: 199). But what, one might ask, makes mechanization necessary, especially in 'labor-surplus' economies?

There are several processes (Rudra et al., 1990: 32). One is that: by allowing multiple cropping in a shorter growing period, the application of biochemical inputs sets up a pressure toward mechanization in order for farmers to cope with the increased time constraint (i.e. farm operations have to be finished on time) (Byres, 1983).[11] That is, farmers resort to mechanization in order deal with sharp seasonal peaks in labor demand (from main crop harvest through second crop weeding time) and the resultant bidding up of wage rates (Lipton: 179). And, as Lipton says, a machine hired or bought for use in the peak season can also be used in other seasons. He agrees that if the use of MVs causes mechanization, this is a direct result of employers' reaction to the labor-using effects mentioned earlier. The post-harvest operation tends to be also mechanized. The high ratio of grain to dry matter of MV grain makes MV husks susceptible to easy shattering, and this gives incentive for mechanical milling, says Lipton.[12]

MV-induced rise in food output has led to low food prices and therefore rises in real wages. But when real wages rise, *given* an over-supply of laborers, employers are able to depress money wages – Lipton's famous 'responsive money-wage deceleration' (214, 219) (I will return to this later). This leads to fall in real wages and thus to the erosion of laborers' consumption gains from extra MV-induced food production. It is not that, Lipton says, GR causes money wages to necessarily fall. It is that the rate of increase of money wages falls.

There is another reason, says Lipton, why wages do not increase much. In many places, due to such factors as subsistence minima, screening and

---

11   Lipton says, however, that the argument that tractorization, etc. causes higher cropping intensity collapses when the inputs of MVs, fertilizers and water are controlled for (pp. 198–199). Besides, incentives for mechanization are buttressed by cheap subsidies.

12   In addition, urbanization of the MV-induced surplus is another problem. '[T]he growing proportion of outputs processed as urban surpluses (the fact that food from villages goes to the city and is processed there for urban consumption) raises the capital/labour ratio in milling, baking, etc.' (Lipton: 187).

REFLECTIONS ON THE TECHNOLOGY – POVERTY RELATION

nutritional efficiency, pre-MV wages have been kept well above the equilibrium (at the point where the supply of and the demand for labor power intersect) (Lipton: 284). The implication of this is that 'even if MVs induce a considerable increase in demand for labour [sic] ... this need not pull up the equilibrium wage above the actual pre-MV rate' (p. 284). What Lipton is saying is that wages are above the level one would expect from the given supply and demand of labor. So when demand for labor increases, wages do not increase because they have already increased (or been higher)![13]

Consider the negative impact of the GR on the poor as buyers of food. MVs do cause an increase in food production. But the poor may not buy the extra food output because they do not have the necessary purchasing power (Lipton: 13). This is a point others such as Varshney (1994) also make, and rightly so. Besides, and arguably in part because of the lack of purchasing power of the poor, the extra food 'might have displaced food imports and raised stocks, but have not substantially increased food availability per person, especially among the poor' (Lipton: 257; Patnaik, 1991). While prices for crops grown and eaten by the poor are allowed to fall, government stocks and replacement of imports are allowed to prevent a sharp fall in prices of crops grown by larger, surplus – producing farmers, as a fall in prices would undermine the incentive for these richer farmers to deliver food and raw materials to urban areas (Lipton: 217–218, 221).[14]

Thus Lipton (and others) express some reservations about the supposed benefits of the GR for the poor. Despite these major reservations, the balance of advantage to a typical 'poor person' in the Third World, from MVs, appears large, if we 'add up' their various effects on such a person as small farmer, hired worker, and consumer (Lipton: 258).

Overall, the negative effects of the MVs are outweighed by their positive effects, he says. In particular, labor-using effects, normally, outweigh labor-displacing ones. Inequality between smaller and larger farmers increases in MV-areas but 'absolute poverty declines' (p. 319). And, to the extent that MV-technology has not delivered on its promise, it is because of the over-supply of laborers, because of *population factor*, that is. The specter of the population haunts the poor.

---

13 Pre-MV-stickiness downwards explains why wages increase little. Post-MV stickiness downwards explains why laborers will not bargain for increased employment at restricted wage rates in place of labor displacing techniques to meet the extra demand for labor, as wage rates cannot fall below the current level (Lipton: 286).

14 But given that Lipton believes farmers should get rewards for risk-taking, he cannot find anything wrong with this.

180   CHAPTER 5

2   The Literature on the Green Revolution and Poverty:
        A Critique of Neo-Malthusianism

Lipton's (and others') idea that the MV-*technology* necessarily has *pro-poor* attributes and can necessarily cause poverty reduction but that if it has not been able to deliver on that promise it is because of *population* problems, is problematic. I want to suggest that underlying this idea is a specific form of neo-Malthusianism. Or, the objective effect of such thinking is resorting to neo-Malthusianism. I define this specific form of neo-Malthusianism as a combination of Malthusianism (the idea that population growth is the prime cause of scarcity and, therefore, of poverty) and technological determinism, which has some amount of pro-poor bias to it. It is true that for Lipton, MV technology interacts with the social aspects such as population and state policy (p. 17). But his framework suffers from inadequate conceptualization of both technology and of social aspects such as population. To the extent that he discusses the non-population aspects of society at all, he always under-stresses and under-conceptualizes them and treats them in an *ad hoc* manner.

    There is a large amount of evidence from his book to suggest that his framework smacks of technological determinism (or indeed, technological reification) in the specific sense of giving much more power to technology that it itself can possibly have. Let me explain this.

a)   Lipton says, if MV technology is pro-poor it is because of the nature of the technology itself. MVs' physical properties are pro-poor.

> Certainly [MVs'] physical properties... MVs' use of more labour and management per acre, their production of coarser and cheaper varieties favouring self-consumption rather than marketing... should be more helpful to small farmers than to big ones. (p. 177)
> [W]ithout the extra employment income and food supplies created by the [extra grain] due to MVs, many of the world's poor would today be poorer still, and millions now alive would have died. (p. 9)
> [M]any millions of poor 'small' farmers would be worse off today if MVs did not exist. (p. 12)
> With rapid population growth and scarce land, the position of landless labour is much worse without MVs than with. (p. 186)

All this textual evidence suggests that, for Lipton, there is a relation between GR technology and poverty reduction at a theoretical level, although the actual extent of poverty reduction in different places and in different times might be less or more.

REFLECTIONS ON THE TECHNOLOGY – POVERTY RELATION

b)   Lipton believes, while GR would necessarily cause poverty reduction, if it has not delivered on its promise, it is partly because of technology as well!

[T]he real poverty problem with MVs arises in the rural areas that they leave out. (p. 147)
Indeed, the MVs have to some extent failed the poor partly because they have not spread enough to offset mechanization or land-hunger, and especially because they have not spread to areas of insecure water supply [these are mainly rainfed areas]... (p. 9)

So, MVs – *both* when they are present and when they are absent – affect the poor.

c)   Lipton recognizes that old, inegalitarian power structures in the village do hurt the poor. But he is also skeptical of the claims made by some Marxists that MVs transform the local power structures and relations of production (p. 324). For, Lipton says, the MV technology is too 'seriable', 'separable' and 'single-unit' for that. It is seriable in that the technology does not have to be used on a farm system as a whole; a piecemeal experiment is feasible. It is separable in that the package can be separated/unpacked. And, it is single-unit in that the adoption does not involve each unit in relationships with neighbors and/or authority structures; how much one gains from the technology does not depend on one's neighbors' or authority structures (p. 316, 318–319).

Thus the MV-technology is an evolutionary one: it does not require the transformation of local power structures (p. 319), which are left intact. This means that the richer people corner more benefit (p. 401), leading to rise in inequality, although absolute poverty can decline.[15] Clearly, for Lipton, to the extent that MVs hurt the poor, that is because *the nature of the technology is such that* it can be used in a context where older power relations do not have to be changed. It is technology that is in the driving seat. It is technology that determines how and whether or not it affects the poor.

---

15   While not changing the local power structures, MVs change *national* power structures, however, and that hurts the rural poor. By increasing production sharply, MVs produced urbanized surplus of food and raw materials and thus adverse internal terms of trade against rural areas. Thus national urban-based power structures got strengthened. Also urban elites do a deal with rural elites who provide the surplus. Because state policy is against the rural areas (farmers and non-farmers), pro-rural poor effects of technology cannot be realized (p. 402). As local power structures are not changed, the impact on strengthening urban, national power structures is larger.

182   CHAPTER 5

So the technology needs to be and can be more pro-poor (e.g. hand-pump; new seeds for millet for semi-arid areas for subsistence farmers) (Lipton: 126, 325). This means the lack of a sufficiently pro-poor technology is a necessary cause of poverty. So the solution to world poverty lies in poverty-oriented, MV-based food agriculture [which] is the *only chance* to provide the growing poor populations of Asia and Africa with livelihoods during the many decades before their widespread industrialization (p. 425; stress added).

Note that for Lipton, it is not *any* technology that would solve poverty, for to say that would be crude, pure neo-Malthusianism. Rather there is a need for a *particular* type of technology, one that is *necessarily* pro-poor, suggesting that Lipton's neo-Malthusianism, unlike neo-Malthusianism per se, has *some* pro-poor bias. To the list of Sen's entitlements of the poor, Lipton adds one more, one that I would call 'technological entitlement':

> Only MV technology *directly available* to the poor – either because unavoidably labour intensive (*yet profitable*), or because concentrated on crops (or areas or assets) that remain in the control of the poor – is, in our judgement, likely to lastingly overcome the *"population threats"* to the poor people's food entitlements. (p. 215; stress added)

It may be noted that Lipton sees here no possible contradiction between labor-intensiveness of a technology and its profitability. Neither does he recognize the possibility of, and the long term structural tendency towards, the poor losing control over their means of production through pauperization and proletarianization,[16] and therefore, not being able to use the technology, no matter how 'pro-poor' it might be. More significantly, and from the standpoint of this chapter, Lipton's framework sees no need for changes in the way food and other goods and services are produced and distributed and in the power relations underlying this production and distribution. Marxist political economy is banished. Technological entitlement is in. In fact, it is very clear that Lipton's framework takes the current private-property dominated market economy for granted and that he, like Amartya Sen and other pro-poor economists, firmly believes in its underlying principle.[17] Technology can be designed

---

16   These are the processes that Marxist political economy of agrarian change has been drawing attention to.

17   He recognizes that '[B]igger farmers can hang on for higher prices [i.e. they do not have to sell their crops immediately and can wait until price rises happen]'. But such price rises 'seldom reflect more than the cost of storage ... and normal profit to allow for price risks' (p. 128), so that big farmers getting higher prices than smaller, needy farmers is justified. Further, Lipton finds nothing wrong with merchants, who buy from smaller farmers, 'insist[ing] on a lower grain price, in part as a reward for risk-bearing' (p. 129).

REFLECTIONS ON THE TECHNOLOGY – POVERTY RELATION

that would avert any need for radical social change that is necessary to eliminate poverty. Lipton, in this sense, is not too far from Borlaug, the biological scientist who received Nobel Prize for *Peace* (*not* for science) for inventing the new seeds and making possible GR that would turn the poor away from the danger of *Red Revolution* in the Third World.

Underlying Lipton's stress on technology is his view that there are 'population threats to the poor' (p. 215) and that population is a primary determinant of unemployment and wages. Let us therefore consider the second aspect of Lipton's neo-Malthusianism: his view about population–poverty relation in the context of MV-use. Lipton asks:

> Are poor people's insufficient gains – even losses – traceable to MVs themselves, and their role in the spread of rural capitalism; or to rising person/land ratios and hence weakening in the bargaining power of workers, small tenants and borrowers. The former position is taken by most (not all) Marxists; the latter by neo-Malthusians... (p. 304)

To know whose side Lipton is on, Marxists or neo-Malthusians, consider this.

> Just as population growth has helped to make growing proportions of the poor dependent on labour incomes rather than on MV farms direct, so it has helped to create a "reserve army" of under-employed adults, *Malthusian rather than Marxian*. The former population effect limits poor people's consumption gains from extra income in cultivating MVs even on small farms. The latter effect, the growing reserve army – by permitting "responsive money-wage deceleration" – reduces the prospects that extra MV-based food availability can help the poor by holding food prices in check. (p. 215; stress added)

Population growth has thus been invested with a massive amount of causal power. Population growth, not class differentiation or profit-driven mechanization or extant class relations impeding economic development that creates non-farm high-wage jobs, thus forcing a large number of people to rely on small parcels of land, and ultimately, to become landless, is the major driving force behind proletarianization, an increase in the number of people dependent on labor-income. This means that the poverty-reducing impacts of MVs through their impacts on small farmers is minimized *due to* population growth. Population not only increases the supply of laborers but also reduces their wage-gains. MV-induced increases in food production lead to lower food prices which in turn cause an increase in the real value of money wage in the first instance. The increased real wage then 'enables or induces many more poor and unskilled workers [whose supply is large because of population growth] to come forward and compete for employment' (p. 214); MVs, says Lipton, '*stimulate* poor people to produce even larger populations of potential workers' (Lipton: 404, 415; stress added). This permits employers to reduce money wages in turn (p. 214).

> [*T*]*he main reason* why wage-rates stagnate and why wage shares decline, is that, with work forces growing fast, extra *demand* for labor due to MVs meets increasing *supply* of laborers prepared... to work at rates barely above subsistence.
>
> LIPTON: 185; stress added

The use of MVs leads to more employment and to larger wage bills. But these benefits are to be shared among many people because of natural population growth and migration to MV areas from non-MV areas. So, 'employment and hence wage receipts *per household* rise less, and may even fall' (p. 186). 'This is not usually "because of MVs" but because of population growth' (p. 186; quotes in original). Thus: 'MVs have had to contend with population-linked factors' such as population growth and induced increases in supply of laborers', which weaken the poor (p. 258; parenthesis added).

There is no doubt that Lipton's framework is neo-Malthusian. But he is somewhat different from a pure, crude, neo-Malthusian. 'To say that with today's population but 1960s seeds, millions of poor people now alive would now be dead, is not to take a crude neo-Malthusian view [which is] that poverty is caused by an imbalance between food availability and population' (p. 338), and that growing populations can be fed from constant land only through technological innovations (p. 211). The latter view is neo-Malthusianism that was behind the GR, as Lipton rightly points out. Lipton differs from a pure neo-Malthusian in part because he does not believe that the only role of technology is growth of more food at a rate faster than the population growth. Technology has also to generate more *employment* which would increase the poor people's *entitlement* to food. Lipton's therefore is a refined form of neo-Malthusianism.

To cut the long story of Lipton's (and others') theory of the GR–poverty relation short: GR and poverty reduction are necessarily causally related (GR has a necessary causal mechanism whereby poverty reduction will happen) but that if poverty has not been reduced as much as it should have been, it is because the technology has not been sufficiently used or been sufficiently pro-poor and because of the population problem. Both these positions are *conceptually* indefensible. The next section will say why.

REFLECTIONS ON THE TECHNOLOGY – POVERTY RELATION

3   Technology, Population and Poverty: A Contingent Relation

What is revealed in studies on technology development or technology – poverty relation, is a narrow conception of technology: what are deeply social processes are attributed to technology as such. It is forgotten that technology as an aspect of productive force always works within the framework of social relations of production (including relations between property owners and relations between them and workers). It is the social relations of production, class relations expressing the social organization of production, that, ultimately, have the primacy over the productive forces.

In a capitalist economy, production is always a production of a use value (e.g. food) *and* production of value and surplus value (or certain amount of surplus labor) (Marx, 1977). Labor is combined with technology and other means of production, and the product is sold as a commodity, which, in value terms, is the sum of constant and variable capital and surplus value ($c + v + s$). So, as an input into production, technology bears the same characteristics as production itself. Firstly, it has use value (it contributes to production), and it is bought and sold as a commodity. Secondly, it is also a means of the final product (e.g. grain, computer, or whatever) absorbing more and more surplus labor. It is a means of increasing exploitation, that is.

In the capitalist context of India, the combination of labor and the new technology has meant an increased final product (i.e. grain). But this increased product needs to be looked at both as a use value (grain to be eaten) *and* as a means of soaking up – bearing or embodying – more surplus labor (since in a given time – e.g. a crop season – a given amount of labor input is producing more than before). The level of wages that labor receives does not necessarily reflect the size of the increased product now possible with the use of the technology. In more general terms, the nature of technology and its effects in a class society reflect these two aspects of technology: the use value aspect and the exploitation aspect of technology. The main aim of technology, when adopted by the capitalist, is not to produce more in order to increase wages and to meet human needs. Lipton, like most others, stresses the use value, the production aspect, of technology (how technology increases production), and not its role in exploitation. In the latter role of technology does an important mechanism of poverty lie.

Technological change in agriculture has a special macro-economic significance in terms of understanding the social relations aspect of technology. The agriculture sector produces food, which is an important item consumed by the working class from which capital must appropriate surplus value. And when less labor time is needed to produce wage-goods including food, other things (real wage and the length of the working day) constant, i.e. when labor productivity rises, more surplus value is produced in its relative form. This is 'the surplus-value arising from the curtailment of the necessary labor-time' and thus a fall in the value of labor power (Marx, 1977: 432). This happens when:

> the rise in the productivity of labour ...seize[s] upon those branches of industry whose products determine the value of labour-power, and consequently either belong to the class of normal means of subsistence, or are capable of supplying the place of those means.
> Ibid.

The value of labor power is also reduced when:

> those industries which supply the instruments of labour and the material for labour, i.e. the physical elements of constant capital which are required for producing the means of subsistence.
> Ibid.

Lipton says, on balance, the MV technology is labor-intensive and can be made more so. But in capitalism, labor intensiveness – ratio of labor input to technological input – depends generally and largely on whether employing a particular technology will increase profits for owners, not on whether that technology will produce employment for laborers. Whether it is an individual capitalist or a collective capitalist, it is not their job to produce jobs. Labor intensiveness of technology also depends partly on class struggle, as the struggle over mechanization in farming (and fisheries) in Kerala shows (see Chapter 3; also Srinivas, 1998).

In Lipton's argument, employers are able to reduce real wages because of an oversupply of laborers (p. 214). But surely the relation between wages and supply of laborers is a contingent affair. I may offer two comments in support of this. (a) Wages are primarily determined by the cost of the production and reproduction of labor power as a commodity; only changes in its price are affected by its supply and demand. (b) The extent of under-/un-employment – the balance between the supply of and the demand for labor – is primarily determined by accumulation and the level of profit. Population growth is not at all immaterial. Indeed, it can, in some circumstances, and for a definite period of time, make the employment situation worse. But it cannot be the fundamental motive force behind that situation. Lipton's money wage deceleration thesis is entirely within the neo-classical framework in which wages are determined by the supply of and the demand for laborers. There is no suggestion in his work that production and wage determination are largely *class*

REFLECTIONS ON THE TECHNOLOGY – POVERTY RELATION 187

issues: that employers use their class power, the power they have over laborers because of their property ownership and control. And to say that population-linked effects destroy the neo-Malthusian optimism about the MV technology (Lipton: 214) is still to be within a populationist paradigm treating population as an independent variable. The capitalist economy, with its law of value, operating historically and at several spatial scales, including the rural/urban, regional, national and global, creates a relative surplus population through replacement of labor by technology, rationalization of work-organization, and class differentiation, etc. This relative surplus population can be used in times of cyclical capitalist expansion and it can be used to undermine the bargaining power of workers during normal times. The relative surplus population – a reserve army of labor – allows capitalists to force a worker to do the work of more than person. The so-called oversupply of labor is largely a class issue: it is class relations between owners and employers that set limit within which population and technology work. Where does this leave us with respect to absolute poverty then?

Absolute poverty means two things: that there are certain absolute needs that one must satisfy (basic minimum food, shelter, clothing, etc.) and that the person lacks the resources to meet those needs. Technology is not the basic determinant of either of these two things. Absolute poverty is a highly concrete issue. Like any concrete issue, this is a product of multiple determinations. It should not be reduced to any one set of mechanisms. Very briefly, absolute poverty can be caused by slow economic growth and by loss of access, or by reduced access, to basic goods and services or to an income. The loss of access to income, or reduced access to income can happen due to unemployment, low wages, low prices of goods produced by smaller property owners, loss of property of smaller owners, and so on.

Reduction in absolute poverty *necessarily presupposes* an increase in the real income of the people living below the poverty-line, however defined. An increase in the real income of the poor will occur when society's income level is increased[18] and when a significant part of that increased income trickles down to the poor through the market process. The real income of the poor can also increase (a) when the poor themselves are involved in growth (e.g. when the *property-owning* poor, i.e. smaller property owners, produce more), and (b) when more employment is created in the economic activities undergoing growth, benefiting the *property-less* poor (i.e. poor laborers).

The poor people can increase their real income as well even *without* an increase in the income of the society. Indeed, faster economic growth by itself

---

18   '[S]low economic growth is generally associated with low impact on poverty alleviation' (Vyas and Bhargava, 1995: 2572; Fields, 1995: 80).

does not reduce poverty significantly (Vyas and Bhargava, 1995; Das, 1995). This is because 'economic growth could affect only those at the upper end of the income distribution and thus make no impact on poverty reduction' (Toye and Jackson, 1996: 56). The poor can increase their real income *without* an increase in the income of the society as a whole if there is a significant amount of redistribution by political means (e.g. redistribution by the state), of: (a) existing income-generating *means of production* to the poor and/or (b) the *incomes* of the non-poor people to the poor (e.g. taxing the rich and using the tax to provide subsidized means of subsistence to the poor).

Thus, the real income of the poorer people will necessarily increase owing to three processes. These processes are: (a) the market-based trickle-down of increased income, (b) the involvement of the poorer people themselves in economic activities in which income is undergoing growth, and (c) the state-promoted redistribution of the existing income-generating means of production and/or of the incomes of the rich. However, whether these three processes will occur is *contingent*. It depends on (e.g.) the balance of power between the poor and the non-poor (Wright, 1995). And when these processes work, the extent to which poverty will be reduced is also a contingent matter.

Now, what is the relation of the use of the GR technology to these three processes? The GR farming does not seem to have any link to state-promoted redistribution except that it has circumvented the need for land redistribution, which has a potential to alleviate poverty (Griffin, 1989: 147). So I will focus on the relation of the GR to the market processes [(a) and (b) above].

The GR technology, like any technology, needs to be viewed as having certain causal power (e.g. the power to produce more). The technology has caused a rise in land and labor productivity, thus creating the possibility for increasing the share of the total product allocated to labor (see Das, 1998a: 125). The power of the technology to increase productivity exists by virtue of: (a) the physical *structure* of the technology itself *and* (b) the *structure* of property relations within which the technology is used. I have referred to Lipton's view that the physical structure of MVs themselves is such that they produce more (and are therefore pro-poor) (Lipton: Chapter 2). So, I will focus on the structure of property relations that Lipton under-conceptualizes and under-stresses in order to focus on population. Property relations are interpreted here broadly as the relations mentioned above: (a) between those who own property and those who do not (at least not to such an extent that they will not have to work for wages), and (b) between property owners (e.g. farmers and sellers of seeds).

Consider the first aspect of property relations. As I discussed in the last section, technologies are combined with labor in the labor process. The labor process takes place within the framework of relations between laborers on the one hand and those who own the means of production including technologies on the other. The labor process has certain specific *effects*. These include not only the physical effects – overall development of productive forces (i.e. a rise in productivity of labor) – but also economic-distributional effects – how much income laborers will earn.

Now these effects of the labor process are always mediated by property relations. For an example: it is the case that the use of the GR technology causes higher productivity by virtue of the internal structure of the GR inputs. But farm-*laborers* may not gain if the larger farm *owners* resort to labor-displacing mechanization. Thus the poorer people *may not* be directly involved in the activities where growth occurs and may not benefit from the increased income of the society.[19] But mechanization is not a necessary condition for labor not to get their share of the increased product that the technology of the GR makes possible. There is a limit to the rise in wages, which, irrespective of the reason for it, beyond a point, actually represents a diminution in unpaid labor and decrease in surplus value:

> as soon as this diminution [of unpaid labor] touches the point at which the surplus-labor that nourishes capital is no longer supplied in normal quantity, a reaction sets in: a smaller part of revenue is capitalised, accumulation lags, and the movement of rise in wages receives a check. The rise of wages is therefore confined within limits....
>
> MARX, 1977: 771

And the pressure on the rise in wages to stop is expressed in specific strategies by capitalists. For example, whenever the wage level reaches a point that cuts the average rate of exploitation and profit, employers use their class power to fight back and take necessary steps to reduce wages (investing in labor-saving technologies; suppression of wage-strikes; deproletarianization[20]). The level of wages crucially *depends* on the rate of exploitation and the attendant accumulation,[21] and on class struggle (Das, 1998a). The relation of laborers'

---

19   But, *pace* Byres (1983), and following Lipton, I would say that it is *not necessary* either that the larger landowners using the biochemical technology will also use labor-displacing mechanization. I insist, once again, that the relation between the MV technology and mechanization, including the so-called adverse effects of the latter on labor, is contingent.

20   This means restricting laborers' freedom to sell their labor power as free agents, as Brass has argued. This occurs in GR areas of the less developed world (as in the advanced countries).

21   The two are related: surplus value that is appropriated (exploitation) is reinvested in production (accumulation).

wages to how much they produce and therefore to the technological input into the labor process is not a *necessary* relation. Workers' wages are not primarily a product of how much they produce. Consider here the fact of near-stagnation in wages in the US since the 1970s, while productivity has risen. 'While productivity grew 64.9 percent in the period 1979–2013, hourly pay for production and non-supervisory workers rose by just 8.0 percent' (Jones, 2014).

Now consider the second aspect of the property relations. This refers to the distribution of property itself (land and money). And the distribution of property *affects* what the *effects* of the use of a technology are on (e.g.) smaller property owners. While the use of the GR technology can *necessarily* cause increased productivity, whether particular people will use the GR technology and other needed inputs is *contingent*. For example: if people do not own (much) land on which to use the technology, or if they have some land but do not have the money to buy the inputs, then they may not benefit from the GR technology. Even if they use the GR inputs, they may not use these in *proper* amounts because of lack of money (and knowledge), and therefore may not significantly augment their income on a sustainable basis to remain above the poverty-line.

Combination of technology with labor and other means of production can enhance productivity. But in a class society means of production are unequally distributed, and employers of labor, rather than labor, have the power to make decisions about the labor process, including the decisions about the labor intensiveness of the technology. Under this circumstance, the income benefits from increased production are necessarily unequally distributed. Absolute poverty, the fact of people not being able to meet their basic minimum needs, is a necessary aspect of this unequal distribution of 'income' in a class context, i.e. the income from employment (wage-income) or from property ownership (income in the form of capital), or from a combination of the two. Those people (smaller property owners and especially laborers) who get less than larger, labor employing, property owners *may* remain in absolute poverty. For some of them, the level of benefits from increased production may be relatively high so they may escape absolute poverty.

The point of my discussion is that whether the GR or indeed any technology will enhance or mitigate poverty is a contingent matter. The necessary effects of technology on society are those which are internal to the structure of the technology itself (in the case of the MV technology the necessary effect is greater yield). Technology as a physical (or chemical) thing can have only *physical/chemical* effects. Its *necessary* effects, as opposed to contingent ones, cannot be *social*. This is true about the GR technology just as much as computers. Technology itself does not, and cannot, have any necessary or inherent pro-poor causal property. That is: it is possible that the GR can reduce/increase poverty but not necessary. One cannot deny that some of the causes of poverty and some of 'the effects of the GR' *are* related. It is only that the relation is not *necessary*. Relatedly, my point is also that the so-called negative economic effects of the GR on poverty cannot be *reduced* to the GR itself. For, these effects are mediated by property relations, including how property owners relate to one another (as owners and buyers of commodities) and to workers whose labor power is bought by (larger-scale) property owners. This means and to repeat, the GR – or any technology – *itself* cannot necessarily hurt the poor. I take a theoretically agnostic view of the relation between technology and poverty. The social effects of the technology – effects of technology on society – are socially mediated, and are especially mediated by the class relations (property relations) within which the technology is used.

Similarly, population's relation to poverty or its relation to GR's impacts on poverty is a contingent affair. The over-supply of laborers and therefore un/under-employment may dampen wages. But at a given point in time, the mechanism of under/unemployment is largely *independent* of population growth, even if population growth can exacerbate the already-existing problem of under/unemployment and low wages. It is a function of class power of employers, of accumulation and attendant level of profit. Oversupply of laborers, under some circumstances, can contribute to the lowering of wages. It can make it difficult for laborers in their political struggle over wages by increasing competition among them (Shrestha and Patterson, 1990; Findlay, 1995). But the oversupply of laborers cannot be the fundamental motive force behind the determination of wages. It is not just that wages are never allowed to continue to remain at a high level for a long duration when there is a *shortage* of laborers in a place. More significantly, if/when a rise in wages undercuts the average rate of profit then the capitalist economy can *create* a relative *surplus* population, the so-called oversupply of laborers, through the replacement of labor by technology.[22] This happened when tractors were introduced in the Green Revolution areas, for example. A relative surplus population is created and allowed to continue to exist, one that can be used when it is needed for production of profit by the labor employing class and to undermine the bargaining power of laborers. It is class in the sense of property ownership and the social relations of private accumulation that set limit within which population has its effects. In other words, the effects of the so-called oversupply of labor, of population growth – like the effects of technology – on poverty are contingent and are therefore an empirical question.

---

22   Notice the high capital intensity of India's urban industries and their decreasing ability to absorb labor, for example.

4 The Green Revolution and Poverty in India: An Empirical Analysis

My empirical analysis is at the level of States.[23] I will compare the poverty situation over time and over space, i.e. across 17 major States in India, in the pre-neoliberalism period. From the standpoint of the GR, I have divided the States into two types. (1) I will call the first type, the more advanced GR States. These are the ones where the land under five major MV food crops (rice, wheat, maize, jowar and bajra) as a percentage of the total cultivated land under these crops is more than the median value for all the States. (2) The less advanced GR States are the ones where the percentage is below the median. (The States' ranks remained unchanged between the mid-1970s and mid-1980s.) In addition to this simple comparison across States over time, I will use correlation analysis to look at the relation between the use of the GR technology and the population factor on the one hand and poverty on the other (see Table 5.1).

The poverty level – the percentage of the rural population below the officially defined poverty line – tends to be lower in the more advanced GR States than elsewhere. So, one might expect a negative association between the use of the GR technology and poverty level, as discussed by Lipton and others. The following Table shows (lagged) correlations between poverty level and the use of the GR technology, at different points in time. Poverty levels for the mid-1970s, the mid-1980s and the mid-1990s are correlated with the use of the GR technology both in the mid-1970s (by when the GR had advanced both in terms of its adoption by smaller owners and in terms of spread to areas outside the original GR areas) and in the mid-1980s (by when the GR had advanced even further).

Table 5.2 shows that in the mid-1970s, there was a moderate degree of correlation between the GR and poverty level. But the relation seemed to have weakened afterwards as seen in the correlations between poverty level in the mid-1990s and the use of the GR technology in the mid-1980s. To the extent that there is any correlation between the GR and the poverty level at all, it is largely because of the fact that poverty levels in the States which adopted the technology earlier were lower than in the States which adopted the technology later. Indeed, in the more advanced GR States of the Punjab and Haryana combined, the poverty level throughout the 1960s was never more than 40% (except for 1967–1968) whereas the all-India poverty level was close to 50% at least

---

[23]   I am aware that using the States, which are huge areas, is problematic on grounds of ecological fallacy, because many of the relations between the new technology, population and poverty work at the intra-State, and especially, the family level.

REFLECTIONS ON THE TECHNOLOGY – POVERTY RELATION

TABLE 5.1   The Green Revolution and rural poverty, 1970s–1990s

	Rural poverty					
	1973/74	1977/78	1983	1987/88	1993–1994	1973/1994
Advanced GR States						
Andhra	48.4	38.1	26.5	20.9	15.92	67.1
Bihar	63.0	63.3	64.4	52.6	58.21	07.6
Gujarat	46.4	41.8	29.8	28.7	22.18	52.2
Haryana	34.2	27.7	20.6	16.2	28.02	18.07
Himachal	27.4	33.5	17.0	16.3	30.34	−10.73
Jammu & Kashmir	45.5	42.9	26.0	25.7	30.34	33.32
Punjab	28.2	16.4	13.2	12.6	11.95	57.62
Tamil Nadu	57.4	57.7	54.0	45.8	32.48	43.41
Uttar Pradesh	56.4	47.6	46.5	41.1	42.28	25.04
Group average	45.2	41.0	33.1	28.9	30.19	33.21
Less advanced GR States						
Assam	52.7	59.8	42.6	39.4	45.01	14.59
Karnatak	55.1	48.2	36.3	32.8	29.88	45.77
Kerala	59.2	51.5	39.0	29.1	25.76	56.49
Madhya	62.7	62.5	48.9	41.9	40.64	35.18
Maharastra	57.7	64.0	45.2	40.8	37.93	34.26
Orissa	67.3	72.4	67.5	57.6	49.72	26.12
Rajasthan	44.8	35.9	33.5	33.2	26.46	40.93
West Bengal	73.2	68.3	63.1	48.3	40.80	44.26
Group average	59.1	57.8	47.01	40.4	37.03	37.3
All-India	56.4	53.1	45.6	39.1	37.3	33.3

Notes: Expert group on poverty, planning commission (presented in NIRD, 1998). Percent change in poverty levels between 1973 and 1994. A negative sign in the final column means poverty level has increased.
SOURCE: NIRD, 1998; AND HTTP://WWW.SCIENCEDIRECT.COM.EZPROXY.LIBRARY.YORKU .CA/SCIENCE/ARTICLE/PII/S0016718501000069#TBLFN2

TABLE 5.2   Correlations between the Green Revolution and rural poverty level, 1970s–1990s

	PV77–78	PV83	PV87–88	PV93–94
GR (Early stage)	−0.677	−0.574	−0.610	−0.563
	(0.003)	(0.016)	(0.009)	(0.019)
GR (Late stage)	–	–	−0.554	−0.439
			(0.021)	(0.078)

Note: GR (Early stage) and GR (Late stage) are measured by: the land under five major MV food crops (rice, wheat, maize, jowar and bajra) as a percentage of the total cultivated land under these crops in the 1973–1976 and 1982–1985, respectively. PV77–78 is the percentage of the rural population below the poverty line in 1977–1978; likewise for other years. Figures in parentheses are p values. Correlation between GR (Early stage) and GR (Late stage) are 0.958 (p = 0.000).
SOURCE: CMIE, 1987; AND NIRD, 1998

for most of the 1960s. The unweighted mean poverty level in the 1960s in the Punjab–Haryana region was 35.87% as compared to 55.21% at the all-India level (as per the data from World Bank, 1997).

A better test of the relation between the GR and poverty would be whether the use of the technology is associated with any poverty *reduction*. Poverty reduction signifies the fact that poverty is a process, rather than a thing frozen in time. So, one would expect that the GR would be correlated with the *rate* of poverty reduction over time rather than poverty *levels at a given time*. There seems to have been a weak positive correlation between the GR in its early stage on the one hand and poverty reduction between the early/mid-1970s and the late 1980s on the other, possibly indicating some weak but favorable impacts of the technology on poverty reduction (Das, 2002). But there are no correlations between the GR in its later stage and poverty reduction. The overall message seems to be that there is no statistical correlation between the GR and poverty reduction. Let us probe this a bit further.

Each of the two types of States – more advanced GR States and less advanced GR States – can be divided further into two types based on the poverty reduction rate. These are: (a) States where poverty reduction has been greater than the median for all States (I will call them more pro-poor States), and (b) States where poverty reduction has been less than the median (I will call them less pro-poor States). We have thus four types of States, as shown in Table 5.3: (I) more advanced GR and more pro-poor States; (II) more advanced GR and less pro-poor States; (III) less advanced GR and more pro-poor States; and (IV) less advanced GR and less pro-poor States.

Table 5.3 shows that among the more advanced GR States, there are States where poverty reduction has been very high and also States which have not performed very well in poverty reduction. Similarly, among the less technologically advanced States, poverty reduction has been both more and less. Very significant poverty reduction (56%) has been possible over the 1973–1994 period in (e.g.) Kerala which is not a major GR area but which is known for the re-distributive policies, including land reforms, implemented by various leftist regimes in power there (see Franke and Chasin, 1991; Heller, 1995; Das, 1999c). Whereas, over the same period, a premier GR State, Haryana, has one of the worst records in poverty reduction (only 18%).[24] This is consistent with the fact that the rate of increase in money wage since 1970 in Haryana has been slower than in several less advanced GR States such as Orissa or Madhya Pradesh (Jose, 1988).

From the standpoint of Lipton's theory about GR's necessary pro-poor causal property, categories II and III are problematic, at least on empirical grounds. Why would poverty reduction be so low in spite of the widespread use of the

TABLE 5.3 Poverty reduction (1973–1994) with and without the Green Revolution

Green Revolution	Poverty reduction	
	Greater	*Less*
More advanced	(I) Andhra, Punjab, Gujarat, Tamilnadu	(II) Bihar, Haryana, Himachal;[a] Jammu and Kashmir, Uttar Pradesh
Less advanced	(III) Madhya Pradesh, Karnataka, Rajasthan, Kerala, West Bengal	(IV) Assam, Maharastra, Orissa

a   Poverty has increased by 10% in this State (this is the only State where poverty has increased).

SOURCE: DATA FROM NIRD, 1998

---

24   There is a debate on the impacts on poverty of the new liberalization policy in India which started in 1991 (see Chapter 4). Many scholars argue that it has had an adverse impact (Dev, 2000; Nayyar, 1996; see, Das, 2000b for a brief critical discussion of this literature). So, let us take poverty reduction between 1973 and 1987–88 (the last year for which comparable data for all States is available for the pre-liberalization period). The overall picture does not change, although there are some changes in actual entries in particular boxes. Several of the more advanced GR States have shown relatively low poverty reduction and there are several States where GR is not advanced but which have experienced greater poverty reduction.

196   CHAPTER 5

TABLE 5.4   Poverty, population growth and population pressure on land

More advanced GR states with greater poverty reduction			More advanced GR states with less poverty reduction		
	Pop. growth	*Pop. pressure*		*Pop. growth*	*Pop. pressure*
Andhra	18.2	3.36	Bihar	22.55	5.94
Punjab	17.36	1.73	Haryana	22.77	1.83
Gujurat	14.89	2.28	Jammu and Kashmir	23.4	4.56
Tamilnadu	13.27	4.58	Himachal	17.5	4.08
			Uttar Pradesh	22.53	3.62
Group average	15.93	2.987	Group average	21.75	4.01
All India	19.71	2.986			

Notes: Population growth: decadal rural population growth – i.e. the percentage rate of rural population growth between 1981 and 1991. Population pressure is defined as no. of persons in rural areas (in 1981) per hectare of gross cropped area (in 1984–1985). All India figures include the 17 States and other smaller States and Territories.
SOURCE: NIRD, 1998; AND BANSIL, 1992

technology (category II) and how can poverty reduction be so large without much use of the technology (category III)?

Is it possible that GR would have caused greater poverty reduction but population growth has been preventing that, an argument which Lipton makes? One way of looking at the population issue would be to look at the population growth rates and population pressure on land in more advanced GR States, including the more pro-poor States and less pro-poor States (type I and II States).

The unweighted average population growth for more advanced GR States with greater poverty reduction is somewhat lower than the average population growth in the more advanced GR States with lower rate of poverty reduction. The pressure of the population on land needs also to be looked at, as Lipton says population pressure in terms of high person/land ratio is a crucial factor that influences unemployment (p. 206). Table 5.4 shows that the unweighted average person/land ratio in more advanced GR States with greater poverty

REFLECTIONS ON THE TECHNOLOGY – POVERTY RELATION

TABLE 5.5   Correlations between the population factor and poverty reduction, 1970s–1990s

	Poverty reduction over		
	1983–1987	1983–1994	1987–1994
Pop. pressure	0.446	0.067	–0.009
	(0.073)	(0.798)	(0.973)
Pop. growth	–0.214	–0.193	–0.173
	(0.409)	(0.457)	(0.506)

Notes: None of these correlations is statistically significant or significant from the standpoint of Lipton's theory. This result is, however, consistent with a widely held view in population geography/population studies that 'there is no significant correlation, positive or negative, between national population growth rates and various measures of development' in the Third World (Jones, 1990: 168). The 0.446 correlation seems to suggest that there is a mild *positive* association between poverty reduction and population pressure.
SOURCE: AUTHOR'S CALCULATIONS

reduction is a little higher than the corresponding average in the more advanced GR States with lower rate of poverty reduction.

5   Conclusion

The upshot of the foregoing analysis is that while the GR seems to be some- what associated with the ratio of the rural population below the poverty line *at a point in time,* there seems to be no association between the GR and the im- portant issue of poverty *reduction.* This is the case whether or not the popula- tion factor is held constant. The GR technology and the population factor, the twin neo-Malthusian mechanisms in which Lipton and others invest so much causal power, seem to have no statistical relation with poverty reduction (at the State level in India). Poverty reduction has taken place both with and with- out technological advancement. And persistence of poverty characterizes both technological advancement and the lack of it.[25]

---

25   Here I am abstracting from the real possibility that even if income and assets are equally distributed, there can be still absolute poverty if the level of development of productive forces is very low (i.e. where the total income of all the people in a place is less than the sum of the differences between the poverty line and each person's income). The use of technology can remove this 'natural' condition of scarcity. But it must be noted that whether technology can deliver even on this front and continue to do so depends on

TABLE 5.6 Poverty reduction (1973–1988) with and without GR

Green Revolution	Poverty reduction	
	Greater	*Less*
More advanced	(I) Andhra, Punjab, Gujurat, Haryana, Himachal, Jammu and Kashmir	(II) Bihar, Tamil Nadu, Uttar Pradesh
Less advanced	(III) Karnataka, Rajasthan, Kerala, West Bengal	(IV) Assam, Madhya Pradesh, Maharastra, Orissa, Rajasthan

Notes: Pop. growth: the decadal growth rate of rural population between 1981 and 1991. Pop. pressure: Number of persons in rural areas (in 1981) per hectare of gross cropped area (in 1984–1985).
SOURCE: BASED ON: NIRD, 1998; AND BANSIL, 1992

The statistical results in the chapter are not inconsistent with some similar existing research (at the State level) (Cook, 1996). These results are also not inconsistent with the case studies seen as a whole. For example, case-studies show that the poor have gained from economic development both in GR areas (Harriss, 1991; Alauddin and Tisdell, 1995; Beck, 1995[26]) and in non-GR areas (Vaddiraju, 1999) and that poverty has persisted in both GR areas and non-GR areas (Das, 1995; Datta, 1998; Kamal, 1998; Paul, 1990).

To the extent that there is an association between poverty *levels* and the GR, this should be accepted with caution. In the first place, in the statistical analysis, I have abstracted from the contribution that the various poverty alleviation programs started by the Indian State since the late 1970s may have made to

---

appropriate social relations, for indeed, social relations can be a barrier to development of and the use of productive forces. Where land and other assets are unequally distributed and continue to be so given the failure of the land reforms policy, and where there is mass poverty and lack of non-farm employment opportunities, the land-owning class often finds it profitable to invest their resources in 'non-capitalist' ventures (leasing out land to land-hungry peasants for high rents; usury, etc.), rather than in productivity-raising technology such as the MVs (Das, 1999b; Patnaik, 1986). Lipton does not discuss this class-embeddedness of the GR technology at all.

26 A more recent publication, based in village-studies, show that the Green Revolution has helped the poor, including in their fight against food insecurity (also, Baker and Jewitt, 2007).

poverty reduction (Vyas and Bhargava, 1995; Das, 2000a). In addition, I argue, the very fact that the state could *not* rely on the GR for poverty reduction and thus started a 'direct attack' on poverty through these policies (e.g. loans to the poor to set up small businesses) (Das, 1998b) is an indirect indicator of the limited impact of the GR. I have also abstracted from the ecological impacts of the GR such as salinization, etc. (Shiva, 1991) as well as its impacts on laborers' health (many laborers in the Punjab lose their limbs while operating machines) (Chandan, 1979). If we 'deduct' these costs of the GR from its so-called benefits, we may perhaps find no relation between GR and poverty level or perhaps we will find a negative one! Abstraction from these issues is a limitation of my study and points to a need for incorporating these in an analysis of the GR–poverty connection.

Secondly, the statistical association which I have presented above does not at all suggest any necessary relation between the GR and poverty levels. Any such claims to necessity are, in my view, conceptually indefensible. Besides, the positive association could just mean that the GR started in the States which had lower poverty levels to start with.[27]

The real test of the relation between the GR and poverty lies in its impact on what happens to the poverty process over time (not just at a point in time) and in different States (not just in some particular places), for poverty is not a thing but a *socio-spatial process*. In other words, the more interesting issue to look at is the relation between the GR and poverty reduction. I have shown that the GR has no statistical relation with poverty reduction. Poverty has been, and arguably, can be reduced without the GR (or for that matter, without any other technology or an increase in the economic output as such). And, in some cases, GR can have some favorable impact on the poor (through its impact on non-farm employment and by other means) (Harriss, 1991). But it is not necessary that that will be the case generally. Given the GR, poverty reduction is possible but not necessary. More generally, technology is neither a necessary nor a sufficient condition for poverty reduction. If the lack of technology was a necessary cause of poverty, one in seven people in the United States of America would not have to live below the line of absolute poverty. While the GR technology does not have any necessary poverty reduction impact, it cannot also be said that it has any necessary poverty-increasing impact, *independently* of social relations within which technology operates. There is simply no necessary relation between technology and poverty reduction, positive or negative. Much of what I have said about technology in its Green Revolution form

---

27   This could be because those who are already well-off are able to use the technology more than those who are not.

applies to technology in its biotechnology form. A transition seems to be occurring from the Green Revolution to the gene revolution (biotechnology). The latter is linked to neoliberal capitalism as we have seen in the previous chapter. Biotechnology companies are pushing for the use of GM (genetically modified) seeds to be used on the ground that with these seeds, cultivators will increase their yields and therefore their income. The arguments in favor of the use of GM seeds are almost identical to those for the Green Revolution (HYV seeds) and therefore can be critically assessed in the way that this chapter does. Like the Green Revolution, the gene revolution is controversial, and for similar reasons (Bownas, 2016; Herring and Paarlberg, 2016). Given that the GMO seeds are extremely expensive to buy (Plahe et al., 2017; Shiva et al., 2002) and that they have to be bought every year (a cultivator cannot save the seeds from the current year for use in the next year), and that the use of seeds requires other chemicals which need to be bought, GMO farmers are going into debt, and some of them are committing suicide. The effects of GMO seeds, like those of HYV seeds, will depend on the overall political-economic or class context in which these seeds are accessed and used (Carroll, 2017). If in India's Maharashtra State, the districts using GM cotton seeds are the districts where numerous indebted farmers have committed suicide, this points to the need to examine the GM technology in relation to the context of class relations within which it works.

The analysis of the GR–poverty relation sheds light on the relation between technology and society, or to use the terminology of Marxist political economy, the relation between social relations and productive forces (especially, technology) (Callinicos, 1988; Cohen, 2000; Liodakis, 1997; *Science & Society*, 2006). The analysis supports, and points to, general theoretical ideas about the class character of technology, that 'technological change and its social consequences are shaped by generalised commodity exchange, investment capital, wage labor and other dominant social forms of our epoch' (Smith, 2010: 203).[28] Technology, as a 'thing' exists and operates, in the context of certain social relations, which shape how technology produces its effects. So, technology is not only a 'thing' but also a relationship. Technological change is important as it can help a society produce more in less time and help human beings transcend some of the barriers that nature imposes. Technology itself cannot solve humanity's problems such as poverty, however, as its effects are mediated by capitalist class relations. For Marx:

---

28   On socio-ecological and political aspects of technological change, apart from Smith (2010), see Tisdell and Maitra (2018), Dasgupta (2018) and Herring (2006). On the gender aspect, see Hansda (2017).

> capital is defined by a profound ontological inversion of means and ends. Human ends are subordinate to the accumulation of money capital as an end in itself, and human flourishing is subordinate to the flourishing of capital. ...From Marx's standpoint, this inversion fundamentally shapes the nature of technology in capitalism
>
> SMITH, 2010: 206

It is in fact no longer sufficient to define technology solely in terms of use-value as 'the equipment, techniques, and expertise that can be applied to produce a good or service' (ibid.). That definition is not false. But it fails to capture the historically specific nature of technology under *capitalist class relations*. This is 'a social order in which equipment, techniques and expertise are generally developed and employed only if it is anticipated that surplus value will be appropriated as a result of doing so'. Under capitalism, 'technology is not primarily a means to the fulfilment of human ends.... Technology is first and foremost a means to capital's end, valorisation' (Smith, 2010: 206).

Because technology works in the context of social relations, technology can be a window on to the understanding of the structure of social relations itself:

> Technology reveals the active relation of [human beings] to nature, the direct process of production of [their] life, and thereby it also lays bare the process of the production of the social relations of [their] life, and of the mental conceptions that flow from those relations.
>
> MARX, 1977: 493

CHAPTER 6

Low-Wage Neoliberal Capitalism, Social-Cultural Difference, and Nature-Dependent Production

Crucial to the neoliberal project have been agricultural exports as a means to earn foreign exchange and to secure fiscal stability.[1] This strategy has led to India becoming a member of a group of nations that Harriet Friedman calls 'New Agricultural Countries' (NACS) (Friedman, 1993: 45). Counterpoised to the Newly Industrialized Countries (NICS) (Brohman, 1996), the emergence of the NACS represent a quintessential strategy of Third World development under neoliberalism, which has occurred, paradoxically, with state support. 'New agriculture' refers to the production of high-value non-traditional crops (e.g. flowers and shrimps) for the world market, as compared to the traditional crops produced under colonialism and during the immediate post-colonial period (Maitra 1997: 247; Watts, 1996: 232–233).

New Agriculture signifies a dialectics of articulation and disarticulation. It *articulates* local social production relations in NACS directly to the global economy – and to its price signals – more closely than achieved during the era of the Green Revolution (the subject of Chapter 5), when national food self-sufficiency was emphasized (Nanda, 1995: 20). So, whilst NACS, such as India, are increasingly specializing in luxury and niche-market crops, fish farming, and animal feeds, developed countries have specialized in the intensive export of heavily subsidized basic wage goods. This trend is indicative of an emergence of a new international division of labor in agriculture (McMichael, 2000). This new division of labor signifies, among other things, the relatively deregulated production of commodities for export, based on a low-paid, unorganized working class that is increasingly deprived of government welfare benefits: in other words, neoliberal capitalism in agrarian/rural contexts. New agriculture practices consequently, and simultaneously, *disarticulate* agricultural production from the requirements of local populations and environments (Teubal, 2000): products of new agriculture are not affordable by the common people, most of whom live under a budget of Rupees 150 or so a day in India.

---

1   An earlier version of this chapter appeared as Das (2014).

© KONINKLIJKE BRILL NV, LEIDEN, 2020 | DOI:10.1163/9789004415560_007

The effects of neoliberalism on agriculture are multi-scalar and place-specific. At the national scale, new agricultural production appears to have resulted in less land being used for food crops cultivation, so much so that per capita food availability in India is down to the level experienced during the Bengal famine of 1943 (Patnaik 1999, 2003). This is occurring in the context of WTO-mandated state withdrawal from public food distribution, employment generation, and input subsidies (Chossudovsky, 1999). Other effects of neoliberalism are particularly important at regional and local scales. Export-oriented units in new agriculture employ substantially fewer people per every dollar invested than does traditional cereal farming. Amongst other effects, this depresses the domestic demand for those mass-produced commodities that help promote industrialization. New agriculture has, also, been shown in many countries to lead to the displacement of smaller farmers (Stonich, 1995) and create new social divisions (Jamieson, 2002). Further, new agricultural practices degrade land so significantly that after a single decade of production, fields are in fact no longer suitable for any productive use, including a return to cereal cultivation. Chemical additives in capital-intensive new agriculture not only contaminate land and water (Barbier, 2004; Bhat and Bhatta, 2004; Flaherty, 1999; Ronnback, 2003) but adversely affect the health of (especially female) workers too (see Sass, 2000).

Like many other countries of the South, India is a low-wage platform of global capitalism. Such a platform works in industries, services, mining, as well as in agriculture, of which aquaculture is an important part. Aquaculture is the fastest growing food-producing sector in the world (World Bank, 2007). Shrimp culture is an important part of aquaculture. Shrimp production is a specific form of new agricultural production.

The burgeoning academic literature on export-oriented shrimp culture in the neoliberal world has shed light on ecological as well as selected economic aspects of shrimp culture, including the conditions of small-scale shrimp farmers. What is generally missing in this literature is a theoretically-informed emphasis on the material–social conditions of wage laborers working on shrimp farms. If shrimp-culture is being promoted, we must understand whether it benefits the men, women and children who produce shrimps as wage-workers. Using evidence from India, I seek to fill this gap by studying shrimp producers *as* wage laborers. When explored through a Marxist approach, the issue of shrimp wage laborers reveals the nature of a specific kind of 'metabolic rift' that is not talked about in the existing literature, a rift that characterizes the relation between wage labor and capital. This approach also shows how place-specific relations of difference along with biophysical conditions of production, influence the more general relations of capitalism, including those of the formal subsumption of labor.

The first section of this chapter briefly outlines the current state of the analysis of shrimp culture and offers Marxist criticisms of this analysis. The second section maps out the contours of a different framework. The third section introduces the geographical context of shrimp culture under study. In light of the conceptual ideas in the second section, I then present the empirical discussion on shrimp farm laborers, including their socio-geographical character, in the fourth and fifth sections. The final section summarizes the empirical findings and draws some conceptual conclusions.

1   Shrimp Aquaculture and the Missing Laborer

The shrimp aquaculture literature has usefully unpacked its ecological and economic aspects and effects. Scholars have studied the ecology of shrimp farming (Vandergeest et al., 1999). Research has shown how shrimp culture has caused the conversion of mangroves (Huitric et al., 2002; Martinez-Alier, 2001) and rice land into land for shrimp aquaculture (Islam, 2009). It has also shown how shrimp culture has led to soil salinization, water pollution, and depletion of soil nutrients (Flaherty and Karnjanakesorn, 1995), all of which contribute to a decline in the yield of staple crops (Ali, 2006). There is little on shrimp labor in this literature, however.

Scholars have also investigated the economic and developmental aspects of shrimp production at local and national scales. The globalization of shrimp culture, which includes trade in shrimps as well as the process of vertical integration within the industry, has already received attention (Goss et al., 2000). While some argue that this globalization process has produced positive effects on exports, income, consumption, nutrition, and equality, others are less sanguine about these effects (e.g. its effect on employment) (see Neiland et al., 2001; also Barraclough and Finger-Stich, 1996). The analysis of the economic aspects of shrimp culture, like that of the environmental aspects, is problematic, however. This is partly because serious theoretical attention is not paid to the issue of labor, or to class, more generally. When the literature looks at the impacts of shrimp culture on income and livelihood, it does not report on the class composition of income or the class character of that livelihood. Does the income of those engaged in shrimp culture come from profit, or from leasing out land for shrimp culture, or from smallholders' self-employment? Or does it come from *wages*? To the extent that there is any indication of the class aspects of income and livelihood, the focus has been on small-scale shrimp farmers in terms of their economic viability and other issues (Pradhan and Flaherty, 2008; Samal, 2003; Vandergeest, 1999). Undoubtedly, these studies have admirably shed useful light on the precarious nature of small-scale shrimp farmers. For example, Pradhan and Flaherty (2008) say that while Indian shrimp culture has benefited the country through increase in exports, it has hurt smaller shrimp farmers (pp. 71–72). Vandergeest et al. (1999: 584–585) are concerned with the viability of smaller farmers in Thailand based on their economic resilience, which is partly enabled by the particular ecology of shrimp culture. Samal (2003) has highlighted the competition for fishing areas (for both capture and culture of shrimp) between poorer traditional fishermen of lower castes and rich businesspersons of non-fishermen castes in one of the largest brackish-water lagoons in the world, Chilika Lagoon, which is located in eastern India.

However, some of this analysis tends to ignore the tendency that 'shrimp farms are witnessing increasing proletarianization' in well-known shrimp areas such as Thailand (Goss et al., 2001: 454). So the labor aspect of shrimp culture is relatively neglected.[2] An assumption underlying the promotion of export-oriented shrimp culture by national and international agencies is that the increased income from the sale of shrimps will allow rural people to buy the food they need which is no longer grown locally or nationally (Weeks, 1992: 7). Shrimp aquaculture is supposed to increase rural people's income through direct sales of shrimps and from wage employment (see World Bank, 2007: 60). But these assumptions are problematic if laborers earn wages that are so low as to compromise their ability to buy food and other necessaries. This I will show is the case.[3]

While acknowledging that sociologists, geographers, and others including those who adopt a political ecology approach, have made an enormous

---

2 However, the wage labor issue is not *entirely* ignored (see Pokrant and Reeves, 2007). Sometimes, it is mentioned in passing but in general it is not given much theoretically informed consideration. Stonich et al. (1997) mention 'a very modest number of low-paying, temporary jobs working on (shrimp) farms' (p. 170), but there is generally no *analysis* of the dynamics of the low-wage regime itself. In their very interesting work, Pradhan and Flaherty (2008: 69–70; also Islam, 2009: 73–74) mention low wages and irregularity of employment, but they do so briefly and descriptively.

3 Also: if shrimp aquaculture is a type of agricultural production, then the kind of attention that has been paid to relations between capital and labor within traditional agriculture by agrarian political economists (Byres, 1999; de Janvry, 1981; see also Buttel, 2001) must be paid to laborers on shrimp farms as well.

contribution towards our understanding of ecological and selected macro-economic/developmental aspects of shrimp-culture, this chapter claims that the story of shrimp-culture (indeed of aquaculture) has been, more or less, the story of the missing laborer.[4] The chapter therefore seeks to make a modest attempt to fill this gap. This chapter will only focus on the themes of wage and working day of laborers on shrimp-farms and in rural shrimp-beheading depots (both of which are rural-based) as well as issues surrounding labor control in the sphere of production.[5]

---

4 While aquaculture work has neglected labor issues, labor studies – including the work of geographers and sociologists – suffer from an important problem. Much of this work has shed light on the conditions of work in automobile industries (Rutherford and Gertler, 2002) and cleaning industries (Aguiar and Herod, 2006) and on how workers' cultural practices are a barrier to getting and keeping a job (Bauder, 2005). There is also interesting research on temporary laborers in relation to labor intermediaries – temp agencies (Peck and Theodore, 2001) and 'labor contractors' (Breman, 1996) – and the regulatory role of the state (Peck, 1996). However, in much of the literature, and reflecting a wider tendency in social sciences, the materiality of capital – labor relation is displaced from its central position by a concern with issues of difference, identity, and unionization (Houston and Pulido, 2002: 404; Hudson 2001: 24; Rutherford, 2010: 774). Indeed, the defining aspect of what is called labor geography and new working class studies (Russo and Linkon, 2005) is the agency of organized labor in the making of the capitalist landscape (Castree, 2007; Herod, 2001: 33–37; Tufts and Savage, 2009) in the aquaculture context, see (Oseland et al., 2012). Of course, the materiality of labor is not entirely missing, but to the extent that it is discussed, it has a few problems. One is that the materiality of labor tends to be studied through a framework that does not require much serious theoretical attention to the issue of class exploitation in the spaces of production. Also, most of the work conducted in labor studies, including the geographic literature on labor, is focused on advanced capitalist countries and their cities. This spatial bias must be corrected. For a critique of the labor geography (type) literature, see Das, 2012a, and chapter 4 in Das, 2017a.

5 The life of a laborer cannot be reduced to how much money she receives and how long she toils every day. There are other important issues. These include: the effects of labor process on the working bodies used as 'a strategy of accumulation' (Harvey, 1998), as well as issues of labor control to which men and women are subjected in the hidden abode of production. In some cases, the labor process also involves a degree or violence against people, especially child workers (see Das and Chen, 2019). It also includes: the discursive dimensions of laborers including their consciousness (which will be very briefly touched on as it relates to the wage-issue) and their 'class-identity' (and indeed various other identities including those that are regional, ethnic and gender-based) (see chapter 10 in Das, 2017a). There is, of course, the theme of class organization (which is stressed in the labor geography literature) (see chapters 11–12 in Das, 2017a).

2 A Labor-Based Approach to Nature-Dependent Commodity Production

Marx's philosophy emphasizes materiality. It also emphasizes relations and their contradictory character or rift-proneness. In terms of materiality, it is important to recognize that conditions for reproduction of life must be continuously produced. And for production to happen, nature and labor are necessary: indeed nature and labor are two sources of wealth (use-values). They are sources of the things we consume. In all forms of society, production requires relations between nature and humans, and relations among humans as they are related to production (these relations are the relations of production). And in a class society, there is always tension – rift – in these relations.

In a social-cultural system of large-scale profit-driven production, more is extracted out of nature in a specific place than is returned to it in that place within a given period of time. This process has been called a metabolic rift, a rift in the system of reciprocal exchanges between nature and society.[6]

That is not the only form of rift. There is a rift in 'human' relations as well. Marx assumes that laborers are paid a wage by the property owners that covers the cost of commodities that are necessary to satisfy their physiological needs as well as the needs that have a 'historical and moral element' (1977: 274–275). This is a useful assumption for investigating exploitation at the level of society, at a given spatial scale over a given period of time.[7] But in a specific place and at a specific time, wages for countless numbers of laborers do not allow them to satisfy their very basic needs, including food.[8] Marx *sometimes* recognizes

---

6 A country's soil nutrients are used to produce agri-commodities which are exported to other countries instead of being consumed and recycled in the place of their production; this causes the metabolic rift (Foster, 2007: 10). It is important to emphasize (pace Foster) that even if there is no export from a country, the metabolic rift can happen if nature is not used sustainably, i.e. if more matter (e.g. trees, or water, or soil nutrients, etc.) is extracted from nature than is given to it within a time period that nature needs to replenish – regenerate – itself) (Das, 2018b).

7 Note that this assumption can be criticized for ignoring unpaid labor performed mainly by women that contributes to the reproduction of labor power sold outside of the home for a wage (see Gimenez, 2005).

8 Marx *sometimes* recognizes this possibility. Indeed, in *Capital* itself, he says that: 'In the chapters on the production of surplus-value we constantly assumed that wages were at least equal to the value of labor power (which is roughly the cost in time of workers' maintenance). But the forcible reduction of the wage of labor below its value plays too important a role in the practical movement of affairs ... In fact, it transforms the worker's necessary fund for consumption ... into a fund for the accumulation of capital' (1977: 747–748). It is this possibility

this possibility, which has not received a lot of attention within political economy perhaps because of the 'Euro-centric'[9] tendency within post-Marx Marxism. In his *Wage, labor and Capital*, Marx says this: while it is true that 'the cost of production of simple labor power [of unskilled labor] amounts to the cost of the existence and propagation of the worker' and that 'The price of this cost of existence and propagation constitutes wages', this statement applies to the *whole* 'race' of laborers, for 'Individual workers, indeed, millions of workers, do not receive enough to be able to exist and propagate themselves' (1976: 27). Indeed, in *Capital* itself, he says that: 'In the chapters on the production of surplus-value we constantly assumed that wages were at least equal to the value of labor power (which is roughly the cost in time of workers' maintenance). But the forcible reduction of the wage of labor below its value plays too important a role in the practical movement of affairs...In fact, it transforms the worker's necessary fund for consumption ... into a fund for the accumulation of capital' (1977: 747–748). There are many reasons why wages may not cover the cost of workers' maintenance. These include: a reserve army of laborers (unemployment/under-employment), caused by constant technological change and independent small-scale producers being converted into wage-labor-dependent people, relative to demand for labor; economic crisis (over-production); and, a balance of power between capital and labor in favor of capital (Marx, 1977; Lebowitz, 2003). When and where wages are low in the specific sense mentioned above, a lot is taken out of 'laboring bodies' (and laboring bodies are a part of nature and have material needs) – in the form of work effort or energy – than is returned to them in the form of wages, resulting in *super*-exploitation, a process not hugely dissimilar to the metabolic rift.[10] In outlining a framework within which to understand these dynamics, one may start with three simple premises.

One is that production of wealth requires nature, and not just labor, as mentioned before. 'Labour is... not the only source of material wealth... As William

---

that the author seeks to investigate in the specific context of the production of the global 'white gold', shrimp.

9   This is 'Euro-centric' for a specific reason: in post-colonial societies, this phenomenon of millions of laborers barely being able to satisfy their bodily (food) needs with the wages they receive from capitalists is much more stark than in advanced capitalist countries of Europe and North America, where the wages received are not only higher, even holding productivity constant (consider per hour wages of a sweeper in India and a sweeper in the US), but are also supplemented with some social benefits from the government.

10 Note that even if wages cover the cost of workers' average needs, there will be still exploitation, a normal level of exploitation. When wages fail to cover workers' average needs, there is super-exploitation.

Petty says, labour is the father of material wealth, the earth is its mother' (Marx, 1977: 134). Capital uses natural forces as it finds them; it also directly transforms these forces to increase their productivity (Boyd, Prudham and Schurman, 2001). An important aspect of nature-dependent production is that it has a degree of inherent unpredictability (ibid.). To these insights must be added another process, one that is generally overlooked in the literature: the biophysical nature of the labor process influences the way labor itself is employed, exploited, and dominated.

The second premise is that labor is the other source of wealth (and indeed, labor is the only source of the capitalist form of wealth as value). Labor takes many forms, the most important of which is wage labor. This occurs where there is a high concentration of land and capital (a process of concentration that began with the original dispossession of peasants) and where the production of use values is driven by the production of value and surplus value. The fact that a large number of people must sell their labor power on a daily basis or for at least a significant part of their living, for an inadequate wage, defines the common fate of much of the global working class. The workplace, the hidden abode of production, and the labor marketplace (the wage relation) crucially affect how people live and work (Carter, 1995; Harvey, 1982: 106–119).

The third premise is that both nature and labor are subjected to relations of rift. Under private enterprise, those who control conditions of production extract more out of the environment in a specific place than they return to it in that place, within a given period of time. This process is called metabolic rift, defined as a rift in the reciprocal exchange between nature and society (Foster, 2007: 10). In the context of a nature-dependent process such as shrimp culture, this rift happens though mangrove destruction and chemical contamination of land and water. Now, laborers (the other source of wealth apart from nature) are *also* subjected to a rift: a lot more is taken out of them than is returned to them. Let us call this the Labor Metabolic Rift (LMR) or the second metabolic rift, to distinguish it from the metabolic rift mentioned above, which can be called environmental metabolic rift (EMR) or the first metabolic rift.

There are three forms of LMR. In LMR 1, capital takes a lot more out of labor than it gives in the form of wages with which to buy the means of subsistence. This is exploitation in its normal sense. This happens *even if* wages are adequate for the normal maintenance of labor. Exploitation in its normal sense can be expressed by presenting what is potentially the best sentence from *Capital* volume 1: 'The fact that half a day's labour is necessary to keep the labourer alive during 24 hours, does not in any way prevent him from working a whole day' (Marx, 1977: 300).

In LMR 2, wages *fall short* of what is needed for the normal maintenance of labor. This is super-exploitation, an above-normal level of exploitation. An extreme form of LMR 2 is LMR 3: the laboring bodies that enter into production are worse in quality than the bodies that had initially entered it. Marx (1977: 342–344) says that under specific conditions, even if workers are paid wages covering the cost of their reproduction, their laboring body (as a means of accumulation) is adversely affected. These conditions include: working longer-than-normal hours (which can reduce the length of the working life of a person by x%, while the daily/monthly wage received during his/her active working life is not increased by x%), a fast pace of work under strict surveillance, working under specific biophysical conditions including the use of hazardous chemicals, night work, and an absence of workplace safety. In its many forms, LMR draws attention to these issues concerning the labor process *as well as* the wage question which concerns the market for wage-labor.

Wages are low and working conditions are objectionable for a variety of conditions that we cannot discuss in detail here. Some of these factors are impacted by the specificity of the production regime, which, in the present context, includes the biophysical character of shrimp production. Very briefly, these conditions include: the level and strategy of accumulation (e.g. certain technologies – mechanical and biological – that are deployed to pump out more surplus value); a reserve army of labor, which reduces the bargaining power of the labor that is employed; the low level of consciousness of workers *vis-à-vis* capital, which adversely affects their bargaining power; and the absence or presence of state support for workers, which also adversely affects their political power. A very important condition for LMR is also the internal differentiation of the working class, based on such relations as gender, race, caste, age, and locational status. This means that: certain segments of the working class are defined as not worthy of the status of a full human being, having one unit of labor power and full citizenship. Such a construct, which is an attack on democratic rights of common toiling people, allows capital to depress their wages below the average, which is already inadequate.

3 The Local, National and the Global Contexts

Shrimp is a major world – commodity produced for a luxury internal and international market. Fewer than 30 countries, the majority of them in Asia, produce shrimp for export to the relatively advanced triad (the US, Japan, and the European Union). Shrimp production increased dramatically (by 650%) from 0.2 million tons in 1985 to about 1.5 million tons in 2002, according to the FAO

LOW-WAGE NEOLIBERAL CAPITALISM, SOCIAL-CULTURAL DIFFERENCE 211

(Food and Agricultural Organization). A major shrimp-producing country, India accounts for 8.5% of world production (ibid.). Commercial shrimp aquaculture became a significant activity in India only in the early 1990s when the economic liberalization program was launched (IAA, 2001). Between 1996–97 and 2005–06, on an average, the area dedicated to shrimp farming was more than 155,000 hectares. The highest concentrations of shrimp farms in India are in the eastern coastal provinces of Andhra Pradesh, Tamilnadu, and Odisha; shrimp culture also happens in six other provinces (IAA, 2001). The empirical material for the present study is drawn from Odisha (shown on the map, Map 1: Orissa's name was changed to Odisha in 2010). Odisha has a potential area of more than 32,586 hectares that can be used for brackish-water shrimp culture, out of which 14,231 hectares in its seven coastal districts have been developed for shrimp farming.[11] In 2005–06, more than 8,000 hectares were being used for shrimp farming in Odisha, where shrimps are produced in ponds as well as within net barricades in the brackish-water Chilika Lagoon. The actual labor process in a pond environment is a little different from that in the lagoon, as I will discuss later.

During the period between 1996–97 and 2005–06, annual shrimp production in India averaged more than 105,000 tonnes. Between 2005 and 2007, India exported frozen shrimp worth one billion US dollars each year, most of which went to the US, Japan, and the EU (these data are from various tables in Indiastat.com, a user-fee-based database). According to Odisha's Directorate of Fisheries, shrimp production increased from 6,805 tonnes in 1996–97 to 9,739 tonnes in 2005–06. Odisha's productivity has been above the all-India average. In 2005–06, frozen shrimp worth US $56.94 million was exported from Odisha, most of which went to the US, Japan, the UAE, and European countries. It should be added that Odisha's shrimp culture is export-oriented like that in, say, Thailand, but its shrimp production is dominated more by wage labor than family labor.

Shrimp culture is being promoted by the state in order to increase export and earn dollars.[12] Odisha is not only an important shrimp-producing state; it is also one of the poorest states overall. Out of every 100 people, 36 cannot read or write. According to the 2011 census, it had a population of 42 million (which

---

11 Only 30% of the area consists of small farms (below two hectares) and 7.5% of the area consists of medium-size farms (two to five hectares). The vast majority of the shrimp aquaculture area (57%) is constituted by farms that are at least five hectares in size. 5.5% of the area is under the control of corporate farms. This information is provided in the India Aquaculture Authority report.

12 Also, with the withdrawal of support from the neoliberal governments for traditional farming, some farmers are inclined to switch capital investment to aquaculture.

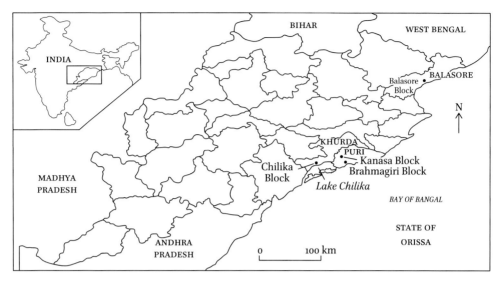

MAP 6.1   Four Blocks located in three shrimp districts
SOURCE: AUTHOR

has increased to about 45 million in 2018), of which 85% lived in rural areas. Odisha is divided into several districts, each of which comprises many Community Development Blocks (or Blocks). These are clusters of villages. The present study was conducted in four Blocks located in three of the seven shrimp districts (Puri, Khurda, and Balasore) (Map 6.1), which account for more than half of the areas dedicated to shrimp production. The empirical analysis in this chapter is predominantly based on the interviews with laborers about their wages and working conditions, although I do not present too many quotes.[13]

4   Working for Less and in Poor Conditions: 'Capital' Negated

There is a wide diversity of workers in the shrimp sector. This chapter deals with workers involved in shrimp farming in Odisha, specifically in the ponds, and in net barricades. It also deals with those employed in 'depots' where

---

13   The research reported in the chapter is based on 75 in-depth interviews and 5 focus group discussions (FGDs) conducted over a period of time (2006–2009) in the four Blocks. 36 interviewees were wage laborers, including 6 women (note that the bulk of the work is done by males), and 3 of the FGDs consisted of wage laborers. The interviewees, selected on the basis of snowballing, also included 29 farmers (as well as 1 FGD) and 14 government officials and politicians (as well as 1 FGD). The majority of interviews were tape-recorded and transcribed. Some were manually recorded.

shrimps are sorted and beheaded. Located in close proximity to the farms, these depots can be seen as a geographical extension of the shrimp farms. The vast majority of laborers work for individual proprietors who own 1–7 ponds. There are less than half a dozen big farms, each of which has 10 to 16 ponds in the fieldwork area in the north. These farms are owned by city-based companies and are run by managers and supervisors on their behalf. I will mainly focus on the conditions that are common to these different kinds of workers, i.e. the workers who work in the ponds, the net barricades and in the depots. The social relations of production within which workers work are those of capitalism.

Shrimp workers work with two kinds of technology: biological (e.g. seeds; chemically contaminated water and medicines) and mechanical (e.g. tractors and spades for earth work; aerating machines; pumps; nets). Workers clear the land, dig ponds, construct and maintain embankments and dykes, release shrimp fingerlings, feed the shrimps, aerate the ponds, guard the farms, and harvest shrimps. Where shrimp culture happens within net barricades, people have to construct these barricades by dipping themselves in water.

Both men and women (including, aboriginal women) participate in earth work to prepare ponds. After the ponds are ready, the work is mainly done by males. Most are children or unmarried young adults. A number of the laborers are mothers, who sometimes bring their little children to the work-sites. They make a little resting place near the ponds for them to play. However, work on shrimp farms is not considered proper for women after the fingerlings have been released into the ponds, except for such work as carrying and breaking ice. Male pond owners do not want to employ women.[14] Women are employed on farms only when men are not available. Besides, working on shrimp farms requires night duty. Staying on the farms at night is not considered safe for women workers.

Most of the laborers are employed on either of two kinds of contract. Those hired on a daily basis do the pond preparation work. They also do the harvest work. The bulk of the work, however, is done by laborers, called 'permanent' staff, who are hired on seasonal contracts. They are employed on the basis of a monthly salary for one season of four to five months. On the few farms owned by city-based companies, which employ up to about 20 people per farm, annual contracts are offered to some people, who do repair work in the off season. Most of the permanent staff live on or near the shrimp-pond embankments. Several people live together in one small makeshift hut. Rainwater sometimes gets inside the huts, making them spend sleepless nights. Many child laborers are afraid to stay in these huts in stormy weather. In one season,

---

14   They fear that women's menstrual blood might affect the water quality in the pond.

two of them died due to lightning in one of the northern villages. Those who work in the net enclosures stay on boats if the enclosure is inside the lagoon, or live in a little hut if it is near the bank of the lagoon.

Permanent laborers are on duty around the clock (or for 16 hours, from 6 a.m. to 10 p.m., in case of company-owned farms). Workers eat and sleep on the farm (or on the boat, in case of the net barricades). These laborers are therefore *working* while eating, cooking, and sleeping. They take turns to sleep. Their 24-hour physical presence makes the theft of shrimps less likely. They stop people from throwing unwanted things in the ponds and protect the shrimps from birds. They have to go under water, even at night, to create waves to make the shrimps move; on big farms, aerating machines are used.

The shrimps have to be fed four times in 24 hours, including twice at night, as per a feed chart given by the owner or the supervisor. If the shrimps are not fed, the laborers are reprimanded. Thus, the biophysical nature of the labor process complements other ways of controlling labor, such as direct supervision (via, for example, the supervisors' gaze; unannounced checks at night) and a bureaucratic method (e.g. the feed chart). The biophysical conditions also have health implications: laborers catch cold and suffer from fever; chemically contaminated water spoils their skin.

Permanent workers receive wages in cash and in kind (i.e. in the form of food). Food comes from the owners' home or is cooked near the pond. In the case of net enclosures, the food is cooked on the boat, and the owner buys the groceries. On company farms, people eat in the company-run kitchen. The vast majority of adult laborers get between Rs. 1,500–2,000 a month for what are practically 24-hour working days. Even discounting the fact that they work while sleeping or eating in their huts, the working day is easily 16 hours. So, the *hourly* wage is Rs. 3–4 (approximately 7 to 9 cents USD). Daily wage workers get Rs. 50–70 a day without food (in 2008–2009). They get a little more during harvest time because of the greater workload. Those working in the net barricades earn a little more (i.e. Rs. 100 or so) because their work is a little harder.

Wages vary from one laborer to another. Women daily-wage earners get Rs. 5–10 less than men for similar work (e.g. earth work). Child workers receive anywhere from Rs. 800–1,200 with food. This is less than what adults get. Larger farms pay a little better than smaller owners. Those workers who are given supervisory duty, who are a little older than ordinary workers (called 'pond boys' on company-owned farms), get Rs. 300–500 more than others. Those who have worked with an employer continuously for more than a season get a little more than the 'first-timers', but even then their wages are not high.

Wages are usually paid *after* the sale of the harvest. As a result, migrants cannot send money home every month. Their family members live on credit,

LOW-WAGE NEOLIBERAL CAPITALISM, SOCIAL-CULTURAL DIFFERENCE

on which they have to pay an interest. Also, many get sick due to the effects of chemicals used in the ponds, so they have to spend money to get better. The net monthly wage (i.e. the gross wage minus the sum of interest payments just mentioned and the money spent on health-care) would be much lower. In all respects, the wage is low.

The wage is low relative to the amount of work performed. It is also low relative to profits made. These profits enhance the lifestyle of the owners. Laborers see or hear about the shrimp farmers' luxurious lifestyle (e.g. their ownership of big houses and motor vehicles). Interviews with owners suggest that a total investment on a one-acre farm, for one harvest of Rs. 300,000, including Rs. 20,000 spent on wages, may generate a total sale of Rs. 450,000. Approximately, this generates a rate of exploitation (profit relative to money spent on wages) of roughly 750% and a rate of profit-on-investment of about 50%. The wage is also low relative to people's needs (i.e. the value of their labor power). An average family needs Rs. 100–120 a day for food (rice or flour, groceries, and vegetables). But laborers do not make much more than Rs. 70–80, and work is not available every day.[15] They produce a delicacy that they can hardly afford to buy. The theoretical assumption in *Capital* that wages cover the cost of production of labor power is empirically negated. Capital extracts a lot more from labor than what it gives labor. Many permanent laborers do not even receive a wage at all or receive only a part of it. This is because of owners' and supervisors' fraudulent tricks. If laborers initially contract to work for the season but leave after a month or so, they are not paid for the days worked. Those who stay on also suffer: employers make deductions from wages saying they incur a loss. Some pay only a part of the arrears and promise to pay the remainder later. Many owners simply delay the payment of arrears. Many employees do not return to claim their arrears.

After the harvest, shrimps are taken to rural depots. As on the farms, there is a gender-based division of labor here. Shrimps are sorted and graded by men. The women's job is to behead the shrimps and to remove legs and shells from shrimps. Many women believe that men cannot sit for hours at a stretch to do this work. The gender division of labor at home may have an effect on that in the workplace.

Unlike men on the farms, women in the depots work for a piece wage. They get paid for filling a bowl with headless shrimps or on a weight basis (see Photo 6.1 below). Daily earnings, usually Rs. 50–70, fluctuate depending on

---

15   In 2004, a family of five in rural India needed approximately Rs. 95 to buy just enough food to provide the minimum of 2,400 calories necessary for normal bodily function (if one does not consume this many calories, one is considered poor) (Patnaik, 2007: 174).

PHOTO 6.1   Women in a shrimp-processing factory in Odisha, India
SOURCE: AUTHOR

how much work they do. Some days can fetch Rs. 100. In the early morning, they go to the supervisors' office to clean the kitchen utensils and sweep the floor, and this work is totally unpaid work. To be able to get the *paid* work, therefore, *unpaid* work must also be performed. Members of a group take turns to do this. *If* they complain or miss a day, they are threatened with the loss of paid work. It seems the household is not the only place of uncommodified, unpaid labor.

In the depots near the lagoon, women do night work. As a focus group discussion and interviews with farmers and politicians confirm, many traditional fishermen, including the husbands of these women, have migrated to cities, as the traditional fishing areas to which the locals had customary access are being increasingly taken over by the larger-scale businesses. So, being in the public places at night may not be safe, given the local conditions (females are usually accompanied by males in public places and at night). Night work is also not good for their health given their duties at home in the day. Also, in the depots, they have to squat for long hours on the wet ground (see Photo 6.1). Their waists, backs, and legs hurt. Their hands develop inflammations and wounds, and even bleed. Their nails are also affected. Like the men on the shrimp farms, they sometimes cannot eat with their hands. They burn newspapers and apply the ash to their wounds for relief. And they do this hard work under the gaze of male supervisors trying to maximize the work effort.

Thanks to the shrimp sector, women shrimp-laborers make substantial financial contributions to their families. This gives them some autonomy and some self-esteem. Although they are unceasingly superexploited, they have not stopped dreaming of a better life: as a woman worker said, she would like to have a house built with bricks, to pay for a good education for her children and to have a savings account in a bank. That the capitalist system has failed to fulfill these simple needs of common people is a cruel fact. There is a flip side, however. It is about the conditions of men. In the southern villages those men who have not migrated do not catch much fish to sell, due to overfishing in the lagoons by rich entrepreneurs, or do not get much wage-work. In the northern region, the use of indigenous migrant workers (and the preference for women laborers in the depots, as in the south), has meant limited work opportunity for men. Sometimes women earn more than their husbands. This creates conflicts, and some women face ill-treatment from their men. Interestingly, the difficult material situation (i.e. the lack of opportunities for earning a living by fishing on one's own account and the low wages offered for wage-work) is forcing a change in male consciousness: some men have accepted the importance of women's financial contribution. This suggests that capitalism seems to have some progressive effect on women's relation with men.

5 Making Sense of Low-Wage Capitalism: From the General to the Locally Specific

Why and how are wages in shrimp culture kept so low? Why are conditions of work so poor? And how are these conditions justified by owners and accepted by workers? Clearly, to make a profit, owners must extract a lot more net product out of workers than what they pay in wages. This is the fundamental aspect of the class relation. It is a power relation. It is a powerful imperative. This affects wages and working conditions directly. This class context also affects wages and working conditions indirectly and in complex ways, some of which are associated with neoliberalism.

First of all, the employment situation is fraught with insecurity. Capitalism is coercive. It is so because the majority are *compelled* to work for a wage for living, and whether they obtain wage-work depends on whether a profit can be made from it. Capitalism becomes doubly coercive where people cannot choose between employers. Shrimp workers accept low wages as there is no alternative (self- or wage-)employment. If they complain, they are told 'someone else will work if you don't'. Neo-liberalization of capitalism (relative withdrawal of government support to workers and poor peasants) has contributed to the situation by reducing (self- and wage-)employment opportunities. Employment insecurity can be acute *in specific places* (e.g. traditional fishing areas where people are losing rights to fishing and are relying on wage-work)[16] where owners have enhanced their power to drive down wages and impose poor conditions. Owners do not employ people continuously in part because continuously employed workers might demand an increase in wages.

The regime of overwork – extraction of a maximum amount of work effort in a given time and for a given wage – is indeed connected to the payment of low wages:

> If one man [working long hours] does the work of 1½ or 2 men, the supply of labour increases, although the supply of labour-power on the market remains constant. The competition thus created between the labourers allows the capitalist to beat down the price of labour, whilst the fall in the price of labour allows him, on the other hand, to force up the hours of work still further.
>
> MARX, 1977: 689

The prolongation of the working day increases the amount of work without increasing the number of workers hired. One does the work of two or three. It is this process of forcing workers to provide excessive amount of labor that keeps the commodity produced cheap and globally competitive. A 45-year-old shared his critical insight:

---

16 Trade liberalization has resulted in layoffs in cities, reducing employment opportunities for migrant rural workers. In rural areas, shrinking state investment in development projects has had a similar effect. When neoliberalism created an opportunity for shrimp exports, rich non-fishermen caste people have displaced poorer traditional fishermen in the Chilika Lagoon who increasingly have to depend on wage labor (rather than the direct sale of fish or shrimps). This adds to local unemployment, puts downward pressure on wages, and thus helps export-oriented capitalist shrimp culture. It is as if neoliberalism (= export-oriented high-value production) has secured some of its own conditions of reproduction (= low wages via unemployment through dispossession and state withdrawal of benefits). For a critical analysis of Indian neoliberalism, see chapter 4 of this book, and also Ahmed (2011) and Patnaik (2007).

> We are working at night. And in the day. But we get one salary. The owner makes money from this. The laborer is working twice over ... The work we do at night for that ... hmmm ... we are not getting any money. The salary we are getting is for the work in the day.

The regime of the long working day is associated with the biophysical character of the labor process. The labor process on shrimp farms is a continuous process; it is like a biophysical assembly line. This means that shrimps have to be attended to for 24 hours continuously for 4–5 months. The labor process overlaps with the biophysical production process, unlike in crop farming. Also, shrimp farming is a little risky: there can be a virus attack, for example, or a sudden rainfall that can change the pond's salinity. Now, the biological nature of the labor process contributes to consent to overwork (in Burawoy's sense). Many, including child laborers, have come to accept this 'infantile' idea, that shrimps are like little growing children needing care and protection.

However, it is *not* because of the nature-dependent and biological character of the labor process as such that laborers work long hours. It is rather the *capitalist* character of this biophysical labor process, and further its neoliberal (unregulated) nature, that is behind the long working day, which contributes to low wages. Surely, shrimps could be looked after in three shifts of eight hours each, but this would increase wage costs and diminish the global competitiveness of the export-oriented sector. A statement from Marx in *Capital* seems to accurately describe the situation: 'As soon as peoples ... are drawn into a world market dominated by the capitalistic mode of production, whereby the sale of their products for export develops into their principal interest, the civilized horrors of over-work' begin (1977: 345).

The strategies of extraction of work effort in the depots that contribute to low earnings are interesting. In the shrimp depots, workers (mostly women) working on the basis of piece wages work very long hours. Their work intensity is enhanced through strict supervision (i.e. bureaucratic labor control). This is also done through the use of biological technology (i.e. technological labor control) when, for example, chemicals are mixed with shrimps to help workers process more shrimps. Work output is also maximized through the piece wage system: the faster one works, the more money, one thinks, is earned. If workers process more shrimps every hour, they will earn a little more, other things constant. However, workers barely receive the equivalent of a daily subsistence wage. The piece-wage system acts more like a labor-control system within the labor process, which allows the entrepreneurs to extract more work from workers, without having to pay more than what would be a daily time-wage. The definition of the piece itself is contested and resolved in favor of the employer.

Workers are given shrimps in specific containers to behead and are paid by the container. Supervisors pack a lot more shrimps into each container than what they would normally contain, and this strategy reduces earnings. Thus the women workers in depots, like their male counterparts on the shrimp ponds, are subjected to capital's fraudulent tricks. No matter how fast women work, they still take home a wage that barely covers the costs of food. Since many of them do not know counting and they are paid once in many days, they generally depend on their supervisors to maintain the account. They say the wages they receive are less than what is due.

The method of wage payment and the form of wage contribute to the difficult situation as well. As mentioned, the majority of permanent workers are paid only *after* the harvest finishes. Women workers in the depots are also not paid daily. Withholding wages increases profits when arrears are not paid. One may not challenge low wages or bad conditions of work because of the fear of losing the arrears. Thus, withholding wages is also a way of making people stick around and work harder. Describing the situation of the *aqua*-laborers through an 'aqua' metaphor, one migrant worker said:

> [Sometimes] we return [home] without any money. We lack the courage to speak up ...Owners are water ... Labor-boys are thirsty. ... If they wish they will give water. Otherwise, not. If they wish, they will pay money. ... Maliks [owners] are locals. Workers are outsiders.

I now turn to what I have called *vulnerable workers*. The idea of difference is crucial here. Capitalist production, of course, requires labor. But the category 'labor' is a complex one at a concrete level, as suggested earlier, both geographically (local vs nonlocal labor) and socially (in terms of social relations of oppression based on gender, ethnicity, and age). Workers as a class that is subject to exploitation by capital become vulnerable workers when they also experience social relations of oppression. A large number of shrimp farm laborers are young adults or children, as young as 14 or 15 years. Farm owners recruit children from their villages by telling them that they are needed just to scare away crows from shrimp ponds; actually, they end up doing all kinds of work that adults do, including handling heavy aerating machines. When it comes to work, they are treated *as if* they are adults, so more work is expected of, and extracted from, them. But when it comes to wages, they are treated *as if* they are children, so wages can be kept at a low level. Younger workers are preferred to older adults because they can work for less (50–100% less). With no wives or children to look after, these young workers can be on duty for 24 hours. Finally, in a society where younger people are supposed to carry orders from, and respect, older people, younger workers, including children working for mature adults (i.e. the owners and supervisors), are also likely to be docile.

Apart from age, gender is another aspect of workers' social vulnerability. Most of the workers in rural beheading depots are women. Traditional gender norms contribute to their super-exploitation. As mentioned already, in many cases, women contribute substantially to family finances. Like women in other places, they must divide their labor time between home and paid workplace (McDowell, 2001). The crushing burden of work at home and in shrimp depots and the fact that their employment contracts are precariously temporary make collective protest against low wages and poor working conditions difficult. Even when they try to protest at times, male managers shout at them. Bear also in mind the fact, noted above, that the husbands of many of these women are not with them. True, their husbands, like their employers and supervisors, behave in a patriarchal manner, including in situations where their wives earn a little more than them. But often husbands *are* a source of support at home. The family is not only 'a place of unequal power and resources'; it is also a centre of 'elementary solidarities', '"a place" on which working-class people put an understandable value' (Barker, 2006: 73). When women protest, their honor can be at stake, especially in the absence of their husbands and in the absence of any workers' organization.

Many owners prefer to recruit migrants, although for initial pond preparation, locals are also hired: in other words *from where* laborers are recruited is important. For one thing, devoid of local social capital (access to social networks), migrants will not easily be able to steal the 'white gold' (that is, the crop of shrimps) and sell it to local friends and relatives. Given the biophysical character of production, ensuring the safety of the product is paramount: if there is a labor conflict, migrants are also less likely than locals to put poison or some unwanted material in the ponds. The biophysical production demands continuous attention, and locals are more able than migrants to leave work to see their family and friends and perform reproductive duties at home or quit before the harvest in search of a better job. It is generally easier to control non-local labor and extract more work effort and pay low wages. Furthermore, migrant workers do not have a permanent address in the villages where they work. They therefore lack access to a social wage in the form of government benefits, which would otherwise improve the relative power of labor. The way in which their labor power is bought in the marketplace further adds to their difficulty. Sometimes, owners and supervisors travel to the villages to look for workers, including young children. If one gets five but needs three, he gives two to another owner who saves on the recruitment costs. If the latter pays lower wages, laborers cannot protest because they have not entered into *direct* negotiation with their employer, nor can they complain to the person who recruited them but is not their employer.

Many migrant workers are from aboriginal communities. To the extent that wage relations *do* exist, wages *are* lower in these areas as compared to the relatively more developed areas of shrimp culture. This is in part because a portion of the value of these workers' labor power is covered by production on their own land or the sale of forest products. Culturally, people from aboriginal areas are perceived by others as having a simple life with a limited number of needs. So low wages have something to do with the low value of the labor power as well, in the uneven space-economy.[17] Thus the use of politically *vulnerable laborers* – migrants, aboriginal people, children and women – is partly responsible for the low-wage regime. These workers' identity has been constructed in a specific way by the wider population. Individual workers of oppressed groups are socially constructed as those who possess less than one unit of labor power (and indeed as people with less than one unit of citizenship, thus not having the rights that others can enjoy), and this fact allows and justifies the payment of low wages to them. Individuals from aboriginal communities are seen as the ones who lead a simple life (they are not 'modern' enough) and therefore need less to survive. So, they can be paid less than others. Marx assumes that the value of labor power is fixed at a point in time in a given country. This assumption needs to be relaxed where the labor market is characterized by a cultural geography, one where social-moral elements of the value of labor power vary between places.

Finally, there is the issue of the specific forms of workers' and employers' consciousness and political action through which the objective reality of the low-wage regime is reproduced. Employers deduct money from the arrears, citing the loss in business as a reason. Whether the loss in business is real or an excuse, workers will not know for sure, given that they, as workers, have no control over how the enterprises are run. But some of them tend to *believe* the owners. This belief may include an underlying feeling of empathy for the owner, a belief to which the biophysical labor process in shrimp farming contributes. Workers see that sometimes ponds are indeed flooded, and that this or that disease strikes. They also hear that the owner is 'exploited' by the seed and pharmaceutical companies. Many workers seem to have *internalized*

---

17   Marx assumes that the value of labor power is fixed at a point in time in a given country: 'in a given country at a given period, the average amount of the means of subsistence necessary for the worker is a known *datum*' (Marx, 1977: 275). This assumption needs to be relaxed where, for example, the labor market is characterized by a cultural geography, one where social-moral elements of the value of labor power vary between places.

the business worries of the employer. There seem to be bourgeois instincts of workers rather than working class instincts.

The capital – labor relation is conflict-prone. Employers and supervisors are conscious that workers *can* protest against their condition. So they employ pre-emptive steps to stop any possible unity among workers. Conscious of their interests vis-à-vis workers', the employers thus deploy a micro-geographical strategy aimed at keeping them separated. Once again, the biophysical conditions of shrimp farming are crucial. Employers rely on these to justify their strategy: if workers from different sites mingle, owners say, a virus may spread from one pond to another. In general, there are serious barriers to workers developing solidarity. They are different from one another in terms of where they are from, their ethnic status, age, wages earned, and the fact that they are working on different farms that are geographically scattered. If the workers were allowed to mingle, these barriers might soften, and this is the unspoken logic of the employers' geographical strategy. The reproduction of capitalism, including the low-wage regime, happens through the reproduction of what Lebowitz (2003: 86) calls 'separation' among workers. Spatial separation is one form.

While workers work for low wages under difficult conditions, there is no union – not even a progressive civil society association – to unite them across space. This compounds laborers' difficulty and adds to employers' power, contributing to the regime of low wages and poor working conditions. Local Left parties (e.g. the Communist Party of India [Marxist] or CPM) are oblivious of the plight of, and political vulnerability of, shrimp workers, as it was clear during an interview with a major CPM leader. In northern Odisha villages, CPM members confine their activities to traditional agriculture in support of paddy farmers. In the southern villages around the lagoon, the communist parties, especially CPM and the Communist Party of India (Marxist-Leninist) or CPI (M-L) are focusing almost exclusively on the dispossession of fishermen from traditional fishing areas. That many of the traditional fishermen have become full-time or part-time laborers has not been registered on the Left radar. I had expected to see Left-based mobilization of laborers. The irony is that during the interviews, many shrimp workers themselves, who are not well-educated, said one after another that they *want* unions. A worker from the aboriginal community seemed to sum up my own analysis:

> Because there is not much work available, we are forced to accept whatever wages owners offer us ... If I bargain with the owner individually, he will not listen ... Laborers want to increase their wages. But the owner ... wants to give low wages. ... It would be good to have a union. People will join it. We want it. ... [But] No one is advising us about a union.

6 Conclusion

In an interesting way, the emphasis on agriculture and the neoliberal approach to development have come together. In the late 2000s, the World Bank's *World Development Report 2008* (World Bank, 2007) suggested that agriculture – commercial agriculture, that is – can deliver economic development and poverty-reduction in the Global South. And, internationally, neoliberal approach to development is promoted by the World Bank and other similar institutions. Neoliberalism (which is the main topic of Chapter 4) includes at least two inter-connected things. One is the state's relative withdrawal from welfare provision (which has implications for the social wage and the balance of power between capital and labor over wages, etc.).[18] Another is the promotion of a regime of relatively de-regulated production which is enabled by trade liberalization and which is based on a politically vulnerable non-unionized (mobile) working class to produce cheap commodities for export. These two approaches – stress on agriculture and a neoliberal approach – come together when export-oriented, de-regulated production of non-traditional agricultural goods from poorer countries (to richer countries but not just to richer countries) is encouraged. Shrimp aquaculture is a very important aspect of this process.[19] Shrimp production is a specific instance of a larger system of production. It is a form of 'New Agricultural Production' (NAP): the production of luxury (or high-value) non-traditional agri-commodities for export (Watts, 1996: 232–233). NAP fits in with, and is a part of, a larger process: neoliberalism, or, agrarian neoliberalism.

Social scientists, including economic geographers and sociologists, have critically analyzed the problems of shrimp farmers and the adverse environmental effects of shrimp aquaculture. But they have generally neglected a crucial dimension: the conditions under which men, women, and children *work* for a wage to produce shrimps. The story of shrimp culture has been, more or less, the story of the missing wage laborer. Drawing on in-depth interviews, this chapter has discussed the conditions of laborers in export-oriented shrimp

---

18   Expenditures on rural development as a percentage of national income have come down from 2.8 in 1993–94 to 2.3 in 1997–98 to 1.9 in 2000–01 (Patnaik, 2007: Table 2). Of course, aquaculture production, like production of other things, can happen within capitalist contexts, which may somewhat vary in terms of political power and working conditions of labor (on a comparison of aquaculture in social democratic and neoliberal contexts, see Phyne, 2010).

19   Note that with respect to aquaculture, there is much import and export within the global South as well (Belton et al., 2017).

culture. It shows how the export-oriented production of shrimps results in the reproduction of a working class that works for abysmally low wages and under very poor conditions.

Production of shrimp – like the production of all things – requires labor. In most cases, this labor takes the form of wage-labor. While all wage-laborers *are the same* at one level in that they all have a specific relation (of exploitation) with capital, at another level, wage-labor *is differentiated* along lines of social relations of gender, age, location and ethnicity. The exploitation and domination of aqua-laborers happens in ways in which capitalist relations[20] are mediated by place-specific relations of difference. The exploitation and domination of aqua-laborers are also shaped by the specificities of nature-dependent production (e.g. the biophysical character of labor process). Just as forces of nature such as land and water are 'exploited' in shrimp-culture, meaning that the shrimp-production process extracts a lot more out of nature than it returns to it, laborers on shrimp-farms are similarly exploited: the wage they receive to produce a 'cheap' commodity for export are less than the net value embodied in the shrimps that they produce. Nature and labor become the twin sources of this cheapness. Akin to the metabolic rift, this is a social rift. The two rifts are parts of the same process: relation between capital and the immediate producer.[21]

Shrimp culture is justified by what Bush (2008) calls 'development narratives' or by 'rhetoric of poverty alleviation'. This kind of development discourse around shrimp-farming is contradicted by the materiality of the real situation:

---

20   The capitalist relations in question may include in specific places what Belton et al. have chosen to call 'Quasi-capitalist operations' in Bangladeshi aquaculture that 'combine the use of labour based on both kinship and market relations' and that 'accumulate some surplus capital through the exploitation of wage labour, which may subsequently be deployed in the pursuit of further accumulation by, for instance, reinvestment in expansion, intensification, or diversification' (Belton et al., 2012: 907).

21   Political ecology of shrimp-culture – or what one may more properly refer to as the *political economy* of the environmental and social context of shrimp-farming – must deal with laborers, or laboring bodies of men, women and children, in a serious and a theoretically informed manner. Indeed, one may say that what is called political ecology as such must be concerned with not only the environment and small scale producers directly interacting with it but also wage-labor relations. Unfortunately, that is not the case. Given an anti-class approach in much political ecology, the political is without its class basis. And given its anti-materialist and idealistic approach, nature is treated as social/mental construction of nature, more or less, devoid of its materiality (for examples of this kind of work, see Castree and Braun, 2001; for a sympathetic critique, see Demeritt, 2002). So both the political and the natural/environmental remain under-theorized. In fact, a large part of what is called political ecology is neither political nor ecological.

those who produce shrimps, like millions of people performing other kinds of work, do not receive a decent wage, and are forced to experience all the three forms of LMR (Labor Metabolic Rift). The inadequacy of wages takes many forms. The 'gross wages' are low. Their *net* wages are also low because of the various hidden 'costs of work' (e.g. delayed payment of wages; deductions from wages; costs of illness that is caused by work). Real wages are low in relation to laborers' basic needs. Relative wages – wages relative to the profit – earned by entrepreneurs are also low (workers are aware of this class inequality in part from the lavish life style of the aqua-entrepreneurs). Laborers are working for more than 16 hours a day in inhumane conditions. Groups of four to five persons are herded together in tiny, unsafe huts that can break in rough weather, for four to five months (shrimp-farming season). To Kautsky's words (1988: 385), they work 'like beasts of burden by day [and are] housed worse than beasts of burden by night'. In spite of laws against child labor, a large number of children are employed who 'are far more defenseless than adults' (Kautsky, 1988: 352). Some of them are effectively unfree laborers, unable to negotiate with the private entrepreneurs over wages and working conditions. The conditions of aqua-laborers discussed here, including the ways in which their lives in the workplace and labor market are controlled, are similar those of the workers subjected to sweatshop conditions more generally (Mezzadri, 2016, 2018; Pattenden, 2016).

The regime of low wages and poor working conditions in shrimp areas, as elsewhere, is caused and reproduced by multiple concrete mechanisms. These include: the precarious employment situation. Increasingly divorced from the means of production such as land and access to water bodies, and without savings or secure long-term employment, workers, including women and child workers, rely on this or that capitalist for their social reproduction. Each owner presumes that the workers whom they employ only for 4–5 months will somehow survive for the rest of the year from family production, meager crumbs thrown at their families in their own villages from the government whose welfare commitment is dwindling, or from the employment by other owners. If employers have to employ certain workers on a more permanent basis, they might have *some* interest in their long-term social reproduction. This is not the case. Shrimp-workers are paid below-subsistence wages. The other concrete mechanisms behind the regime of low wages and poor working conditions include specific strategies on the part of the employers: deliberate delay in, and withholding of, the payment of wages; strict labor control regimes including use of chemicals maximizing work effort; the fraudulent tricks of employers; and capital's power to impose and define the 'piece' and the 'wage' in the piece-wage system, even in the face of occasional protests. Interestingly, these are some of the processes that Marx talks about in *Capital* volume 1.

There are also several subjective processes that reproduce low-wage capitalism. These include the specific form of working-class consciousness that suggests a form of empathy for the 'suffering' employers. This is a form of consciousness – a bourgeois consciousness of workers – that overlies an incipient 'anti-capital' consciousness, or consciousness in its 'embryonic form' as Lenin says in his *What is to be done?* (Lenin, 1977a: 113). Underlying workers' empathy for employers who pay low wages and commit what Marx would call 'fraudulent tricks' (cited in Lapides, 2008: 145, 208) is the mistaken idea that wages are paid to a laborer out of the sale of products of her labor. According to this idea the magnitude of wages depends on the actual price at which the employer is able to sell the shrimps, so if shrimps sell for less, wages will be less. Shared by both employers and laborers, this idea contributes to the reproduction of capitalist relations. Marx criticized it thus:

> Let us take any worker; for example, a weaver. The capitalist supplies him with the loom and the yarn. The weaver applies himself to work, and the yarn is turned into cloth. The capitalist takes possession of the cloth and sells it...Now are the wages of the weaver a share of the cloth..., of the product of his work? By no means. Long before the cloth is sold, ...the weaver has received his wages.
>
> MARX, 1976: 18

Therefore, 'Wages are not a share of the worker in the commodities produced by him. Wages are that part of already existing commodities with which the capitalist buys a certain amount of productive labour-power' (Marx, 1976: 36). The *fact* that wages are being paid *after* the shrimp-harvest is sold – note that this already represents delayed payment of wages – contributes to this *illusion* in the minds of workers.

Workers' spontaneous consciousness is generally contradictory. While there is evidence of illusion as just mentioned, there is also evidence that workers are conscious of the fact that their situation is objectionable, unjust and injurious. While many workers are conscious of the need to be organized against these conditions, some show more passive resistance. This is indicated by one person when he said (and it is worth repeating): 'No one should work in shrimp-culture in his or her life'. What if a large number of workers believe in this? What if local branches of Left parties suddenly have their veil over their eyes removed? Unfortunately, the reality is that the locally-based Left parties have failed to do anything to mobilize workers and raise the workers' consciousness. All this suggests the need for an investigation of the *absence* of workers' anti-capital agency, even in a trade-union form.

One can see that each of the processes underlying the low-wage regime discussed above is connected to the politics of wage-labor relations, i.e. to the issue of the balance of power between capital and labor. Even such economic factors as unemployment causing low wages are not just economic factors: unemployment makes political resistance against low wages difficult to launch, and hence wages tend to be low. But employers know that workers *can* resist. That is why they take pre-emptive steps to stop any possible unity among workers.

The relations between capital and labor are being mediated by specific social relations (and constructions) of gender, age, and ethnicity (one of whose local forms is 'tribality'). These are utilized by employers to create a vulnerable workforce, which makes it possible to superexploit without much political trouble. Importantly, relations between capital and labor are also mediated by the geographical character of labor. Generally, a social wage (e.g. government welfare) and local 'social capital' can tip the balance of power between the employer and the employee slightly, in favor of the employee. Migrant workers, however, are denied this advantage. At one level, capital's laborers do not have to be migrants or women or children. But in actual practice, in specific places and times, social difference makes a difference to capital.

It is also important to notice how the relation between capital and labor operates through the biophysical nature of the labor process. This happens in many ways. The shrimp production process is nature-dependent: it can be affected by unpredictable rains and floods. Shrimps can catch diseases. We need to, however, connect the nature of the nature-dependent production to its social (capitalist) nature. Consider how the unpredictability of the biophysical process as well as the fact that the production process is continuous (i.e. shrimps have to be looked after for 24 hours) contribute to a form of consent to the regime of long hours and difficult (night) work in the mind of laborers: people are made to believe that shrimps are like children, can become sick, and need to be constantly looked after through long hours of work. The biophysicality of the labor process acts as a mask to hide its capitalist character. It also acts as a form of labor control: if shrimps have not been fed well throughout the night at proper intervals, the employer will know this from a specific form of the physical movement of shrimps.[22] Aqua-labor is controlled in other

---

22   This form of labor control is in addition to other mechanisms being used: direct supervision; and 'bureaucratic' methods such as feed charts.

ways as well. For example, women laborers' work intensity is sought to be enhanced through the use of chemical technology when, for example, chemicals are mixed with shrimps to help the laborers de-head them faster. Ensuring the safety of the biological product (shrimp) is paramount; this leads the employers to hire nonlocals who are easier to discipline and who have limited ability to inflict Luddite style class revenge (e.g. by harming the shrimps in the event of a labor dispute). The biophysical process also affects laborers' health, producing what Fracchia (2008) would call the 'body in pain'. The men, women and children, who produce a popular delicacy for the national and global markets, cannot even eat with their hands the simple food (rice, etc., and not shrimp) that they can buy with their meager wages. Their hands have blisters due to the use of chemicals at the production and beheading sites. It is as if each shrimp, a commodity, records in its body the annals of low wages, unending night shifts, and long hours of work as well as the unfulfilled desire of the poor laborers, men and women, to enjoy a socially acceptable level of living.

Workers' conditions are of little concern to owners, however. If one worker is crippled, another can be hired. There are substitutes in plenty. There is a great deal of labor power in situ, whose production has no cost to individual employers. But if one shrimp is below the expected size or if it dies, what is lost for ever is value and surplus value (i.e. the amount of labor used), which have no substitute. When a use-value (e.g. edible shrimps) produced by the worker is lost, the value is also lost, and with that, any surplus value in it is also lost. If shrimps are not healthy, owners cannot sell them in the global market for an expected profit. So the health of the non-human living creatures is of much greater interest to the moneybags than the well-being of human beings. Human labor, in its metabolic relation with nature, produces shrimps, but shrimps, when turned into commodities, and the commodities for export, become more 'valuable' than human beings and their labor. A general point to note is that: the capitalists' interest in living beings is not because of their respect and care for life-forms, even if some of them could be animal rights activists, but because certain life-forms support the value-form of production, i.e. the production of value and surplus value.

Like many other export commodities from the countries of the periphery, shrimps are being produced dominantly under social relations of global capitalism.[23] This is capitalism based on formal subsumption of labor (which is the

---

23   And the story of shrimp laborers cannot be entirely their story. Indeed, their story is also that of most laborers producing other commodities for export in the periphery; it may be recalled here that euphoric accounts of export-oriented industrialization were even used

topic in Chapter 3), a mode of capitalist production based on long working days and the payment of low wages (i.e. wages that do not even cover subsistence needs). Formal subsumption of labor comprises what I called earlier in this chapter LMR 2 and LMR 3 (as well as LMR 1).[24] Wages and the working day are touching their physical minimum and physical maximum respectively. In the context of global demands for reduced state intervention in national economies, Third World comparative advantage supposedly lies in 'cheap' environmental and labor resources. 'Cheap', however, only signifies the relationship between exchanged commodities; hidden are the material realities of production, including the state's vital complicity, which permits such commodities to appear in the world market as 'cheap'. It is also unlikely that the low-wage regime described here is specific to the spatial context under study. It is likely to be common to most shrimp-exporting poorer regions in the world.[25] Export-oriented capitalist production of succulent shrimps results in, and is based on, the reproduction of a working class in its crippled state[26] that nonetheless continues to ensure the production of this global commodity. To the extent that natural resources and labor are used to produce subsistence goods for export to richer countries (more or less, of the imperialist bloc), this process potentially contributes to the decline in the value of labor power in the richer countries and higher rate of appropriation of surplus value in its relative form there.[27]

The conditions of work that low-wage aqua-workers experience as reported in this Chapter are similar to those of workers studied by other scholars. Basile (2013) discusses the low-wage capitalism in the context of the industrial district for silk production in rural South India. Pattenden (2016) talks about the harsh labor control regime in rural South India. Mazzadri (2016) reports

---

against radical development theory, which sought to analyze the limits of the extent to which capitalism could benefit workers in the periphery in a genuine sense.

24   The concept of subsumption is not always applied in a way Marx used it, as we have seen in chapter 3. In a study of aquaculture in China, Huang (2015: 403) says: the 'stage of "formal subsumption" [is] when agri-capital operates discretely through the monopoly of "inputs" and allows the continuation of individual labour'.

25   Economic globalization – development of the world market – is very democratic: it has a tendency to create a situation where all the human beings who must work for a wage, more or less, work and live under similar inhumane conditions.

26   The exact nature and magnitude of this state – in terms of mortality and morbidity and overall physical and mental health conditions – must be the topic of a separate detailed discussion.

27   This also represents the imperialist transfer of value (see Smith, 2016).

sweatshop conditions in garment production in multiple cities in India, shedding light on the interconnection between processes of class formation and patriarchal norms in globalized production circuits. Mazzadri's observations on the capitalist exploitation of women, including its effects on their bodies, reflect the conditions of child and women workers reported in this Chapter. Similarly, just as aqua-workers produce a high-value product which they cannot afford to consume, Mies's (2012) lace-workers produce a high-value product which they cannot use: Mies examines the ways in which women are used by capital to produce luxury goods for the Western market and simultaneously not counted as workers or as producers in their fragmented workplaces. Instead they are defined as 'non-working housewives'. This is similar to the fact that the perception of child workers being necessarily and always a secondary source of financial support for their families is a justification for why they are paid low wages in aqua-culture in the areas that I study. Bannerji (1995: 31) makes a general point: 'There is a direct connection between lower value of the labour [power] of women in general ... and the profit margin'.

Relevant here is Marx's (1977: 164) notion of commodity fetishism where relations between commodities produced (in different places) replace relations between people producing these, both in reality and in our consciousness, and where it appears as if being bought and sold for a profit is in the very DNA of a thing such as shrimp.[28] That a dollar can buy – or that a certain amount of a product can be exchanged for – several counts of cheap foreign shrimps, this relation of exchange, is not written in the body of this commodity-shrimp, how-much-ever we may twist and turn and pinch these edible creatures. Much rather, this relation of exchange is based on specific social relations under which the laboring creatures producing this commodity live, work and suffer. These are the social relations of property and of production, the class relations. These relations signify the fact that common men and women do not have control over social production, which is why the following is also a fact: the objective material interest of every laboring person is in buying as many counts of shrimp (or as much of any other commodity they need) for every dollar they have, which represents a certain amount of labor-time that

---

28   The argument is not that if people just understand that shrimps and other similar commodities are produced under inhumane conditions, these conditions will disappear and that there will be no commodity fetishism.

they themselves have sold under conditions that they, just like aqua-laborers, do not control. These conditions are given by the extant class relations, whether in India or elsewhere. And these class relations are defended by the state. In the next chapter, we will examine the class character of the Indian state, and whether it has been able to alleviate the conditions of workers.

CHAPTER 7

Class Relations, Class Struggle, and the State in India

It is a truism that in order to understand the economic issues such as poverty and development that confront India (or any other country, for that matter), one must investigate the nature of the state, for the economic is a deeply political matter and the political is 'concentrated economics'.[1,2] It is not surprising that the state in a large, under-developed capitalist country such as India, has been the subject of much discussion. To gain an adequate understanding of the state, it is important to unpack the class context of the state, both in terms of class structure and the struggle of the lower classes who are not only exploited but are also social oppressed. And then there is the institutional materiality of the state itself, including its democratic and territorial form, that needs to be stressed. Like all relations, the relations between the state and its class context are potentially contradiction-ridden and the reasons for this need to be examined.

This chapter contains seven sections, of which the first examines how the Indian state has been examined by scholars and what is problematic about their views, setting the context for an alternative view of the state. Sections 2–3 show how the state has been influenced by its 'base' in the dominant classes, and how the relations between property-owning classes and between them and the upper bureaucracy work. Section 4 discusses the relation between the state and lower classes. Section 5 deals with the state-form (territorial and liberal-democratic form) and lower-class struggles. Implications of the politically contradictory nature of state intervention in relation to uneven development and neoliberalism are outlined in Section 6, while Section 7 contains a brief conclusion.

1 Existing Views on the Indian State: A Critical Review

Rudolph and Rudolph (1987), and indeed, many others who have followed them, look upon the state as a third actor which has seemingly marginalized

---

1 An earlier version of this chapter appeared as Das (2007).
2 Lenin (1921) says: 'politics is a concentrated expression of economics...'.

© KONINKLIJKE BRILL NV, LEIDEN, 2020 | DOI:10.1163/9789004415560_008

both capital and labor and plays an autonomous role.[3] There is a Marxist counter-part of the autonomous state: Lockwood (2014) argues that the Indian state is an autonomous agent as it is a part of production relations. However, the state autonomy approach, especially, that of the Rudolphs, substantially under-estimates the dominant class bias of the state. Bardhan (1998) characterizes the state as an 'above the fray' arbiter between dominant classes, responding to the interests of these 'classes'.[4] Adopting a problematic approach to class (within so-called analytical Marxism), this view does not say much about the actual exploitative class relations and the role of the Indian state in reproducing them.

Chibber (2003) seeks to conduct a class analysis of the Indian state. He says that: contrary to common belief, in the early years of post-colonial India, the Indian capitalist class did not embrace state planning, and that it did not allow the construction of a developmental state, which could have disciplined the capitalist class as in East Asia. The capitalist class accepted, and benefitted from, import-substituting industrialization, which ensured protection from external competition, and the capitalist class received subsidies from the state, but it thwarted state initiatives to regulate industrial activity which were thought necessary for rapid industrial transformation.

Chibber thus seeks to counter the perception that the Indian state was socialist before neoliberal policies began. It was not, he rightly says. The capitalist class was in favor of state intervention but it did not want to be told how to use the resources it received (Chibber and Usmani, 2013: 207). That class wielded tremendous power in making the state do what it wanted (e.g. scaling back the power of the planners). The Indian state always supported capital but its modalities of support changed. During Nehru's times, the state gave resources to the capitalist class as a whole but kept individual capitalists at arm's length. The state kept its instrumental autonomy, in other words. The planners thought that capitalism was necessary for development but capitalists were not to be trusted in the halls of power. After the mid-1980s, business class's proximity to policy-making grew. As well, the business houses which were new and which did not have much link to the state became more vocal and demanded liberalization.

It is not clear to me why any Marxist would expect the capitalist class to subordinate itself to the state to any significant extent and without complaint, except in exceptional cases.[5] Whether or not the Indian capitalist class refused

---

3 For recent reviews of the Rudolphs's work, see: Sarangi (2017), and Sinha (2016).
4 This is the standard neoclassical argument (see Caparaso and Levine, 1989).
5 These cases include South Korea. American imperialism used Korea (and Japan) as a battlefield against communism, so the USA supplied resources and bore the cost of their military

to be controlled and disciplined by the Indian state via the latter's planning mechanisms, becomes an important question, not for Marxists, but mainly for those – from the Right on the political spectrum – who take, and who took, the claim at its face value that the Indian state was a socialist state. Marxists do not need to be convinced that ultimately it is capital that decides what the state does or does not do and that the Indian state was – and is – an out-and-out capitalist state. And a capitalist class that funded the architect of anti-colonial struggle (Mr. Mohandas Gandhi) was not going to give away what it achieved (i.e. getting rid of some of the foreign shackles on its growth) by having to obey the disciplining rules of the new state at the cost of its interests, beyond a tolerable limit.

There are several other problems with Chibber's 'class' view of the state. (1) The state-class relation cannot be understood adequately within a framework such as Chibber's that abstracts from (a) the *totality* of the relations between the proprietary classes and the classes they exploit, *including in rural areas*, and (b) the global situation (e.g. imperialism's connection to an economy, both during colonial times and after formal de-colonization, a connection that imposes limits to economic development processes in the periphery). Chibber's view is more or less an instrumentalist view of the state. However, whether the instrumental control over the state happens – whether or not the capitalist class and/or its individual members direct the state and write its documents or initiate a legislation, and so on – is, more or less, beside the matter, as far as defining the capitalist character of the state is concerned. (2) To say that the state failed to become a developmental state because it failed to develop its political capacity to discipline the capitalist class, is to explain one political process in terms of another political process (Chibber, 2006), so the approach is more politicism that characterizes liberal/left-liberal thinking, and less class-analysis. In a capitalist society, it is normal to expect that the capitalist class would thwart being controlled, unless there are strong counter-vailing mechanisms (e.g. war; imperialism, etc.). What needs to be explained is why in certain cases the capitalist class agrees, however temporarily, to being controlled or why it can be controlled against its wish? (3) To say that India did not become another East Asia because appropriate state policies could not be in place is to assume that state policies as such could develop the productive

---

protection. American market was opened to exports from Korea. What the Korean case illustrates is this: individual members of the capitalist class could be persuaded to listen to the state (and thus regulate their tendencies towards anarchic competition) because the state, operating in an international environment that was made favorable by imperialism, ensure conditions for profit-making.

forces under capitalism, as if relations between capital and labor domestically and the imperialist context in which such relations exist, do not matter, i.e. as if the capital-labor relation in India, and imperialism as the global-level class relation between the big business of militarily powerful advanced countries and direct producers of India and similar other countries, do not create obstacles (limits) to the development process, whether in farming or industry in the periphery. The relationship between the state and class, or between the state and the capitalists, cannot be seen just from the standpoint of whether state can, or cannot, promote the development of productive forces. The matter of economic development is only partly determined by the success of state policy. To assign a greater role to state policy in capitalist development is another piece of liberal/left-liberal thinking that seeks to support the agenda of the reproduction of capitalism in slightly modified form (e.g. regulated capitalism). (4) Chibber's class analysis of the state implies a critique of the neoliberal ideas (that the state was socialist, that its socialist interventions were behind slow economic growth, and therefore the state must let private players do what they want), but that critique is from the standpoint of a left-liberal/social-democratic, or capitalist-state-developmentalist, framework like the one he prefers. In contrast, class analysis of the state must be from a thorough-going Marxist angle. The Marxist angle is one that prioritizes the relation between proprietary classes, and between them and the exploited classes, and sees the state and the capitalist class, more or less, as two arms[6] of capital-as-a-class-relation, within which disagreements, including over who should listen to whom and how much, are intra-family matters.[7]

As if to echo Chibber's views, Harriss (2013: 212) makes the following claim: 'failures of planning in India had to do with the attempt at combining it with accommodative democratic politics that actually gave power to the big bourgeoisie and to the dominant landowning peasants, who were able in effect, between them, to hold the state to ransom'. Harriss adds: 'The power structure of the Indian state still constrains redistribution', in spite of 'a second democratic upsurge' (i.e. protests by lower and middle castes). So here the implication is that it is democracy – politics – that has given power to the capitalist

---

6   In terms of agency, the two arms are: state actors (top officials and politicians) and members of the capitalist class organized in informal groups and chambers of commerce, etc. It is interesting that members of the capitalist class who authored the Bombay plan – the Indian capitalists' manifesto – also joined the National Planning Commission (Chandra, 1999: 217).

7   According to Naseemullah (2016), the Indian state is not weak or captured but internally divided and thus disarticulated, because of a deep and enduring political conflict between those who wish to use the state as a tool to transform society and those who see it as a means to preserve the current social relations.

class. Such a view under-conceptualizes the structural power of the capitalist class.

In the neoliberal approach to the state, the state apparatus invariably appears as oversized and too powerful.[8] This in turn permits it to be characterized as a barrier to the development of free enterprise, an approach which licenses the view that a minimalist state will be the one to ensure prosperity (see Tendulkar and Bhavani, 2007). However, as argued in Chapter 4, this minimalist apparatus, the neoliberal Indian state, is actually a maximalist one: it intervenes where and when necessary, so as to facilitate the exploitation of workers and small-scale producers by capital, whether domestic or foreign, rural or urban.[9]

In the institutional approach, the Indian state is seen in terms of the policy process, (i.e. in terms of what it does), and in terms of the differences between the branches of the state (Sinha, 2011: 50). But the question of the conditions of the existence of the state and of its power, which is expressed in its policy-making, remains under-theorized. Sinha says that the state is not to be seen as a homogeneous entity that constrains the bourgeoisie. The state is to be seen as segmented and porous: regional elites, provincial governments, the associations of the big business, bureaucracy of the federal government, all lobby for policies in their favor. Similarly, Sundar (2011) argues that every Act (law) of the state is ultimately a product of governmental bureaucracies, reflecting the *state's* imperatives at a point in time (e.g. to check Naxalism), and is subject to the acceptance of government officials at different levels, if it is to be implemented, even if 'there are interstices through which people can express their legislative power' (p. 187). In other words, for both Sinha and Sundar, the state is an autonomous institution whose roots in class relations are under-theorized.

The Indian state has also been examined by scholars who are, to varying degrees, influenced by the cultural turn (postmodernism/post-structuralism/post-colonialism) (Corbridge, 2001; Corbridge et al., 2004; Gupta and Sharma, 2006; Kaviraj, 1992, 2011). For exponents of this approach, the state is discussed in terms of its 'fragility' and 'fluidity', and of the meanings attached to it by citizens, including by villagers. Building on ethnographic studies, scholars point to 'the ways in which state institutions, practices, and discourses interact with cultural registers and modes of practice that lie outside formal institutional structures, thereby extending the influence of state institutions into everyday life but also transforming the experience of the state in the process' (Witsoe,

---

8 This is not to be confused with the concept of the 'over-developed' state (Alavi, 1972; also Saul, 1974).
9 On different aspects of the state under neoliberalism, see Sarmah and Barua (2014).

2011: 74; see also Premchand, 2017). They show how "the state" actually manifests itself within local contexts. They argue that there is a:

> need to take more account of the ways in which political practice shapes people's experience of the state – a move that necessarily leads to an awareness of the multiple ways in which the state is imagined.
>
> WITSOE, 2011: 74

They say that there are 'the specifically postcolonial ways in which state power is experienced in India, although wrought with insidiously direct forms of oppression and violence'. The ways in which the state works 'have also opened spaces for potentially radical democratic challenges to established power based on very different concepts of popular sovereignty and "social justice"' (ibid.).

The state is thus a collection of 'people' just as society itself is an aggregate of 'people', some of whom are poor or lower-income groups and interact with and 'see' the state.[10] The on-going and local-level interaction – inter-penetration – between the state and those who are called citizens is emphasized (Kruks-Wisner, 2018).[11] Out of sight in this conceptualization is the class character of the 'people', 'citizens' and 'state actors'.[12] The state's caste character is stressed.[13] But once again, the class relations underlying caste are cast away (see the excellent Marxist work on caste by Singh, 2014, who argues that the

---

10　The concept 'people' is always designed to hide class differences, especially when used interchangeably with 'the nation'. These Weberian categories, of 'people' who 'see' the state, are consistent with the Weberian view of the state as a mere organization. Class is doubly banished: from 'sight', and from those who do the seeing.

11　For example, Kruks-Wisner (2018) examines 'citizen-state relations, asking who makes claims on the state for social welfare, and why. The frequent, but varied ways in which citizens engage in claim-making reflect the state's deeper local penetration and, simultaneously, the increasing porousness of social and spatial boundaries. The state, through decentralization and a proliferation of social welfare programs, has become more visible while citizens have become more mobile, leading to a greater frequency and intensity of citizen – state encounters. Under these conditions, ... social and spatial exposure fosters claim-making. Those who traverse boundaries of community and locality are more likely to make claims on the state and to do so through a broader array of practices than are those for whom such boundaries remain more rigid' (p. 157).

12　On a critique of the culturalist framework, see Mannathukkaren (2011).

13　There are various studies on caste, from the standpoint of the state. Mosse (2019) talk about how caste has been studied in social sciences, including in terms of the effect of affirmative action policies in public-sector education and employment. De Zwart (2000) says that caste exists not as a fact of Hindu life but because of colonial and post-colonial governments: the government defines social categories (or official constructions) under

secret of caste lies not in Hindu religion but in political economy).[14] In the cultural approaches, the citizens who are supposed to be interacting with the state are not passive agents, and that is good, but citizens are seen as contesting, not the class aspects of the state and society but only/mainly relations of subordination or the relations between the governed and those who govern, and such contestation happens often outside of the sphere of formal rules and structures.[15] The underlying notion of the state is that it is merely a power relation, but why is there a need for state actors to exercise power relations and in whose interests they do so? Might there be a relation between power relations and the class character of the state?

This literature complements the macro, national level structuralist treatment of the state, in which the state appears to be disembodied and working without the involvement of social agents. But it comes at a cost: this literature, influenced by the post-turn (or the cultural or discursive turn) is largely silent on the materiality of the state, on its solidity, its coherence, all of which come mainly from its class logic. It is the latter which one should be able to infer from, and which in turn shapes, everyday interaction.

Linked to this literature is the recent social capital approach (Das Gupta et al., 2004; Krishna, 2002) which seeks to chart a middle path between the class (= societal) view of the state and a perception of it as 'autonomous'. Those who

---

which people must register in order to qualify for the material benefits such as jobs and education, a fact that has made these constructions real in their consequences.

14   Witsoe (2011: 74) says that: 'the experience of "the state" in India is *intimately* connected with the experience of caste, the changes associated with the politics of lower-caste empowerment have transformed the ways in which people imagine the postcolonial state'. Witsoe (2011) also says: 'The specificities of what could be meaningfully termed "postcolonial governmentality" in India are reflected in the ways in which these techniques of governance – exercised in relation to development discourse – are combined in practice with relations of dominance and subordination articulated in relation to caste, forming a hybrid mode of governance wherein the exercise of violence outside of the legitimated routines of "the state" is a standard aspect of political life. It is therefore not surprising that caste identities have profoundly shaped the ways in which people imagine the state, and vice versa' (p. 75).

15   Chatterjee (2004) argues, in India's postcolonial context, there is a distinction between the civil society of the elites (the realm of formal structures and rules which are inhabited by bureaucrats, technocrats and academic people, etc. imagining and interacting with the state) and the political society. The state's interaction with the majority happens within political society which comprises networks and groups, like slum dwellers' associations and (caste) mafias, whose very existence is predicated on illegality. 'Following this logic, one can differentiate between elite conceptions of "the state" emphasizing law-bound institutions of governance imagined as separate from "society" and imaginings of the state generated from political society' (Witsoe, 2011: 74). The class origin or the class aspect of caste is neglected.

240   CHAPTER 7

hold this view maintain that relations of complementarity and synergy exist between on the one hand state officials, who are relatively insulated from dominant class pressures, and on the other the poor majority. The former are thus able to help the latter secure development inputs and benefits from an otherwise unsympathetic state. Such an over-optimistic view has been criticized by Das (2005) and Fine (2001). Here it is sufficient to note that, like the 'everyday state' literature, this view under-theorizes the class character of the state, and is therefore too sanguine about its development role vis-à-vis the poor.

Against such views is a historical materialist class-theoretic interpretation of the Indian state, which is deployed here. Just as political-economic processes discussed in earlier chapters are class processes and concern class relations, so do the fundamental aspects of the state. As I have said in Chapter 2, what is necessary is an emphatic reassertion of the validity of class analysis, now out of academic fashion, with particular reference to the formation, reproduction and agency of the state. Such an approach stresses that the state cannot but reflect – and is thus driven by – class interests, albeit in ways that are sometimes contradictory (Das, 2006). Even in apparently structurally autonomous quotidian behavior and relations, therefore, the material fact of class is the most important social context affecting the conditions under which lower classes (i.e. workers and small-scale producers of different castes in urban and rural areas) live and work.[16] Capitalist relations, along with what are taken to be 'pre-'/'non-'capitalist relations in rural areas where they exist, define this class context. Scholars in the 'post-tradition' are mistaken to *focus* on the formal and informal relations of political power between those who rule and those who are ruled. Such relations are not unimportant, theoretically or politically. But they need to be seen within the context of the relation between those who control society's productive resources and those who do not. This is the context which shapes the class character of the state, which in turn shapes its relation with those who are ruled. As Marx explains in *Capital* volume 3:

> The specific economic form, in which unpaid surplus-labour is pumped out of direct producers [i.e. specific ways in which class relations work], determines the relationship of domination and servitude [or, the relationship between rulers and ruled], as it grows directly out of production

---

16   Indian capitalism, like capitalism in other ex-colonial contexts, emerged out of the interaction between pre-capitalist society with capitalist colonialism. So there are classes other than workers and capitalists; as well, capitalism exists with pre-capitalist mechanisms in specific localities, and this situation affects the nature of the state (Mazumdar, 2016: 232).

itself and, in turn, reacts back on it as a determinant. ... It is in each case the direct relationship of the owners of the conditions of production to the immediate producers ... in which we find the innermost secret, the hidden basis of the entire social edifice, and hence also the political form of the relationship of sovereignty and dependence, in short, the specific form of the state in each case.

MARX, 1991: 927; parentheses added

However, there is more to the relation between class and the state than indicated above. The fact that the relation between classes shapes the state's relation with society in the general way that it does as indicated above:

does not prevent the same economic basis – the same in its major conditions – from displaying endless variations and gradations in its appearance, as the result of innumerable empirical circumstances, natural conditions, racial [or caste] relations, historical influences acting from outside [e.g. imperialism], etc. from showing infinite variations and gradations in appearance, and these can only be understood by analyzing these empirically given conditions.

MARX, 1991: 927–928; parentheses added

This is the perspective that is deployed here in this chapter. The class relation shapes the relation between the rulers and the ruled, and the latter relation, in turn, shapes the class relation, within a system of relations in which the class relation, ultimately, is fundamental. And the relation between classes and the state itself is shaped by various empirically-existing conditions, including mechanisms of social oppression (e.g. caste, gender),[17] external connections such as economic globalization, and so on. The class character of society and of the state does not (and cannot) operate in a vacuum: it is accordingly reproduced and impinged on – among other things – both by ideologies and practices of caste, ethnicity, religion, nationality, regionalism and gender, and by the political form of the state itself, which includes the democratic form and its geographical (e.g. federal form).[18] Since capitalism is the dominant mode of production in India, the state is predominantly a capitalist apparatus, and as

---

17   While many Indian feminists accept Marxists' class theory of the state, they also add that the Indian state is also patriarchal (Menon, 1999: 12).

18   On the state's relation not only with caste but also with ethnicity, nationality, regionalism and gender, see Beteille (2007), Chakrabarti (2001), Kumar (2017), Mohanty (2004), and Singh, 2014. On the state's democratic form, see Austin (2003), and on its geographical form, see Das (1998b), and Sinha (2003).

such an agent of capitalist development nationally and locally.[19] For this reason, the state and rural/urban capital are the two arms of what is an overarching capitalist social relationship. The actions of both capital and the capitalist state – class struggle from above – are in turn influenced politically by struggles conducted against them by lower classes.[20]

2 The Indian State and Its Class Base

It is a truism that classes which control the means of production also control state power. By controlling state power, these classes become, in turn, politically dominant.[21] The dominant classes are, in political terms, the fundamental 'support base' of the state and, in economic terms, its most important beneficiaries (two arms). The state protects their property rights when these are challenged, thereby protecting their political interests. It guarantees the reproduction of their accumulation project, the way in which wealth/value is generated, thus protecting their economic interests as classes, although specific members of these classes may lose out from this or that policy[22] or specific members of these classes may derive special benefits from certain policies because of their close connection to powerful actors within the state

---

19   As we have seen in Chapter 3, the view that Indian social formation is semi-feudal is held by many scholars (Bhaduri, 1973, 1983; Byres, 1996), and has been subjected to severe criticisms by Brass (2002) which I agree with. Also, simple fact is that capitalism – at least in the sense of formal, if not real, subordination of labor under capital – dominates non-capitalist class relations (where they exist) in the Indian social formation, including the 'rural social formation', which is politically managed by a capitalist state.

20   Mao, for example, defined these classes thus: 'poor peasants have to rent the land they work on and are subjected to exploitation, having to pay land rent and interest on loans and to hire themselves out to some extent'. And the worker 'as a rule owns no land or farm implements, though some do own a very small amount of land and very few farm implements. Workers make their living wholly or mainly by selling their labour power' (Mao, 1961).

21   'Because the state arose from the need to hold class antagonisms in check, but because it arose, at the same time, in the midst of the conflict of these classes, it is, as a rule, the state of the most powerful, economically dominant class, which, through the medium of the state, becomes also the politically dominant class, and thus acquires new means of holding down and exploiting the oppressed class', as Engels said (cited in Lenin, 1977c: 16).

22   They lose out because the perception by the state elite of the interests of specific capitalists may not exactly fit in with those of the latter, and also because of struggles within the state of capitalist fractions, including those based in specific regions and in rural areas. In these struggles, some capitalists but not others lose.

or to a party in power or because their enterprises are seen by the state as important to the nation, and so on.

As usually understood in the Indian context, the two main proprietary classes holding state power are urban capitalists and large rural landholders.[23] In this coalition, urban capitalists, especially the larger owners of capital with national and, under the neoliberal dispensation, international scale of operations, who exploit nominally free wage-labor, are not merely dominant but also increasingly so. Equally well known is the fact that the urban bourgeoisie has demanded, and benefited from, state policies, and such a favorable relationship had to be justified in the post-1917 and post-1947 situation on the basis of the *ideology* of socialism. Indeed, this relationship was cemented in the early years of independent India.

The Bombay Plan[24] was formulated in 1944 by the leaders of the big business (Birla, Tata, etc.), who also funded the anti-colonial struggle (Mukherjee, 2015). It envisaged a doubling of per capita income in 15 Years from 1944. Given its economic weakness, the big business authors of the Plan wanted the state to pay for infrastructural developments and the development of basic industries which were not profitable for the private enterprises (and which also needed bulky investment, something the private sector did not generally have). A manifesto of the Indian capitalist class, the Bombay plan was a document on what is to be done, from the standpoint of the interests of the capitalist class.[25] It connected the interests of the state, the masses and the capitalist class, within a whole, and this was the strategy of state-assisted capitalist development. The Plan did recognize inequality, in its own class interest though: inequality restricted the domestic market. So it allowed the state some redistributive role, but it made sure that egalitarian reforms (land redistribution) did not challenge the right to private property (this meant that class-based shackles on industrial development remained) (Prashad, 2015: 33).

Drafted in the last years of the World War II, which had prompted state interventionism in Britain itself, the 15-year Plan of the capitalists aimed to ensure that the new post-colonial state would protect Indian capitalists'

---

23   This is contrary to the view both that the state is a neutral arbiter between classes/groups, and that the state is controlled by 'intermediate classes' located between the exploited and the dominant classes. Note that while 'capitalist' signifies a relation of exploitation, 'landowner' usually indicates the nature of the property owned (that is, land) and says nothing about the form of exploitation that the landowner is engaged in.

24   It was formally known as 'A Brief Memorandum Outlining a Plan of Economic Development for India', or 'a Plan of Economic Development'.

25   The Indian capitalist class had made much progress under colonialism, even though colonialism constrained its growth (see Chandra, 1992 on pre-1917 Indian capitalism).

interests vis-à-vis foreign capitalists (foreign competition) and domestic labor (Prashad, 2015: 32). The Plan even suggested that some measures of coercion were desirable (i.e. coercion vs anti-capitalist elements such as labor), and Nehru, a bourgeois-democrat, agreed to this (Prashad, 2015: 37). Yet, formulated during a time when the communist/democratic-socialist Left was organizing the masses and when the Russian Revolution of 1917 was fresh in people's memory, the Plan was shaped by the belief of capitalists that a policy of egalitarian reforms was 'the most effective remedy against social upheavals' and that 'socialist demands could be accommodated without capitalism surrendering any of its essential features' (Chandra, 1989: 384).[26]

So, the Plan was prepared to accept a 'temporary eclipse' in 'freedom of enterprise' in the interest of national development and even made friendly references to the Russian experiment (Sarkar, 1983: 408). The Plan even quoted the economist, Pigou, that socialism and capitalism were converging and that a dynamic economy needed to mix the best features of both (Guha, 2012: 134). Of course, it would be foolish not to believe that capitalists would listen to the state much less than they said they would, and that they would want to milk the new state (in a process of 'post-colonial' primitive accumulation) as much as possible in spite of all their love for the new independent nation for which they apparently fought. There was some kind of partnership between the two arms of capitalist relation: a partnership between the capitalist class, whose leaders authored the Bombay plan as their manifesto, and the top bureaucrats and the enlightened bourgeois politicians of the capitalist state, generally connected to the Congress party, which was financially and intellectually supported by the capitalist class and which made sure that anti-colonial struggle, i.e. the struggle against national oppression, did not grow over into a challenge to the private property, and class exploitation. The bureaucrats and politicians made use of capitalists' expertise, etc. (capitalists joined various committees of the state), and capitalists made use of the state. All this was done in the name of national development and anti-imperialism. Nothing major was done which would pose any fundamental obstacle to the fact that capitalist private property remained in the hands of the capitalists and that the vast majority would face a choice between starvation on the one hand and the sale of their labor power (as wage-earners), or the sale of the product of their labor (as small-scale producers) at a price that cannot even ensure a decent level of reproduction of their lives, on the other hand.

---

26   On the working class struggle and the potential threat of communism in pre-colonial India (see Bahl, 1995; Basu, 2004; Chandavarkar, 2009; Chowdhuri, 2007; Sahay, 2006).

CLASS RELATIONS, CLASS STRUGGLE, AND THE STATE IN INDIA

In India, as we have discussed in Chapter 3, the capitalist form of exploitation is the dominant form of exploitation which is based on economic – and not extra-economic – coercion. This, in turn, allows the state to have a degree of autonomy vis-à-vis specific fractions of the capitalist class, an autonomy that allows the state to possess the flexibility with which to ensure the reproduction of the conditions of capitalist accumulation. Of course, there is nothing to guarantee that the state will succeed in doing what it is possible on its part to do. As well, nothing that has been said above means that there are no other processes which will shape the relation between the state and capital.

The Indian state firmly protects, not private property rights (consider the rights of self-employed peasants that are being crushed by the state), but capitalist property rights. An organic intellectual of the capitalist class, Gurcharan Das (2012: 158), writes: 'Capitalism depends on the right to property, which is one of India's advantages', especially since 1991, but, of course, the capitalist class demands that the state 'needs to do more to strengthen that right' (ibid.). This is necessary for the capitalist class to, for example, enlarge its property-base at the expense of self-exploiting small-scale property owners.

Of course, mere defense of private property would not be enough. The state has to promote capitalist economic development, which is a means of money-making for the capitalist class. The Bombay plan itself shaped the post-colonial state policies in relation to economic development.[27] Domestic markets were automatically protected, and state-owned industries provided cheap capital goods and state-owned banks continue to heap cheap money or indeed free money (loans given are pardoned) on private businesses. Close ties with the

---

27   Chibber says that the capitalist class did not embrace state planning, and that explains why industrial development did not happen. This is a little problematic. 1) It is mistaken to assume that correct developmental policy – including the disciplining of the capitalist class by state – *in itself* can result in the development of productive forces, especially in a very large and poverty-stricken low-income country such as India; there are obstacles to economic development that emanate from existing class relations that need to be transformed. 2) His thinking does considerably under-stress the fact that the capitalist economy was much more regulated in the early years than in more recent times. 3) For Chibber, it is a (neoliberal) myth that a weak bourgeoisie was shaped by developmental planning, a myth from which followed the claim that if industrial development did not occur, the blame must be on the state, a claim that was conducive to neoliberalism. For me, both the neoliberal myth and Chibber's critique of the myth share a common ground: the absence of a fundamental challenge to capitalism as a class relation, whether it is aided or un-aided by the state. To imply that capitalism is regulated or must be regulated by state power is not necessarily to challenge capitalism as such; whether that challenge happens depends on the dynamics of class struggle and on the matter of which class controls state power.

state allowed big business to ensure monopoly control of contracts (Prashad, 2015: 33). Concentration and centralization of capital went on.

Private sector companies (as well as public sector companies which have helped the former grow) have benefited enormously from the huge reserve army of labor in rural and semi-rural areas, which has been kept alive at near-subsistence level through various so-called development policies. In this respect, the strategy of locating industries in 'backward' (= aboriginal/semi-rural) areas in the name of promoting rural and/or regional development has been crucial. Recently, the neoliberal method of primitive accumulation encouraged by the state, including the sale of not only public sector companies – some of which are located in aboriginal/semi-rural areas – but also the land of indigenous peoples and other small-scale producers, to the urban capitalists at below-market prices, has deposited an enormous quantity of investible resources in their hands.[28] Indeed, those members of the capitalist class who have enjoyed close relations with influential politicians and bureaucrats have benefited hugely from this process.[29] There are some who think that the bourgeois class really had a bad time before the neoliberal times. Consider however what a former CEO of CII (Confederation of Indian Industries) says about those times: 'some of the larger business groups thrived within this system of controls by exercising their own influence and pre-empting capacities' (T. Das, 2018: 2) which constitute what Herring (1999) calls 'embedded particularism' (state's links to specific capitalists) that was responsible for what he calls 'India's failed developmental state'.

Members of the other arm of dominant class in India are the top ten percent of rural landholding families. They are involved in the appropriation of capitalist profit: mainly from farming, but also from non-farming activities, such as rural transportation and construction. These rural landowners appropriate ground rent, as well as mercantile profit and usurious interest. However, the actual mix of their portfolios may change from place to place, from time to

---

28 The post-colonial neoliberal state in India has acquired land on behalf of private companies by virtue of eminent domain' as outlined in the colonial-era Land Acquisition Act 1894. Several amendments to the 1894 Act have broadened the purview of the public purpose clause and have facilitated more state intervention in land acquisition on behalf of capitalists. The New Act of 2013 has expanded the ambit of public purpose to include public-private-partnership projects (Mallick, 2018; see also Chakravorty, 2016).

29 Therefore, the idea that free market policies will result in less corruption is no more than neoliberal propaganda. Interestingly, while every capitalist makes use of the state to accumulate their wealth, in public they and their well-paid intellectual supporters keep emphasizing how the free market – the invisible hand of the market and everyone obeying the law of dharma of the market (i.e. doing what is in one's self-interest and not cheating) (G. Das, 2012) – makes a nation prosperous.

CLASS RELATIONS, CLASS STRUGGLE, AND THE STATE IN INDIA 247

time and from one member of the landed class to another. To some degree, the specifically capitalist elements of this class emerged in part due to what was predominantly a bourgeois land reform that removed some erstwhile pre-capitalist fetters (Das, 1999c; Djurfeldt and Sircar, 2017). The capitalist class in rural areas has benefited not only from the policy of exemption of taxation on agricultural incomes, but also – and more importantly – from the Green Revolution (discussed in Chapter 5), which was promoted by the state policy of providing cheap inputs and price support (Nanda, 1995). The economic importance of what may appear to be 'non-capitalist' elements of the dominant landowning class is an effect of the fact that the state considers it legitimate for them to extract extremely high rents (in cash, labor or kind), and charge usurious interest rates (which can be 50–60% a year) on loans.[30] These forms of exploitation are legal according to Indian bourgeois constitution (although bonded labor, which is widely used in rural areas, is not).[31] The rural propertied class still exercises substantial political power, through which it protects both its accumulation project and the sources of its capital/wealth.[32]

---

30   It is not clear why the level of rent/interest *per se* determines the nature of class relations, that is, whether these are capitalist or not (Das, 2001c: 164). Does the payment of wages below the value of labor power – which happens when the supply of labor outstrips demand – make the payment, and therefore the capital/labor relation, pre- or non-capitalist? To the extent that the nature of the state is conditioned by the relations of exploitation (whether and to what extent these are capitalist), and to the extent that the capitalist nature of the mode of exploitation is underemphasized (as in the much of the Indian mode of production debate), the capitalist nature of the state (which also happened to receive very little attention in that debate) will be also diluted.

31   Although the social base of the state is said to be formed by a coalition of proprietary classes, the state is a bourgeois state. According to Kaviraj (1988), this can be explained in three different senses. First, the logic of capitalism, no matter in what juridical form it appears (the public or the private sector), economically and politically subordinates the economic and political reproduction of 'non-capitalist' modes of production where they exist. That is, the society is dominated by the capitalist class, or a coalition dominated by that class. Second, the state-form is a parliamentary democratic one that 'arranges disbursing of advantages in a particular way; and the democratic mechanism works as a useful sensitive political index as to when the distribution of disadvantages, which is bound to happen and intensify in a capitalist economy, is becoming politically insupportable' (Kaviraj, 1988: 2430). And third, the state ensures the domination of the bourgeoisie and helps, through capitalist planning, in the reproduction of capitalist relations (Kaviraj, 1988: 2430).

32   Varshney (1994) almost reduces the power of 'the rural' and the countryside to the power of commercial farmers. Strictly speaking, rural power is that exercised by propertied class plus that of lower classes. Varshney correctly identifies some of the limits to the power of commercial farmers, but he misses the point that the real limit is that posed by the countervailing power of the lower classes.

Another beneficiary of state policies is what might be termed 'state elites', composed of high-ranking members of the bureaucracy plus senior officials engaged in the industrial management of public sector enterprises. In a country like India, where the overwhelming majority of the population are illiterate or primary school drop-outs, 'the educated elite' according to Bardhan (1998: 52), 'enjoy a high scarcity value (a rent) for their education and profession. By managing to direct educational investment away from the masses, they have been able to protect their scarcity rent', which is seen in their salary increases and perks. State elites have benefited considerably from the expansion of educational and administrative functions and the nationalization of industries, which created jobs for managers in the public sector, and subsidized collective consumption (which has actually made some of them members of an expanding consuming class). In the era before neoliberalism, the 'process of implementation of (policies) often generates rental income from disbursement of permits and favors which accrues to the bureaucratic elite' (Bardhan, 1998: 51). More recently, with neoliberalism, these elements have benefited – illegally – from the sale of public assets, the state-promoted method of primitive accumulation. In short, state elites have economic resources, as well as social and cultural capital. Since they occupy crucial positions in the state apparatus, they use state's 'autonomy' to implement policies in their own interest, akin to exercising powers of patronage. As long as the myth of state 'autonomy' circulates, this will confer an advantage on those who administer the economic resources and implement policies.[33]

At the local level, state elites (officials, and political leaders, especially, of ruling parties) represent the worst face of state power. Forming an alliance with the economically dominant classes at this level, they corner much of the development benefits that are supposed to go to the poor. Their high-handedness complements and reinforces that of the proprietary classes, not least because of the way urban capitalists disregard the legitimate trade unions rights of workers, and rural landowners keep rural sections of the lower classes in relations of servitude and 'hold' state power quite literally (they are the state itself in many areas). In effect, such actions blur the boundary between the state and the dominant classes at the local level.[34] All this renders problematic the sanguine social capital theory of the state, which pins hope on state – society synergy as a possible source of progress where lower classes are concerned.

---

33   Mukherji (2017, 2008) discusses how state autonomy in the form of state officials/ technocrats' autonomy matters, even if the state is weak.

34   The story of the 'hermeneutic divide' between the local/village-based and centrally-based officials is too well known to be narrated here (Kaviraj, 1992).

CLASS RELATIONS, CLASS STRUGGLE, AND THE STATE IN INDIA 249

3 A Coalition/Alliance of Proprietary Classes

An obvious question to ask is why is the urban bourgeoisie said to find it necessary to share state power with landowners? Why is a *coalition* of large-scale exploitative rural landowners (the landed) and the urban-industrial bourgeoisie said to exist in a social formation where capitalism is the dominant mode of production and exchange?[35]

One needs to understand the economic and political importance of the landed. The landed includes those landowners who exploit the masses by appropriating ground rent (and sometimes, usurious interest) or surplus value or a combination of the two. The relation between the landed class and the direct producers, whether it is based on ground rent or surplus value, is a relation of not only economic exploitation but also political power. The masses depend on the landed for a little piece of land on rent, on loans, and for wage-employment (in farming and non-farming activities). This dependence is economic. It can also have political effects: how much independence can the masses whose lives depend on the landed class, have, when they themselves are thoroughly unorganized? So economic control over the masses *is* a source of political control. When the masses produce products (which, more or less, take a commodity form) for the landed (indeed, for rural capitalists as such), in the *same* process is reproduced a relation between the two classes, a relation that is economic and political (as well as cultural/discursive).

Besides, landowners actively exercise *de facto* control over the state apparatuses (e.g. police; civil administration that does some developmental work) at the local scale through electoral and other mechanisms, especially at the local/provincial scale.[36] Rural property owners – and rural capitalists as such – are

---

35   The 'coalition' concept in the sense in which it is used in the literature means that there are fundamental class differences (as well as overlaps of interests) between landowners and urban capitalists. Implicit in the concept is the idea, which is problematic and resonates with the semi-feudal thesis, that the nature of the surplus appropriated by landowners is in a fundamental way different from that extracted by urban capitalists. It can be argued much rather that state power is held by a single bourgeoisie, composed of an urban component and a rural one. There are differences between individual capitalists and groups of capitalists, yet we do not use 'coalition of urban capitalists' in characterizing state power. So why *coalition* of landowners and urban capitalists? Strictly speaking, we should talk about the Indian capitalist class, a fraction of which comprises the rural capitalists, a part of whose income comes from ground rent.

36   The Indian state is described as the capitalist-landlord state by many on the left (it is also described by Maoists as semi-colonial and semi-feudal). What is stressed in these various (confusing) characterizations is that the state redistributes value from smaller (national

not just a proprietary class. Rural politicians, who have an enormous control over the local administration, generally come from that class and/or from strata that are closely related to that class. They control and discipline the rural masses and punish them where necessary, through a judicious mixture of elections and extra-economic coercion and ideas, which are usually very regressive. The ideas that circulate in rural areas and that shape the thinking of the masses (for example, ideas about how to respond to society's problems; who to vote for, what should be the perception of the state?) are, typically, the ideas of the propertied class (from rural areas and also, increasingly from the cities)or are those that reflect the interests of this class. The rural property owners, including those who appropriate the surplus in the form of rent and interest and in the form of profit, are not just a class of economic exploiters. They are also social oppressors. The men, women and children who are economically exploited are also those who are socially oppressed. Usually, the large-scale property owners are not Dalits, but the direct producers often are. The property owners are typically men, but direct producers are both women and men. So the full force of caste and gender relations is made use of to control and shape the masses: not only to exploit them, but also to keep them subjugated. The rural masses (including those who have small plots of land), as a potential ally of the urban working class, are an enormous potential threat to the propertied class, whether in rural or urban areas. What makes them a potent force is not just the fact of their class-anger rooted in them being exploited and oppressed. It is also their number, given the fact that the majority of the people – majority of the direct producers – live in rural areas, unlike in, say, other parts of the Global South (e.g. Latin America). Given their potential as a threat to the propertied, it is important that they be prevented from launching any attack on the class character of the state or indeed on the urban capitalist class. The

---

or regional) enterprises to monopoly and overseas businesses, and that it protects relations generating ground rent, which hurts capitalist development. This is actually a critique of the excesses of the state activity (as opposed to its normal activity). This is because of a fractionalist approach to the state. As just mentioned, the Indian state is in my view best characterized simply as capitalist state. This is because it supports and reproduces, over any overt/covert class resistance, three things. First, the institution of private property and – most importantly – the form of capitalist private property. Second, and therefore, it supports the relations of exploitation between capital and labor in rural and urban contexts. And third, it supports capitalist accumulation, in the form of formal and real subsumption. Its support for ground rent is a consequence of its support for private property, without which ground rent as such could not exist. Therefore the state-promoted reproduction of the relations of ground rent, including 'pre-' or 'non-'capitalist forms where these exist, is predominantly a consequence of the state being capitalist.

urban bourgeoisie indeed needs the rural propertied class in a large, dominantly-rural country such as India, to control the masses. The rural propertied class is therefore regarded as functional to the political interests of the bourgeoisie.

The act of controlling and disciplining the rural masses by the rural propertied class also delivers an important *economic* advantage to the urban bourgeoisie: food and agri-materials consumed by industries are produced cheaply, because rural workers are remunerated well below the value of their labor-power and rural petty producers sell their products at a very low price, so the rural commodities are very 'competitively' priced. This kind of economic advantage is not something that would be possible at the existing level of the development of the productive forces without the sort of control that rural property owners have over rural toilers. Besides, the continuing existence of rural landlords helps reproduce the idea of private property ownership and thereby the idea of capitalist private property, and this is beneficial to the urban capitalist class. So in terms of the defense of private property and in terms of the defense of the capitalist market (note that both rural and urban property owners benefit from market transactions), they have the same interest. As well, any strong action (e.g. a properly-implemented land reforms policy) against the large-scale rural landowning class (whether they appropriate rent or profit and interest) would hurt the economic interests of the urban bourgeoisie because, as, the latter itself has been involved in the exploitation of peasants through its links with the rural landlord class and though its mercantile and usurious operations in villages, as just indicated (see also Davey, 1974: 102). It is important to note that just like most sections of the urban bourgeois class, the rural land-owning capitalists have also supported the liberalization of trade that the urban capitalists have demanded, because the rural capitalists, generally speaking, have eyed making money from unregulated markets and from the exports of farm-products.

Some analyses include top state elites as a part of the coalition of classes holding state power. In line with his neoclassical economic approach, Bardhan (1998: 51) maintains that 'if physical capital can be the basis of class differentiation, so can be human capital in the form of education, skills and technical enterprise', which these top bureaucratic elites possess.[37] The latter have close links to intellectuals in India and abroad, and as a top bureaucrat in the rural

---

37   As Bardhan mistakenly thinks, the idea of the physicality of capital is consistent with a class approach. That approach to capital is firmly within mainstream, neoclassical economics (Fine, 2001).

development ministry of central government once informed me, 'all these IAS (Indian Administrative Service) officers want to be top class intellectuals, thinkers'. These bureaucratic elites also have connections with business groups, both in India itself and in the Indian diaspora, and thus constitute an important support base for the Indian capitalists at home and abroad. But are they part of the dominant class coalition? Not bourgeois in a productive sense, state elites have been affiliated to the bourgeoisie in cultural and ideological ways. It was in this sense that Nehru called himself a bourgeois. But they have had a degree of autonomy.

Even before independence, state elites were the repository of the intelligentsia, working out a development theory for Indian capitalism, often restraining more intensely bourgeois objectives and formulating policies that appeared to be more reformist and universal. They viewed 'their society as in need of basic change' (Kohli, 1987: 25), and charted a path of capitalist development that sought to resist, within limits, imperialist pressures, in a way that is consistent with the bourgeois conception of 'national' development. State elites are not wholly independent of capital, however, since its logic sets the limit within which state elites formulate specific strategies of accumulation and specific development discourses, both of which project the interests as well as the ideas of state elites. These ideas have included, at one time, belief that India should follow an independent capitalist path after 1947 and, more recently, the idea of neoliberal development. Much planning/policy discourse accordingly comes from these state elites who are always in interaction with the organic intellectuals of the capitalist class working in the academia, media, private consultancies, etc. This is effected through the various institutions/apparatuses of the state, and through their rules, procedures, discourses and strategies (see Baviskar, 2003; Ferguson, 1994; Williams, 2004) to which certain intellectuals contribute. In short, there is an ensemble of state institutions/apparatuses (e.g. National Institute of Rural Development; the Nehruvian Planning Commission or its present dwarfed neoliberal avatar), procedures, discourses and tactics of development – a Foucauldian might call this 'developmentality of the state' – that allows the state elites to govern the people, to exercise power over the millions of development-hungry, illiterate and semi-literate Indians in rural areas (and in impoverished urban spaces) in the name of development, although Foucauldians forget that these mechanisms do not of themselves *create* the power of state elites. The origin of that power is dominantly in the *class* nature of society and of the state.

I have mentioned the intellectual aspects (Bardhan calls these human capital) of the state bureaucracy. I should elaborate on this point. While one must acknowledge that the bureaucracy has included some very smart thinking minds from time to time, there are reasons to worry about its overall intellectual capacity which functions as the repository of knowledge that the state deploys to rule. One does not need to be a Weberian to unpack some of the reasons for this. The minimum requirement to be an IAS officer is an undergraduate degree, although a large number of officers are perhaps post-graduate drop outs. The quality of higher education in social sciences and humanities is simply poor and getting poorer. The content that students learn – memorize – is a set of ideas that are designed to support/justify an inegalitarian social order, and especially, a capitalist order, an order that is also oppressive of lower castes, of religious minorities, and of women.[38] To be an officer, one of the major requirements is memorizing a vast amount of raw information (e.g. who won the Olympic prize in sport x, in year y, from country z?): so what students do – i.e. memorizing – to get their under-graduate degree in order to be eligible for taking the recruitment examination, is what they do to get the job of an officer too. Many officers come from science and engineering backgrounds, and the nation does need officers with such backgrounds. But it is not clear how socially sensitive, both intellectually and practically, those people are. Given the way the officers live and work (generally pushing files, taking orders from politicians who often take orders from the business class), and indeed given the pressure of work, it is not clear if there is any significant scope for developing one's intellectual abilities whereby one can understand people's problems in a way that is scientific and critical.[39] Although they are known as civil servants, they are, more or less, uncivil masters of ordinary people: in a truly colonial style, the officers are perceived as mini-kings, and many of them probably perceive themselves as such (as brown sahibs).[40] To the extent that this is true, it is not even clear if they feel that they lack any knowledge, and if they do, they can always get someone by using their power to write a few things for them, just as politicians and prime ministers appear to be erudite by delivering speeches

---

38 That the scientific temper is being tampered with in recent times is a separate issue.

39 An approach is scientific when it is backed by evidence and reason, and not by belief, intuition or myth. An approach is critical when it is critical of the unequal power relations – between the property owners and the property-less or between the rich and the poor, between the oppressors and the oppressed, and between powerful state actors and ordinary citizens – and of how a society treats the physical environment. And, an approach is critical when it is critical of the ideas that support the exploitative and oppressive relations and the undermining of the material basis of society in the natural environment.

40 On Nehru's critical attitude towards the top bureaucratic layers (ICS/IAS), see Davey (1974: 224).

which are written by hired speech writers, etc. Let's assume that intellect is necessary for state-policy and it exists and that state-policy can contribute to the solution of people's problems. Then how is it that the Indian state is run by thousands of intellectually-capable men and women who are overseeing a society that fails to meet the basic needs of the vast majority, and is increasingly curtailing democratic rights of people? Given that the vast majority are suffering as much as they do, can one conclude that: there is limited intellect within the top layers of the bureaucracy or that policies are formed without being backed up by much intellectual work/rationale (consider demonetization that has hurt millions) or that to the extent that top layers of bureaucracy have a stock of intellect, it is ignored in policy-making, and that this is done in order to support an exploitative and oppressive order? When will 'the bureaucratic caste' understand that whether or not they have any intellectual abilities, they are, more or less, irrelevant as far as any significant improvement in the conditions of the toiling masses is concerned, because in spite of their self-grandeur about their intention to help the masses, they are tethered to the proprietary classes and their political representatives, both to serve these people and in their own interest (see Das, 2013b)? But surely, they are very relevant as far as ensuring conditions for exploitation and subjugation of the masses is concerned. In this sense, the top officers are close allies of the proprietary classes, and are a major obstacle to the self-emancipation of the toilers in whose name they administer.

Whether they have much 'human capital' or not, state elites *qua* elites are not a class, so they cannot be considered a part of the class coalition holding state power.[41] Unlike rural propertied class and urban capitalists, state elites cannot transfer property to their heirs. It is the ownership/control of the means of production that decides who ultimately has power in a society and the state.[42] State elites have a certain degree of autonomy, but this they exercise mainly on the basis of the fact that they coercively and ideologically defend capitalist property relations and implement capitalist accumulation projects: hence their activities – including rent-seeking – must be seen as contingent on

---

41 The idea – common in the 'political economy' literature – that state elites are a dominant class, and the idea – common in the neoliberal literature – that the activities of state elites are a reason for India's low level of development, are two sides of the same coin. The problems of society are located in the political realm, rather than in the sphere of class relations of exploitation. To accept that the state elites are a dominant class is also to accept that 'the rule of full-time corps of non-propertied officials is an unavoidable feature of modern society' (Post, 1999: 146).

42 In the African literature, state elites controlling the public sector industries and business are called a state bourgeoisie or a managerial bourgeoisie (Leftwich, 2000: 91). Pedersen (1992) says that Indian bureaucracy is not a class.

a state the structure of which is designed to pursue capitalist class interests. State elites qua state elites are *not* a class, and cannot therefore hold and exercise state power on their own behalf no matter how much they seek to elevate themselves.[43]

The dominant class-base of the state changes over time. Since the late 1960s, there has been a proliferation of members of the capitalist class (Chandrasekhar et al., 1999).[44] In more recent times, capitalist elements among the landed have become more powerful (Chattopadhyay, Sharma and Ray, 1987) and have been connected to urban capitalists. Under neoliberalism, there is greater corporate control over agriculture, and greater interaction with the landed through such mechanisms as contract farming. Also, a result of the competition between big corporations (domestic and foreign) and smaller-scale enterprises has been that many of the latter companies get slowly eliminated, causing an increasing level of centralization of the means of production in line with Marx's thinking (Marx, 1977: 777).[45] This same trend also manifests itself in another form within agriculture: the rising inequality in some areas of the distribution of operational land (land owned plus land leased in minus land leased out). So the class base of the state is narrowing in the sense that it is increasingly dominated by a powerful domestic urban bourgeoisie and rural property-owning class which are also linked to international circuits of capital, and as such, they are the main beneficiaries of the neoliberal globalization policy of the Indian state.[46]

4   The Indian State, Lower Classes, and Lower-Class Struggle

The above section outlines a more-or-less familiar story within political economy, one about control by elements composing the dominant classes over state power in India. But this is only one half of what is a larger story. A problem

---

43   The political implication of this is that replacing one set of state actors with another leads to no fundamental changes in the conditions under which workers and peasants live.

44   This suggests that: thanks to certain state intervention in the 1950s–1980s, new kinds of capitalists came into being (this constitutes the proliferation of the capitalist class), and then a changed capitalist class makes new demands on the state (e.g. liberalization).

45   This is something Patnaik (2001) has also commented on.

46   Also the top state elites as a 'consumption class', whose emergence state policies in the era before neoliberalism helped, along with the rural and urban propertied class, have acted as a great pressure for the liberalization of imported luxury items. They have also prompted the use of country's resources for the production of luxury non-wage goods, including new agricultural products (flowers, shrimps), a process which has further contributed to what Samir Amin has called 'disarticulation' of the economy.

with much radical theorization of the state and its class character has been its structuralist nature, and its near exclusive stress on the interests of the dominant classes.[47] This is un-dialectical. In a dialectical analysis of class, there are no capitalist interests or landowner interests that exist in abstraction from those of the lower classes. Rather obviously, class is a relationship of exploitation and power between classes. What the state is and does, and why, must accordingly also be investigated from the standpoint of the lower classes, and especially in terms of their struggle against the state and the propertied classes, no matter how weak and constrained that struggle is. In this dialectic, the fact that the Indian state is engaged in reproducing the political and economic interests of 'those above' does not go unchallenged by 'those below'.[48]

Class struggle is therefore not merely important but crucial to an analysis of the state. Accordingly, how the Indian state is perceived by the lower classes, who compose about 70% of the population is an essential part of the equation. As is well known, in the rural context, poor peasants and agricultural laborers are subordinated by a wide variety of regionally-specific production relations, extending from sharecropping and other kinds of tenancy arrangements, structuring conditional access to small plots of land, through to local/migrant/ seasonal forms of landless employment. Those compelled to rely mainly or wholly on the sale not of the product of their labor but rather of labor power itself are exploited by property owners, who appropriate surplus labor mainly in the form of profit. In the urban context, barely 10% of wage-earners have access to a regular wage and pension benefits. Everyone else is precariously employed.

For a large proportion of wage-workers, their employment is confined neither to given areas nor to one specific pattern of work. Forming a reserve army of labor, the size of which is swelling partly thanks to neoliberalism, they are also subject to exploitation by urban capitalists on a seasonal basis, when they migrate to towns and cities in search of off-farm work. Such workers are often paid below the value of labor power. In many instances they are deproletarianized (Brass, 1990, 1999, 2003) in the sense of not having the freedom personally to sell their own labor power, their only commodity.[49] Despite lip-service

---

47   For example, the Indian mode of production debate had very little to say about class struggle.

48   The critical approach which focuses simply on the power of the dominant class is therefore unhelpful from the standpoint both of lower-class interests and of macro-level change. Nilsen (2008) reflects on the possibilities for the state to function as an enabling space for the struggles of subaltern social groups.

49   This includes arrangements whereby migrants are recruited by a labor contractor, who then sells their labor power to a rich peasant or agribusiness enterprise.

to the eradication of bonded labor, this kind of unfreedom is a relation that the Indian state has failed to eliminate.[50]

Given the unequal distribution of resources, and the attendant exploitative conditions, class struggle is immanent. There is always a potential for struggle even if the potential is not always realized or manifested explicitly.[51] The history and geography of Indian society, like all class societies, is thus also a story about both the fact of and forms taken by lower-class struggle, a point underlined by numerous studies (Desai, 1986; Dhanagare, 1991; Mukherjee, 2004; Pathy, 1998; Shah, 2000; Singharoy, 2004).[52] The ideological impact of such class mobilization and agency in the specific context of the countryside, and especially struggle by poor peasants, is such as to have prompted Arvind Das (1982: 1) to observe: 'The spurts of writing on the agrarian question in India have quite remarkably followed the ebbs and tides of peasant movements'.

Forms of class struggle from below vary and are often place-specific. One can observe four inter-connected forms. The first is the struggle by proletarian and semi-proletarian elements as full-time or part-time wage-earners against capital, both in urban and in rural areas.[53] This 'from below' struggle also includes struggle against localized pre-capitalist exploitation. More importantly, the lower-class struggle, which is generally in the form of strikes (work-stoppage), is against the formal and real subsumption of labor under capital: that is, it is against low wages, oppressive labor practices, long hours and poor working conditions, precarity, and the introduction of, or subordination to,

---

50   Of a little more than a billion Indians, 836 million people – 82 per cent of whom are Dalits, the Scheduled Tribes, the Other Backward Classes and the poor Muslims – earn less than 20 rupees a day (note that a kilogram of rice costs more than 10 rupees in the market). If the sort of the economic distress that afflicts the vast majority that is indicated by the above statistic does not show state failure, then what does? (Of course, the state has been very successful in ensuring that India has one of the highest number of millionaires and billionaires in the world.)

51   It is in this sense that class-in-itself is not entirely separate from class-for-itself.

52   See also the publications of the two major left-wing parties [CPI and CPI(M)], plus the various annual publications of peasants and laborers associations (including All Indian Kisan Sabha) affiliated to these parties. One does not have to approve of the theory underlying these struggles, or the tactics involved (the use of violence by armed squads), to appreciate the fact that generations of activists have given up everything in their lives to organize the lower classes/castes and fight against oppressive and exploitative conditions.

53   Recent literatures on class struggle include: Bhowmik, 2014; Dutta, 2018; Heller, 1996; Miyamura, 2010; Nathan, 1999; Pattenden, 2018, and Sheth, 2014. Chandramohan (1998) examines some of the theoretical explanations of agrarian unrest.

labor-saving technology, and so on.[54] Of necessity, this sort of struggle also becomes one aimed at the state which supports the propertied class against 'from below' agency undertaken by workers and small-scale producers. The poor people in rural and urban areas do fight for concessions from the capitalist state, including in its role as an employer and provider of things that contribute to social reproduction.[55] Workers as a class have intra-class divisions: they are divided on the basis of job security, occupation, wage-level, location, etc. So their struggles include the struggles on the part of the informal labor (Agarwala, 2013) and not just the formally employed labor.[56] The fact that a large proportion of those who must depend on the sale of labor power for a living does not have access to regular employment has an implication for class struggle: some fight against the employers for higher wages (trade union struggle) and others fight against the state for pro-poor policies (struggle in the political sphere). Besides, the trade union struggle itself also takes the form of political struggle when trade unions demand a government-mandated minimum wage of Rs. 18,000 and linking the minimum wage to inflation.[57] Also, workers have not only struck work; and they have also defended the public sector (and fought against their privatization); and they have also built production and service-provision coops as a means of building working class power (Kerswell and Pratap, 2019).

---

54   Consider the numerous accidents at work in rural areas, some of which are fatal (Nag and Nag, 2004), including those caused by tractors over-turning, one case of which I observed on a farm just outside of Delhi in the summer of 2007. The absence of any safety regulations is the main cause of these accidents.

55   Subadevan and Naqvi (2017) talk about how the urban poor seek to get concessions by pursuing informal and formal strategies.

56   Herring and Agarwala (2006) say that informal workers organize differently that stably employed workers. 'First, because capital takes the form of constantly changing employers, who may even be unknown at the point of production, worker organizations take their demands to the state, rather than to capital. Second, demands for expansion of citizenship rights focus on welfare benefits (such as health and education), rather than workers' rights (such as minimum wage and job security). Third, because neither employers nor workplaces remain constant, informal workers organize around the neighborhood, rather than on the shop floor. These strategic changes have an impact on class identification: a unique class identity that simultaneously asserts workers' informality and their position within the working class. Informal workers employ a rhetoric of "citizenship" and mobilize votes to institutionalize rights' (p. 346).

57   Meyer (2016) says that only those workers who are in powerful structural locations, such as transportation and distribution workers, are in a position to take the economic route while the swelling ranks of the precariat have turned instead to the political sphere to press their demands for a better standard of living.

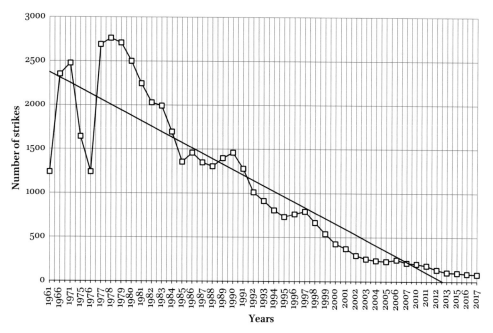

FIGURE 7.1 Number of strikes
SOURCES: HTTPS://THEOPENDATA.COM/SITE/2012/03/STRIKES-AND-LOCKOUTS-IN-INDIA/; HTTPS://WWW.RESEARCHGATE.NET/FIGURE/INDUSTRIAL-DISPUTES-IN-INDIA-19952006_TBL1_235622522; HTTPS://WWW.FINANCIALEXPRESS.COM/ECONOMY/FEWER-STRIKES-LOCKOUTS-IN-LAST-3-YEARS/1072233/; LABOUR BUREAU. 2015. SHIMLA: GOVERNMENT OF INDIA

I have mentioned in Chapter 4 the fact of regular workers' strikes in India, including under neoliberalism that began formally in 1991. My point has been to stress that workers have not been passive, even under neoliberalism which is supposed to have discouraged workers' struggle. Let us have a slightly long-term view of strikes. (1) There has been a decline in the number of strikes since the 1960s and 1970s, so the decline did not happen only since the onset of neoliberalism in mid-1980s and early-1990s (Figure 7.1). This requires an explanation which cannot be offered here. (2) Associated with the decline in the number of strikes has been a decline in person-days (called man-days, in official documents) that are lost due to the strike, which is a measure of the costs inflicted on the capitalist class. The decline in person-days is less steep and more uneven than the decline in the number of strikes (Figure 7.2). (3) However, and this is surprising, the ratio of person-days lost to the number of strikes has been increasing over time, especially since the onset of neoliberalism (Figure 7.3). As Kumar (2018) says, in the years between 2014 and 2017 only, there was a

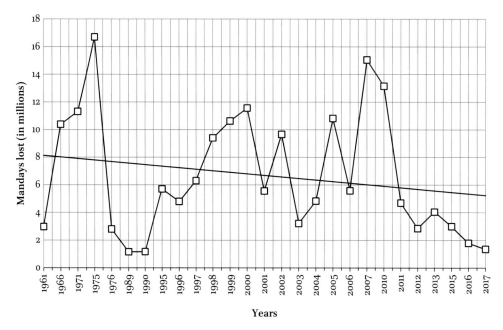

FIGURE 7.2 Mandays lost (in millions)
SOURCES: HTTPS://THEOPENDATA.COM/SITE/2012/03/STRIKES-AND-LOCKOUTS-IN-INDIA/; HTTPS://WWW.RESEARCHGATE.NET/FIGURE/INDUSTRIAL-DISPUTES-IN-INDIA-19952006_TBL1_235622522; HTTPS://WWW.FINANCIALEXPRESS.COM/ECONOMY/FEWER-STRIKES-LOCKOUTS-IN-LAST-3-YEARS/1072233/; LABOUR BUREAU. 2015. SHIMLA: GOVERNMENT OF INDIA

loss of 7.34 million person days, costing Rs. 14,350 million, including Rs. 5,500 million in 2017 only.

The second main form is 'from below' struggle against primitive accumulation:[58] the state assisting with, or facilitating, what Lenin called 'depeasantization' – smallholders being stripped of their means of production; the privatization of common property and public sector resources, again with the connivance of the state; and the withdrawal by the state of benefits meant for the poor.[59] Here again 'from below' agency targets the state (and not just the propertied classes) for its support for primitive accumulation – for example

---

58 There is a large amount of literature on protests/struggles against dispossession (see Levien, 2018; D'Costa, 2017; Nielson and Nilsen, 2016; Nilsen, 2010, 2016; Steur, 2014).

59 Marx discussed these processes with reference to England (Marx, 1977: Chapters 25–28). Modern interpretations of primitive accumulation are found in De Angelis (2004) and Harvey (2003), among others. On a critical analysis of Harvey's re-conceptualization of Marx's (and Luxemburg's) primitive accumulation, see Das (2017b).

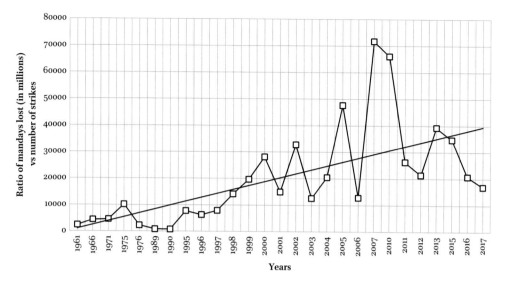

FIGURE 7.3   Ratio of mandays lost (in millions) versus number of strikes
SOURCES: HTTPS://THEOPENDATA.COM/SITE/2012/03/STRIKES-AND-LOCKOUTS-IN-INDIA/; HTTPS://WWW.RESEARCHGATE.NET/FIGURE/INDUSTRIAL-DISPUTES-IN-INDIA-19952006_TBL1_235622522; HTTPS://WWW.FINANCIALEXPRESS.COM/ECONOMY/FEWER-STRIKES-LOCKOUTS-IN-LAST-3-YEARS/1072233/; LABOUR BUREAU. 2015. SHIMLA: GOVERNMENT OF INDIA

when it privatizes the commons.[60] Connected to this form of struggles is the struggle, launched by small-scale commodity producers for better farm prices and lower farm inputs.[61]

In addition to these two forms of class struggle – aimed at capital and its state – there are other kinds of conflict that have their roots in class inequality: that are opposed to ecological degradation,[62] and gender/caste/ethnic/national

---

60   Lake Chilika is Asia's largest brackish water lake. For thousands of traditional fishermen and women, it is a common property resource, which they use to obtain their livelihood. The state is now allowing agribusiness enterprises to use parts of the lake for export-oriented shrimp production. This hinders open access to the lake for traditional fishing, and by polluting the lake, results in the depletion of the fish-stock adversely affecting the economy of the traditional fishing community. All this has triggered a massive and often militant movement, helped by the local left (CPI M-L/Liberation). Its targets are capitalists, some of whom are high level state officials themselves, and the provincial state apparatus.

61   Of course, this struggle is often led by large-scale, capitalist farmers (on famers' movement, see Brass, 1995; Gupta, 2002).

62   See Guha (2002) on the environmental movements. On movements in aboriginal areas, see Sinha (2002) and Singh (2002); on the Dalit movement, see Omvedt (2002); on

oppression. This is the third form of lower-class struggle. Indeed, adverse environmental change and non-class forms of oppression have, arguably, a disproportionate impact on the poor than on the better-off sections. To the degree that the propertied classes and the state bolster – either overtly or covertly – 'non-class' forms, moreover, they become the target of agency aimed at such oppressions. These are the struggles in which lower classes participate, although whether they do so always because they are conscious of the role of capitalism in the creation of ecological problems and social oppression, is doubtful.[63]

The fourth form of the lower-class struggle is one that is most clearly 'political': for the democratization of the state. Workers and small-scale producers join with the broad mass of the population in this kind of agency, not least because they are the ones who often experience in its most overt form the corrupt practices and patronizing attitudes of state elites, the 'brown sahibs' who treat them like slaves.[64] In so far as the undemocratic nature of the state – its lack of accountability to the lower classes in terms of policies, programs, and politics – derives from the fact that the main role of this apparatus in a society

---

women's movement, see Lingam (2002.) On the relation between the Marxist movement and the caste movement, see Teltumbde (2016) who says that there is an increasing divergence between the two. See Omvedt (1993) on the new social movement in relation to class agency.

63   These movements are portrayed as empowering alternatives – what Corbridge terms the 'politics of the feasible', echoing the words of the British Conservative Rab Butler (for whom politics was 'the art of the possible') – to 'bad' narrow-minded class-based leftist struggles (Omvedt, 1993). These movements often engage in the politics of neo-populism/ nationalism of the kind usually associated with the political right, such as the BJP. But these movements can have left-leaning elements in certain contexts. Indeed class based actors have been involved in these movements, and those involved in the latter – for example, Medha Patkar – sometimes show direct support for class struggles. Nilsen (2008) discusses accumulation by dispossession (in the Narmada Valley) in the larger context of the political economy of state-led capitalism in India, where state development strategies have in large part functioned as vehicles for the expropriation and enclosure of vital productive resources in favour of the country's dominant proprietary classes. But there are limits to the extent to which social movements can use the state as a neutral arbiter by ignoring the 'constraints' imposed by proprietary classes.

64   Attitudes towards corruption can be ambivalent. It is generally the case that leaders of communist parties are less corrupt than other leaders, and yet, apparently, some voters in Kerala think that if a leader is not corrupt they might not be able to help. I learnt this from my conversation with Professor Mohanakumar. Similarly, Witsoe (2011: 82–83) records that in the context of villages in Bihar in the 1990s: 'many people supported politicians not only despite perceptions that they were corrupt but also precisely because they were perceived as corrupt and therefore capable of using their positions for the benefit of their supporters'.

CLASS RELATIONS, CLASS STRUGGLE, AND THE STATE IN INDIA   263

that is capitalist is to reproduce capitalist-class dominance over the direct producers, struggles over democracy are centrally linked to the fact of class. In more recent times, struggles against the attack on democratic rights have focused on the attacks on religious minorities from fascistic forces.[65]

Apart from these four inter-connected forms of struggle of lower classes against various forms of injustice that more or less emanate from the capitalist character of the society and the state, the lower-class politics also takes forms that directly reproduce and support the unjust conditions of their own existence. Partly given the constraints that class structure imposes on lower-class politics and partly because of ruling class strategies to weaken potential lower-class opposition, the lower classes have engaged in various forms of politics that are ultimately not in their immediate or long-term interest and that are shaped by their false consciousness: providing support to parties of the right on the basis of identity politics of nationalism and religion; being a part of a clientilistic structure in which some powerful property-owners-cum-politicians provide limited assistance to lower classes in return for political support (e.g. votes) from them;[66] and constantly reposing faith in the bourgeois parties and indeed in the state as such as the set of institutions that one can appeal to for the improvement of one's conditions.

5   State Form, State Policy, and Class Struggle

That such struggles are waged by 'those below', means in turn that both the propertied classes and the state find it necessary to make concessions.[67] Many

---

65   It is important to stress that the map of lower-class struggles includes an inter-connected chain of struggles – the struggles against dispossession, disenfranchisement, and stigma or disrespect (Nilsen and Roy, 2015). Whether subalternity is the underlying factor underlying these struggles is a different matter.

66   Pattenden (2011) says that: owing to fiscal decentralization to gram panchayats, some members of the dominant class have control over the financial resources spent at the local scale, which they use to gain support from workers: this process reproduces new patterns of workers' dependence upon the dominant class. This points to how class state relations are played out at the local scale.

67   Of course, these concessions are used by capital (and state elites) for its own benefit, generating demand for commodities (farm implements, fertilizers, cattle for small producers). State elites also benefit, since implementation of these policies is a source of bribes and influence. In terms of urban labor, the state has sometimes initiated pro-labor legislations not as a direct response to actual struggle but as a preemptive response to avoid having to face such struggle (on this see Teitelbaum, 2013). Yet, according to Teitelbaum (2006), workers are more united and powerful than assumed.

scholars have maintained that important anti-poverty policies, including agrarian reform programs, have indeed been the result of 'from below' class struggles (Desai, 1989).[68] Even such accumulation projects as the Green Revolution were driven in part by the fear that actual or potential famine conditions during the 1960s might constitute a threat to the political order from the lower classes.[69] It is undeniably the case that the Green Revolution was in part offered as an *anti-poverty* policy. Similarly, the recent policy aimed at ensuring 100 days of employment to those seeking manual work in villages – the National Rural Employment Guarantee Programme – for which the political left fought, is another example of concession by 'those above'.[70]

It is a mistake, however, to assume that the *only* response the Indian state can make to 'from below' struggle is a conciliatory or defensive response: giving concession. The state frequently launches 'from above' class struggle in support of capital's economic interests and in the interest of maintaining political order. This comes in many forms. One is the commodification of 'commons', or common property resources that pre-dated capitalism and were an important component of direct producers' subsistence. Commons also take the form of state provided subsistence (for example, subsidized food for the poor), an achievement won as a result of grassroots struggle by lower classes.[71] State actions aimed at commodifying the commons are designed to further two ends: not just promoting capitalist development but also preventing – or pre-empting – any move towards the project of *transcending* capitalism and

---

68   The Hindu (2007) reported that the Janadesh March on October 28, 2007, when thousands of rural poor and landless arrived in Delhi to press their demands, the Union government announced on October 29 the setting up of a National Land Reforms Council. The latter would take a 'holistic approach' to land reforms and will come out with a National Land Reforms Policy.

69   There are, of course, other interpretations as to the driving force behind the Green Revolution programme. An external one was identified by Cleaver (1972), who maintained that overproduction of chemical inputs by agribusiness, destined for the US markets, meant that these enterprises looked to foreign markets in the Third World as an outlet for their commodities. Hence the Green Revolution package (chemical inputs and irrigation).

70   Arjun Sengupta, Chairperson of the National Commission for Enterprises in the Unorganized Sector, candidly connected class struggle to state policy. His words (cited in Dhar, 2007) were as follows: 'We must realise that the voiceless groups have now started to assert themselves by seeking their rights. This (social engineering in the form of universal employment guarantee) is one way of doing it. The other way would be through naxalism (or more generally, 'from below' struggles). This is the dynamics of the situation that is pushing us towards a more inclusive economic development'.

71   This policy has been watered down (Swaminathan, 2000).

CLASS RELATIONS, CLASS STRUGGLE, AND THE STATE IN INDIA 265

the capitalist state.[72] Another is a direct attack on working conditions in the form of policies that support exploitation of workers and small-scale producers by the property-owning class. And of course, when all else fails, repression is the response to class struggle.

Class struggles must additionally be seen as being influenced by the *form* taken by the Indian state, and not just by its actions. Hence the class character of Indian society, and the grassroots struggles arising from this, influence the nature of the state *form*, which in turn influences state *actions*. There are two dimensions to the state form: democratic and territorial. To begin with, therefore, is the double impact – as outcome of grassroots conflict and on the shape of such agency – of the fact that the Indian state currently exhibits a liberal democratic form.[73] Indeed, given severe forms of inequality and high level of poverty within the country, perhaps nowhere else in the world is the degree of the gap between substantive economic inequality and formal political equality as great as it is in India. This gap is decreasing though to the extent that the state-form is increasingly being more illiberal.

The existence and reproduction of the democratic form of the state itself must be seen partly as a product of continuing struggles by the lower classes in conjunction with other strata for democracy in the face of strong anti-democratic pressures from society.[74] The latter emanate from landlord elements that remain powerful in the countryside. More importantly, they also derive from the current nature of capitalism that depends increasingly on

---

72   One can even go further. The suppression by the Indian state of rural labor struggle against capital has, ironically, made it more vulnerable to capital. Among other things, this has enabled rich peasants, commercial farmers and agribusiness enterprises to conduct 'from above' forms of class struggle, including the reproduction and/or reintroduction of unfree labor (or what Brass calls deproletarianization). Misrecognizing the latter as evidence for the 'pre-' or 'non-capitalist' nature of the agrarian labor process has led to the epistemological confusion within the left about the nature of class contradiction. 'Feudal' or 'semi-feudal' landlords replace agrarian capitalists as the main target of 'from below' agency, and conflict between capital and labor gives way to a struggle between the broad masses and 'semi-feudal' landlords. Capitalism is as a result categorized as a desirable development, to be introduced by a 'progressive' bourgeoisie. This ideological mystification – arising from the fact that contemporary capitalist reality in rural India 'folds within itself a certain degree of falsity', to borrow a phrase from Eagleton (1999) – has contributed further to the disempowerment of agricultural labor and poor peasants.

73   India is unusual in this regard. It is similar to western developed countries in that the state has a liberal democratic form, but dissimilar in that a vast majority of the Indian population is dependent upon farming.

74   Although capitalism is compatible with liberal democracy, it does not necessarily need this.

various coercive measures that characterize primitive accumulation.[75] Threats to formal democracy also come from those (e.g. fascistic forces) who are opposed to gender equality and minority religions. Given the size of India, maintaining territorial and political order in half a million villages, 500 cities and thousands of towns amidst much deprivation is a difficult task for the class-state, which must constantly recycle/reinvent discourse about caste and religion so as to maintain order through the activities of political parties on the right and center of the political spectrum.

A liberal democratic capitalist state must not only promote accumulation but also legitimize this support by seeming to act on behalf of the whole nation, a strategy bolstered by making concessions. Arguably, the latter include the democratic form itself, which helps the state deflect or soften class antagonism by means of periodic elections. A secular form of religion for the masses, the capacity to exercise the vote at regular intervals provides lower classes with the illusion that it is they who exercise control over the state and the dominant classes. Not only does this fuel the hope that they gain material benefits from electoral patronage, but it also perpetuates the belief that if not this party/leader then the next one in power will address their problems.[76] The fetishistic worship of democracy is widely prevalent among the poor citizens and scholars. Indeed, thanks to the efforts of the state via educational institutions and publicity, etc., most people do not understand the following simple fact. Just as people are free to work for this or that capitalist employer but not free not to work under the control of a capitalist employer for a wage, similarly, people are free to choose this or that capitalist party, but not free not to vote for a capitalist party to power or a party that will fundamentally work within the constraints of capitalist property relations. Freedom to choose a party in elections, free or not, will not bring freedom from miseries: this is not understood by most people.[77]

The existence of the democratic form, of course, does not mean that it is the only form of class rule: indeed, when necessary the state will and does use coercion, increasingly so against the lower classes if they resist its accumulation policies beyond a certain limit. What is interesting to note is that the use of *coercion* against the lower classes is justified through the *democratic* form. Whichever party is in power, whether it is the 'centrist' Congress or the rightist

---

75   As Mandel (1969) notes, the state exercises coercion 'for maintaining the material interests of the strongest section of the exploiters'.

76   This is obviously a very different kind of hope to that referred to by Mandel (2002).

77   Roy says (2018) that India's democracy provides the country's poor with unique opportunities for political engagement and that the poor people are not, therefore, excluded from politics.

BJP (they are actually two factions of what could arguably be seen as a united party/front of the bourgeoisie, at least as far as economic policies are concerned), they tend to use violence against the lower classes if what the latter demand fundamentally challenges the dominant class elements. In fact, even the left front government has used repression against ordinary people protesting against the violation of their rights.[78]

When the state form is democratic, coercion is not seen as what it is – namely, suppression of lower classes by a class state acting on behalf of dominant class interests – but rather as what it appears to be. That is, it is merely seen as wrongful action carried out either by this or that political party in furtherance of an incorrect policy, or by officials/politicians who are misinformed as to what is really required. A corollary is that such agency by the state is in effect mistaken, an anomaly that can be rectified by changing the party in power, its leadership, or bureaucrats and officials carrying out the orders.[79] This is akin to Marx's theory of commodity fetishism, an ideological inversion (Ollman, 1993) whereby 'the relationships between producers [...] take on the form of a social relation between the products of labour' (Marx, 1977:164,165), when 'the definite social relation' among producers themselves assumes 'the fantastic form of a relation between things'. Similarly, what actually is a coercive relation between classes, enforced by the capitalist state, is mistakenly seen as a relation between voters/citizens on the one hand and parties, political leaders, and officials on the other. This is a relation that cannot be eliminated until the state is directly and socially regulated, in much the same way as commodity fetishism, as Rubin (1973) says, cannot be removed until labor power is directly and socially regulated.[80]

At the same time, however, excessive coercion can adversely affect political legitimacy of the parties in power and even of the state itself. In response to the numerous class struggles over the land issue during the 1960s, the federal government of India stated: 'It will be unrealistic to seek lasting solutions to a socioeconomic problem (i.e. unequal distribution of land)...through coercive measures alone' (Government of India, 1986). Thus the state is required to balance three processes: (i) accumulation; (ii) legitimation through material and non-material concessions, including the democratic form; and (iii) coercion.

---

78 Police have killed peasants resisting dispossession in CPM-ruled West Bengal and Congress ruled Andhra Pradesh.

79 The view that the state is an autonomous institution – popular among Weberian theorists – is consistent with this perception.

80 It is not just the rural poor who subscribe to this kind of reification. Both the postmodern 'left' and liberal political theorists do the same, as a result of which they endorse non-governmental organizational politics, aimed at putting pressure on the local-level state actors to change their ways.

The actual intervention over a period of time and over space must be seen as a mix of these three, the nature of which depends on the intensity of class struggle both inside and outside the state, as well as on the requirements of accumulation and the nature of a particular political regime that manages the affairs of the state.

The democratic state form also influences the shape taken by class struggle itself. On the one hand, it dissolves what are *classes* into *individuals* and – further – into *individual voters*. By giving opportunities for full expression to religious, casteist, ethnic and regional identities, the state fragments the lower classes into members of electoral groups, into supporters of this or that party (or fractions thereof), irrespective of their class position and interests, thereby weakening the power and agency as lower classes. Currently, democracy has enabled the property-owning class – including those who use unfree labor and are therefore *un*democratic in a substantive sense – to 'capture' specific parts of the state through liberal *democratic* elections. In some areas of India, therefore, proprietors are still able to compel lower class/caste members to vote as they (the landed) would like. Through their control over specific parts of the state – especially at the local/regional level – property owners appropriate the resources allocated by the state to the poor. On the other hand, by ensuring a limited degree of free association and speech, and through electoral procedures and the 'rule of law', the state in its democratic form has indeed allowed rural and urban workers who form the majority of the population, to voice limited opposition to economic exploitation and political domination. Within limits, they are permitted to exert pressure on the capitalist state to create conditions that favor the lower classes.[81]

The democratic state form has thus allowed competition between political parties which has contributed in varying degrees to the politicization of lower classes, and to the implementation of policies on their behalf such as land reform. Although much attention has been paid to competition between mainstream parties – see, for example, Chibber and Nooruddin (2004) – less has been said about the competition between these and leftist parties (see Bardhan and Mukherjee, 2005; Echeverri-Gent, 1995) and almost nothing about the competition *between* leftist parties. The latter is an important feature of India's liberal democracy, no matter how faulty democracy is and reformist many of

---

81   On the topic of how people's struggles have resulted in some developmental outcomes, see Williams (2009). It should be noted, however, that democracy, rather obviously, has not resulted in much reduction of substantive inequalities (Heller, 2000). It should be noted that the scope for egalitarian development has been shrinking within the neoliberal-capitalist phase that began since the early 1990s, which is why the state's response to lower-class struggles has been one of repression and ideological manipulation (e.g. the use of identity politics; lies, false promises, etc.), regardless of the political-party-regime.

CLASS RELATIONS, CLASS STRUGGLE, AND THE STATE IN INDIA   269

these parties are. It was the *inter-communist* party competition – not electoral competition or democracy as such – and the consequent extraordinary combination of parliamentary and direct-action strategies by the two left parties that it fostered in Kerala, that was responsible in part for a higher degree of implementation there of 'radical' tenancy reforms.[82]

Many commentators, including Amartya Sen (1999), assume that by encouraging competition between parties and allowing a free press, democracy will lead to the implementation of pro-poor policies. He says that what the government does can be influenced by public pressures from below (Dreze and Sen, 1995). But much depends on what issues are politicized. What is, or is not, politicized depends on the visions and pre-occupations of *opposition* parties. Non-communist *opposition* parties do not *oppose* ruling parties on crucial issues such as payment of compensation to landlords in the land reform laws or privatization of state-owned companies or India's subjugation to the imperialist military-economic framework. In other words, on class-related issues that do matter to the lower classes, opposition parties do *not* matter. Parties in power and parties in opposition do not oppose the fundamental interests of the business class. Both ruling and opposition parties work within the framework of a state that supports the fundamental interests of the propertied classes and share an anti-lower-class ideology which, in turn, contributes to the depoliticization of the crucial issues. Dreze and Sen ignore the fact that the ideology of the propertied classes and the coercive character of the state, among other things, influence what enters into political debates and what does not. Sen's view is problematic because it is silent about the class character of the parties/regimes, which manage the common affairs of the state, which, in turn, manages the common affairs of the capitalist class. Sen's optimistic prognosis, which I mentioned in Chapter 2, cannot answer the question why it is that crucial development issues – such as unequal distribution of means of production (particularly land), extreme forms of income inequality, absence of high-quality and free state-provided health-care and education, and employment for all at an inflation-adjusted living wage – do not become important election issues, and are not much debated by competing mainstream parties (Das, 2001a). Democracy can help in the promulgation and implementation of policies favorable to the lower classes, but within limits. If these classes are to secure significant access to economic resources, including land, in the

---

82   It is significant that, with the exception of isolated pockets, these two left parties have more-or-less given up on extra-parliamentary actions. The resulting vacuum, in terms of class politics, has been filled in some areas – and especially in eastern India – by the parties/formations that are influenced by Maoism.

democratic process – so as to enjoy the health and educational freedoms which Sen rightly thinks all human beings should – then this at least requires the severe curtailment of political power exercised by dominant proprietary classes. And for this to happen, democracy must also involve competition and polemical struggle as well as a degree of collaboration between/among left parties, and democracy must allow genuine struggle between them and mainstream parties. Yet, the fact that remains that the (bourgeois) democratic state form itself poses severe limits to the capacity of lower classes to gain enough power to be able to secure resources from governments that must promote capitalist interests.

The other dimension of the state concerns its territorial or geographical form.[83] It is commonly agreed that the federal nature of the Indian state has meant that individual states possess some autonomy in framing and implementing policies (and this is especially so with respect to agriculture, police, education, health, etc.). A federal bourgeois state-form emerged mainly as a product of two processes. First, the struggle between members of the bourgeoisie at regional and national levels, over issues such as regional markets and labor reserves (Kosambi, 1957). And second, a similarly regional struggle conducted by lower classes (Vanaik, 1990). This territoriality of the state form provides regional components of the dominant class (regional bourgeoisie) of middle and higher castes some leeway, enabling them to pursue their class and caste interests by influencing the state at sub-national levels.

This form also creates – albeit unintentionally – spaces within the state structure that lower classes are able to use to their advantage within limits. It is this combination of territorial state form and class struggle that, in a context of uneven development nationally, results in regionally specific bourgeois-political-economies throughout India. The latter vary from regimes dominated by traditional landlords from the upper castes – such as, for example, Madhya Pradesh and Orissa – to one where their dominance has been challenged by capitalist farmers and rich peasant groups from middle caste backgrounds. Lower classes/castes are to a greater or lesser extent accommodated (Gujarat and Maharashtra being instances of the former, Bihar and Uttar Pradesh of the latter), while in yet other sub-national states their interests are better

---

83   The geographical form of the state includes: the central level; the provincial/State level; the local level (e.g. village or taluka or the district) interaction between state institutions and common citizens (mainly lower classes); relations between the central level and the provincial level; relations between provinces; relations between the local level and provincial/national levels; and relations between the different levels (especially, provincial and national levels) and the global-scale processes and institutions (Das, 1998; Sinha, 2011; also see Jacob, 2015).

CLASS RELATIONS, CLASS STRUGGLE, AND THE STATE IN INDIA   271

represented, such as in Kerala. And there are similar variations within a province in terms of organization of lower classes and (institutionalization of) Left power.

Under certain conditions, therefore, lower classes 'ruling' at the sub-national level can formulate and implement area-specific policies that reflect their interests. Wherever this has occurred in the past – Kerala, West Bengal and Tripura, being obvious examples (Desai, 2003; Kohli, 1987; Heller, 2000; Pillai, 2003) – the following developments have resulted:

a) The political legitimization of struggles by workers and small-scale producers in rural and urban areas, no matter how limited that acceptability is. This outcome is underlined by the decision of leftist governments not to allow the police to interfere in confrontations involving landlords and tenants in Kerala during the era of land reform;[84]

b) The mitigation of class exploitation through anti-poverty policies in a relatively uncorrupt manner and social sector investment;

c) A political decentralization which empowers lower classes at the village level;

d) A stable environment where accumulation based on private property can proceed.[85]

Of significance has been the limited expansion of trade-union rights and, particularly, of broad civil rights and the legal prohibition of extra-economic coercive practices by landowners, at least, during the early period of the left regimes. Similarly important is the fact that at a sub-national level the left has facilitated the construction of an agrarian 'accumulation strategy'. For example, the devolution of power to lower classes has enabled – within limits – the provincial state to 'discipline' erstwhile landowners. As a result, there has been a decline in the share of the crop taken as rent, in the incidence of eviction, and some land has been redistributed. Limited financial support has also been provided to small holders (Bhattacharyya, 2001). What all this demonstrates, albeit tentatively, is that even a moderately reformist development strategy entailing redistribution of economic resources is in the end a reflection of the local balance of class forces: where state apparatuses are governed by left

---

84   For example, in Kerala the 'new police policy' prevented intervention in agrarian disputes in all cases except when life was in danger. Much the same happened in West Bengal during the 1960s when Mr. H. Konar was the land reform Minister in that state.

85   One should note that the last aspect of the left's social-democratic type regime (ensuring capitalist accumulation) sets limit to what can be achieved in terms of the first two. And indeed, the importance of the first two aspects has been reduced over time in the provinces where the Left has been in power.

parties, and where the left is well organized, lower-class input into these policies has been greater and the implementation of these policies in their interests has been better.

The lower classes have been able to win some concessions through their parties (Left parties). However, since 2009, these parties (which are, more or less, social-democratic in practice) have experienced drastic electoral decline, and this is partly related to neoliberalism as discussed in Chapter 4. Two things should be said about this. The political power of the Left cannot be reduced to electoral success or defeat, however. While the Left's mobilizational power may not be evident at the national scale, that does not mean that it is not powerful in specific areas within the country or a province. The fact that the Left is not that powerful at the national and provincial scales is used by right-wing people to say that the Left is irrelevant, that it is dead. And such a conclusion helps to *legitimize* right-wing policies and thinking.

While capital – labor relation is everywhere, the ways in which that relation is experienced are locally rooted. This is the case in the West (Cox, 1988) and in India (Das, 2001b). In terms of the ways in which labor markets generally function, they are quite localized. Similarly, relations between landlords and moneylenders on the one hand and small-scale producers as tenants and debtors on the other hand, are locally rooted: their relations are experienced within geographically circumscribed areas. If Left politics – organization of lower classes – has to succeed, it has to begin in specific areas, and then scale up to higher geographical levels such as district, province, etc. In other words, Left organization has to be multi-scalar.

Indeed, state power in India is exercised at multiple scales. In the rural context, these are: central level (Delhi); States/provinces; districts within a State; sub-districts/tehsil within a district; development block within a tehsil; cluster of villages (Panchayat) in a development block; revenue or administratively defined single villages; and wards/neighborhoods/hamlets. In terms of urban India, there are: central level (Delhi); States/provinces; cities with their mayors, etc.; wards/neighborhoods within a city, and so on.

While left/radical/Marxist politics has lost some of its power at the Central and provincial scales, there are literally hundreds of wards/hamlets, cities, village-clusters or development blocks, villages, etc. where Marxists and radicals are relatively powerful, and they are exercising their power, however limited, to make the state and employers do what they would otherwise not do. That there are serious limits to what Left parties can achieve – and these limits are partly because of their limited ideological compass as mentioned in Chapter 3 – is a separate topic (see Chapter 13).

6   The Indian State and the Class Contradictions of Economic Development

In view of its class character, the state is rather obviously a contradiction-ridden entity, and this in turn problematizes its development role. One consequence of having to manage conflicts is that the Indian state has been unable to play the same kind of developmental role (building infrastructure for agricultural and for industrial development) as the East Asian state (Amsden, 1998).[86] Another is the outcome of tax avoidance or evasion by the dominant classes: the shortfall in state revenues means that state expenditure is concentrated in specific regions. This creates a basis for regionally uneven economic development, which complements the inherent tendency towards uneven development under capitalism.

The most important outcome of this uneven economic development is, as noted earlier, a corresponding geographical unevenness to grassroots struggles (lower-class struggles).[87] Regional variations throughout India in terms of economic development shape the form and intensity of class conflict, along with factors such as the caste-class correlation, the nature and quality of lower class leadership, and the degree of left-wing unity.[88] This effect of uneven development is a geographically fragmented process of class formation and struggle, which is an important contributory factor in the weakness of a 'from below' challenge to the state at the national level, where the power of the dominant classes is concentrated and protected.

---

86   One should be careful not to over-stress this point: it is problematic to assume that the state under capitalism could play a positive role in promoting development on a sustainable long term basis, rural or urban. The positive role of the nation-state in, for example, East Asia has been overstated, and its negative role correspondingly understated (Burkett and Hart-Landsberg, 2003).

87   The state responds to unevenness of class struggle through a spatial fix. Urban workers, for example, tend to be more organized than rural workers, which permits income deflation through unfavorable terms of trade to operate against agriculture (Patnaik, 1995:168). Class struggle in the urban areas reinforces this spatial fix, accentuating the rural-urban disparity. There are contradictions, however, as squeezing the countryside (and this really means squeezing its lower classes) creates the problem of agrarian backwardness which can be a fetter on industrial development.

88   It must be said that some of the most courageous left movements lack a coherent rigorous radical theory (applicable to the Indian social formation as opposed to its component local formations). Accordingly, they suffer politically from problems of empiricism (their views about society and tactics change according to locations) and from associated localization of the movements they lead (see Nathan, 1999).

When seen in terms of development policies for the lower classes/castes and in relation to class struggle, therefore, the Indian state is, once again, a deeply contradictory entity. If lack of grassroots power contributes to poverty, the process of regionally uneven development fostered by the capitalist state reproduces and entrenches that powerlessness: the state must therefore be seen as an important cause of lower-class poverty. This is one of the many reasons why one should be critical of those – among them postmodernists, supporters of NGOs and advocates of social capital – who regard decentralization of state power as part of the solution to poverty and underdevelopment, rather than as part of the problem.[89] Looked at differently, the issue of decentralization is one about the scale – and thus the efficacy – of opposition to the capitalist state.

In India, as elsewhere, scale is indeed central to the success or failure of the class struggle. Of significance, therefore, is the fact that the vast NGO sector, much favored as an 'alternative' form of development, grows out of, and is in tune with, neoliberal policies of the state (Petras, 1997). For its part, the neoliberal state is highly supportive of most NGOs, which act as its development subcontractors. While the left movement seeks to organize and formulate policy at the national and provincial levels, much NGO activity by contrast is resolutely small-scale, in terms both of issues addressed and the area covered. Although the work carried out by a few NGOs is of benefit to the poor, this kind of piecemeal approach to poverty tends to reinforce the fragmented nature of grassroots opposition to capitalism and its state, and to provide the latter with a semblance of ideological legitimacy, by fulfilling an ameliorating role (= 'survival') within the existing system.[90]

The three processes outlined above – the near-abrogation by the state of its development role, the sub-contracting of micro-level 'survival' projects to NGOs, and the organizational weakness of multi-scalar class-based opposition in the face of poverty and inequality – raise once again the following political question: can the Indian state face a legitimation crisis? In this context, the following points can be made.

To begin with, it is important to recall that, from the standpoint of lower classes, the colonial state did not discharge a developmental role; in part,

---

89   On the decentralization debate, see among many others Veron et al. (2006). On non-party grassroots politics (which does not aim to control power through electoral or by other means), see Kothari (2002), and Harriss (2011c).

90   Harriss (2011c) says that in neoliberal India, there is the popularity of a new politics: this is based in communities, not workplaces, on voluntary associations in civil society and not political parties, and on social movements and not trade unions (p. 91). The new politics excludes the poor as active agents. The organizations may work for the poor, but they are not of the poor (p. 92). New politics is against the state and not against the employer (p. 103).

CLASS RELATIONS, CLASS STRUGGLE, AND THE STATE IN INDIA   275

therefore, the post-1947 state in India gained a degree of ideological legitimation from its promise to foster economic development, a break with the approach of the colonial state. About this Partha Chatterjee (1993: 203) observes:

> The new state represented the only legitimate form of the exercise of power because it was a necessary condition for the *development* of the nation. [...] (it) acquired its representativeness by directing a program of economic *development* on behalf of the nation.

Accordingly, the legitimacy of the state in the era of Independence 'had to flow from ... the historical necessity of an independent state that would promote national *development*' (Chatterjee, 1993: 205; emphasis added).[91]

Like the earlier colonial state, however, the current neoliberal state in India is not fulfilling (and as importantly, not being seen to fulfill) a developmental role. Hence the development process – both the material benefits and discourses/rhetoric of development including such slogans as *garibi hatao* (eradicate poverty) – no longer discharges for the state the legitimizing role to the same extent it did earlier, in the more optimistic decades following Independence.[92] This is certainly true of the way the state is 'seen' by 'those below' in many parts of eastern India, where there exist very strong radical militant organizations of the rural poor. There the reduction in spending by the neoliberal state on anti-poverty policies – a process termed the selective retreat of the state – has indeed eroded its legitimacy in the eyes of the vast majority of the rural population in terms of promoting development. For lower classes, therefore, the state is not perceived as a 'caring' state to the same extent it was earlier, both materially and discursively. If capital says to labor 'perform or perish', cannot labor say the same to capital's state?

The potential legitimation crisis arising from the failure of the state to fulfil its development role – i.e. to act as a 'developmental state' – also has a scale aspect. Previously, and however misguidedly, citizens in the vast rural periphery subscribed to the belief that that higher-level state institutions really

---

91   Some scholars say that the colonial state was characterized by a dominance without hegemony while the postcolonial state is characterized by a passive revolution (Chatterjee, 2017).

92   Roy (2018) says that poor people are central to Indian politics in that the poor engage with their elected representatives, political mediators and dominant classes in varied ways in order to advance their claims, and that public policy and political parties, and development plans and elected representatives derive their legitimacy in the name of the poor. The point is: if the poor (lower classes) can be a source of legitimacy at one time, they can be a source of its opposite – the crisis of legitimacy – at another time.

wanted to help the poor, and that it was only the local scale officials/politicians that were mismanaging the resources.[93] A villager confirmed this to Akhil Gupta (2000) in the following manner: 'Although the government has many good schemes, the officials in the middle eat it all'. I too have come across this type of responses from the lower classes in Orissa as well in my research on the state, social capital and poverty (Das, 2005). Thus the potential crisis of legitimation used to be confined largely to the local state. Now, however, with central government – even the judiciary at the provincial and national scales – openly espousing neoliberalism (and its twin, authoritarianism), all levels of the state apparatus are vulnerable in this respect.

Of additional relevance is that the ideological illegitimacy of the colonial state derived from its being 'other' economically: that is, it was seen as serving the external ('foreign', 'non-Indian') interests in furtherance of which it licensed the exploitation of Indian workers and peasants. The ideological legitimacy of the post-1947 state, and a central emplacement of Indian nationalist discourse, emanated from the fact that it would be independent of an international capitalism. Hence the legitimacy of the Indian state 'had to flow from the nationalistic criticism of colonialism as an alien and unrepresentative power' (Chatterjee, 1993: 205). The point is that now – and once again – the state is creating the conditions for the transfer of profits to the foreign capital: indeed, the neoliberal Indian state is actively encouraging international capital to exploit its own lower classes, a process in which domestic capitalists – urban and rural – are invited to participate. Under neoliberalism, capital has no nation. Even capitalists from a poor nation such as India, in pursuit of profit, are investing capital in the richest countries such as Canada, the US and the UK, and indeed thousands of dollar millionnaires from India are leaving India (6000 left in 2016 and 7000 in 2017). To this has to be added the fact that many smaller business units are going under because of neoliberal competition and withdrawal of state protection, thereby narrowing the class/social basis of the capitalist state. The nationalistic dream – the idea that there is a nation and what the state does is good for the nation – may be on the way out. If the concept of nation has any significance, it must, first of all, be the 'nation' of workers and small-scale producers, yet the neoliberal state is increasingly alienating itself from *this* 'nation'. And this is why, there is a need to construct another nation, one that is based on religious etc. identity. This strategy creates internal enemies of the fake nation (e.g. religious minorities and politically progressive

---

93   For a similar case of mistrust in the local state combined with trust in the central state, in the context of China, see So (2007). On the 'development state' in Latin America, see Petras and Veltmeyer (2007).

people defending democratic rights), so the real nation is divided and weakened and does not concentrate the real enemies of the nation. The real enemies are (a) the capitalist class in whose interest policies are being formed by all kinds of governments, and (b) all those who support this class and all those who are creating disunity within *the nation of toiling masses* in the name of religion (hard or soft Hindutva), and by using a false sense of history, and so on.

Another contributory factor in this delegitimization process is that action by the neoliberal state is perceived to lack rationality. The colonial state was exporting wheat from India to the UK when in India itself the population did not have sufficient food to eat. In a similar vein, the neoliberal state is now seen as irrational in promoting the production of luxury commodities, such as flowers, shrimps and animal feed for export to imperialist/rich countries, when millions are malnourished and hungry at home.[94] The state-promoted export of these new agricultural commodities is itself based on cheap labor and cheap land. 'Cheap', however, hides the ecological and social conditions under which these commodities are produced by peasants and workers, many of whom are lower-caste women. Cheapness is not a characteristic innate to India, either to the (tattered) bodies of its workforce or to its (degraded) nature, both of which are deployed by neoliberal capitalist accumulation (this issue is discussed in the last chapter).[95]

The perceived difference between the colonial state and its post-1947 counterpart – a crucial ideological one – thus no longer holds.[96] This is because the state is no longer able to sustain even the fiction of carrying out policies designed to benefit large swathes of the Indian polity – the 'people' who form 'the nation', in other words. The failure is more drastic with the turn to neoliberalism, and to right-wing politics associated with the rise of BJP as a hard-right governing party. In fact, the neoliberal state-form and state intervention (the state's relative withdrawal from welfare-provision, and a certain degree of control over the business class) were justified on the basis that the neoliberal state is good for the masses but as we have seen, this has turned out to be a lie. Neoliberalization has hurt the masses, including by dispossessing them of their small-scale property, so the neoliberal form of the state cannot have the legitimacy in the minds of the ordinary people.[97]

---

94   As others have argued, per capita food availability has declined to levels experienced during the 1943 Bengal famine (Patnaik, 2002, 1999).

95   See Harvey (1998) and Smith (2007) for discussions about the body, nature and capitalism.

96   There are many other aspects of the difference between the colonial and the postcolonial state than those discussed here (see Murphy and Jammaulamadaka, 2017).

97   Chacko (2018) says that there is a long-term crisis of the state because successive governments have been unable to establish legitimacy for the post-1990s policies of

While neoliberalism is deeply against the interests of the masses, the state and the business class justify neoliberalism on the ground that it helps and will help the poor. Apart from the differences/contradictions between the colonial state and the post-colonial state, there are important differences/contradictions between the pre-neoliberal state and the neoliberal state. While the personnel of the state before the mid-1980s, often drawn from lower strata of society (e.g. petty-bourgeois strata), maintained some distance between them and the capitalist class, now the personnel of the state revel in their connections with, and take pride from their work for, the business class. The social legitimacy of the state clearly is at stake because the state, at least, has to give the appearance that it is neutral, that it is for everyone, for all classes. But maintaining such an appearance is difficult because a distinctive change in the class character of the personnel of the state, as Prabhat Patnaik (2018) eloquently describes, prior to neoliberalism:

> The State personnel drawn from the ranks of the petty bourgeoisie were generally skeptical about, and even to a degree hostile to, the capitalist class and were committed to State capitalism which they also saw as a means of self- advancement in the new situation of de-colonization. The State was a bourgeois State, laying the foundations for capitalist development. But the motivation, the ideological inclinations, and the class background of the State personnel ensured that the State had a degree of autonomy both vis a vis imperialism and also vis a vis the domestic capitalists.

However, something has changed with the turn to neoliberalism:

> The "neo-liberal State" too is a bourgeois State like the *dirigiste* State, but the personnel of the former differ fundamentally from the personnel of the latter, not just in their ideological predilections, which are closely aligned to the views of the Bretton Woods institutions, *but also in their being deeply enmeshed with the world of finance and big business.* What we find in today's State personnel is not just a different set of ideologues, World Bank ideologues, as distinct from the Nehruvian ideologues that manned the *dirigiste* bourgeois State, but a set whose motivation is no different from that of the big bourgeoisie and financial interests and

---

neoliberalization. Similarly, Levien (2013) argues that while the pre-neoliberal state dispossessed small-scale producers like the neoliberal state does now, the latter has been unable to achieve the ideological legitimacy of its predecessor, leading to more widespread struggles against state-enabled dispossession.

CLASS RELATIONS, CLASS STRUGGLE, AND THE STATE IN INDIA

which therefore has no compunctions about being closely integrated with the latter.[98]

This is something Harsh Mander (2016), a former top civil servant also remarks on:

> in my time no official would be seen spending time with businesses. If an official socialised with the rich and the powerful, the official was considered someone who lacked integrity. Today you can claim to be doing it in the name of nation-building and advancing the economy.

As a result of this, there has been an 'undermining of the social legitimacy of the State', and this 'especially in the context of the tremendous increase in wealth and income inequalities associated with the pursuit of the neo-liberal strategy' (Patnaik, 2018).

Whether all these structural conditions will actually result in a legitimation crisis, and to what extent, will, of course, depend on how the lower classes and their political parties and their organic intellectuals at home and internationally, respond to these conditions politically.[99] And to the degree that the crisis does take shape, much also will depend on how the state reacts, in particular its deployment of coercive power at its disposal, and in turn how lower classes respond to this. There is also a possibility that the crisis of the state will be manifested as the crisis of parts of the state.[100]

---

98   Patnaik adds: 'The matter relates not just to anti-poverty programmes. The personnel of the neo- liberal State have little interest in running the public sector, which is one reason why the public sector becomes financially unviable over time, and provides grist to the mill of those who want it privatized. Even normal government functions are not carried out by the bureaucracy, which is more interested in networking with patrons in the world of corporates and foreign donors, or in attending World Bank-sponsored training programmes, than in the nitty-gritty of administration. More and more government functions as a result are "outsourced" to private agencies, which promises profits for all'. (Patnaik, 2018). It is however important not to over-emphasize this change in personnel which concerns instrumentalist control of the bourgeois. It is the capitalist class character of neoliberalism that has led to the state being managed by bourgeois personnel (people who either include members of the bourgeoisie or who are shaped by bourgeois ideas and aspirations), and that in turn is responsible for the on-going reproduction of the capitalist-neoliberal order.

99   For a different view of the crisis of the Indian state, one that stresses ethnic politics, see Mukherji (2014).

100 According to Kaviraj (2011): governments, bureaucracy, army, etc. – the parts that make the state – are seen by people as corrupt or inefficient or dreaded, while the state 'as a powerful regulatory idea' continues to exist in their mind, an idea that is involved in every

7 Conclusion

In the analysis of the state, including the state in a specific country, the class character of the state is generally obscured or mystified. To do a class analysis of the state often prompts a charge of analytical bias (because the state is assumed by most to work as a neutral agent), as well as the charge of economism and 'classism'. The latter charge implies that a class analysis of the state reduces the state to class relations and to its economic imperatives, and thus ignores non-class social relations such as caste and gender, etc.

The main aim of this chapter has been to implicitly respond to these charges and to explicitly re-assert the class character of the state. It is a truism, albeit a crucial one, that class relations and the attendant material conditions constitute the most important context for all forms of intervention by the state and for the very form (territorial and political form) of the state itself. Of course, within this class context other social relations – i.e. those of caste, religion, ethnicity, region and nation – operate and influence the state and its class character at a concrete level.

So reasserted in this chapter is the class view of the Indian state. Because capitalism is the dominant mode of production in India, the state is a capitalist state, and thus an agent of capitalist development, both in pre-neoliberal and neoliberal times, and both in rural and urban areas. The relation of partnership between the two arms of capital relation – the state and the capitalist class – has been justified in terms of two major ideologies: one is of state control and socialism, and another is one of free market (and its twin, communal-hyper-nationalistic authoritarianism). Ideology does not mean total lies. Ideology refers to ideas that are partly true and partly false and that contribute to the reproduction of an exploitative and oppressive order (Eagleton, 1991). The ideology of state control over the business world in India in the early years of the post-1947 period was not entirely a lie. There *was* a degree of state control. There was a degree of state intervention on behalf of the masses. Even the ruling class understood from the very beginning (since the 1940s) that a small degree of state control and a small degree of pro-poor re-distribution is a remedy to potential social upheaval. In the neoliberal times, the ideology of free market has justified serious intervention in the interest of capital while it seeks to make common people believe that it lacks the resources to help them in any

---

demand for justice. In other words, there is no crisis of legitimacy of the state, although its parts have 'lost some of their legitimacy, in a rising tide of undirected and uncontrollable social aspiration ... There is no end in sight of the Indian society's strange enchantment with the modern state' (p. 46).

significant manner. In other words, the state has always worked, more or less, in the interest of the capitalist class (see Sen, 2017; Das Gupta, 2016). Its policies (as well its form – federal-liberal-democratic form) have been accordingly influenced by the interests/actions of the dominant classes, although they have also been, to some extent, shaped by the lower-class struggles, actual or potential.

Like any capitalist state, the state in India must sustain the myth that capitalist accumulation (which goes by the name of 'growth') benefits not just the already-better-off entrepreneurs, and that the poor also gain some advantages from it. The myth needed is that the exploiters (misnamed as employers and wealth-creators) and the exploited benefit from the same process. The legitimacy of the post-1947 state derived in no small measure from two assumptions: that, unlike colonial government which served 'foreign' interests, it would serve domestic ones; and that, to this end, it would promote economic development from which the nation as a whole benefited. Increasingly, however, the distinction between the pre-1947 and post-1947 development projects is being eroded, as the neoliberal state not only facilitates the dispossession and exploitation of the poor by international and domestic capital, but also encourages the latter to undertake export-oriented cultivation. Farm crops are once again being seen to be produced mainly for an elite (= 'foreign') market, much as they were during the colonial era. This can contribute to the broader process of delegitimizing the development state, a situation which in turn intensifies class struggle 'from below', and the repressive 'from above' response by the neoliberal state protecting the interests of the capitalist class in India.

Because of a continuing failure on the part of the state to promote development in the interest of workers and small-scale producers and because of its current neoliberal policies supportive of domestic and foreign capital, this apparatus may face a legitimation crisis, especially in rural areas and in urban slums. Might the economic crisis of accumulation, including crisis of livelihood, and the legitimation crisis of the state (or its political crisis), lead to a larger crisis, i.e. a crisis of democracy itself and of the bourgeois system as a whole, which might be manifested as the strengthening of fascistic tendencies? Whether the potential for such a systemic crisis, that affects both the ruling class the masses, will be realized depends on how the lower classes and their organizations respond to the situation politically. Indeed, the topic of how the lower classes fight for their rights and how the state responds, is an important one. This will be discussed in the next two chapters.

CHAPTER 8

Class Dynamics of Poverty, State Failure, and Class Struggle

Historical materialism views human society through the lens of class struggle, a concept that, unfortunately, is unfashionable today.[12] This historical materialist view conjures up several significant ideas. One is that: humans *make* their own history, as Marx asserts on the opening page of his *Eighteenth Brumaire* (Marx, 2000: 329). But what does making history (and geography) really mean? It means, among other things, creating something that would not otherwise exist, in the absence of purposeful (collective) human interventions (Callinicos, 2004). A more specific instance of intervening in the world is fighting against its various forms of injustice. Though a critic of most tenets of historical materialism, Giddens (1981: 224), echoes Marx, to some extent, when he says: 'unless drugged or beaten – and usually not even then – human beings fight back [against oppression], for a part of being a human agent is to know that … one has the capability of exercising agency'. Marx and Engels had a more explicitly *class-specific* version of this view, when they wrote in 1847 in the *Communist Manifesto*, emphasizing *class* rather than just *human* agency: the oppressed classes – plebeians, slaves, serfs and workers – 'stood in constant opposition' to their oppressors, in the quest for justice (Marx and Engels, 1977: 108–109). This is an idea repeated in a letter written in 1879 to German activists: 'For almost 40 years we have emphasized that the class struggle is the immediate driving power of history … we, therefore, cannot possibly co-operate with people who wish to expunge this class struggle from the movement' (Marx and Engels, 1982: 307). For historical materialists, therefore, making history means that existing conditions of life are not acceptable because they are exploitative and oppressive, and that new and better conditions of life can, and must, be created, and that they can only be created through political struggles against the class/ classes responsible for the existing conditions. The act of making history (and geography) in a class-society *is*, ultimately, class struggle. In this precise

---

1   An earlier version of this chapter appeared as Das (2009).
2   Historical materialism includes what David Harvey famously calls historical-geographical materialism, which is a geographically-inflected historical materialism. The latter takes seriously the issues of space (geographical unevenness), place and scale (Harvey, 1996).

© KONINKLIJKE BRILL NV, LEIDEN, 2020 | DOI:10.1163/9789004415560_009

sense is the history of society the history of class struggle, as stressed in the opening lines of the *Communist Manifesto*.

Implicit in the class view of society is an interesting dialectical connection. This connection is between the conditions of existence and class struggle. Conditions of existence include what Marx (2000: 425), in *Preface to the Critique of Political Economy*, referred to as 'material productive forces' and 'relations of production' (and the empirical effects, such as various forms of deprivation emerging partly from the contradiction between the two). Because these conditions are exploitative, they *require* (necessitate) class struggle for their transcendence, and they *prompt* (make possible) class struggle for this purpose. The second aspect of the dialectic is that: these conditions not only prompt class struggle, but also condition, or set limits on, class struggle (i.e. class struggle from below, the class struggle of the oppressed). For, humans make history not as they choose but under the historical-geographical conditions transmitted from the past (Marx, 2000: 329; Harvey, 2000: 47).

The conditions under which people live can now be interpreted more broadly than usual. They must be seen as encompassing not only material conditions, but also ideas that people produce in the process of living under, reflecting on, and struggling against, the material conditions. These ideas can include the ideas that signify disrespect towards certain groups, and ideas that prompt people to support or to fight oppression. An idea can act like a material force when many people have it, as Marx said. Plekhanov, widely regarded as the father of Russian Marxism, said: 'once the forms of [people's] consciousness have sprung from the soil of social being, they become a part of history' (1971: 116), a history that 'weighs like a nightmare on the brain of the living' (Marx, 2000: 329). The conditions of existence include not only ideas but also the state that seeks to create order (Lenin, 1977b: 11). As discussed in the previous chapter, the state seeks to create an order not only by interventions in support of the dominant classes, but also by *repressing* exploited classes and seeking to elicit their consent to the system's reproduction, including through selective bribes. State policies often take the form of 'development', on the ground and on paper. These must be construed partly as a form of class struggle from above, launched on behalf of the propertied. The chapter focuses on the first aspect of the dialectic, in the historical-geographic context of India (i.e. how conditions of existence create political spaces for class struggle). It will only briefly discuss the second aspect.

The anti-imperialist struggle in the less developed world embodied a great dream. This was a dream that *post* independence, the unjust conditions of existence created by colonialism would be removed, and that people would live a better life. They would eat more and better. They would live a life of dignity.

This dream remained unfulfilled, more or less, at least for the most disadvantaged classes, groups and regions. 'Spaces of hope' that millions of villages represented, became spaces of despair. New exploitative conditions were produced, while old conditions were left intact by the post-colonial state and new ruling classes (in a way not dissimilar to what Fanon feared). The cross-class nationality struggle soon gave way to class struggle from below, 'now hidden, now open fight' (Marx and Engels, 1977: 109).

The struggle by common people takes different forms in different countries and places. In the Indian context, one of these is the Naxalite movement. It is so called because it started in the Naxalbari region of the West Bengal province. The Naxalite movement is a part of the worldwide Maoist movement.[3] Even if one is broadly critical of the movement, it is possible to say that 'it has been the principal defender of the poorest and most deprived against their class oppressors and the politicians, bureaucrats, police and paramilitaries backing them at various levels' (Vanaik, 2011: 102). Since the late 1960s, it has undergone a scalar transformation: from a local flare-up to a regional, and some might say, a national-scale movement. It has spread to 40% of the country's geographical area. Some form of the movement exists in about 20 of the country's 29 provinces, including 223 districts out of a total of 640; in 2003, only 55 districts were affected (Ismi, 2013) (see Map 8.1).

Sumanta Banerjee (2017), a sympathetic commentator on the Naxalite movement, says that the Naxalite/Maoist armed struggle is the longest surviving revolutionary movement in the history of peasant resistance in India. Shah and Jain (2017: 1215) say that: the Naxalite movement is 'the world's longest standing revolutionary struggle' (see also Mukherji, 2012: 5). The former Prime Minister of India, Dr. Singh, of the centrist Congress Party, the traditional party of the Indian proprietary classes, called the Naxalites the single biggest national security threat.[4] The BJP government, the right-wing government in power now, is very aggressive towards Naxalism. The study of radical movements claiming to *change* the conditions of existence in the world is an opportunity to *interpret* the conditions that prompt them in a way in which lessons can be drawn to facilitate the act of changing the world, even if the lessons might not be liked by participants and supporters of a given movement. The Naxalite movement, including its geography, is also a window on an Indian countryside in perpetual developmental crisis.

---

3   Often, by the term 'Maoist', some refer to the activities of the CPI (Maoist). I use the term 'Naxalite' and 'Maoist' as a generic category to refer to the class-based social movement in India that is ideologically informed by Maoism, which originated in Naxalbari, and which includes activities of CPI (Maoist).

4   This prompted The Financial Times to say 'A spectre is haunting South Asia – the spectre of Maoism' (quoted in Callinicos, 2010).

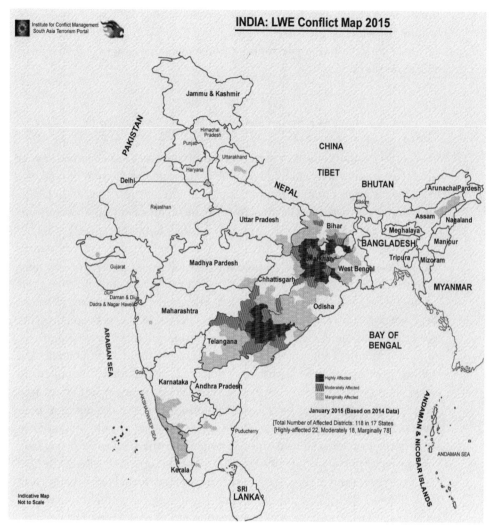

MAP 8.1 Geography of the Maoist Movement
Note: The darker the areas, the more active is the Maoist movement.
SOURCE: HTTP://WWW.SATP.ORG/SATPORGTP/COUNTRIES/INDIA/DATABASE/LWE_CONFLICTMAP2015.HTML

This chapter briefly looks at some of the material conditions in India's rural areas in relation to Naxalism, from the 1960s to the present time. The remainder of the chapter has four sections. Section 1, which follows this Introduction, discusses how relations of class and social oppression have created difficult conditions of living for the rural poor. I also briefly consider the failure of the post-colonial capitalist-landlord state to counter these conditions, thus suggesting that state's failure itself is an aspect of poor people's life. It is the unjust conditions of living that have created a situation 'ripe' for class struggle, one instance of which is the Naxalite movement. Its growth and spread are dealt with in Section 2. Section 3 presents a critique of the movement. A final section concludes the chapter.

1 Class Dynamics, State Failure and Poverty in Rural India

The material conditions of existence of the rural masses are structured by relations of production including relations of unequal distribution of land, the main means of production. They are also influenced by relations of social oppression based on gender (partly signifying the relations of reproduction) and caste/ethnicity. During colonial times, the British imperialists created highly unequal agrarian class relations. A significant aspect of this was an extremely unequal distribution of land: by the time they left, fewer than 12% of families owned 65% of all land.[5] During the nationalist movement and after, there was a demand for a more egalitarian agrarian order from peasants, many of whom were organized by the communists. But to maintain the class unity of the movement, nationalist leaders did not pay serious attention to this demand. After formal independence, the post-colonial state sought to implement land reforms that would make agrarian relations more egalitarian. The policy did not achieve much success. More than a decade after the British left, about 40% of India's land was owned by 5% of rural households, who did not farm their plots personally. Pauperized small holders began selling plots of land to meet their subsistence expenditures. Inequality in the ownership/control over land continues: in 1995–96, approximately 7% of families operated 66% of the land (GOI, 2007:109), and in 2003, less than 10% of families owned more than 56% of land (Bhalla, 2006: 34). On the other hand, the number of landless households, or families who were near-landless (owning less than 5 acres) has been increasing (albeit rather slowly): in 2003, these families constitute 90.4% of rural households, an increase of more than 20% since the mid-1950s (Bhalla, 2006: 34). Lack of land, the basic source of subsistence, is particularly severe in the case of socially marginalized groups, the Scheduled Castes (SCs) and Scheduled Tribes (STs): 90% of the former and 70% of the latter possess less than 5 acres, or are landless. Land ownership is a major determinant of income (and power): in the 1990s, a large farmer (owning more than 25 acres), who is likely to earn most of their income by using tenants for a rent and/or who employs daily-wage laborers, earned more than 7.5 times the income of a landless wage-earning household (which is approximately 11,000 Rupees) (Shariff, 1999: 28).

---

5   The data are for 1953–54, the earliest year for which data on land distribution are available.

CLASS DYNAMICS OF POVERTY, STATE FAILURE, AND CLASS STRUGGLE   287

Those who deny the significance of private property (specifically, private property that allows its owner to exploitat the labor of others) as the major determinant of material conditions should take note of this simple statistic. It is not without reason that the demand for the abolition of capitalist private property is the factor that distinguishes Marxists from all other progressives, as Marx argued.

Associated with an unequal land distribution is the presence of rental exploitation. In the 1960s, many landlords cultivated their land by leasing it to poor peasants (i.e. those who did not own much land and who had to work for others as tenants and/or for a wage). Landlords demanded high rents. Landowners would also impose levies on tenants to bear the cost of ceremonies in their houses. Peasants performed free forced work on landlords' land and for their households. Many of these practices still exist, although on a smaller scale. There are still at least 40 million bonded laborers, and close to 90% of them are Dalits or tribals (Human Rights Watch, 1999); there are also close to 100 million child laborers (who are effectively unfree laborers, many of whom are subjected to physical violence by their employers) (Das and Chen, 2019). The bonded laborers cannot choose who they work for, how long, and for how much.

In the 1960s, landowners also had their land cultivated by nominally free, hired laborers, paying below-subsistence wages. Hired labor is now occurring on a much larger scale than in the 1960s in most States. More and more people depend on the sale of their labor power for living, although they rarely have paid employment for more than 200 days in a year. They live as long as they work, and they work as long as they live. For, there is neither personal saving nor pension for old age. On the other hand, minimum wage laws are hardly implemented. In 1989, in Bihar's Jehanabad district, a hotspot of agrarian struggles, minimum wages were paid in only 16% of the 933 villages (Louis, 2005: 5372). In 1999–2000, the real wages of agricultural laborers was only 25.48 rupees for males, which was lower than the average minimum wages of 14 States (Rupees 44.13) (Singh, 2002: 70). Agricultural laborers, like poor peasants, and all those involved in petty production (e.g. tribals), are the most food-insecure. This is partly because food prices have increased relative to their earnings, while the Public Distribution System (PDS) of the government, which is supposed to provide subsidized food, has been ineffective (Singh, 2002: 72). The collapse of the PDS has recently prompted villagers in Bihar's Bhojpur district, another area known for class struggle, to burn their ration cards protesting the fact that they are not receiving subsidized food. There are many places, such as Orissa's Kalahandi district, where millions of tonnes of food are stored in government food-stores, while locals are forced to eat mango seeds. One does not need to employ the strategy of deconstruction to construe that these seeds are not good for health. Of course, state officials with university degrees, including of the coveted IAS (Indian Administrative Service), maintain that the local indigenous population eats these seeds because of poor eating habits. What is to be questioned is these officials' own habit growing out of their responsibility to manage the unjust social system, the habit of adding insult of salt to already festering class-inflicted wounds. This is a habit that coexists with another habit, that of being subservient to the property-owning classes and their political masters, partly, in their own career interests.

Indeed, in some places, people eat the rats that fatten themselves by eating the grains stored in government stores overflowing with food. Monkeys feast at some of these stores, while humans starve nearby. It seems that animals are better off than millions of human beings in India.[6] This, of course, might not be extra-ordinary to academics, including many fascinated by ANT (actor network theory), and other theoretical gimmicks of the comfortable petty bourgeoisie, who deny ontological dualities.[7] The situation described above points to this irrefutable inference from a Marxist standpoint: continued separation of direct producers from means of production (e.g. land) and means of consumption (e.g. food) is necessary in reproducing their dependence on capital (including landed capital), and this dependence lies at the heart of class relations.

It is true that wages of agricultural workers have risen somewhat. But their wages are much lower than what is required for a decent living. The rate of growth of their wages is also lower than that of wages in the rural non-farm sector. More importantly, it is also lower than the rate of growth of labor productivity which benefits landowners (Singh, 2002: 70). Thus agricultural workers not only live in a condition of absolute poverty, but also in relative poverty, relative to other workers and to property owners. And their poverty – and indeed, poverty of other categories of the toiling mass – are partly because the price of labor power is low, the price of the product of labor sold by small-scale producers is low. All this is in a situation where there is much uneven development between areas and sectors (see Sainath, 2001: 158) and where there are few welfare benefits from the state.[8]

Low agricultural wages, lack of suitable and plentiful non-farm employment, and poor income on tiny holdings, mean that peasants must depend on private moneylenders for their credit needs. The annual rate of interest charged by them is 50% or more. In the 1960s, 'of the estimated total number of 16.3

---

6 That in recent times, under the patronage of right-wing groups and their government, cows in India have higher status and respect than some of the oppressed groups in the country is an interesting development.

7 This is the idea that human beings are qualitatively different from non-human animals, even if they are both living beings, and that human beings' needs must be prioritized over the animals'.

8 In fact, because wages are low, many people are forced to work as small-scale producers.

CLASS DYNAMICS OF POVERTY, STATE FAILURE, AND CLASS STRUGGLE 289

million agricultural labor households..., 63.9% of the estimated were indebted' (Banerjee, 1984). In 2003, the figure was still high at 49% (GOI, 2007: 73). An average farmer's debt was equal to her/his household's total spending over two years (ibid.). Since 1983, the percentage of the total debt incurred from private moneylenders has been increasing (Bhalla, 2007: 317). To the extent that there was institutional credit (e.g. from government owned banks) for rural areas, most (close to 90%) was monopolized by larger farmers, rather than made available to poor peasants and landless laborers (Varma, 2002: 65). In recent times, institutional sources of credit are drying up under neoliberal capitalism. This is why private moneylenders are more important as a source of credit than in the 1960s, when Naxalist movement began. Apart from large landowners and moneylenders, traders are another class, on which poor people's lives are dependent, including in aboriginal areas. They buy farm and forest products from tribals, as well as economically insecure peasants, at a cheaper-than-market rate, and sell them at a higher rate. Enjoying the support of many politicians, traders hoard the essential commodities such as rice, wheat, pulses and sugar, and increase the prices way beyond the level workers and poor peasants can afford. Unable to pay their loans due to crop failure and/or decline in profitability of farming, thousands of peasants, including many from the better-off section, are committing suicide: 182,936 between 1997 and 2007 to be precise (Sainath, 2009). This means more than 18,000 a year. In other words, one farmer commits suicide every half an hour. (Note that these figures exclude female farmers committing suicide: because they do not own land (their husbands do); they are not considered farmers in the official statistics.) Many farmers are jailed because of default on their loans.

Conditions of life are, dominantly, but not exclusively, determined by class relations. The charge that historical materialists reduce everything to class is a most disingenuous ideological propaganda by academic pluralists and relativists, whose main motive is to under-value class, and banish class struggle from intellectual and political practice by playing identity politics. Marxists maintain that class relations are experienced through, and reproduced by, caste (or race), ethnicity and relations of reproduction or gender (Callinicos, 1993; Gimenez, 2005) that compound the injurious effects of class. All Dalits, tribals and women are not landless laborers. But when someone is a Dalit, a woman, and a landless laborer, or a petty producer from an economically backward and politically neglected region, her condition of life is even more miserable. In addition to suffering class-based exploitation and dispossession from the land, the toiling masses – poor women, tribals and low caste people, including *Dalits* – are also subjected to social discrimination and political marginalization. Poor people live under constant threat to their dignity (*izzat*) and political rights. Caste oppression is rooted in class exploitation (e.g. agrarian class relations) and contributes toward the reproduction of class relations, sometimes more directly and sometimes less so. Until recently, low caste people, even if they had the money, could not buy the clothes they want, cannot walk in upper caste neighborhoods wearing footwear or carrying an umbrella, and cannot sit on a cot in the presence of upper castes. Nor can they take upper caste surnames. Nor can students of lower castes sit on front benches in class-rooms (Nathan, 1999). In July 2009, upper caste people in a village near Patna beat up a Dalit woman for listening to popular Hindi songs on a mobile phone. Caste influences the division of labor and access to assets. This is seen in the 'continuing confinement of lower castes to the ranks of agricultural laborers' (Nathan, 1999: 162).[9] In many villages, low caste people (mainly women) have to trudge long distances to fetch water, for they are not allowed by the upper caste people to take water from the public ponds or wells near their huts. This creates a difficult situation in times of drought: low caste women are not allowed to use wells located in upper caste hamlets. India remains a caste society or, more accurately, a class-caste society.

Poor people are not only oppressed by caste, but also gender relations. In rural areas, the economic disparity between men and women appears to be greater than in urban areas. Not only are women more likely to be unemployed. Their daily wage rate is also much less than that for males. Given the continuing preference for male children in a patriarchal society without provisions for old age security, female feticide and infanticide, as well as the neglect of female children, continue. The result is that the female male ratio for the population as a whole is well below unity (Dreze and Sen, 2002: 230) and that the ratio for children (0–6 years), in particular, is extremely low and declining (945 in 1991, to 927 in 2001, and 919 in 2011).

Women from lower castes and from poor peasants and working-class backgrounds have little control over their own bodies. Their body is a means for the cheap production of wealth for the landed and for their sexual enjoyment. Their body is also a means/weapon of class struggle in their hands. When low caste laborers demand higher wages from higher caste landlords, the latter feel 'threatened that a "low man" [is] ... challenging their privileged position' (Frankel, 1990: 122). This explains why they commit atrocities against the Dalits, including Dalit women. An ideological condition of existence of the class system is that the exploited class 'looks upon the requirements of [the existing] mode of production as self-evident natural laws', as Marx remarked towards the end of *Capital*, vol. 1 (1977: 899). This ideological precondition for reproduction of the class system begins to be undermined when exploited people view the existing conditions of life (i.e. the class relations and the state that reproduces these) as changeable and challengeable, and actually start

---

9   This conclusion is based on Prasad's study of Bihar villages under the influence of Naxalites.

CLASS DYNAMICS OF POVERTY, STATE FAILURE, AND CLASS STRUGGLE   291

challenging them. This, in turn, prompts a counter-challenge, class struggle from above, which uses caste and other non-class relations to intensify the offensive. Let me cite just two instances. A Dalit farm worker in Tamilnadu was forced to drink urine for complaining to the police about trespass against a caste Hindu; in another case, two Dalits were forced to feed each other human excreta because they stood by another Dalit in his battle with a local elected leader (Kumar, 2002: 157). Between 1981 and 1999, on average, an atrocity (e.g. rape, murder, arson, etc.) was committed against three Dalits every hour.[10] In the State of Bihar, the response of upper caste landlords to the political assertions of Dalit laborers and poor peasants has taken the form of private landlord armies that ruthlessly suppress the low caste poor fighting for their legitimate rights.[11] Massacres of the lower classes of low castes by landowners of upper (and sometimes middle) castes are highly gendered, showing how class, caste and gender are interconnected at a concrete level, *within the context of class relations*.[12] For example, landlords subject low caste women to the most barbaric mutilation and murder, to stop them from giving birth to children who, landlords fear, would become Naxalites (*Liberation*, 2003).

Thus millions of people who depend entirely or partly on the sale of labor power suffer from multiple forms of deprivation and live under the clutches of capitalists, landlords, usurers and merchants, who make use of caste and other forms of non-class oppression. The state has sought to intervene in four major areas in addressing problems of rural distress and deprivation. These are: land reforms (1950s–), the Green Revolution (1960s–), cheap credit to the poor (1970s–), and providing wage-employment (2006–). These policies have failed in most places, for most of the people who need them.

In terms of land reforms, the state failed to restrict the amount of land owned or controlled by the larger landowners, including the pre-capitalist landowners. It could not reduce the rental exploitation of peasants. The total amount of land distributed in the whole country amounted to less than 5% of total gross cropped area. The agrarian question – social obstacles (e.g. non- or pre-capitalist class relations) acting as a barrier to capitalist development – that was to be

---

10   Interestingly, 'The conviction rate of cases of atrocities against the SCs/STs [is] less than 30 per cent against the average of 42 per cent for all cognisable offences under the Indian Penal Code' (Dhar, 2009). This shows the casteist nature of the Indian state.

11   One of these, the Ranvir Sena (army), was formed in 1994 to respond to the new assertiveness of the farm laborers with more effective repression, through the creation of a professional militia with better training, weaponry and leadership. The Sena enjoys the protection of much of the political elite across party lines (Kumar, 1999).

12   Intersectionality is definitely not the tool with which to examine the relation between class and social oppression, and one reason why, as I see it, is that the intersectionality approach does not have any theory of inter-section (see Science & Society's symposium on intersectionality) (Science & Society, 2018).

resolved at the national scale, through state interventions, remained unresolved. Having failed to destroy landlordism, the state resorted to a technological fix to the agrarian question in the mid-1960s. It did so by providing technological support in the form of the Green Revolution in specific areas. Much of the benefit from this policy, which was in no small measure prompted by US imperialist interests in the sale of modern inputs in India, was monopolized by the same larger landowners whose power the land reforms policy was supposed to undermine but left intact. This class used the technology to increase productivity. The smaller owners did not have much financial capacity. Nor did they have a sufficient amount of land to benefit from the new technology. Capitalist landowners resorted to mechanization. This deprived laborers of any gains they might have otherwise enjoyed. Representing a technological fix to India's rural distress, the Green Revolution came to be associated with multiple forms, or layers, of social-spatial inequality. These included: inequality between employers and laborers; between larger owners (i.e. capitalist farmers/landlords) and smaller owners; between landlords and semi-proletarians/tenants; and between Green Revolution areas (in which the state deliberately concentrated its efforts at promoting agrarian capitalism) and non-Green revolution areas.

As the Green Revolution could not reduce poverty, in the late 1970s – early 1980s (a topic explored in a previous chapter), the state launched the Integrated Rural Development Policy (IRDP). This aimed at giving small loans to poor people to start income-generating activities – setting up small shops, starting dairy businesses, using improved farm implements, etc. This policy, more or less, was also a failure. In the capitalist system, the use of its resources must be justified mainly on the basis of the profit-logic. This logic put severe limits on the amount of money the capitalist state could commit in the form of pro-poor policies, such as the IRDP or PDS, *relative* to (a) the massive need of the tens of millions of the poor whom the system marginalizes (e.g. peasants increasingly losing access to land; people without secure employment for a living wage), and (b) the massive need to appease, bribe and subsidize capitalists to invest in specific areas and sectors. It is also not easy for 'penny capitalists' – semi-proletarian entrepreneurs to whom the state gives a small loan to invest in business – to accumulate 'capital' and benefit from it. Given a choice between converting a meagre state loan to 'capital' (or a means of creating self-employment, more accurately) and using it to buy food just to live, they would just choose the latter. This they did (Das, 2000). The law of dialectics says that Rs. 500,000 can be capital but not Rs. 500. The fact that it is difficult for starving poor people to be entrepreneurs did not occur to the apologists of capital and anti-poor officials and politicians, sitting in far-away and comfortable places, who were, and still are, eager to promote market relations in every nook and cranny of the country. And, the limited money that the state could commit did not even reach the intended beneficiaries. Officials and politicians work in an utterly undemocratic manner and have unscrupulous links to traders and landowners. Therefore, much of the IRDP money ended up in the pockets of the local officials, or with the traders supplying the assets needed for the income-generating activities (e.g. animals; farm implements) (Das, 2000). That small bits of money given to individuals or to groups of individuals (especially women), and possibly via NGOs, can be empowering has become conventional wisdom, including among so-called critical social scientists. This shows the extent to which the fetish of the market has colonized the consciousness of the politicians, bureaucracy and petty-bourgeois intellectuals.

Partly due to the pressure from the parliamentary left, the state started, in 2006, a new policy of employment creation, known as National Rural Employment Guarantee Scheme or NREGS. Its aim is to provide at least 100 days of guaranteed waged employment a year to every household whose adult members volunteer to do unskilled manual work at the legislated minimum wage. Reports suggest that, like the IRDP, a large part of the money meant for this policy has gone to the politicians, officials and property owners (e.g. contractors), except in those few areas where the poor people are able to exercise constant vigilance over the implementation of the scheme (Khera, 2008; Liberation, 2008; Rai, 2007). Because the policy, if properly implemented, can hurt the economic elite a bit by tightening the labor market, it seeks to sabotage the policy (Roy, 2015). Provisions of the act are routinely violated. For example, the delay in the payment of wages lasts for weeks and months; laborers are not paid the mandated unemployment insurance if they are not provided wage-work when they demand. There is also not enough money provided for the policy to work (to give *everyone* wage-work at a decent living wage as and when they need it): once again, the capitalist system puts limits on how much can be committed in the form of any anti-poverty policy. The actual amount spent on the poor depends on the balance of class forces. But there are severe structural limits, ideologically expressed through such constructs as 'budget deficits go up' or 'government assistance makes people lazy'. Note that these are expressed by the members of same class, directly or through their spokespersons, who have no qualms about milking the state (the fiscal stimulus as a bribe, or corporate welfare, from the state) to get out of an economic rut that is entirely of their own making. This signifies that hypocrisy, like most things in life, has a class character.

The major interventions of the post-colonial state have failed to significantly improve the conditions of life of the poor created by class (and other) relations. The main, if not the sole, reason for this is the class character of the state itself. For example, the abysmal failure of the land reforms legislation can be attributed to two major factors connected to class relations (Das, 1999c). First, as in other similar post-colonial countries, and as discussed in Chapter 7, large landowners in India share state power with the urban bourgeoisie: this means that state policies were dominantly in the interests of these classes and their international patrons. *Given* the absence of alternative opportunities to make profit, caused by the overall imperialist framework in which the country operates, these landowners' class interest was in the ruthless exploitation of people with little or no land: exploitation of poor peasants via rental extractions and (increasingly) of laborers at via the payment of below-subsistence wages, sometimes under unfree conditions. Heavy rental extraction meant that peasants had insufficient resources to invest in land. Super exploitation of peasants (and laborers) also reduced the size of the home market. Besides, given the opportunity to earn revenue through these means of super-exploitation, property owners had little incentive to invest in land to increase labor productivity. Thus, to the extent that one can at all isolate national-scale factors of underdevelopment from imperialism,[13] class relations acted as a fetter on the development of productive forces, at least in specific regions.[14] This under-development of productive forces contradicted capitalists' interests in higher rates of profit which would have come from a higher level of the development of productive forces resulting in the production of cheaper farm products for food and raw materials combined with a growing home market allowing large-scale production in the cities. So, landowners were potential 'enemies' of the urban capitalist class. The *economic* interest of the capitalist class, domestic and foreign, was such that it would not have had any problem if the land reform legislation had completely or significantly destroyed the pre-capitalist class (except that some elements of the urban capitalist class were also involved in forms of exploitation in villages that were not quite capitalist). Such legislation would also have improved the material conditions of peasants and rural laborers. But the *political* interests of capitalists were such that they could not go against the feudals type. What Marx said in 1852 (in an article in New York Daily Tribune) about the then-British bourgeoisie, is relevant to their Indian counterpart now: 'They prefer to compromise with the vanishing opponent [i.e. the feudals] rather than to strengthen the arising enemy [i.e. the working class], to whom the future belongs, by concessions of a more than apparent importance.

---

13   Imperialism is defined here 'as a form of class relations: relations between metropolitan bourgeoisie and Third World workers/peasants', as it is enabled by the powerful states of the imperialist countries and by the actions of the elements of the bourgeoisie of the less developed countries (Das, 2001c: 168).

14   This does not mean that the dominant reason for India's under-development lay in the so-called pre-capitalist or semi-feudal class relations per se. Indeed, many of the so-called feudal relations are not semi-feudal but capitalist at a lower stage of development.

CLASS DYNAMICS OF POVERTY, STATE FAILURE, AND CLASS STRUGGLE 295

Therefore, they strive to avoid every forcible collision with [them]' (Marx, 2000: 361). The landowners, including the *pre-capitalist* elements of this class (e.g. former *rajas, zamindars,* etc. who were supporters of imperialism) were powerful in specific regions. They perform the important role of controlling the rural masses, including laborers, whose anger against landlordism could be potentially directed at the bourgeoisie of the country as well as at the imperialists. So, the bourgeoisie, and the state on its behalf, could not afford to hurt the landowners' interest too much by implementing land reforms. Second, those who were directly or indirectly responsible for the implementation of the legislation, including judges, came from the landed class or represented their interests.

If large landowners' farms were broken and their land was consequently redistributed among poorer peasants and the landless, and if the latter were provided technological and financial support by the state through cooperatives, land productivity would have increased, putting money in their hands creating a home market. This did not happen. This could not happen. This is because of the overall balance of class forces, within the country and internationally (i.e. influence of imperialists). Promises of land reforms on paper (and insignificant material benefits here and there) were just used to quell the resentment of the masses. These must be seen as what they are: as class struggle from above, to pre-empt any class struggle from below.

The Green Revolution, in a sense, represented a continuity with the earlier program (i.e. the land reforms), although these two programs are seen by many as different. This continuity reveals the class character of the state. The land reform legislation protected the class interests of the propertied families (landlords, capitalist farmers, rich peasants), who were allowed to possess land beyond the legal ceiling-limit (i.e. any amount of land they could hold on to). The Green Revolution placed new means of production (e.g. the new technological package; state capital in the form of subsidized loans, etc.) *precisely* in the hands of the same class and allowed it an opportunity to accumulate capital, unfettered *and* untaxed. Neither the land-reforms nor the Green Revolution did anything to undermine the economic and political power of large property owners (many of whom also invested in non-farm activities such as transportation, trading, etc.). They continued to govern the conditions of existence of the poor. That radicals had expected otherwise (that bureaucratic land reforms would be progressive and the Green Revolution would bring about technological change, and empower poorer peasants with proper state support), without any radical change in balance of class forces, signifies their fascination with the national progressive bourgeois thesis and the idea that the nation-state in an imperialized country can help bring about radical long-term rural transformation in property relations and in the level of development of productive forces. On the other hand, given the state's class character, the daily activities of the state must be insulated from the constant monitoring of it by the masses. Without their popular participation in the everyday workings of the state, including ways in which pro-poor policies are implemented, government funds meant for the poor are squeezed on their way from the national and provincial scale state apparatuses, to the local government officials/politicians. Like landlords, government officials and politicians are utterly insensitive to the problems of the poor (Corbridge and Harriss, 2000: 201–202; Subramanian, 1998).

In the post-1991 period, not only have the newly introduced government programs for the poor largely failed, but also earlier programs have been diluted (in several States). There is a clear connection between this and neoliberal capitalism, partly imposed by imperialism. For, one of the (contradictory) aims of the latter is to shrink mass income and consumption at home in order to enable cheap exports and repayment of debt to imperialist finance capital (see Patnaik, 1999) and to reproduce India as a low-wage platform of global capitalism.[15] Since the inception of neoliberalism, rural development expenditures, as a ratio of the net national product, have dropped, as mentioned earlier (Patnaik, 2007: 155). Among other things, this has led to a reduction in the creation of employment opportunities. The little help available from the government in the name of the economic reforms with a *human* face[16] has not been enough to counter the inhumane effects of neo-liberalism (on rural income, employment and access to land). The dilution of the development program is also seen in the case of the land reforms laws. The legal restriction on land ownership is considered by domestic and foreign capital and their political and ideological supporters to be an institutional constraint on the flow of agribusiness investment to rural areas of the country. Indeed, India is known for its wide diversity of climates favorable to the production of various commodities which cannot be economically produced in cold climates of imperialist countries (Patnaik, 1999). The existing ceiling on land is seen as a constraint also on acquiring agricultural, homestead and forestlands for a variety of agricultural as well as non-agricultural purposes including export-oriented capitalist industrialization (Special Economic Zones or SEZs) (Pushpendra, 2000).

The SEZ phenomenon, which has even infected the Left governments, signifies a pattern of peripheral capitalist industrialization which requires both (a) *dispossession of peasants* and (b) extra-ordinary level of *exploitation of laborers,*

---

15 Shrinking income and consumption of the toiling classes is the characteristic aspect of neoliberalism *everywhere* (including in imperialist countries), not just in peripheral countries. This means that there is a potential basis for international solidarity of working class and peasants against capital, including its neoliberal *avatar*, everywhere and at all scales.

16 The fact that ruling class and the state use this phrase indicates that they admit that economic reforms are inhumane.

including some of the erstwhile peasants, now rendered landless, who work in these SEZs for low wages and without the usual façade of legal rights. Land is acquired minimally as a space on which to put constant capital. It is acquired more for speculation by predatory capital. To the extent that land is used for actual production process, the existing land reform legislation is being diluted to facilitate the transfer of land from peasants to big business, who invest capital to produce commodities for export and for local elites (e.g. golf courses; holiday resorts; luxury houses; 'luxury crops' such as flowers), the commodities that the rural masses cannot afford to consume, thus immensely contributing to inequality. Global capitalism is producing new needs, and new means of satisfying these needs, as it must. It is also (re)producing a class of poor peasants and workers which cannot meet these needs. With no land for household production, with no/little social security from the state, and with not much alternative and regular employment opportunities within a reasonable commuting distance for a living wage, vast sections of the rural and semi-rural (as well as urban) population are subjected to ruthless exploitation including the use of coercive labor relations. The degree of exploitation increases with the extent to which commodities are produced for export. Export-production, especially of luxury products, generally, means that the local workers and semi-proletarians are not a market to rely on. Anyone who has actually observed areas of export agriculture or SEZs will know this to be true.

The unequal land distribution, mentioned earlier, to which the land grab under neoliberalism contributes, means that, in the absence of plentiful non-farm employment at a decent wage, the majority of the landless and near-landless population represents the vast reserve army of labor for domestic and foreign capital. The reserve army of labor has been produced from colonial times through the devastating impacts of British manufactured exports to India on her industries. It has been swelling, thanks to new imperialist mechanisms imposed by World Bank, WTO, etc. (e.g. liberalization of trade). The reserve army, which Harvey (2003), unfortunately, treats as capitalism's other, has far-ranging implications: it contributes to the backward nature of peripheral capitalism. For, a disproportionately large reserve army (without any social security from the state) undermines conditions of class struggle against low wages and long hours of those employed, especially when workers are divided along lines of caste, gender, ethnicity and location (migrants vs locals).[17] In turn, this, more or less, dampens the normal imperative on the part of

---

17   The reserve army also raises the level of exploitation of the currently employed through the mechanisms of low wages and overwork, despotically imposed by capital, and this reduces employment opportunities of those who are a part of the reserve army, as Marx

capitalists to go for technological innovation. The implication is that millions of people remain in technological backwardness with extremely low level of labor productivity and of cooperation at work, as well as spatial isolation. For every Bangalore, there are thousands of under-developed villages and small towns which are literally in darkness. People work with rudimentary technology on farms and in factories and without the benefits that large-scale production provides. The vast majority have been living in half a million villages. 63% of villages with a population of 1000 or less are not even connected by a road (GOI, 2005: 199). If the spatial system is a productive force (Cohen, 2000: 51), one can imagine how under-developed India's villages are.

The effects of class relations and relations of oppression and state's failure to counter these have created a situation of declining food availability for the poor,[18] land alienation (especially in aboriginal areas) and farmers' suicide.[19] Available statistical data on poverty reveal some crucial aspects of rural living conditions from the early 1960s.

1.   The official poverty line is based on 'inadequate absolute standards' which do not reflect 'norms of dignified human living' (Mehta, 2002: 34). It is best seen as a 'line of hunger'. Even so, the percentage of poor people in the total population went from 38% in 1960–61 to 54% in 1968–69, years of the original launch of Naxalism. In the 1970s and 1980s, as many as 320 million, on an average (more than 40% of the total population and close to half of the rural population), were in official poverty in any given year (GOI, 2003: 92). Thousands have perished from starvation or starvation-related illnesses. Close to 6 out of 10 children are malnourished (Shariff, 1999: 94). The life of villagers is cut short due to lack of proper food and medical help. In the 1980s–1990s, rural life expectancy was not even 60.

2.   As late as 1999–2000, there were 260 million people living below the official poverty line, including 193 million rural poor: this means that more than one in every four Indians, and nearly a third of its rural population, was in official poverty (GOI, 2003: 92).[20] Utsa Patnaik's (2007) very useful

---

argued in chapter 25 of *Capital* volume 1. What follows is that those who are employed *and* those who are not, are both impacted by the capitalist system.

18   The daily net availability of foodgrains (food production plus import minus export) per person has gone down from 510 grammes in 1991–92 to 470 grammes in 1994–95 to 434 grammes in 2001–02 (Patnaik, 1999: Table 12; 2007: Table 4).

19   The incidence of farmer suicide in Andhra Pradesh is one of the highest in many of its districts most associated with Naxalism.

20   In 2011, there were 276 million poor people in India (they lived on $1.25 a day in PPP terms).

CLASS DYNAMICS OF POVERTY, STATE FAILURE, AND CLASS STRUGGLE 299

analysis lays bare the class nature of poverty statistics and the class-prejudice of its ideological producers, the apologetics for big capital, who are dressed up as professors of the science of economics.[21] She shows that in 1999–2000, the per capita rural poverty-level expenditure which commanded food quantities giving 2400 calories (the minimum necessary for the normal functioning of the body) is Rs. 19 a day, and that 74.5% of the rural population consumed below this level (2007: 141, 189). (The figures for 1983 and 1993–94 were 70% and 74.5% respectively). 3 out every 4 Indian villagers have been in absolute poverty according to her. And, this means that the potential support base of movements for justice among poor people is simply huge and potentially threatening to the state which is why the state is increasingly turning coercive.

3. A villager is more likely to be poor than an urban person. A villager also does not have access to the collective consumption items (e.g. hospitals and educational institutions) that a city dweller has.[22] This partly explains why rural areas are so explosive politically.

4. The percentage of the rural population that is poor in the States affected by moderate or heavy Naxalism is generally above the all-India average (Table 8.1; column 3).[23]

5. The average monthly per capita expenditure of rural poor households and the overall level of rural development tend to be lower in all major Naxal-affected States than the all-India average (Table 8.2).

6. The official poverty level for Dalits and tribes, the groups Naxalites are most closely associated with, tend to be higher than for others; this is the case both at the all-India level and in the major Naxal-affected States (Table 8.1; column 1–2).[24]

---

21 Her scrutiny of official numbers suggests that the number game is not totally useless and that one can challenge the conventional analysts by playing their own rules of the game.

22 The percentage of the rural population that is officially poor is 27.09; the urban figure is 23.62 (GOI, 2005: Table 3.1). The rural infant mortality is 66 while the urban infant mortality is 38 in 2003 (GOI, 2007: 19). The relative infant mortality gap between rural and urban areas – the ratio of the rural infant mortality rate to the urban infant mortality rate – indeed increased between 1995 and 2003.

23 The united Andhra Pradesh is an exception. Before its division in 2014, it was the largest among all Naxal-affected States. It should be noted that poverty level is expected to be very high among the indigenous population in Andhra districts where the Naxalite movement is strong.

24 Of course, there are numerous areas where the level of developmental distress is high (e.g. higher than the national average) and, yet, there is no Naxal activity. Naxals have been active only in *some* of the distressed areas. The point is that where the level of distress is low, the Naxal-type movement is likely, showing that the Naxalite movement does

300 CHAPTER 8

TABLE 8.1   Rural poverty (1999–2000) among most oppressed groups in selected Indian
States

	Percentage of the poor among		
	Dalits	*Scheduled Tribes*	*All groups*
Andhra Pradesh	16.5	23.1	11.05
Bihar (1)	59.1	58.7	44.03
Madhya Pradesh (2)	41.2	57.1	37.06
Orissa	–	73.0	48.01
West Bengal	34.9	50.1	31.85
All States (3)	35.3	44.2	
All-India (rural) (4)	26.5		

Notes: (1) includes Jharkhand; (2) includes Chhattisgarh; (3) all states = % of poverty among
SCs or among Tribes in rural India as a whole; (4) poverty ratio for rural India as a whole.
SOURCE: RADHAKRISHNAN ET AL., 2004, IN GOI, 2005

2   The Naxalite Movement as a Form of Lower-Class Struggle

> Maoism is spreading very rapidly across the Indian subcontinent. Genu-
> ine Marxists should be studying this phenomenon and drawing appropri-
> ate conclusions from it.
>
> JACOB SECKER (in a letter to *Socialist Worker*, UK, 2006)[25]

Thus a large proportion of the national population has not enjoyed a life of
economic security and dignity since independence from colonial rule. Because
of the unjust conditions created by class reproduced through, and reinforced
by, highly undemocratic relations of caste and patriarchy, and because of the
failure of the so-called *democratic* state, often praised by imperialist states as a
model for the Third World, to significantly mitigate the effects of these
conditions, a massive political space for potential radical movements for justice has been created. The Naxalite movement is a particular instance of radicalization of exploited masses, which will be discussed below. Indeed, given
the conditions of existence, as described above, one really wonders: why it is

---

not hang in the air: it is materially rooted. But objective conditions do not guarantee that
a radical movement will occur, least of all, a given *type* of movement (e.g. Naxalism).

25   https://socialistworker.co.uk/art/8691/Letters.

TABLE 8.2   Monthly average per capita expenditure of poor people (Rupees) in 1999–2000 in selected States

	Poor	Composite Index of rural development
Andhra Pradesh	215	99.3
Bihar (1)	269	70.1
Madhya Pradesh (2)	250	86.8
Orissa	248	93.2
West Bengal	281	103.2
All India	282	115.8 (unweighted average of all States)

Notes: (1) includes Jharkhand; (2) includes Chhattisgarh.
SOURCE: GOI, 2005

that people do not revolt more often, more intensely, and in more areas, than has been the case? There is not enough space in this chapter to consider this question in any detail. An important question: what are the proximate factors behind its occurrence and continued existence? A correct understanding of the second, more specific, question may throw some light on the more general, first question.

The northern parts of India's West Bengal province[26] have a long history of peasant and worker struggles. Although short-lived, the first peasant organization in the country was formed in north Bengal itself at the All Bengal Peasant Conference of 1925 (Samanta, 1984: 21). From the early 1950s, a radical section of the Communist Party of India (CPI) organized peasants, most of whom were sharecroppers, in the Naxalbari area of West Bengal's Darjeeling district. In the period 1958–62, local peasants' associations, led by the Communists such as Charu Mazumdar, called for the harvesting of crops by peasants, arming them to protect their crops, and self-defense against police attacks (Banerjee, 1984). Such peasant activities in Naxalbari coincided with simmering troubles within the then-undivided communist party. In 1964, the party split into the 'pro-Soviet' CPI and the 'pro-China' Communist Party of India (Marxist) or the CPI(M). In 1967, these parties formed a United Front government in Bengal in coalition with some bourgeois parties. The formation of a Left-led state government increased the peasants' expectations for immediate relief.

---

26   This area is strategically important as it is not far off from Bangladesh, Nepal, and China.

On March 2, 1967, in Naxalbari, Bigul Kishan, a sharecropper, armed with a court order, had gone to till his land. He was attacked by the landlord and his hoodlums. The police did not take any action. The fact that the incident occurred just a month after the formation of the United Front government was seen as indicative of the futility of hoping that a Left-oriented government would help the peasants. This perception fueled further militancy. Fifteen to twenty thousand poor peasants, in about two thousand villages, were enrolled as full-time activists, supported by the urban educated youth (Jalal, 1995). Peasant committees were formed in every village. They were transformed into armed guards carrying traditional weapons such as bows, arrows and spears. They occupied land. They seized the crops from landlords' land. They burned all land records which had been used to deceive them. Peasant committees also passed death sentences on oppressive landlords, looted guns from them, and set up a parallel administration in the villages. They cancelled debts owed to moneylenders who were asked to return the mortgaged properties to the original owners. They established daily wages for farm laborers. They also fixed prices of essential goods in the big shops (Banerjee, 1984). From March to May 1967, feudalism was driven out of a 300-square mile area. Peasants' control over the area was complete: no outsider could enter without their permission. The exercise of political power, and control over territory, went hand in hand. With some justification, Naxalbari could be considered India's little Paris Commune.

The peasant movement turned violent when landlords resisted the seizure of their land and crops. Police action followed clashes between landlords and peasants. Following the killing of a policeman on May 23, 1967, a major police action was launched on 12 July by the State government, with full support from the Central government. The police killed nine people, including two children, as well as six (aboriginal) women, who played an important role in the movement (Damas, 1991: 84). The Naxalbari movement in the area was temporarily defeated.

Places stand for processes (Pred, 1984). What happens in a place triggers similar processes in other places. Even if what happened in Naxalbari was temporary, it became a beacon for class struggle in many other places. Naxalbari as a place multiplied itself, so to speak. Unlike other peasant movements, Naxalbari had a wider significance. It was a product of and a catalyst in a conscious process of building a new Marxist-Leninist party. The building of a new party was a consummation of the process of the 1964 split within the undivided communist party, and this in turned ensured that the tiny spark in Naxalbari that lasted only for three months developed into a prairie fire across much of India for decades (Sen, Arindam, 2017).

According to Government reports, 5424 agrarian agitations occurred between 1967 and 1970 (Shah, 1990: 291). A Coordinating Committee, and later a party, called the CPI(ML) – Communist Party of India (Marxist-Leninist) – was formed on April 22, 1969 by dissidents from the CPI(M). It got encouragement from the then Chinese Communist Party. Its aim was to coordinate localized struggles into a mass movement. Thus the CPI(M) was split into the CPI(M) and the CPI(ML). Naxalism is associated with the latter, CPI(ML). Government repression continued. By 1973, nearly 40,000 members or sympathizers were in jail.

All social movements[27] are informed by one or another ideological framing, consciously or not. The Naxalite movement is a part of a larger trend in which social movements are shaped by Maoism in the global South (Dirlik, 2014; Kumbamu, 2019). The CPI(ML) itself split many times into multiple factions, each claiming to be the true party. In post-Naxalbari times, the movement split into some 40 M-L groups engaged in fights for the expansion of their areas of influence. These groups have now consolidated into three main M-L streams, although a large number of other groups still remain outside. All M-L groups owe their origin to events in Naxalbari and are guided by their interpretation(s) of Marxism-Leninism-Maoism. They all view Indian society as semi-colonial (i.e. as under clutches of imperialism) and semi-feudal. According to them, the Indian state is controlled by imperialists, comprador bureaucratic bourgeoisie and feudal landlords. They agree on the need for a democratic revolution to destroy feudal economic and social-cultural relations, because for them the main contradiction in society is between feudals and the masses (and not between capital and labor). Therefore, their political mobilizational energy is spent dominantly on peasants (although they do make references to workers in their literature) who would geographically encircle the cities and capture power. The M-L movement is divided mainly on the basis of their tactical approach towards the balance between parliamentary and extra-electoral politics. Some [e.g. CPI (Maoist)] almost exclusively focus on armed struggle and are underground;[28] while others, such as Kanu Sanyal's group, use mainly over-ground methods and run mass organizations. Groups such as CPI(ML) Liberation use a combination of both underground and overground methods; they participate in elections (Banerjee, 1999: 203–204).[29] CPI(ML) (Liberation), a registered political party, is now cooperating, in electoral and extra-electoral struggles, with mainstream communist parties.

---

27   I am using (radical) social movements and class struggle interchangeably in this Chapter.

28   CPI (Maoist) has spread itself from the Telengana region of Andhra Pradesh to the tribal-dominated districts of adjoining Maharashtra, Chhattisgarh, Jharkhand, and Orissa.

29   Liberation has its bases primarily in Bihar and pockets of influence in Uttar Pradesh, West Bengal, Assam, Tamilnadu and Punjab and Orissa.

In terms of the Naxalite leadership, it is traditionally in the hands of petty-bourgeois or middle class people (see Routledge, 1997). They include: school teachers, students and skilled workers. Some of the leaders (including Mazumdar himself) do indeed come from peasant background. Women and Dalits are less likely to be in leadership positions. Many of the Naxalite leaders come from urban areas and are of younger age (this was especially the case in the 1960s in West Bengal). They have a sense of self-sacrifice. They speak the language of the poor and live like, and with, them. Naxalites dream of a better society. Shah (2017: 53) writes: 'It is, perhaps, the very hierarchies of Indian society that have produced some of the world's most committed pursuers of a more equal society'. Shah says the Naxalites 'came across with dignity, as equal human beings, over time making them a part of an extended family in the region' (p. 54).

Although the movement has been heavily repressed by the state, it exists in large number of almost a third of India's districts. One reason for this are the objective material conditions discussed in section 2, including dispossession.[30] Another reason is that Naxalites are able to provide some help to the poor to cope with, and fight against, many of these conditions. They have tried to ensure justice through direct means. The dedicated cadres have initiated 'social changes in their areas of control' (Banerjee, 2006: 3159).[31]

3   A Marxist Class-Theoretic Critique of the Naxalite Movement

Yet, as Banerjee (1999: 222) says, '[I]n terms of spatial growth', the Naxalite groups have 'virtually lost their original pockets in West Bengal', and 'have failed to extend their influence beyond their traditional bases', mainly located in the eastern half of the country. Why? Why is there a gap between (a) the potential social and spatial influence of a movement for justice such as that led by Naxalites, given the widespread unjust conditions of existence, and (b) its actual sphere of influence? Could it have a *larger* following, socially (in terms of classes, for example) and geographically, than it has traditionally had? What are its limitations, including of that segment which exclusively focuses on the

---

30   Braud (2015) says that in the contemporary round of globalization, the forcible seizure of land from the Scheduled Tribes in a process similar to primitive accumulation, explains the Naxalites' continuing appeal.

31   Naxalites' developmental activities will be discussed in more details in the next chapter.

CLASS DYNAMICS OF POVERTY, STATE FAILURE, AND CLASS STRUGGLE 305

armed struggle? The critique presented below will be from a Marxist class perspective.[32]

Focused on the oppression and exploitation of peasants by landlords, the movement is, generally speaking, not powerful in the areas of strong rural capitalism, where wage-workers are subjected to a high level of exploitation both within agriculture and outside (retail, transportation, construction, etc.). It is generally confined to areas where the development of capitalist relations of exploitation is relatively stunted. A certain segment of the Naxalite movement (CPI Maoist) is almost totally confined to the areas demographically dominated by tribals, who constitute less than 10% of the total population of the country. This strategy is not sufficiently sensitive to class differentiation in the aboriginal population (Duyker, 1981). It also leaves out vast sections of economically distressed people, especially the non-aboriginal poor peasants and laborers. The Naxalite mobilization is also generally absent from urban areas (Banerjee, 2017; Sagar, 2006: 3178). This means that the movement is weakly integrated into the class struggle of the non-agrarian working masses.

There is, in my view, a major theoretical reason for all this, which I will *briefly* discuss and aspects of which are ignored in the critical assessments of the movement. Firstly, Naxalites view what are in effect *capitalist relations at a low level of development of productive forces* as some kind of feudal relations of exploitation (or 'semi-feudalism'). This explains why the extent of feudal-type exploitation is overestimated and why, therefore, politically, the movement is confined mainly to economically backward agriculture-dominated areas, ignoring vast swathes of the country reeling under *capitalist*, and increasingly, neoliberal capitalist, exploitation. The Naxalite movement, *like the mainstream communist* movement which it criticizes, believe in a two-stage theory of revolution (a pre-1917 Leninist strategy transcended by Lenin's own *April Theses*, that is systematically ignored by most Indian marxists): a democratic revolution (against feudals) first, and a socialist revolution sometime in the future. The Naxalite movement and the mainstream communist movement are more similar that most people think. The Naxalite movement, like the mainstream Marxist movement from which it separated, is *not* a socialist movement; it is not a movement for socialism. The Naxalites' fight, effectively, amounts to a fight for a better bourgeois society cleared of vestiges of feudalism and without unfree labor relations. Their struggle is for an authentic system of (liberal) democracy, one without autocratic and bureaucratic

---

32   For a critical discussion on Naxalism from a post-colonial perspective, see Seth (2006).

distortions, before any fight against capitalist relations as such can begin.[33] Their ideological-political focus on what they call semi-*feudalism* will continue to keep millions of toiling people outside of their influence, including the reserve army of labor under capitalism. Their lives are adversely impacted by the bourgeoisie, including its so-called 'national' faction.[34] Naxalites' influence – and indeed, the influence of any movement – will be limited *unless* the fight against localized feudal practices (which the Naxalites are right to point to) becomes a part of the fight against the capitalist system *as such*, whether the 'bearers' (Marx, 1977: 92) of that system are national, monopoly or imperialist capitalists. Places where unfree/bonded laborers are used by property owners to make money, leaving ordinary people to starve, and places where employers use modern technology to make large profits, are both parts of the same system. These two kinds of place represent spatially uneven development *under capitalism* (discussed in Chapter 3) and do not require a *temporally uneven* (i.e. two-stage) political strategy. A correct and non-teleological understanding of capitalism and uneven development *within* poor countries such as India is at the heart of the matter here. This understanding Naxalites seem not to have. They seem not to have understood this: capitalism does not promote modern progressive development always and everywhere, so the low level of economic development cannot be automatically seen as existing because of pre-capitalism, or because of relations that are not really capitalism (see Chapter 3). Of course, the Naxalite movement uses such terms as the working class as the agent of revolution, socialism, Leninism, etc. but these terms are used more as an *ideological justification* for their inadequate theory and inadequate practice than anything else.

I have said earlier that conditions of existence have an important influence on the fundamental ideas about these conditions which in turn become a part of conditions of life. And ideas created under certain conditions in one place can travel to another place where these ideas are applied by people without giving due thought to the conditions in which they think and intervene. In

---

33 According to a major Naxalite stream – CPIML (New Democracy): 'The Indian Revolution, taken as a whole, passes through *two distinct stages* of historical development, i.e. the people's democratic and the socialist revolution'. This is the two-stage theory. And in terms of who will participate in the first stage of the revolution:
    'The people's democratic revolution under the leadership of the working class will establish a democratic dictatorship of the working class, the peasantry, the urban petty bourgeoisie and the *national bourgeoisie* under the leadership of the working majority of the Indian people'. The new, people's democratic state will ensure the '*Protection of Industry and trade of national bourgeoisie*' (http://www.cpimlnd.org/party-documents; italics added) (accessed on August 10, 2009).

34 The 'national' faction will be a part of their people's democratic state.

Chapter 1 of *Capital* volume 1, Marx (1977) says that Aristotle said great things about exchange but given the unequal slave society he lived in, he could not develop his ideas about value that underlies the equal exchange of commodities.[35] The Maoist thought that underlies Naxalism commits a kind of 'Aristotelian error' (or, a semi-Aristotelian error). This involves creating ideas about world-society based on what is happening within the narrow confines of a given society. Let me explain.

Consider the following conditions. Capitalist production co-exists with a vast peasantry which is exploited on the basis of rental and usurious extractions. Capitalist property owners resort to unfree labor relations including those based on extra-economic coercion. They also make use of vulnerability of migrant workers. Some of them make use of unfree labor, because it is can be cheaper and can be subjected to discipline more than free labor.[36] It is these sorts of conditions, when not seen in relation to what is happening globally and when not interpreted on the basis of adequate Marxist theory, that give rise of what is called Maoism, including the idea of semi-feudalism.[37] As a set of ideas, Maoism can then travel to another place and another time (for example, modern capitalist India), in the minds of some people. It has. The material conditions in Mao's peasant-dominated China (along with some conjunctural political conditions such as defeats in the city) might have prompted him to not think about (a) the urban wage-labor as the agent of revolution and (b) the idea of revolution against the rule of the capitalist class as opposed to

---

35   Marx (1977) writes in *Capital* vol. 1: 'What is the homogeneous element, i.e. the common substance', which, for example, 'the house represents from the point of view of the bed, in the value expression for the bed? Such a thing, in truth, cannot exist, says Aristotle. But why not? ...Aristotle himself was unable to [understand the fact that in] the form of commodity-values, all labour is expressed as equal human labour ...because Greek society was founded on the labour of slaves, and hence, had as its natural basis, the inequality of men and of their labour powers. The secret of the expression of value, namely, the equality and the equivalence of all kinds of labour' required a new material condition which was 'a society where the commodity-form is the universal form of the product of labour, hence the dominant social relation is the relation between [persons] as possessors of commodities' (pp. 151–152).

36   Marx's general theoretical assumption was that capital-as-a-whole (or capitalism) requires nominally free labor, but surely, *specific capitalists* do not mind at all using unfree labor if by doing so they can reduce the cost of production.

37   Of course, one should not think that mere observation of material conditions can explain the emergence of a specific theory that explains such conditions adequately. If that were the case, everyone in capitalism would become a Marxist armed with the theory of value and surplus value. But it is true that unless capitalism is fully developed, a theory of revolutionary scientific socialism would be impossible. Theory intervenes between material conditions and one's understanding of those conditions.

the revolution against feudal oppressors. These conditions might have, in part, given rise to the over-emphasis on peasants or small-scale self-employed property owners (in isolation from the urban working class) as the main agents of revolution.[38] Perhaps the specific conditions made him commit the Aristotelian error of sorts.

Now, these *ideas* have been influencing what are called Maoist political strategies in our times. One might ask: what makes India's Naxalites – and Indian communists as such – not to see that there is a much greater prevalence of wage-labor in modern-day India, which is a part of a world that is decisively capitalist. And does such recognition (dominance of wage-labor and of capitalist form of private property and of exploitation) not have serious implications for communist politics, including the fact that wage-workers allied with the non-exploiting peasants on coming to power, cannot but transcend capitalism, which means that a process of democratic revolution cannot be separated from socialist revolution? Aristotle did not live in a society dominated by value relations, so he could not theorize value. But Indian Naxalites live in India which is dominated by the capitalist law of value, and where the vast majority of direct producers are exploited on the basis of the appropriation of surplus value (in absolute or relative form) and yet, the central focus of their politics – like that of mainstream communist politics – is not fighting capitalist class relations (wage-slavery) as such.

So, Naxalites do not say 'no' to capitalism as such (they do not intend to and they do not need to abolish capitalist class relations, although they use anti-capitalist and socialistic terminology), for according to them, India lacks the dominance of capitalist production relations. India, for them, is still a semi-*feudal* (and semi-colonial) country.[39] They must then agree that the suffering of the masses is not fundamentally caused by capitalist class relation. A *democratic* capitalism, i.e. a capitalism which is free from neo-colonialism and feudalism and which uses free labor always and everywhere, is yet to exist, according to them. Such a capitalism must first be made to exist under the tutelage of Maoists. Many 'conscious capitalists', capitalists with a conscience, and

---

38   When the movement began, the Chinese communist party praising it said this in July 1967: 'The Indian revolution must take the road of relying on peasants, establishing base areas in the countryside, persisting in protracted armed struggle and using the countryside to encircle and finally capture the cities. This is Mao Tse-tung's road' (quoted in Bagchi, 2017).

39   As mentioned earlier, the Naxalite view that Indian society is semi-colonial/semi-feudal is conceptually inadequate (Basu and Das, 2013; for a critique of this view from the standpoint of concrete conditions in parts of the red corridor, see Shah, 2013). Yet, it cannot be denied that feudal practices persist within state apparatuses and within civil society and that India is increasingly under the onslaught of imperialism.

their ideologues (e.g. Amartya Sen; Vandana Shiva; many Aam Aadmi party supporters) would like to address the problems which Naxalites talk about and fight against: social and geographical inequality, corruption, poverty, landlessness, illiteracy, social discrimination, fraudulent practices of businesses, crony-capitalism, etc.[40] For example, a part of their protest against mining capitalists taking away people's land is the idea that they can control capitalist businesses in a more people-friendly way. Even Arundhati Roy, who is an enthusiastic supporter of Naxalites, and who believes in going beyond communism and capitalism, and who is no Marxist, thinks that Naxalites' industrialization policy is 'woolly' (2011: 210). Thus, in terms of Marxist class theory, Naxalism is very problematic.

Associated with their problematic view of the class character of India is their view of revolutionary agency, which is their second big theoretical problem: if capitalist exploitation is not the dominant form of exploitation, then wage-labor cannot be main agent of revolution. For them, rural oppressed classes (peasants, including Adivasi peasants) can lead a revolution. This view mistakenly conflates the capacity for revolutionary action with the degree to which a group is oppressed and poverty-stricken (e.g. peasants and adivasis). They seem oblivious of the fact that: the most oppressed group may not be the most revolutionary group (against capitalism). They also forget that: the peasantry are stratified into different classes including a class which exploits poor peasants/laborers and that the peasantry are geographically dispersed in thousands of villages. The non-exploiting independent peasants do have the ability to fight against exploitation and oppression by landlords, moneylenders and state officials but they cannot lead a revolution against the system of private property relations as such. Peasants' class instinct is generally proprietary; it is not coherent and collectivist as the class instinct of the urban proletariat potentially is. This fact is demonstrated by cadres of the Naxalite movement. Kunnath's Maoist respondent, Raju Bhai, very much wanted a piece of private property, as did the hero of the celebrated Indian novel, *Godaan* (the Gift of a cow). Any future success of the movement will be limited by its denial of the dominance of, and therefore, the need to remove, capitalist class relations as such. Its success will also be limited by its actual neglect of the role of the wage-earners in factories and offices as the pre-eminent anti-capitalist force, whose interest lies in their political independence vis-à-vis all sections of the business-class (compradore or not). In class terms, the Naxalite movement is *not* as

---

40   Mazumdar said in 1970 that the majority of the business-people would support the People's democratic revolution as they are a large part of the national bourgeoisie (in Banerjee, 1980).

310   CHAPTER 8

threatening, as the state and some intellectuals think it is. However, by producing the image that it is the single biggest security threat and by labelling *any* movement for justice as Naxalite, the state is using its fight against movement(s) such as Naxalism as an excuse to eliminate any opposition to class rule, including the possibility of the Naxalites' fight for democratic capitalism from becoming a fight against capitalism as such.

There is some relation between Naxalite's theory of class society and their view of how to launch class struggle. Naxalites emphasize extra-economic coercion aspect of exploitation, and not economic-coercion that is the hallmark of the capitalist value relation. This view – coupled with their view of liberal democracy (discussed below) – is partly behind the stress on military struggle within a segment of the movement. The violence practiced by Maoist revolutionary squads, as a part of the Naxalite movement, must be seen as problematic. The ruling class and its state are not Gandhians. So the class struggle below cannot be Gandhian. It is true that the Indian state uses violence to crush people's movements for justice. This is the reality. 'Indian Maoists have at least addressed this reality, even if inadequately, and their very success in sustaining themselves among the poorest is testimony to the partial efficacy of taking up arms. However, for a segment of the Naxalite movement, what should be at best a defensive posture, politically subordinated to a more sophisticated strategy for long-term transformation, has unfortunately become the main strategy itself' (Vanaik, 2011: 107). The issue, therefore, is not whether violence can be used for a defensive cause. The issue is whether violence – and that too, secretive violence by individuals – can be the central method of class struggle. It cannot be.

The Naxalites' armed action is being used by the state as a justification for killing Naxalite supporters who are among the organic leaders of the exploited classes.[41] Such killings by the state are weakening the movement (Banerjee, 2017). The practice of violence affects the political culture of the movement. First, in many areas, anyone who challenges the government about its inactions and who fights for legal rights (e.g. payment of minimum wages), runs the risk of being labelled a Naxalite. And, the 'Naxal label' means punishment. Once one is labelled a Naxalite, it is difficult to return to normal life, relatively free from suspicion, fear and death. So people depend on the party to help them deal with the police and the courts. Thus, many people may remain in

---

41   They are killed by landlord armies supported by mainstream political parties. They are also killed by state's military forces or by state-sponsored civilian militias.

CLASS DYNAMICS OF POVERTY, STATE FAILURE, AND CLASS STRUGGLE 311

the party because they need its protection, and not necessarily because of ideological commitment (Bhatia, 2006: 3181). In the absence of ideologically committed cadres, the social and geographical expansion of the movement suffers. Secondly, there is a culture of intolerance amongst Naxalites towards those holding a different political view, including parties and leaders of the parliamentary left and even those of fraternal Naxalite factions. And the tension is often resolved through violent encounter. This strategy undermines conditions under which intellectual and political efforts can be made towards broad and principled 'Left unity' (a united front within which movements of proletarians and semi-proletarians march separately but strike together) that the radical resolution of the unjust material conditions demands (I am here abstracting from the fact that even if such a united front happens, the two-stage theory of revolution that binds all the elements of the front, including the Naxalites, and the political practices that theory will inform, will be an enormous obstacle to a socialist revolution) and constitute a crisis of revolutionary leadership.

Continuous armed conflicts between state forces and a part of the Naxalite movement have also drastically reduced the space for other forms of struggle (non-violent struggles) and thus compounds the problem that arises out of the movement's neglect of the urban working class. The stress on violent methods on the part of certain sections of the movement does dilute the emphasis on whatshouldbedone:democraticallyorganized,proletarian,political-ideological education and organization (see Haragopal, 2017).[42] As Lenin (1978: 11) said in *Revolutionary Adventurism*: 'without the working people all bombs are powerless, patently powerless'.

Political power of the masses to challenge the whole capitalist system does not come from the Maoist 'barrel of the gun'. Nor does it come from 'semispontaneous consciousness' (of peasants, etc.) (cf. Guha, 1983). The latter is, more or less, a reaction to desperate conditions needing some urgent change. But revolutionary consciousness is a different matter: it reflects the imperative of destroying the relics of capital's history (e.g. feudal landlordism) and of transcending the capitalist system along with undemocratic and imperialist ways in which that system operates. Such a consciousness, including among sections of the peasantry, has to be *actively* worked for, both through education and

---

42 Speaking about the section of the Naxalite movement that prioritizes armed struggle, Haragopal (2017) says that whether the movement will succeed in achieving its goal (i.e. new democracy) will depend on whether it prioritizes political mobilization over its military strategy (see also Murzban, 2014; and Mukherji, 2012 for critiques of Maoist strategy of using violent methods of struggle). Interestingly, like most commentators on Naxalism, Haragopal does not challenge Naxalism's two-stage theory of revolution.

struggle. Such a process must not at all denigrate class consciousness (of peasants and others) in its 'embryonic form' (Lenin, 1977a: 113), including the consciousness which is the raw material of, and which is expressed in the form of, the Naxalite movement.

As I have said, Naxalites' view of liberal democracy is linked to their view of class struggle and the use of arms. A sympathetic analyst of the movement, Professor Mohanty (2006) says that a part of the Maoism-inspired movement has not fully recognized the importance of the liberal democratic process. One can also say that the movement – especially, the segment that emphasizes arms struggle – has not fully understood the *educative* role of practice (i.e. struggle). Liberal democracy is a form of bourgeois-class rule and yet it exists because the masses struggle for it and demand it. It is not a mere concession from the ruling classes; they would be happy to suspend it when doing so is in their interest. This is in fact happening now, as we will see in our discussion later on fascistic tendencies. To paraphrase Marx's second famous Thesis on Feuerbach (Marx and Engels, 1977: 13), whether the state and the ruling classes can meet the radical demands of the exploited classes cannot be (just) a '*scholastic* question'.[43] It is to be resolved in practice, i.e. through their own struggles for radical demands, and, therefore, it is 'a *practical* question'. Democratically-organized mass movements are necessary in struggling to get some material concessions from the state and the propertied classes. Naxalite areas are among the poorest in the country. There are, therefore, numerous things to struggle for, including: publicly provided schools, electricity, water and health centers (Bhatia, 2006: 3181). There is a need for struggles for a living wage and the right to employment and for free transportation. 'However, these issues get eclipsed since most of the Naxalite groups do not wish to engage with the present government except as an enemy' (Bhatia, 2006: 3181). This is because, in my view, Naxalite leaders possibly assume that the *theoretical* knowledge about the state (what it can and cannot do) that *they* possess is shared by the *masses*. This is a serious epistemological lapse. The bourgeois democratic process, within limits, offers to social movements for justice, some limited possibilities for exposing the patently undemocratic practices and developmental failures of the state and ruthless exploitation by the ruling classes (domestic and foreign). It is useful in educating the masses about the limits to what is possible

---

43   Some feminists and anti-caste thinkers believe that the state is not as inflexible as Marxists think because it can meet a variety of *their* demands (see Gudavarthy, 2005: 5417).

Marxists have made the theoretical argument that: the state will not cross some well-defined limits in terms of meeting the demands of exploited classes. Those who are not convinced by this *theoretical* answer may find the answer in and through *practice* (= struggle).

CLASS DYNAMICS OF POVERTY, STATE FAILURE, AND CLASS STRUGGLE 313

within the system and about alternative anti-capitalist, anti-feudal demands. The process of struggle for concessions creates a condition for building solidarity and promoting class-consciousness, at multiple scales, among the exploited classes. They must emerge as agents of their self-emancipation *in the process of* fighting for these concessions at multiple scales. One, of course, does not have to believe that the state can or will meet these demands, but the masses must discover the limits to what the state can do partly in practice, i.e. in the process of making their demands.

Finally, the movement has been said to have paid in-adequate attention to gender and caste issues *in practice*. It has sought to respond a potential problem here. Celebrating the 50th anniversary of the movement that began in Naxalbari in 1967, and presenting a history of the movement, Bhattacharya, who is a major ideologue of the Naxalite movement and a leader of the CPI(ML) says:

> Naxalbari was a great moment of radicalisation of the Indian communist movement. It gave rise to a new paradigm of class struggle that is not confined to the economic realm or the parameters of parliamentary politics, but committed to fight out oppression and injustice in every sphere of social existence. Issues of caste and gender, race and nationality, language and culture found their rightful place in this new praxis of class struggle.
>
> BHATTACHARYA, 2017

The Naxalite movement does emphasize the fight against non-class oppression. Yet, some critics say, patriarchal attitudes and practices persist within Naxal organizations (Mohanty, 2006: 3164). Women are almost negligible in leadership positions. The movement seeks to 'create new casteless, classless communities where women will be equal to men' but it is 'most often led by men from elite backgrounds' (Shah, 2017: 55). Shah adds: 'In the Maoist case, although many Adivasis and, in some areas, women joined the revolutionaries, the higher-caste leaders not only failed to give sufficient space for the nurturing of lower-caste, Adivasi and women leaders, but also seemed to neglect the fact that the societies they worked amidst had more egalitarian gender relations than the ones from which they had come' (ibid.). The hard and dangerous work of handling guns is mainly done by Dalits or people from the lower castes, and those who get killed belong mostly to these sections (Bhatia, 2006: 3180). Tribals, Dalits and other low caste people comprising the bulk of their support base 'are not [yet] adequately represented in the upper echelons of the party leadership' (ibid.). Culturally, while 'song writing, tune setting and writing of poetry [generally] ...centred around the SC (Scheduled Castes) and OBC

(Other Backward Classes) *wadas* in the villages, ...writing theory and speech making still remained an upper caste phenomenon' within the movement (Ilaiah, 2004: 238).

4   Conclusion

Making history, from a class standpoint, means that existing conditions of life are not acceptable because they are exploitative and oppressive, and that new and better conditions of life can, and must, be created through political struggles against the class/classes responsible for the existing conditions. The act of making history (and geography) in a class-society *is* class struggle. This chapter is about class and class struggle in the historical-geographical context of post-colonial India. It discusses how relations of class as well as caste- and gender-based social oppression have created extremely difficult conditions of living for workers and peasants in rural and aboriginal areas, which the post-colonial capitalist-landlord state has, more or less, failed to significantly mitigate. The conjunctural combination of unjust conditions of living and the failure of the state to significantly alleviate these conditions has created a situation ripe for *class* struggle, one instance of which is the Naxalite movement, a part of the world-wide Maoist movement.[44] Its growth and spatial spread have been uneven in time and space. The movement has much appeal among the poor in many areas. This, like other similar movements, 'are explicit rejections of both the right to commoditize and appropriate natural resources and the exclusion from development of peoples in poor areas containing natural resources' (Herring, 2013: 131). The Naxalite movement, along with other such instances of political action by the masses (e.g. trade union struggles mentioned earlier), suggest, once again, that the masses are not passive victims of exploitation and oppression.

The Naxalite movement is rooted in material conditions of existence, social-cultural as well as economic. It has fruitfully combined class politics (albeit in a rather limited manner) as well as those of cultural oppression. Thus the Naxalite movement shares important characteristics of what Veltmeyer (1997) calls 'new peasant movements' in his research on peasants in Latin America. Many people within the state agencies, and many middle class people, do not

---

44   Gomes (2015: 106) says: 'the story behind the Maoist Conflict in India is a story of grievances arising out of feelings of exclusion of various forms. We see how the underdeveloped districts and districts with higher land inequality are more prone to conflict'.

CLASS DYNAMICS OF POVERTY, STATE FAILURE, AND CLASS STRUGGLE 315

fully understand Naxalites' pro-poor ideological significance. Partly influenced by a militaristic thinking, they homogenize the movement associating it exclusively with violence, and treating Naxalites merely/mainly as armed thugs, without any political and socio-economic program of development for the poor.[45]

However, the Naxalite movement does suffer from serious problems which emanate from its inadequate class-based understanding and class-based practice. The material conditions of deprivation are produced dominantly by the specific ways in which capitalism works in the concrete conditions of India, which include remnants of feudalism, and liberal democracy, within the system of global capitalism. The Naxalites have not fully and consistently understood this: that the most important reason for rural distress, and indeed the distress of the majority of the country's population, is the *capitalist* character of the system, which is also mainly responsible for state's failure to mitigate some of the adverse effects of the system on the poor. Because of the Naxalites' inadequate understanding of the system's dynamics, their dominant focus has been mistakenly on the rural/agrarian issue (in backward regions) and on its so-called 'semi-feudal' shell. This has meant that the movement has, more or less, been disconnected socially from the working class and spatially from urban areas, the main theatres of accumulation and exploitation by both domestic and imperialist bourgeoisie.

It is not popular to say this, but the reality is this: class is the most fundamental determinant of life. The ways in which class relations work in a historical-geographical situation, including through relations of gender and caste/ethnicity, etc., tend to create unjust conditions of existence. These conditions necessitate, prompt as well as influence class struggle, whose success in any given time and place is not guaranteed. Inspired by Maoism, the Naxalite movement, like other movements for justice, originated and continues to exist because of the extremely unjust material conditions of existence of millions of ordinary working people. The continuation of the movement is due also to the Naxalites being able to provide some relief to the suffering masses and help them stand up for their rights (as discussed in the next chapter). Yet, inadequate class-analysis and inadequate political practice, along with state repression, have limited the success of the movement.

---

45   Of course, a segment of the movement is itself no less responsible for such a perception as it too seems to be eager to propagate armed struggle (Gupta, 2006: 3172).

CHAPTER 9

State Repression as Class Struggle from Above

When the state is not responsive to ordinary people's needs, and when the normal operation of the economic system does not meet their needs, what do they do?[1] They engage in struggles, small or large, covert and overt, legal or illegal, against the state and against the economic system, protected by the state. India is known not only for the dual failure – state failure and economy's or market's failure – and associated poverty and inequality and social oppression. India is also known for its history of popular struggles against all forms of injustice.

Rural class struggle informed by Maoism is one of these struggles, as we have discussed in the previous chapter. It has mobilized poor people against sections of the propertied class (e.g. landlords, traders; mining companies) for social justice in India. The movement has conferred limited benefits upon the poor in some places. It is not averse to using violence to get these benefits and to stop them from being taken away. The Indian state seeks to violently repress it, killing thousands. Anyone suspected of having any links with the Naxalite movement, and especially, with that faction of it which the state has banned, can be jailed or killed. This raises wider conceptual questions about the relation between social movements (movements against injustice) and the state. Why does a liberal-democratic state kill its own citizens?

It must be made clear at the outset that a critique of the Indian state's violent response to the Maoist movement does not *at all* mean an endorsement of how Maoists understand society and seek to change it. This chapter takes the position that: long-term structural changes in society require active self-emancipatory participation of politically conscious masses in cities and villages in social-political mobilization against exploitation and injustice, and that emphasizing violent methods of destruction as a strategy, cannot construct conditions for social justice, even though such methods may yield short-term localized results.

The first section of the chapter briefly and critically discusses the existing conceptual literature on state repression of social movements, and presents a preliminary attempt at an alternative approach to the topic. The next two sections provide some empirical evidence, including from newspaper reports,[2]

---

1 An earlier version of this chapter appeared as Das (2017).

2 The use of newspaper reports in the social movements research has become a popular source (Earl et al., 2004); their online availability as a 'cyber-common-property resource' has

© KONINKLIJKE BRILL NV, LEIDEN, 2020 | DOI:10.1163/9789004415560_010

STATE REPRESSION AS CLASS STRUGGLE FROM ABOVE   317

which supports this approach: while the second section looks at the state's ideological-repressive response to the movement, the third section examines why the state deploys violent means against it. The final section draws out some conceptual implications of the discussion.

1   State Response to 'Social' Movement: A Conceptual Discussion

There is a large literature on why social struggles/movements occur in rural areas (Anderson and Seligson, 1994; Castells, 1983; Houtzager, 2000; Oslender, 2004; Page, 1975; Skocpol, 1982) and in society at large (Auvinen, 1997; Dudley and Miller, 1998; MacCulloch, 2005; Miller, 2000; Morris, 2000). This chapter focusses on the state's response to social or people's movements: in particular, its violent response (della Porta, 1996, 2014; Hess and Martin, 2006; Ondetti, 2006;[3] Fominaya and Wood, 2011; Ortiz, 2013). Among the various explanations, I will deal with two: state form (i.e. whether it is liberal-democratic) and social nature of protesters.[4]

Lack of democracy – democratic state form – is said to cause state repression. In democracies, agents of repression are less able to function without some form of civilian oversight, which compels them to exert greater effort in justifying their action (Davenport, 2004: 542).[5] Repression may hurt politicians'

---

  contributed to this trend. Of course, this common property resource is increasingly in danger of being controlled by capitalist companies in their own interest.

3 The last two sources consider how unjust state repression can engender social mobilization.

4 There are other explanations as well. For example: it is argued that repression can also make individuals realize that the state has the monopoly of force within society and thus pre-empt future anti-state resistance (Davenport, 2004). Also argued is that state's repressive activity in the past enhances its possibility at present. '[O]nce specialized agencies of state coercion are in operation, elites are likely to calculate that the relative costs of relying on coercion are lower... Moreover, directors [of repressive agencies] may ... recommend [or initiate] violent "solutions" to suspected opposition... as a means of justifying ... [their] continued existence' (Gurr, 1986: 160). It has also been said that elites who have used violence to gain power (or for national consolidation) will use violence to remain in power, as they believe that their past success in the use of violence will repeat itself (Gurr, 1988: 52). Thus state's (state actors') interests and state structure (especially its repressive structures) explain state's repressive activity. This view has some merit, but it is problematic. Just the fact that specialized agencies and methods of coercion exist does not mean that the state will use these against a given social movement.

5 It should be noted that: in some cases where mass movements have used peaceful means to challenge the state, and succeeded in changing public opinion in favor of the movement and against state policy, particular governments have had to exert greater effort in justifying their repressive actions, because the social movement has been a kind of educator of the public, and a shaper of public opinion.

prospect of returning to office. Democracy creates spaces for non-violent methods of resolving conflicts through political parties and elections (Henderson, 1991). Effective democracy also provides citizens – at least those with political resources – the tool to oust potentially abusive leaders from office (ibid.). The democratic state can also use non-coercive measures – concessions/reforms – to meet challenges from internal opposition (Gurr, 1988: 55). '[T]he more libertarian a state is, the less intense its violence can and tends to become' (Rummel, 1984: 443; 1985). A libertarian state guarantees not only basic civil liberties and political rights but also economic freedom. Indeed, if the state regulates economic affairs less, there will be less violence: 'the more government, the more violence' (Rummel, 1984: 461).[6]

In sum, the liberal argument is that: democracy pacifies. But this argument suffers from several problems. That democracy provides citizens the tool to oust potentially abusive leaders from office (or to force them to change their policies significantly) assumes the following: people's resistance is in a form that is approved by the state, and that electoral participation is an effective way of redressing inequalities. But most importantly the 'democracy pacifies' argument fails to properly recognize the constraining effect of private property relations (combined with a market-mode of resource allocation and use) on the exercise of democratic rights of ordinary people and on state's power to address their problems by giving meaningful material concessions. State repression of those protesting austerity points to this fact. As Dryzek (1996) argues, business demands on the state, whether in India or the USA, restrict state's political options, more or less, to those that support capitalist interests, even if these are anti-democratic and hurt the interests of the majority. Further, repression may not hurt chances of returning to office if *all* major political parties agree on the legitimacy of repression of given movements for social justice, and they *will* agree if they believe in the sanctity of private property and free markets. Further, to say that a state which controls economic affairs less will be less violent is to suggest that we should expect a saintly state and peaceful society. Instead, the 'more' capitalist the state becomes in its day-today activities, the less scope it has, to meet the demands of ordinary people, and therefore the more violent it tends to be in response to these demands.

People's democratic right is a valuable gain (Bobbio, 2005) obtained/ sustained through struggle. A capitalist society with liberal democracy is better

---

6 Thus democratic institutions eliminate the desire for repression by opening up the political system to citizens, the need for repression by providing other mechanisms of influence, and the capacity for repression by curtailing the freedom of coercive agents (Davenport, 2004: 539; also Schatzman, 2005).

than one without.[7] But democracy, which is a form of class rule, generally does a good job of amicably resolving material-ideological conflicts that are *internal* not only to the ruling classes (e.g. conflicts among various fractions of ruling classes over access to state support for them or over how to manage the capitalist system) but also to the political elite of different political parties, an elite that is broadly supportive of these classes. Democracy may cause a time lag between a movement's beginning and onset of repression. But it is unlikely to stop the state from using repressive measures against a radical social movement that challenges certain aspects of class relations (e.g. unequal distribution of land) and certain effects of these relations (e.g. poverty, etc.).[8]

In the second explanation of state violence, protesters using non-institutional and confrontational tactics[9] are seen by the state as a greater threat, so they face greater repression than the dissidents not using these tactics (Davenport, 2004; Poe and Tate, 1994). These kinds of protest provide authorities with a legitimate mandate to sanction them as a law and order measure. But this explanation is also inadequate: peaceful protests (e.g. Occupy protests) have been routinely repressed, if they go beyond the limit of what the state and the ruling class will tolerate.[10]

An alternative explanation of state repression of people's struggles must these two approaches as points of departure. It must, at the minimum, look at the class character of the state and of mobilizations/protestors. First the latter. One must recognize two things here. For one thing, it is the subordinate strata of proletarian and semi-proletarian *classes,* who have little (informal) access to state power, that tend to use non-institutional tactics. For another, these classes or class-strata are considered a serious threat not just because of the *way* in which they rebel (i.e. the non-institutional method of protest) but because of *what* they rebel against: the fact that they rebel against what the state must

---

7   Maoists (and others) realized this during the mid-1970s when civil liberties were suspended in India.

8   On contradictory empirical effects of capitalism on human rights, see Burkhart (2002).

9   The word 'non-institutional' refers to direct action and extra-electoral methods.

10   Further, the chances of repression are said to be greater when the threat comes from subordinate protestors because they are said to collapse under pressure owing to their limited retaliatory power (Stockdill, 1996 in Earl, 2003). Failure of the attempt to repress will invite public ridicule, so easy targets – subordinate protestors – are more prone to repression. Thus, protests that are threatening (because they use non-institutional tactics) and that are weak (because they cannot retaliate easily) will be most prone to repression (Earl, 2003: 54). Research indeed shows that events in which subordinate groups participate are more likely to invite police action (Earl et al., 2003). But the reason for this may not necessarily be that that they are weak and have limited retaliatory power (India's Naxalites have much retaliatory power). Instead of their weakness, we must stress the class character, and therefore, class power, of the subordinate protestors.

protect (i.e. aspects of the private property system such as dispossession, super-exploitation, etc.).

In understanding why the state represses social movements, one must stress the class character of the state as well.[11] Whatever else it may be, 'the state is an organ of class rule, an organ for the oppression of one class by another; it is the creation of "order", which legalizes and perpetuates this oppression' within a given territory (Lenin, 1977b: 11). Its most fundamental objective is to protect exploitative private property relations and sustain/promote the associated mechanisms of accumulation (Das, 2006; Draper, 1977: 251). Class relations are fundamentally coercive, even under capitalism which celebrates individual freedom. For example, the reproduction of capitalist class relations (including the market-imperative) is based on the continuing separation of laborers from means of production. This separation has to be reproduced continuously. People are dispossessed of their land (and indeed access to common property and state's limited benefits), and often through state and private force. This happened during Marx's times (Marx, 1977: 874–876), and this happens now (Donnelly, 1989; Farid, 2005; Harvey, 2003).[12] People have to work under the 'despotic' control of property owners as well (Marx, 1977: 477, 548–550), surrendering much of the fruit of their labor to capital. This despotism often takes the form of violence against the masses, including proletarian and semi-proletarian women.

Every movement or mobilization is not directly against the existence of private property relations as such. A movement can fight against the ways in which these relations work or against the actual effects produced by these relations. For example, they can be against property owners not paying (minimum) wages or against the extension of the working day much beyond the normal. When laborers have the right to get minimum wages and employers

---

11   By state I refer to a set of institutions which exercise monopoly over the means of violence and whose main aim is to control the subordinate classes and protect the private property rights of the exploiting classes. The state, which appears to be neutral and to represent political equality, is rooted in substantive inequalities. This does not mean that all institutions of the state (e.g. police, army, judiciary, legislature, executive, various local branches of the state) work necessarily in tandem at a given point in time, nor that every single action of the state is pro-capitalist (in an immediate sense). There is a wide range of views on the state. Some have debated the state as an autonomous entity (Skocpol, 1985), a tool for the powerful classes (Domhoff, 1990; Mills, 1959), and as a structure of relations that work to create conditions for accumulation (Poulantzas, 1968). Others have discussed the state as an ensemble of representations, processes, and practices (e.g. Lemke, 2007; Mitchell, 1999; Sharma and Gupta, 2006). For recent reviews of ideas about the state, see Pressman, 2006.

12   Capitalism is also coercive in another sense: having been separated from access to means of production, people must depend on the uncertain labor market to find work, and if they don't, they starve; and this reliance on property owners must be reproduced by the state through coercive enforcement of private property relations (Marx, 1977: 272–273).

have the right to set the wage the way they want, or whenever peasants have a right to live and work in an area and companies want that area for factories or to extract minerals, it is often the case that '[b]etween equal rights, force decides' (Marx, 1977: 344). And, this force is generally (and in the last instance) the force of the state used on behalf of the property owners. The regime of low-wages is coercively reinforced. If lower classes challenge the right to private property, or the ways in which property owners accumulate wealth/income, this would be framed by the state as non-negotiable or difficult-to-negotiate. So, the movement faces violence. Whether the *mode/form* of such a movement is non-institutional/confrontational/violent is generally immaterial as far as the cause of state violence is concerned. The *content* of the movement, its class content, is moot. And the state being democratic or not is largely beside the point.

It would be inaccurate to state that the state rules only by coercion. It does not, as Gramsci has suggested. Sometimes it does introduce measures to alleviate the negative *effects* of private property relations and of mechanisms of class-based accumulation. Decentralized governance which moves the government administration to people's doorsteps, some redistribution of income and assets, employment creation through public works, and so on *are* implemented by the state. The state does this often in response to (violent and non-violent) movements.[13] Development measures of the state are a relatively cheap means of earning legitimacy. Legitimacy comes from the mere introduction of the measures (measures on paper, the very discourse of measures or of development). It also comes from their limited implementation, the actual concessions (e.g. developmental benefits). Many measures do remain on paper or under-implemented because their implementation will hurt the economic elite (for example, a significant rise in wages that is mediated/enforced by the state will adversely affect profits of capitalists, and state-enforced land redistribution without compensation to big landlords will affect the interests of landlords).[14] If a movement of subordinate strata fights for the implementation of pro-poor policies beyond a *given limit*, the state tends to make the movement a target for attack. Whether there is liberal democracy and whether protesters are violent is, once again, beside the matter. These two factors can, generally, only shape the magnitude of state violence and how quickly the state violence comes as a response.

---

13   The relatively autonomous role of an enlightened state leadership cannot be ruled out.
14   This is the case, according to some, even if in the conflict between the government and the Naxalite movement, the government programs make 'civilians more willing to support the police because it improves the relationship between the government and the people' (Khanna and Zimmerman, 2017: 132) and can, if effectively implemented, potentially mitigate violence (Dasgupta et al., 2017).

And finally, we must bear in mind the scalar character of the state in relation to effects of democracy on repression. Both economic reproduction of class relations and state's support for these relations happen at different scales. There are property owners (e.g. landowners; mining business) whose economic operations are more locally oriented, and others which are more nationally and globally oriented. State activities also exist at different scales: local, provincial and national (Cox, 1990). Challenge to capitalist relations and the state happen at different scales, therefore. A *nation*-state may be liberal-democratic as indicated by its national constitution and by social-political practices at the national scale, but at the *local* scale state institutions may be much less democratic. This partly reflects interests of ruling classes at the local-scale and the ways in which their interests support, and are supported by, undemocratic relations of gender, racial and caste inequalities. The argument that democracy reduces violence must be tempered by the fact that at the local scale there may be very little democracy in practice and therefore any resistance against the state, violent or not, will tend to meet with violent response from the state. Of course, the actual level of violence depends on the place-specific balance between state power and the power of the subordinate classes/class-strata.

This power balance is often upset in many places. The northern region of West Bengal State in India was such a place. Like many other regions of India, it has a long history of peasants' and workers' movement (Kennedy and Purushotham, 2012). From the early 1950s, a radical section of the Communist Party of India (CPI) organized peasants in West Bengal's Naxalbari subdivision of Darjeeling district. This is when the Maoist movement began and spread to other parts of the country. We have discussed some aspect of the movement in the previous chapter. In this chapter, the focus is on state's response to the movement.

2   The Indian State's Response to the Naxalite Movement

The Indian state has responded to the Naxalite movement by mainly two means: a developmental means which aims to produce consent of the affected masses to the legitimacy of the state, and a non-developmental (coercive) means. The deployment of the non-developmental means is supported by the third form of state response: an ideological struggle against the Naxalite movement. Ideologically fighting against the movement, the state is keen on 'bracketing the Naxalite movement with the terrorism of ... different religious, ethnic or linguistic varieties' (Banerjee, 2002). At one time, the Home Ministry described Naxalism as a 'more formidable threat than (posed by) Islamic

STATE REPRESSION AS CLASS STRUGGLE FROM ABOVE

fundamentalist groups'.[15] The state describes the movement: as a 'menace', and as 'left-wing *extremism*'. It engages in the domestic othering of the Naxalite area of influence ('the Red Corridor') as 'unpatriotic', 'undemocratic', a 'diseased zone' (Malreddy, 2014).[16] For the state:

> The perversion of Naxalism has to be traced to its very roots in the ideological concepts like class struggle and class violence and a demonology created by them. It is this demonology that then leads to terrorist acts...It is easy to understand that these concepts and the acts of violence that flow from these concepts have no sanction whatsoever ... in Indian philosophy and culture... Naxalism is a crime against humanity.
>
> GOI, 1998

In a speech in 1998, India's Home Minister belonging to BJP (Bharatiya Janata Party), a Hindu Right party, said that Naxalism is a 'particularly dangerous challenge to the rule of Law, to the Constitutional order, to the nation's *internal and external security* and to the supremacy and legitimacy of the Indian State itself' (GOI, 1998).[17] He added: Naxalism 'has blurred the distinctive nature of a war on the borders by making every street and every home a frontier of the nation. ... Naxalism is an enemy of the Indian dream [dream of an India free from hunger, fear and corruption]' (ibid.). In April 2006, addressing a day-long meeting of chief ministers of the provinces hit by Naxalism, the then Prime Minister, Mr. Singh, of the Congress Party, said: 'It would not be an exaggeration to say that the problem of Naxalism is the single biggest internal security challenge ever faced by our country' (quoted in *Rediff*, 2006). It is also a threat

---

15   http://www.dcrcdu.org/dcrc/Navalakha.doc.

16   Malreddy (2014) says that Indian state's response to the Maoist insurgency has been ideologically shaped by the 'new terrorism' discourse of Western powers, following the absolutely condemnable terrorist attack on the US; this discourse 'others' Islamic terrorism as a trope of a 'civilizational clash' between East and West.

17   Given the fascistic right's deep antagonism towards left forces, the onslaught against Naxalites continues under the Hindu-nationalist government in power now, which is a major threat to democratic rights of ordinary people (Das, 2016). BJP's Home Minister Rajnath Singh says he can finish the Maoists in '3 years' (by 2016) by flooding Chhattisgarh with troops. The Rightwing BJP government will not be any less authoritarian than the centrist securalist government of earlier times. 'The only change from the so-called "security and development" approach of the [earlier] regime, is the "securitise and communalise" approach of the BJP and its associates, illustrated by the recent announcement that "non-Hindus" would not be allowed into Bastar villages and the plan to develop sangh parivar-scripted "local histories" of adivasi areas'. (Sundar, 2014b). Sundar adds: 'what we have is not an anti-Maoist plan but an anti-adivasi plan since it is they who will bear the brunt of the government's onslaught'.

to democracy and to 'our way of life' (ibid.). Thus in the eyes of the state, the Naxalite struggle is ideological and is against the nation's cultural tradition. According to both of the biggest parties of the capitalists and landowners (the Congress and the BJP), Naxalism is a threat not to the oppressive practices of certain property owners but a threat to the *nation as a whole*, and one that exists every*where* within the national space. In other words, the Naxalite threat is scaled up: it is 'nationalized'. This allows the state to exaggerate the level of threat it poses, so that consent can be produced to the national-scale mobilization of military forces against the movement.[18]

Extraordinary police powers and the draconian laws have been used against Naxalites (SAHRDC, 2002). The Prevention of Terrorism Ordinance (POTA) of 2001 was promulgated during the BJP rule. It has now been repealed under public pressure. When civil society activists toured six districts of Jharkhand State between January 29 and February 3, 2003, they found that most of those arrested under POTA were cultivators, students or daily wage-earners. A majority of them were booked because they had provided food to Naxalites or possessed Naxal literature. When asked how a Naxalite is identified, a senior police official told reporters: 'Anyone caught with a copy of the Communist Manifesto or Mao's Red Book becomes a suspicious character. We then watch him and often find clinching evidence'.[19] A police officer said to Arundhati Roy (2009): if people in the forests have malaria tablets and Dettol (an antiseptic and disinfectant liquid) bottles which come from outside, they must be Maoists, and his 'boys' kill them. State killing of Naxalites continues (Figure 9.1 below). Between 1994 and 2014 (October end), security personnel have killed 29,904 Maoists/Naxalites, producing an annual average death of 1424, or 4 deaths a day (one every 6 hours).

'Encounters' are usually faked by the police to cover up the torture and subsequent murder of Naxalite suspects and sympathizers. These are extra-judicial killings by the liberal-democratic state. In many areas, hundreds of young men attend the police stations every week. Sympathizers of Naxalites are picked up at midnights (Murali, 2003). The state has deployed civilian militias which have been involved in rape, torture and displacement of aboriginal people. The Operation Green Hunt – a massive mobilization of paramilitary forces – is on. Militarized zones are produced in parts of India: 'Today Jharkhand [a province in eastern India] is a fully militarized zone. There are over a hundred bases

---

18   In more recent times, the state has threatened intellectuals who sympathize with Naxalism.

19   A Human Rights Watch Briefing Chapter for the 59th Session of the United Nations Commission on Human Rights March 25, 2003 available at: htttp//hrw.org/un/chr59/counter-terrorism-bck4.htm.

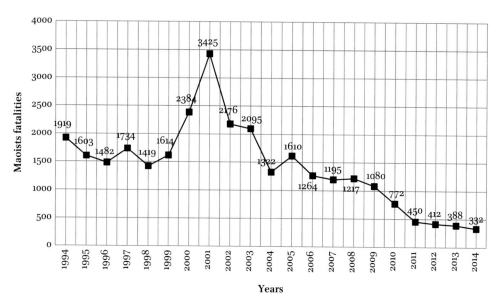

FIGURE 9.1 Fatalities of Maoists in India (1994–2014)
SOURCE: DATA FROM AN AUTHORITATIVE SOURCE, HTTP://WWW.SATP.ORG/

with a total of 50,000 official paramilitary troops involved in military action. There are Indian Army bases, too, but these are not involved in direct action yet' (Dias, in Ismi, 2013).

State violence is reinforced by, and complements, the direct violence of the wealthy class. In many parts of the country, members of this class hire private force (including goons) to attack anyone who challenges their super-exploitative practices (and upper-caste hegemony). They also have easy access to the police which is often bought with money and/or political connection. If industrial and mining businesses have private security force, landlords have their own armies. Violent activities of landlords and business people are often not penalized by the state. The legal process is more or less on sale: if one does not have money, it is impossible for one to get justice from the courts.

3   Why Does the State Repress the Naxalite Movement?

Why is there so much state repression, in a society which claims to have, and which, undoubtedly, does have, some elements of a liberal-democracy and which boasts of a spiritual culture of non-violence? One answer is that Naxalites use violent methods. This is to some extent *true*. Naxalites squarely place violence – armed agrarian struggle – on the agenda as a justifiable means to fight the Indian state with the objective of a radical transformation (Banerjee, 2002). They challenge the state's monopoly of violence, and assert the right of its opponents to resort to violence against the propertied classes and the state.[20] Some Naxalite groups (e.g. CPI-Maoist) have continued their near-absolute commitment to violence. But this is not true about other groups. For example, the CPI-ML (Liberation), says: 'we do not subscribe to any theory of "excitative violence" and still less to "individual assassination"'. But 'the rural poor cannot be denied their right to organise their own resistance forces to counter the attacks of landlord armies' (Arvind Das, 1997).

The Naxalite violence is real. In many areas of the country, 'The local administrators, especially the policemen are afraid to venture out of the main towns or their homes and offices' (Ray, 2002). And, in other areas, local level officials pay Naxalites money out of the development funds (e.g. 30 per cent or so) in exchange for peace (Shah, 2006; Srivastava, 1997). Numerous members of the legislature, and regional and local politicians are provided round the clock security in view of the Naxalite threat. Apart from rich traders and landlords, more than 225 political leaders, including those of parliamentary Marxist parties, were killed by a Naxalite outfit (People's War Group or PWG) only in Andhra Pradesh between 1993 and 2003 (Hindustan Times, 2003). As Figure 9.2 shows, security personnel have been regularly killed by Naxalites. Between 1994 and 2014 (end of October), Naxalites have caused 9424 security personnel deaths, producing an annual average of 452 (or more than one a day).[21]

That the Naxalites use violence, and therefore the state is violent towards them, is only a part of the story, however. There is another reason for state violence: Naxalites' political-development activities and political mobilization of people through these activities constitute an economic threat to certain types of private property owners, and a political-ideological threat to capitalist state power, as explained below. In many areas, poor people (especially, aboriginal people) are either led by Naxalites, or receive sympathy from them (see Harriss, 2011a). Naxalites articulate grievances against what the state has done (e.g. expropriation of people's land) and against what it has not done (e.g. its failure to satisfy people's basic needs). Naxalites construct an alternative

---

20 Charu Mazumdar, the architect of the movement, said that distributing land of 'feudal classes... among the landless and poor peasants... cannot be done peacefully. ... In today's era ... we cannot organize peaceful mass movements. ... Because the ruling class will not, and is not giving us any such opportunity' (in Banerjee, 1980: 26–27, 78).

21 As in the previous figure, this number excludes the civilian deaths in the incidents, for which Maoists/Naxalites must be co-responsible along with security personnel. The number of security personnel killed is one fourth the number of Naxalites/Maoists killed by security personnel.

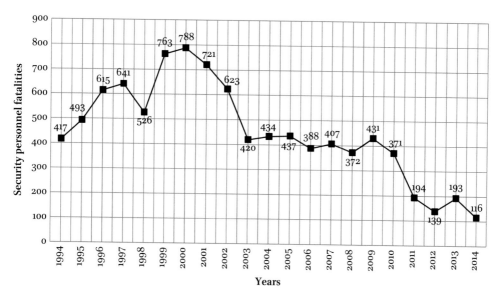

FIGURE 9.2 Security personnel fatalities in India (1994–2014)
SOURCE: DATA FROM AN AUTHORITATIVE SOURCE, HTTP://WWW.SATP.ORG/

landscape of development in socially-spatially marginal areas, within their limited means (Table 9.1). This landscape includes a variety of developmental activities which might put many NGOs to shame.

Where domestic or foreign big business is seeking to control the natural resources (e.g. minerals; land), Naxalites mobilize the aboriginal[22] peoples, as a part of a broader coalition of forces, against the land grab. The Naxalite left mobilized the tribals against land grab for the Posco steel project in Odisha (CPI-ML, 2011) Odisha. In some non-aboriginal areas as well, where attempts have been made to trample on the land and water rights of poorer people to promote capitalist development, Naxalites have fought against such attempts (e.g. the SEZ cases in West Bengal). In my own research I have seen the CPI(ML) Liberation mobilizing the fishermen castes around Orissa's Chilika lake, where the traditional fishing rights are being violated by rich investors of

---

22 Although I have stressed the aboriginal status of the people that Naxalites have mobilized, it is my view that the aboriginality itself is not necessarily the main cause of their sufferings. The cause of their suffering is their class background (e.g. the fact they are property-less or are gradually losing their property through market and extra-economic mechanisms; their reliance on a precarious labor market where wages are low). Their experience of class relations is reinforced by their aboriginal status which explains their discrimination in the economic sphere and the fact that the state has failed to give them the benefits that they deserve and that are claimed to be provided to them.

TABLE 9.1   Naxalite development activities

– Building/maintaining irrigation infrastructure	– Education
– Community kitchen	– Health-services
– Land distribution among the poor	– Crime-control; administration of justice
– Abolition of bonded labor	– Implementing minimum wage policy
– Stopping exploitation of aboriginal women	– Punishing corrupt officials
– Fighting for fishing-community's right to fish	– Relief-measures
– Protection of peasant-tenants against eviction	– Making politicians declare their assets
– Protesting displacement of (aboriginal) people caused by capitalist development projects	
– Making sure low caste laborers/peasants can vote without fear	

SOURCE: VARIOUS NEWSPAPER REPORTS AND ACADEMIC SOURCES

non-fishermen caste.[23] They provide protection to forest-dwellers against oppression by government officials who themselves behave as coercive landlords (Balagopal, 2006: 2185–2186; Roy, 2011). With their help, aboriginal people can enjoy access to state-controlled forests in some areas. The Naxalites also mobilize the masses against the destruction of their environment by capitalist development (see Kujur, 2006).

Naxalites have taken up issues of fixing prices for forest produce collected and sold by aboriginal communities, including by mobilizing them to strike for a higher price. In many areas under their influence, the price of *tendu* leaves (that are used to make country cigarettes), for example, did increase from Rs. 2–3 for 100 bundles (each bundle has 50 leaves) in the early 1980s to Rs. 80–100 by the mid-1990s.

In some places, the granaries of landlords are ransacked, and records of peasants' debts to moneylenders burnt. Naxalites occupy the ceiling surplus land (the land owned by landowners beyond the legal limit) and defend it by using force, if necessary, and distribute the land among the poor.[24] Naxalites have also secured minimum wages fixed by the State government for laborers

---

23   That the traditional Left has also played some role in slowing down neoliberalization (and in forcing the state to implement some pro-poor measures) is un-deniable.

24   By early 1990s, a group of neo-Naxalites formations in Bihar had distributed 14,000 acres among the poor (Sunday, 1992). In Andhra Pradesh alone, PWG is believed to have distributed half a million acres of land to poor people according to Prakash Singh (1995: 108). Naxalites have also taken land from the government (e.g. Forest department) and given it to the poor as well. The CPI Maoist itself has distributed 300,000 acres of forest land between 1986 and 2000 (Roy, 2011: 74).

STATE REPRESSION AS CLASS STRUGGLE FROM ABOVE

(Behera, 2002; Louis, 2005; Wilson, 1999: 340). They are involved in the protection of rights of agricultural tenants and have fought to abolish bonded labor.

Naxalites have worked against social oppression. The viciously patriarchal dowry system has become less of a problem in many Naxalite areas (Bhatia, 2006). In Andhra Pradesh, PWG campaigns against gambling and prostitution (Singh, 1995: 112). Kunnath (2006: 116) reports that from the mid-1970s the Naxalite movement took up Dalit grievances and organized struggles against caste and class oppression. Not surprisingly, Dalit communities, along with those from the aboriginal communities, formed the primary support base of the movement. Naxalites have managed to roll back powerful upper caste militias in some areas. The social basis of CPI-ML (Liberation), in Bihar, has been centered on the Dalits' struggle for dignity (as well as for land and wages). They have organized separate anti-caste mass organizations, and fought for socio-economic benefits, including the reservation of jobs for lower castes in the private sector (Gudavarthy, 2005). Inter-religious and inter-caste marriages are being promoted. Parents and relatives who oppose such alliances are educated about the need to change their outlook (Bhelari, 2003). One Naxalite outfit (MCC) arranged at least 2,000 such marriages in Chatra District (in Jharkhand State).

Many Naxalite groups participate in elections. As Arvind Das (1987) writes, the setting up of Voters' Protection Committees by CPI-ML (Liberation) aims to ensure that the low-caste, poor people can vote without fear. Naxalites also mobilize people to demand that politicians announce publicly their assets both before and after becoming members of legislature, a demand that has led to the police shooting down many Naxalites (Misra, 1994). Punishing corrupt state officials, who eat up the government money meant for the poor, is another part of the Naxalite development agenda. They have organized rallies against crimes, corruption and communalism.[25] They run schools, health systems, and community kitchens (Navlakha, 2006: 2188; Chaudhuri, 2001). They propagate progressive ideas and educate people about the ills of the system (e.g. corruption; anti-people nature of development) through cultural activities (e.g. dance and songs). They force doctors to attend to patients, and make truant teachers teach classes.

---

25 One reason why the Hindu fundamentalists are against the Naxalites is that they are an obstacle to the Hindutva forces trying to Hinduize the aboriginal people and turn them against, say, Christians.

Thus Naxalites have produced an alternative landscape of development at the local/regional scale, however limited the developmental benefits for the poor may be. This landscape is an economic, political, and ideological threat to the state, and therefore *this* fact is a major explanation of state violence. The alternative landscape of development hurts the economic interests of ruling classes (e.g. when employers are forced to pay minimum wages or to surrender land), whose interests the state is to protect.[26] They also hurt the economic interests of the state directly when, for example, state-owned forests are taken over by poor people. Nearly 10.03 million hectares of forests in the country – which is about one seventh of the forest land – are said to be under the Naxalite political-military control. This has caused a loss of revenue. Naxalite 'disturbances' happen in a large area which is rich in minerals, which are worth billions of dollars (bauxite deposits in Odisha State only are worth $4 trillion, and this is more than three times India's entire annual gross domestic product). Any restriction imposed by the Naxalite on the use of this area – whether Naxalites are stopping the entry of mining companies or whether they are 'taxing them'[27] – hurts the economic interests of big business and of politicians/ officials associated with it. Interestingly, on 18 June 2009, Indian Prime Minister told the parliament: 'If left-wing extremism continues to flourish in parts which have natural resources of minerals, the climate for investment would certainly be affected' (quoted in Roy, 2009). Economic interests of rural property owners are also hurt: this occurs when the ceiling-surplus land of landlords is taken away for redistribution among the poor, when individual oppressive landlords who lease out land to poor peasantry for high rent and/or employ rural laborers at low wages are disciplined and are forced to grant concessions.

In all these ways, the Naxalite developmental activities are an economic threat to the state and ruling classes, which is why the state responds to it in a violent way, irrespective of the political party that is in power. When ruling classes fight to defend their interests (e.g. mining rights; payment of low rural

---

26   Consider how police killed 16 Dalit laborers on March 9, 2001 in Bhawanipur village in Mirzapur district, Uttar Pradesh province. The demands around which they fought under the Naxalite leadership were access to land, minimum wages and work. All the 16 had come from neighboring villages and were shot dead by police. A senior police officer told the People's Union for Democratic Rights that 'it is justified if they die or get killed. They are criminals'. Their crime was that as Dalit agricultural workers they dared to organize themselves and fought for their rights and that they, of course, were organized by Naxalites. Indeed, calling/labelling any democratic radical social movement Naxalite has become a convenient way of justifying state repression. http://www.dcrcdu.org/dcrc/ Navalakha.doc.

27   The movement levies 'taxes' on companies, which are used for development and possibly on arms.

wages and high rents, etc.), or when the state fights in defense of ruling class interests, Naxalites fight back, which invites (further) state violence.[28]

Naxalites' alternative development landscape is not just an economic threat; it is also a political threat. This is in two ways. One is the fact that the alternative development landscape can cause – and has caused to some extent – a potential transformation of the poor from being passive citizen-subjects to active class-subjects or from being merely local-scale political actors to political actors at provincial and national scales.[29] This happens when the movement makes demands that are legitimate/legal, but given the class character of the state (as discussed in an earlier chapter), the state finds it 'difficult' to implement these demands (e.g. land redistribution; irrigation of farm-land; payment of minimum wages). Such a political transformation can happen and does happen when, for example, the movement actually constructs an alternative development landscape by mobilizing common people to construct irrigation reservoir or to force local traders to pay more for the forest produce, or to take ceiling-surplus land from landlords and distribute it among the poor, and so on, and when it uses political power to defend that alternative landscape. Politically, Naxalites have tried to 'help the adivasi peasantry or Dalit laboring classes in some very backward regions to emerge as an independent political force' freed from the influence of landlords and traders (Gupta, 2006: 3173). While the Naxalite developmental activities can potentially organize the poor, and transform them politically, the state's agenda, however, is different: the state de-politicizes (and divides) the exploited classes (as Poulantzas, 1968 argued decades ago). The state does this by converting citizens to passive clients of its limited benefits/services and which citizens, the majority of whom have limited economic ability to pay, have to pay for. Or, when the state promotes any politicization, it is very limited 'politicization', in which people join voter-queues once every few years. They do so, as atomized individual citizens (groups of citizens divided on the basis of their loyalty to this or that bourgeois party), not as class-subjects, and the best that they as voters can achieve is to get rid of one party of the minority (the property-owning class) for another

---

28 The laws with which repression occurs bear the stamp of class. The colonial legal system set up to repress the anti-colonial resistance is used against radical social movement now. 33% of Indian Penal Code provisions (designed during colonial times) pertain to offences against property (Kannibaran in Subramanian, 2004).

29 If peasants have a 'merely ... local interconnection', and if 'the identity of their interests forms no community, no *national* bond, and no political organization among them, [and thus if] they do not constitute a class' (Marx, 1967), they are not so much of a threat to the state. Note that strictly speaking, Marx is not right: to be a class, it does not have to be politically organized. Classes objective by virtue of objective relations and processes, and irrespective of whether they engage in politics.

party of the same minority. Any greater politicization which challenges the proprietary classes and politicians/officials about their undemocratic actions is not, and cannot, be on the state's agenda, given state's own class character.[30] To the extent that Naxalite developmental activities can cause a high level of politicization of the masses, it attracts state violence.

There is another threat from Naxalites' development activities, which is closely related to the threat from the politicization issue. The idea that the capitalist state is formally separated from the proprietary classes (Wood, 1995) does not hold in many areas. India may be a liberal democracy in Delhi and on the pages of the constitution, with its characteristic separation of political power from economic power. At the local scale, things are different: businesses and landowners directly use political power and means of violence in order to enforce exploitation, making a mockery of the bourgeois separation of the economic from the extra-economic. Here the authority of the state is that of, for example, the landlords, mining businesses, and other businesses. Their class interests are fixed in geographically circumscribed areas and cannot be moved. The state machinery often comprises of a non-official apparatus of moneybags and landed interests, traders, and their private armies. In this case, 'the local state' generally sides with the rich upper caste property owners in their dispute with the lower caste (or aboriginal) landless poor (Roy, 2002) and with other sections of the propertied-class. The Naxalites undermine the political (= extra-economic) power that the ruling class utilizes to enforce *economic* exploitation. For example, in many districts in Bihar where Naxalites are active, 'The price of labor [power] in the "flaming fields" is determined by the balance of forces between the armies of [landlords of] the upper castes (usually with police support) and the armies of the laboring poor' (Corbridge and Harriss, 2000: 206; the last bracket is in original). Naxalites side with the laboring poor in their political struggle. What all this means is this: any struggle against property owners and moneybags, for economic benefits (e.g. lower rents; higher wages; higher prices of commodities produced/sold by poor people) tends to become an extra-economic or political (and often military) struggle against the state which, however, claims monopoly over extra-economic coercion, and any struggle against the state for some economic gains hurts the interests of property owners.[31]

---

30   It should be noted that: the alliance of proprietary classes that holds state power includes landlords and urban bourgeoisie, and that landlords play an important political role of keeping the rural masses under control, and any direct threat to landlords will not easily be tolerated (see Chapter 7).

31   Landlords appropriate a large share of the state-resources supposed to be used for the poor. The more the poor claim, the less the landlords get, so the latter lose economically. And the more the poor receive from the state, the less favorable becomes the balance of

STATE REPRESSION AS CLASS STRUGGLE FROM ABOVE

That the Naxalite movement, including that part of it which has been banned, is doing something for the masses is widely shared, even by agencies of the government. Sundar (2006), who is a Sociology professor at Delhi University and who does not support Naxal violence, says that the movement does show 'more commitment to people's development than the government' (p. 3190). Prakash Singh, who worked in Naxalite areas as a senior police officer, wrote: 'shorn of polemics, it (Naxalite movement) represents the struggle of the ...social and economic survival [of the poor]'. As Sarkar and Sarkar (2016: 891) say:

> Even the rudimentary services established by insurgents frequently outstrip those provided by the state. For instance, the Naxalites have attempted to address historical issues such as caste-based discrimination and landlessness that the Indian state has ignored, suppressed, or exacerbated.

As well, an expert group appointed by the erstwhile Planning Commission of India said that in terms of day-to-day activities, the movement 'is to be looked upon as basically a fight for social justice, equality, protection, security and local development' (in Banerjee, 2008a).

The Naxalite alternative development landscape – the fact that the movement has tried to help the poor – has posed, potentially and in reality, an ideological threat to the state as well, and not just an economic and military threat. The late Samir Amin (2005) says: 'in spite of tactical errors of judgment' the Naxalite offensive, 'has reawakened revolutionary awareness among the peasantry in vast areas ... of India'. As mentioned, Naxalites make 'difficult demands' on the state. Most of their demands – including the demand that aboriginal communities' land be not alienated without the consent of the people – are *legal* from the standpoint of the bourgeois laws. They are bourgeois-democratic demands, which, if met, would make the system a little more tolerable for some time. Through the national constitution and through its laws at national and provincial scales, the state has promised various measures for the poor (e.g. education, land redistribution, freeing bonded labor, and minimum wages) which, more or less, remain on paper. The implementation of these measures by the state will hurt the ruling class interests in one way or the other. But Naxalites demand that the state implement these. And when the state fails, they implement the legal measures, and if/when necessary, through the use of force. By forcing the state to implement its own measures and sometimes implementing these measures themselves where necessary by force (e.g. claiming

---

power between them and the propertied class in the class struggle, so landlords lose politically.

land held by landlords beyond the legal limit and giving it to poor people), Naxalites show in practice that the state, the so-called trustee of development (Cowen and Shenton, 1996), is no longer able to derive legitimacy and pacify poor people merely from its discourse, i.e. from the fact that it can write/utter a pro-poor development policy. Written or spoken words do not satisfy the need for food, for that need is not just an idea. Naxalites' development activities – and those organized by other progressive groups – indicate to some people that there is an agency which is somewhat anti-state but which can do things that the state is supposed to do but fails to do. The movement is forcing the state to see that the poor will not always accept the gap between 'development proper'[32] (that the post-colonial state has been promising), and 'development on paper'. The movement is taking steps to ensure that the poor will use arms to wrest concessions and to defend the limited gains that they have achieved through struggle. By providing palpable benefits to those who are poor, dispossessed, disrespected and neglected, however limited these benefits are, the movement gets their support (their consent), including to their violent means. And the state is in danger of losing poor people's consent in many areas.[33] What is the state's loss is Naxalites' gain. The state does not and will not tolerate the Naxalite movement gaining consent of the people, however. If the state loses consent of people to it, then its claim over (and actual practice of) monopoly over violence, its dominant form of survival, is undermined, and with that the control of the ruling class over economy and society is gone. There is an inverse relation, in many areas, between the amount of consent the state gets and that which the Naxalite forces (and indeed other such forces) get. If the geographical territory of the country is seen as an ideological surface indicating the distribution of support for the state as opposed to anti-state forces, that surface has numerous potholes, representing anti-state sentiments. These hidden potholes are more powerful than hidden land mines (that some Naxalite forces use – and once again, I do not support this at all). Their size and number can expand very quickly, given the right conditions. That is the fear of the state and of the ruling class.

In Naxalites' areas of influence, common people do believe that Naxalites are doing something for them, something that the state has not been able to do. For example, the Dalits of Dumari village in Bihar, where Kunnath (2006) conducted his fieldwork, did not object to the militant character of the Maoist campaign against the landlords and the local state, and they indeed 'wanted the Maoist armed squads to remain in the area as they feared that

---

32   This refers to promises of development in government documents.
33   The traditional Left, which, when in power, has pursued similar policies to the mainstream parties at least since the 1990s. So it is losing people's faith and consent too.

the landlords would re-establish their domination if the Maoist arms were withdrawn' (p. 205). Once a landless laborer bonded to a middle-caste landlord family in Dumari, Rajubhai (Kunnath's respondent) grazed his master's cattle in exchange for 25 rupees per month and food. Daily 'humiliation, overwork and abusive words' were the staples on which he was compelled to subsist, yet he felt that 'silence was the best option' (p. 112). However, once the Maoists arrived, Rajubhai attended their secret meetings in the paddy fields, led the Dalits against a particularly oppressive landlord, and eventually became the commander of a Maoist armed squad (p. 113). The Maoist squad fought pitched battles with the landlords' army and were able to beat the landlords into submission so landlords could not be as violent as before (pp. 113–115). Interestingly, district-level econometric research shows that Naxalite activity has a dampening effect on the level of violence (violent crime and crimes against women), and that poverty attracts Naxalism (Borooah, 2008).

Because of their pro-poor material interventions, the Naxalites are able to mingle among masses and get their support, thus multiplying the effect of their revolutionary violence against injustice and state violence, which is why they are a threat to the state. They have a degree of support of the ordinary people in the areas of their operation (Haragopal, 2017). As Sarkar and Sarkar (2016: 891) say:

> By addressing these issues [people's problems], the Naxalites are able to project themselves as the champions of oppressed communities, while highlighting the state's apathy or antagonism, and effectively cultivating the perception that the state is the enemy. In such conditions, even if the state successfully stems insurgent activity, persisting and unresolved local grievances and popular support for insurgents are likely to bring about a re-emergence of insurgency.

That there is a threat of an alternative development landscape by Naxalites – the idea that a war is going on over consent/legitimacy – is inadvertently corroborated by none other than the Police Chief in charge of a region most guarded by the militarized Naxalite movement: 'I can fight the Naxals but not *Naxalism*. That has to be done only through development' (quoted in Chakrabarti, 2009, p. 376; italics added).[34] One can gauge the depth of ideological – discursive – conflict between the state working on behalf of the

---

34 Some part of the security establishment is unwilling to accept that Naxalites are winning people's consent through their good deeds. 'It is wrong to say that they have taken up people-oriented schemes' said Neeraj Sinha, senior police officer in Garhwa district in Bihar province. 'They are changing their strategy only to save their skin' (in Bhelari, 2003).

ruling class in the name of development, etc. and common people living in aboriginal areas. The state has been heavily investing in the construction of roads. Ordinarily, roads are an ordinary thing – who can be against roads? But roads have become a political thing. Without roads, natural resources cannot be extracted by the ruling class, nor can the state fight the Naxalites who have some control over the areas where resource extraction is happening or can happen. Roads are justified as a development work, as something that will benefit the masses by bringing schools and hospitals, etc. Ordinarily, roads should. But consider this report on how some people in Chhattisgarh see the roads in Naxalite areas, and in particular how and why they show their opposition to state's view of development via road construction:

> The villagers here ... are vehemently opposed to the state's definition of development. *"Humare paas na gaadi hai na ghoda, sadak humare kiss kaam ke?*(We neither have an automobile or a horse, why do we need concrete roads?)" asks the *sarpanch* [an elected leader] of one village... The villagers claim the entire focus on roads has been to further militarise the region. "Earlier it was Salwa Judum, now the vigilante group has manifested itself into an even more offensive District Reserve Guards (DRG). They come here, loot our ration, and ill- treat the villagers. Almost every house has at least one man or in some case even women arrested from our village".
>
> SHANTHA, 2018

The fact that an alternative development landscape posing a multi-pronged threat to the state is an important reason for state's violence is performatively proved by the state itself. Not only does the state burn villages and kill/harm Naxalites and their (academic) sympathizers. It also *destroys* the landscape of development constructed by them. An observer noted: the 'police and paramilitary forces destroyed a big irrigation bund [an embankment] near Mahboob Nagar ... [in Andhra Pradesh] built by voluntary labor *since the inspiration came from the Naxalites*. Police also destroyed five bus stops in Karim Nagar and Warangal district *since they were built by sympathisers of the Naxalite movement*' (reported in Frontier, undated). Such an act of destruction allows the state to continue to frame the movement (and other similar movements for justice) merely as a violent and anti-people movement. But the same act of state-led destruction is also strongly suggestive of the ideological (not – or not just military) threat that Naxalites pose and indeed, any similar radical movement against injustice inflicted by the system on common people would pose – to the capitalist state the main job of which is to protect the fundamental interests of the property-owning, exploiting class.

STATE REPRESSION AS CLASS STRUGGLE FROM ABOVE

4   Conclusion

Let us briefly see the Naxalite movement through the lens of the literature on social movement/protest, which uses the language of *cultural frames*, *mobilizing structures* and *political opportunity* structure (McAdam, McCarthy and Zald, 1996). Clearly, ideological framing, or representation of the Naxalite movement as terrorist, as a menace, as a security threat, as ultra-left extremism, along with state's own democratic shell (liberal-democratic form), give some legitimacy to the state to repress.[35]

And this is not just specific to India (see Pion-Berlin, 1989 on Latin America). A part of the state's ideological framing is the coercive agencies' ethos that Gurr (1986) had identified. In the Naxalite case, this is the fact that they are a communist movement and that a communist movement is automatically seen as a threat to security of the capitalist state (Subramanian, 2004). This ethos, supported by many middle class people, helps state repression. Further, the state has access to its own expanding *mobilizing structures:* network of police and paramilitary agencies, police informers, anti-Naxalite civilian militias that the state supports, all of which, of course, complement the private coercive means available to the propertied classes. Here it is important to mention how state-supported research calls for more state violence against Naxalism. For example, Gupta and Sriram's (2018: 339; cf. Sarkar and Sarkar, 2016) publicly-supported research (from police headquarters) says that:

> at lower levels of security expenditure in the violence affected area, an increase in security expenditures leads to an increase in violent incidents (rather than a decrease); and only at higher levels of security expenditure in the area, an increase in security expenditure leads to a decline in violent incidents. Therefore, it is useful for the policy makers to start with higher security contributions than lower. However, if higher contributions are not forthcoming immediately, then security contributions should be continuous for long enough to see the desired impact.

In other words, the relation between the magnitude of state's violence (as indicated by the security expenditure) and the incidents of Naxal violence follows an inverted U-curve. Most importantly, the political-economic-ideological threat from Naxalites offers the *political opportunity* for repression.

There is no doubt that Naxalites use violent methods. One should also remind oneself that: landlords and some business houses use daily violence

---

35   See Thomas (2012) for a discussion on how the Naxalite movement has been framed in different ways (including as a law and order problem).

against ordinary people whether through their own security agencies or through state's coercive forces used as their own private property; Hindu mobs burn Christians' houses, destroy mosques and massacre Muslims, and Islamic terrorists kill innocent Hindus in a society where bourgeois democracy is turning to the right; landowners from higher castes also kill toiling men and women from lower castes (see Nandy, 2003: 124–125). Yet, Naxalite violence is seen as *the greatest* threat to the state by both of the biggest parties of the bourgeoisie, and to the class order that the state must protect. This is *because* their violence is against: actions of specific sections of the property-owning class (e.g. landlords, traders, mining companies), the excesses of the capitalist class system, and functioning of state personnel and laws that *support* the exploitative property owners, including by violent methods. It has been argued that 'repressive forces are themselves the most consistent initiators and performers of collective violence' (Tilly, 1978: 177; della Porta, 2014). In the case of the Naxalite movement, its violence is prompted by state violence (and by violence from the sections of the property-owning class itself).[36] If this is the case, then the idea that the state is violent towards Naxalites just because they are violent is inadequate, if not entirely untrue. State violence is rooted in its own class *content* and in the class content (character) of the Naxalites. It does not primarily come from their *mode* of fighting. The physical threat from Naxalites is not the only reason for state violence. The state uses, and will use, violence against the Naxalite movement because the state must defend the interests of sections of the propertied class that the movement is fighting against. And state violence, in turn, prompts Naxalite violence in certain cases, and which in turn prompts state violence.

Holloway advocates the 'emphasis ... on saying "No", refusing, puncturing capitalist command and (within that) constructing *alternative ways of doing things*', '*the immediate creation of an alternative society*', the creation of 'autonomous spaces', and thus saying 'yes' as well (Holloway, 2005: 271–272; 269; stress added). The Naxalite movement says both no and yes. They say no to *some* aspects of dominant power relations. They say yes to constructing alternative modes of living *within* capitalism. And that is a threat to the state.

In terms of its actual practice, the alternative development landscape that the Naxalites seek to produce conforms to the post-Marxist (e.g. Gibson-Graham, 2006) idea of production of post-capitalist spaces within capitalism. Arguably, the movement is a part of worldwide tendency of lower classes in

---

36   Mohanty (2017) says that violent reaction by the state might make the elite feel less insecure, but eventually such a strategy will be counter-productive because the people at the receiving end – those who have been alienated, exploited and displaced – take up arms against the state. Rather than being intimidated and killed, the oppressed communities (e.g. adivasis) need autonomy and support from the government, Mohanty says.

the capitalist periphery struggling for land, culture, democracy and employ-ment (Chatterton, 2005; Hristov, 2005). They are not just an agency of *resistance* (backed by *force* where necessary); they also play a positive, albeit limited, developmental role. In a sense the Maoists are mimicking state practices of governmentality (Sundar, 2014a), or rather what one might call 'state's develop-mentality'. The latter can be seen as developmental governmentality, which signifies the deployment of developmental activities and state's developmen-tal discourse (false promises of development) to discipline people and shape their consciousness that in turn legitimizes the capitalist state. Naxalites pro-mote an alternative developmentality which produces consent of common people to Naxalism, and thus potentially enhances their politicization. This can produce a serious threat to the state. State violence is partly directed at *destroying* this threat.[37]

The state generally functions as one arm of the structure of private – property relations, and intervenes on behalf of the propertied classes. Whatever else the state is, it is, above all, an armed body of people, separate from ordinary toiling masses who are the majority (workers and poor peasants). The state is basically an institution of class violence, functioning on behalf of the ruling classes, and against these ordinary people.[38] The state uses violence against ordinary citizens if they fight against: (a) this *structure of private property rela-tions*, (b) the *mechanisms* through which this structure works (e.g. competitive drive for profit, rent and interest; dispossessing people of their land in order to ensure access of the business world to people's resources), (c) and the *concrete effects* of these mechanisms (e.g. extreme poverty; ecological destruction). The

---

37   For Sarkar and Sarkar (2016): 'Even the rudimentary services established by insurgents frequently outstrip those provided by the state. For instance, the Naxalites have attempt-ed to address historical issues such as caste-based discrimination and landlessness that the Indian state has ignored, suppressed, or exacerbated. By addressing these issues, the Naxalites are able to project themselves as the champions of oppressed communities, while highlighting the state's apathy or antagonism, and effectively cultivating the per-ception that the state is the enemy. In such conditions, even if the state successfully stems insurgent activity, persisting and unresolved local grievances and popular support for in-surgents are likely to bring about a re-emergence of insurgency. Counterinsurgencies must provide the services and address the issues that insurgents have taken up. In addi-tion to larger development initiatives, these efforts must include attention to small-scale local grievances. If the state is unable to address this range of grievances at least as effec-tively as the rebels, it is less likely that counterinsurgencies will be successful in the long term' (p. 891).

38   It is true that the state also contains workers and that many of its day-to-day activities (including non-military) are run by ordinary people. But these people have very little au-tonomy: they are constrained by state's policies which are structurally 'designed' to serve the ruling class interests. As well, the ordinary state workers usually have to do as the higher echelons of the state ask them to, and the higher echelons, which share ruling classes' interests and/or ideologies, work generally in the interest of these classes.

state uses violence against ordinary citizens if they fight against the powerful *agents* of the state (e.g. parties; officers, police) who support these relations/mechanisms. The form of political movement of the masses does not matter much. Its content – its class content – does. That is: whether ordinary people are engaged in peaceful mobilization or whether they use a degree of violence (in self-defense), is generally beside the point. This is always the case. And when inequality level rises, the mask of democracy that a state wears is increasingly difficult to wear. There are 245,000-dollar millionaires in India, while 92 per cent of the adult population has wealth below $10,000. In this country a farmer kills himself every half an hour because he cannot pay the bills, and a child under five dies every 15 seconds because of lack of food and health-care, and the economic elite regularly kills/harms people for exercising their democratic rights including fighting against low wages and dispossession of the only thing they have (a small piece of land). In such a country, state violence against ordinary people and those who politically mobilize them *is* an intervention on behalf of the ruling classes and their political spokespersons, whether or not the mobilization of ordinary people is violent.

Launching class struggle from above on behalf of the propertied classes, the state impersonates guerilla tactics of a section of the Naxalite movement to fight it (Sundar, 2014a). By doing so, it is turning what I would call the 'homo sufferer' (working masses) into Agamben's 'homo sacer': those people who one could kill without being guilty of committing murder. In India's so-called red corridor,[39] there is an important contradiction: the red corridor's monetary value is multiple times the nation's annual income, and yet it contains the world's most impoverished people (especially among low castes and aboriginal communities). The state is trying to 'resolve' this kind of exceptionally intense contradiction, and the contradiction between a small elite and the majority of the population, by creating a (quasi-) 'state of exception', 'a legal civil war that allows for the physical elimination not only of political adversaries but of entire categories of citizens who for some reasons cannot be integrated into the political system' (Agamben, 2005: 2). This civil war is the class struggle from above, launched by the state, against the masses, i.e. the lower classes (workers and poor peasants, including those who are from the adivasi and Dalit backgrounds).

As Spacek (2017), a Canadian researcher, says: 'force and development have become conceptually blended and hybridised in practice, leading to a colonisation of statecraft by policing and violence' (p. 176). The consequence of

---

39   This part of the red corridor may represent an 'emergent system of dual authority in which the demarcation between official and insurgent governance is blurred' (Spacek, 2014).

development as war is the emergence of architectures of force across the conflict zone; architectures which have become, metaphorically, the forward operating bases of the state. The result has been a significant increase in the construction of policing facilities in previously ungoverned spaces as well as the fortification of existing police infrastructure. Throughout the [Naxal] region, the roads and towns have become dotted with barricaded, walled police compounds replete with sentry posts. Large areas of land in the major cities have been turned over for the construction of police cantonments and police lines. The government has also established, modelled on centres in the North-East, "schools of jungle warfare and counter-insurgency" directly in the conflict zone. Civil infrastructure is in the process of being colonised by the state. Educational facilities have become sites of war-making and, in many instances, have been physically altered, reflecting a hybrid logic of social service delivery and violence (p. 176).

As a result of all this:

> the state's presence has become more visible and militarised. Development and the spread of the state is materialised through architectures of force that function both as militarised nodes of state power and sites from which to dominate space. On the surface, it would seem that the militarisation of space fundamentally clashes with the developmental and constitutional frameworks that structure the official rhetoric of the state on insurgency. Arguably, however, it does not.
>
> Ibid.

The reason for this is that: 'The police have become the developmental agents in the [Naxal] region, responsible for carrying out infrastructural and social service delivery. They are the primary agents of the state', a state that is operating on the basis of 'architectures of force and spaces of violence' (p. 176). So, in so far as carrying out developmental activities is about producing consent to the legitimacy of the state and to the class rule that the state defends,[40] and in so far as the coercive organs are the agents of developmental activities, the boundary between coercive and consent-making state activities is blurred.

The state is able to engage in violence against Naxalites by producing an epistemological exaggeration: a political-geographic overestimation of the threat to the state, a knowledge-claim, a ruling class ideology, which would justify the increased level of violence by the state. By saying that the Naxalite threat can be anywhere anytime, the state of exception can potentially be

---

40 Singhal and Nilakantan (2016) say that state's developmental activities are about the battle over hearts and minds (of the oppressed).

produced anywhere anytime within the nation. The border moves inside, so the military can be engaged.[41] That this feeds into, and is supported by, right-wing, hyper-nationalist groups and individuals, is another matter.

There are three forms of violence (Zizek, 2008). Symbolic violence is 'embodied in language' and which is imposed through 'a certain universe of meaning' (Zizek, 2008: 1–2). The state labelling the Naxalite movement as a menace, as criminal, as unpatriotic, etc. is symbolic violence. The state's tendency to see any social justice movement as Naxalite or as having some Naxalite influence, and therefore as (potentially) violent that needs to be repressed, is also an act of symbolic violence. In September 2018, the state arrested five well-known social justice activists, labelling them 'urban Naxals'[42] for their alleged connection to the Naxalite movement (The Hindu, 2018a). The deployment of the construct of 'Urban Naxal' is a means of expanding state's battle against the Naxalite movement to the cities. This urbanization of state's fight against Naxalism is also a form of an all-out war against *any form* of dissent that the state cannot cope with or tolerate.[43] Someone who is seen as an enemy of *the state* is equated to an enemy *of the people* in order to justify penal interventions. This seeing does not see that the state works on behalf of the fundamental interests of a tiny minority of the population, propertied classes, and that it even works at the behest of certain individuals or fractions belonging to the propertied classes. This way of seeing things does not see that the act of exploitation by the capitalists and landowners – this act deprives the toilers of their right to the product of their labor and subjects them to unceasing miseries – is not a crime, while fighting against such exploitation in ways that the state sees as inappropriate is a crime. Why? The state must create its enemy, its other, to justify its own existence, the main purpose of which is to keep in check the state's real enemy (nation of workers and peasants, the majority of the population), whose interests are antagonistic to the ruling class-minority which the state must protect. The state cannot *overtly* declare the majority of the nation as its enemy

---

41   Azam and Bhatia (2017) say that the level of violence by the state against Naxalites has a significantly positive impact on violence committed by Naxalites themselves and that the provincial governments trigger an insurgency with the intention to acquire control of some economic assets with the help of the central government. As a result, India democracy seems to face a serious challenge in reconciling its thirst for natural resources and the economic growth sustained by these resources, with its founding humanistic values (ibid.).

42   Urban Naxals are supposed to supporters of Naxalism while active Naxals are actually engaged in struggles in rural areas.

43   The construct Urban Naxal supports, and is supported by, another right-wing construct: anti-national (anyone who asks difficult questions about the undemocratic and pro-capitalist character of the state is branded as anti-national).

but its actions treat the majority as the enemy or as if it is the enemy: *anyone* who resists the class rule and its effects is labelled a Naxalite and can be harmed, whether or not they have anything to do with Naxalism. So the state has *de facto* launched a war against the enemy within, against the majority of the people, via its war against the localized Naxalites (and similar others sites of radical resistance). Just as the state is generally a false protector of common people's interests, the enemy it constructs is also false, or not as true as portrayed by the state.

Symbolic violence can create a condition for what Zizek calls "subjective violence", which is the violence performed by "a clearly identifiable agent" (Zizek, 2008: 1, 10). This agent can be the agent of the ruling classes (their security agents or hired hoodlums) or of the state apparatus. State's subjective violence is reinforced by, and complements, the subjective violence by the ruling class, and to which Naxalite movement responds by its own subjective violence.

Systemic violence refers to the 'catastrophic consequences of the smooth functioning of our economic and political systems' (Zizek, 2008: 2). This is the violence that prompts the other two forms of violence. Class rule is behind systemic violence and the state supports the class rule. The state is launching a violent war on people because they are fighting against systemic violence (i.e. they are fighting against a war on their livelihood and on their democratic right to protest injustice). State violence against Naxalites is an instance of a general violence, a violence that is necessary to thwart all forms of actual/potential opposition to systemic violence (i.e. to class rule). The government claims that its troops are there to counter the Naxalites, but in actuality its aim is to intimidate into silence all kinds of democratically-organized movements such as people resisting land grabs or fighting police repression. By creating drastic panic among people and curtailing common people's freedom, the state makes it possible for corporations to be free to 'suck out the minerals and forest resources' (Dias, in Ismi, 2013).[44] One form of freedom (bourgeois freedom) comes at the expense of another (freedom of the toilers). Between two equal freedoms, it is the freedom that can be backed by greater violence that wins.

What state violence – the *de facto* 'everywhere-endless-war' against its own people fighting for justice – means is this: while a 'society' will not tolerate violence against the state, it will very easily tolerate violence against the body and soul of its common citizens, including little children who are malnourished, who have to work as bonded labor abused by labor contractors and employers (see Das and Chen, 2019), and who are assaulted by security people, in Naxalite

---

44   I am grateful to Professor Sheila Delany for drawing my attention to this article.

areas.[45] Why do the counts of security personnel killed while fighting against some segments of the Naxalite movement more important than the counts of the little children dying premature death because of the failure of the state to provide for better conditions of life?

Someone can argue that all states, when challenged by non-state forces, will behave the same way as the Indian state is doing in response to the Naxalite challenge. He/she might ask: would a socialist state (a state that comes to exist just after a revolutionary overthrow of capitalism) allow people to challenge it in the way that the Naxalite movement does? The answer is no. But there is a difference. All societies have a minority and have a majority. In class divided societies, the minority are the ruling class and the majority are the exploited classes.[46] All states of class societies, including capitalism, are states of, and for, a minority (the class of exploiters that controls society's productive resources) and against the majority. The capitalist states use violence to suppress the toiling exploited majority. That is very undemocratic. A socialist state is different, however: it would be the first state that is the state of the majority (workers and peasants) who need the state to stop overthrown classes from returning to power. Therefore any challenge from the overthrown properties classes, who constitute a tiny minority, will need to be crushed by the state on behalf of the people. That response of the state is not comparable to the fact that a capitalist state violently crushes an opposition from the masses (the majority) to it in the interest of the minority (exploiting property owners). The question is not: how does the state respond when it faces a challenge? The class character of the state and the class character of the challenge to its power are important to keep in mind. State violence to preserve the privilege of a minority is not the same violence that may be necessary to preserve the economic and political power of the vast majority.

This chapter has been critical of state violence in India, the scope of which has been *expanding*. There is another aspect of the reality which cannot be denied. This is that the Naxalite theory and strategy are self-*limiting* (Das, 2010, 2015). This is for various reasons, as we have discussed in the last chapter.

---

45   'Due to increasing police combings and diminished accountability, news of security forces burning villages or sexually assaulting children have become all too common... A survey by the Ministry of Women and Child Development also found that 38 percent of aboriginal children below 5 year of age are underweight and 44 percent have stunted growth' (Chowdhury, 2018).

46   'The owners of capital, the owners of the land and the owners of the factories in all capitalist countries constituted and still constitute an insignificant minority of the population who have complete command of the labor of the whole people, and, consequently, command, oppress and exploit the whole mass of laborers, the majority of whom are proletarians, wage-workers, who procure their livelihood in the process of production only by the sale of their own worker's hands, their labor-power' (Lenin, 1919).

Firstly, there is the fact that the Naxalite movement is *not* fundamentally against the totality of capitalist class relations. The Naxalite movement is also problematic in that, whether or not it uses violence, it mistakenly treats the peasantry (or, the rural poor) as the main revolutionary agent rather than an ally of the urban working class. The deployment of anarchic and secretive violence by certain segments of the movement, whom Jal (2014: 76) calls 'born-against anarchist', is against the principle that the masses can only self-emancipate themselves and that they will do this on the basis of their political organization and organized action, and not on the basis of secretive violence.[47] But if the state can inflict violence on a movement which is not particularly anti-capitalistic and if it does not mobilize urban workers, one can imagine how violent the state will be in relation to a movement that is fundamentally anti-capitalistic and that mobilizes the main revolutionary agent (the working class) to fight for a socialist society characterized popular democracy in every sphere of life, and not for a better – more democratic – form of capitalism.

We have seen that state repression is particularly likely when social movements target private property relations and accumulation projects of the property-owning class that cause ordinary citizens to suffer. Whether these movements are violent, and whether the state is a liberal democracy is a contingent matter. The liberals' argument that democracy pacifies the state collapses when one considers how repressive the liberal-democratic state is towards a movement such as the Naxalite movement, even if this movement is not seeking to go beyond capitalism. The response of the state to the Naxalite movement is symptomatic of a wider tendency across countries, including India: states are turning to authoritarian methods to suppress dissent. This is because with rising inequalities and given the crisis-tendencies of capitalism, states are increasingly unable to buy legitimacy by granting benefits, however limited, for the benefit of the majority. The states are increasingly unable to respond to the fact that there is a fundamental contradiction between big business's interests in profit and interest, and working masses' interest in obtaining access to food, shelter, health-care, education, culture and sustainable environment. The pacifying effect of democracy that some social movement theorists stress will work if the ordinary people remain pacified and do not exercise their (class-)agency and their right to dissent, in word and action, in the face of exploitation and oppression and wait indefinitely for some benefits from above

---

47   Much recent research draws attention to the fact that Naxalites kill many civilians based on their assumption that they are police informers (Vanden, 2018). There is a parallel between this and the fact that: 'The government's bid to crush Maoism has involved a frontal assault on sections of the latter's social base, which remains the most oppressed in Indian society' (Vanaik, 2011: 106).

(e.g. state, NGOs, etc.). But, if ordinary people have to remain pacified, what value does democracy indeed have?

The Indian state sees the Naxalite movement, especially, the activity of the more militant section of it (CPI-Maoist), as the greatest threat to itself and to democracy, and this is in part because the Naxalite movement does use physical force against oppressive elements where necessary and possible. But is the Naxalite movement really the main danger to democracy? It is not. The main anti-democratic force is not the Naxalite movement (sometimes called the Far Left) but it is the Far Right. So when the government labels the Naxalite movement as a force against democracy, it is taking a dangerous stance:

> The government's stance is ... dangerous because it receives legitimation from a whole array of intellectuals, academics and media figures, endorsing the idea that armed Maoism is "enemy number one". This is plainly ludicrous. The principal danger to Indian democracy comes not from Naxalism but from the forces of Hindutva, which have carried out violence and brutality on a scale that dwarfs anything armed Maoism has done. The forces of the Hindu right have succeeded in institutionalizing themselves within Indian civil society in a way unmatched by the whole of the left, mainstream or Maoist; its political and cultural vehicles have been legitimized as an acceptable part of the mainstream. For example, the instigators and apologists for the 2002 anti-Muslim pogrom in Gujarat – figures such as Chief Minister Narendra Modi – are not only unpunished, but lauded as statesmen.
>
> VANAIK, 2011: 106

Therefore, we must turn to the Far Right now, which is the real threat to democracy and an obstacle to lower-class struggle, and to much more. Indeed, this is how those who are associated with the Naxalite movement see – and must see – the Far Right.[48]

---

48   A major ideologue and leader of the Naxalite movement, Bhattacharya (2017) said this: 'Today when the Sangh brigade in power with their Hindi-Hindu-Hindustan agenda is desperate to bulldoze India under the twin wheels of corporate plunder and communal polarisation, the radical energy and resilience of Naxalbari could perhaps never be more needed'. A former Naxalite leader, V. Rao, said: 'We had fought against feudal lords and a bourgeois system to create a class-less society. We did not achieve success, but our objectives are more relevant in the present context when a BJP-RSS government is trying to divide the country and society on religious lines', adding that they are 'real enemies of class struggle' (quoted in Indian Express, 2017). Abhijit Mazumdar, a leader of CPI(ML) Liberation and son of Charu Majumdar who was the founder of the Naxalite movement, said: 'From the class struggle of 1960's, the focus has shifted to the RSS-BJP combine. If we have to fight against the communal divide, we have to widen the class struggle' (ibid.).

CHAPTER 10

Capitalist Development and Liberal Democracy under a Right-Wing Regime

Thus far we have talked about the capitalist character of India's political economy and of its politics.[1] A simple fact is that India's political system and its political economy have failed to meet the needs of the masses. Such a failure has prompted struggles from below: these have included not only trade union struggles and numerous political protests but also the Maoist struggle that has been going on in a quarter of the country's territory. This is the context in which to examine the threat to the democratic and social rights posed by right-wing forces in India, as a form of ruling class struggle 'from above'.

The Bharatiya Janata Party (BJP), an extreme right-wing party led by Narendra Modi, won India's 2014 general election partly by promising development or *vikas* for all (and also by stoking hatred against non-Hindus). On May 25, 2018, Mr. Modi, the supreme leader of BJP, said this on Twitter: 'On this day in 2014, we began our journey of working towards India's transformation'. He added: 'Over the last four years, *development* had become a vibrant *mass movement*, with every citizen feeling involved in India's growth trajectory. 125 crore Indians are taking India to great heights' (italics added).

Major promises made by the party in power – about bringing back black money (unearned money), creating 10 million jobs a year, and so on – have turned out to be false promises, but the government keeps repeating them. The government spends millions on publicity to make common people believe to be true what is not true, and, in particular, that good days (achhe din) are upon them.[2] Yet, many have started understanding the real intentions of the right-wing government, which are both communal (religious-sectarian) and pro-business, and therefore, against the toiling classes. Among those who initially fell for emotionally-charged appeals from the right-wing forces supporting the government, to national and religious pride based on distorted representations of the past (and present), many are now understanding that what is really important is access to decent employment and standard of living, social peace, and so on, and that false pride cannot meet such needs. One should ask, and many *are* asking: To what extent has development really happened under the

---

1   An earlier version of this chapter appeared as: Das (2018a).
2   The party's 2014 slogan was '*Achhe din* aane waale hain' (good days are coming).

© KONINKLIJKE BRILL NV, LEIDEN, 2020 | DOI:10.1163/9789004415560_011

right-wing government? If Mr. Modi says he and his people began their 'journey of working towards India's transformation', one might ask: how exactly has India been transformed? Transformed from what into what?

This chapter is the first in the series of four chapters on the extreme rightward turn in India's political economy and politics, characterized by the rising strength of political-social forces exhibiting certain fascistic traits. Using data from media, and national and international institutions, this chapter empirically examines India's economic, social and political development under its right-wing regime. The remainder of the chapter has 5 sections. In Section 1, I discuss the economic development record of the BJP government. In Sections 2 and 3, I show, respectively, how the ultra-rich are gaining enormously, and how the poorer segments are, more or less, losing under this government (2014–2019). In Section 4, I show the government's record of political development, including democracy and social harmony. In Section 5, based on the information from a national survey and other data, I discuss how the dismal record of development is slowly getting registered in the minds of common people who are getting disillusioned with the government. This disillusionment is an embryonic consciousness against right-wing thinking and policies, but whether it will further develop and how, no one can tell. In the final section, I provide some conceptual and general reflections on the government: in particular, I reflect on whether its dismal record of development is coincidental or whether it stems from its inherent right-wing nature. I also reflect on the internal connection between government's economic and non-economic character. I reason that the Right-wing government is right-wing for a reason: it is right for the business class.

1 BJP Government's Record on Economic Development at the National Level

Economic growth – increase in per capita Gross Domestic Product, or GDP per capita – is one of the indicators of economic development. Other things constant, a situation of rising GDP per capita is better for common people than one where it is not rising. There is little to suggest that economic growth has been stellar since 2014 (even if the calculation of GDP has been mired in controversy). If anything, the numbers have declined. The lackluster performance in terms of economic growth is in spite of the fact that the new government, installed in May 2014, enjoyed three advantages: a recovering global economy post 2008 crisis, and falling oil prices, due to which the country received a bonanza of 6 lakh crores in revenue; as well, the government has also had an absolute majority in the parliament.

LIBERAL-DEMOCRACY UNDER A RIGHT-WING REGIME

An important aspect of development is physical infrastructure, which the government has rightly stressed. The number of electrified villages has increased since 2014. Of course, that does not mean that all or even the majority of people in a newly-electrified village have access to electricity: barely 7% of the villages newly electrified under the new government have 100% household connectivity. A village may be connected to the electricity grid but may not have access to power for most of the day, and even if there is power, all villagers may not be able to afford to buy power. Similarly, 36 million Liquefied Petroleum Gas (LPG) connections have been issued over the last two years; yet, millions of families do not have the resources for refills. The picture with respect to the construction of national highways has been generally positive: 4,410 kilometers in 2014–2015 and almost 10,000 in 2017–2018. Of course, one should bear in mind that while the target was to construct 41 kilometers a day, the actual achievement has been no more than 23 per day. 120,000 kilometers of rural roads were built during the 2014–2017 period, and this is a remarkable achievement, but it is a false claim made by BJP that this achievement is an all-time high.[3]

Development is more than about an increase in income/wealth or about an increased availability of infrastructure (including *bijli, sadak* and *pani*)[4] although it is necessary. An alternative indicator is the Human Development Index (HDI). HDI takes into account income as well as education and health conditions. India's index did not improve significantly (in spite of the fact that the previous government had made some social sector investment): on a scale of 0 to 1, the index was 0.609 in 2014 and 0.624 in 2015, and increased to only 0.636 and 0.640 in 2016 and 2017 respectively. Relative to other countries, India's HDI rank was 130 in 2014, and it remained the same in 2017.

2   The Winners under the BJP Regime: The Capitalist Class
       (and the Richer Elite)

Where the government is generally doing a good job is for the business class, which played a critical role in installing it, including through secretive election funding and the dissemination of pro-BJP ideas through the compliant and communalizing media that the business class controls. Consider the World

---

3   'In the period 2008–11, rural road construction was 157,631 kms with 2009–10 being a peak year with 60,117 kms of roads constructed. Year 2008–09 was also higher than 2016–17' (Jawed, 2017).

4   *Bijli, sadak* and *pani* are respectively electricity, roads and water.

Bank's Ease of Doing Business Index. This index indicates improvement in the business environment in terms of whether regulations for business activities, including labor-related regulations, are simpler for business and are in its interest. India's rank has moved up from 142 in the 2015 report to 100 in 2018 and 77 in 2019 (the years refer to the years of publication of the World Bank reports) (Figure 10.1). India's performance during the first four years of the right-wing pro-business government in terms of easing business regulations has been spectacular: India jumped 65 spots during this period. This means that the business people find it easier to do business without having to worry about government restrictions. The fact that the business class is benefitting from the government is also indicated by the fact that India's stock markets have been doing rather well.[5] More than any other section of the population, it is the business class which is experiencing *achhe din* (good days).

In serving the business class, the ultra-nationalist government has been giving away the nation's financial resources in the form of loans from public-sector banks to the private sector (Figure 10.2). The loans issued from nationalized banks are becoming non-performing assets (NPA): by mid-2018, the total size of bad loans had ballooned to nearly 10 trillion Rupees, three times more than in 2015. Like its predecessor, the BJP government continues to write off the loans that the big business owes to public-sector banks; the number of write-offs has increased substantially between 2014 and 2016 (Figure 10.3).[6] As well, the government's watch on capitalists is so relaxed that bank fraud has become standard practice. For the period from 2013 to March 1, 2018 there were 23,866 cases of fraud, each of 100,000 Rupees or more (*The Hindu* May 2, 2018). In addition to the write-off of loans and the abuse of the nationalized banking system by the big business allowed by the government, is the fact that the Income Tax Department has begun writing off 500,000 billion Rupees of tax arrears by corporate defaulters, on the ground that their economic health is not sound.

---

5 Sensex and Nifty are stock market indices in India, which, respectively, represent Bombay Stock Exchange (BSE) and National Stock Exchange (NSE). Now, 'Equity benchmarks BSE Sensex and NSE Nifty have advanced nearly 40 per cent since Modi took over as Prime Minister. The 30-share Sensex jumped to trade at 34,344 on May 23, 2018 from 24,716.90 on May 26, 2014. During this period, the index hit an all-time high of 36,443 on January 29 this year, while the Nifty surpassed the 10,000 mark for the first time ever' (Oberoi, 2018).

6 Note that the NPA problem has arisen at least in part because the current BJP government – like Congress-led governments – has made banks keep lending to India's business houses (including the businesses that are politically connected to them) to support a flagging economy (Kumara, 2018a).

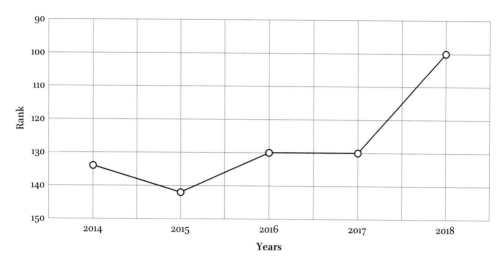

FIGURE 10.1   Ease of Doing Business Index 2014–2018
SOURCE: DATA FROM HTTPS://EN.WIKIPEDIA.ORG/WIKI/EASE_OF_DOING_BUSINESS_INDEX

All these pro-business actions have adverse implications for the country's overall economy. The banking sector woes have indeed 'caused a collapse in availability of credit to industry which then spiraled into low investment by the private sector and consequently low fixed capital formation' (Chakravarty, 2018). This will not have a positive effect on employment-creation. Writing off unpaid loans means socializing them. When businesses make money, it is theirs. When they incur losses and cannot return the loans taken from society, the losses belong to society! The fact that the government gives all kinds of presents to the big business (write-offs of loans or tax arrears, etc.) means making the toiling masses 'pay through increased taxes' (including through the regressive GST) as well as 'social-spending cuts for the cash infusions needed to strengthen the banks' balance sheets and preparing them to be sold off to big business (Kumara, 2018a). When the nationalized banks' resources dry up in the fraudulent way that they are, these banks' ability to serve the ordinary people (both in terms of amount of lending and the cost of sending) will be compromised.[7] While the loans to the big business are waived, any talk of loan waivers to farmers in distress is seen as a threat to India's credit-worthiness by the rating agencies. The story does not end there. Farmers are being sent to jail

---

7   Besides, such frauds will have a serious impact on the economic health of the banks, and this will be used as a justification to privatize them, i.e. to hand them over to the business class which is responsible for the bad economic health in the first place.

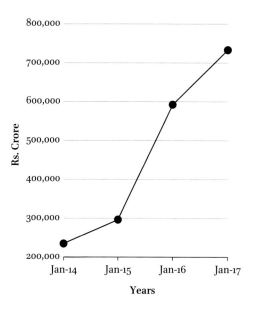

FIGURE 10.2 Public sector banks' gross NPAs in Rs. Crore, 2014–2017
SOURCE: DATA FROM HTTPS://WWW.FIRSTPOST.COM/
BUSINESS/BANK-NPA-TREND-IN-7-CHARTS-BAD-LOANS-
AT-STATE-RUN-BANKS-MAY-BE-PEAKING-SELECT-PRIVATE-
PEERS-SEE-RISE-4218813.HTML

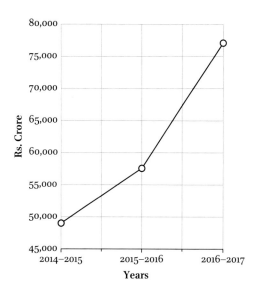

FIGURE 10.3 Loan write-offs (Rs. Crore), 2014–2017
SOURCE: DATA FROM HTTP://INDIANEXPRESS.COM/ARTICLE/
BUSINESS/BANKING-AND-FINANCE/PSU-BANKS-WRITE-OFF
-RS-55356-CRORE-IN-SIX-MONTHS-BAD-DEBT-4966594/

LIBERAL-DEMOCRACY UNDER A RIGHT-WING REGIME

for defaulting on their loan repayment. Arvind Subramanian who served the BJP government as the former Chief Economic Advisor for almost 4 years, declares that writing off the corporate sector's bad loans makes good economic sense, saying 'this is how capitalism works' (cited in Sharma, 2017).

It is widely known that India's ruling elite has been pursuing a policy of privatizing state-owned companies since the early 1990s. But as with many other pro-business measures, the current right-wing BJP government with its brute electoral majority, has gone much further than the Congress governments. BJP even targets for privatization highly-profitable companies. Even if workers have had little say in how these companies are run, these companies are products of the labor and savings of millions of common people; these companies also provide some security to their employees. Yet, the government seeks to sell off government-controlled companies to private hands in order to allow the latter to make huge amounts of money on them. As well, an aim of the right-wing government is to dismantle whatever social protections the state-owned companies 'provide against low-wages, mass-sackings and deleterious working conditions so as to further undermine the social position of the working class as a whole and thereby make India even more attractive to investors' (Kumara, 2018a). By selling off state-owned companies, the government will also reduce the fiscal deficit and make the international rating agencies happy. It will also use the money from the sale of the companies for investment in cash-starved state-owned banks so they can lend to private businesses, and for building infrastructure as per the needs of the capitalist class.

In any case, there is a massive looting of the state by the ruling class going on.[8] The business class is not only taking resources from the state without an equivalent (consider cheap sale of state companies, or non-performing assets of state-owned banks). The blatantly pro-business character of the BJP government is indicated by the ways in which it goes about selling off state-owned companies to private businesses: the whole matter is left in the hands of the private businesses themselves.[9] This means that the *private* businesses will decide how they will loot *society's* resources. The ruling class is also using society's resources to produce and to protect its own private wealth, without paying the full cost of those resources (consider tax rebates and tax-write-offs by

---

8   One can call it 'looting of the state by the state' which is the state of the capitalist class, working on its behalf and in its interest.

9   'The rapacious big business interests animating the Modi government's privatization drive are exemplified by its appointment of Reliance Mutual Exchange Traded Fund, an investment fund owned by the billionaire Anil Ambani, to serve as the "consultant" and "expert" overseeing the quick, partial or complete privatization of ten giant and highly profitable [public-sector companies]' (Kumara, 2018a).

the government). If Britain looted Rupees 91 lakh crores (Rupees 91 trillion) at current rates over 300 years from India, one can compare very well the amount of loot of India's resources by the Indian (and foreign) capitalist class, fully assisted by politicians and bureaucrats, in the name of development and transformation (Shankar, 2018). The process of such a loot, which began under Congress with the full support of BJP-in-opposition, has intensified under the current BJP government, whose major policies are a package of presents for the business class.

The package provided for business by the government includes the things just mentioned. It also includes the government's anti-labor policies such as allowing employers to hire and fire freely (more on this below), not increasing minimum wages, using coercion to break unions and social resistance, and so on. This allows business to super-exploit workers by paying them minimal wages and benefits. So, the BJP's promise of *sabka saath* and *sabka vikas* (Together with all, Development for all) is in reality *corporates ke saath, corporates ke vikas* (Together with corporates, Development for corporates). It is no surprise that the number of India's dollar billionaires was 109 in 2014 and this has increased to 136 in 2017 (Figure 10.4). The BJP regime has made little difference to the continuing tendency towards the concentration of wealth, with the share of India's wealth held by the top 1% growing under the BJP government, from 49% to 58.4% between 2014 and 2016 (Figure 10.5). The richest people are increasing their share of the nation's health faster under this government than before: in 2017, a whopping 73% of the new wealth generated went to the richest 1% of the population. This means that under this so-called nationalist government, only 27% of the wealth created in 2017 went to the bottom 99% of the nation. OXFAM (2018) observed: 'In the last 12 months the wealth of this elite group increased by Rupees 20,913 billion. This amount is equivalent to [the] total budget of Central Government in 2017–18'. It is clear which nation, or which part of the nation, the nationalist government really cares about.

The BJP's populist claim that it would bring back black money from overseas and deposit 1.5 million Rupees in every citizen's account has melted into thin air. Of course, many of the super-rich have black money abroad.[10] But the strong ties between the government and the business class – through electoral funding mechanisms, for example – protect the rich. One of Mr. Modi's promises was: 'I have decided if you bless me and give me the opportunity I will bring back all the black money'. This lofty promise has melted into thin air.

---

10   'A report by US-based think tank Global Financial Integrity (GFI) estimated that $21 billion in black money was taken out of India in 2014 alone' (quoted in Arun, 2017).

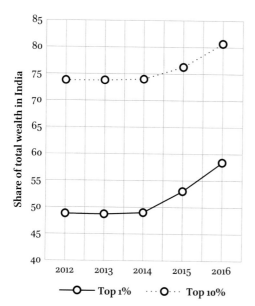

FIGURE 10.4   Share of wealth held by Top 1% and 10% in India, 2012–2016
SOURCE: DATA FROM HTTPS://WWW.LIVEMINT.COM/MONEY/MML9OZRWAACYEHLZUNIMNO/THE-RICHEST-1-OF-INDIANS-NOW-OWN-584-OF-WEALTH.HTML

One should note that the ultra-rich stratum, including the business class, and the political class (law-makers/politicians) overlap: the ultra-rich become politicians, and politicians become the ultra-rich. According to the Association for Democratic Reforms (ADR): 'the average assets of the 46-member Council of Ministers [which was sworn in 2014] is Rupees 13.47 crore…Of the 44 ministers analysed, 40 (91 percent) are *crore patis*'. Note that more than 92% of Indians have assets that are worth Rupees 600,000 or less. ADR further reveals: 'Four of Modi's ministers have declared more than Rupees 30 crores worth of assets' (Pereira, 2014).

One might briefly refer to a few policies of the right-wing government to show its pro-business character. One is demonetization. At 8 pm on November 8, 2016, the government made a sudden announcement invalidating all Rupees 500 and Rupees 1000 currency notes as of midnight of that day. It set a December 31 deadline for depositing the withdrawn currency bills into bank accounts. It fixed a daily Rupees 4,000 limit (later reduced to Rupees 2,000) for the exchange of old notes for new currency. Explaining the demonetization scheme,

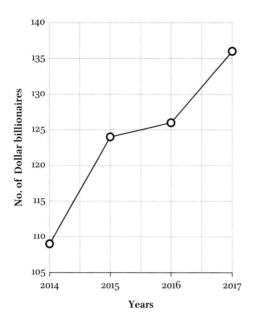

FIGURE 10.5   Number of U.S. Dollar billionaires in India, 2014–2017
SOURCE: DATA FROM HTTPS://WWW
.STATISTA.COM/STATISTICS/324237/
INDIA-NUMBER-OF-BILLIONAIRES/

Modi said: 'To break the grip of corruption … we have decided that the currency notes presently in use will no longer be legal tender from midnight tonight' (quoted in Financial Express, 2018). The government had said that Rupees 5 lakh crores (Rupees 5 trillion) of illegally-held money, or black money, would be eliminated. Yet, 99.3% of demonetized currency returned to the banks. The rich people – 148,000 account holders – deposited more than Rupees 8 lakh of demonetized currency each, amounting to a total of Rupees 4.89 lakh crores into the banks. No action has been taken to ensure that these rich people's money is legally acquired.

The aim of demonetization is not really to fight corruption but to ultimately help the business class. How? First, demonetization has allowed the government to inject the desperately needed cash into the banking sector which will lend to the private sector. Note that the banking sector is burdened with non-performing assets because of defaults by the business class, and has therefore cut down on new business-lending, producing adverse effects on economic growth. Besides, the demonetization scheme has forced millions to open bank accounts. This constitutes a method of modernizing India's backward capitalist economy, by strengthening the Indian bourgeoisie's banking system and its reach; note that the BJP government has already made clear that one of its principal goals will be to privatize large parts of the banking system (Kumara and Kumar, 2016). As well, this policy has benefitted a segment of *the capitalist class* that deals in e-transactions (digital money). While demonetization has been broadly (even if not straightforwardly) in support of the business class, it has hurt the laborers and farmers (as mentioned below).[11]

Another major pro-business intervention is in the area of labor laws. Bypassing the parliament, the BJP government issued a notification in the government *Gazette* that 'Fixed Term Employment has now been introduced irrespective of the industry', thereby amending the 'Industrial Employment (Standing Order) Act, 1946' (Kumara, 2018a). This regressive change in labor laws means that Indian businesses can hire workers on a 'non-permanent' basis, for any length of time, whether for days, months, years, or the duration of a project. The 'fixed-term' does not mean any job security: an employer can indeed terminate a worker's contract at any time on the ground of changed business conditions. The laid-off worker is not entitled to severance pay or compensation. The government justifies such a regressive change by saying that companies can now hire workers on short-term contracts without having to use outside labor contractors and that workers hired on 'fixed-term' contracts will receive the same wages and, on a pro-rata basis, the same benefits (except severance benefits) as permanent employees. These are supremely spurious claims. First, the government has not prohibited employers from using labor contractors and temporary work agencies to hire casual workers by paying them wages and benefits far below those paid to regular workers. It has simply broadened employers' options for hiring workers who can be easily dispensed with. Second, the Indian Labor Ministry hardly enforces minimum wage, health and safety and other work standards anyway, which means that the legal guarantees of equal pay are essentially meaningless (Kumara, 2018a).

3 The Losers under the BJP Government: The Toiling Masses

In a capitalist society such as that of India, wealth is, ultimately, generated by the labor of common people who have to work for others for a wage and who receive only a small part of what they produce. The extraction of wealth is also based on the use of the nation's natural resources. Not only is the environment

---

11 This is the case even if some of them may have had a sense of satisfaction seeing and/or thinking that the demonetization has hurt the rich more, including by members of them having to stand in queues for depositing and withdrawing their money.

depleted as existing environmental regulations are dismantled, but there has been little improvement in the conditions of workers. The employment situation is simply desperate. According to *IndiaSpend,* an average 213,000 jobs have been created every year in the 2014–2017 period. This is a far cry from the 10 million jobs a year promised by the BJP government.[12] That the government has failed on the job front is corroborated in a national survey in May 2018 where 57% of voters said that finding jobs in their area had become more difficult during the past 3–4 years; this figure was 49% in January 2018 (Lokniti, 2018).

A wage-earner's economic living standard depends, more or less, on the number of hours and days employed, and the wages received per hour or per day. Not only are employment opportunities scarce and jobs precarious, but nominal and real wages have remained also low, showing little sign of improvement under the BJP government. According to a recent Reserve Bank of India report, rural wage laborers experienced high wage growth between 2007 and 2013, partly due to improvements to the rural employment program under the previous government (which was under the Congress), but that growth rate in rural wages has declined during the 2014–2018 period under BJP's rule, in part because the momentum of the rural employment-generation program has been dampened (Kundu, 2018). This is confirmed by data for rural wages: from 2008 to 2013 (prior to BJP's rule), in nominal terms, wages increased by 15%, but during the BJP's tenure, this rate has fallen to just a third of the previous rate (*Indian Express,* 2018).[13]

The promise of creation of self-employment through schemes such as the Mudra Yojana (Money Scheme) which provides small loans to small-business people is simply deceptive: the average amount of loan has been less than Rupees 50,000; with such a small amount one can never set up an enterprise that will generate revenue for a family to lead a life beyond poverty. Barely 1% of all

---

12   It should be noted that, during the 2014 general election campaign, the BJP had criticized the Congress Party for '10 years of jobless growth' and promised jobs and development, if voted to power.

13   During the latter period, the average number of person-days for each household employed under MGNREGS dropped, as did the number of households getting 100 work days a year.

   51.7 lakh families got 100 days of employment in 2012–2013 and 46.6 lakh families got 100 days of employment in 2013–2014. But it has drastically come down to 24.9 lakh families in 2014–2015 and a dismal 20.45 lakh families in 2015–2016.

   The Modi government has cut the financial allocation under MGNREGA. While the Congress-led government spent Rupees 39,778.27 crore and Rupees 38,552.62 crore on the scheme in 2012–2013 and 2013–2014, respectively, the spending went down to Rupees 36,033.81 crore and Rupees 34,226.80 crore in 2014–2015 and 2015–2016 respectively (INC, 2017).

mudra loans are substantial amounts (i.e. at least 5 lakh Rupees) (Mohammad, 2018).

Given the highly unsatisfactory situation with respect to employment and wage growth, it is not surprising that the majority are not doing that well. With more than 70% of the new wealth generated going to the richest 1%, the 670 million Indians comprising the poorest half of the population saw a paltry 1% increase in their wealth. While the richest 10% of Indians controlled 80.7% of nation's wealth in 2016, the bottom 50% owned a mere 2.1% (Chakravarty, 2016). According to the Indian brokerage firm Ambit Capital, while India's annual per capita income is a miserable $1,850, for the poorest half of the population, it is just $400. By contrast, the top 1 percent (i.e. 13 million people), earns $53,700 annually (Kumara, 2017). The per capita income of India's poorest 50 percent is substantially lower than the per capita income of Afghanistan ($561), a country devastated by decades of US imperialist-fomented wars, including the current 16-year American occupation (ibid). While the trend of increasing inequality preceded the Modi regime, the control of the ultra-rich over the nation's wealth has increased faster after 2014. With the ultra-rich doing as well as they are, there is no sign of the relative position of the majority improving at all.

The BJP government has emphasized the importance of development in the form of: *sabka saath and sabka vikas*, or in other words, inclusive development. This is a laudable goal. But does the government promote this? Luckily, there is a new development index that seeks to capture this interesting idea. Designed by the World Economic Forum as an alternative to GDP, the Inclusive Development Index (IDI) reflects more closely the criteria by which people evaluate their countries' economic progress. The IDI is based on: growth and development (GDP per capita; labor productivity; life expectancy and employment); inclusion (median household income; income and wealth inequality, and poverty rate); and intergenerational equity and sustainability (public debt level; carbon intensity of GDP, etc.) (World Economic Forum, 2018). India's IDI score was 3.38 in 2017 and slipped to 3.09 in 2018 (Norway, the top country, has a score of 6.08). Among the developing economies only, India's IDI rank was 60 in 2017 and it slipped to 62 in 2018.

When unemployment continues to be a major issue and when wage growth is slow, it is not surprising that millions cannot meet their basic needs. According to the Lokniti 2018 survey (referred to earlier), the percentage of people who are not able to fulfil all of their needs and face some or much difficulty has increased from 53% to 67%, just between January and May 2018. Another indicator of the miserable situation of the vast majority is the agrarian crisis: in rural areas, where most people live, the agrarian distress continues, with farmers not getting a remunerative price for their crops. Between 2014 and 2016, 36,362 farm-dependent people committed suicide, meaning two cases of suicide every hour. So, on the agrarian crisis front, there has been little improvement.

Conditions of farmers and workers were made worse due to demonetization. It paralyzed single-worker 'businesses', which are owned by numerous poor families, comprising 80% of the country's 52.85 million enterprises (Kumara, 2017). It also caused millions of urban workers in small businesses to be thrown out of work, at least temporarily, as the small businesses rely mainly on cash transactions (ibid.). Demonetization affected rural areas badly. A Ministry of Agriculture report said: 'India's 263 million farmers live mostly in the cash economy' (meaning that they do not use electronic transactions), and that demonetization came at a time when they were selling autumn crops or sowing winter crops, and that that is when they needed a lot of cash which demonetization removed from the market. The report also said that 'millions of farmers were unable to get enough cash to buy seeds and fertilizers for their winter crops. Even bigger landlords faced a problem such as paying daily wages', so workers suffered (quoted in Nair, 2018).

A country that aspires to be an economic power must meet the most basic needs of its poor, and especially, the need for food. Yet, hunger is rampant. The Global Hunger Index (GHI) study combines indicators that measure the extent of undernourishment in the population and the extent of undernourishment and mortality of children under five. The GHI ranks countries on a 100-point scale, with 0 being the best score (no hunger) and 100 being the worst, although neither of these extremes is reached in practice. The hunger index and scores for India are getting worse. In 2018, India was ranked 103 out of 119 countries.

4   BJP Government's Record on Protection of Democratic Rights

There is an *undeclared* emergency in India. This is an undeclared war on freedom of speech and assembly, in the name of *vikas*, patriotism, nationalism, Hindu pride, and so on. Journalists or indeed anyone who dares to criticize the BJP government and the militant-communal forces which support it, are subject to verbal or physical assault or online-trolling from their supporters. There is an attack on scientific attitude towards nature and towards society, including its history.

Consider the 'Democracy Index'. This index is based on five categories: electoral process and pluralism; civil liberties; the functioning of government; political participation; and political culture. Based on their scores (on a scale of 0 to 10, where 10 = best) on a range of indicators within these categories, each country is given a composite score. Although there is still a democratic tradition in India, the degree of the country's democratic character is shrinking, as seen in changes in this index (Figure 10.6). A free press is an important part of democracy. The degree of press freedom is, more or less, decreasing as well (Figure 10.7). This is corroborated by the assault on journalists who dare to speak the truth and to criticize wrong actions/thinking of the government and of the (militant-communal) forces.

The new government had promised to eliminate corruption through increasing public awareness, e-governance, etc. What is the reality? Corruption is reduced when, other things constant, common people have the freedom to keep an eye on politicians (especially of the ruling party) and government officials. A society where the rule of law is not well adhered to, where the rule of law is whatever the right-wing forces think it is, and where there is a threat to freedom of press and secular civil society organizations, from right-wing violent mobs and from the state institutions steeped with right-wing ideas, such a society will not lower the level of corruption within the government institutions and at the interface between them and the business-world. As far as everyday corruption is concerned, a survey – by the Centre for Media Studies – reports in 2017 that 43 per cent of households feel that the level of corruption has increased in the preceding year. This is petty corruption, something that households face in their day-to-day life.

The Transparency Corruption Perception Index uses a scale of 0 to 100, where 0 is highly corrupt and 100 is very clean. India's corruption score has remained unchanged at 40. In 2015, the score was 38. India is among the 'worst offenders' in terms of graft and press freedom in the Asia Pacific region, according to Transparency International. Since 2015, India's world ranking in terms of corruption has been getting worse. India's corruption level in the public sector seems to be not getting better, in spite of the government's promise to provide clean governance, in spite of its promise of *sahi niyat*.

Secretive election funding by corporates (through electoral bonds), a policy that is promoted by BJP, is a major form of corruption made legal: a company will not give millions for nothing to a ruling party and/or provide material and ideological-social support to its vote-garnering forces masquerading as cultural organizations. A corporate, or a group of corporates, can buy *an entire policy package*, and not just this or that specific intervention on behalf of a company (e.g. buying a piece of government land for less than the market price by paying some politicians and officers a lot of money), and when an *entire policy* is bought, that is corruption but is not seen as that. It is quite likely that the total donations to BJP controlling the current government are several times the donations to all the other parties put together. One of the best ways to show that

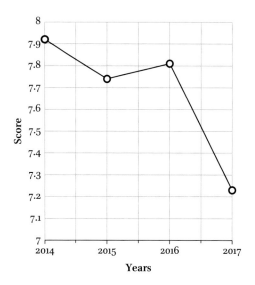

FIGURE 10.6   Democracy Index 2014–2017
Note: Score is out of 10; higher score = greater freedom
SOURCE: DATA FROM HTTPS://WWW.SUDESTADA.COM.UY/CONTENT/ARTICLES/421A313A-D58F-462E-9B24-2504A37F6B56/DEMOCRACY-INDEX-2014.PDF; HTTPS://WWW.YABILADI.COM/IMG/CONTENT/EIU-DEMOCRACY-INDEX-2015.PDF; HTTP://FELIPESAHAGUN.ES/WP-CONTENT/UPLOADS/2017/01/DEMOCRACY-INDEX-2016.PDF

a party is non-corrupt is for it to tell the public who is funding it and how much. BJP will not do this. In fact, it has made it impossible for the donation for the 2014 elections to be investigated.

A society that does not respect the rights of women and children is a society with which there is something terribly wrong. In this context, it is important to note that, the number of crimes committed against women in big cities has been increasing under the BJP regime, from fewer than 38,500 to more than 41,500 between 2014 and 2016 (NCRB, 2016).

Similarly, as workers and as petty producers, Dalits (the communities occupying the lowest positions in the oppressive caste hierarchy in Hindu society) are most exploited, and as ordinary citizens, they are most oppressed. Instead of ensuring their democratic rights and dignity, there is increasing violence against them, because their views and practices do not conform to those of the upper-caste elite which supports the government. The number of crimes committed against Dalits in big cities has risen from 1,470 to more than 1,600 (NCRB,

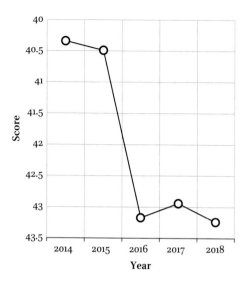

FIGURE 10.7 Press Freedom Index 2014–2018
Note: Score out of 100. A smaller score on the report = greater freedom of the press as reported by the organization
SOURCE: DATA FROM HTTPS://RSF.ORG/EN/RANKING/2018; HTTPS://TIMESOFINDIA.INDIATIMES.COM/WORLD/REST-OF-WORLD/IN-WORLD-PRESS-FREEDOM-INDEX-INDIA-RANKS-133RD/ARTICLESHOW/51941837.CMS; HTTPS://TIMESOFINDIA.INDIATIMES.COM/INDIA/PRESS-FREEDOM-IS-INDIA-IN-DECLINE/ARTICLESHOW/64009855.CMS

2016). According to NCRB, 40,801 cases of crime against scheduled castes were registered in the country as a whole in 2016, compared to 38,670 cases in 2015, an increase of 5.5%. Similarly, 6568 atrocities against Adivasis were recorded in 2016, compared to 6276 in 2015, a rise of 4.6% (Varma, 2018b).

> These two most oppressed sections of society together make up about 25% of India's population. The manuvadi and Brahmanical approach of the Sangh Parivar [the family of Hindu-communal groups] towards these sections is primarily responsible for their increasing marginalisation in the years against Modi rule.
> Ibid.

It is not surprising therefore to hear one BJP leader say this about Dalits:

> To us they are like a side dish, a pickle. You need a finger-lick (of the pickle) between mouthfuls to get your food down. But they can never be the

main course. It is ok to interact with them, in party offices. But our cultures are too different to sit down with them at home.

ANANDAN, 2018

Their *haath* (hand) is needed as workers and as voters, but their *saath* (their company) is shunned because they are perceived to be very low on the caste hierarchy. Uttering the name of Mr. Ambedkar, while having nothing to do with his ideas or practice in support of democratic rights of the oppressed, is one of the most hypocritical things a party and its leaders (and their paid-for savvy speech-writers) can do. That sort of strategy might result in some votes from some disillusioned Dalits (and aboriginal people), but it will do nothing to improve their economic and social conditions. Words do not fill a stomach. Empty words are worse at doing that job.

The incidents of communal violence have increased during the tenure of the BJP government (Figure 10.8). The victims generally receive little protection from police or other officials who must, generally, obey the party in power, and many of whom are themselves developing a communal attitude. Between 2014 and 2017, there was one communal incident, on an average, every 12 hours. In the communal incidents 389 people were killed (between 2014 and 2017) and 6,969 were injured (in 3 years from 2015). On the rise are incidents of violence by cow-vigilantes who illegally act against those who deal in and/or eat beef, and for whom cows' lives are, apparently, valued more than human lives. Targeting Muslims and *Dalits*, these incidents have increased from fewer than 5 in 2014 to more than 35 in 2017 (Figure 10.9). Varma (2018) reports that an 'estimated 700 attacks have taken place on churches, clergy, carol singers, Christmas and Easter events and missionaries across the country in the past 4 years' (2014–2018). Not surprisingly, India's record is getting worse in terms of what is called the Social Hostilities (religious unrest) Index:[14] In 2014, this was 7.9, which increased to 8.7 in 2015 (10 = worst). Even the sphere of personal life and love is not beyond communalization. A Muslim man having a Hindu partner is accused of engaging in 'love jihad': it is 'a supposed form of religious warfare by which Muslim men lure Hindu women away from their faith' (Bhatia, 2017). Even movies where such a relationship is shown are threatened with boycott.

---

14   The Social Hostilities Index looks at 13 indicators including crimes motivated by religious hatred, mob violence related to religion, communal violence, religion-related terrorist groups, using force to prevent religious groups from operating, the harassment of women for 'violating' religious dress codes and violence over conversion or proselytizing (Rukmini, 2017).

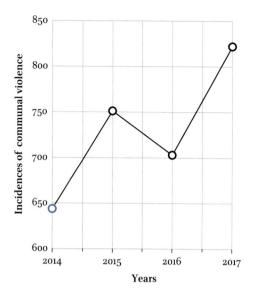

FIGURE 10.8   Incidences of communal violence, 2014–2017
SOURCE: DATA FROM HTTPS://WWW.FIRSTPOST.COM/
INDIA/INDIA-WITNESSED-822-COMMUNAL-INCI
DENTS-IN-2017-SAYS-CENTRE-111-KILLED-2384-IN
JURED-IN-VIOLENCE-4338217.HTML; HTTPS://WWW
.FIRSTPOST.COM/INDIA/COMMUNAL-VIOLENCE-ROSE-
BY-28-FROM-2014-TO-2017-BUT-2008-REMAINS-YEAR-OF-
HIGHEST-INSTANCES-OF-RELIGIOUS-VIO
LENCE-4342951.HTML

5   People's Response to False Promises

The Modi government has spent Rupees 4,806 crore on publicity of its achievements in its four years of rule, from 2014–15 to 2017–18. Writing in 2018, Varma (2018) revealed that Modi's BJP government had indeed spent more than double the amount on publicizing its achievements than was spent by *two* United Progressive Alliance (Congress-led) governments. Varma observed that this 'barrage of publicity through all media platforms is meant to create the illusion that the Modi government, which won the 2014 election promising *Achhe Din* [good days] for Indians, has fulfilled its promises'. Taken from taxes and other imposts, the money spent on publicity could have been spent on people's well-being.

The money is spent on illusions aimed at smudging the gap between what the ruling class and its government actually do for the people on the one hand and the life that people actually experience on the other. But the people's objective experience of life and government is registered in their consciousness. There is a limit to how much and how long such propaganda can maintain the

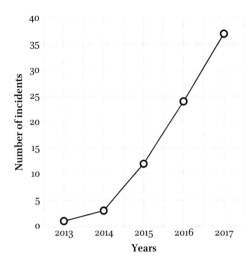

FIGURE 10.9   Hate crime: cow vigilante violence, 2013–2017
SOURCE: DATA FROM HTTP://DATA.INDIASPEND.COM/

falsehood. When not many jobs are created, when wage rises are stagnating, when the rich are getting obscenely richer, when farmers are not getting a fair price for their produce and hard work, there is likely to be disillusion with the government. Admittedly, this happens, however inadequately, unevenly, slowly and contradictorily. If a section of the population had supported the BJP which made lots of promises, the level of its support for the party and its government has begun declining. Of course, what might happen during the 2019 election, when BJP resorts to communally-charged emotional appeals to nationalism, is a different matter.

Given its failure to deliver on its big promises made just to garner votes, one way the BJP government has sought to maintain and bolster electoral support is religious hatred and hyper-nationalism. But the people are no longer so accepting of this zealotry, just as they are no longer accepting of the false economic promises. Many now understand that the issue of religious division between Hindus and non-Hindus is not the cause of their problems. Many now understand as well that as a nation India is not under attack from the forces that the BJP's so-called nationalist forces say it is; that is, religious minorities or indeed anyone who dissents from the party and its government. The evidence for this realization is seen in several areas. For example, since 2014, the BJP has been losing one election after another, and its vote share has been declining. In a by-election in Kairana, Uttar Pradesh, held on May 28 and May 30, 2018, the

BJP lost its own seat. Using its normal electoral engineering practice of raking up emotional issues concerned with religion or religion-based nationalism just before the election, the Hindu-nationalist party had attempted to consolidate Hindu voters by using the 'issue' of a photograph of Jinnah, the founder of the Islamic State of Pakistan, in Aligarh Muslim University in North India. However, this negative jingoism was countered by opponents who focused on real issues: 'What will be the poll agenda in Kairana by-election: Jinnah or *ganna* [sugarcane]?' This intervention on behalf of sugarcane farmers resonated with a perception that the BJP's invocation of the Jinnah photograph was by a party insensitive to the issues that really mattered in an area where sugarcane is the main cash crop and where delayed payment from sugar mills is the main issue. *Ganna* mattered: a coalition of Muslims, *Dalits*, Jat farmers and people from OBC background (Other Backward Class, a group of socially and educationally disadvantaged castes) highlighted livelihood issues, showing the BJP's divisive politics of religious identity was really a non-issue. Lies and false promises were trumped by the facts of real-life experience and hardship.

This also seems to be a message of the multi-round massive nation-wide survey referred to earlier, in which the decline of support for the BJP is highlighted: 'The survey found that there isn't a single major issue on which the Modi government is rated positively now' (Lokniti, 2018: 6). The BJP campaigned in 2014 declaring that it would promote development. Interestingly, 51% of those surveyed considered it had done little developmental work, while 64% felt it had not been able to address farmers' concerns and 61% felt it failed to control rising prices (see Figure 10.10). While the BJP consistently claims it believes in *sabka saath* (Together with all) and that it is not communal, its actions have been quite different, with 52% of those surveyed considering it had not maintained religious harmony. The BJP campaigned against the Congress Party in 2014, declaring it corrupt. Yet, 55% of those surveyed thought that the BJP government itself had been unable to curb corruption. In fact, three in five considered the Modi administration a corrupt government.

Given all these failures, one is not surprised to find the Lokniti survey (2018: 7) comment that: 'Overall, 44% of the voters thought that the country was headed in the wrong direction'. According to the survey, only '35% felt otherwise'.

Modi also promised *sabka vikas* or inclusive development but only 30% believe there has been *sabka vikas* in the government's time in office and the proportion of voters who do not believe development has benefitted everyone is increasing. The BJP-led government's claim of development of all is no longer convincing to people, as shown in the Lokniti (2018) survey. In May 2018, only 30% of voters believed development has been for all sections – the rich and the poor – a decline from 39% in January 2018. Meanwhile, a far greater percentage believed that the development promised by the BJP in 2014 had benefitted only the rich (up to 42% in May 2018 from 36% in January 2018), while about 22% believed there has been no development at all. This means that 64% of voters have a negative view of development under the BJP regime. This perception is in line with rising inequality between the rich and the poor and the failure of the government to address the unemployment problem, as mentioned above. It is hardly surprising that the level of support for the BJP-led government has been declining among middle and lower classes (see Figure 10.11).

In response to the government's failure to address caste oppression, in part due to the BJP's upper caste biases, the level of Dalit support has been falling (see Figure 10.12). In May 2018, only 22% of *Dalits* supported the BJP. This is 9% lower than in January 2018 and is down 2% on the 2014 Lok Sabha election. Three in five *Dalits* (60%) and over half the *Adivasis* (indigenous or aboriginal communities) (54%) said that they were dissatisfied with the concern shown by the Modi government towards growing crimes and atrocities against them. The BJP's pro-rich and pro-urban biases also mean that it has failed to address farmers' concerns, which is why their support for BJP is diminishing. This is reflected in the May 2018 Uttar Pradesh by-election and Lokniti survey results (see Figure 10.13). This is also reflected in the fact that in November 2018, thousands of farmers marched to Delhi protesting against the BJP government. Called the 'Farmers Liberation March', and organized by the All India Kisan Sangharsh Coordination Committee (AIKSCC), a joint front of 208 farmers organizations, including Left-led organizations, this is the fourth such rally in one year. Farmers are demanding a special Parliament Session to pass laws on debt waiver and higher prices for their produce.[15]

In the light of the various failures of the government, the percentage of people who are dissatisfied with it has been rising, and the difference between the percentage of people who are satisfied and the percentage of people who are not satisfied has now reached zero (Figure 10.14).

During the 2014 Lok Sabha election campaign, as widely known, Modi had promised to bring *achhe din* (good times). The proportion of voters who thought that he had failed in bringing *achhe din* has been increasing. In May 2018, more than half were still waiting for *achhe din* (see Figure 10.15).

---

15   This huge rally as a powerful political response to the real economic miseries of common people stands in marked contrast to ongoing attempts by communal forces to whip up support for a law to allow the construction of a Ram temple in Ayodhya.

LIBERAL-DEMOCRACY UNDER A RIGHT-WING REGIME 369

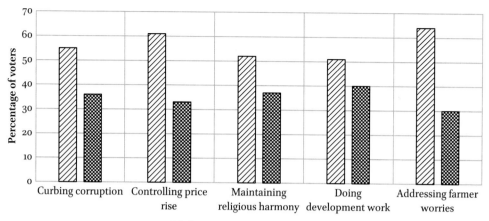

FIGURE 10.10 Voters' perception of the Modi Government's record (in 2018 May)
Note: Respondents were asked: 'Has the Narendra Modi-led Central government done a good job or a bad job with regard to the following?'
SOURCE: DATA FROM LOKNITI SURVEY, 2018

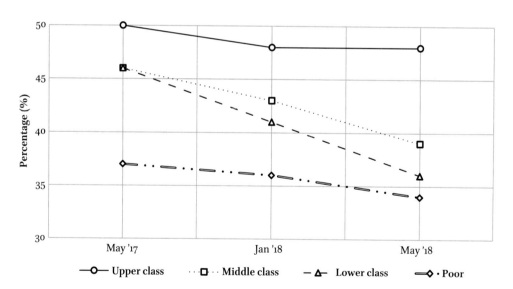

FIGURE 10.11 Percent of support for the BJP-led government
SOURCE: DATA FROM LOKNITI SURVEY, 2018

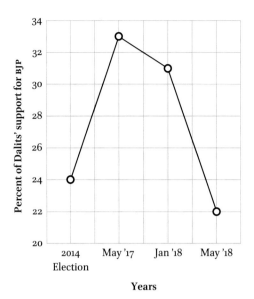

FIGURE 10.12   Percent of Dalits' supporters for BJP
SOURCE: DATA FROM LOKNITI SURVEY, 2018

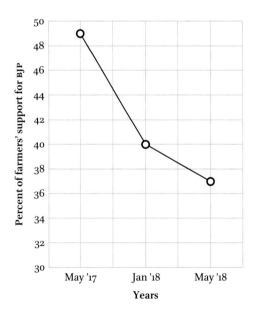

FIGURE 10.13   Percent of farmers' supporters for BJP
SOURCE: DATA FROM LOKNITI SURVEY, 2018

In May 2017, 39% said they would vote for the BJP in the event of a snap national election. By January 2018, the figure dropped to 34%, although that was still an increase from the 31% who voted for BJP in 2014 election. By May 2018, there were more people in the country who did not want the Modi-led government to return to power after the next election than those who did. Nearly half (47%) of all respondents in the Lokniti's May 2018 survey said that the government did not merit another term in office. Only 39% thought it deserved another chance after the 2019 election.

The anti-government sentiment was found to be especially strong among religious minorities. About three-fourths of Muslims, three-fifths of Christians and well over half of Sikhs indicated that they did not wish to see the Modi government back in power in 2019. This is not surprising given the Hindu-nationalist government's dismal record on communal harmony.

Interestingly, the Lokniti survey found that a sizeable section of voters from the majority Hindu community also had an anti-government sentiment, with 42% of Hindu voters anti-government and 44% pro-government. Out of all Hindu communities, *Dalits* and *Adivasis*, who have been victims of violence and atrocities since 2014, were found to be strongest in their opposition to the government at 55% and 43% respectively. They were followed by dominant OBC communities (Upper OBC castes), with 42% opposed to the government (Lokniti, 2018: 13).

6 Conclusion

Under the Modi government, as we have seen, the country's average level of income has been high (by India's standards), even if it is not increasing particularly rapidly. There has also been some improvement to physical infrastructure since 2014. Yet, overall, the record of development during the BJP regime has been an epic of dismal failure. This is the case, especially if we consider the issues that affect the lives of the masses such as: unemployment and under-employment; low wages; increasing concentration of wealth and income; agrarian crisis; and increasing attack on democracy and secularism and attendant communalization of society and polity. The ultra-rich has had *achhe din*. But the vast majority of people of different castes and religions live and work under economic and political conditions which, generally speaking, have not been improving. They have had *bure din* (bad days).

According to the Prime Minister (or his erudite speech writer), *development* has become a vibrant *mass movement*. This is only in written or spoken words, however. One indirect indicator of the overall failure of the government is in

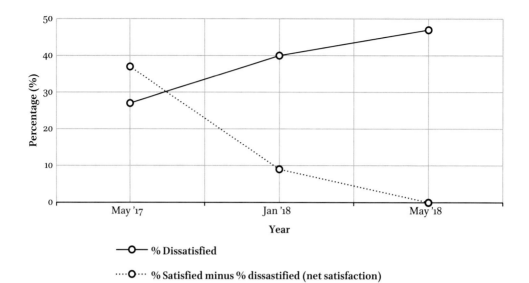

FIGURE 10.14   Percentage of voters dissatisfied/net-satisfied with the BJP government
SOURCE: DATA FROM LOKNITI SURVEY, 2018

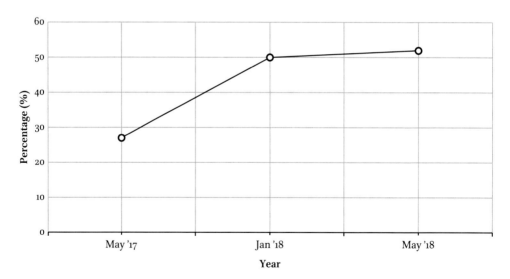

FIGURE 10.15   Percentage of voters who think Mr. Modi has failed in achieving *achhe din* (good times)
SOURCE: LOKNITI SURVEY, 2018

fact the amount of money it spends on publicity. People are not experiencing development as much as BJP would like them to believe. So, it is spending millions on publicity on creating illusions.

Words *are* important. Yet, word ≠ world. There is development, but of the ultra-rich and not for the masses. Development as a mass movement is a beautiful idea. Development *should* become a mass movement. But it *will* become a mass movement when *masses*, democratically self-organized, *move* to take control over their lives. Development *will* become a mass movement when the masses (toiling workers and small-scale producers) control how nation's resources are used – i.e. when *they* are able to decide and say that nation's resources, which are, more or less, products of their *own* labor interacting with nature, are used to satisfy *their* needs, and *not* the needs of the business class for profit, *not* the needs of the political class for accumulating election funding, personal financial fortunes and power, and *not* the needs of the pliant bureaucratic and intellectual layers for their pecuniary and other privileges.

It might be argued that while the situation is not all that good, things can be better in the near future. There are no grounds for such an assumption, however. In fact, the BJP government's failure has a *necessary* character, because of its class and social (religious-sectarian and upper-caste) biases. Controlled by a right-wing party, the government is brazenly pro-big business and panders to a narrow, upper-middle class urban segment of highly educated technical personnel, who, in turn, churn out pro-BJP and communal propaganda and hyper-nationalism meant to dupe the masses, including by using social media. The overall economic orientation of the government is indicated by 'Modinomics'. Modinomics is India's version of 'Reaganomics', which is a product of right-wing economists representing the interests of the big business, both domestic and foreign, and given official approval by Modi, and his political advisors. Conservative American David B. Cohen, who served in the George W. Bush administration, praised Modi, saying that, like Reagan, he 'is an unabashed proponent of free market economics'. He added:

> As one who lived through Reaganomics, I believe that Modinomics can be the perfect antidote to the kleptocratic crony socialism that has kept India from realising her vast economic potential. If India's natural entrepreneurial dynamism is ever fully unleashed, the sky will be the limit.
>
> COHEN, 2014

Modinomics is, fundamentally, an anti-people package of pro-market, pro-business policies. It includes 'privatisation, cuts in food and fuel subsidies and a new sales tax [GST], a tax that is the most regressive way to get revenue as it hits the poor the most' (Roberts, 2017). Its aim, and its effect, are to create the conditions for enabling profits for the corporates through a combination of inter-connected processes: super-exploitation of the masses on the basis of flexible labor policies; extreme austerity, increasing people's vulnerability; reducing corporate tax liability; and surrendering society's natural and financial resources and state-owned enterprises to private business-owners. Modinomics is a vision of the most extreme form of neo-liberal capitalism that Indian state embarked on (see Das, 2015; also Chapter 4 of this book).

The multiple failures of the government can be tied to its blatantly right-wing nature. The government is *right*-wing for a reason: it is *right* for the business class, a class which is on the *wrong* side of history.[16] It is right-wing because its fundamental aim is to serve the business class. It therefore cannot be expected to do much that is right for wage-earners, farmers, the poor and small-scale entrepreneurs, in any systematic, logical and long-term manner, *even if* some in government may have good intentions and even if some crumbs may fall, and do fall, to the people in exchange for political support.

To judge a government's policy requires one to consider, for example, the extent to which the things (or use-values) it provides its common citizens have a commodified or de-commodified character (see Polanyi, 1944/2001; also Block and Polanyi, 2003). The more de-commodified the things are, the better it is for the majority, simply because the majority do not have a lot of money in their hands. One must ask: is water or education or healthcare of good quality provided to citizens in adequate amount by the government as a free use-value or, at least, at a minimal price, relative to the income of the people? From the standpoint of the majority, the purpose of a government is to provide an *antidote* to the ravages of the market, at least as far as the consumption of basic necessaries is concerned. However, true to its right-wing economic policies, what the BJP government, led by the party of the trading and business class, calls 'development' is a tradeable thing, a commodity. The so-called developmental benefits are market-mediated and even corporate-mediated and constitute the mechanisms for the creation or expansion of the market for commodities to be produced for a profit.[17] This is exactly what the neoliberal-capitalist state does. What use are electricity wires or LPG connections if people have no money to pay for electricity and LPG? What use are roads if these roads siphon off natural resources and the surplus of an area to other places,

---

16   The shelf-life of the business class is long over. The progressive character of the business class is a thing of the past. It is the proletariat that is objectively the rising class (see Das, 2017; see Chapters 10–11 of this book on the relation between the proletarian struggle and the fascistic movement).

17   Consider the much-hyped insurance for farmers and how insurance companies are salivating over the profits available.

especially, big cities, the main seat of capital? What use are roads if these roads take one to the places where there is neither decent wage-work nor free or subsidized government-provided services? Something that is as simple as a road or electricity which everyone needs, comes to have 'metaphysical subtleties', when this 'very trivial thing' (Marx, 1977: 163) is seen in the context of the commodity-driven society that this right-wing government is intent on strengthening.

For the mathematically inclined, the impact of the BJP government can be rendered as: $I_{BJP} = I_{EP} + I_{CP} + (I_{EP})(I_{CP})$, where the impact of the BJP (I_{BJP}) on people is the sum of the impact of its right-wing economic policy (I_{EP}), its communal policy of authoritarian-communalism-hyper-Hindu-nationalism (I_{CP}), and the interaction between the two.

Common people are directly hurt by BJP's development policy and economic thinking, buttressed by right-wing economists, including some from the US, who had previously been marginalized. The communal-authoritarian policy that divides people and that crushes the right to dissent also directly affects the masses, in part by undermining their potential for resistance against the economic and the political elite. And given that BJP's economic policy is implemented in a context of communal-authoritarianism supported by vigilantism and mob violence, the adverse impact of the economic policy is magnified: its adverse impact is greater than what it would be if BJP was not *both* communal and economically right-wing.

If you are a Dalit or from a religious minority or indeed a woman who wants to live like an ordinary citizen with all the rights that men enjoy, then your life is one of fear. If you are someone who is against the regime of unreason, religious obscurantism, and on-going attacks on secular ideals, and who is courageous enough to speak the truth, then your life is one of fear as well. The world's largest democracy has been reduced to this. The question is why? Why is this turn to the extreme right-wing thinking and practices which are indeed characteristic of a fascist*ic* movement?

CHAPTER 11

Towards a Political Economy of Fascistic Tendencies

As we have seen in the last chapter, India is experiencing something like a national emergency. This is in the form of persistent attacks on the basic democratic rights of ordinary citizens, by hyper-nationalist Hindu-supremacist forces, which are supported by, and which support, a right-wing political party (Bharatiya Janata Party or BJP). Religious minorities, especially, Muslims, have become 'near-exact equivalent of the Jew' (Sarkar, 2016: 143). The right-wing forces are bent on creating a Hindu state, where religious minorities will remain subservient to the majority religion, and where Dalits (ex-untouchables) will continue to be oppressed by the higher castes in the Hindu social order. The Hindu-nationalist forces are targeting not only religious minorities and Dalits, but also Leftists as well as rationalists and secularists, who oppose their Hindtuva (Hindu-ness) ideology.

The rise of the BJP is a part of the world-wide right-wing bourgeois political trend moving on (or towards) a 'fascistic path'.[1] Fascistic forces are not a thing of the past as far as developed liberal-democratic countries are concerned, which is where they began in early parts of the 20th century. Their threat is very much present right now, including in the US. On April 6, 2018, a former Secretary of State of the US warns in *New York Times*: 'fascism – and the tendencies that lead toward fascism – pose a more serious threat now than at any time since the end of World War II' (Albright, 2018). And, there are fascistic forces in the less developed world as well. During the times of European fascism, there was 'a time when the entire bourgeois democracy in each country believed that fascism was possible only in the backward countries which had not yet graduated from the school of democracy' (Trotsky, 1940). And there are scholars (Vanaik, 2017) now who believe that fascism is not possible in less developed countries, as I will discuss later. I will argue that there *are* 'fascistic

---

1 This is reflected not only in anti-fascist movements happening in different places, but also in the growing attention being given to the topic in academic debates and discussions (e.g. Anievas et al., 2014; Baker, 2005; Banaji, 2016a; Chacko and Jayasuriya, 2018 and the special issue it introduces; Dobkowski, and Walliman, 2003; Kallis, 2003; Mann, 2004; Mason, 1995; Neiberg, 2018; Panitch and Albo, 2016; Patel and McMichael, 2008; Paxton, 2004; Rieman, 2018; Robinson and Barrera, 2012; Saull, 2015). There is also a large amount of discussion in newspapers, magazines, and blogs.

© KONINKLIJKE BRILL NV, LEIDEN, 2020 | DOI:10.1163/9789004415560_012

tendencies' – as a form of bourgeois politics or an extreme tendency toward the breakdown of bourgeois politics – in both richer and poorer countries. Just as the idea that private property is an eternal thing produces the view of capitalist class society as the natural order of things, similarly, the view that capitalism will always have a democratic system makes many people under-emphasize the danger of the collapse of the democratic set-up, which can lead to a fascistic threat. To the extent that such a danger exists, whether it is in rich countries or in poorer countries such as India, the question is how do we understand the threat as we face it, from the standpoint of removing it? This chapter and the next seek to explain fascistic tendencies.

The remainder of this chapter is divided into four sections. Section 1 deals with some definitional/conceptual issues concerning fascism. Section 2 introduces the topic of the fascistic threat in India and sheds light on its importance of the threat to India's Left and progressive culture. Section 3 deals with the political economy of fascism and fascistic tendencies, at a general theoretical level, but with an eye towards India. This section relates the fascistic tendencies to class society, to capitalist class-society and to India's capitalist society, in terms of *economic* as well as *cultural-political* processes, and in terms of society's *structural* conditions and class *agency* involved in the fascistic movement.[2] The focus of this chapter on the political economy aspects of the fascistic tendencies sets the context for the next chapter which discusses the bourgeois-political dynamics of the fascistic movement in India. The final section concludes the chapter.

1 Fascism and Fascistic Tendencies: Some Conceptual Issues

1.1 *Very Briefly, What Is Fascism?*
There are two forms of bourgeois rule. One is the democratic system. There is no doubt that bourgeois democracy is 'a great historical advance in comparison with medievalism' (Lenin, 1977c: 28). Marxists in fact 'demand the extension of ... bourgeois democracy' as a tool for working class organization, *in order to prepare the people for revolution* for the purpose of overthrowing ...the exploiters' (ibid.: 59; italics in original). Liberal democratic rights that have been won and sustained through mass struggles do provide *some* opportunities to the masses to express their interests and ideas, within limits, as compared to the opportunities available under feudalism or fascism. Yet, the bourgeois

---

2 In discussing the class agency aspect, I build on chapter 25 of Marx's *Capital 1* and Aijaz Ahmad's excellent work.

378   CHAPTER 11

character of liberal-democracy should not be underestimated at all. It is, more
or less, the case that:

> the exploiters inevitably transform the state (and we are speaking of de-
> mocracy, i.e., one of the forms of the state) into an instrument of the rule
> of their class, the exploiters, over the exploited. Hence, as long as there
> are exploiters who rule the majority, the exploited, the democratic state
> must inevitably be a democracy for the exploiters.
>
> LENIN, 1977C: 35

Liberal democracy, as a form of class rule, fully protects the interests of the tiny
economic elite (say, top 1–5% or so) versus the masses (bottom 60–80% or so)
who constitute the vast majority. Liberal democracy is much more useful for
resolving conflicts between members of a given class (e.g. between two landlords, two capitalists, two workers, etc.) than between two antagonistically-
related classes. As Lenin (1918) says, 'the ruling party in a bourgeois democracy
extends the protection of the minority only to another bourgeois party, while
the proletariat, on all serious, profound and fundamental issues, gets martial
law or pogroms, instead of the "protection of the minority"'. In a class society,
there cannot be equality between classes, and without economic equality, democracy as equal rights is of limited value. Liberal democracy – bourgeois democracy – is, ultimately, sustained on the basis of the deployment of coercive
measures and violence against the masses, or the threat of violence against
them. There is indeed also always a threat to existing democratic rights of common people. Just because a state currently tolerates democratic rights that
does not mean it will always do so. In fact,

> whenever the proletariat comes forward as an independent force the
> bourgeoisie shifts over to the camp of the counterrevolution. The more
> audacious the mass struggle all the swifter is the reactionary degenera-
> tion of liberalism. No one has yet invented a means for paralyzing the ef-
> fects of the law of the class struggle.
>
> TROTSKY, 1939

This brings us to the second form of class rule: authoritarianism. Under certain
conditions, authoritarianism can be transformed into a fascist/fascistic rule.
Today no country has a fascist rule, if by fascism we mean the following:

> When a state turns fascist,… it means first of all for the most part that the
> workers' organizations are annihilated; that the proletariat is reduced to

an amorphous state; and that a system of administration is created which penetrates deeply into the masses and which serves to frustrate the independent crystallization of the proletariat. Therein precisely is the gist of fascism.

TROTSKY, 1944

The gist of fascism and its task consist in a complete suppression of all workers' organizations and in the prevention of their revival.

TROTSKY, 1932d

Some say that fascism is a political movement. 'Fascism ... is the ideology of nationalism upheld by an anti-democratic and totalitarian state', says Mackel (2010). But fascism is not an ordinary political movement. Fascism is authoritarianism. But it is different from Bonapartism, although fascism does have elements of Bonapartism.[3] 'Fascism is not merely a system of reprisals, of brutal force, and of police terror' (Trotsky, 1932i). It is a ruling-class-based intervention: it is class struggle from above, effected on the basis of threat and practice of violence against the masses, in order to protect capitalist class relations and to promote capitalist accumulation strategies. Trotsky continues:

Fascism is a particular governmental system based on the uprooting of all elements of proletarian democracy within bourgeois society.

In the course of many decades, the workers have built up within the bourgeois democracy, by utilizing it, by fighting against it, their own strongholds and bases of proletarian democracy: the trade unions, the political parties, the educational and sport clubs, the cooperatives, etc.

The task of fascism lies not only in destroying the Communist vanguard but in holding the entire class in a state of forced disunity. To this end the physical annihilation of the most revolutionary section of the workers does not suffice. It is also necessary to smash all independent and voluntary organizations, to demolish all the defensive bulwarks of the proletariat...For, in the last analysis, the Communist Party also bases itself on these achievements.

TROTSKY, 1932i

---

3 '[It is wrong to say that] fascism is simply a repetition of Bonapartism. There is an element of Bonapartism in fascism... Without this element, namely, without the raising of state power above society owing to an extreme sharpening of the class struggle, fascism would have been impossible' (Trotsky, 1940).

A political project such as fascism needs a class agency. Fascism's class agency is made up by: the petty bourgeoisie, old and new, and sections of the wage-earning class and the under- and unemployed, supported by sections of the propertied class (more on this later). Fascism is an authoritarian political movement against the masses, by the masses, on behalf of the ruling class.

1.2 *Fascism Not Possible Anymore?*

If fascism is, more or less, what we have just described it to be, it is clearly a dangerous thing. It is a serious threat to democratic rights. This means that it is also a serious threat to social-economic rights of the masses, as without access to democratic rights, they cannot demand social-economic rights. But some have argued that given strong liberal democracy in rich countries, and given capitalism's resilience, there is a very weak chance of fascism happening there (Vanaik, 2017: 297, 284). Vanaik (2017) says that Marxists have underestimated: 'the strength and durability of bourgeois democracy after 1945', and this underestimation is the 'natural correlate of an obverse error – the overestimation of the 'structural crisis' of capitalism' (p. 299).[4] The idea that capitalism is in structural crisis is out of line with the fact of the 'remarkable productivity of late capitalism and its ability to learn from mistakes (preventing anything a repeat of anything approximating the Great Depression)' (p. 299).[5] The kind of social-economic dislocation that caused fascism in Europe is nowhere present now. 'Decades after the end of the long boom (itself never anticipated) the prospects of fascisms coming to power within remain dim', Vanaik says, although there are newer and stronger authoritarian pressures (p. 300). There is also little reason to expect fascism to come to the Global South. Firstly, 'Why should foreign capitals having controlling positions in the dominant class-coalitions or ruling-class alliances of specific developing world countries want to encourage, not just the authoritarian option, but the specifically fascist one?' (p. 302). Besides, crucial to the functioning of multinational companies is their control of knowhow and not so much of markets or of resources (p. 301). Secondly, the fascist option made sense in a context where there was a powerful systemic threat to the rule of capital from the working class (especially where the possibility of its rapid mass radicalization existed) (p. 303). But in

---

4 This view is very close to Chibber's (2017) view that capitalism is not in crisis but neoliberalism is.

5 For Vanaik, because Marxism has under-emphasized capitalism – financial capital's – dynamism, it has over-emphasized inter-imperialist rivalry and war, which had triggered fascism in Europe in the 20th century. The most important feature of expanding capitalism has been technical innovation (Vanaik, 2017: 301). Political stability through democratic/semi-democratic system and the preservation of capitalist relations are much more important to the imperialist project (Vanaik, 2017: 312, 300–302).

our times the tendency is towards de-radicalization of the working-class movement. Thirdly, while fascism is based on the squeezing of the middle classes in rural and urban areas (i.e. proletarianization), that is also not happening now in the less developed world: 'the assumptions of the classical Marxist theories of fascism have been shaken' (p. 305).[6] Fourthly, there is a discursive obstacle to fascism: the memory and awareness of what the historic experience of fascism has meant and the practical experience of prolonged bourgeois democracy are powerful vaccine within the working class (and even the petty bourgeois) against the fascist temptation' (Vanaik, 2017: 306). All in all, Vanaik says, 'In post-colonial societies, the political vehicles of religious fundamentalism or religious nationalism are not fascist formations but, at most, potential formations' and that 'the conditions for the realization of that potential do not exist, and are not likely to surface' (p. 324). As far as India as a post-colonial country is concerned, 'there is no convincing economic rationale for emerging fascism, though there may be for emerging or deepening authoritarianism' (p. 302). Besides, the organized working class does not see communalism as representing fascism; only many of their communist leaders do (p. 334).[7] 'While the fascist state in India would necessarily be Hindu nationalist, the Hindu communal and nationalist state would not necessarily be fascist' (p. 324). There are, of course, several conceptual problems with the thesis that fascism, or something close to it, cannot come to the Global South, as suggested below; and that thesis has to be counter-posed, *empirically*, to what is happening in Brazil under Bolsonaro in 2018.

1.3 *From Fascism to Fascistic Tendency/Tendencies*

Fascism must be seen as a historical process. This is in two inter-related senses. One is that it is a stage in the cycle of capitalism. It is a particular historical system of capitalist reaction. Bourgeois politics progresses through certain stages, and fascism is the last one (here no linearity is implied, however).

> we must differentiate three historical stages: at the dawn of capitalist development, when the bourgeoisie required revolutionary methods to

---

6 In most of the Global South, there is the fact of persistence of the peasantry. In the towns, the middle classes have usually had little pressure from below, from a working class. The relative size of this middle class is much larger in the South than in the early industrializing countries at a comparable stage (p. 305).

7 Note that the word communal is used in India not in its usual western sense, which is associated with commons (e.g. communal property, communal living, etc.). 'Only in India does the word "communalism" refer to a malignant ideology and violence prone practice – even a form of "fascism" – which justifies itself in the name of religious difference' (Ahmad, 2013: 6).

resolve its tasks; in the period of bloom and maturation of the capitalist regime, when the bourgeoisie endowed its domination with orderly, pacific, conservative, democratic forms; finally, at the decline of capitalism, when the bourgeoisie is forced to resort to methods of civil war against the proletariat to protect its right of exploitation.

The political programs characteristic of these three stages: *Jacobinism*, reformist *democracy* (social democracy included) and *Fascism* are basically programs of petty bourgeois currents.

TROTSKY, 1932a

Thus fascism is, first of all, a stage in bourgeois politics representing the breakdown of the democratic system (see Figure 11.1 below).

There is another sense in which fascism is to be seen historically: it is that in any given society, traits of fascism and those of democracy can be combined in various proportions, however temporarily. This aspect of the historical character of fascism exists given the 'the law that governs the displacement of one social system by another, even though they are irreconcilably inimical to each other' (Trotsky, 1932d). Indicated here is a stage of potential transition to fascism proper:

during a given period, between the democratic and the fascist systems, a transitional regime is established, which combines the features of both... There are periods during which the bourgeoisie leans upon both the Social Democracy and fascism, that is, during which it simultaneously manipulates its electoral and terroristic agencies... But such a condition of the state and of the administration is temporary in character.

TROTSKY, 1932d

During the transition period: there cannot be further reforms of capitalism in the interests of masses, but 'neither Communism nor fascism is ready as yet to seize power' (Trotsky, 1932d). There is thus a tendency towards the crisis of bourgeois politics.

I approach the crisis of bourgeois politics as fascistic tendencies from two inter-related philosophical viewpoints. One concerns the distinction between tendencies and outcomes (and the related distinction between appearances and underlying reality): a mechanism – i.e. a way of acting or functioning of an object – exists necessarily by virtue of the nature of an object (i.e. the internal relations which constitute the object and its relation to other objects, within a system) and the effects of the mechanism (when it is active) may be mediated by – and even temporarily countered by – other mechanisms and by contingent

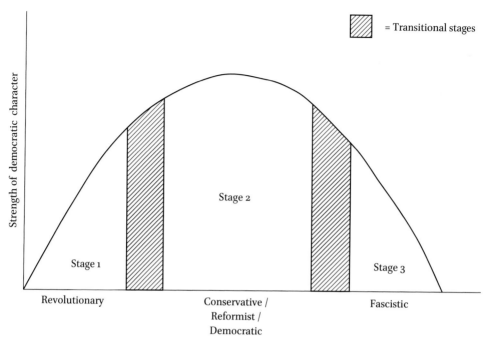

FIGURE 11.1 Curve of capitalist politics
SOURCE: AUTHOR

conditions (see Sayer, 1992: 106), although what is called a tendency is ultimately more powerful than what is called a counter-tendency (Carchedi, 2010). This philosophical view shaped Marx's theory of capitalist crisis caused by the rate of profit to fall with the rising organic composition of capital. The second perspective informing my view of fascism says that:

> understanding anything … requires that we know something about how it arose and developed… our notion of anything [must] … include, as aspects of what it is, both the process by which it has become that and the broader interactive context in which it is found.
> OLLMAN, 2003: 13

This is the perspective of Marx, the dialectician, who studied capitalism of his time not just from the standpoint of what it was but also from the standpoint of where it was going (given its internal tendencies), what it was tending towards (e.g. development of monopolies; globalization; recurrent and intensifying crises, etc.), even if many of the things he thought characterized capitalism were going to be materialized to a greater extent in the 20th century than during the time when he was writing about it.

When I say fascistic tendency (tendencies), the term/concept refers to mechanisms (processes/relations), which exist by virtue of the capitalist-class society, and which, under certain conditions, can result in a fascist government/ state. There is a tendency towards the breakdown of bourgeois democracy, and 'The workers are aware that democracy is suffering shipwreck everywhere, and that they are threatened by fascism even in those countries where fascism is as yet non-existent' (Trotsky, 1940). While India or any other country does not have a fascist regime, there are fascis*tic* movements and fascistic governments, as in the US of the late 1930s–1940s, and in many countries such as India and the US in contemporary times. There *are* fascistic *tendencies* (mechanisms/ forces/processes) which *can* produce a fascist outcome (i.e. fascist state) when favorable *conditions* are present. Fascistic tendencies can exist in a society which is not fascist. The transitional phase is obviously different from the stage where there is full-fledged fascism, but there are similarities: fascists aim 'at the domination of the traditional bourgeois parties in the name of the "strong state"; this is a fascist trait characteristic of the movement and of the regime' (Trotsky, 1934a). A party, an organization or a mob can be fascist – or almost fascist (fascistic) – without there being a fascist state. A mob or an organization can be fascist (almost fascist) within a broader movement that is fascistic, that shows fascistic tendencies. Fascism not only represents a stage in the history of capitalist politics. It itself develops in stages, like all processes do.

> [There] is no reason to argue that unsuccessful fascist parties are less fascist than successful ones. The German Nazi Party did not suddenly become fascist when it achieved success in the polls, it was already fascist before 1930. What made it fascist was its ambition to become a mass reactionary party.
>
> RENTON, 2007: 106

It is important that we call a thing by its right name.[8] 'Names are used to distinguish between concepts; concepts, in politics, in turn serve to distinguish among real forces' (Trotsky, 1932g). Fascism, fascistic tendencies, authoritarianism, Bonapartism, etc., need to be carefully used. I distinguish fascism from authoritarianism and fascistic tendencies (the mechanisms that can produce

---

8   Implied here is a tripartite relation: among (a) the real (what exists independent of the thinking mind), (b) what is reflected in our mind, as a mental image, which (c) is then given a name (a conventionally chosen sound). What is important is we get our concept right (Sayer, 2000).

fascism). Sometimes, I use the term fascistic tendencies to refer to the bearers – embodiments – of these processes and relations such as a given organization or a party. Of course, whether a group calls itself fascist or (Hindu-)nationalist is beside the matter, just as whether the bourgeoisie calls itself an entrepreneur class or the middle class cannot hide its class character. Whether the working class *sees* fascistic tendencies or mere communalism is really beside the point.

Even if the fascist movement today is not a mere replication of the fascism of the earlier times (say, 1930s), fascism – or strong tendencies towards fascism – has some common traits. According to Rieman (2018), the West is facing a threat of fascism which is the form of modern mass politics that actively cultivates people's worst irrational sentiments including resentment, hatred, xenophobia, and fear, and that mobilizes ignorance and prejudice by nurturing and flattering them.

A former Vice President of the US, Mr. Wallace, wrote an article in 1945, entitled 'The danger of American fascism'. In this article, several of its traits are described that are relevant to the contemporary fascistic tendencies including in India under the Modi regime:

a. spouting populist themes but manipulating people and institutions to achieve the opposite;
b. pretending to support ordinary working people, and paying lip service to their welfare;
c. demanding free enterprise, but speaking for monopoly;
d. putting money and power ahead of human beings;
e. distrust of democracy because it stands for equal opportunity;
f. claiming to be super-patriots, but wanting to destroy constitutionally-given liberty;
g. super-nationalists' pursuit of power by deceiving citizens and playing to their fears;
h. needing and using scapegoats;
i. harboring an intensity of intolerance toward other races, parties, classes, religions, cultures, regions or nations than those fascists represent;
j. using lies to promote civic division, which then justifies authoritarian crackdown;
k. poisoning the channels of public information;
l. never wanting to present the truth to the public but to use the news to deceive the public;
m. giving currency to snide suspicions without factual foundation;
n. directing all deceit towards the final goal of capturing political power and using state power and market power and thus keeping the ordinary people in eternal subjection. (Wallace, 2017)

The fascistic movement/project (fascistic tendency) is implemented differently in different countries and yet the fascist movement in one country (e.g. India) shares some traits with the fascist movement in other countries. Talking about India and the West, Patnaik (2017) writes that the fascist movement there has these attributes:

> the propagation of a "supremacism" ("white supremacism" in the West, "Hindu supremacism" here); an apotheosis of unreason (manifested in "supremacism" and the projection of a "messiah"); a grassroots movement (which distinguishes it from mere authoritarianism) and an alliance with big capital.
>
> PATNAIK, 2017b; see also DESAI, 2002

Fascism (in the sense of a fascist state or fascistic tendencies that can produce such a state) is a form of bourgeois class-politics. It is a political-ideological *mass movement* that seeks to rescue *capitalism* from its crisis (i.e. from its failure to develop productive forces and meet people's needs, and consequent economic slowdown) by employing *authoritarian* measures against ordinary people and against religious or ethnic minorities or indeed against any person/group/organization, and especially the Left, which seeks to protect the democratic and economic rights of ordinary people, including minorities (see Renton, 2007).

2 A Short Introduction to the Fascistic Movement in India

In India, BJP, which is the political head of the fascistic movement and whose current political leader is Modi, is a part of the Sangh Parivar ('family of organizations'), a collective of Hindu-nationalist groups/movements that propagate fascistic ideology and engage in fascistic political activities. The Sangh works under the ideological mentorship of RSS (Rashtriya Swayamsevak Sangh, or, National Volunteer Organization) established in 1925, the same year India's communist party came into being.[9] RSS is probably the world's largest voluntary organization. It is probably the world's largest cadre-based organization. Its own trade union federation is the largest in India. A fascist organization, RSS employs paramilitary uniforms and armed voluntary corps. It has borrowed the ideology of nation and race from Nazi Germany and adapted this to India (for a brief history of RSS, see Basu et al., 1993).

---

9 See Upadhyay (2018) on how the RSS builds its trade union organization.

BJP combines its forces with, and rides on the back of, its 'cousin', the communal-fascist RSS and other elements of the fascistic Parivar. BJP stands for, and is a part of, a *fascistic movement with Indian characteristics*. This is recruiting its cadres from middle class and semi/un-employed people and the wage-earning class, by making use of the discourse of the Hindu religion, of the idea of Hindutva (Hindu-ness).[10]

Given that I talk about *fascistic* tendencies, it is important that RSS's class character is emphasized. It is mistaken to believe that the RSS, the ideological guru/mentor of the BJP, the new national party of the Indian capitalist class, is merely a communal force with little respect for democratic rules, that it is mainly or merely a cultural-political force against bourgeois democracy. The RSS, the center of the fascistic movement in India, is, above all, an *anti-communist* force. It is not only against bourgeois democracy, but it is also against proletarian democracy, i.e. against the organs of the proletarian democracy (e.g. proletarian parties, etc.). The RSS has been anti-communist historically, for its origin. It has been spreading its reactionary ideas through its own organizations and through the friends/supporters in Congress and other non-left parties. In October 1949, when Mr. Nehru, the first Prime Minister of India, who was fundamentally a secular person (and far more secular than most in the Congress party he led), was away in the United States, senior Congress leaders said they would allow RSS members to join the party. Welcoming the move, the RSS said: 'It is the end of the Congress war on the Sangh. It is a right step in the direction of national consolidation', and that with 'Communists out to enslave Bharat to Russia and Socialists still trying to find their feet', commented the RSS in its journal, 'mutual goodwill and co-operation between the Congress and the Sangh is the surest guarantee of national unity in this hour of crisis' (quoted in Guha, 2018). In the early years of post-colonial India and in the aftermath of 1917, RSS leaders offered their services to Nehru's Congress, saying that RSS was 'the only way to meet the challenge of communism', and that it is RSS that provided the only ideology which can harmonize and integrate the interests of different groups and classes and thus successfully avoid any class war (ICL, 2014). RSS began building trade unions with the overt goal of fostering

---

10 There is much literature on the link between neoliberalism and Hindutva (Desai, 2011; De and Saha, 2002). It is being recognized that neoliberal capitalism is expanding the middle class, which, in turn, is the base for the fascistic movement. The hegemonic aspirations of the middle class, including its newly-created elements (such as those in the IT industry), have taken the form of a politics of reaction, blending market liberalism and political and social illiberalism (Heller and Fernandes, 2006). Chacko (2018) says that the BJP is not only pro-corporate but also pro-neo-middle class. It recreates the middle and 'neo-middle' classes as 'virtuous market citizens' who view themselves as entrepreneurs and consumers but whose behavior is regulated by the framework of Hindu nationalism.

harmony between capitalists and laborers. This fascistic organization also set up a party called Jan Sangh, which became in 1980 what is called BJP.[11]

With the elevation of Modi to the political leadership of the right-wing movement – Modi who used Gujarat under his Chief Ministership as a laboratory for communal and neoliberal capitalist interventions – RSS has got a shot in its arm: 'Modi's "achievement" in India consisted in effecting... an alliance between the RSS and Indian big capital' (Patnaik, 2017b). Not only has RSS openly associated itself with Hitler, it has also declared itself as openly anti-communist and a reactionary-*bourgeois* force.

Independent India's communal-fascistic movement has evolved over time. One can think of four stages.[12]

1947–mid-1970s: This was the time of Nehruvian socialism (read: state-directed peripheral capitalism), partly informed by the Bombay Plan referred to in Chapter 7. There was also a formal commitment to democracy and to secularism. Given weak material foundations, the basis for democracy, which always requires the state being able to provide material concessions in response to lower-class struggles, was weak. And for similar reasons, secularism as a part of democracy (in the sense of the respect for the rights for religious minorities) was also weak. Not only was it the case that 'Hindu nationalism was already an important stream in the wider flow of anti-colonial cultural nationalism', in that religious symbols were widely used in the anti-colonial struggle (Vanaik, 2017: 329). It was also the case that the fascistic movement, which had a very minor role in the anti-colonial struggle, had been against secularism, even if secularism, in India, means 'equal respect for all religions in the conduct of the affairs of the state' (Ahmad, 2013: 8).[13] Yet it is also true that RSS's attempt to collaborate with Congress is not successful, thanks to the presence of Nehru

---

11   For a short history of the BJP, see Basu (2013). On the BJP's post-2014 resurgence, see Palshikar et al. (2017). It should be stressed that, and as I have said, according to some (Vanaik), Indian communalism cannot be seen in terms of the concept of fascism. However, there is a literature that seeks to interpret communalism on the basis of that concept (Banaji, 2013; Harriss-White, 2003; Krishna, 2003). See also De Mello (2018): he relates the fascistic situation to what he calls Indian sub-imperialism (on the dangers of the countries of BRICS playing a sub-imperialist role, see Bond, 2014).

12   This brief historical discussion below is partly based in Ahmad, 2003.
      Also, it should be said that it is arbitrary to begin with 1947. There are distinct colonial roots of communalism. For example, in reaction to British imperialism during the 19th and 20th centuries, Indian Muslims and Hindus imagined and invented their separate and distinct religious communities and communal nationalisms. These were institutionalized in the subcontinent's political systems by the British government in collaboration with Indian politicians (Stern, 2000).

13   It should be noted that the word secularism has different meanings. Among many texts on secularism, see Thapar (2016). The original European meaning (the separation of the state from religion, which means that the state will not be influenced by religious beliefs

TOWARDS A POLITICAL ECONOMY OF FASCISTIC TENDENCIES 389

who was not only a major supporter of secularism and scientific temper, but who also commanded respect because he played a major role, with Gandhi, in the anti-colonial struggle.

Mid-1970s–late 1990s: This period coincides with the decay of the Nehruvian consensus on India's commitment to *state-directed* capitalism (called socialism by the Right), which included some control over capitalism.[14] This period also coincides with a weakening commitment to secularism and democracy.[15] In 1976, the Indian constitution was amended, officially making it a secular

---

of citizens or of those who conduct state affairs) is a different one from how secularism is used in India.

In India, secularism means 'equal respect for all religions'. This is the 'socialist approach to religion with Indian features'! However, how can believers treat each other as equal believers worthy of mutual respect? For Hindus, Islam is inferior, and for Muslims, Hinduism is inferior. In fact, 'equal respect for all religions in the conduct of the affairs of the state would necessarily lead, especially in the context of the corruptions of liberal democratic politics, to greater respect for the religion of the demographic majority whose votes count for more, whose privileged classes command much more money and power, and among whose middle classes new kinds of religiosity are now rampant. In India, the demographic majority of those defined as Hindus by the state itself is so overwhelming that the state must necessarily favour Hindus in its secularism regardless of which political party is in power; between the Congress and the BJP, there would necessarily be a difference of degree, thanks mainly not to different ideologies but to the differences in the constituency blocs that each wishes to address' (Ahmad, 2013: 8–9).

According to Chandra (2008: 2), the European definition of secularism as the separation of state from religion is a universal definition, and is held in India, and Mohandas Gandhi agreed with it. So 'to talk of any Indian definition of secularism which would deny this is to deny secularism' (ibid.).

'India is a land of religions', and from this arises 'another specific feature of secularism in India'. This is that: 'The state should have equal regard for all religions'. The two meanings are the same thing, Chandra says: 'the doctrine of the state neutrality towards religions takes the form of state extending equal opportunities to the followers of all religions and to atheists' (Chandra, 2008: 2–3).

14   On the topic of the shift from Nehruvian secular democracy to the recent right-wing, communal times, see: Frankel, 2005; Khilnani, 2017; Niclas-Tolle, 2015; and Corbridge and Harriss, 2013.

15   The commitment of the state to secularism has not been that strong from the beginning. For Aijaz Ahmad (2013) (and Perry Anderson): in India and for the Indian state, 'secularism [is used] as a legitimating ideology', or more specifically, 'the Indian state... is a Hindu communal state that uses secularism as its legitimating ideology'. Ahmad argues that: 'the Indian state is in large measure a communal state that can accommodate all sorts of communalisms, including notably the Muslim one, but it is predominantly a Hindu communal state simply because Hindu communalists are far more numerous and powerful than all the other communalists combined. ... [The] Indian state can live with communalism perfectly happily so long as communal violence is minimized, because such violence, like any other violence in public affairs, creates a law & order problem [and is a threat to capitalist property]' (Ahmad, 2013: 8–9).

state, even though the constitution prohibits the slaughter of cows, an animal which many Hindus consider sacred. Yet, in the mid-1970s (1975–1977), a national emergency was declared suspending the democratic rights, and this was a response to, among other things, working class struggle (e.g. railways strike). There was a massive anti-emergency movement led by an alliance of non-Marxist (petty-bourgeois) socialists and some fascistic elements as well as Left forces. This movement against the attack on liberal democracy as well as post-emergency Janata government legitimized the fascistic elements (e.g. RSS) which actually represent a more dangerous attack on democracy than the Emergency. Jan Sangh, the right-wing political party that the RSS had set up in 1951 became what is now known as the BJP. Concurrently, the decline of the Congress Party, which had a formal commitment to secularism, began, but the non-Congress opposition, including the fascistic elements, were not able to provide a stable non-Congress alternative either, creating a space for a non-secular national-scale alternative. The demise of 'communist regimes' in the world also created an adverse climate for the Indian communist movement so whatever limited ability it had to fight the BJP did not materialize. The Indian ruling class turned to the imperialist US with the political support of all non-communist parties, nominally secular or not.

In 1991, the ruling class embarked on neoliberal capitalism in response to the crisis of state-directed capitalism which overlapped with the days of the Congress party's dominance. Institutionalization of politics of religion happened, with a tacit agreement between the Congress and some fascistic forces (laying the foundation stone for the temple in 1989; and destruction of the 16th-century Babri masjid (mosque) located in the city of Ayodhya, in 1992, which was not stopped by any part of the state, whether the Congress party or the coercive agencies, and this showed the non-secular character of the state as such, and not just as a party). *The Hindu*, a progressive newspaper, published an editorial on December 7, 1992, which it republished on December 7, 2918 (*The Hindu*, 2017). The following lines from the editorial are worth reading in today's context:

> It was religious fanaticism at its ugliest in Ayodhya yesterday, with the country's worst fears coming true in the nightmarish spectacle of the brutal destruction of the 450 year old Babri Masjid by thousands of frenzied kar sevaks [people who offer services for free to a religious cause]. The disputed mosque was razed to the ground with a barbaric savagery reminiscent of the crude traditions of settling scores in medieval history. The demolition of the Masjid has delivered a lethal blow to the image of a secular and democratic India.

The BJP and its militant allies, the RSS, the VHP and the Bajrang Dal stand exposed as having brought on this horrific denouement even *as the essentially destructive and fascist nature of its strategy and tactics* [italics added] cannot be in doubt any more. The BJP's claim to be a defender of the national interest lies in shreds today.

...what is vital is to recognise that this is a defining moment in India's history, a moment at which the country can be plunged into a dark abyss of primitive emotions threatening to erase four decades of a successful track record of a progressive secular democracy.[16]

The peaceful change of government from one fraction of the proprietary coalition to another fraction, through elections continues, and the vast majority of people continued to vote in national and provincial elections, showing that liberal-democracy continues to have much legitimacy in the minds of common men and women. Neoliberalism also creates a situation where all parties pander to business interests, so some have to play a politics of identity (including religious identity) to attract voters in a competitive electoral field (more on this in the next chapter).

Late 1990s–2014: A new and stable power bloc of the Indian Right arose with the BJP-led government at the national level elected. The Indian ruling class moved closer to an alliance with imperialism as a junior partner, a process which all non-Left parties support. The commitment to neoliberalism and globalization of economy also deepened. The capitalist class operating in India came to have a trans-nationalized segment, which, like the other segments, demanded a good business climate (de-regulation, austerity, wage repression, etc.). The Congress served as the formally secular face of the neoliberal capitalist class while BJP served as its communal face. All-non-Left parties have colluded with BJP. Evident was an increasing communalization of popular consciousness, on the basis of the mass work by RSS and its infiltration into state ideological and coercive institutions. India increasingly became a national security state, demonstrating fascistic tendencies.

---

16   The Hindu (2017) goes on to say: 'All the secular political forces must rally to the defence of the country and pull it back from the brink. A first step would be to rebuild the destroyed Babri Masjid as a gesture towards the minority community and as a reaffirmation of an unwavering commitment to the vision of a democratic India, free of any kind of bigotry'.

2014–present: With the BJP coming to power in 2014, the fascistic movement has experienced a boost. Led by the RSS, the fascist movement has indeed been making good use of electoral methods to mobilize the masses and to win support for their cause. In early 2019, the BJP is in power in a larger number of States on its own or with an alliance partner (Map 11.1). It is now the dominant party of the ruling class, and it supports, and is supported by, imperialist capital and its states. Many secular-minded leaders from Congress think that another election win by BJP in 2019 will produce irreversible damage to India's secularism.[17]

The fascistic movement continues to attack not only liberal-political forces that defend secularism but also the Left. The increasing political significance of the fascistic movement under BJP's political patronage is indicated by the fact that when for the first time in Indian electoral history, there was a direct electoral face-off between the Left and the BJP in March 2018, BJP won. This was in Tripura, a small State in North-East India. Even though the Left garnered 45% of the votes (down from 48.11% in 2013), the BJP, with its alliance partner, won the majority of seats with a vote-share of 50.5%. BJP did so by using money and muscle power, by swallowing up politicians of the Congress party, which is a traditional and non-fascistic party of the property-owning class, and by selling the dream of what it calls development. Within less than a month of the declaration of the Tripura election results, the violent attack on the communist movement in Tripura by the fascistic movement has taken the following forms: 'Nearly a thousand Left cadres have been physically targeted, 1699 houses have been ransacked and looted, over 450 shops burnt, over 800 Party offices have been attacked, looted and some burnt down and 134 offices of Left mass organisations have been captured and occupied by the BJP. Indiscriminate arrests and foisting of false cases against the Left cadre continue'. (CPI(M), 2018). In fact, soon after the results were declared, two statues of Vladimir Lenin were taken down by the fascistic mob.[18] The Governor of the State, who

---

17   A prominent Congress leader who is also an author of many books says: 'If they (BJP) win a repeat in the Lok Sabha [in 2019], our democratic constitution as we understand it, will not survive as they will have all the elements they need to tear apart the constitution of India and write a new one…That new one will be the one which will enshrine principles of Hindu Rashtra, that will remove equality for minorities, that'll create a Hindu Pakistan and that isn't what Mahatma Gandhi, Nehru, Sardar Patel, Maulana Azad and great heroes of freedom struggle fought for' (quoted in Times of India, 2018).

18   Interestingly, one of the most prominent statues of Lenin in India, at Esplanade in the center of Kolkata, remains in place even though the Left is no longer in power.

TOWARDS A POLITICAL ECONOMY OF FASCISTIC TENDENCIES

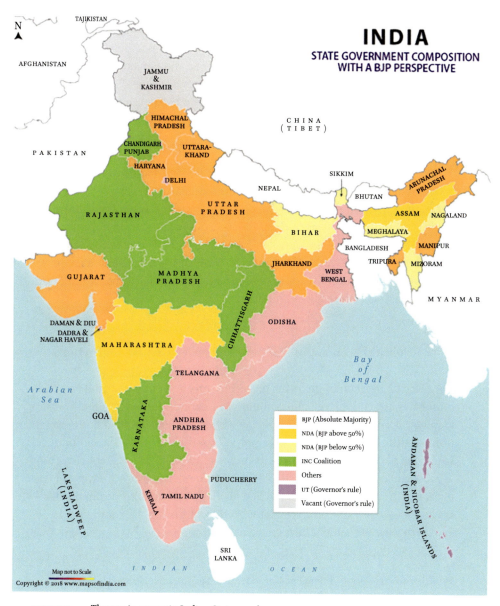

MAP 11.1 The BJP in power in Indian States, early 2019
SOURCE: HTTPS://WWW.MAPSOFINDIA.COM/ASSEMBLYPOLLS/STATE-ASSEMBLY-LEADING-PARTIES.HTML

should ordinarily be above party politics, justified this criminal vandalism by saying on Twitter: 'What one democratically elected government [the reference is to the communist government] can do another democratically elected government can undo. And vice versa'. All these and similar actions demonstrate the right-wing's deep disrespect for democratic values. Political violence against ideological opponents is one of the main means of acquiring influence and governmental power, for the BJP.

The election result in Tripura is being seen by the right-wing movement as its definitive victory over the Left, politically and ideologically, and this should be seen in the light of what I have said above about the anti-communist character of the RSS. Recall there was here, for the first time, a direct contest between the Right and the Left in which the Left lost. This election result will, no doubt, add to the obstacles to the communist movement (and not just to the cause of protection of democratic and secular values). The question is: what is to be done about the fascistic threat (the topic of the penultimate chapter)? Answering such a question presupposes an understanding of the nature of fascistic threat itself (the topic of this chapter and the next).

3   Political Economy of Fascistic Tendencies, Globally and in India

The fascistic movement involving discriminatory and violent attitude towards minorities, including religious minorities, cannot be seen merely as an ideological/cultural process. Cultural ideas exist under definite material conditions, even if these ideas cannot be simply reduced to the material conditions. So when one of the most prominent historians of India, Chandra (2008) says that 'Communalism is basically an ideology', that 'Communalism is … a way of looking at politics and society … around that ideology' and that the 'communal leaders and ideologues are primarily interested in spreading the communal belief system or ways of thought', he is only partly right (pp. 7–8).[19] When he says that

---

19   For an explanation of communalism in terms of ideas, but not ideas based in India but in the West, see Ranganathan (2018). According to him, the recent rise of the far right, communalism and nationalism in India are better understood as a continuation of Westernization. He says that India has long traditions of philosophies that take the job of reasonable living to be one of distinguishing our thoughts from our attitudes. Moreover, not only did Indian thinkers not endorse anything like the *logocentric* conflation of thought and language, they from the very earliest times treated disagreement and dissent as the proper mode of public interaction. Ranganathan argues that Hinduism is unique among religions in not being reducible to any core teachings or tradition. Rather, it constitutes the disagreements of philosophy with South Asian resources.

'Other aspects of communal activity are secondary and follow from the basic communal ideology', and that 'Communal ideology and not specific policies lie at the heart of a communal party', he is not even half right (pp. 7–8). Fascistic tendencies, including when the targets are religious minorities, are only partly ideological.

Similarly, when Simeon (1986) says that communalism is the Indian version of fascist populism and racist nationalism, the fascistic tendency appears to be mainly a political phenomenon. When one says that 'Fascism invades the public sphere with controlled mobs' and that it 'represents an assault on *politics*, a replacement of democratic dialogue by violent intimidation...' (Simeon, 2016: 154), one is un-dialectically (one-sidedly) stressing fascism as a merely *political* phenomenon.

Unlike Simeon, there are those scholars (e.g. Vanaik) who, as we have seen, deny that there is a fascist threat in India. They are 'much more likely to see the principal danger as residing not in something that lies *behind* Hindu communalism, or in some fascist core *contained within or hidden in* Hindu communalism, but as Hindu communalism *itself*, as the specific manifestation of the politics of cultural exclusivity and radical right-wing reaction' (Vanaik, 2017: 335; italics added). In other words, for these scholars, what appears on the surface is all that there is. There is nothing – or nothing much – *behind* it. In this alternative approach, the focus is on 'politicized Hindutva's deep roots and growth in civil society, well beyond the question of its capacity to appropriate the state' (ibid.: 335). Vanaik (2017) says: 'In a sense, the phenomenon is *more deep-rooted* than fascism, *more enduring* and *more difficult* completely or comprehensively to destroy' (p. 335).

Several problems with this denial of the fascistic threat approach should be noted. (1) What is being claimed is that India is experiencing merely a threat of communalism, an attack on the rights of religious minorities, but not a threat to liberal-democracy as such. (2) In this approach, as well, the threat of communalism is not because of any crisis of capitalism, so there is no material root for the on-going right-wing political activities. The latter exist because of such things as the decline of a specific kind of politics (e.g. Nehruvian project of socialism, secularism and democracy). It is 'the decay of the post-colonial project as originally defined that best explains the subsequent rise of reactionary authoritarian populism embodied in the Sangh combine' (ibid.: 329). In other words, the decline of Nehruvian *ideas and politics* – a centrist-populist ideological and political framework – has caused the rise of communal politics.[20]

---

20   In this vein, Nigam (2010) says that in times of crises, Nehruvian secular-nationalism has shown itself to be fundamentally Hindu in its latent assumptions. In its pursuit of a

All in all, whether the problem at hand is the threat of fascism (as in Simeon, etc.) or whether it is the threat of communalism, politics explains politics. Politics is the explanan, and politics is the explanandum.

Fascism or fascistic tendencies *are* ideological/cultural and political. But is there not a material reality *behind* their ideological and political character? In the middle ages, Catholicism might have appeared to be the dominant mode of life just like politics in ancient society did, but then 'the Middle Ages could not live on Catholicism, nor could the ancient world on politics', as Marx (1977: 176) said in a famous footnote in Chapter 1 of *Capital*, vol. 1. In fact, it is the mode in which people gain their livelihood – i.e. the 'production and reproduction of life' and the class relations within which that happens – that, ultimately, determines, and that is, ultimately, indeed expressed in the form of, certain ideological and political practices, including, for example, how powerful religious ideas are to people's worldview, and how religious strife is made use of politically to gain material advantages. And, of course, ideological and political practices in turn influence their content: the production and reproduction of material conditions of life. Fascistic tendencies need to be seen in relation to the entire totality of capitalist class relation (including in terms of capitalist economic and political processes). Let us say that fascism is, at the minimum, a certain relation between the ruler and the ruled, a relation that is undemocratic in the extreme, that receives some political support from some sections of 'the ruled' (typically, politically backward sections of the lower classes) and that seeks to destroy the resistance of the politically advanced sections of the lower classes against class exploitation and domination, as well. Then that relation (fascism or tendencies towards it) has to be explained mainly in the relation of production (i.e. in the class relation), and its various necessary outcomes in terms of the accumulation of wealth. We may recall from Marx's point from Chapter 6 of his *Capital*, vol. 3 that: it is in 'the direct relationship of the owners of the conditions of production to the immediate producers', that we find 'the hidden basis of the ... the political form of the relationship of sovereignty and dependence' (Marx, 1991: 927). Marx's point is also that politics in class society is ultimately class politics. In *German Ideology*, Marx and Engels (1978) say:

---

national culture, it produced the dominant culture as the norm, marginalising minority cultures. Corbridge and Harriss (2013) make a potentially useful generalization when they say that Nehruvianism has been challenged by two revolts of the elites: economic liberalization and Hindu nationalism. These revolts have been challenged, in turn, by various movements, including those of India's lower and middle castes ('Backward Classes'). As it will be clear in this and the next chapter, economic liberalization and Hindu nationalism are deeply inter-connected. Once again, politics is understood, more or less, in terms of politics, and that too elite politics. Out of view is the operation of *capitalist* economy and *capitalist* politics.

all struggles within the state, the struggle between democratic, aristocrat-ic and monarchy, the struggle for the franchise etc., etc. are merely the illusory forms in which the real struggles of the different classes are fought out among one another. (p. 54)

Marx also says that while politics is based on economic matters, politics also reacts back on economic matters. In a letter, Engels clarifies the 'materialist conception of history' that he and Marx had developed:

the *ultimately* determining element in history is the production and re-production of real life. Other than this neither Marx nor I have ever as-serted. ...The economic situation is the basis, but the various elements of the superstructure – political forms of the class struggle and its results, to wit: constitutions established by the victorious class after a successful battle, etc., juridical forms, and even the reflexes of all these actual strug-gles in the brains of the participants, political, juristic, philosophical theories, *religious views and their further development into systems of dogmas* – also exercise their influence upon the course of the historical struggles and in many cases preponderate in determining their *form*. There is an interaction of all these elements in which, amid all the end-less host of accidents..., the economic movement finally asserts itself as necessary. Otherwise the application of the theory to any period of his-tory [or to any country] would be easier than the solution of a simple equation of the first degree.

ENGELS, 1890; *italics* and parenthesis added

No political or ideological project hangs in the air. 'We must be able to discover under the political form the economic and social content' (Trotksy, 1974: 34). The right-wing project, including Hindu-supremacism, *is* an ideological-political – cultural-political – phenomenon. But it is more than that. The Hindu right-wing project is a class project, more than anything else. If bourgeois poli-tics takes fascistic form as opposed to the democratic form, a major part of the explanation must lie in the class relation of bourgeois production and ex-change, in the miseries that the capitalist system produces for the common people, and the resultant political struggles and defeats of the lower classes. That is: the major explanation of the fascistic form of bourgeois politics must lie in bourgeois political economy and bourgeois politics.[21] There are multiple aspects of this.

---

21   The right-wing attack on rights is not merely an attack on one form of bourgeois political-ideological framework on another form of bourgeois-ideological framework. If it was merely so, it would be just an intra-family battle – a battle between those bourgeois forces

3.1 *Capitalist Exploitation, Dispossession and Immiserization*

Common people in all the countries of the world, whether India or the USA, face numerous pressing problems: low wages, un-/under-employment, insecure employment, forcible loss of access to land or other means of livelihood, crisis of rural economy, ecological degradation, lack of quality health care, education and shelter, etc.[22] These social problems, which are affecting common people like natural forces, are basically caused by the way the political-economic system works, by the totality of the relations between the basic classes. Supported by the capitalist state, nation's resources are controlled by a tiny minority (the ruling class). And actively aided by the state, the ruling class makes enormous profit by (a) exploiting workers (i.e. by paying them a very small part of the net product they produce, and often paying a wage that does not even cover the average cost of maintenance, and converting the surplus value thus produced into fresh installments of capitalist private property), and (b) using various methods of primitive accumulation in its modern forms (dispossessing small-scale producers, and by robbing society of its common financial resources whether these are in the form of un-returned loans from state-owned banks, or non-payment of taxes, etc.).[23] Income and wealth inequality is rising. The bottom 60–70% are living a precarious existence, given low wages, and insecure employment and growing unviability of small-scale producers in an increasingly competitive world with diminishing government support for them. Besides, millions are experiencing oppression and exclusion based on caste, race/ethnicity, gender, and religion. In short, there is an on-going attack on people's living standards, which is caused by the fundamental nature of capitalism and which is exacerbated by its neoliberal form.[24] Such an attack is reinforced by various mechanisms of social oppression.

In the less developed countries such as India, the normal effects of capitalism on the common people are more extreme than in more developed countries (even if this does not mean that the rate of exploitation – s/v, or the ratio

---

who are committed to democracy and secularism and those bourgeois forces who do not. The BJP is not just attacking secular and democratic values and practices of, say, the Congress party, the traditional party of the bourgeoisie. The BJP is also attacking social and democratic rights of the toiling masses. It is not only against liberal-democratic-secular bourgeois formations. It is also anti-communist.

22 Nearly half of the world's population – more than 3 billion people – live on less than $2.50 a day (any discussion based on the paltry $1.25 poverty line is absolutely meaningless), and more than 70% of the population live on $10 a day.

23 Chatterjee (2017) says that the most recent period of Indian history has seen marked by an attempt to create a new hegemonic bloc based on Hindu majoritarianism under conditions of rapid primitive accumulation and competitive populism.

24 The neoliberal form of capitalism drives the neoliberal policies of the state, irrespective of which party controls the governments.

of surplus value to value of labor power – in less developed countries is necessarily higher than in more developed countries). In the less developed countries, there is a backward form of capitalism. This form of capitalism potentially undermines the basis for democratic conduct. State officials and politicians 'oversee' a type of capitalist production which is not only based on a massive amount of dispossession of small-scale property owners (e.g. peasants) and privatization of state-owned enterprises and resources, but also on the regime of low wages and long hours.[25] It is not a capitalism where in the sphere of production the main method of surplus appropriation is based on systemic technological change aimed at increasing productivity of labor. The dominance of this form of capitalism has traditionally marked the more developed countries. When capitalism is based on formal subsumption of labor, it is hardly conducive to very democratic relations between state (officials) and citizens and between employers and employees. When profits come more or less from the naked exhaustion of the body of direct producers (or from their dispossession of property) rather than from increased productivity of their labor based on systemic logic of technological change in every sector and subsector, and when the very basic needs are not met by capital or the state, the relation between 'sovereignty and dependence', or the relation between the ruler and the ruled, tends to become a *coercive* relation, even if one is not tied to a given employer through extra-economic means.[26] One must also note that like in many other countries, India's capitalism has been experiencing a massive jobless growth and economic slowdown (especially, in manufacturing and farming). The relation between increase in GDP and an increase in employment has been becoming weaker and weaker: as Figure 11.2 below shows, the curves for GDP increase and employment increase are diverging more and more over time.[27] The unemployed people can be disruptive and need to be repressed, from the standpoint of the capitalist class and the state elite.

Similarly, when accumulation of money is based on the big business taking control over state-owned resources and over small-scale private property and collectively-owned property, what happens is a contradiction between two

---

25   Such a regime is called formal subsumption of labor as a form of capitalist class relation as we have discussed in Chapter 3.

26   This necessarily does not mean that economically advanced societies in the West are paragons of democracy. Democracy is a form of class rule, and class is the most important form of inequality. But between two class societies, the state in one can be a little more democratic than another.

27   In the 1970s and 80s, when GDP growth was around 3–4%, employment growth was about 2%, says Dr. Amit Basole, the lead author of a recent study. 'Currently, the ratio of GDP growth to employment growth is less than 0.1'. That means that a 10% increase in GDP results in a less than 1% increase in employment (reported in The Hindu, 2018b).

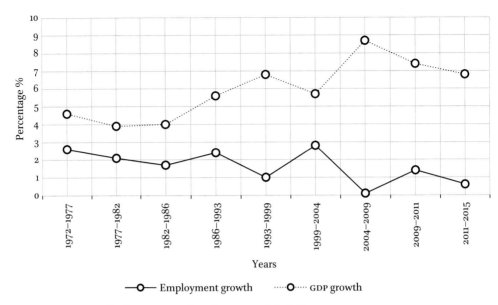

FIGURE 11.2 Employment growth and GDP growth in India, 1972–2015
SOURCE: DATA FROM *THE HINDU* (2018)

equal rights. This the contradiction between the right of the big business to take control over property which is not in the domain of private-sector capitalism on the one hand, and the right of the common people to use the small-scale or collectively-owned property and to enjoy the advantages of state-owned property on the other hand. Between two equal rights, it is the force of the big business, including its trans-nationalized segment, reinforced and supported by the state, that counts. Any opposition from peasants and ordinary citizens against privatization is met with repression. As well, the right of the common people to enjoy state-provided services and use-values contradicts the right of the big business – especially, the financialized segment – to see reduced fiscal deficit, a contradiction that triggers opposition. And as opposition grows, there is need for more repression. A fascist/fascistic state supplies those the means of repression.

Capitalism affects the layer of petty bourgeois families adversely, and not just workers. Whether in Germany after World War I or in the India of today, the capitalist system ruins 'some layers of the petty bourgeoisie' while it creates 'others anew: around the factories, artisans and shopkeepers; within the factories, technicians and executives' (Trotsky, 1933b). Economic crisis hits 'the artisans, the peddlers, and the civil employees' (ibid.). 'The economic crisis in agriculture' under capitalism is 'ruining the peasantry' (ibid.). 'The decay of the middle strata did not necessarily mean that they are made into proletarians, inasmuch as the proletariat itself ... [is] casting out a gigantic army of chronically unemployed' (ibid.).

Exploitation, oppression, dispossession of petty bourgeois producers and immiserization/inequality do not go un-challenged in any society. Ordinary people – workers, farmers, etc. and socially oppressed groups such as Dalits – are engaged in recurrent protests and struggles. There is a strike every week in one or another part of the world. It is true that people are reacting to the *effects* of the operation of the capitalist system rather than to the existence of the system itself. It is true that people are not class-conscious enough to adequately trace their problems to the root, i.e. the capitalist system operating through mechanisms of social oppression. Yet, people do engage in struggles. It is true that these strikes and struggles, which are often confined to specific workplaces or sectors or areas, have not been escalated to take on state power and the rule of capital as such, but that is not a reason to overlook the militant tradition of workers, peasants and oppressed groups, nor is there a basis for one to say that Left parties organize them to merely let off steam, i.e. to calm the anger of the people.[28] The intensity of strikes has increased (as indicated by increases in persons and person days lost per dispute) in India, even if the number of disputes has decreased, and strikes remain a major risk factor for the business world (Figures 11.3 and 11.4).

If a worker comes to work, there is a cost: she/he has to be fed and sheltered, which means they need a wage. If a worker stops work (as in a strike or a protest against low wages, unfair working conditions and casualization of work), there is also a cost to the employer, as his/her labor is withheld leading to the cessation of production.[29] There is a pressure on enterprise-owners to reduce *both* kinds of cost, which emanate from the economic and political logics of capitalism. To reduce these costs (by driving down wages and by making it difficult for people to strike), the enterprise owners need help from their political cousins (political party leaders). So, fascist/fascistic politics comes in handy.

3.2 Ruling Class Counter Response to Lower Classes: Coercion and Consent

The ruling class cannot exist without exploiting wage-labor and without maintaining the separation of common people from the means of production (the ruling class must continuously engage in dispossessing people of their access to commons and/or their individual property and/or state's resources). This

---

28 Saying so is resorting to functionalism: explaining an event merely in terms of its functions/effects.

29 The one-day strike in India in September 2016 reportedly caused a damage of more than $2.5 billion to its capitalist economy.

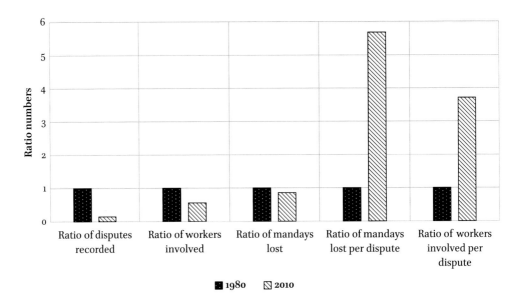

FIGURE 11.3 Increasing intensity of strikes in India
Notes: In the figure above, all the numbers (i.e. number of disputes, workers involved, mandays lost, and mandays lost per dispute and workers involved per dispute) for 1980 are taken as 1, and accordingly the numbers for 2010 are converted into a ratio, by dividing the 2010 numbers by the 1980 numbers. One can see this ratio has decreased for the incidents of disputes, workers involved and mandays lost, while the ratio of mandays lost *per* dispute and the ratio of workers involved *per* dispute (indicating intensity of disputes) has increased.
SOURCE: DATA FROM AIOE/FICCI (N.D.)

especially happens, if these resources are needed by the ruling class, and/or if these resources being in the hands of the common people significantly reduces their dependence on wage-labor. Exploitation and dispossession, however, prompt opposition from common people, (covert or overt), which, in turn, requires a ruling class response. One form of response is the use of coercion/repression, including an attack on democratic rights. This is from above (state agencies and policies). This coercive response occurs from below in the form of vigilante groups and lynch mobs organized/supported by fascistic forces, and private security forces and even criminals recruited by the members of the propertied class. Another response is making the lower classes consent to the system and thus weakening the lower-class opposition to the system. Note that it is not just the fact that the whole system of capitalism-in-crisis, that is increasingly failing to meet people's very basic needs, is justification on the basis of the production of consent and deception. It is also the case that to the extent that repression is used against lower-class opposition to the capitalist system, that repression also requires justification, which requires production of consent.

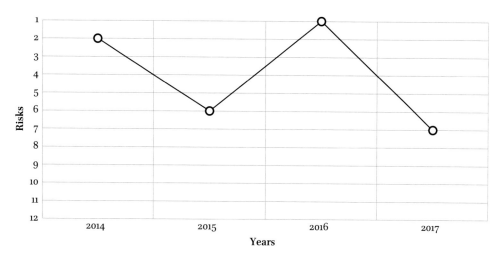

FIGURE 11.4 Corporate perception of risk from trikes, closures and unrest
Note: On a scale of 1 to 12 (there are 12 sources of risk), 1 = the most important source of risk
SOURCE: DATA FROM AIOE/FICCI (N.D.)

Consent is sought in many ways. It is sought on the basis of emotional appeals to various forms of identity politics including that based on nationality, religion, etc. (the pursuit of identity politics dominates over struggle against capitalism). These appeals also divide the opposition to capitalism and the state. Consent is also sought on the basis of giving limited material concessions as well as sheer deception. Deception involves the deployment of lies that can be religious/mythological lies. Deception also involves secular lies which include false promises of pro-poor policies which the government *knows* it will not be able to deliver. Both secular and religious/mythological lies are used in a capitalist society.

> Developed bourgeois ideology is rationalistic and directed against mythology. The radical bourgeoisie tried to make do without religion and build a state based on reason rather than tradition. An expression of this was democracy with its principles of liberty, equality and fraternity. The capitalist economy, however, created a monstrous contradiction between everyday reality and democratic principles. A higher grade form of lying is required to fill up this contradiction. Nowhere do people lie more politically than in bourgeois democracies. And this is no longer the objective "lying" of mythology, but the consciously organized deception of the people, using combined methods of extraordinary complexity. The technology of the lie is cultivated no less than the technology of electricity.

> The most "developed" democracies, France and the United States, possess the most deceitful press.
> TROTSKY, 1927

As we see from the foregoing discussion, there is a chain of causal links and internal relations: these connect (a) exploitation and dispossession which characterize the capitalist society and which produce concrete adverse effects on lower classes, (b) opposition to exploitation and dispossession which then prompts (c) state's various responses on behalf of the ruling class such as the strategies of repression, consent-making and deception via lies and politics of identity based in religion, etc. (Figure 11.5 below).

I will elaborate on these ideas. The working people's fight-back, actual and potential, needs a counter-response from the economic and political elites who manage the capitalist economic-political system. The counter-response to people's fight-back comes in many forms. One is to allow some oppositional

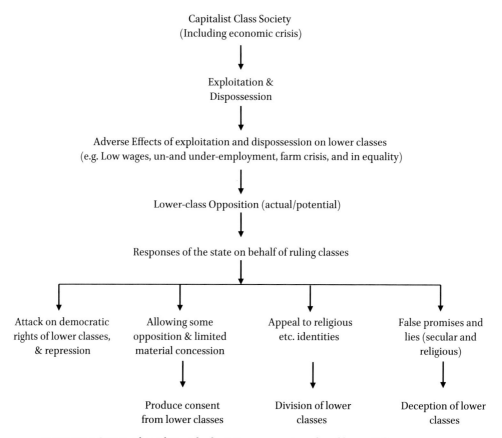

FIGURE 11.5 Structural conditions for fascistic movement produced by capitalism
SOURCE: AUTHOR

activity to occur in order to stop people from being angrier, and to grant some concessions. From the 1950s for several decades, this was a strategy in many countries, including in India, and this produced a certain degree of consent to the system – to 'the reformed democracy'. Since the onset of neoliberal form of capitalism, such a strategy is less likely as income deflation for the majority is a necessary part of the neoliberal capitalism, which means that the states have reduced ability to provide economic concessions to the masses. States' inability to provide concessions contradicts the common people's democratic rights – especially, them having the right to organize and make demands. Of the many 'negative' forms of counter-response is an attack on democratic rights such as the right to form (independent) unions, the right to free speech, etc. as well as attack on the social rights (e.g. reduction in already-limited welfare benefits). These attacks weaken the bargaining power of the masses and make it difficult for people to exercise their democratic rights. This fact – and especially, the attack on labor rights – happens irrespective of which party – whether they are more democratic or more fascistic – is in power.

Another form of the counter-response from ruling-class forces is the use of identity politics. To distract attention from people's miseries, to weaken people's fight for equality and for a better life, bourgeois and petty-bourgeois class forces, their politicians and their organic intellectuals, divide the masses on the basis of social and geographical identity (e.g. caste; race; identity; location – migrants/refugees vs locals; regionalism expressed as demand for new provinces to be carved up from existing ones). Note that while the capitalist class can benefit from the politics of hatred, the latter can also be dis-functional if it creates too much of a law and order problem undermining the business climate, why is why: 'even influential layers of the bourgeoisie fear the fascist experiment, precisely because they want no convulsions, no long and severe civil war' (Trotsky, 1931a) (more on this in the next chapter).

3.3   *Special Role of Religion as a Mechanism of Deception*
Increasingly, religion as a basis of identity politics is used in such countries as India: when employers/owners and workers of a given religion are united in the name of religious loyalty, such an action is directly counter-posed to class politics which draws attention to, in theory and practice, the fundamental and irreconcilable interests between these classes.[30] Often religious identity is used in tandem with other identities such as those based on caste and aboriginality.

---

30   To the extent that the ideology of the politics of religion exists as a process in a way that is relatively autonomous from class relations and of capitalism, the bourgeoisie does not mind using such politics, where it exists, to manage any potential or actual opposition to its rule and to further its own economic interests.

Religion – like everything else – has to first exist for it to be used, although reasons for its existence (origin) may not exactly be the reasons for its continued use.[31] Its existence is deeply, if not reducibly, rooted in material conditions. Religion (e.g. Hinduism, Islam, Christianity, Buddhism, etc.) – in the forms of religious texts, sayings, myths, rituals, etc. – expresses, however imperfectly, the depth of human beings' suffering, whether it is caused by society or nature. Religion also expresses people's complaints/protests against their suffering. Religion popularly expresses – albeit in contradictory and inadequate ways – some aspects of the potential of humans, including their potential to have a degree of freedom from what neuro-scientists such as Davidson (2012) call afflictive emotions such as excessive anger against individuals, sadness, egoism and anxiety (from which Marxists and non-Marxists suffer) and to nurture wholesome qualities such as kindness, agreeableness, love and altruism. Both kinds of emotions arise in the brain, and positive emotions can be cultivated, including on the basis of some methods prescribed in world's major religions such as Buddhism and Hinduism (ibid.). Religion also expresses the humankind's eagerness for, a more humane world.[32] Religious texts/traditions may indeed contain important ideas, however, 'utopian', about what a good society might be. We can offer a couple of examples. From the Russian vantage point, here is Zetkin:

> Among the Russian small peasants, there are old and deeply felt traditions of indigenous village communism that have not entirely died away. They have been sustained and reinforced by primitive religious feelings

---

31   There has been a large amount of literature on religion from a Marxist perspective. A sample literature includes, apart from Marx and Engels (1964), the following: Avakian, 2008; Boer, 2009, 2011, 2012, 2013, 2014; Page, 1993; Saxton, 2007. Texts on religion in the Indian context include: Chattopadhyaya, 2013; and Habib, 2015.

32   This potential and this eagerness, as expressed in religious discourses and practices are products of objectively-existing relations: humans' relation with nature signifying their struggle to control it, and their relations with one another, including relations of conflict and harmony. Indeed, '*Man makes religion*, religion does not make man. Religion is, indeed, the self-consciousness and self-esteem of man... Man is *the world of man* – state, society. This state and this society produce religion, which is an *inverted consciousness of the world*, because they are an *inverted world*. Religion is the general theory of this world, its encyclopaedic compendium, its logic in popular form, its spiritual *point d'honneur* [point of honour], its enthusiasm, its moral sanction, its solemn complement, and its universal basis of consolation and justification. It is the *fantastic realization* of the human essence since the *human essence* has not acquired any true reality. The struggle against religion is, therefore, indirectly the struggle *against that world* whose spiritual *aroma* is religion. *Religious* suffering is, at one and the same time, the *expression* of real suffering and a *protest* against real suffering. Religion is the sigh of the oppressed creature, the heart of a heartless world, and the soul of soulless conditions. It is the *opium* of the people' (Marx, 1843).

TOWARDS A POLITICAL ECONOMY OF FASCISTIC TENDENCIES

> that view all property as ultimately from God, as God's property. These sentiments are nourished by the propaganda of Tolstoy's followers, Social Revolutionaries, Narodniks, and many religious sects. And these beginnings of communist understanding are systematically encouraged and promoted by the measures of the proletarian state.
>
> ZETKIN, 1922[33]

Interestingly, similar religious feelings that view all property as God's property existed in India as well. Consider *Isa Upanishad*, a religious-philosophical text written by some insightful people who probably lived in a pastoral society 2500–3000 years ago (note that during those times, secular and religious ideas used to co-exist in a given text or in the minds of particular thinking persons). This text *begins* with what can be called a 'primitive'-communist type view of society, a society without private property. It says that: everything is owned by the supreme controller; one may enjoy what is allotted to one by that supreme controller but one should not encroach upon others' property.[34] Of course, such a view is not rooted in a scientific conception and is therefore utopian, but nonetheless it captures human beings' lofty aspirations for a better society. While the Hindutva people are proud of Hindu ideas *and* deeply worship private property, they should know that texts such as *Isa Upanishad* imagine a society without private property. It is human beings who create religion to help them cope with a world which is difficult and over which they have not much control. Indeed, objective conditions of alienation from one's own self, one's fellow human beings, from material conditions and access to resources, produce certain religious beliefs and practices (just as the same conditions of alienation and suffering, when scientifically thought through on the basis of the philosophy of materialist-dialectics, prompt production of socialist ideas). Religion as a set of ideas and practices can shape people's thinking, which in turn can, under certain conditions, prompt people to kill/hurt others in the name of religion. As long as objective conditions exist for the need for religion, religion will exist. So, freedom to satisfy that need, i.e. freedom to practice any religion, as long as it is more or less a private affair and does not affect state's actions, is an essential part of democracy, as are the need to protect the views and practices of religious minorities, the freedom to criticize religion from the

---

33 Commenting on this paragraph John Riddell (2009) says about Zetkin: 'she expresses a thought that I have not found elsewhere in world communist literature of the time'. On the idea that ancient Indian texts have atheistic and secular elements, see (Sen, 2005).

34 *Isavasyam idam sarvam yat kim ca jagatyam jagat, tena tyaktena bhunjitha, ma gridhah kasyasvid dhanam* is the first few lines of the Isavasya Upanishad. One might split the lines into parts like this: *isavasyam idam sarvam* – everything is owned by *isa*, the supreme controller. *Tena tyaktena bhunjitha* – you may enjoy what is allotted to you by Him. *Ma grdhah kasya svid dhanam:* but do not encroach upon others' property.

standpoint of science, and the freedom not to have any religion. Such freedom is under attack now, as a part of the attack on democratic rights.

Religion itself may not necessarily lead to politics of religious hatred any more than differences in skin color necessarily produce politics of racism. Yet, fascistic forces make use of people's need for religion (or indeed need for a similar sense of belongingness based on other identities), to divide a nation along the lines of religion, race, etc. and promote the political hegemony of given religious and ethnic groups.[35] This goes against the tradition of people of different religious beliefs and ethnicities generally having lived together peacefully in many countries, including India, the US, and many European countries.

As a form of class society which is a society of alienation and inequalities, bourgeois rule, at an abstract level, can exist without, say, religious (or racial) discrimination. But in reality, in many cases, that is not the case. The ruling class and its ideological and political representatives use religion (along with other similar tools) to divide people and to divert their attention from their own failure to meet people's needs.[36] Religious ideas, generally, do not represent, in any systematic way, the ruling class as being responsible for the miseries of the masses. Usually, problems that people face are said to be due to their own personal (moral) failings or acts of some unseen powerful agency (gods, etc.). Religious ideas make people rely not on their collective political action against their exploiters/oppressors and the state, but on supernatural forces and their own moral rectitude to fix their problems.[37] The ruling class makes use of many religious ideas to make people passive, in other words.

The 'need' of the ruling class to use identity politics whether it is based on religion or race (or indeed geography) for all these purposes is real. Trotsky (1933) wrote about the connection between fascism (national socialism) and race. By mainly replacing race with religion in his original lines, these lines

---

35   Not all religious belief leads to the politics of religious hatred but such politics where it exists 'is rooted in a sense of religious identity and in how these identities... are manipulated for political purpose, material advantage, violent competition and all the rest. Religion per se cannot be held responsible' [for the politics of religious hatred] (Ahmad, 2013: 7).

36   The poison ivy of communal politics can only thrive in a class society. It will not thrive in a class-less society or it will not have the force it has in a class society, as a class-less society is based on harmonious development of productive forces to allow for the inclusion of everyone in social progress, and on mutual solidarity rather than mutual alienation and competition.

37   Millions of Indians still take the help of religious ideas and practices to get cured of their physical and mental illnesses.

could be translated into a message to describe the fascistic tendencies in India to a large extent.

> In order to raise it above history, the Indian nation is given the support of the Hindu religion. History of India is viewed as the emanation of the Hindu religion. The qualities of the Hindu religion are construed without relation to changing social conditions. The theory of religion, specially created, it seems, for some pretentious self-educated individual seeking a universal key to all the secrets of life, appears particularly melancholy in the light of the history of ideas. On the plane of politics, communalism [i.e. political use of religious divide] is a vapid and bombastic variety of chauvinism. As the ruined landlord class sought solace in the gentility of its blood, so the mass of pauperized petty bourgeoisie and lumpen-proletariat and similar other sections befuddles itself with fairy tales concerning the special superiorities of Hindu religion and its symbols such as the holy cow. Worthy of attention is the fact that the leaders of the fascistic movement, like most Indians, are not native Indians but inter-lopers from other parts of Asia.

That the ruling class does have a need for the use of identity politics whether it is based on religion or race (or geography) is indeed real. What is also a fact is that it has the ability to do so. This is because the ruling class, more or less, controls the means of communication of ideas among the masses, which are now-a-days both electronic and non-electronic.[38]

3.4 Lower Classes' Alienated Need for Identity Politics and Irrationalism

The need of the ruling class for religion and other such identities to calm and control the masses coincides with the masses' own material and social-psychological need for religion and other forms of social identity. People resort

---

38 As is widely known, Marx and Engels (1978: 64–65) famously say: 'the class which is the ruling *material* force of society, is at the same time its ruling *intellectual* force. The class which has the means of material production at its disposal, has control at the same time over the means of mental production, so that thereby, generally speaking, the ideas of those who lack the means of mental production [such as workers and lumpen proletariat, etc.] are subject to it. The ruling ideas are nothing more than the ideal expression of the dominant material relationships, the dominant material relationships grasped as ideas.... The individuals composing the ruling class possess among other things consciousness, and therefore think. ...[They] rule also as thinkers, as producers of ideas, and regulate the production and distribution of the ideas of their age: thus their ideas are the ruling ideas of the epoch'. The ruling class ideas are produced not just by the ruling class intellectuals but also by elements of the ruling class itself, and these elements do disseminate reactionary ideas directly.

to such things as religion to cope with a hostile and difficult class-society that fails to meet their needs. If there is scarcity of resources in society, a common-sensical view is that a certain social-cultural group (e.g. a given religious group) is responsible for this, whether or not that view is backed by evidence and reason. People of a particular religion (or a caste or race) identify themselves with those from the same religion (or a caste or a race) in their daily lives. This has a material basis. For example, if a wage-earner is to get one of the few available jobs or if a small-scale producer is to sell some product in a highly competitive market, increasingly dominated by big business, a network based on a social identity (e.g. religion, caste, race, etc.) becomes helpful. Religion can be a powerful coping mechanism: belief in an all-powerful supreme being who will help in times of crisis or belief in the idea that life will be better after death, are comforting, and can obviate the need for political resistance. Besides, social identity can become a source of a psychological satisfaction which, for example, a rich Hindu shopkeeper and a poor Hindu wage-worker may enjoy by thinking that they belong to one religion. Such a sense of psychological satisfaction matters especially when people are experiencing material insecurity. Of course, such feeling of identity prompts supremacist ideas: 'my religion is the most natural religion, and yours is the most artificial', or 'my caste is superior to yours', or 'this is my country in which you have no place'. And such feelings cause political friction among followers of different religions or castes, etc. In the process, the real friction – the conflict between common people on the one hand and big business and its state on the other – is replaced by friction among common people themselves, a friction that is more or less illusory.

The task of using religion (or a similar such thing) by the ruling class to weaken potential and actual lower-class opposition to the social order becomes easier in societies (e.g. those in the global periphery) where pre-modern, pre-capitalist ideas and practices have not been eliminated due to an incomplete bourgeois-democratic revolution, and where therefore these ideas and practices are 'combined' with those of advanced capitalism, a process of 'combined development' that means, as suggested in Chapter 3, 'an amalgam of archaic with more contemporary forms' (Trotsky, 2008: 5).

As mentioned, not everything in what are called religious texts is about religion, as there are philosophical ideas about human beings and nature, etc. in these texts. But a lot of what goes on in the name of religion represents irrational thinking, the thinking that is not, and that cannot be, backed by scientific evidence. Capitalism creates a need and an opportunity for irrational thinking, and thus for the use of religion and similar things (e.g. race) to weaken lower-class opposition to the existing social order, and thus feeds into the ideological basis for fascistic tendencies which thrive on irrational and anti-scientific thinking. This happens both in rich countries and in poor countries such as India. The following lines, even if they talk about a very developed stage of the fascist movement in the 1930s, can be interpreted as *something* that reflects the contemporary reality in India and elsewhere very well:

> Fascism has opened up the depths of society for politics. Today, not only in peasant homes but also in city skyscrapers, there lives alongside of the twentieth century the tenth or the thirteenth. A hundred million people use electricity and still believe in the magic power of signs and exorcisms [and one might add, going to miracle-making gurus; cow urine and the fact that plastic surgery existed in ancient India as proven by the elephant-headed god, Ganesh].[39] ...What inexhaustible reserves they possess of darkness, ignorance, and savagery! Despair has raised them to their feet fascism has given them a banner. Everything that should have been eliminated from the national organism in the form of cultural excrement in the course of the normal development of society has now come gushing out from the throat; capitalist society is puking up the undigested barbarism. Such is the physiology of... [fascism or strong fascistic tendencies].
>
> TROTSKY, 1933b; parentheses added

As mentioned, the dominant condition for fascistic tendencies is capitalism. This is the case especially when capitalism experiences economic crisis, as indicated by a slow economic growth leading to un-and under-employment and a government inability to provide welfare. By creating extreme inequality and by failing to satisfy the needs of the masses, the system (or, those who manage the system) makes some people believe in, and act on, their illusory needs such as the need for pride based in religious identity, which trump real needs (e.g. need for decent employment, etc.). This, in turn, creates a situation where a section of the population is mobilized to pursue the illusory needs. As well, for the same reasons (economic crisis, inequality, etc.), the state becomes increasingly authoritarian, and its liberal-democratic foundation begins to shake, because the system cannot meet the political demands from a large section of the population

---

39   It is possible that cow urine or any other animal's urine or some such thing has medicinal properties. And just because it might have been mentioned in some ancient texts that have religious content, that itself does not necessarily mean that such things have no usefulness. *However*, before their usefulness is *scientifically proven*, this cannot be taken as true on the basis of religious belief. From the vantage point of a class society, which creates condition for religion, there is also nothing inherently wrong with a group of people treating an animal as sacred, in the sense of being worthy of special admiration and worship, but it is deeply problematic when that belief is used to create political antagonism between (a) people who hold such a belief and (b) people who do not hold such a belief, and to hurt the latter group which poses no material threat to the former, when that belief shapes the affairs of the state and when that belief is given the same epistemological significance as evidence-based ideas based on reason.

412   CHAPTER 11

for a better life. Under certain conditions (e.g. relative weakness of resistance), political authoritarianism can take an extreme form. This, when supported by a segment of lower-class population, can produce fascistic tendencies.

3.5   *Agents – Foot Soldiers – of Fascistic Movement*

Capitalism indeed does not only create the *structural* condition for fascistic tendencies by producing economic problems for the masses, who then blame their conditions on an enemy (e.g. religious minority; refugees). Capitalism also creates the *agencies* through which the fascistic project, including its violence aspect, is carried out. Here the role of petty bourgeois elements is important as fascistic movement's storm troopers or foot soldiers. This is because they are crushed by big capital so much so that they are only owners in a nominal sense, with their debts often outstripping the current monetary value of their property:

> The main army of fascism ... consists of the petty bourgeoisie and the new middle class: the small artisans and shopkeepers of the cities, the petty officials, the employees, the technical personnel, the intelligentsia, the impoverished [and pauperized] peasantry.
>
> TROTSKY, 1931a

It is true that what is called the petty bourgeoisie 'is characterized by the extreme heterogeneity of its social nature' (Trotsky, 1932c), and that 'ideologically it scintillates with all the colors of the rainbow' (Trotsky, 1932c). While 'At the bottom it fuses with the proletariat and extends into the lumpenproletariat', whose ranks expand thanks to capitalist crisis, 'on top it passes over into the capitalist bourgeoisie' (Trotsky, 1932j). The petty bourgeoisie 'may lean upon old forms of production but it may rapidly develop on the basis of most modern industry (the new "middle class")' (Trotsky, 1932j), including in what is now called information technology where workers are so alienated in the workplace that they resort to such things as religion (as a mechanism to cope with mental stress), a fact that, in turn, makes many of these people directly or indirectly support the agenda of soft Hindutva and some may even support the strident political movements based on religion. Research conducted by the social anthropologist Carol Upadhya of the National Institute of Advanced Studies, Bangalore, conducted among IT professionals in Bengaluru in the early 2000s, finds that:

> the price of their new-found wealth is the inability to maintain social and family relationships or even to have a meaningful existence outside of work... [this] lack of a sense of social connection or community may

account for the fact that a large number of IT professionals attend courses offering 'fast food' packaged spirituality....

Quoted in DESHMANE, 2017

Capitalism stokes the anger of the petty bourgeoise, including small scale producers, leading them to demand an authoritarian rule, falsely believing that that is the solution to their problems. 'The sharp grievances of small proprietors never out of bankruptcy, of their university sons without posts and clients, of their daughters without dowries and suitors, [demand] ... order and an iron hand' (Trotsky, 1933b).

Fascism penetrates the proletariat from below and from above. Many classstrata such as 'Salaried employees, the technical and administrative personnel, and certain strata of the functionaries [government officials]' (Trotsky, 1932h) which were democratic can go into the fascist camp and 'are capable of drawing in their wake... a stratum of the labor aristocracy' (Trotsky, 1932h), and all this is indicative of the fact that fascism is 'penetrating into the proletariat from above' (Trotsky, 1932k). Then there is penetration of fascism into the proletariat from below:

> Considerably more dangerous, however, is... [fascism's or fascistic movement's] possible penetration from below, through the unemployed: No class can long exist without prospects and hopes. The unemployed do not represent a class, but they already compose a very compact and substantial layer, which is vainly striving to tear itself away from intolerable conditions.
>
> TROTSKY, 1932k

Important to the fascistic mass-movement are certain layers of the reserve army that Marx (1977) talks about in *Capital* volume 1.

One category of 'the relative surplus population is the stagnant population. This forms a part of the active labour army, but with extremely irregular employment. Hence it offers to capital an inexhaustible reservoir of disposable labour-power. Its conditions of life sink below the average normal level of the working class...It is characterised by maximum of working time, and minimum of wages' (p. 796). Another relevant layer is 'the lowest sediment of the relative surplus population' which 'dwells in the sphere of pauperism'. This layer includes 'vagabonds, criminals' etc.; in other words, 'the actual lumpenproletariat'. The lowest sediment is filled with those who are: 'the demoralised and ragged' and many other layers of the unemployed population (p. 797). When the reserve army expands (in part thanks to on-going primitive accumulation, privatization of state-owned companies, and migration of the poor

414 CHAPTER 11

from the villages), it puts pressure on wages of those who are employed. This has a series of cultural implications that Marx does not consider, and which should be considered in order to shed light on the relation between capitalism and fascistic tendencies.

Thanks to the reserve army,

> the wage is so depressed that a proper proletarian culture is hard to sustain and many from inside the proletariat itself tend to get lumpenized: living partly by labour and wage within the capitalist system, but also supplementing it often with earnings generated by wit and, at times, even crime.
>
> AHMAD, 2013: 19–20

Not just that:

> the army of the unemployed is so vast, so permanent, that an innumerable number of them just stop seeking that kind of work, fall out of the capitalist system properly speaking, partaking of no labour that creates surplus value, falling into the underbelly of a pseudo-economy that runs parallel to the real economy and is governed by no rules, not even of exploitation, and where one can earn anything from a daily living to a fortune to a sudden death simply by going from one wager to another, often taking wit and/or crime in one's stride.
>
> AHMAD, 2013: 20

This sort of material processes has real effects on consciousness.[40] 'A stable life of productive labour gives one pride, or at least a grounding, in what one does' (ibid.: 20); besides, 'The life of value-producing labour is lived in a community of others who do the same' (ibid.: 20). This is not the case with the un-and under-employed. With them:

> lack of [their]... productivity, that sense of who one is, robs one of pride in oneself [and] that pride must somehow be regained, even if it is by

---

40 Breman (2016) talks about how pauperism is produced under Indian capitalism: the non-laboring poor who never had, or have lost, their ability to take care of themselves; the footloose labor driven away from the village for lack of work but also driven back 'home' again when they are thrown out of their casual employment; and, finally, an urban underclass redundant to demand, experienced by the better-off as a nuisance and brutally evicted from their slum habitat. These elements are a potential basis for the fascistic movement.

TOWARDS A POLITICAL ECONOMY OF FASCISTIC TENDENCIES

harming others, be it by way of crime or by that purported non-crime that is communalism itself, with all its violences.

Ibid.: 20

As well:

the life of the lumpenproletariat is by its nature one that creates no community out of any shared conditions of labour but must always work within collectivities that are tentative, transitional and forever in need of getting re-invented out of the emergencies that individuals in this quasi-class face all the time. Bereft of class belonging, they are prone to temptations of community-belonging to caste, religion or whatever – a kind of belonging far more abstract than the concrete belonging to a community of labour.

Ibid.: 20

So a chance to be recruited into communal politics and similar endeavors often gives them the much-needed purpose of life, which is reinforced by a sense of religious belongingness, though it is a fictive sense of 'belonging to a real community'. And, 'In the process, the aggressivity of posture that is so important for sheer survival in lumpen life can get easily transferred to communal/fascist kinds of organized violence' (Ahmad, 2013: 18–19).[41]

There is indeed a direct relation between communal and fascistic mobilization on the one hand and criminality on the other, and especially, a criminality which not only satisfies a social psychological need (for a feeling that one is doing something in life) but which also can generate material reward (e.g. some income; some loot from sectarian riots; even a post in the fascistic party organization or its Ministry).

The culture of the lumpen (and similar other) elements that is conducive to the politics of hate is not entirely governed by its economic conditions of capitalism, however. Relevant here are also political processes in capitalism, which mediate in the relation between the economic conditions and culture. Firstly, the class of people which has nothing but its labor power to sell – the working class, including those who are currently not employed – needs democratic rights to be able to put organized pressure on the capitalist class and its state

---

41   It is not surprising that, as Ahmad (2013: 3) says: 'Bulk of the storm troopers for any fascism or any religious inflamed violent conflict, and in ethnic cleansing always come from among those' who are victims of (a predatory) capitalism and 'who have been spiritually destroyed and morally disoriented by the cruelties they suffer in their everyday life'.

for an increased private wage and increased social wage (government benefits), so it can have an adequate access to food, shelter, etc. that it needs. However, to be able to avoid having to give any concession, the capitalist system must curtail working class' democratic rights. This is why the force of identity politics is a measure of the fact that people's level of progressive consciousness – that they are members of a democratic secular republic, with certain rights irrespective of their religion or any other identity, that they, as workers and peasants, have some rights and can demand certain things based on their collective strength – is extremely low. The content of such a politics of identity (religious identity) can take authoritarian and then fascistic forms. Secondly, when there are vast segments of the working class who have no hope of regular employment and which have indeed no experience of employment, they have no *need* for democratic rights to put pressure on the employer: they *have* no employer. They have no taste *of* democracy. They have no taste *for* democracy. When millions of people in a society have no need for, and experience of, democracy, this potentially creates a condition for fascistic tendencies. They can easily become pre-disposed towards becoming storm troopers for fascistic tendencies. This shows that sheer criminality and undemocratic attacks on others who, generally, are like them in class terms (e.g. people belonging to religious, etc. minorities) can indeed be a source of some reward. So ultimately, the politics of religious and other forms of identity, including in its fascistic forms, are rooted in material conditions and their class form (and especially, the capitalist class form).

Indeed, when millions live in poverty and misery in an increasingly unequal society, then:

> Extreme religious faith and ethnic nationalism are often all that gives their lives purpose and dignity. Many, with good reason, believe that colonialism, capitalism, multi-national corporations and their own indigenous leaders have all harmed them. Thus, they return to fundamentalist beliefs of their ancestors or are susceptible to political manipulation....
> DOBKOWSKI and WALLIMAN, 2003: 13

It is simply wrong to say that the actually-existing proletariat are not or cannot be conservative in their political attitudes. Workers as a class are progressive, but only potentially. In their daily lives, individual workers and groups of workers can have reactionary attitude, partly thanks to worsening economic conditions and partly thanks to the absence of political education from the communist and progressive movements. Even if some of them have the memory of Nazism, that memory is no vaccine against their belief in fascism or fascistic ideas at all (pace Vanaik). Marx knew this. Trotsky said:

> The workers are by no means immunized once for all against the influence of fascism. The proletariat and the petty bourgeoisie interpenetrate, especially under the present conditions, when the reserve army of workers cannot but produce petty traders and hawkers, etc., while the bankrupt petty bourgeoisie effuses proletarians and lumpenproletarians.
>
> TROTSKY, 1932k

There is one more dimension of capitalism that potentially connects it to fascistic tendencies. Capitalism is driven by the logic of accumulation for its sake, by the incessant pursuit of wealth in its abstract form (money). Such a regime of production will not survive without incessant consumption. Thus capitalism creates cultural attitudes whereby people see themselves as consumers of commodities chasing their own 'well-being', and they do so partly to counter their alienation-from-one-another in the workplace and in the labor-market. But in the process, they lose their ability to empathize with fellow-human beings' suffering, signifying their alienation from other people. If, as the neuroscientist, Richard Davidson says (2016; also 2012), generosity (altruism) is one of the four aspects of human mental well-being, a trait that many religions, including Hinduism and Buddhism, emphasize, clearly people are losing their ability to be generous. Among many contingent manifestations of such lack of empathy and of such a high degree of alienation is the fact that not only does a large segment of the population engage in sectarian-fascistic violence that kills thousands of innocent people but also is such violence tolerated by others in their everyday lives.[42]

4   Conclusion

In understanding the rise of fascistic forces, one has to keep in mind Marx's theory of politics in class society. It is in 'the direct relationship of the owners of the conditions of production to the immediate producers', in which we find the hidden basis of 'the political form of the relationship of sovereignty and dependence' (Marx, 1991: 927). He also says that: 'all struggles within the state' – for example, struggles over democracy, etc. – 'are merely the illusory forms in

---

42   It is also interesting that such sectarian violence is condoned/supported by some politicians as reaction-to-an-action, an idea that mistakenly physicalizes the human being. Such physicalization of human beings actually contradicts the religious belief in the name of which people engage in sectarian violence: a part of the religious belief is that there is more to the human being than their physical body.

which the real struggles of the different classes are fought out among one another' (Marx and Engels, 1978: 54). Avoiding economic reductionism, Marx asserts that while politics is based on economic matters, politics also reacts back on economic matters.

The rise of the BJP is a manifestation of a global phenomenon that is expressed in India: the global phenomenon is the fact that the big business facing an economic and social crisis is resorting to social reaction, politics of hatred, and authoritarianism (both authoritarianism from above – the state; and authoritarianism from below – rightwing forces). The increasing strength of right-wing forces, including the rise of the BJP as the political head of these forces in India, has been engendered by four mechanisms, three of which – and these are mainly political-economic mechanisms, are discussed in this chapter.

a. The first is the crisis of global capitalism, the crisis that is manifested in India. Associated with this is the crisis of post-colonial bourgeois-nationalist-developmental-statism (i.e. crisis of post-colonial national capitalism), and the attendant crisis of livelihood of common people. The bourgeois system of the world and India's backward capitalism operating within the influence of imperialism and imperialist institutions, have been simply incapable of meeting the basic needs of the toiling classes. Masses are subjected to exploitation (and indeed, super-exploitation) and dispossession and immiserization. To the extent that imperialism shapes the lives of common people in India (and similar other countries in the South), one can say that fascistic tendencies are 'the expression of the most slavish dependence on foreign imperialism' (Trotsky, 1974: 34).

b. The combination of exploitation, dispossession, and immiserization requires legitimization/justification in the minds of the masses. As well, that combination prompts potential and actual opposition. A ruling class response is authoritarianism, that also requires justification. There is thus a need for double justification (or consent from the masses): the system of exploitation/dispossession/immiserization needs justification, and the coercive response to the lower-class struggle against the system also requires a justification. There is a need for the weakening of the lower-class opposition too. The ideology of religion – religious divide between Hindus and religious minorities – and associated Hindu-nationalism, provides such justification. It also divides the masses along the lines of religion and fake view of nationalism that considers vast sections of the population anti-national. Deployment of religion and religion-based politics is supplemented with lies and false promises, to obtain consent to the system, and this, in a liberal-democracy, includes obtaining votes for fascistic political outfits. All in all, a structural space is created for increasing strength of fascistic forces, which have been existing in India since 1920s.

c. Capitalism not only creates the space for fascistic forces, but also a need for these forces. Capitalism also produces a class-agency for the fascistic project. It produces a reserve army of labor and pauperized small-scale producers (who are on their way to becoming completely propertyless), the elements of which, in a poor economy without social benefits (or with very limited benefits) from the government, are vulnerable to lumpenization and criminality. Having been 'spiritually destroyed and morally disoriented by the cruelties they suffer in their everyday life', these victims of (neoliberal) capitalism, not surprisingly, form the bulk of the fascist storm troopers (Ahmad, 2013: 4). There are vast sections of the population whose needs are not met by capital or the state, and they blame their situation on, for example, minorities.

Just because capitalism creates a need for fascistic forces and just because capitalism creates lumpen elements that can be used by the fascistic project, that does not necessarily mean there will be fascistic forces in *active operation*. The bourgeois-*political* dynamics of the rise of fascistic tendencies will be discussed in the next chapter.

CHAPTER 12

Bourgeois-Political Dynamics of Fascistic Tendencies

A fuller understanding of fascistic tendencies must take us beyond the sphere of the political-*economic*, which was more or less the focus of the last chapter. We must pay attention to the sphere of politics in a bourgeois society. The political dynamics of the fascistic tendency have been different in different countries. Focusing on the Congress and the BJP as two faces of bourgeois politics, I will now deal with the fascistic tendencies as they are manifested in the *concrete political situation* in India, in the light of the *general* discussion of the political economic dynamics of the fascistic tendencies, in the last chapter.

The Congress Party, and the Communist parties (which are social-democratic *in practice*) constitute the combined forces of the 'Center' and the Left, and can be called, with *some* justification, 'reformist democracy'. I will begin, in Section 1, with the Congress Party as the traditional party of the bourgeoisie. I will, as well, briefly mention the failure of the Left which has supported the Congress against the BJP. I will discuss how it is that the various failures of 'reformist democracy' – the failures on the economic front and the failures to protect democracy and secularism – have produced a situation for the right-wing forces to become stronger, electorally and otherwise. In Section 2, I relate the rise of the BJP as a part of the fascistic movement, to the logic of capital, including in its neoliberal form, and to the capitalist class. The relation between the capitalist class and the fascistic movement is not straightforward, as communal tensions can affect the business climate. The BJP has intelligently responded to the mild business concerns about political tensions. In Section 3, I will deal with the multiple ways in which the BJP as a part of the fascistic movement has been garnering support, electorally and extra-electorally. In Section 4, I show how the BJP – and the fascistic movement – is a contradictory process. The final section concludes the chapter and sets the context for a discussion on how to fight the fascistic movement.

1 The Failure of 'Reformist Democracy' to Weaken Fascistic Tendencies

Coming out of the anti-colonial movement which it led, the Congress party has hitherto been the traditional party of the post-colonial bourgeoisie. It 'was

© KONINKLIJKE BRILL NV, LEIDEN, 2020 | DOI:10.1163/9789004415560_013

built by a multi-ethnic coalition of middle [Congress party] class elites in alliance with small rural landholders', and the coherence of these groups' class interests 'facilitated the emergence of a strong party espousing an inclusive and programmatic nationalist ideology' (Tudor, 2013, discussed in Clarke, 2017: 581; see also Chibber, 2010). Such an ideology 'allowed it to downplay and depoliticize other potentially relevant lines of difference in India, including those dividing regions, linguistic groups, and castes. The combination of its inclusive, nonsectarian version of nationalism and its coherent distributive coalition gave it a stable base on which to build a postcolonial democratic nation' (p. 585).

But the influence of the party within its own lower-class and socially oppressed base has been in decline (as has that of the Left) in part because of the fact that neo-liberal capitalism has forced it to pander to ruling class interests at the expense of those of lower classes (Figure 12.1). Demagogically presenting itself as a champion of the lower-classes (and Hindus), the BJP has now (almost) displaced the Congress as the new dominant party of the capitalist class, a process that has slowly happened over time. In fact, the BJP's electoral acceptability – in terms of vote share – has been increasing over time even if unevenly (Figure 12.1).

One might ask: how different and similar are these two political 'arms' of the capitalist class (i.e. the Congress and the BJP)? The Congress plays the religion card to win elections.[1] More specifically, it often deploys soft Hindutva.[2] It has failed to protect secularism. For example, it has failed to hold accountable those responsible for: the carnage of Sikhs in 1984, in Delhi, and of Muslims in 2002, in Gujarat. It has failed to stop the demolition of the Babri mosque in

---

1 The Congress party has 'nurtured and supported' the Shiv Sena, BJP's right-wing cousin, 'for over two decades from the mid-sixties to the mid-eighties. In the early phase, this support was given to break the Communist hold over the trade union movement in Mumbai; in the later phase, it was to settle factional scores within the Congress itself' (Dhawale, 2000: 1–2). Congress and RSS also do not belong to two different planets: 'The RSS ... has often come out in appreciation of the [Congress party] when it feels the tactical interests of Hindu communalism demands it. The RSS would ideally want the major national party to become Hindu oriented. In 1987, a powerful RSS leader said: 'We are not anti-Congress. Our founder leader was a Congressman. Our organisation is opposed only to the Congress policy of appeasing the minorities' (Karat, 1992; parenthesis added).

2 In its election campaigns in Madhya Pradesh to be held in December 2018, the Congress is planning Ram yatra. Its politicians, including its national President, openly and publicly display their religiosity and show that there are devotees of this or that Hindu god (Ghose, 2018). As well, 'the Congress Party is busy trying to showcase its 'soft Hindutva' ideology. Days before the Election Commission's poll bugle, Congress president Rahul Gandhi went on a temple, mosque, gurudwara run across MP. ...In its manifesto too, Congress played the soft Hindutva card to woo Hindu voters, traditionally seen as the BJP's vote bank. The manifesto promised to build *gaushalas* (cowsheds) in every gram panchayat, set up new *adhyatmik vibhag* (department for spirituality) and open new Sanskrit schools across the state' (Dutta, 2018).

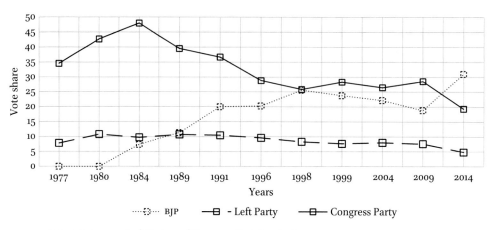

FIGURE 12.1 BJP, Left Party, and Congress Party's vote share, 1977–2014

1992 in Uttar Pradesh by the Hindu-communal forces. It has also failed to stop the forced migration of hundreds of thousands of Hindus from the Jammu valley, and deaths of hundreds of them in the hands of Muslims. It has failed to stop the deaths of civilians, many Hindus, during the Khalistani movement in the Punjab. During the Congress rule, in 1976, Indian constitution was amended, officially making it a secular state, and yet the constitution prohibits, on religious grounds, the slaughter of cows, an animal which many Hindus consider sacred. However, the Congress will *generally* not go against the principle of secularism *to the extent that* the BJP will and does. Its politics is not dominantly based on the politics of sectarian hatred. Besides, within the Congress, there *are* intellectual forces of liberal democracy and secularism (e.g. Shashi Tharoor, Mani S. Aiyar), and some of its senior leaders even think that a stronger electoral Left, even if it is their political rival, is good for democracy.

As far as economic policies – the policies concerning capitalist development – are concerned, there is relatively little difference between the BJP and the Congress, although the Congress can be slightly more pro-poor than the BJP can ever be as a matter of principle. Both are enthusiastic supporters of bourgeois class relations. Both support neoliberal forms of capitalist accumulation. The BJP and the Congress are two factions of the dominant bourgeois political formation. If anything, the BJP is 'the right-wing of the Congress'. The Congress has failed to significantly raise people's living standards, including of minorities. There have also been corruption scandals involving the leaders of the Congress and the members of the business class. The Congress has also not protected liberal democracy always: it declared national emergency suspending democratic rights in the mid-1970s.

If the Congress has failed to protect social and political rights, the Left has not succeeded much either. Like other regional off-shoots of the Congress in power (regional parties), the Left has, more or less, implemented the same neoliberal capitalist economic policies in the States where it has been in power (this is not to deny that the Left has invested in the social sector in its States and has tried to act as Left-Congress to some extent). Focused more on electoral battles than on extra-electoral mobilization, the Left has not organized its basic class forces (workers and small-scale producers) on a large enough scale to enable them to challenge communal thinking and practice and the on-going attack on their democratic rights. Indeed, failing to develop common people's class consciousness is one of the most important failures of the Left. It has tried its best to keep the BJP out of power several times, but it has not used the breathing space thus achieved to adequately mobilize its class forces against both capitalism, including in its neoliberal form, and communalism.

To repeat, the Left has been undeniably committed to secularism and protection of minority rights. Yet, before, during, and after the 1992 mosque demolition (the latter definitely signaled an attack on democracy and secularism, from the fascistic forces and which enabled the political rise of these forces), 'at this decisive moment in modern Indian history, the parliamentary left could not even carry out a counter-mobilization against the onslaught of communalism' (Vanaik, 2011: 102).

2 The BJP, the Fascistic Movement, and (Neoliberal-Peripheral) Capitalism

In this section, I will discuss the symbiotic relation between the capitalist class and the fascistic movement. I will then discuss the various ways in which the entire family of fascistic forces has pursued an agenda that is pro-capitalist as well as a communal, in the extreme.

The capitalist economic logic includes the fact that capitalist property relations need to be protected and that conditions for capitalist profit need to be ensured. Any political party – from the Right, Center and the Left – that manages the collective affairs of capital and of its state must reproduce the economic logic of capitalism. Given the economic logic of capitalism, the Congress and the BJP, the two main parties of the capitalist class, are very similar in terms of economic policies. They must support – they must be embodiments of – the capitalist economic logic. The BJP as a capitalist party has to pursue capitalist development like the Congress does. While in power, like the Congress, the BJP has indeed implemented neoliberal capitalist policies, and while in opposition, it has also supported such policies. This is the political effect of the economic logic of capitalism.

Thanks to the *neoliberal* capitalist strategy reflecting the demands of the capitalist class, the strategy that the Congress Party ushered in and that all parties including the Left have supported, capitalist economic growth has caused a greater un/under-employment, income-deflation for the masses, and rising inequality, with a top tiny class massively benefitting from economic growth and the vast section living in misery (see Figure 12.2 below). The miserable situation of the masses, aggravated by the inability of the state to provide for them in a less developed economy, has created a support-base for the BJP's agenda over the last 4 decades or so: this has allowed the BJP to lie that it can do things differently. The situation has also enabled the BJP and its family to produce their storm-troopers who come from angry petty bourgeois people and from un/under-employed people.

It should be noted that the economic failure of the Congress is not just a political failure, the failure of a political party. It is a part of the failure of the entire bourgeois system of politics which is subordinated to the crisis-ridden bourgeois political economy operating within the capitalist world market. Given the pressure of the world market and imperialist institutions, maintaining a protected economy for long was going to be difficult anyway, especially given the balance of power between the capitalists and the masses in a peripheral-capitalist country being heavily tilted towards the former. It should also be noted that while capitalism constrains political parties, the constraints are never absolute. Capitalism sets limits within which political parties can autonomously act. Depending on the balance of power between classes that is reflected in their programs, they can be more or less pro-people, once again within limits. Under the political pressure of the Left and progressive forces, the Congress was able to introduce, for example, a rural employment program, which the BJP has not been keen on implementing as strongly as the Congress as we have seen in Chapter 10. That fact reflects their slight differences in relation to the welfare of the masses (and slight differences between them and Left parties). These are differences in degree, however.

As far as common people are concerned, and considering the Congress' overall character (including on the economic front and in relation to secularism and democracy), the perception is that there is little economic difference between these two parties. This is partly signified by the fact that perhaps there is not

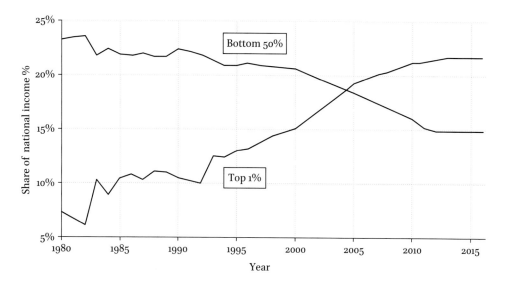

FIGURE 12.2 Income inequality in India, 1980–2015
SOURCE: HTTP://WIR2018.WID.WORLD/FILES/DOWNLOAD/WIR
-PRESENTATION.PDF

much qualitative difference in the nature of electoral support for either of the parties: people who support for Congress today may support the BJP tomorrow, and vice versa (Figure 12.3 below). There are States where both the BJP and the Congress have received high vote shares (Gujarat, Rajasthan, Madhya Pradesh, Chhattisgarh, Himachal Pradesh, Uttarakhand and to some extent, Karnataka as well – the States in the upper right corner of Figure 12.3). There are States where both parties have received limited amount of electoral support in the form of vote shares (e.g. Tamil Nadu, Bengal, Andhra, Telangana, Maharashtra, Bihar – the States in the lower left corner of Figure 12.3). In fact, the vast majority of States (i.e. taking into account what are known as major States), fall in either of these categories (and this has political implications, as we will see).

There is no doubt that the BJP, as a part of the fascistic movement, is fundamentally a capitalist party. The fascistic forces are not just based in certain reactionary *ideas*. They have a deeply material character. There is no doubt that RSS, the ideological guru and mentor of the BJP, is not just an anti-democratic and communal force, but also it is a deeply *anti-communist* force. Anti-communism animates the entire fascistic movement, and that is an attraction for the capitalist class. In contrast, the Congress can be slightly conciliatory towards the Left.

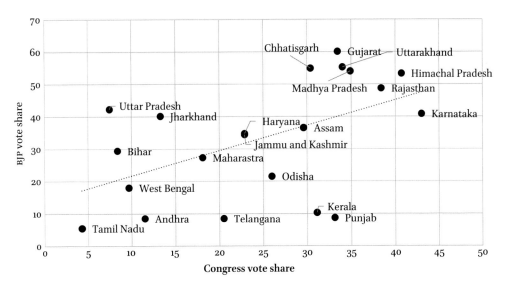

FIGURE 12.3 Congress vote share vs BJP vote share in India's general election, 2014

RSS is not only the motor force behind fascistic ideology that justifies a reactionary political project of the Hindu state as well as anti-people and pro-business economic policy (in spite of fruitless references to such empty terms as Gandhian socialism, Swedishi, etc.). It seems that much like the Christian missionaries who laid the groundwork in the past for the European colonial-capitalists and their political representatives, to colonize countries, the Hindutva missionaries (e.g. the RSS cadre) are helping the BJP now to colonize the space of India's secular-democratic fabric and to inflict a fascistic agenda on the country, in the interest of the capitalist class and to appease some politically backward obscurantist elements in the population.[3] RSS's groundwork that gets the BJP votes includes coercion and consent: brutal attacks on minorities, secularists, democrats and communists, as well as ideological brainwashing and charity work. Often the charity work has a direct ideological function promoting fascistic ideas.[4]

---

[3] For the BJP, the secularism of non-BJP parties is 'Pseudo-secularism' which it basically defines as 'the practice by all parties which denies the essentially Hindu character of the country and therefore pampers the minorities and appeases minority communalism for garnering votes'. So what the BJP calls pseudo-secularism is equal to minorytism. For it, 'Genuine secularism requires recognition that Hinduism is the cultural essence of Indian society and its binding force', and therefore, 'only acceptance of Hindutva could make one a genuine secularist – what it calls positive secularism. Any defence of legitimate minority rights becomes minorityism' (Karat, 1991: 4).

[4] Consider the RSS-funded network of schools in rural areas, that takes advantage of the complete collapse of state-funded education. That the RSS has infected the minds of millions of

Underlying the different factors behind the BJP's post-1980s popularity, is the fact that sections of the ruling class itself (the bourgeois and big landlords), have shifted their moral, intellectual, financial and political loyalty to the BJP from the Congress, often willingly, and sometimes unwillingly.[5] The reason is that it does not matter whether the BJP and its foot-soldiers kill Muslims and secularists and communists; if the ruling class elements can benefit from the BJP's authoritarianism that helps its implement neoliberal capitalist policies and that curtails the freedom to criticize pro-capitalist policies, why not support it? It is not surprising that: in 2009, Anil Ambani said that 'Narendrabhai has done good for Gujarat and imagine what will happen if he leads the nation. A person like him should be the next leader of the country' (quoted in Karat, 2014: 7). Similarly, Sunil Mittal, head of the Bharti group, echoed Ambani: 'Chief Minister Modi is known as CEO, but he is actually not a CEO because he is not running a company or a sector. He is running a State and can also run the nation' (ibid.). These words from the ruling class proved to be prophetic, as Mr. Modi indeed became the Prime minister in 2014.

Indeed, what use-value is the facade of secularism Hindu fundamentalist forces allow the moneybags to amass a lot of money? We have seen that the business class economically profits from the labor of workers and small-scale producers and politically 'profits' from a right-wing government unleashing 'the reserve army' of the forces of reaction that divide and intimidate any potential anti-capitalist force (and thus playing a role that is complimentary to that of police, etc.).

However, the relation between capitalist economy and the right-wing character of capitalist politics may not always work in favor of the capitalist class in a straightforward way, and indeed, under some circumstances, the capitalist class can present some limited counter-vailing mechanisms to right-wing-ism. As mentioned earlier, communal violence can destroy property, including capitalist property. It can also create a law and order issue that can undermine the business climate (in a communal riot, people may not go to work, and they may reduce/stop the purchase of commodities, and both of these facts will

---

children is clear. In 2004, reports surfaced of high-school textbooks in Gujarat, which was led by Mr. Modi for years, that admired Nazism and fascism. In a section called 'Ideology of Nazism', the textbook said Hitler had 'lent dignity and prestige to the German government', that he 'made untiring efforts to make Germany self-reliant' and that he 'instilled the spirit of adventure in the common people' (Schultz, 2017). To cite another example: when 25 mostly upper-middle-class students at a private French school in Mumbai, a city that is home to fascistic tendencies, were asked to name the historical figure they most admired, nine of them picked Hitler. That India's cultural atmosphere is demonstrating fascistic traits is clear.

5 Writing just before the 2014 general election, Karat (2014) said: 'Whatever the outcome of the election, there is no doubt that Hindutva is witnessing a second coming, and that there is a shift among the big bourgeoisie in favour of the right-wing communal party, the BJP' (p. 3).

adversely affect business profit). And the law and order situation is already getting worse, as shown in the recent killing of a police officer by Hindutva forces. This is the logic here: when a *culture* of mob lynching is encouraged within, and by, the fascistic movement, this culture can easily spread. It can hurt and discipline not only its usual targets (e.g. Muslims), but also the security personnel if they dare to do their duty by investigating lynchings or other such atrocities by the fascistic forces.[6] So domestic capital and global capital can put *some* restraints on the right-wing party by using such mechanisms as words of warning, and threat of producing a bad image about the investment climate.

Domestically, certain members of the ruling classes (e.g. Godrez or Bajaj) have been concerned about communalism, and it is possible that some of them – as individuals and not as bearers of the economic logic of capital – do care about secularism as a value (see Gurcharan Das, 2012). The global capital is also concerned about the law and order situation that communalism can create. In November 2015, Moody's Analytics asked Modi to keep the BJP members 'in check or risk losing domestic and global credibility' (quoted in Kumar and Jones, 2015). The reason is not that the global business cares about the protection of democratic rights as such; in fact, Modi, who was an international pariah because of his role in Gujarat riots, was warmly and widely embraced, by imperialist capital and politicians and was accorded high status at global capital's family gathering at Davos.[7] Much rather, the reason is pecuniary. Moody Analytics warned that 'the belligerent provocation of various Indian minorities has raised ethnic tensions' and that an increase in communal violence and increased opposition in parliament to such violence mean that 'debate turns away from economic policy' (quoted in Kumar and Jones, 2015). Moody criticized Modi for not implementing economic reforms fast enough. Spending time on fomenting communal tension against minorities is not endorsed by global capital because it draws attention away from policy-making in favor of capital. So the right-wing dispensation responded positively at the time, however temporary or muted the response was.[8]

When sections of the domestic capital have showed their uneasiness with communalism, Hindu supremacists arm-twist them into supporting them: in one case, they put pressure on a major national trade organization of the capitalists (Confederation of Indian Industry) to retract their statements of concern

---

6   The growing mob culture is threatening the constitution and putting the life of police inspector at a greater risk of losing life while performing professional duty. The inspector was the Investigating Officer in a 2015 lynching case that killed a Muslim person.

7   Modi has wanted to refurbish his image by making numerous foreign trips.

8   The BJP's chief and Modi's right-hand man, Amit Shah, asked Haryana Chief Minister Khattar and a few other politicians to temper their communal appeals so as not to impede the implementation of the BJP's economic 'reform' agenda (Kumar and Jones, 2015).

about communalism. It is possible that the BJP will listen to capitalists' 'warnings' and positively respond to the uneasiness about communalism. But there is a limit to the extent to which the BJP can keep its forces in check. This is because to serve capitalists, the Party has to win, and to win the party depends on these reactionary forces during election time and at other times. And, as long as the law and order situation can be maintained through the *intensification* of state- and vigilante-violence, killing of minorities and anti-reaction dissenters might be just fine, from the standpoint of capital. Besides, not all communal-fascistic action is in the form of coercion or killing. A large part of this is in the form of spreading communal and hyper-nationalistic ideas on the basis of the fascistic capture of cultural-educational institutions (e.g. universities and research centers), and that does not concern the business class as that does not create communal tension on the street as yet. Money wins. Capitalists are in competition with one another, and a special relation with a ruling party can enhance one's competitive advantage. Which capitalist would want to be on the wrong side of a party, given that the party can benefit him/her in a big way? Besides, many of the capitalists involved in the $40-billion-dollar Hindu-spiritual market and promoting soft Hindutva are directly and indirectly supportive of the fascistic tendencies.[9] For global capital, India is a low-wage platform for making money (especially, given that the average wage is much lower than in China where living standards double every 13 years, as Roberts, 2018 reports, while India is obsessed with trivial cultural identity issues), and with its cheap labor and cheap natural resources and its state-owned companies for sale, global capital might not be too critical of the forces of capitalist reaction in India (unless there is another India-like territory in terms of profit-making opportunities but one where the political-sectarian tension does not exist).

---

9 'While keeping the business of spirituality centre stage and claiming to retain a non-political and ideological stand, these spiritual entrepreneurs and their outfits [selling spiritual advice, herbal health products mentioned in religious scriptures, etc.] have actually been effective in becoming platforms to promote "soft Hindutva" to a large and influential captive audience. The rise in religiosity and conservative tendencies within Indian society appears to have only aided the efforts these platforms have made to push forward soft Hindutva' (quoted in Deshmane, 2017). Also: 'Ramdev's admirers and followers get more than medical advice: they also get a lesson in Hindu traditionalism and Hindu pride. Interspersed with yogic postures and medical virtues of herbs and food items, Ramdev offers a steady harangue against Western culture, Western medicine, and Western corporations. He equates the promotion of the physical health and well-being of Indians with the promotion of *desh ka swabhiman* (national self-pride) through a revival of its ancient sciences. He has made no secret of his association with the Sangh Parivar: a picture of him doing the RSS ... salute at a convention of the women's wing of the RSS is available in the RSS weekly, *The Organiser*. But Ramdev's open embrace of Hindu right-wing ideas has not diminished the enthusiasm of the masses, which is a strong indication of how normal and ordinary the world view of Hindu supremacy and revival has become' (Meera Nanda quoted in Deshmane, 2017).

But we have seen that capitalist reaction is everywhere. There is a race to the bottom here as well. Given that there is capitalist reaction in all major countries, India will not lose out easily in the eye of global capital for unleashing the forces of reaction. Capital, ultimately, does not care about democracy or secularism. Ultimately, it cares about money, about profit and interest, and about the preservation of capitalist social relations. In this, different fractions of capital are the same, except that while foreign money capital and the trans-nationalized segment of Indian capital are more mobile, capital invested in mining, manufacturing and large-scale agribusiness is a little less so, which means that the law and order situation created by communal tension might affect these relatively-immobile fractions a little more than it would other fractions of capital.

Thus the right-wing forces, led by the BJP, like the Congress itself, deliver the business class what it wants, and in the process, have garnered the support of this class. And where/when this class has murmured a bit about the religious tensions that are created by these forces, the concerns of the business class have been temporarily heeded in a subdued manner or more or less ignored.

3 Political Techniques of the Fascistic Movement

It is to be reiterated that the political character of the right-wing forces including the BJP must be seen from the standpoint of capitalism's logic and from the standpoint of similarities and differences between the BJP and the Congress as two political parties of the bourgeoisie. There are two inter-related points to be made. (1) Capitalism has not only an economic logic but also a political logic to support the economic logic: there is a need to weaken any potential/actual opposition to the rule of capital. And as we have seen, this is where specific political techniques are important in reproducing capitalist rule. (2) It is the case that the economic problems created by capitalism and the failure of the Congress Party to help people to cope with these problems, have created a structural space for fascistic forces to rise. But to assert this is not enough. The structural space for fascistic forces has to be actively made use of. And these forces *have made use of* the opportunities by employing specific political – cultural-political – techniques. These techniques include demagogy (lies; false promises). These also include, and importantly, violent measures, suppression of dissent, and making emotional appeals to people on the basis of religion, and nation. I will discuss these techniques below.

3.1 *Demagogy*
The extreme form of demagogy – associated with the populist character of fascistic tendencies, defines the BJP. It comes to power by appealing to the masses, by exploiting their resentment against existing economic and political elite

and by promising lots of good things, including millions of job and assistance for farmers and unearthing of unearned income (black money as it is called in India) and distributing it among common people. But the party delivers little because it has to satisfy its real boss: big business. To some extent this resonates with German fascism.

> Fascism in power is least of all the rule of the petty bourgeoisie. On the contrary, it is the most ruthless dictatorship of monopoly capital... Fascism succeeded in putting them [the middle classes] at the service of capital. Such slogans as ... the elimination of unearned income were thrown overboard immediately upon the assumption of power.
>
> TROTSKY, 1933b; parentheses and ellipses added

As just mentioned, it is the economic failure of the Congress to significantly raise people's living standards, including of minorities (Muslims are among the poorest among the different communities in India after decades of 'reformist democracy'), and to ensure that benefits of capitalist economic growth are distributed in a reasonably fair way, that has allowed the BJP to practice demagogy to attract voters: the demagogic BJP chants the mantra of development (read: free market capitalist development). It seeks to garner votes by making promises that it knows it can never deliver.

It should be stressed that whether during the election time or during another time, the promise of development is more ideological than material. Its main aim is to obtain consent (in the form of votes) so that the government can implement a twin agenda: (a) pro-market, pro-business, neo-liberal, economic policies that are buttressed by (b) an unashamedly communal strategy of dividing the masses along religious lines, ensuring that any significant opposition to (neoliberal-)capitalism is blunted. Of course, some minor developmental (redistributive) concessions (e.g. social services from the RSS; toilets or cooking gas cylinders from the government) that can hardly improve people's living conditions significantly and on a sustainable basis, *are* made to certain sections of the population. Demagogy cannot work in thin air.

The Congress has also been vulnerable to corruption scandals involving its leaders and the members of the business class that the party is keen to serve. This has prompted the BJP to practice demagogy on a different front: the BJP chants its other mantra – good 'governance'. It wants people to believe that it is a cleaner variant of the corruption-ridden Congress, even if it is not (as we have seen in Chapter 10). In reality, that term (good governance) means that the BJP can make the decisions concerning capitalist involvement – and this includes giving away people's land and public money, etc. to the business class (domestic or not) – without being much worried about the due process and the impacts of such decisions on the people and the environment. More broadly, for the BJP: good governance means the centralization of power in the hands of Prime Minister's Office and at the federal level at the expenses of the provinces; pro-business governmental interventions including transfer of society's resources and public loans to private businesses at below-market rates; and close relation between businesses and political leaders/officials so investment clearances are made with inadequate screening of the impacts of investment on society and environment, or without proper public input. The BJP's 'governance talk' complements its 'development talk' very well.

3.2 Sectarian Appeal to Religious Identities

The RSS and other elements of the fascist parivar recruit their cadres from middle class and semi/un-employed/under-employed people and from some wage-earners, by making use of the discourse of the Hindu religion and the idea of Hindutva (Hindu-ness).[10] Hindutva is euphemistically called a way of life to make it appear non-religious.

Resorting to politics of religious identity helps the BJP to *distinguish* itself from the Congress, in order to sell itself in the voter market as a different and a unique political commodity. The Congress, once again, is not immune to the politics of sectarian hatred. But playing the politics of difference based in religious identity is the *differentia specificia* of the BJP, or of the entire right-wing movement of which the BJP is a part.[11]

It *is* a fact that people have a need for religion and religious consciousness, given conditions of suffering, as we have seen. The BJP takes advantage of this

---

10 Plausibly, 'an urban, upper caste, middle class, socially conservative Hindu' might be 'spontaneously oriented toward accepting the Hindutva proposition that what is unique about India, and therefore its defining feature among nations, is that the great majority of its citizens are Hindu, and Hindu culture must therefore be accepted as national culture; those who do not accept this culture as the normative culture of India are really not Indian in the deeper sense' (Ahmad, 2013: 11). Underlying such a conservative belief is another belief: that religion is the defining trait of a culture. 'And this belief can go together with ideas of Religious Tolerance, Sarva Dharma Sambhav, the belief that Hindus are tolerant, liberal, peace-loving by nature, and that national disunity comes from others who are much too narrow-minded, fundamentalist, socially backward etc. So, when we ask ourselves whether or not communalism could ever become not just a majoritarian ideology but in fact something of a common sense for millions upon millions of people – possibly the majority of Indians – the answer would probably depend on which version of communalism we have in mind' (ibid.: 12).

11 In fact, the BJP's project is based on the coalescence of three kinds of hatred against or distaste for: religious minorities, a progressive economic policy benefitting the working masses, and democratic conduct/values. On the topic of the oppression of Muslims in India, see Jamil (2017).

fact. People are being 'encouraged' and forced by the right-wing forces to subscribe to a communal ideology, which purports to describe and explain society's major problems in terms of a combination of two things. (a) One is a (bodily/mental/spiritual/economic) individualism: the idea of a strong, hard-working, nation-loving, individual with the right morals and with a sense of economic entrepreneurship based in private property. Individuals with these traits are said to be necessary to solve society's problems. (b) Another is religious identity: every aspect of society is seen from the standpoint of the Hindus versus non-Hindus divide.[12] India's problems are because of what non-Hindus do now or did in the past, and implicitly, because of what the Muslim-dominated Pakistan did or does. If one puts (a) and (b) together, the right-wing manifesto for national development points to the importance of cultural-nationalistic and economic individualism: love your Hindu nation, hate non-Hindus unless they do/think exactly as Hindus want, and have the right morals as sanctioned by Hindu scriptures, and be a hard-working entrepreneur (even if that means selling tea and pakoras). With respect to the Hindu – Muslim divide, it should be added that, according to the right-wing forces, all things associated with living Muslims or with the India ruled by the kings who practiced Muslim religion are inherently bad, and all things associated with those who are Hindus or with ancient India are inherently good, even if it is the case that both Muslims and Hindus came from what is now called India or even pre-1947 India and that *all* the epochs of the Indian society, like all societies, have had both progressive and regressive features in terms of economic development, class relations, cultural changes, and so on and therefore should be both celebrated and critiqued. Concomitantly, the BJP also seeks to change people's way of thinking from one that is based on empirical-historical evidence and on reason, to a way of thinking that does not care (much) about evidence and reason, and that treats beliefs and myths as empirical evidence.[13] If in Hindu mythology, a god G was born in place P,

---

12   This means that: society's problems are mainly seen as those that are created by the divide between religious groups and by the lack of Hindu-nationalist pride and unity, by the wrong things that minority-alien religions have apparently done to the majority group, and that solutions to the problems are claimed to lie in the supreme cultural-political dominance of a united majority religion (Hinduism). The majority religion is considered to be the only original religion of the nation, as compared to all other smaller religious groups which are alien religions having come from outside. It is also believed by majority-communalists that India's past is like no other country's and is always superior to other nations, and that major scientific achievements of the West, including plastic surgery, can all be traced to India's history.

13   What is true in the world is, more or less, independent of what is made out to be true, on the basis of power relations one has. It is true that the earth revolves around the sun, that

434   CHAPTER 12

then that god is a real person, and that place is a real place which must be defended against its use by non-Hindus. It also seeks to encourage a way of thinking that is un-critical and conformist, and that seeks to assert, at all cost, the
supremacy of Hinduism. Any historical or contemporary event that glorifies
Hinduism, as the Sangh Parivar sees it, and that respects Hindu *sentiments* as
the Parivar sees them, is both real and good, and needs to be defended. To the
extent that fascistic supporters of the BJP have any critical attitude, it is mainly
directed at the critics of their own conservative and un-scientific views about
society, economy, and history.

3.3   *The Fascistic Idea of the Nation*
The nation is seen by fascistic forces, ultimately, as the territory of the
majority-religion (Hinduism). The aim of these forces is to seek to establish a
Hindu *rastra* (state), a state where Hindus will have rights and non-Hindus will
have no rights or very limited rights. As Golwalkar, a Hindutva ideologue and a
former head of the RSS, expressed it, "in this land, Hindus have been the owners, Parsis and Jews the guests, and Muslims and Christians the dacoits [ban-
dits]". It provocatively asked: "... do all these have the same right over the
country?" (cited in Guha, 2006). Non-Hindus can only live in a way that is subservient to Hindus, culturally and politically.[14] It is not anti-national in the eyes
of the BJP or of the fascistic movement as a whole, when its government gives
away to big business-owners, *nation*'s land, or nation's state-owned companies
that have been built on the contributions of the ordinary *working people of the
nation*, or indeed money from *nationalized* banks to rich investors who do not
return the money, and who indeed flee the country with their un-earned money, while the government is watching. It is also not anti-national in the eyes of
the fascistic movement when the government prostrates before the American
imperialist military strategy, making Indian soil available for refueling US

    Madhya Pradesh is to the south of the Himalaya mountains, and that Aryans came from
    outside of what is currently called India. All this is true even if political control over schol-
    ars and over their professional organizations, and violent means may be used to make
    people believe otherwise. There is a difference between what is true and what people
    think is true, and between what people normally believe to be true and what people are
    forced to believe as being true. Resorting to unreason and making people accept unrea-
    son as reasonable is a hallmark of fascistic tendencies.

14   Following the Godhra riots in which hundreds of Muslims were killed by Hindutva-
    fascistic mobs, at a meeting in Bangalore in mid-March, 2002, the RSS adopted a contro-
    versial resolution titled 'Godhra and After' in which Muslims were cautioned that they
    would only be safe in India if they won the 'goodwill' of Hindus. By 'Hindus', the resolu-
    tion, of course, meant the RSS. 'Let Muslims realise that their real safety lies in the good-
    will of the majority', the resolution stated (Varadarajan, 2009).

warplanes.[15] This is because all this is done to serve the interests of the nation as the right-wing Hindutva brigade *sees it*.[16]

3.4 *Violence/Intimidation and Intolerance towards Dissent*

Slowly creating a consent to the fascistic agenda is not enough. Resorting to intimidation and violence is necessary. RSS cadres are adept at making *ad hominem* and physical attacks on those who challenge them intellectually or politically.[17] Intense (religious) passion and higher decibels of one's speaking, with a touch of masculine aggressiveness, decide the truth status of the words spoken by these people. The idea of Hindutva is used by fascist forces to criticize any person, whether a Hindu or non-Hindu, who does not favor the use of religion for politics and who may be critical of certain ideas and practices sanctioned by Hindu religion. Ominously, violence is often justified on religious grounds: in one case, after killing a Muslim man by accusing him of cow slaughter, the fascistic RSS justified this by saying that: 'Vedas [Hinduism's oldest scriptures] order killing of the sinner who kills a cow. It is a matter of life and death for many of us' (quoted in Bhardwaj, 2015). The fascistic movement makes use of violence to force conformity on people to Hindu morals and practices, the morals and practices of what is defined as the majority group that forms the nation.

In communal violence, organized by the fascistic leaders, various communalist vigilante groups are involved.[18] These foot-soldiers of Sangh Parivar

---

15 'Under Modi, India has emerged as a veritable frontline state in Washington's drive to encircle, strategically isolate, and prepare for war against China. The Modi government has parroted the US line on the South China Sea, where the US has repeatedly conducted provocative "freedom of navigation" exercises, supported Trump's war-mongering against North Korea, and expanded cooperation with the leading US allies in the Asia-Pacific region, Australia and Japan' (Kumara, 2018b). As well: 'India has opened its military ports and airports to US battleships and warplanes, and taken advantage of the Trump administration's support to recklessly escalate tensions with its regional nuclear-armed rival, [Muslim-dominated] Pakistan' (Kumara, 2018b).

16 Fascistic tendencies know only one form of nationalism and bulldoze over all different kinds of nationalism and are deliberately oblivious of the fact that: 'There can be the fascist nationalism of Nazi Germany [which is similar to Indian fascistic nationalism], the imperialist nationalism of the United States, the revolutionary nationalism of communists who led wars of liberation in such diverse countries as Vietnam or Angola; there can be secular Arab nationalism, and there can be clerical nationalism of contemporary Iran'. (Ahmad, 2013: 11).

17 A student activist from JNU said to me: 'RSS people will give us blankets in the night and beat us up in the day', meaning they can be very nice but when you argue with them, they will beat you up. A major human rights activist and former professor in a major Central University said this to me: 'RSS people, when they join a public debate, always make personal attacks on, and shout at, those who challenge them, because that is their overall strategy, but in private they might apologize'.

18 This is, of course, happening in a context where Hindutva has infected everyday life (Berti et al., 2011).

who conduct the lynchings and killings of minorities, communists and people who do not follow their communal ideology or practices, are administratively and politically protected – and are indeed aided by – the BJP-in-power.[19] Once in power, one's words speak the truth: what one says becomes true. One's blatant lies can be words of absolute truth. After ordering the police not to protect the Muslims against a Hindu mob or encouraging a Hindu mob to kill innocent Muslims, one can tell naked lies that one has nothing to do with Muslims being killed. It is not surprising that as fascistic-communal forces are gaining ground, communal incidents – incidents involving conflicts between different religious groups – are on the rise (see Figure 12.4 below). An extreme form of violence that is resorted to is burning people of minorities background alive, as it happened in Gujarat where, for example, a Congress Member of Parliament from the Muslim community was burnt alive.[20] Another is rape, including of children.

Violence is used not only against religious minorities. It is also used against lower castes who are oppressed by, and who therefore resent, Hindu ideas and practices, and against women who may wish to not obey traditional Hindu morals. Despite its rhetoric and active work to woo scheduled castes, tribals and other socially oppressed groups. The BJP is a party, which aims to defend all aspects of the moribund in-egalitarian Hindu society. It is profoundly hostile to the social emancipation of oppressed groups such as women and Dalits, whose oppression has been justified by a set of ideas, if not all ideas, within Hinduism (Karat, 2004: 13). Of course, the BJP seeks to increase its level of acceptance by giving limited concessions to some oppressed groups, including religious minorities. The BJP as a political party *has* had some adherents from religious minorities. This is due to a strategic reason: to broaden its mass base. As long as Hindus' supremacy is recognized, the BJP does not mind granting minor concessions, in part to gain wider consent to its reactionary rule. This strategy includes selective co-optation of leaders of religious minorities and

---

19 '[The] pogroms that engulfed Gujarat in 2002 [included] a spate of "spontaneous" violence that was calculated to generate mass support through communal mobilization'; it was characterized by the complicity of state institutions (Banaji, 2016d: 224). I should say, however, that the idea of complicity of state institutions is becoming hard to justify, given that the boundary between the state and the fascistic Sangh Parivar is being terrifyingly blurred.

20 'Burning people alive has sinister advantages and a macabre logic not available to the usual forms of killing. It can be easily executed by organized groups with tacit support or acquiescence of their community, used to wipe out large numbers indiscriminately, poses no danger to the perpetrators and helps to create an internal climate of terror...' (Ansari, 2011: 135–136).

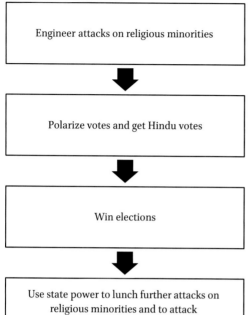

FIGURE 12.4
The fascistic logic of religious-sectarian riots during election season
SOURCE: AUTHOR

lower castes.[21] It has included some minority leaders within its umbrella by offering some political and material rewards. And some minority people may have been forced by circumstances (e.g. threat of majority communalism) to accept the BJP.[22]

Resorting to communal violence (including the use of lynching mobs) becomes a means of dividing and intimidating the toiling masses and of diverting attention from the BJP's failure to improve people's economic conditions, a failure that is a given because of its utterly pro-business character.[23] So the

---

21 'The BJP manifesto promises to look after the welfare of the Muslims, their educational and economic status and promote Urdu. All this is possible, if the Muslim minority recognizes that Hindutva is a way of life which they must come to terms with' (Karat, 2004: 6).

22 Karat (2004) writes that a section of the Muslim community 'is now veering around to some sort of accommodation with the BJP. Though a small section, it is a portent of things to come. One motivation is simply the search for the crumbs of office and the opportunist quest for minor concessions which is seen in persons like Arif Mohd. Khan joining the BJP, or, the Delhi Jama Masjid' Imam's new-found softness for the BJP. The other is a resigned acceptance of living under conditions of majority dominance – what the RSS chief Sudarshan graphically described as living on the goodwill of the majority' (p. 6).

23 'The more the regime's failure in the economy and social welfare sector manifests itself, the more it resorts to open communalism, encouraging violence against Muslims and

business class is happy with the BJP, even if its hands are colored red by the murders of minorities, democrats, secularists and communists. Money has no color or religion.

Intolerance towards those who share different views is a hallmark of fascism and of fascistic tendencies. Fascistic forces in India and elsewhere have an antipathy towards intellectuals (of Marxists and other progressive varieties).[24] Within limits, and in certain respects, the fascistic movement shares a space with identity politics, and its attendant idealistic, irrational thinking has taken a religious and nationalist form in India. Fascism also targets many of the promoters of identity-based, social-constructionist academic thinking, who may be somewhat championing the rights of the socially oppressed groups, or at least, of the more privileged layers in these groups.[25] A major object of fascism's ideological hatred is Marxism, however, even if the movement hardly has the intellectual tools with which to critically engage with such a powerful body of thinking as Marxism. Important to note is the fact that India has one of the biggest communist movements in the world (even though it is weak, relative to the task at hand). Marxism – in terms of Marxist theory and Marxist movement – is the most consistent supporter of the democratic and secular discourse, of scientific attitude, and of the objective interests of the toiling masses. Fascism – or fascistic tendency – comes to exist as the most strident and complete opposite of Marxism. When Marxism is fought against and marginalized,[26] then what one gets is its polar opposite (fascism). Marxism is for socialism and against capitalism. It is internationalist, and against parochial inward-looking nationalism, while it celebrates the accomplishments of a nation as a part of the family of nations, and criticizes everything that happens in a nation that is against social and democratic rights of common people of that nation and of

---

      Dalits (Arun Jaitley, the finance minister, can in parliament hold beef-eating a worse crime than the lynching and murder of Muslims)' (Habib, 2017).

24   About the fascist movement of his time, Trotsky said: 'The leaders of the movement are liquidating "intellectualism" because they themselves possess second- and third-rate intellects, and above all because their historic role does not permit them to pursue a single thought to its conclusion. The petty bourgeois needs a higher authority, which stands above matter and above history, and which is safeguarded from competition, inflation, crisis, and the auction block. To evolution, materialist thought, and rationalism – of the twentieth, nineteenth, and eighteenth centuries – is counterposed in his mind national idealism as the source of heroic inspiration' (Trotsky, 1933b).

25   This sort of thinking has been promoted by certain academic trends since the 1980s mainly to counter Marxism theory and politics. On the relation between the attack on secularism and certain styles of academic thinking (e.g. post-modernism), see: Baber (2006), and Nanda (2007).

26   Marxism is marginalized in academic circles, media, political movements, and popular (online and offline) conversations. It is fought against by people who give in to idealism and politics of identity.

other nations. And Marxism is for popular democracy, and against authoritarianism. Fascism could not be more different from Marxism in all these respects.[27] It is not surprising that 'Hitler gave himself the ambition to be the 'destroyer of Marxism', and that it was this goal which made him and his movement fascist, even before the party had achieved significant size' (Renton, 2007: 106). It should be stressed that Hitler, the rabid anti-Marxist and anti-communist, continues to inspire the fascist movement in India as elsewhere.

3.5 Mobilization of Foot-Soldiers and Supporters

The fascistic movement is not ordinary Bonapartist authoritarianism. It includes violent grassroots organizations of certain class-fractions or class-strata: urban petty bourgeois people; un-employed and semi-employed people; some sections of the working class and of upper-caste landowning class. Their material interests are not met by the capitalist system. Steeped in hyper-nationalistic ideas, they angrily turn themselves against their socially constructed or perceived enemies (minorities; and Marxists and even liberals, who reject their identity politics and who reject their undemocratic intolerance). These forces are engaged in what Gramsci would call a war of attrition (see Roberts, 2011). The fascistic movement is a cadre-based movement from which the BJP benefits electorally.[28]

The task of mobilizing the foot-soldiers gets easier given that for many people (who are of petty bourgeois background and who are un/under-employed), being a part of the fascistic movement is a source of material reward including from criminal activities that we have talked about earlier. For many, being a part of such a movement is also a source of social-psychological satisfaction (emanating from a sense of belongingness to a religious community).[29] Participating

---

27   Perhaps one common ground between Marxism and fascism is that both are rooted in mass movements but with completely opposite purposes.

28   As Vanaik (2018) writes: 'the BJP's biggest asset remains its massive cadre base, which includes foot soldiers willing to wreak violence on command. The rise of the far right is a worldwide phenomenon, but nowhere else is there a force like the Sangh, which has had an unbroken existence of over ninety years and a width and depth of implantation in civil society unmatched in any other country. The BJP and the Sangh, the broader family to which it belongs, represent a far-right force with undeniable neo-fascist characteristics. Apart from the BJP and RSS, the VHP (World Hindu Council) is the other main pan-Indian body. It is the 'overlord' for cultural-religious activities, with mutually beneficial links to the leaders of numerous Hindu sects. VHP muscle and money help these sects to grow, thereby enhancing the aura of their leaders, who duly call on their devotees to support Sangh campaigns, programmes and electoral candidates'.

29   Whether such a belongingness actually exists across a large country such as India, and how strongly it does, is a different question. The fictional character of such community feeling, of such belongingness, should be stressed. Ahmad (2013) brilliantly writes: 'the

in communal riots might give the economically desperate lumpen elements a sense of satisfaction that they are capable of doing something in life. The BJP takes advantage of people's need for religious beliefs in an alienating world and of the fact that for some people their economic insecurity appears to be alleviated by a sense of agency and empowerment. This sense is created when what one does/think has some palpable effect: killing fellow-citizens, destroying monuments, aggressively lobbying to change Muslim place names to Hindu names, and so on.[30] Besides, 'Hatred against the Muslim minority has been systematically inculcated in such a manner that violence of barbaric proportions against them is not only widely condoned but also even enjoyed by certain sections of the Hindu communities' (Ansari, 2011: 135–136).

But the foot-soldiers of the fascistic movement fail to understand that they are putting an axe on their own feet, and that are merely pawns in the larger a communal-corporate game that is ultimately against their own economic and democratic interests as citizens. Mistakenly called *fringe* elements, these forces are *central* to the whole communalist-fascist enterprise: they help the BJP garner electoral support by polarizing votes along religious lines. So the BJP government cannot but support them. The BJP forces incite the right-wing mob and then justify the criminal violence committed by describing it as spontaneous reaction to the alleged action of a perceived enemy (e.g. religious minority, or communists or rationalists), a justification that is based in the physicalization of human beings that I have referred to earlier.[31]

---

way we frequently speak of 'Hindu community', 'Muslim community' etc. strikes me as purely fictional; it is very doubtful that Muslims of Kashmir and Muslims of Kerala share very much more than some religious rituals, a handful of founding texts of Islam, and a common fear of Hindu communalism. And, it is equally hard to believe that Christians of Nagaland and of Kerala are all members of a Pan-Indian Christian community. The idea of there being a Hindu 'community' across regions, castes, occupations etc. is ... absurd. ... And yet, in all our discourses of politics and policymaking the existence of such homogeneous, pan-Indian religious communities is simply taken for granted as if this was a self-evident fact. This fictive identity has been superimposed upon real society by self-serving politicians, mullahs and mahants, self-serving and cynical politicians, and the state itself which, like the colonial state, much prefers dealing with 'community representatives' than with class politics' (p. 7).

30   'It is perfectly plausible that a Kar Sevak [an RSS worker], pulled out of the miseries of the lumpenproletariat and brainwashed with glorious ideas of Hindu heroic duty to liberate Lord Ram's Janmbhoomi, may indeed fancy himself a hanuman in the army of Ram as he climbs up to a dome of the babri masjid in order to pull it down. Religion is not responsible but it is not entirely innocent either. The less religion there is in society at large and the more strictly it is separated from all forms of political life, the less violent and persistent communalism would be' (Ahmad, 2013: 7–8).

31   'The reaction of this murderous incident [in which Hindutva forces killed Muslims in a riot in 2002] in Gujarat was natural and spontaneous. The entire Hindu society cutting across all divisions of party, caste and social status reacted....' (quoted in Varadarajan,

Apart from on-the-ground foot-soldiers (e.g. various vigilante groups), the BJP, the political vanguard of the fascistic movement, receives help from a variety of inter-connected sources: the *babas* (spiritual masters) selling/offering tips, based in religious texts, for mental and spiritual peace and sound physique; the so-called intellectuals with dubious academic credentials but with loyalty to the Hindutva-fascistic movement, who have suddenly come out of nowhere, some of whom having been made the managers of educational institutions,[32] and RSS cadres (who are highly disciplined and austere and who truly think what they are doing is in the interest of the nation as they see it). There are also a few party spokes-persons who regularly show up on TV channels, who seem to know everything about everything and who forcefully champion the views of the right-wing forces, trying to make up for their intellectual deficiency by using emotionally charged words about the nation and Hinduism and facts from mythology treated as historical evidence. The BJP uses all these resources, apart from the media and secretive funding from the business class, to shape the manner in which people think about society and history and act in their daily lives. The ideas of the ruling class and of those who manage its affairs politically gradually become ruling ideas.

In appealing to majoritarian-sectarian identity (Hindutva) and in mobilizing its foot-soldiers, the BJP, in pursuit of a reactionary-bourgeois project, has little regard, however, for bourgeois institutions, including institutions of law and order.[33] This is evident from the following words of the then Prime

---

2009). 'The first use of this morally perverse 'Newtonian' logic of action and reaction to justify the killing of Muslims after Godhra was made by Modi in an interview to Zee Television on 1 March, even as the violence was at its peak. And ironically, it wasn't so much a reference to the burning of the Sabarmati Express as to press reports that former Congress MP Ehsan Jafri – who was lynched by a Sangh Parivar-led mob at his residence in Chamanpura, Ahmedabad on 28 February – had fired at the mob in order to try and disperse them. Modi said that Jafri's 'action' of firing had infuriated the mob and that the massacre which followed was a 'reaction'. Since his remark generated a huge controversy and led the Gujarat information department to deny that he had said any such thing, it is worth reproducing his exact quote: 'What is happening is a chain of action and reaction. What I want is that there should be no action and no reaction'. Asked about the violence which erupted throughout Gujarat on the day of the VHP-sponsored bandh, he said: 'It is natural that what happened in Godhra day before yesterday, where forty women and children were burnt alive, has shocked the country and the world. The people in that part of Godhra have had criminal tendencies. Earlier, these people had murdered women teachers. And now they have done this terrible crime for which a reaction is going on' (quoted in Varadarajan, 2009).

32 This is just like the Moghul tax collectors who were made land owners by British colonialists.

33 Jaffrelot (2011) says that in the post-Nehurvian period, the simultaneous and related rise of Hindu nationalism has put the minorities and secularism on the defensive, and in many ways the rule of law is at risk too.

Minister of India, Mr. Narasimha Rao (of the Congress), during the time the fascistic forces demolished a 16th century place of worship for Muslims. Upon hearing the news on 6 December that the mosque has been destroyed by Hindu activists, Mr. Rao expressed himself thus in a speech:[34] 'While this [demolition] was going on, the local authorities and the police appeared to be standing as mute spectators'.[35] Mr. Rao continues:

> This dismal picture of inaction and dereliction of duty was because of orders from the Chief Minister of U.P. [who was of the BJP] not to use force...
> In the context the Supreme Court held that 'the demolition of Babri Masjid in brazen defiance of the order of this Court is indeed a challenge to the majesty of law and the Constitution. ... The Demolition is an unprecedent attack on the secular foundation of democracy, the authority and dignity of this Court. The Court thus stands betrayed as never before'

The kind of foot-soldiers that the fascistic movement mobilizes can be indirectly garnered from Table 12.1 below. It shows partisan response to the demolition of the mosque on December 6, 1992, an event that is definitely a watershed in the history of post-colonial bourgeois India's record on secularism: the table shows that a very high percentage of supporters of BJP and its allied parties thought that the demolition of the mosque was actually justified, relative to supporters of Congress and the Left. While 40.7% of the BJP supporters thought the act was justified, only 22% of all voters thought so (the numbers were much lower at 9.1% for Left supporters and 16.5% for Congress supporters).

It should be said that while Mr. Rao, the then Prime Minister, appears to lament the demolition of the mosque and seems to be helpless, the same Mr. Rao mobilized all the energies of the state to change India's economic regime from dirigisme to de-regulation, against opposition from below. Why was he

---

34 His speech is reproduced in Singer (2012: 173).

35 The direct and indirect effect of the communal mobilization on the security apparatus is clear from the following lines from Vanaik (2018): 'In the late eighties and early nineties, during the 'Rama's Birthplace' campaign – the Ram Janmabhoomi, in which right-wing Hindu groups fought to build a temple on the site of the old Babri Masjid in Ayodhya, Uttar Pradesh, claiming the mosque was located where the god had been born – Indian Army chiefs made clear they would not take responsibility for protecting the mosque because Army *jawans* were overwhelmingly Hindus whose battle cries were invocations of Lord Ram. (The Indian Army exhibited no such qualms when it came to military assaults on the Sikhs' Golden Temple in 1984 or the Muslim shrine of Charar-e-Sharif in Kashmir in 1995.)'.

BOURGEOIS-POLITICAL DYNAMICS OF FASCISTIC TENDENCIES

TABLE 12.1   Partisan response to the demolition of Babri mosque in 1992 (in %)

	Congress	BJP+	Left	Total
Response				
Unjustified	42.9	25.7	54.9	38.1
Justified	16.5	40.7	9.1	22.7
Not heard about it	32.6	22.2	26.9	29

SOURCE: NATIONAL ELECTION STUDIES, CSDS, DELHI 1996, QUOTED IN MITRA, 2011: 128

powerless in one instance and powerful in another is a question to ask.[36] Besides, while the fascistic forces disregarded the courts, army, police, etc., the following question should be asked: would the same courts, army and police, etc. allow 'a mob' of workers take over a factory to manage it by themselves in order to meet their daily needs, or a multi-story residence of a member of the super-rich for their own use? The demolition of the mosque and similar other fascistic actions such as lynchings of non-Hindus suggest that it is not just the BJP but the entire bourgeois political system that is thoroughly compromised when it comes to the defense of secularism and democratic rights.

3.6   The Tactical Constructions of the Individual Icons, from the Past and the Present

From time to time, within the fascistic movement, certain lesser-known individuals are elevated to a status of wider acceptability, and this is done in the same process which deliberately downgrades other individuals. The process involves making some people acceptable who are otherwise not acceptable, and making some people unacceptable who are otherwise acceptable. The fascistic movement has made an ideological use of those who are dead and who might have had nothing (much) to do with communal ideology, as their own. Individuals from Sardar Patel, to Bhagat Singh to Bhimrao Ambedkar and Subhas Bose, all freedom fighters, are shamelessly and hypocritically constructed as the BJP's own. Doing this is necessary in part because the fascistic movement which hardly had a record of fight against the British, has had no

---

36   It is clear that 'Congress Prime Minister Narasimha Rao did nothing to stop the campaign that would defy the Constitution, with impunity, by demolishing the Babri Masjid in Ayodhya in 1992 – demonstrating the de facto sovereignty of the forces of Hindutva in defying the law' and he did this for a simple fact: 'fear of offending "Hindu sentiment"' (Vanaik, 2018).

444 CHAPTER 12

widely-accepted and legitimate icon from the anti-colonial movement. On the other hand, blatantly communal leaders, whom most Indians cared little about, have been resurrected as leaders of the (Hinduized) nation. To repeat, individuals who have nothing to do with communalism but who are widely respected are made a part of the ideological family of the fascistic project while the deeply communal leaders – both Indians as well as non-Indians such as Hitler – are elevated to a high status in the minds of the people and/or made more acceptable than they normally are. As a part of the same process, certain individuals – from the center and the left – are deliberately denigrated or ignored: Nehru and Gandhi as well as Lenin and Marx (note: Marx and Lenin are bad in part because they are aliens, but Hitler of Germany, who continues to shape the Indian fascistic thinking, is not considered to be an alien).

Then, at one time, Mr. Vajpayee (a BJP leader who became a Prime Minister) was constructed as a moderate face of Hindutva, so he could make appeal to the masses based on his (poetic) charisma. Currently, Mr. Modi has been elevated to the position of the supreme leader. A small-time RSS person a few decades ago, he has been constructed as someone who is a strong leader, with oratory skills and mass appeal. This is an illusion that has also fed into the so-called Modi wave, which is created by the media and disseminated by it among an accepting section of the public.[37] Both Mr. Vajpayee and Mr. Modi are even seen as statesmen, even if, for example, a massive carnage of Muslims occurred under their tenure.

Individual personalities *are* important in any political project. It is very difficult to implement a fascistic movement without individuals with fascistic or deeply authoritarian traits. Modi is effectively the current leader of the fascistic movement. Nandy (2002) says that Modi has a fascistic personality:

> More than a decade ago, when Narendra Modi was a nobody, a small-time RSS *pracharak* trying to make it as a small-time BJP functionary, I had the privilege of interviewing him ...It was a long, rambling interview, but it left me in no doubt that here was a classic, clinical case of a fascist.

---

37 'The announcement of Modi as the leader of the BJP's [2014] election campaign saw a massive and sustained campaign in the corporate media, both television and print, to project Modi on a development and good governance platform. This unprecedented campaign is a result of the total backing of the corporate sector, which owns the bulk of the mass media in the country. At the same time, the corporate media have blacked out the communal aspects of the BJP campaign and the big role the RSS is playing in the campaign. ...This campaign explains the genesis of the "Modi wave", which is then repropagated by the very corporate media that created it. The impact and the appeal that Modi has among educated youth and sections of the middle classes in various parts of the country is a result of this media campaign' (Karat, 2014: 8–9).

I never use the term 'fascist' as a term of abuse; to me it is a diagnostic category comprising not only one's ideological posture but also the personality traits and motivational patterns contextualising the ideology.

Modi, it gives me no pleasure to tell the readers, met virtually all the criteria that psychiatrists, psycho-analysts and psychologists had set up after years of empirical work on the authoritarian personality. He had the same mix of puritanical rigidity, narrowing of emotional life, massive use of the ego defence of projection, denial and fear of his own passions combined with fantasies of violence – all set within the matrix of clear paranoid and obsessive personality traits. I still remember the cool, measured tone in which he elaborated a theory of cosmic conspiracy against India that painted every Muslim as a suspected traitor and a potential terrorist. I came out of the interview shaken [thinking that] ...for the first time, I had met a textbook case of a fascist and a prospective killer, perhaps even a future mass murderer.

While individuals *are* important in any political project, it is important that individuals be seen as always operating within social relations which are manifested through the individuals.

The king is king only because the interests and prejudices of millions of people are refracted through his person... [The] leader is always a relation between people, the individual supply to meet the collective demand...Not every exasperated petty bourgeois could have become Hitler [or Modi], but a particle of Hitler [Modi] is lodged in every exasperated petty bourgeois.

TROTSKY, 1933b; parentheses added

Following Marx, I assume that ultimately, 'individuals ... are the personifications of economic categories, embodiments of particular class-relations and class-interests'. One should not 'make the individual responsible for relations whose creature he socially remains, however much he [or she] may subjectively raise himself above them' (Marx, 1977). There are objective political economic processes and class relations that underlie the fascistic movement, as discussed earlier, within which certain individuals' authoritarian personality plays an important role.

3.7   *Normalization of the Fascistic Movement*

Interestingly, it is the ideological success of the RSS–BJP forces that many have forgotten that the Indian state had banned the RSS several times (in 1948, 1975 and 1992). RSS is now taken to be a normal organization, like any other, with which one can have exchanges. Some people might believe that 'I voted for the BJP because the Congress did not do anything'. This statement mistakenly assumes that the BJP, hitched to the fascistic RSS, is a normal party in a democratic set-up, that it can be one of the choices for voters.

In spite of its reactionary traits, the BJP is indeed seen by millions of ordinary citizens (even if still a minority of the country, though a large minority) as well as by sections of the economic-political elite in India (and in imperialist countries), as a political party like any other. This is indicative of the weakness of Left-democratic culture, and of the strength of communal-political thinking of which the fascistic movement is to be credited for. This kind of thinking – that the BJP and RSS are normal organizations in a liberal-democratic system – is actually infecting all-non-Left parties, so much so that they are happy to accept former BJP- and RSS-leaders in their fold.[38] In a sense, non-BJP, bourgeois parties have contributed to the acceptability of the discourse and the political practice that the BJP stands for. Bannerji (2006) says that RSS has made use of media, including transmission of TV serials (e.g. Hindu epics such as Ramayan and Mahabharat) to promote Hindutva. The idea that the BJP is a party like any other is an illusion that has been accepted by many voters. This illusion has been helped by the media, which is, more or less, the propaganda channel of the different fractions of the ruling class, and which is increasingly communalized.[39] The fact that leaders/spokespersons of the BJP, RSS and

---

38   Indeed, many non-BJP parties, including even Congress, welcome 'middle-level leaders and activists of the BJP when they leave their parent party due to some disgruntlement, mainly of not getting tickets, by the Congress and other bourgeois parties' such as the Samajwadi party and the RJD (Karat, 2004: 1). Karat goes on to make this insightful comment: 'This approach indicates a serious misreading of the BJP and the game plan of the RSS. In class terms, the BJP has been the rising force getting increasing support from significant sections of the ruling classes. For such a party which is bent upon legitimizing the Hindutva agenda, it is actually beneficial if there is greater political promiscuity. Politicians from the non-BJP stream joining the BJP gives its respectability and those from the sangh combine joining other parties helps to make its politics less untouchable' (ibid.). Karat continues: 'the spectacle of Kalyan Singh joining hands with Mulayam Singh and then returning to the BJP fold in the space of three years; Laloo Prasad Yadav nominating a known VHP man in Muzafarpur and a Babri Masjid demolitionist in Gaya; or the Congress leadership beaming at the arrival of a defector from the BJP are not symptoms of the weakening of the BJP but the facile acceptance of the BJP as another bourgeois party, though fortunate enough to be in power at the Centre'. What all this shows clearly is that with respect to secularism, the bourgeois-secular parties are only vacillating allies of the Left.

39   One may remind oneself of Bhagat Singh, the non-sectarian freedom fighter, here: 'The real duty of the newspapers is to educate, to cleanse the minds of people, to save them from narrow sectarian divisiveness, and to eradicate communal feelings to promote the idea of common nationalism. Instead, their main objective seems to be spreading ignorance, preaching and propagating sectarianism and chauvinism, communalising people's

other members of the family propagating Hindutva, have gained a place on TV channels and academic platforms (including in Science congresses) demonstrates how normalized the fascistic tendencies have been, especially, in the minds of urban middle 'classy' people and other strata.[40] Such a process of normalization was achieved partly by the BJP hiring a PR firm (Washington-based, APCO) to obliterate the bad things that it does and to hype up its false promises to make them appear more real than they are (Banaji, 2016b: x). The fascistic cause has also obtained support from the diaspora elements who seem to be more 'communal-patriotic' outside of the country than when they were inside. The Hindu-diasporic elements, like the new middle class elements in new sectors such as the IT industry, seek to fill their 'cultural vacuum', their lack of connection to society from which they have come from, by turning to 'godmen' and religious teachers, as Chris Fuller and John Harriss suggest (quoted in Deshmane, 2017), and this has contributed to the BJP's cause.[41]

3.8   Electoral Tactic

The fascistic movement is not just interested in remaining a movement. It is interested in using elections to capture state power, and use state power to further the fascistic agenda. Now, how does its electoral strategy works?

It has become a common electoral practice to incite the sentiments of the religious minorities and act against their interests, engineer a communal riot (especially where its base is weak or its acceptability is in decline), polarize votes and win elections, so several months prior to a major election, communal riots happen or conditions for these riots are deliberately created by the fascistic elements (see Fig. 12.4).[42] Such a strategy, the aim of which is to garner

---

minds leading to the destruction of our composite culture and shared heritage' (quoted in Habib, 2018).

40   A retired professor of political science once told me that there was a need for leftists to engage with and inform the Right-wing people about the leftist views. Such an approach to fascists is different from the non-platform approach (Renton, 2007): fascistic people who have no respect for democratic values, cannot be allowed a platform for discussion.

41   'Indians settled abroad, clinging to obscurantist versions of their religion in an effort to salvage their identity in an alien context, have thrown their weight – and funds – on the side of reaction in their home country' (S. Gopal quoted in Singh, 2010: 86). Interestingly, many of these people are highly educated Indians living in modern cosmopolitan and multi-cultural and multi-religion cities like Toronto, New York, Dallas, etc.

42   'The Godhra train incident in March 2002 provided Narendra Modi with the perfect opportunity to sponsor massive "retaliation" against Muslims' (Ahmad, 2013: 10), and such a retaliation by galvanizing conservatives Hindus boosted BJP's electoral strength. The latter was used to attack the interests of the ordinary people, whether Hindus or Muslims, through the BJP's 'neoliberal-predatory' capitalist policies originally in Gujarat, and later, at the national level, following the 2014 general election. There is a parallel here with US imperialism: the US used the 9/11 as a pretext, as an opportunity to launch a new round of

Hindu votes, may be combined with some demagogic promise of economic help, which hardly comes.[43]

And when the party comes to power, two things happen. First, RSS and other elements of the Sangh Parivar get support from the BJP being in power, to expand its (i.e. RSS's) tentacles inside the apparatuses of the state, including educational and coercive institutions, which is why any illegal and undemocratic activity by the *Parivar* can go unpunished. Second, violence against the minorities continues as a means of the expansion of the communal-fascistic influence (and in opposition to secular forces including of the Left),[44] and this is possible because the attackers know they will be, more or less, protected by the government (Figure 12.5).

By deploying all these techniques, the fascistic movement led by the BJP has been growing in strength. This has had a palpable material effect of the communal-fascistic-bourgeois movement that is also blatantly anti-communist. This can be seen from the standpoint of the fascistic forces' relation to the business class and to the masses. In India's contemporary conservative climate – which has been in the making since at least the late 1980s and which is characterized by the emergence of the BJP, as a party of the Right (a blatantly pro-business party) – what is good for the business class is seen by this authoritarian party as being good for the nation (all one needs to do is hide the interests of the business class by such talk as 'development'). Indeed, seven things have come together as different elements of the deadly fascistic tendency which have made the BJP such a strong bourgeois party with a communal agenda: *nation*, interests of the *business class*, *development*, governance, *Hindu religion*, and an *authoritarian political party*, that is rooted in a *mass movement*. Several conflations exist. The interest of the nation is the interest of the business class. And the territory of Hindu religion is the nation's territory, as Hinduism defines the soul of the nation. This means that: the interests of the *business class* are the interests of the nation, which is defined as the nation of Hindus (all those subordinated to Hindus), and the interests of the Hindu nation are the interests of the business class. Business interests are also hidden behind the screen of *development* and *governance*, both of which the government is apparently pursuing in a manner it sees fit. If one says anything against the government's pro-business policies (or any other policies that adversely impact ordinary people and minorities), or against the undemocratic

---

imperialist-military attack. On the connection between electoral competition and communal riots, see Jairath (2014).

43 The BJP does treat Hindus – and especially those who subscribe to Hindutva – as a vote bank, even if it has criticized Congress for engaging in vote bank politics.

44 Fascistic violence is justified on the basis of hurt sentiments: perceived insults, including to tradition, religion, nation, etc. is used as a pretext for mob violence (Simeon, 2016: 161).

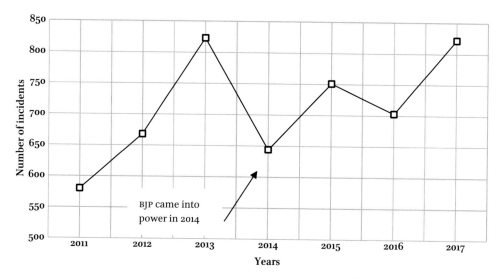

FIGURE 12.5 Incidents involving conflicts between different religious groups in India

aspects of the majority religion or against the empirically false claims of Hindutva ideologues, one is considered anti-national. One has to accept, it seems, that whatever the right-wing authoritarian Hindu-nationalist government does is for the nation.[45]

The *ideology* of the homogenous nation is used to support pro-business policies and thus has a *material* effect: for the ruling class, fascistic tendencies are a blessing (even if not in an entirely unproblematic way). The nationalist ideology has a material consequence for the masses as well, but in a diametrically opposite way. For the masses, it means material sacrifice at the altar of *vikas*. The BJP asks for sacrifices from masses for the nation, which, for it, stands above the masses and their exploiters. In concrete terms, the fascistic notion of the nation means this: 'in the interest of the nation, give your hand and land for industrialists', and 'do not ask for higher wages or better working conditions from your employers'. The notion of nationalism held by the fascistic brigade is a religion-driven mental state (a Hindu nation) rather than one that signifies the nation as the nation of the toilers of different religions, genders, and castes, so the BJP's notion of nationalism is such that it cannot be used as a tool in the fight against the capitalists who exploit the toilers, whether they are Hindus or Muslims or Christians. The BJP's notion of the nation is

---

45 When Arun Jaitley, a prominent leader of the BJP and the current finance minister, says that 'freedom of expression cannot be at the expense of the nation', he is demanding in effect that people should "sacrifice" their freedom of expression, which is their fundamental right, for the sake of this metaphysical concept of a "nation" (Patnaik, 2016: 6).

also not the nation as a people oppressed by imperialism, so such a notion of the nation cannot be mobilized against imperialism either; and yet the Hindutva movement hypocritically calls itself nationalist.[46] The fascistic-nationalist movement is not only palpably pro-capitalist but also is it shamelessly subordinating the interests of toiling masses living in India to imperialism.[47] This is the real treachery, and this is the real treason, as far as the toiling tormented majority are concerned.

4   The Contradictory Character of the BJP

What one thing, or what one process is, is because of its relations to many other things and processes. The world is the world of internal relations. In dialectics, of all the different types of relations, contradiction is the most important relation (Ollman, 2003). Lenin (1914b) says: 'The splitting of a single whole and the cognition of its contradictory parts... is the *essence*... of dialectics'. And contradiction permeates the body of internal relations. The current situation in India and the world is one of major contradictions.

a.   The contradiction between productive forces and production relations is ultimately behind the economic crisis of capitalism, which is expressed in the fact that the economic growth rate, rise in productivity and the rate of increase in the creation of jobs, etc., all suffer. Productive forces are being fettered by capitalist social relations of competition, profit-making, and exploitation.

---

46   When anti-imperialist nationalism is undermined, this opens an opportunity for communalist-fascistic nationalism: 'In its relations with the global economy', the Indian state 'no longer represents the Indian people and their interests to the world; the principal task that the neoliberal state in India has assigned to itself is that of transmitting the interests and orders of international finance capital to the Indian people. And this is so despite the surviving but utterly hollowed out institutions of representative electoral democracy. In this situation, the state must in practice abandon the kind of secular nationalism that had been the basis of our anti-colonial movements, and a powerful Right-wing gets into high gear to redefine Indian nationalism in religious, obscurantist, High Brahminical terms which offer no resistance to imperialism' (Ahmad, 2013: 21).

47   The Hindutva brigade, actually, had no/little role in the anti-colonial struggle itself that created the nation that we see now; in fact, the fascistic movement offered to cooperate with the colonial powers, treating the Muslims as the real enemy. According to Vanaik (2017), RSS is not fascist because it supported colonial power or did not fight against it. He says: 'That the 'ultra-nationalism' of the RSS and Hindu Mahasabha never led it to participate in the National movement for independence from British colonial rule, or even openly to espouse anti-imperialism, has always been an embarrassment of sorts for those labelling them as fascists' (p. 312).

b. The economic crisis becomes the social crisis (or social and ecological crisis) in that capitalism simply fails to create enough opportunities to meet the social-ecological needs of the masses (there are hunger and malnutrition and rising inequalities; and there is massive environmental degradation).

c. In capitalism, there is a contradiction between economic inequality (property owners and property-less) and political equality (all citizens are equal before law).

d. The latter contradiction now comes to coexist with another contradiction. This is within the sphere of bourgeois politics. When economic and social crisis creates a condition for authoritarianism, the formal political equality – the formally democratic character of relations between the rulers and the ruled – is undermined: some citizens (a religious majority; people with right-wing views) are politically privileged relative to other citizens (religious minorities; people who dissent from the system). The right-wing party makes use of grass-roots right-wing forces to intimidate, repress and divide the masses, and makes use of state's repressive forces (e.g. police; investigative agencies such as Central Bureau of Investigation in India, etc.) against minorities and progressive forces and indeed against even opposition bourgeois parties. This means that there is a contradiction between formal political equality and actual political *inequality*.

e. Further, when a right-wing party comes to power promising to address people's problems and thus respond to the economic and social crisis of capitalism, but fails to do anything (much), a further political contradiction is created. This is a contradiction between policy-promise and policy-outcome, and thus between words and reality, which will potentially fuel the resentment of the toiling masses. Resolving this *political* contradiction further reinforces the tendency towards the use of authoritarian methods, in the absence of a sufficiently strong Left movement, an absence that reflects a contradiction of its own (contradiction between the severity of economic-political problems of the masses and the weakness of the Left movement relative to the task at hand).

The rise of the BJP represents the crisis not only of bourgeois economics but also of bourgeois politics: the bourgeois system, and therefore, the bourgeois ruling class, has, simply, failed to secure not only social rights but also democratic rights, including rights of religious minorities. So the blame for the current situation – attack on democratic rights and the growing strength of fascistic forces – must be at the door not only of the BJP and its supporting forces, but also the bourgeois class itself. That is why the fascistic threat is a class project, and not merely a political-cultural project. The contradictory aspect of that class project is this: while the ruling class is increasingly losing its right to be the ruling class, the masses are not yet ready to say 'we cannot take it anymore'.

In other words, what all this signifies, and points to, is a strong tendency towards the breakdown of the liberal-democratic shell of India's (peripheral) capitalism. The current situation is one of a series of contradictions in the economic, social, and political spheres. And because the contradictions are those that are of the bourgeois system as a whole, they cannot be resolved by capitalism and its political system, even if it is managed by a party such as India's BJP, which is seen as, and which claims to be, a strong party, led by a strong leader.

5   Conclusion

The increasing strength of right-wing forces, including the rise of the BJP as the political head of these forces in India, has been engendered by four mechanisms. Three of these mechanisms are discussed in the previous chapter. These are mainly political-economic mechanisms.

The first is the crisis of global capitalism, the crisis that is manifested in India. The second is the combination of exploitation, dispossession, and immiserization requires legitimization/justification in the minds of the masses as well as an authoritarian response. And then there is the fact that capitalism produces a vast reserve army of labor and pauperized small-scale producers, the elements of which, in a poor economy without social benefits (or with very limited benefits) from the government, are vulnerable to lumpenization and criminality.

However, just because capitalism creates a need for fascistic forces and just because capitalism creates lumpen elements that can be used by the fascistic project, that does not necessarily mean there will be fascistic forces in *active operation*. The political has a relative autonomy. The bourgeois-political dynamics of the rise of fascistic tendencies are discussed in this chapter.

The failure of bourgeois politics as well as Left politics – indeed, the failure of the entire bourgeois political system – to defend democracy and secularism is a crucial process contributing to the rise of the BJP. The whole determines the parts and the parts influence the whole. The Congress and the BJP are two faces of Indian bourgeois politics, both promoting neoliberal capitalism, and the BJP using the religious divide to distinguish itself in the election market. There has indeed been the decline of the relatively secular bourgeois national party (the Congress) and attendant 'capital flight' from the Congress to the BJP. It is as if the following has happened: as Nehruvianism (semi-statist developmental model with very muted elements of social democracy), in part influenced by the Bombay plan, saved the Indian bourgeoisie from the any threat of struggle from below (any communist threat, potential and actual) in the post-1917 period, the fascistic threat came in its turn to liberate the bourgeoisie from Nehruvianism, in a condition where a strong Left movement is absent.

Much of what we see in India and elsewhere in terms of fascistic tendencies can be captured by these lines except that we are not talking about fascism but fascistic tendencies: 'Fascism is a product of two conditions: a sharp social crisis on the one hand; the revolutionary weakness of the ... proletariat on the other' (Trotsky, 1931a).[48] The proletarian has been kept weak due to bourgeois-reformist organizations of every type and by the communist parties which have failed 'to unite the workers under the banner of the revolution' as well as by the far left tendencies to do much to organize the workers (Trotsky, 1931a).

The 'turn of the fascist regime arrives' when 'the "normal" police and military resources of the bourgeois dictatorship, together with their parliamentary screens, no longer suffice to hold society in a state of equilibrium' (Trotsky, 1944). Then 'Through the fascist agency, capitalism sets in motion the masses of the crazed petty bourgeoisie, and bands of the declassed and demoralized lumpenproletariat – all the countless human beings whom finance capital itself has brought to desperation and frenzy' (Trotsky, 1944). But during a transitional stage, such extreme measures are not yet necessary. Normal resources play the dominant role, supplemented by fascistic forces. But the latter forces play a consent-generating role: deploying lies and brainwashing about what a nation means, about the Hindutva, etc., to make people believe in the fascistic vision. The petty bourgeois fascist forces also seek to undermine ideas about labor and proletarian movement.[49] The proportion of assistance that capital mobilizes from the normal resources (e.g. state's police forces) as opposed to fascist sources can also change depending on the severity of crisis and strength of the anti-capitalist forces. But (already) the division between the normal forces and the fascistic forces is getting blurred because of the increasing penetration of fascistic ideas and practices inside the state. This means that

---

48   'Fascism is ... the final link of a specific political cycle composed of the following: the gravest crisis of capitalist society; the growth of the radicalization of the working class; the growth of sympathy toward the working class and a yearning for change on the part of the rural and urban petty bourgeoisie; the extreme confusion of the big bourgeoisie; its cowardly and treacherous maneuvers aimed at avoiding the revolutionary climax; the exhaustion of the proletariat, growing confusion and indifference; the aggravation of the social crisis; the despair of the petty bourgeoisie, its yearning for change, the collective neurosis of the petty bourgeoisie, its readiness to believe in miracles; its readiness for violent measures; the growth of hostility towards the proletariat which has deceived its expectations. These are the premises for a swift formation of a fascist party and its victory' (Trotsky, 1944).

49   'The passage to fascism, on the contrary, is inconceivable without the preceding permeation of the petty bourgeoisie with hatred of the proletariat' (Trotsky, 1934a).

elements inside the state' normal coercive forces are sympathizing with, and even supporting, the fascistic forces, who, in turn, protect these elements from any potential threat of punitive action from what is left of bourgeois democracy and its constitutional rules.

The increasing strength of right-wing forces represents a most extreme form of the latent tendency towards an attack on democracy, the tendency that exists in capitalist societies when there is massive inequality and where the most basic needs of the masses remain unmet while a tiny class basks in obscene amount of wealth and income, under conditions of capitalist economic crisis. The tendency is expressed when capitalism is no longer a progressive force, when it is constantly in crisis, when the working class poses a threat to its class rule, while it fails to transcend the capitalist class relation.[50]

The ruling class comes up with a solution to its crisis-ridden life by resorting to fascism or fascistic tendencies. Fundamental to the worldview of the forces playing the politics of hatred against religious and other types of minorities, is the idolization of *free market economics* in the interest of the business class, and of *authoritarian politics*. Authoritarian politics is necessary to implement free market economics in the interest of property-owning classes. This is especially so in an unequal, poverty-stricken, relatively backward society like India where millions of people are not only subjected to economic miseries caused

---

50   What this means is that when capitalism is due for overthrow but is not overthrown morbid symptoms appear. In his last article, Trotsky said this in response to those who say that 'contrary to Marx's prognosis fascism came instead of socialism'. 'Nothing is more stupid and vulgar than this criticism. Marx demonstrated and proved that when capitalism reaches a certain level the only way out for society lies in the socialization of the means of production, i.e., socialism. He also demonstrated that in view of the class structure of society the proletariat alone is capable of solving this task in an irreconcilable revolutionary struggle against the bourgeoisie. He further demonstrated that for the fulfillment of this task the proletariat needs a revolutionary party. ... [The] opportunism of the summits of the working class, subject to the bourgeoisie's influence, could obstruct, slow down, make more difficult, postpone the fulfillment of the revolutionary task of the proletariat. It is precisely this condition of society that we are now observing. Fascism did not at all come "instead" of socialism. Fascism is the continuation of capitalism, an attempt to perpetuate its existence by means of the most bestial and monstrous measures. Capitalism obtained an opportunity to resort to fascism only because the proletariat did not accomplish the socialist revolution in time. The proletariat was paralyzed in the fulfillment of its task by the opportunist parties. '[There] turned out to be more obstacles, more difficulties, more stages on the road of the revolutionary development of the proletariat than was foreseen by the founders of scientific socialism. Fascism and the series of imperialist wars constitute the terrible school in which the proletariat has to free itself of petty bourgeois traditions and superstitions, has to rid itself of opportunist, democratic and adventurist parties, has to hammer out and train the revolutionary vanguard and in this way prepare for the solving of the task apart from which there is not, and cannot be, any salvation for the development of mankind' (Trotsky, 1940).

by capitalism but are also fighting against their miseries, and who therefore have to be suppressed/managed through authoritarian means, if the business class has to be kept happy. The ideology and practices of free market economics and authoritarian politics are dressed up by right-wing demagogic leaders, as, for example, development and good governance, respectively, and sold to voters in the election market. These two catchwords – development and good governance (or similar terms) – resonate with common people who are economically poor and who are also subjected to bureaucratic apathy. These terms are used, along with hyper-nationalism based in the idea of the supremacy of an ethnic group or a religion (e.g. Hinduism), to help produce/spark a *mass movement*. In short: blatant free market economic ideas and policies,[51] rabid religious nationalism, and authoritarian intolerance towards rational dissent: all these come together, support each other, and produce a grassroots movement. This is the best way to describe it all: fascist/fascistic tendency (see Figure 12.6). I describe the Indian situation as one which has fascistic tendencies but which is not yet fascist.[52]

Make no mistake: the BJP is not an ordinary political party. Yet, the fact that it is an ordinary party is the perception among wide layers of the population. This is a perception that has been slowly produced, over decades, by the corporate media, sections of the middle class and of the business world, so much so that the views of this party and its fascistic supporters including RSS ideologues on a given topic have become a part of polite, civilized and public discussions on television channels, in classrooms, conferences, and elsewhere. This shows how far to the right public life has moved in India.

The BJP's goal is to see an India that is not only 'Congress-free' ('Congress-mukt') (because the Congress has generally tried to 'defend' secular values) but also 'Left-free' ('Left-mukt') or indeed 'communist-mukt'.[53] This shows that the right-wing forces are much more than mere Hindutva-nationalist forces. Their threat is much more than the threat to secularism and bourgeois democracy. They are fundamentally capitalist, anti-proletarian, anti-communist forces whose fascistic aim is to destroy not only the democratic-secular ethos of the nation but also those militant organizations of the class-conscious masses, of

---

51   In the advanced country, free market economics inside a country can co-exist with protectionism; in poorer economies, free market economics is appealed to both inside a country and globally (liberalization of import and export, for example).

52   Fascistic tendencies in terms of mechanisms that *can* produce a fascist or a fascist type state, and in terms of fascistic organizations.

53   'In their victory speeches made at the BJP headquarters in New Delhi after the results of the Tripura elections were announced, Prime Minister Modi and the President of the ruling party promised to free India of communists...a "Communist-*mukt Bharat*". Modi declared that it was an "ideological victory" over the communists'.

workers and peasants of India that do not preach class unity between the exploiter and the exploited (to the extent that the fascistic movement wants).

The BJP makes use of whatever elements of the democratic system it can use to subvert the values of the democratic system itself in the service of a communal-bourgeois agenda and to establish a system where political power is always in the hands of the majority-religion. It acknowledges the existence of minority religions as long as the latter lie low and do not assert their rights or challenge members of the majority religion.[54] It is worth repeating that the BJP is at the center of, and political head of, an ideologically-driven mass movement that is rooted in small-scale producers and un- and under-employed people and politically backward elements in the working class, a movement that attacks democratic and social rights of workers and peasants. This fascistic movement is like an auto-immune disease in which the body's own immune system kills the cells of the body by mistakenly treating them as foreign and harmful. It is a movement *by* common people *against* common people.[55] While the working class is the strongest defenders of the democratic rights (in part because it needs these rights to mobilize itself), some elements of this class turn themselves against other elements, mistakenly treating the latter as anti-national and harmful. And such divisions within the working class and indeed among the small-scale producers, benefit the bourgeoisie and the parties representing its interests. True to its right-wing nature, the BJP pursues neoliberal policies to create opportunities for national and imperialist capital. It subordinates India to US or any other form of imperialism, in spite of its demagogic, hypocritical discourse about nationalism; it would indeed justify such subordination to imperialism on the ground that that makes the nation stronger militarily. The BJP along with the fascistic movement is a threat to everyone who is committed to the culture of decency and civility in public discourse, to democracy, secularism and to the principle of rational dissent.[56] It is against the basic class interests of the majority of the population.[57] There

---

54   It is true that the 'majority of Muslims have punctually sought a secular electoral alternative' but then this fact is 'not because they are particularly secular in their own outlook', but 'because they expect greater security for themselves in a secular dispensation.'; indeed, Muslims can be as communal as Hindus (Ahmad, 2013: 16).

55   The foot-soldiers of the fascistic movement as a mass movement are ordinary people and that movement by supporting capitalism works against the ordinary people.

56   In fact, in a typical fascistic style, prominent members of the Sangh Parivar, including the BJP, represent any criticism of their statements and practices as illiberal and as intolerant; they paint themselves as victims.

57   Interestingly, when the Shiv Sena, the Right-wing organization as a part of the communalist-fascist family, campaigns against Biharis coming into Maharastra for wage-work, it does not distinguish between Hindu Biharis and non-Hindu Biharis (Ahmad, 2013: 18).

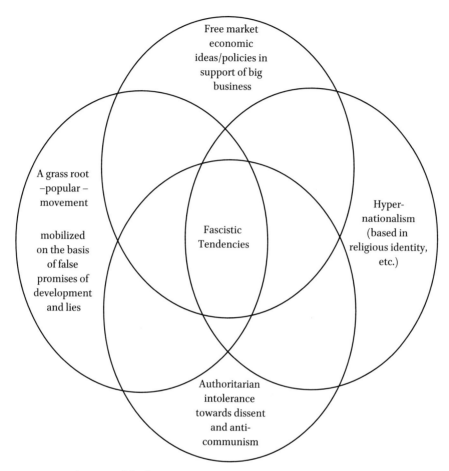

FIGURE 12.6 Anatomy of the fascistic movement
SOURCE: AUTHOR

is no doubt that the bourgeois political rule in India – as in many other countries of the world – is taking an increasingly fascistic form, even if India does not as yet have a fascist state, the 'finished product' that has finished elements of democracy. When a robber with a weapon is running towards us from a distance, we may not see him fully and we may see his silhouette only, but that

---

And this 'illustrates how easily a communalism can move back and forth between the religio-fascist form of Hindutva and the sub-national, ethno-regional posture of Marathi exclusivity' (pp. 18–19). So, the problems of Maharashtra are seen as being caused by migrants and not because of capitalism and the uneven development it produces.

does not mean that he is not running towards us and that we are not in imminent danger.

It is less true to say that the BJP is a communal party that just happens to support the business class. It is truer to say that the BJP is fundamentally a bourgeois party that makes use of communal hatred to attain political influence and in the process serves bourgeois interests (as well as some reactionary interests of a bigoted section of the citizenry). Communalism (religious-sectarian hatred), or antagonism based in religious difference, may have a degree of autonomy with respect to capitalism or with respect to capitalism as it exists at a given point in time. But once it exists, capitalism makes full use of it and feeds into it.

The BJP, like similar parties elsewhere, is a party with a mission: to destroy the deeply-cherished values of a civilized society. When all parties more or less aspire to satisfy the demands of the business class, then in the competitive market for votes, it helps if a party can make use of dangerous gimmicks such as religious pride and hyper-nationalism to package itself as a unique commodity in the electoral market. The BJP is a national party that is not only pro-business but also communally divisive, a party that crushes not only economic rights but also democratic rights of toiling masses. While the BJP government defends the interests of the top 1–10% by not restricting the greedy pursuit of profit, it hurts the economic interests of the masses *and* undermines their power to fight back. While all recent governments have, more or less, done the same, the BJP's method is much more dangerous: it makes use of religion, hyper-nationalism and historical distortions in order to divide the masses. It resorts to authoritarianism to weaken those who oppose it and its policies, bypassing parliament and harassing critics. It now seems a common BJP strategy to engineer a communal riot, polarize voters and win elections based on hatred and fear.[58] And once this communal party is in power, there are further communal attacks as the perpetrators know that they will be directly or indirectly protected by the BJP. Communal riots often give a sense of satisfaction to the economically desperate lumpen elements created by capitalism, making

---

58 In fact, it is widely known that the BJP came to prominence from obscurity on the basis of demolishing a centuries-old mosque in Uttar Pradesh by mobilizing its right-wing Hindu-fundamentalist forces in mid-1990s. In more recent times, in the recently concluded Karnataka elections in May 2018, a major reason it garnered votes was that it created Hindu-Muslim tensions and communal violence, in coastal Karnataka. It is also mobilizing its forces to build a temple for Lord Ram in the place (where there was a mosque which the communal right-wing forces demolished in 1992) in order to stoke communal tension in the run-up to the 2019 federal election.

them believe that they can do something in life. But many of them are, more or less, unaware pawns in the larger communal-corporate 'game'.

A part of the blame for this tragic situation must be on the Left itself. The Left defines the current stage of Indian revolution as a democratic revolution, a stage at which an important task of the Left is to protect the democratic rights of minorities. Yet, what we see is the fiercest attack on democratic rights from communal-fascistic forces. At the same time, it is also the case that the fascistic forces have come to constitute a very powerful obstacle to the Left movement, including in the bastions of Left influence.[59] And, the relative weakness of the Left is partly responsible for the increasing strength of the fascistic forces. These forces are a clear threat to the communist movement on the ground, as we have been seeing in Tripura and Kerala (and also in West Bengal), where communists and their offices are being physically attacked. So, the fascistic forces will have to be stopped, and stopped right now. The question is how?

---

59 Note that the appearance of communal politics has split Left's political energy between the fight against neoliberal policies and the fight against communalism.

CHAPTER 13

Forward March of the Right and the Relative Weakness of the Left: What Is to Be Done?

The bourgeois political rule in India – as in many other countries – is taking an increasingly fascistic form, even if India does *not* have a full-fledged fascist state. The rise of the BJP, the political 'head' of the fascistic movement in India, has been engendered by a multiplicity of mechanisms, which are, more or less, rooted in bourgeois economy and bourgeois politics. The fascistic forces constitute a very powerful obstacle to, and reflects relative weakness of, the progressive and the Left movement. In several parts of India, communists and their offices are being physically attacked, and communists are being killed or harmed by the fascistic forces. So, the fascistic forces will have to be stopped immediately. These forces must be the target of an all-out fight, a fight on economic, political and ideological fronts.[1] The question is how, and what role the Marxist Left has in this?

This penultimate chapter begins with the Marxist theory of Left politics (Section 1). It argues that the Marxist Left must mobilize its *basic classes* (skilled and unskilled workers, self-employed small-scale producers, and unemployed people) with help from politically progressive ('de-classed') intellectuals, against the fascistic brigade, in the *extra-electoral* sphere, as a part of the struggle to transcend the capitalist class relations that are at the origin of the fascistic tendencies. This should be *the dominant approach* to fighting the fascistic movement. On the basis of their large numbers as well as rallies and general strikes, and local-level people's committees, Marxist forces must take the lead, where possible, in countering the fascistic movement and stop it from physically intimidating people.[2] It must be stressed that the Marxist movement is the most principled opponent of fascism. This was understood by Hitler.[3]

---

1 In some ways, the BJP is to the Indian communist movement what the Tsar rule was to the Russian communist movement, and must be treated accordingly.

2 Actually, the BJP has done one good thing: by putting the Left in the same category as Muslims and Christians, as the threat to the nation, it has treated the Left as a friend of minorities. That strategy is potentially making the fight against fascistic tendency a part of the fight against capitalism.

3 Hitler said: 'Only one thing could have stopped our movement – if our adversaries had understood its principle and, from the first day, had smashed with the utmost brutality the nucleus of our new movement' (quoted in Renton, 2007: 113).

© KONINKLIJKE BRILL NV, LEIDEN, 2020 | DOI:10.1163/9789004415560_014

In the light of the basic Marxist principles, the relative strength and weakness of *actually-existing* Left politics in India are discussed in Section 2. It deals with the question of what is to be done *now* to undermine the fascistic threat? If the fascistic forces return to power in 2019, a huge amount of irreparable damage will be done both to the democratic movement and to the communist movement. The Indian Left – all the Left parties from the right to the left – must mobilize its forces extra-electorally against the fascistic movement at local, regional and national scales. But to the extent that the electoral arena is also an important area of struggle in a liberal democracy, some might argue that the Left, given its relative electoral weakness, will have to have some temporary 'understanding' with 'reasonably secular' non-left political parties (*without* being a part of any governmental front and with its full organizational autonomy). Such a proposal potentially contradicts the principle that the Left politics must be independent of bourgeois forces. Section 3 then turns to what I will call *Lenin's theory of temporary revolutionary compromise,* hoping that this will help us critically assess the possibility of, and necessity for, a temporary compromise between Left forces and secular non-Left forces, in order to thwart fascistic tendencies *now* and thus *advance* class struggle. The last section concludes the chapter. It returns to Marx to remind the Left that the fight for democracy (including the fight for the rights of religious and other minorities) is only a beginning on a long march towards a socialist society, one that is democratic in the political sphere as well as the economic sphere. Whether the Indian Left's theory and practice are in line with Marx's principles is a different matter.

1 A General Theory of Left Politics in an Age of Fascistic Threats/Tendencies[4]

Capitalism is the root cause of the attack on democracy and on the living standards of the masses. Capitalism does not grant democratic rights and economic concessions without a fight for these by the masses, and no matter how contradiction-ridden capitalism is, it will not fall without class struggle. Whether it is state-directed capitalism or neoliberal capitalism, workers and small-scale producers will have to engage in a united battle to defend and deepen democratic rights, including the rights of religious minorities, and to get some concessions for an improvement in their living conditions, as a part

---

4 This section is informed by Das (2017: Chapters 11–12), and Das (2019).

of the fight for a new society beyond capitalism. There is no other way out of their problems:

> The revolutionary dialectic has long since pointed the way out and has demonstrated it by countless examples in the most diverse spheres: by correlating the struggle for power with the struggle for reforms; by maintaining complete independence of the party while preserving the unity of the trade unions; by fighting against the bourgeois regime and at the same time utilizing its institutions; by relentlessly criticizing parliamentarism – from the parliamentary tribunal; by waging war mercilessly against reformism, and at the same time making practical agreements with the reformists in partial struggles.
>
> TROTSKY, 1932b

One might even entertain the possibility of entering into a compromise with the hangman. Not always, but under certain conditions:

> To support the hangman in every action directed against the workers is a crime, if not treachery: that is just what the alliance of Stalin with Chiang Kai-shek consisted of. But if this same Chinese hangman were to find himself engaged tomorrow in a war with the Japanese imperialists, then practical fighting agreements of the Chinese workers with the hangman Chiang Kai-shek would be quite permissible and even – a duty.
>
> TROTSKY, 1932l

Of course:

> The possibility of betrayal is always contained in reformism. But this does not mean to say that reformism and betrayal are one and the same thing at every moment. Not quite. Temporary agreements may be made with the reformists whenever they take a step forward.
>
> TROTSKY, 1929

Workers should fight for concessions to improve their conditions within capitalism. The struggle for reforms can – and must – include the struggle for the conditions of struggle, i.e. the 'political freedoms, the right of assembly and association, and the freedom of the press', etc. (Marx, 1871a). The fight against capitalism does require a fight for the conditions for that fight. And in our times, the Right-wing, fascistic, hyper-nationalist forces are the most potent conjunctural obstacle right now to the fight against capitalism.

The struggle for reforms is necessary because without this struggle, workers' conditions will be worse: 'capital, if not checked, will recklessly and ruthlessly work to cast down the whole working class to ... the utmost state of degradation ...' (Marx, 1976: 54). The struggle for economic and political reforms can create: 'elbow-room for development and movement' (Marx's letter to Kugelmann in Marx, 1868a). It is problematic to say that one should not struggle for a rise in wages on the ground that 'to struggle to increase one's wages or to prevent their decrease is like recognizing *wages*' (Marx, 2010: 327; italics in original).

The struggle for reforms, in economic and political spheres, can not only cause some improvement of people's conditions. This can also contribute to the development of their consciousness, as they learn about economy and polity on the basis of their agitational experience.[5] As '*the tribune of the people*', a Marxist party/movement must: 'react to every manifestation of tyranny and oppression, no matter where it appears, no matter what stratum or class of the people it affects; who is able to generalise all these manifestations and produce a single picture of police violence and capitalist exploitation' (Lenin, 1901). Lenin elaborates the idea of the tribune of the people thus: '*Any and every* manifestation of police tyranny and autocratic outrage' [is] a means of "drawing in" the masses' into political struggle' (ibid.). The cases of tyranny and oppression include:

> *the flogging of peasants, the corruption of the officials* and *the police treatment of the "common people"* in the cities, the fight against the famine-stricken and the suppression of the popular striving towards enlightenment and knowledge, the extortion of taxes and *the persecution of the religious sects*, the humiliating treatment of soldiers and *the barrack methods in the treatment of the students and liberal intellectuals.*
>
> Ibid.; italics added

In the Marxist theoretical perspective pursued here, Marxist parties, retaining their organizational independence vis-à-vis bourgeois forces, must mobilize workers and small-scale producers (e.g. poor peasants) for a multi-pronged struggle. Firstly, it is a struggle against the curtailment of democratic rights. These rights include: the right to free speech (online and offline) and public assembly and to form a trade union and to engage in political resistance,

---

5 Marx at times appeared to be more sanguine than necessary about his view of the role of the struggle for reforms in generating anti-capitalist political consciousness.

without intimidation from the state or private forces.[6] The democratic rights also include the rights to: practice any religion one wishes; eat whatever food one chooses (beef or not); love and marry whoever one wants to; and be free from caste, gender, linguistic, ethnic, and geographical discrimination, and from remnants of feudal oppression. An important democratic right to struggle for is the right to receive an education that not only respects scientific temper, secularism,[7] and international solidarity with peoples of other nations and respect for their culture, but also encourages students and the wider citizenry to (a) celebrate the scientific successes of a nation, including those that might be recorded in its ancient and modern non-fiction and literary texts, as well as its literary and mythological accomplishments,[8] and (b) to develop an evidence-based, critical attitude towards one's history, culture, and the political-economic system.[9] Democratic rights cannot be respected where certain groups defined on the basis of religion or caste or race or gender, have inferior rights than other such groups.[10] The fascistic forces are crushing or curtailing all these democratic rights, so a lower-class mobilization is necessary against such curtailment, on the basis of the strength of communist workers.[11]

6   These include: moral police of the Right; private armies or goons of landlords/capitalists and politicians; and Hindutva vigilante groups.

7   The Left's demand must be: no one – no religious leader – should be allowed to use religion and religious places for political activity.

8   All social groups, including indigenous communities, who happen to practice different religions, have made contributions to society. These contributions are recorded in their religious and secular texts and which exist in their oral traditions. In earlier times, when society had a rather limited amount of control over natural forces, religious ideas (including deification of nature) had a special significance which is why some secular ideas about society, nature and the mind were embedded in what are dominantly religious (and mythological) texts. One can always examine these ideas, based on modern science and modern theory of society, to look for scientific and proto-scientific insights in those ancient texts, distinguish them from mythological and purely religious ideas, and where possible further develop them, and reject the unscientific ideas that exist.

9   It is interesting to note that Buddhist ideas about meditation, embedded in what are religious texts, have now been, more or less, corroborated by neuro-scientific investigation (Davidson, 2012). It is also important that a text which is mythological (in which it might be written that god x and goddess y were born in place p_1 or place p_2) should not be treated as one that is historical.

10   One's own religious preference must be, more or less, a private affair, and the state must not show any preference, or loyalty, for any specific religious group. The state must ensure that minority religions are protected against discrimination from the majority religion. The state must not also tolerate violent attack on majority religious groups from minority religious group.

11   One can say that the number of people supporting fascism or fascistic groups electorally (and otherwise) is increasing or large, relative of those who support communists. But this is a mistaken comparison. 'Yes, they have received many votes. But in the social struggle, votes are not decisive. On the scales of election statistics, a thousand fascist votes weigh

FORWARD MARCH OF THE RIGHT AND THE RELATIVE WEAKNESS

Secondly, workers and small-scale independent producers led by the Left must fight against the attack on their living standards, expressed in the form of government austerity, deplorable working conditions, repression of wages, and growing economic inequalities. The masses must make not only immediate demands but also transitional demands.[12] And the concept of the transitional demands must be suitably expanded to include both economic (and political) concessions and ecological sustainability.[13] In the process of organizing such struggles over democracy – these include struggles against fascistic threat to democracy – and over economy, and through imparting ideological education and mobilizing people on the basis of immediate and transitional demands, the Marxist parties must, gradually, help the basic classes transform the reformist (trade unionist) consciousness into class consciousness proper, which means this: given that wealth and income (profit, rent and interest) come, ultimately, from the fruits of labor of workers (and from dispossession of petty-producers), the fundamental interests of these classes and those of the ruling class cannot be reconciled, and therefore capitalism has to go; it also has to go because capitalism is incompatible with long-term ecological sustainability.

This process of development of consciousness will prepare the basic classes to fight for a state, controlled by proletarians/semi-proletariat, in an alliance with small-scale independent producers, for new society. This is a society: where all remnants of feudal/'semi-feudal' relations are destroyed and bonded labor relations completely annihilated, and land[14] is equitably distributed

---

as much as a thousand Communist votes. But on the scales of the revolutionary struggle, a thousand workers in one big factory represent a force a hundred times greater than a thousand petty officials, clerks, their wives, and their mothers-in-law. The great bulk of the fascists consists of human dust' (Trotsky, 1931a).

12 *Transitional demands* stem 'from today's conditions and from today's consciousness of wide layers of the working class and unalterably leading to one final conclusion: the conquest of power by the proletariat' (Trotsky, 1938). These are the demands that are much more radical and progressive than immediate and partial demands (e.g. a little rise in wages; demand for democratic rights) reflect masses' needs (e.g. employment and decent living conditions for all; workers' control over businesses) which, if met, will undermine capitalism. The transitional demands aim to raise the level of class consciousness to revolutionary consciousness.

13 In fact, the fight for ecological sustainability can be seen as a fight for a form of social wage, an ecological social wage (Das, 2018b).

14 This includes land held by non-toiling large-scale landowners. This also includes land and other natural resources (water bodies; forests) that are now held by industrialists in excess of their need and which were taken away from peasants or from control of the state or the village community, with inadequate compensation and with the help of force and/or cronyism.

466   CHAPTER 13

among actual toilers who are also provided financial help from the state and
many of whom may be organized into cooperatives voluntarily. As well, this is
a society which is democratic in economic, political and cultural spheres, one
where, among other things:

a)   the process of democratic change, under the proletarian leadership, is
     uninterruptedly[15] extended to gradually socialize (democratize the con-
     trol over) major means of production and private finance and means of
     transportation and communication that are owned by domestic and im-
     perialist capital;

b)   markets that may exist in certain limited spheres initially are state-
     controlled, and ecologically sustainability is promoted;

c)   exploitation of wage-labor and forcible dispossession of small-scale pro-
     ducers are dis-allowed, with the latter receiving assistance from the state;

d)   all able-bodied people engage in productive work with a decent wage and
     job security for all irrespective of gender, racial, religious, etc.
     backgrounds;

e)   surplus labor that is performed by toilers, and land and other natural re-
     sources, does not exist in their capitalist form; and

f)   the development process focuses on the satisfaction of material and cul-
     tural *needs* of men, women and children, rather than on the pursuit of
     profit for a few (top 1% or so).[16]

---

15   'Uninterruptedly' does not necessarily mean 'all at once' or 'suddenly'. It means minimiza-
     tion of the period during which a proletarian state has to supervise a society dominated
     by capitalist class relations, because such a state of affairs would signify the contradiction
     between political power of proletarians over the state on the one hand and economic
     power of capitalist over means of production on the other. 'Uninterruptedly' and 'gradu-
     alism' are not necessarily mutually contradictory. 'Non-gradualism' does not mean 'more
     revolutionary'. Here are some relevant lines from Engels's (1848) 'Principles of commu-
     nism'. 'Do you intend to replace the existing social order by community of Property at one
     stroke? Answer: We have no such intention. The development of the masses cannot he
     ordered by decree. It is determined by the development of the conditions in which these
     masses live, and therefore proceeds gradually'. 'Will it be possible for private property to
     be abolished at one stroke? No, no more than existing forces of production can at one
     stroke be multiplied to the extent necessary for the creation of a communal society. In all
     probability, the proletarian revolution will transform existing society gradually and will
     be able to abolish private property only when the means of production are available in
     sufficient quantity'.
     Engels continues to say that communist action will involve:
     'Gradual expropriation of landowners, industrialists, railroad magnates and shipowners,
     partly through competition by state industry, partly directly through compensation in the
     form of bonds'.

16   All societies must perform surplus labor (labor that is more than necessary to meet the
     current needs) and must produce a surplus product. Surplus product will be necessary in
     a non-capitalist society not only to build future productive forces (e.g. new bridges and

When even the limited forms of democracy that capitalism allows are being increasingly questioned in words and in practice in a process that is extending into fascistic tendencies, and when the limited form of assistance from the state that is available (in the form of meagre pro-poor intervention) is being withdrawn/shrunk by fascistic (and other) forces, and when the very small amount of the asset-base that petty producers have is being taken away, there should be class-based mobilization by organizations of workers and small-scale producers, under the leadership of Left parties. I am abstracting from the question of what kind of Left parties can achieve such a task.[17] An important aim of such Left-led mobilization must be to confront, as non-violently as possible, the fascistic/communal forces, including on the street, as a part of the fight against capitalism. Masses must be made aware of the three levels of their struggle, i.e. the struggle against the attack on democratic rights, including from fascistic forces, the struggle against the attack on living conditions, and the struggle against capitalist class relation itself.

The fight against fascistic tendencies is a defensive fight, so it has to be a part of a fight for more. Even if this fight succeeds, its success will be inevitably transient just as success in obtaining economic concessions will be temporary. This is because the ugly head of fascistic tendencies will rise (and the attack on living standards will continue) as long as there is capitalism, along with its eternal tendency towards crisis and uneven development, and the attendant need to deceive and divide the lower-class opposition. So, the fight against fascistic tendencies must gradually develop into and be a part of, a fight, by Left-led workers and small-scale producers, for a socialist state and socialist society. The Left has to help the masses understand that genuine long-term success in achieving democratic rights and qualitative improvements in living conditions cannot be achieved within capitalism, that concessions received today can be

---

new roads, etc.) but also to make sure that those who are not able to work (children and pregnant women, retired workers) can satisfy their needs and can meet new needs that enrich the quality of life, spiritually and in other ways. When the major part of surplus labor takes the form of surplus value (roughly, capitalist profit, capitalist interest and capitalist rent, apart from taxes paid to capitalist state, much of which returns to property owners through various policies), we live in a capitalist society. Capitalist surplus labor is thus a surplus product in a 'quantitative' sense *that has a class character*: it is the surplus product produced by direct producers, made possible by development of productive forces, that is appropriated by the ruling class.

17   On many occasions, they, while maintaining their organizational independence, will have to combine their forces with non-communist workers and non-communist small-scale producers to fight for democratic rights and economic concessions (as, for example, in a nation-wide general strike) and against fascistic tendencies.

taken away tomorrow and that significant reforms in a country are produced generally as byproducts of revolutionary struggles in that country and/or in other countries from which they can spread.

2   Left Forces in India: Their Strength and Weakness

India's social-economic and political situation is dangerous for the toiling masses. What is urgently needed therefore is the political mobilization of the multi-caste, multi-religion, multi-regional working class and poor peasants of the vast diverse country against all factions of the capitalist-landlord propertied classes and their political formations. Such a mobilization must defend secularism, democracy, against the attack on these from fascistic forces, and national sovereignty vis-à-vis imperialism. And such a mobilization must be not for a democratic capitalist society whatever that bourgeois-democracy is euphemistically called, but for a workers' and poor peasants' government. It is only such a government that can root out the seeds of the on-going attack on secularism and democracy, and that can help the masses gradually construct socialism. Masses must be conscious of the fact that it is only such a government that can guarantee that the toiling masses enjoy a decent standard of living and practice proletarian (bottom-up) democracy, and that people live in harmony with one another and with nature. Needless to say that such a mobilization in India must be a part of the mobilization at greater geographical scales for socialism in one country is a reactionary and fake idea.[18] These principles must be always kept in mind. They constitute the lighthouse during the long and tortuous journey towards socialism.

We must also bear in mind that:

> the class war takes place on the soil of history, and not in the stratosphere of sociology [or 'bald sociological abstraction']. The point of departure in the struggle against fascism is not the abstraction of the democratic state, but the living organizations of the proletariat, in which is concentrated all its past experience and which prepare it for the future.
>
> TROTSKY, 1932e[19]

---

18   The fight against capitalism in India, to succeed and to deepen, can only be a part of a world-regional (e.g. South Asian) and an international fight, because capitalism is an international system.

19   We must also not forget that: 'in politics, as in all other serious fields, one must know well: what; when, where, and how. Also, it cannot hurt to understand: why' (Trotsky, 1932l).

FORWARD MARCH OF THE RIGHT AND THE RELATIVE WEAKNESS

Fascistic attacks are happening in India, and the BJP is expanding its influence, not only because of (a) the failure of the ruling class to satisfy the needs of the masses, whose living standards are under attack while ruling class is accumulating a massive amount of wealth, and (b) the 'secular' political representatives of the ruling class to defend democracy and secularism (as indicated by the decline of the Congress). Fascistic tendencies are progressing also because of the weakness of Left forces[20] (manifested partly in their geographical confinement to specific parts of the country), relative to what is necessary to conduct the democratic, trade unionist, and socialist movements.

If fascistic forces, that are always the handmaiden of capital (or its hegemonic fractions), are not stronger than they are, and therefore, if India does not yet have a *fascist state*, this is also partly because of the relative weakness of the Left movement, so perhaps there is, ironically, an advantage of political backwardness. This is because: The Left (the bloc of communist parties), does not yet present the spectre of communism/socialism as a serious threat. Instead given their overall political vision, they are merely fighting against the remnants of landlordism, for a more equal distribution of farm-land, and against the attack on living standards of workers and peasants from a specific form of capitalism (neoliberal capitalism and/or a capitalism dominated by specific fractions of capital). These fights *are* absolutely relevant. Yet, it can be seen that the Left is fighting for a particular progressive form of democracy, which also means that it will be the political shell for a particular form of capitalism (a more egalitarian and a more economically developed capitalism) for an indefinite period, under the supervision of a new class-alliance than what exists now. So, in a sense, communists are not really a big threat to the principle of capitalist class relation itself in India now or in the future, as they were in certain advanced capitalist countries in the 1930s, in the aftermath of 1917. Unlike in Germany on the eve of fascist ascendancy, as the CPI(M) General Secretary himself acknowledges:

> In India today, the ruling classes as a whole have not yet come to the conclusion of abandoning the present form of parliamentary democracy, notwithstanding the severe stress and strain that it is under. On the other hand, the threat of the immediate seizure of power by the proletariat is not on the agenda today. Finally, this is also because the stage of the

---

20   From now on (and unless indicated otherwise), I use the term Left to mainly refer to the various formally organized streams of the Marxist Left in India. When I am not talking about India I sometimes use the word 'Left' to indicate the Left that is necessary to mobilize the exploited classes and oppressed people against capitalism and for socialism.

revolution in India [according to all communist parties which have any real presence] is democratic, while in Germany it was Socialist.

YECHURI, 1993: 5; parenthesis added

In fact, *in practice*, and not just in theory, the Left is also not a serious threat to capital*ists* in India, whether big or not, given that when in power at the provincial level, it woos capitalists for investment and to create jobs. And therefore fascistic forces are not yet confronted with the task of having to defend capitalist *property relations* and *fundamental class interests of capitalists* against any significant organized proletarian political opposition. Nonetheless, the fascistic forces, given their inherently pro-business character, are responding to the need to sustain capitalist accumulation at a high rate, and counter the declining rate of profit.[21] Such a need can be met in part by thwarting any potential or actual mass and class struggle against the employers-financiers-traders-landowners combine, including against the super-exploitation of labor and mindless dispossession of small-scale producers. And, such a need of the ruling class is expressed in the form of attempts by extreme Right-wing elements within the bourgeois class to turn to several methods. Resorting to the fascistic movement is a major one. The conjunctural co-existence of the 'relative weakness' of the fascistic movement (i.e. the fact that the fascistic tendencies have not yet captured *state* power fully) and the relative weakness of the Left, can make the Left oblivious of an important ontological fact: that the existence of a thing and its higher levels of development are different *and* are united by a *common* underlying characteristic. And ignoring such an ontological fact can create the illusion about the non-seriousness of the threat from fascistic forces to democracy and to the communist movement.

We should recapitulate two facts here. Firstly, fascistic forces do exist mainly because of a potential and actual ideological and political struggle against certain effects of capitalist accumulation and crisis, a struggle much of which is led by the Left. Established in the same year as the Communist party of India, the RSS, as mentioned earlier, is anti-communist from its origin. Secondly, because the threat to capital is not strong enough from the Left (in a global climate of relative decline of the Left), the need for a fully-fledged fascistic state has not yet arisen on capitalist-economic grounds.[22] If the Left was so strong

---

21   According to Roberts (2016), like many other BRICS countries and advanced countries, Indian capitalism has been experiencing a declining rate of profit.

22   Such a state of affairs is also because the fascistic forces themselves are not yet strong enough, even electorally, *relative to* the challenge from the totality of secular-democratic forces. This is partly evidenced by the fact that they can be electorally defeated, or heavily weakened, by the unity of the forces that are reasonably secular.

FORWARD MARCH OF THE RIGHT AND THE RELATIVE WEAKNESS 471

that it would pose a threat to capitalist property but not strong enough to take power, the existing fascistic movement could turn into a fascist regime, or to something very close. These two facts are because of a common factor: the relative weakness of the Left movement, a fact that has received much attention recently, including in popular circles.[23] And this concrete situation of the weakness of the Left needs to be briefly explained.[24]

One may start with mainstream communist parties [e.g. CPI and CPI(M)]. Along with their partners within the Left Front, they have launched many struggles for reforms and have remained an important part of India's progressive political culture.[25] This is reflected in the fact that among the lower-income people ('very poor') and among unskilled workers and agricultural workers, a proportionately higher percentage of them votes for the Left parties than for other parties (Table 13.1). For example: if 7.5% of all voters voted for

---

23 The recent literature on the Left which discusses its weaknesses, among other aspects of its history, includes: Banerjee, 2012; Bidwai, 2016; Chakrabarty, 2015, 2014; Crowley, 2014; Das and Mahmood, 2015; Josh, 2011; Kersell, 2018; Maitra, 2011; Prashad, 2015; Vanaik, 2011; and Vidyasagar, 2005. See Suniraj and Heath (2017) and Williams, 2009 on how the CPM has received support from disadvantaged groups. On the actual workings of left governments, there is a large amount of literature including: Heller, 1999; Kohli, 1987; Oktem, 2012; Lofgren, 2016; and Mallick, 1994. The criticisms of the communist Left have come from various theoretical and political strands even within what can be broadly called Leftist. For example, there are differences between a Bidwai and a Vanaik on the one hand and an Anjan Chakrabarti on the other. Anjan Chakrabarti (2012) says that: the problem with the communist movement lies in their commitment to state-centric politics and a vanguardist party structure that comes at the expense of advancing the Marxian project of nonexploitation, fair distribution, and democracy. While one criticism is that communist parties are less communistic and more social-democratic, others say that they are probably not even social democratic (for example, Herring (2013) says that it is increasingly unclear that platforms of left parties coincide with the interests of subordinate classes).

24 In this discussion, I include three streams, abstracting from a fourth group: individuals and non-party organizations who are Marxist (although this group has some overlap with my third stream). There are also many individuals and groups who are sympathetic to Marxism and who are involved in grass-roots mobilization of the exploited and oppressed groups and of those who are adversely affected by the massive environmental damage caused by capitalism.

25 They include not only Forward Bloc and Revolutionary Socialist Party (and sometimes, Socialist Unit Center of India), but also, and more recently, CPI(ML)-Liberation. The latter is a (militant) party with roots in the Maoist/Naxalite movement that began in 1967, and combines electoral and extra-electoral work mainly focussing on rural areas. See Kotovsky (1992) and Tharamangalam (1992) on the role of communist parties in organizing workers and peasants (see also Mannathukkaren, 2011; and Heller, 1999).

472 CHAPTER 13

TABLE 13.1 Percentage of voters who voted for various parties/alliances (in national elections
in 1996 and 2004)

1996 Election

	Congress+	BJP+	Left Front
All India average	27.5	24.9	7.5
Very poor	29.6	16	11.3
Unskilled worker	30.6	17.0	10.8
Agri- and allied worker	28.4	17.8	8.9
Scheduled caste	31.6	14.4	11.0

2004 Election

	Congress+	BJP+	Left Front
All India average	39.5	37.9	6.4
Very poor	42.9	32.8	7.5
Unskilled worker	42.6	27.4	8.0
Agri- and allied worker	43.4	36.6	6.8
Scheduled caste	39.7	25.9	8.8

SOURCE: ORIGINAL DATA FROM CSDS (CENTRE FOR THE STUDY OF DEVELOPING
SOCIETIES) AND ELECTION COMMISSION OF INDIA, QUOTED IN MITRA, 2011: 118–119

the Left in 1996, among the sections that are defined as 'very poor', a much
higher percentage (11.3%) voted for the Left. This is in stark contrast to the
Right: if 24.9% of all voters voted for the BJP and allied parties in 1994, from the
'very poor' category, only 16% voted for them. The Left's support base is indeed
disproportionately among the very poor, agricultural workers, unskilled workers and scheduled castes.

Based on the above numbers, one can calculate what I will call the relative
popularity quotient (RPQ) of a party/alliance, relative to specific groups of voters, by using this formula: Percentage of voters from a social group which votes
for a party/alliance divided by the percentage of all voters who voted for that
party/alliance. If the ratio for a party/alliance is greater than 1, that means that
a disproportionately higher percentage of a given social group supports that
party/alliance. If the ratio for a party/alliance is less than 1, that means that a
disproportionately lower percentage of a specific group supports that party/
alliance. The higher the ratio, the higher the RPQ. One can see that the RPQ for
the Left is not only very high as compared to the Right (BJP+); it is also

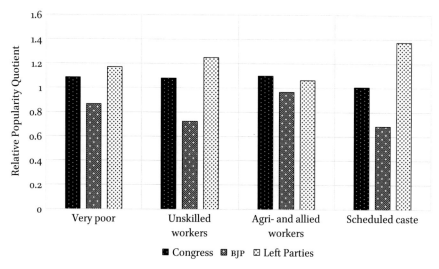

FIGURE 13.1 Relative popularity quotient among lower classes and Dalits (2004 national election)

(generally) high as compared to the Congress as well. The RPQ for the Left for, for example, 'very poor' and for 'unskilled workers' was 2.34 and 2.11 times the RPQ for the Right for these categories, in 1996, although the RPQ for the Left for some of these groups did come down in 2004 (Figures 13.1–13.2).

India's Left and progressive culture would be poorer without the mainstream Left. Yet, they have spent far too much time on elections and on managing the bourgeois-state apparatuses at local and provincial levels. As a result they have failed to transform what are merely democratic consciousness and trade union consciousness of workers and small-scale producers to what is called class consciousness proper, or socialist consciousness. The idea of the struggle for socialism – with which development of class consciousness is associated – is hardly raised in the Left discourse and Left political work.[26] The ideological and political work of the Left is, more or less, shaped by the assumption that, as mentioned earlier, the goal of communists is merely to have a more democratic and more egalitarian capitalism for an indefinite period.[27] The language of socialist vision and the struggle for socialism is as scarce as

---

26 A former veteran communist, Mr. Jyoti Basu, had said in 2008: 'Socialism is a far cry. Socialism is our political agenda and it was mentioned in our party document but capitalism will continue to be the compulsion for the future' (The Economic Times, 2008).

27 Once a well-known communist leader said this to me about West Bengal before the fall of the Left front from power: the Left Front needed to establish capitalist industries first to create a working class, and it would then fight against capitalism.

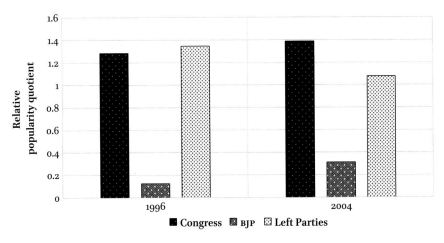

FIGURE 13.2 Relative popularity quotient for Muslims (2004 national election)

water in the Rajasthan desert.[28] What is plenty in evidence is the combination of electoralism and trade unionist consciousness, like water in Cherrapunji. It is being forgotten that the effect of the fight for democratic rights and economic concessions is greater when these take place within the framework of a struggle against capitalist property relations as such, and when a large section of those who engage in these fights has what is called class consciousness proper. The level of ideological education of members and followers of major communist parties is not very high. Obsession with the desire to win many seats in the elections is associated with reformism: a communist party can win many seats to manage a bourgeois apparatus only by making too many compromises with the system and thus by sacrificing the goal of class struggle. Besides where it has been electorally successful and managed to control state power at the provincial and sub-provincial scales, it has pursued capitalist, even neoliberal capitalist policies, so the objective of developing cadres' class consciousness through electoral battle is further undermined. Electoral success and attendant electoral consciousness (= political form of trade union consciousness) has thus come at the expense of class-consciousness which is what the Left should be promoting.

What about the Maoist-inspired Left which is seen as existing to the left of mainstream Left parties? As discussed in two earlier chapters, this segment of

---

28 This applies to even to the class-conscious workers, and perhaps, to most of the communist leaders.

the Left involving many self-sacrificing people who are passionate about the defense of the right of the poor, has also launched many valiant struggles, especially in rural areas and in areas dominated by the culturally rich but economically exploited and politically oppressed indigenous communities living in what can be called, with some justification, 'internal colonies' (see Das, 2019b). But much of this Left – especially, the more militant part of it – is, more or less, isolated from the political mobilization of urban workers, given their belief in the peasants as being the most revolutionary class.

Then there are little groups to the Left of mainstream and Maoist communist parties. They provide excellent analyses of the current situation that actually emphasize the need for the struggle for socialism, by employing insights from revolutionary Marxism.[29] However, the actual influence of these groups on the politics and consciousness of people has been almost non-existent thus far. In other words, the high quality of their intellectual analysis is not matched by their actual political interventions on the ground. This unfortunate state of affairs is in part because right from their origin [consider the history of the Bolshevik Leninist Party of India (BLPI)], this stream of Marxist movement in India (as in many other countries) has shown a tendency towards extreme fragmentation (and indeed unprincipled entrysm) and towards also sectarianism. There are little groups, some of them based in India and others being branches of international organizations. In many instances, when some of them seek to intervene ideologically in the Indian communist movement, they have a tendency to see no distinction between the Left movement and what is plain bourgeois politics, so much so that every instance of electoral (or non-electoral) defeat of the Left becomes an occasion for a small 'celebration' on their part. Some of their criticisms of the Indian Left, including the fact that it

---

29   Their Marxism, includes, and rightly so, the ideas not only from Lenin (including the Lenin of *April Theses*) but also ideas of Luxemburg and Trotsky (and all those who have tried to develop the ideas of these classical thinkers in the more recent times). It should be noted that the last two figures, Luxemburg and Trotsky, and especially, Trotsky, are consistently and systematically ignored – and indeed, blacklisted – by theoreticians and leaders of mainstream communist parties as well as by Maoists, indicating their own version of sectarianism. When a progressive publisher sent to one of the major communist parties a few books on Trotsky, a party representative complained about this, citing political differences between the party and Trotskyism. When the person was requested later to return the books, the publisher was promptly informed that the books had been bought already by some people from the party's book-shop! A communist movement must pay careful, honest and critical attention to the entire Marxist tradition. To do so would be a more holistic view of Marxism than what is often practiced by major parties/movements and Marxist scholars. Such a holistic and non-sectarian view, by reducing some of the (avoidable/non-basic) differences, will contribute to the success of any communist movement (see Das, 2019 on the need for a non-sectarian approach to class struggle).

is not militant enough, are legitimate. Some are not. Consider the following. If there is no Left-led movement in an area or a sector or a work-place, the Left is criticized by some of these Far Left groups, and rightly so. But these groups do not say why *they themselves* do not organize the workers and peasants or why they have not been able to be in a position to organize these classes, despite the fact that these groups or their predecessors have existed for 70 years or so. Further, when workers go on a strike, they are praised for their militancy by these small groups, while forgetting that the strikes are organized by the Left. And, in fact, when the Left does organize strikes and protests, and the Left does this numerous times, it is accused of merely containing the anger of the masses and is thus supportive of the bourgeois system. The Left is also criticized on the ground that it is intentionally confining the strike in one workplace to that place and that it is not mobilizing workers from across workplaces. Of courses, left-led strikes have often been confined to particular places, and that is a problem. But if doing so was the necessary part of Left's strategy, how has it been organizing nation-wide strikes and region-wise farmer movements, and so on? Often the word 'Stalinist' is used by many of these small groups to describe the Indian Left movement. 'Stalinism' is an analytical-political category (Das, 2018c). Is using 'Stalinism' mainly as an abusive-descriptive term, like the abusive use of 'sectarianism' by the Left movement for the Far Left groups, not potentially harmful to the socialist political and trade union movement? The Indian Left movement is Stalinist in its origin and in terms of its dubious theory of revolution (and I have presented my criticisms of its theory of revolution in Chapter 3 and elsewhere). But one must ask: how does the incessant and automatic invocation of 'Stalinism' and spontaneous hatred for and fear of anything to do with the existing Left movement, benefit the Marxist cause, including in the trade union sphere, to be promoted by socialists, who 'have no interests separate and apart from those of the proletariat as a whole' and who 'do not set up any sectarian principles of their own, by which to shape and mold the proletarian movement' (Marx and Engels, 1848)?

Some of the 'negativist' criticisms of the Indian Left's 'reformist' struggles by small Far Left groups, which are mainly propaganda groups, are almost akin to the type of criticisms of working class actions that is indicative of what Marx called 'political indifferentism'. It says that, for example, a struggle against a wage strike is bad because it supports wage-slavery under capitalism or that the struggle for state funding of primary education is bad because primary education is inadequate, or that getting concessions through struggle is bad because it means compromise with the system. Marx himself countered this sort of criticisms (Marx, 1873; see Das, 2019 for a longer discussion on this matter).

The center of gravity (the organizational basis) of some of these groups is also not deeply and extensively immersed in Indian politics and history, so what they say about the Indian society is not rooted in their *active struggles* on the ground.[30] This isolation from active struggles partly explains the sectarian tendency of these groups, which feeds into their isolation from active struggles. Nonetheless, it is important to reiterate that many of the criticisms of the bourgeois society and of Left politics from this Marxist stream, however inadequate, are examples of serious Marxist work and unflinching committment to socialist revolution. And India's Left culture would be also impoverished without these criticisms. India's Left culture will be impoverished in the absence of comradely and critical dialogues between this stream and other streams, which might, in the future, create the possibility of a tactical united front of separately existing Left parties to fight against fascism and other aspects of capitalism and against capitalism itself. But ultimately, the existing Left parties must transcend their limiting view of society and revolution whereby they are wedded to the idea of a democratic revolution and not a socialist revolution as a part of South Asia-wide and global process. This is a most fundamental obstacle to a serious communist movement.

The totality of the Left political landscape is therefore one that is politically rich. It is probably richer than in many western-advanced capitalist countries, which is why an average western intellectual would not even believe that India has such a fertile panoply of leftism. Of course, it has all sorts of problems including those that concern the determination of Indian society's class character, and the determination of the stage of revolution, the nature of the united front strategy. One need not go into these issues here.

Given the over-all left-political situation as briefly described above (i.e. the relative weakness of the Left, given the low level of class consciousness among the masses), it is difficult to see how the struggle for a workers and poor peasants' state can begin *at this very moment*, without being idealistic, voluntaristic and adventurist,[31] especially given that fascistic forces are literally out there to

---

30 Some of these groups lack a dialectical approach to the relation between class exploitation and non-class oppression, including caste and religion, etc. They agree that class relations and struggle against class relations have primacy. From this right premise, they draw the wrong conclusion that non-class relations are effectively not important in the struggle against class.

31 It is adventuristic when one raises the slogan of revolution without prior ideological and political preparations and without the majority of the workers saying yes to a call for revolution (as Lenin says). Marx was called a traitor by some of his contemporaries for cautioning against adventurists. 'Marx, Engels, and Willich worked together on a league and refugee matters through the summer of 1850, but a rift began developing over strategy... Although Marx had put aside all theoretical work since 1848 in favor of political agitation and opposition journalism, it was becoming apparent to him that a revolution was *not*

physically destroy the Left and progressive movements. But it is also not clear how it is that outside of a framework of the struggle for socialism, there can be a fight to completely and permanently eliminate the fascistic tendencies – a fight which is much more than electorally getting rid of the BJP from power: as long as there is capitalist class relation, there *is* an underlying tendency towards the society both shunning its democratic shell, turning towards fascism, and attacking the living standards of the masses. The fascistic tendency is one that may not always manifest itself, and when it is manifested, it may not always be strong enough to take state power. But this is a tendency that is inherent to capitalist class relation, which produces crisis and misery for the majority. The preparation that is necessary to make a demand for a socialist state must be made sooner than later, and an enormous conjunctural obstacle has to be cleared for that to happen: the clearing of that obstacle must be seen as a part of the tortuous, non-linear, process of the fight for socialism.

3   The Indian Left and the Two Forms of the Fight against Fascist Tendencies

The fight against fascist tendencies, once again, cannot merely seen as a fight to replace the BJP with a more secular government nor can the fight against fascistic tendencies be merely confined near-permanently to be a fight for a capitalist society that has no trace of feudalism, that is more democratic, and less unequal and where the state intervenes on behalf of the poor and regulates private businesses. In fact, the fight against fascism and against neoliberal attack on living standards can only be seen as twin inter-connected steps towards, and as a part of, the protracted fight for socialism. Clearly, capitalists do not mind doing business with, and actively supporting, undemocratic and authoritarian forces and even *fascistic* political forces, whether these forces have slaughtered religious minorities or crushed democratic rights or are striking at the root of national unity. This fact is a reason enough to assert, and to tell the masses now, that capitalism itself has to go. Capitalism will go only when the Left – class-conscious toiling masses organized by the communists – overthrows it.

---

imminent. Willich, however, ... believed the [communist] league, despite its small numbers, could through sheer force of will trigger an uprising, and he disagreed with Marx's dawning conclusion that massive social change was more than likely years away. For his part Marx argued that certain things were necessary for a successful revolution... According to Wilhelm Leibknecht, ...Willich and Barthélemy began plotting against Marx: "They called Marx a traitor and said traitors must be killed"(Gabriel, 2011).

Such a class politics requires a much stronger Left, which in turn requires greater organizational strength, attempts at expanding its political hegemony, and the struggles in the legal and extra-parliamentary spheres (Chakrabarty, 2015). It also requires principled Left unity [note that there is effectively very little substantive difference between CPI and CPI(M)]. Such unity must produce a gradually expanding united front of Left forces as representatives of workers, semi-proletarians and peasants, the forces which may remain separate organizationally and which may engage in polemical battles for theoretical and political clarity as long as they need to, but they must strike together in action. It must deploy the full spectrum of parliamentary and extra-parliamentary methods, with the primacy given to the latter. In the fight against fascistic forces, what should be targeted are not only the political and cultural views of these forces (their attack on democratic rights and secularism, their hyper-nationalism, etc.) but also, and this is very important, their pro-business economic and pro-imperialist, policies. Once again, two aspects of fascist movement, communal authoritarianism with fascistic tendencies and idolization of free market economics, serve national and imperialist capital, and go together. Both of these must be fought together. It is idealist and politicist to say that merely an educational attempt to make people's way of thinking less communal, and a mere fight for secular politics, can succeed in fighting fascistic tendencies, without there being a simultaneous fight against policies that the fascistic government implements in the interest of capital.

The electoral sphere is indeed one of the spheres in which class struggle – and indeed struggle for 'social justice' – happens. There are many dimensions to the struggle within the electoral sphere. The latter is important given that liberal democracy is a shell of Indian capitalism and that it has also deep roots in people's consciousness thus contributing to the legitimacy of the system. Unlike in advanced capitalism, the vast majority of voters vote in India. Winning a few seats in the parliaments/assemblies, etc. gives the Left a chance to make its voice of reason heard against fascistic tendencies and against an attack on people's livelihood. An important part of the protracted process of class struggle in the current conjuncture is an attempt to stop a fascistic party from coming to, and/or from retaining, power and from making use of state's resources to attack social and democratic rights of ordinary people and to destroy – or at least severely weaken – the communist movement. Among various forms of bourgeois government, some forms are more conducive to class-mobilizational work by the Left than other forms, so the Left cannot be neutral to which forms of bourgeois government exist, just as it cannot be neutral towards whether capitalism is peasant capitalism or landlord capitalism or whether in a capitalist society wages are lower or higher or whether school education for children is state-funded or not. A government that is run by

480 CHAPTER 13

fascistic, communal and hyper-nationalistic elements, a government that attacks democratic rights *as well as* living standards of people, is the least conducive to class-based movements. One can see this when communists are killed or hurt, statues of communist icons are demolished, when communist offices are ransacked. It is worth repeating this: the process of fighting for a new society must include the fight for the conditions for that fight itself. The Left must fight for these conditions. And only the Left can fight for these conditions in a consistent way. So, it is necessary to fight electorally even if the priority has to be given to the extra-electoral fight to be conducted in opposition to all bourgeois forces. However, electoral success has to be seen dialectically, from the standpoint of the law of transformation of quantity into quality and vice versa.[32]

One might ask (and people do ask this question): why will the voters vote for the Left, given (a) that Left leaders do not generally engage in corrupt behavior which means that they cannot help people make money,[33] and (b) the Left does not get enough votes to be able to run the government so they do not control the purse to provide material help.[34] They have no money themselves to give away in support for votes. These arguments must be listened to and countered. In my view, it is not necessary for the Left to be in government in order for it to be with the masses, to speak on their behalf, to be relevant to their lives (in fact, the more the Left is embedded in governing bourgeois state

---

32   Too little of electoral success would deny the Left access to the parliament and assemblies to represent its views, and it would also deny the Left the chance to feel the pulse of the masses. But if the level of electoral success becomes too much, it can lead to the Left capturing power at, say, the provincial level (or being a part of a national government). This can also be politically problematic, even if the Left is able to alleviate some of the economic miseries of the masses. It can, generally speaking, come to power in a bourgeois system only by making too many compromises with the system, and this fact can blunt the edge of class struggle of its basic classes, because their fighting instincts must somehow be kept in check in a capitalist system, in order to allow a certain level of accumulation of money in the hands of capitalists who are free to move across provinces. This will be the case whether the Left is a partner of a popular front (a bloc of capitalist parties and left parties) or comes to power on its own. And such a control over class struggle would lead to the loss of popularity of the Left among its basic classes. And if the Left, while in power, does engage in too much struggle against employers and traders, then capital will leave (and/or will invest less), leading to unemployment and low wages, which, in turn, will lead to the loss of its popularity among its basic classes.

33   Note that even common people do not mind making a little money from the government sources through corrupt means.

34   A vote for a left party in Kerala is effective but it is wasted in Gujarat, Herring (2013) says.

apparatuses, the less relevant it becomes to the masses).[35] The Left mediates between the masses and the resources of society as a whole that are controlled by the government, the resources that constitute the commons. They include natural commons such as land, forests and water bodies, as well as state-owned resources built on the basis of contributions from ordinary people (state-owned companies providing secure jobs and state benefits in the form of de-commodified use-values). The Left must fight against the commons being given away to capitalists. It must fight for greater access of ordinary people to the existing commons and for an expansion of the existing commons (e.g. expansion of the public sector enterprises and subjecting them to increase democratic control by manual and mental workers; and public provision of services such as education and health-care, sports facilities, theatres, parks, museums, and libraries). Besides, the Left must mobilize people to (a) have a better share of their own product that is taken away by the capitalists in the form of high profit, interest and rent, a process that the state supports, and (b) reduce taxes on them and increase taxes on the super-rich. And the Left must mobilize people around transitional demands that connect immediate demands to the struggle for a socialist society, the demands which include such things as employment for all for a living wage. More specifically, the Left must show its practical relevance to the masses in at least four ways:

1. by mobilizing the masses to win concessions from employers, traders, bankers and landowners on the basis of strikes and protests;

2. by mobilizing the masses to win concessions from the government at all levels (center and State), in the form of progressive policies to meet people's needs, including the policies which reflect the needs of the masses *whether or not the system says it can meet them*;[36]

3. by making sure that the policies introduced under the pressure of the Left are actually implemented, and reach the masses in a transparent, non-divisive, and non-corrupt way, including at the city and village level

---

35   Given the venality of the bourgeois electoral process, in which votes are bought by many parties and sold by many voters, the Left *is* at a disadvantage. But then it is better that the Left should not obtain votes from such voters. In fact, the use of money power in elections must be an issue that the Left should campaign as a part of its fight to deepen democracy.

36   These include: food security, secure employment for all, inflation-adjusted living wages for men and women, increase in the relative wage, or the reduction in inequality between what masses get and what property owners take from the fruits of the labor of the masses, better prices for petty producers and protection from unfair dispossession from their small-scale property, freedom-from debt; free time (reduction in working hours); pension; socialized and universal access to publicly provided quality health-care, education, housing, transportation and culture.

(this would make sure that the policies announced by a government do not serve as an ideological tool as false promises);[37] and

4. by being able to impart education to the masses to develop solidarity among them – education against practices of discrimination based on religion, gender, caste, etc. – and to protect the democratic rights of the socially oppressed groups.

There are thus objective reasons why the Left can have political relevance by winning concessions for the masses, as a part of its struggle for socialism, to the daily lives of the masses and why it can obtain some level of electoral support, even in areas where its presence is not traditionally very strong. [38] But it is clear that merely implementing, or advocating for, progressive policies is no recipe for undermining the fascistic forces.[39] The spread of communalist-fascistic

---

37 False promises amount to lies, the aim of which is to merely calm and deceive the masses (who have also been deceived by non-fascistic bourgeois governments). Fascistic tendencies specialize in promising to deliver good things for the poor people, better than any other alternative political movement (bourgeois-democratic or leftist), without meaning to do anything or much, and in the process, they recruit sections of the masses into, and gain support for, their mass reactionary movement. They cannot deliver what they promise because doing so will hurt the basic interests of capital which they are servile supporters of.

38 Of course, one might say that if the Left is able to do all these to obtain concessions for the masses, why would they be interested in the fight for more (socialism)? The answer is: through struggle for reforms on the basis of immediate and transitional demands and on the basis of ideological education, the Left will help the masses to get more than what the masses would get without any struggle, but no matter how strong the fight for concessions is, the system will never meet the masses' need to any significant extent and on a long-term basis (concessions are also reversible). The fight for concessions, including for things that the system will never agree to (e.g. secure work for all with a living wage and with access to socialized and free quality health care and quality education), will reveal, to some extent, the true nature of the system (i.e. its structural 'bias' against the needs of the ordinary people), and such a fight for concessions, combined with Marxist education in theory and history, will radicalize the masses and prompt them to demand a (stadial) transcendence of the system. It is not enough that Marxist leaders and intellectuals know that there are limits to what the system can deliver. Masses must realize that these limits exist, based on their practice (and some theoretical reflection). Of course, to this one can counter-argue by saying that if the Marxists know that there are limits to reforms, would common people not be demoralized by fighting for these reforms? That counter-argument holds only if the fight for reforms happens without an ideological education which says explicitly to the people that there are such limits and that one should not expect much from the capitalist society.

39 In Tripura, the Left has tried to implement pro-poor policies, within the class and institutional constraints, but this was not enough to stop BJP from winning in the 2018 assembly election. In spite of progressive policies (progressive, that is, relative to blatantly bourgeois regimes in other States such as Gujarat, a laboratory for communal-fascistic-neoliberal-capitalist policies) implemented by the Left Front in Kerala, Kerala has seen a growth of right-wing fascistic forces.

ideology can counter the effects of progressive policies, so an ideological struggle against communalism and fascistic ideas *is* important. Of course, merely fighting against the attack on such ideology is not enough – especially in a country where almost 3 out of 4 people do not have access to an adequate amount of food. Besides the communal-fascistic ideology is rooted in material concerns of the ruling class, which are incompatible, ultimately, with those of the masses. The fight against the fascistic tendencies must be linked to the fight for economic concession, and both of these fights must be a part of the fight against the capitalist class relation itself. In fact, the arrival of fascistic tendency as a part of, and as a response to, capitalist crisis and reaction, and the resultant miseries for common people, is a great opportunity for the Left to say this to the masses (at least, to relatively politically advanced workers and peasants, in the first instance): the ruling class and its political parties are failing not only to meet economic needs but also they are failing to support basic democratic values, and therefore must be overthrown.

Once again: the Left must mobilize its basic classes (workers and small-scale producers) in extra-electoral activities, to fight for democratic rights and secularism and to fight for economic concessions, as a part of, and as steps towards, the fight for socialism. It must also engage in electoral struggle but that must be seen as *only a small part* of its overall political work, a prime aim of which must be the development of democratic-secular consciousness, and of trade union consciousness, and then the transformation of these forms of consciousness into communist consciousness or class consciousness proper. It is this Marxist perspective that must shape Left's approach to the electoral fight against fascism. In the remainder of this section (Section 3), I am going to present a less revolutionary approach as a thought experiment, only for readers' critical reflection, but this is an approach which, in my view, is utterly inadequate and problematic.

As mentioned earlier: unity of Left forces – all forces that are basically guided by Marxist theory of class society and of what is to be done – is fundamental to the task of fighting the fascistic forces electorally (and also extra-electorally). What is also needed is the unity among all secular, non-fascistic forces, including bourgeois forces: in as many constituencies as possible, as many secular-minded parties/movements as possible must be united against the BJP and its allies, before, during, and after the elections, and inside the parliaments/assemblies and outside. There should be as wide a secular front against communalism as possible, a front that is at the same time, to the left of the BJP and the pre-BJP governmental regime, in terms of economic policies. How this can be done is a different matter. One way to think about this is as follows.

There are at least a dozen regional parties in India that are relatively 'secular' in the sense that they do not employ the communal card as consistently

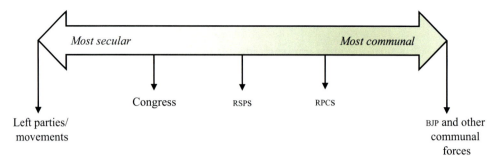

FIGURE 13.3 Scale of secularism
Notes: Where, RSPS: Regional parties, which are relatively, if not unwaveringly, secular. RPCS: Regional parties, which are currently a part of the electoral front dominated by the Hindu-communalist, BJP but which are formally not a part of the Sangh Parivar
SOURCE: AUTHOR

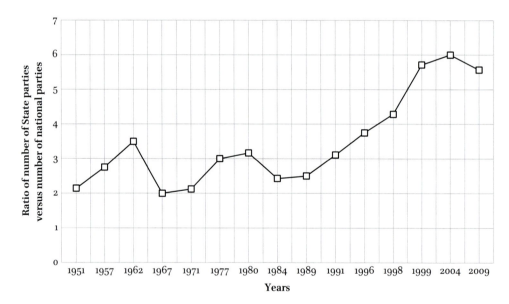

FIGURE 13.4 Ratio of number of State parties versus number of national parties as listed by ECI, 1951–2009

and as forcefully as the way the BJP does, and they are not fascistic as the BJP and the saffron family are: BJD, RJD, BSP, SP, JMM, DMK, AAP, TMC, PJC, etc.[40] (see Figure 13.3 above). Regional parties are basically parties that represent the

---

40   BJD = Biju Janata Dal (from Odisha); RJD = Rashtriya Janata Dal (from Bihar); BSP = Bahujan Samaj Party (mainly from Uttar Pradesh); SP = Samajwadi Party (mainly from Uttar Pradesh); JMM = Jharkhand Mukti Morcha (from Jharkhand); DMK = Dravida Munnetra

FORWARD MARCH OF THE RIGHT AND THE RELATIVE WEAKNESS 485

TABLE 13.2 Percentage of voters voting for a parties/alliances (in 1996 and 2004 national elections)

1996

	Congress+	BJP+	Left Front
All voters	27.5	24.9	7.5
Muslims	35.3	30.1	10.1

2004

	Congress+	BJP+	Left Front
All voters	39.5	37.9	6.4
Muslims	54.8	11.8	6.9

SOURCE: ORIGINAL DATA FROM CSDS (CENTRE FOR THE STUDY OF DEVELOPING
SOCIETIES) AND ELECTION COMMISSION OF INDIA, QUOTED IN MITRA, 2011: 118–119

interests of land owners, better-paid sections of the salaried stratum or the 'professional class' living/working in a province; and, importantly, the regional bourgeoisie – the fraction of the bourgeoisie whose scale of operation is more or less sub-national/regional and which faces competition from big bourgeoisie.[41] Over time, the electoral importance of regional parties is rising: their number relative to the number of national parties is rising (Figure 13.4). The regional parties, *may* be called, with *some* justification, what Lenin called parties of small proprietors. In many ways, the secular regional parties are regional counter-parts of the Congress. Some of them are actually regional offshoots of the Congress, which is why there is generally an inverse relation between the strength of the Congress and that of regional parties, irrespective of the strength of the Left.

The Left has, generally, been the most principled fighter against the curtailment of democratic rights and against the attack on secularism. It is perhaps not an accident that in 1996, while 7.5% of all voters voted for the Left, 10.1% of all Muslim voters voted for the Left (in 2004: the corresponding figures were 6.4

Kazhagam (from Tamil Nadu); AAP = Aam Aadmi Party (mainly from Delhi); TMC = All *India* Trinamool Congress (mainly from West Bengal); PJC = People's Justice Centre (in Tamil Nadu).

41   Note that the distinction between the two is not necessarily clear-cut, as regionally operating smaller firms are connected to nationally-operating larger firms, as suppliers and in other ways.

and 6.9). As a contrast, while 24.9% of voters voted for the BJP and allied parties, only 3.1% of Muslim voters voted for them (in 2004: the corresponding figures were 37.9 and 11.8) (see Table 13.2).

Based on the above numbers, one can calculate the relative popularity quotient (RPQ) of a party/alliance, relative to Muslims, by using this formula: Percentage of Muslim voters who vote for a party/alliance divided by the percentage of all voters who voted for that party/alliance. If the ratio for a party/alliance is greater than 1, that means that a disproportionately higher percentage of Muslims supports that party/alliance. If the ratio for a party/alliance is less than 1, that means that a disproportionately lower percentage of Muslims supports that party/alliance. The higher the ratio, the higher the RPQ. One can see that the RPW for the Left is not only very high as compared to the Right (BJP+); it is also high as compared to the Congress. The RPQ for the Left was about 11 times the RPQ for the Right in 1996, although the RPQ for the Left did come down a bit in 2004 (Fig 13.1).

In so far the Left is committed to secularism, one that is partly expressed in the support of Muslims for the Left, and in so far as it is a great reservoir of democratic-secular consciousness, the Left, acting as *the tribune of the people in the Lenin sense*, and maintaining its organizational independence via a vis bourgeois parties, must help establish a national-level coordination committee (a political discussion platform, or some such thing) for the fight against communalism and fascistic tendencies. A part of this process, from an electoral angle, should be an attempt to establish a federation of regional parties, to which the Left should provide any intellectual and other forms of help as required. From the Left standpoint, the unity among regional parties must be based on at least three commitments. One is the commitment to secular politics: the regional parties must be opposed to conducting politics in the name of religion, and they must be opposed to discrimination against any group based on religion, whether it is majority religion or minority religion. Where these parties (e.g. the BJP, BJD, BSP, TMC) were in an alliance with the BJP in the past and have opposed the BJP since, they must critically review their past practice, draw the lessons, and publicly re-forge their commitment to secularism and to non-cooperation and non-alliance with the BJP. Second, millions of people are attracted to the Right-wing BJP because of the failure of economic policies of the Congress, so the regional parties, if they wish not to be eaten up by the BJP (and the BJP does, and can, eat into regional parties' support base), must be committed to people's welfare, which would also require a commitment to place *some* political restriction on the power of capitalists and landowners to amass limitless wealth, including at the expense of peasants and aboriginal people's access to land and natural resources. Enduring opposition to secularism, in the short and medium terms, cannot be possible unless it is based on the opposition to Right-wing economic policies hurting the masses, i.e. unless such opposition is based on progressive economic policies.[42] Once again, free market economics and authoritarian communalism rooted in a mass movement, are two sides of the same coin, whether or not some free marketers oppose communalism and whether or not some communalists support some amount of state control and state support for the poor. Third, regional parties must be committed to a *supra*-regional, i.e. a national vision. They cannot operate at the center (federal level) *merely* as a motley of regional parties. The collectivity of *regional* parties must have a *national*-scale vision of how to make sure that: (a) India remains a secular-democratic nation with a reasonably independent foreign policy until recently (especially in relation to imperialist countries) and a policy of good relations with neighbors, and (b) it remains a country where federalism – equitable, democratic, relations between the Center and the States – matters. If voted to power, the regional parties must think and act *as if* they are parts of a national party – i.e. as a *federation* of regional parties, which, collectively, will seek to improve conditions of people of India as a whole (its workers and peasants, and various oppressed groups such as indigenous communities, women, Dalits, religious minorities, etc.) and not just in their particular States where these parties rule or have an influence, although they will maintain their own regional identities. In fact, such a *regio-national* approach of regional parties is increasingly necessary given that development of one State is linked to, and dependent on, development in another State, because of the flow or movement of people, investment, water, polluted air, etc. *across* State boundaries.

So, all in all, the national federation of *regional* parties must be based on their *common* commitments to the people of India, the commitments, which have only *regional* manifestations.[43] The three commitments of regional parties

---

42 Regional parties' election manifestos actually do contain some welfare measures for ordinary people, and this is made possible partly because agriculture, education and health are State subjects, over which State governments have much control. Yet, it is also true that regional governments have been active in taking away the land of peasants and aboriginal people to give it to big business (to their regional branches) for a tiny amount of money, and often the money spent on welfare is a small part of the very little amount of money that companies pay in return for the vast amount of wealth they receive. This is a part of the process that links provincial capital and global capital: as Parthasarathy (2015) says: 'Provincial capital and peasant politics ally with global capital, and take advantage of the opening up of new regional and global trade routes which account for urban practices in metropolitan cities, and the processes of urbanization in the countryside' (p. 835).

43 Without those commitments, even if these parties defeat the BJP once, the latter will come back with a vengeance, citing the fact that the regional parties are not (much) better for the masses than the BJP, economically.

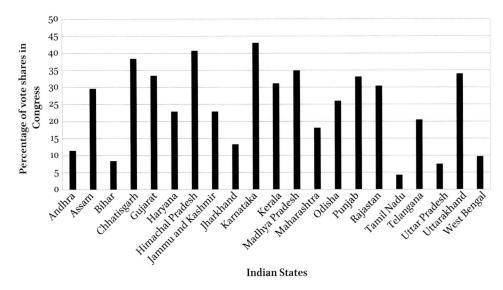

FIGURE 13.5 Congress Party's percentage of vote shares in the 2014 general election in India
SOURCE: AUTHOR

that are just mentioned indeed overlap with Left's own values: secularism, pro-poor policies, and a multi-scalar approach.[44] So they may create a condition for some amount of tactical and short/medium term – not strategic and long-term – cooperation between the regional parties and the Left.

What about the approach of the Left to the Congress, which has been a topic of debate within and outside of the Left? The Congress is not a paragon of secular values.[45] But it cannot go to the extent that the BJP goes to, in attacking secularism. Like most regional parties, the Congress does not have a fascistic agenda. And it is the only non-BJP party, which has a modicum of *pan-Indian* presence; this is in terms of its vote share if not in terms of its actual presence in the Parliament (i.e. seats won) (see Figure 13.5 above).

The Congress could be the main anti-BJP national force and must receive support from all secular forces, both from the Left and outside, in those States where a major regional party is not contending for power, and where the Left is also weak. However, for this to happen, i.e. for the Congress to avoid competition from non-BJP secular parties and to enhance its electoral success

---

44 The latter (i.e. a multi-scalar approach) includes going beyond the narrow confines of a region.
45 Yet, 'it would be a mistake to write off the Congress … as one irredeemably compromised by its failure to uphold secularism' (Banaji, 2016c: 237).

against the BJP, it must change its hyper-neoliberal approach to development (which it, more or less, shares with the BJP). It must adopt an approach that gives much more emphasis to the bottom 70% of the population than it normally has; it must be publicly committed to significantly addressing the issues of: growing inequality and the billionaire raj, the agrarian crisis, employment security and a decent standard of living in cities and villages, and ecological problems. The Congress must do this if it wishes not to be eaten up and/or be dominated by the Right-wing BJP. And this means that: the Congress must be less subservient to the business class, and it must give up its obsession with trickle-down economics, the idea that when the business class increases its income and when the national economic growth rises, conditions of the less-well-off will automatically improve. To get support from other parties, including Left parties, any tactical support from the Congress cannot be based on the following: the Congress shares with the BJP its Right-wing economic policy, and it fights against the BJP merely on the ground that the BJP is communalist. To adequately fight the BJP and to be a partner in the fight against the attack on secularism, the Congress cannot be merely a more or less secular BJP.[46] The extent to which and the durability with which the BJP's electoral support can be dented, and thus the wings of the fascistic movement's political ambition can be trimmed, depends crucially on how economically progressive the anti-BJP front is (whether this front is called a secular-democratic front or a movement against the fascistic movement). The extent and the durability of the fight against the reactionary capitalist politics as fascistic tendencies, presenting themselves partly in the form of the authoritarian repression of democratic rights of religious minorities, depends on how *anti-capitalist* – and how pro-people – the fight is, and *how united* the Left is, and *how independent* it is organizationally vis-à-vis bourgeois forces.

Whether it is the Congress or the federation of regional parties, all parties must be willing to have a vision of development that counters the BJP's model of free-market-based development, which hurts the ordinary people, including those who are foot-soldiers of the fascistic movement itself. The Left must advocate for this, only to unite anti-BJP forces (i.e. the forces of the fascistic movement) in order to stop them from taking control over governmental power, even if these parties will not go beyond a limit in pursuing a non-neoliberal, pro-people developmental path and even if these parties will not support any

---

46 Note that the Congress, already, is no paragon of secularism; it practices, for tactical reasons (for electoral exigencies), a version of Hindutva, and many people supporting the Congress have a soft corner for Hindutva's followers, and/or are erstwhile the BJP supporters/leaders.

serious attack on capitalist private property. The degree of Left's reliance in these bourgeois forces to fight fascistic tendencies is not a constant phenomenon. It happens on the soil of class struggle: the more the Left gets stronger in the process of mobilizing people, the less reliant it will be on some bourgeois forces in order to fight the bourgeois-fascistic forces. Mere talk of secularism is not enough. It is not enough for people to be protected against attacks on their political freedom, including religious freedom. They need to experience freedom from hunger, from farm debt, from job-insecurity, etc. The business class must be *politically forced* by all secular forces, by the masses from below, to grant significant economic concessions (such a process will potentially show the real limit of the liberal-democracy to the masses). And the apparatuses of the Sangh parivar must be actively weakened, with popular support on the ground, aided by the secular-democratic government.

The Left must not be a part of a national governmental front, which is inevitably a *bourgeois*-democratic front, no matter how secular it may become. It must be outside of the front and provide only temporary tactical support (critical support), in its fight against the fascistic tendencies. The Left must demand pro-poor policies from the secular-democratic front and insist on their implementation when introduced. And it must carry on its extra-electoral, mobilization against capitalists and large-scale landowners, maintaining its organizational independence. This means that beyond a point, the secular bourgeois parties will not be the friends of the Left; they are only its temporary allies. Being a part of the national popular front would be an enormous barrier to Left's extra-parliamentary class politics which should be the main form of Left politics. And all these aspects of the struggle against the fascistic movement, including the need to work with some bourgeois forces, must be transparently and publicly explained to the ordinary members of the working class and the class of small-scale producers.

India is a large and geographically diverse country where social and political conditions vary enormously. The fight, within the electoral sphere, against fascistic forces will therefore have to be somewhat different in different States. Basically, the aim should be to minimize divisions among the non-BJP voters (the 69% or so of voters who did not vote for it in 2014). Where the Left is weak and has little chance of winning a seat it may consider giving tactical support to the party or bloc of parties that are anti-BJP. In the constituencies, where the Left is relatively strong (in its traditional areas of support), publicly acknowledging its past mistakes and recommitting itself to the basic interests of the masses including non-dispossession of their property, the Left must campaign against neo-liberal capitalism and communalism, against all contending parties, on the basis of its mass and class movements, to retain and regain its electoral base.

There is an objective condition for a front that is reasonably secular-democratic, with a progressive economic policy. On the one hand, only 31 per cent votes were cast for the BJP at the 2014 general election. This means that merely 20 per cent of the eligible voters, or, 14 per cent of India's population, supported it. In other words: potentially, 86% of India, 80% of eligible voters, and 69% of the people who voted *did not* support the BJP. Note that even in Tripura 57% of voters did not vote for the BJP. This massive subjective force can produce the conditions for the struggle for democracy, secularism and progressive economic agenda. This is the struggle of the 69% versus 31%, or indeed 86% versus 14%. And the 31% (or 14%) includes many people who voted for the BJP not because they accepted the BJP's vision, and especially its Hindutva politics, but because the Congress, the BJP's economic other, disappointingly failed to meet their needs; there was no credible secular and economically progressive national alternative on offer.

On the other hand, there are millions of ordinary people who vote for Left parties (at least 25 million people voted for Left parties at the last election). The CPM and CPI together have 1.7 million Party members, and mass and class organizations of CPM only have a total membership of 70–80 million men and women. In a large majority of Left-oriented constituencies, Left parties are major forces (in terms of electoral support); they have lost partly because of the faulty electoral system (the first-past-the-post system). The Left parties' vote share in West Bengal is nearly as much as the BJP's vote share at the Center.[47] Apart from Left-oriented unions, there are progressive civil society organizations, including those of artists and writers, associated with the Left. There are secular-minded people inside smaller non-Left parties including the parties that came out of the non-Marxist 'socialist' movement. There are secular-minded people in AAP which is a middle class party, with support from poor people, a party that came out of the grassroots movement against corruption within the government. The class-conscious workers in those parties may provide some support to the secular-democratic front.

Any political project requires intellectual ideas. In spite of a recent Right-wing turn in academia, partly due to the pressure from the Sangh Parivar, India has one of the largest concentrations of progressive intellectuals in the world.

---

47   Even in Tripura where the Left lost (in March 2018) after being in power for decades, 45% of voters voted for the Left.

They are committed to scientific and secular values. They think from the standpoint of the masses. The intellectual power of the Sangh Parivar is nowhere close to the intellectual might of the Left (and, indeed, of the Left and democratic forces). The community of Left scholars based in India, without whom fascistic-communal culture would be stronger than it is, has a point of view on important topics confronting India. The Left's viewpoint on different topics far outshines any comparable point of view of the fascistic movement, which has an anti-intellectual trait.[48] The Right-wing movement simply has no counter-parts of the Left luminaries in India, living or deceased.[49] The force of the Left will be stronger if one includes Left scholars working on India but living outside of India. Left scholars working on India have produced important analysis of a wide array of issues.[50] There is indeed an intellectual deficit in the Right-wing movement, one it seeks to fill by non-intellectual means: capturing power and forcing their regressive ideas which defy reason and evidence, on people through political and violent means.[51] But the intellectual might of the Left and progressive forces is not enough to fight the fascistic movement, including its attack on progressive intellectuals and secular education.

4   Such a Big Compromise?: Return to Vladimir Lenin

The 'thought experiment' presented in the last few pages, i.e. the idea that the Left should help establish an economically progressive front of secular

---

48   The Italian dictator, Mussolini, in 1934, called for an end to 'intellectualising' and he thought that the 'sterile intellectuals …are a threat to the nation'; Hitler as well, a year after, exalted the inner voice, heart and faith etc. of the German people over 'hair-splitting intelligence' (quoted in Sarkar, 2016).

49   They include: Aijaz Ahmad (who until recently worked in India), Javeed Alam, Venkatesh Athreya, Amiya Bagchi, Amit Bhaduri, Sumanta Bannerjee, Dipankar Bhattacharya, Anjan Chakrabarti, Neera Chandhoke, Bipan Chandra, C.P. Chandrasekhar, Kunal Chattopadhyay, A.R. Desai, Jayati Ghosh, A.K. Gopalan, Dipankar Gupta, Irfan Habib, Rohini Hensman, Murzban Jal, P.C. Joshi, K.P. Kannan, Brinda Karat, Prakash Karat, D.D. Kosambi, Ashok Mitra, Manoranjan Mohanty, EMS Namboodiripad, K.M. Pannikkar, Prabhat Patnaik, Utsa Patnaik, Archana Prasad, Pradhan Prasad, V.K. Ramachandran, Ashok Rudra, Ranabir Samaddar; Kalyan Sanyal, Sumit Sarkar, Mohit Sen, K.M. Shrimali, R.S. Sharma, Dilip Simeon, Randhir Singh, Romilla Thapar, Sitaram Yechuri, Achin Vanaik, and so on.

50   These include: colonial oppression; colonial resistance; pre-modern history; economic, regional and class inequality; imperialism; economic under-development; agrarian crisis; poverty; technological change; unemployment; gender oppression; caste oppression; ecological change; nature of democracy; growing authoritarianism in politics and culture; and nationalism.

51   This is why the Right-wing is relishing the Tripura election result. But an election victory will itself not necessarily deliver an intellectual victory.

bourgeois parties and/or provide tactical (critical) support to it, in order to fight fascistic tendencies, is clearly in contradiction with the principle that the Left should mobilize its own forces, independent of bourgeois forces. After all, if the Left's fight is against capitalism and for socialism, how can it be with any *bourgeois* force? Such a contradiction, potentially, exists even if Left's electoral-political work must be subordinated to its extra-electoral work aimed at raising class consciousness through education and political organization and struggles. Besides, various regional parties have been with the BJP from time to time and have not been consistently secular, and as we have seen non-BJP, non-Left parties have had no problem accepting into their arms leaders from the BJP camp. They are also *bourgeois* parties, pursuing capitalist and neoliberal policies. In fact, regional-bourgeois parties have converging interests with larger-scale bourgeoisie and with the BJP. This is partly because the regional bourgeoisie wishes to benefit from the neo-liberalization that the BJP promotes, including by directly entering into competitive deals with national and global capital. The latter also opens branches in the States, to which regionally-based small-scale capitalists are linked through the supply chains.[52] Also how can the Left have any relation with the Congress, which is a blatantly neoliberal capitalist party, like the BJP is?[53] In the name of protecting secularism and fighting fascism, if the Left fails to defend social-economic rights which are under attack by both BJP and non-BJP parties with near-equal severity, then what would be left of the Left? Has the Left not supported bourgeois coalitions since the 1970s in order to keep the BJP at bay, and in spite of that how has the BJP come to power with an absolute majority? There is also indeed a real danger that workers and peasants affiliated to the Left parties will be politically subordinated to the bourgeois parties who will hold power and with whom the Left will be cooperating, however tactically. If the Left is in an electoral understanding with bourgeois parties to fight communalism, and when these parties pursue policies that attack people's living standards, how and to what extent can the Left counter-attack these policies/parties?

---

52 'It is this changed position of the regional bourgeoisie which has led to the convergence of interests between the BJP, a representative of the big bourgeoisie, and the parties representing the regional bourgeoisie. At the political level, in many states, the regional party is the main rival of the Congress and therefore the alliance with the BJP is expedient as it provides additional support against the Congress in electoral terms and secondly it enables its entry into a coalition government at the Centre which can be utilized to consolidate its position in the state. Secularism is a barrier which can be breached when class and political interests converge' (Karat, 2004: 3).

53 This question is a little problematic on the ground that the Left itself has acted like the neoliberal Congress in the provinces where it has been in power. Geographical scale cannot be an excuse for inconsistency: one cannot advocate for more progressive policies at the national scale and less progressive policies at the provincial scale. Luckily, the Left is rethinking its land acquisition policy.

These and similar questions and their underlying theoretical standpoint cannot be evaded at all in order to fight an imminent danger, the danger of fascistic tendencies. The aim of a theoretical principle is to unpack what is happening and why, and to guide political action. A fight to abolish landlordism must be conducted in such a way that the masses (workers and poor peasants) are mobilized independent of the capitalist class as it has lost its anti-landlord fighting qualities, given its fear of the working class. As a general principle, the fight against the capitalist class relation must be conducted in a way that is independent of any fraction of the capitalist class (e.g. progressive or national, etc.). The fight against fascistic tendencies must obey the same principle. But given the serious threat that the fascistic movement poses to the communist movement against capitalism and to common people's democratic rights and living standards, could one argue that the fight against the fascistic movement must be a part of the fight to create the conditions for the fight against capitalism and therefore must be a part of the fight against capitalism. I do think that in a long and winding journey towards socialism, if the Left is not to remain mainly an abstentionist political propaganda machine or an organization with only negligible ability to influence national political affairs, one cannot automatically reject all possibilities of conditional and revolutionary temporary compromise with non-Left non-fascistic forces. This is so especially when the subjective forces of the Left have lagged behind the progress of bourgeois reactionary forces and when one enemy is holding a gun and another is holding several dosages of poison, both of which can kill the toiling masses and their political movement. But what does such compromise as a political practice really mean? To answer this question, one must ask another question: what 'alternative' *theoretical* standpoint does that *practice* presuppose? More specifically, is a temporary compromise with some secular-democratic bourgeois forces justifiable? And to answer this question, we need to read about that practice of temporary revolutionary compromise from someone who is, arguably, the Marxist theoretician and Marxist politician *par excellence* of the 20th century. This is Vladimir Lenin whose statues, as mentioned earlier, fascistic forces brought down immediately the BJP's first-time win in Tripura, dislodging the Left and this shows what is going to come. Let's briefly consider what I will call *Lenin's theory of temporary revolutionary compromise.*

4.1   Definition and Typology of Compromise

In an article entitled, 'On Compromises', Lenin (1917) says this: 'The term compromise in politics implies the surrender of certain demands, the renunciation of part of one's demands, by agreement with another party'. In thinking about any compromise, Lenin (1920) says in *"Left-wing" communism: an infantile disorder*, 'the greatest efforts are necessary for a proper assessment of the actual

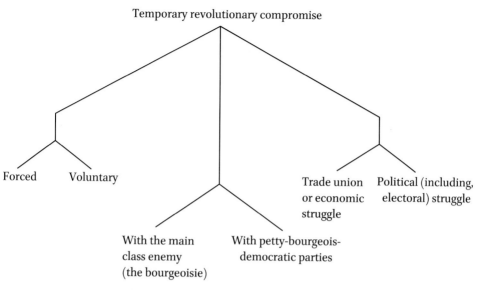

FIGURE 13.6 Types of temporary revolutionary compromise
SOURCE: AUTHOR (BASED ON LENIN'S TEXTS)

character of this or that "compromise"'. Such an assessment will be helped by the acknowledgment that compromises are of different types (Figure 13.6 above). From one vantage point, compromises are forced or they can be voluntary. The first type – forced compromise – is a compromise that is caused by objective conditions but that does not minimize devotion to carry on class struggle: 'compromises are often unavoidably forced upon a fighting party by circumstances' (ibid.). The voluntary type of compromise is one that is caused by the action of traitors to the working class. Lenin eloquently explains the difference between objective and voluntary compromises:

> Every proletarian – as a result of the conditions of the mass struggle and the acute intensification of class antagonisms he lives among – sees the difference between a compromise enforced by objective conditions (such as lack of strike funds, no outside support, starvation and exhaustion) – a compromise which in no way minimises the revolutionary devotion and readiness to carry on the struggle on the part of the workers who have agreed to such a compromise – and, on the other hand, a compromise by traitors who try to ascribe to objective causes their self-interest ... their cowardice, desire to toady to the capitalists, and readiness to yield to intimidation, sometimes to persuasion, sometimes to sops, and sometimes to flattery from the capitalists.
> LENIN, 1920

Voluntary compromises cannot be allowed by the Left but compromises that are imposed by objective conditions such as lack of funds or outside support (for a local struggle) or the relative weakness of the subjective force relative to the enemy's strength, can be, *under certain conditions*.[54] From the second vantage point, the compromise may be with the main class enemy, i.e. the bourgeoisie, and or with 'nearest adversaries', the petty-bourgeois-democratic parties. And, from the third vantage point, compromises can be in trade union struggle (economic struggle) or in politics (political struggle) (more on this below). Compromises in economic struggle can be objective or voluntary, so can compromises in political struggle. Explaining compromise in politics, Lenin (1920) says:

> In politics, where it is sometimes a matter of extremely complex relations ... between classes and parties, very many cases will arise that will be much more difficult than the question of a legitimate "compromise" in a strike or a treacherous "compromise" by a strike-breaker, treacherous leader, etc.

4.2 Nature of Temporary Revolutionary Compromise in Politics

We will focus on compromise in politics. In the course of the struggle to transcend the capitalist society and establish a new, genuinely democratic society, circumstances force the Left to make compromises in the political sphere. Therefore, it is important to bear in mind that: 'The task of a truly revolutionary party is not to declare that it is impossible to renounce all compromises' (ibid.). Engels says against the Blanquist communards, it is mistaken to believe that 'we want to attain our goal without stopping at intermediate stations, without any compromises, which only postpone the day of victory and prolong the period of slavery' (quoted in Lenin, 1920).[55]

Lenin was scathing in his criticisms of some German communists who thought that 'All compromise with other parties ... any policy of manoeuvring and compromise must be emphatically rejected' (ibid.). To launch class struggle, which is protracted and complex, against the bourgeoisie, nationally and globally, 'to renounce in advance any change of tack, or any utilisation of a

---

54 Further, as Lenin (1920) explains in *Leftwing communism*: 'In the practical questions that arise in the politics of any particular or specific historical moment, it is important to single out those which display the principal type of intolerable and treacherous compromises, such as embody an opportunism that is fatal to the revolutionary class, and to exert all efforts to explain them and combat them'.

55 So, 'It would be absurd to formulate a recipe or general rule to suit all cases. One must use one's own brains and be able to find one's bearings in each particular instance' (ibid.).

FORWARD MARCH OF THE RIGHT AND THE RELATIVE WEAKNESS 497

conflict of interests (even if temporary) among one's enemies, or any conciliation or compromise with possible allies (even if they are temporary, unstable, vacillating or conditional allies) – is that not ridiculous in the extreme?' (ibid.).

Echoing Lenin's point that the fight against capitalism requires some temporary agreements and a degree of principled unity among proletarian groups, Trotsky (1933a), whose views on the topic we began the chapter with, says:

> No successes would be possible without temporary agreements, for the sake of fulfilling immediate tasks, among various sections, organizations, and groups of the proletariat. Strikes, trade unions, journals, parliamentary elections, street demonstrations, demand that the split be bridged in practice from time to time as the need arises; that is, they demand an *ad hoc* united front, even if it does not always take on the form of one. In the first stages of a movement, unity arises episodically and spontaneously from below, but when the masses are accustomed to fighting through their organizations, unity must also be established at the top.[56]

---

56 Here are some examples of compromise Trotsky gives: 'The Jewish bourgeoisie in Czarist Russia represented an extremely frightened and demoralized part of the entire Russian bourgeoisie. And yet, insofar as the pogroms of the Black Hundreds, which were in the main directed against the Jewish poor, also hit the bourgeoisie, the latter was forced to defend itself. To be sure, it did not show any remarkable bravery on this field either. But due to the danger hanging over their heads, the liberal Jewish bourgeoisie, for example, collected considerable sums for the arming of revolutionary workers and students. In this manner, a temporary practical agreement was arrived at between the most revolutionary workers, who were prepared to fight with guns in hand, and the most frightened group of the bourgeoisie, which had got into a scrape' (Trotsky, 1932f).

The Bolsheviks more than once proposed to the Mensheviks and Social Revolutionaries in 1917: 'Take the power, we will support you against the bourgeoisie if it should resist' (Trotsky, 1932g). During July and August 1917, Kerensky, then head of the government, was in fact fulfilling the program of Kornilov, the commander-in-chief of the army. ...On August 26, Kornilov broke with Kerensky because of the latter's vacillation, and threw his army against Petrograd. The status of the Bolshevik Party was semi-legal. Its leaders from Lenin down were either hiding underground or committed to prison...These persecutions emanated from Kerensky's government... What course did the Bolshevik Party take? Not for an instant did it hesitate to conclude a practical alliance to fight against Kornilov with its jailers – Kerensky, ... etc. Everywhere committees for revolutionary defense were organized, into which the Bolsheviks entered as a minority. This did not hinder the Bolsheviks from assuming the leading role: in agreements projected for revolutionary mass action, the most thoroughgoing and the boldest revolutionary party stands to gain always. The Bolsheviks were in the front ranks; they smashed down the barriers blocking them from the Menshevik workers and especially from the Social Revolutionary soldiers, and carried them along in their wake (Trotsky, 1932j).

4.3 Why Is Temporary Revolutionary Compromise Necessary and Possible?

Let us consider the matter of temporary compromise from the standpoint of: nature of the class enemy and nature of the working class.

The matter of class has many aspects, which exist at different levels (Das, 2017). Class interests exist at one level. Their political representation by parties exists at another. What happens at the level of the political representation of objective class interests has some autonomy relative to, and therefore, cannot be reduced to, the level at which objective class interests exist. The class enemy of the working class, and indeed every class, is both unitary and fragmented in terms of its interests and consciousness, etc.

In so far as all bourgeois parties support capitalists and landlords, they are the same class enemy for the Left. But these parties support the ruling classes in *different* ways. Some parties – like some sections of ruling class – may be more secular-minded than others.[57] Some may be *slightly* more pro-poor or pro-worker, pro-peasant, than others. In terms of the political representation of ruling class interests, there are two facts. First, different interests of the ruling class (with its multiple fractions) are represented by different parties.[58] Second, these parties, to remain in electoral competition, which is their self-interest, if not for any basic *principle*, will represent the given interests of the ruling class differently, and in ways that are conflictual, within limits.[59] Some of these ways may partially overlap with the Left's agenda (e.g. an increase in the wage) than other ways. These two facts concerning the political representation of the ruling class constitute an objective reason why temporary compromise by Left is *possible*:

> The more powerful enemy can be vanquished only by exerting the utmost effort, and by the most thorough, careful, attentive, skilful and *obligatory* use of any, even the smallest, *rift between the enemies..., any conflict of interests among* .... the various groups or types of bourgeoisie ..., and

---

57 Consider how Gurucharan Das, an organic intellectual of the capitalist class, is wanting that a blatantly pro-capitalist party which is secular be established.

58 More generally, every class is represented by a party, or, more commonly, by a set of parties, because of internal subjective and objective differences within a class. A given class has different class-strata: while at one level their interests are common, at another, they have conflicts, which are reflected at the level of political representation of class interests by parties.

59 These limits mean the following: all parties must support capitalism and private property, and within these limits, specific political parties can pursue their interests that may be relatively autonomous of ruling class interests, and sometimes may even slightly deviate from ruling class interests (in profit-making, etc.) in the short term.

also by taking advantage of any, even the smallest, opportunity of winning a mass ally, even though this ally is *temporary, vacillating, unstable, unreliable and conditional.*

> LENIN, 1920; italics added

Lenin (1920) warns: 'Those who do not understand this reveal a failure to understand even the smallest grain of Marxism, of modern scientific socialism *in general*' (ibid.; italics added). Once again we must remind ourselves about Marx's point about the need to prove truth in practice.[60] And in line with Marx, Lenin (1920) says this:

> Those who have not proved *in practice*, over a fairly considerable period of time and in fairly varied political situations, their ability to apply this truth [i.e. the truth about the need for temporary revolutionary political compromise] in practice have not yet learned to help the revolutionary class in its struggle to emancipate all toiling humanity from the exploiters. And this applies equally to the period *before* and *after* the proletariat has won political power. (Parenthesis added)

Let's turn to the nature of the working class in relation to the need for compromise. The working class is potentially the most revolutionary agent. There is no Marxist party/movement without this class. No anti-capitalist revolution is possible without this class, apart from this class, over the head of this class, or with a substitute for this class and its organization. Yet, although it is an objective reality, the working class does fall short, ideologically and politically. This class is deeply politically divided, in part because of the uneven level of consciousness within this class. The level of class consciousness and political preparedness of the working class has to be much improved; that the largest trade union is the one led by the fascist organization (RSS) indicates this. The working class's consciousness is shaped by the ways in which capitalism operates on the basis of competition, individualism, commodity fetishism, etc. It is also shaped by the ideas and interests of non-proletarian classes within capitalism. As Lenin (1920) says:

> Capitalism would not be capitalism if the proletariat *pur sang* were not surrounded by a large number of exceedingly motley types...'. [These

---

60   'The question whether objective truth can be attributed to human thinking is not a question of theory but is a practical question. Man must [ultimately] prove the truth – i.e. the reality and power, the this-sidedness of his thinking in practice' (Marx, 1845; parenthesis added).

types exist] intermediate between the proletarian and the semi-proletarian (who earns his livelihood in part by the sale of his labour-power), between the semi-proletarian and the small peasant (and petty artisan, handicraft worker and small master in general), between the small peasant and the middle peasant, and so on, and if the proletariat itself were not divided into more developed and less developed strata, if it were not divided according to *territorial origin, trade, sometimes according to religion*, and so on. (Italics added)

This is especially true in countries such as India experiencing belated capitalist development.

Fascism – the fascistic tendency – operates not in the abstract two-class mode of capitalist society, but in a society where there are different classes and class-strata between capitalists and workers. As Trotsky says: fascism – or in our times, the fascistic movement – penetrates the proletariat from below (through the unemployed) and from above (through the middle class people such as salaried employees, etc.). The political implication, as Lenin says, is this:

> From all this follows the necessity, the absolute necessity, for the Communist Party, the vanguard of the proletariat, its class-conscious section, to resort to changes of tack, to *conciliation and compromises with the various groups of proletarians, with the various parties of the workers and small masters.*
>
> Ibid.; italics added

So: temporary compromises *in the electoral sphere* are objectively *necessary* because the working masses are divided and not class conscious (enough) and concomitantly, the Left is relatively weak, at a given juncture. Compromises are *possible* because there are conflicts of interests within the economic elite and within the political elite (i.e. among various parties).

In line with Lenin's theory, I would argue that compromises in the electoral sphere, which do pose ideological and political risks (of subordinating workers and peasants to bourgeois forces), are justified *only when* the following criteria are met (making the temporary agreement as a part of the revolutionary struggle highly conditional).

First, compromises are unavoidable or forced by conditions (e.g. Left is weak relative to, say, fascistic forces, so it needs allies in some cases). The compromises that the Left can allow cannot be because of Left leaders' 'cowardice, desire to toady to the capitalists, and readiness to yield to intimidation, sometimes to persuasion, sometimes to sops, and sometimes to flattery from the capitalists' (Lenin, 1920). Second: compromises, ultimately, contribute to the political project of raising the level of consciousness of the masses and advancing the goal of the communist struggle against (a) capitalism's adverse consequences for the masses, and against (b) the capitalist class relation as such. As Lenin says, tactics of temporary compromises are applied only 'to *raise* – not lower – the *general* level of proletarian class-consciousness, revolutionary spirit, and ability to fight and win' (Lenin, 1920). Third, Left forces maintain their organizational and ideological independence versus non-left parties and movements. The principle of independence must permeate the spirit of united front action:

> [Y]ou must never dare to merge, mix, or combine your own party organization with an alien one, even though the latter be most 'sympathetic' today. Undertake no such steps as lead directly or indirectly, openly or maskedly, to the subordination of your party to other parties, or to organizations of other classes, or constrict the freedom of your own agitation, or your responsibility, even if only in part, for the political line of other parties.
>
> TROTSKY, 1928

The Left will always have the right to criticize, and to politically go against (mobilize its classes against) its temporary allies when their policies attack living conditions of ordinary people.

Fourth, the Left's *dominant* focus is on extra-parliamentary mobilization, including for economic concessions, of workers and peasants, and *not* electoral battles. The point of temporary agreement is not to resort to confine class struggle only to the parliamentary/electoral sphere. 'A parliamentary agreement against fascist predominance in the ... [parliaments] etc., would constitute merely one component part of' the fight against fascism or fascistic tendencies. 'Naturally the Communist Party would prefer to resolve the whole question at one blow outside of parliament. But preferences alone are not sufficient where the forces are lacking' (Trotsky, 1932g). So:

> Compromises are admissible and, under certain conditions, obligatory. The whole question lies in what aim the compromise shall serve; how it looks to the masses; what its limits are. To confine the compromise to the [parliamentary fora], ... means to sink completely into parliamentary cretinism.
>
> TROTSKY, 1932g[61]

---

61 Trotsky continues: 'The situation is completely different when the [communist] party sets itself the task of the systematic and planned struggle for the Social Democratic workers on the basis of the united-front policy' (Trotsky, 1932g).

Once again, 'The task of a truly revolutionary party is not to declare that it is impossible to renounce all compromises, but to be able, *through all compromises*, when they are unavoidable, to remain true to its principles, to its class, to its revolutionary purpose, to its task of paving the way for revolution and educating the mass of the people for victory in the revolution' (Lenin, 1917).[62] The point of political compromise is not to arrive at, and settle for, a capitalist society that is slightly tolerable and that just needs to be managed by the Left forces forever. The compromise in question here is revolutionary compromise (compromise as a part of, and with the purpose of, advancing long-term goals of class struggle), like Luxemburg's revolutionary reforms or reforms as the 'means of the class struggle', whose goal is revolution (Luxemburg, 2009: 129), the compromise that is *temporarily* necessitated by the force of *circumstances* relative to the strength of the Left forces, in order to advance the long-term *revolutionary* goal, the goal of transcending capitalism and not to help sustain capitalism *sans* fascistic tendencies. Therefore: 'Naïve and quite inexperienced people imagine that the permissibility of compromise *in general* is sufficient to obliterate any distinction between opportunism…and revolutionary Marxism, or communism'. In fact, 'the entire history of Bolshevism, both before and after the October Revolution, is *full* of instances of changes of tack, conciliatory tactics and compromises with other parties, including bourgeois parties!' (Lenin, 1920). Lenin says that

> It is entirely a matter of *knowing how* to apply these tactics in order to *raise* – not lower – the *general* level of proletarian class-consciousness, revolutionary spirit, and ability to fight and win.
>
> LENIN, 1920

Fifth, any temporary compromise with less revolutionary forces must be mindful of the usefulness of the united front tactic. Here is Trotsky on this point:

> Assuming a defensive position means a policy of closing ranks with the majority of the … working class and forming a united front with the Social Democratic and nonparty workers against the fascist threat.
>
> TROTSKY, 1930

---

62   'To agree, for instance, to participate in the Third and Fourth Dumas was a compromise, a temporary renunciation of revolutionary demands. But this was a compromise absolutely forced upon us, for the balance of forces made it impossible for us for the time being to conduct a mass revolutionary struggle, and in order to prepare this struggle over a long period we *had* to be able to work even from *inside* such a "pigsty"' (Lenin, 1917).

FORWARD MARCH OF THE RIGHT AND THE RELATIVE WEAKNESS

And the task of such a united front is to fight fascism and it is also 'the task of the systematic and planned struggle for the Social Democratic workers on the basis of the united-front policy' (Trotsky, 1932g).

However, there should not be a united front fetishism.

> we in no way advocate lapsing into a united-front fetishism. An agreement ... remains in effect so long as it serves the practical goal for which it was concluded. If the reformists begin to curb or to sabotage the movement the Communists must always put to themselves the question: is it not time to tear up the agreement and to lead the masses further under our own banner?
>
> TROTSKY, 1932g

So, a temporary compromise may be struck by the Marxist Left only when these conditions are met. Of course, what form that compromise will take is a different matter. Now, one might assess the relevance of Lenin's theory of temporary compromise for the Indian conjuncture where there is *right now* a fascistic mortal threat *to the very existence* of the actually-existing Left movement: note the BJP's aim is to see a 'Left-free India', 'Communist-free India'. Note also that the largest trade union belongs to the fascistic RSS.

The idea of United Front applies, originally, to the idea of the unity of masses, of workers. 'The united front is to unite the Communist and Social Democratic working masses [and non-party workers] and not to patch up an agreement with political groups that are without the masses' (Trotsky, 1932j).

India does *not* have this conjuncture. The equivalents of Germany's social democratic party, or of the communist party (which almost led a revolution in Germany), do not exist in India, thanks to the weakness of the various Marxist streams, including the Far Left. The existing communist parties are effectively social-democratic parties (see Heller, 1995; Chakrabarty, 2015). And, there is no social democratic party, although there may be elements of social democratic *policy* in multiple bourgeois parties that are primarily driven by bourgeois-political formations' need to obtain votes, which, in turn, provide them access to the state to be used in the interests of the bourgeois strata and in the interests of the bourgeois political elite. Workers are not concentrated in working class parties. The working class parties – the communist parties – are not strong enough to meet the challenge of fascistic tendencies on their own. The majority of working class men and women of different castes and religions, do not belong to a communist party or to a non-existing social democratic party, but are members and supporters of bourgeois parties, including bourgeois-fascistic parties. The bourgeois parties all have workers as their members but that does not make them workers' – social-democratic – parties. This explains why it is that in pursuit of a short-term goal (i.e. electoral defeat of fascistic forces), a united front of communist parties and groups and of non-Party-affiliated Marxist groups and individuals, on a tactial basis, is needed. These parties may enter into some understanding with the parties of small scale producers (or, in Lenin's words 'small masters'). Any agreement with the Congress, the traditional party of Indian capitalist class, should be avoided in the fight against fascistic forces, except perhaps in an extremely exceptional case. It must be immediately said, however, that whether it is the Congress or the parties of small masters, they are thoroughly compromised as far as the fight for secularism and democratic rights is concerned, and therefore any agreement with them by the Left must be a rare occasion.

One might argue that there are some objective conditions for some electoral cooperation among Left and non-Left secular forces representing small-scale masters not only because of an imminent existential threat from fascistic forces to the Left, but also because of potential and actual conflicts between the BJP and the non-Left forces. In liberal democracy, there is electoral competition among bourgeois parties, representing interests of bigger capitalists and regional capitalists, and landowners. A non-BJP party may not necessarily be genuinely interested in protecting secularism. To merely exist as a party,[63] it must compete with the BJP. To compete with the BJP and to represent the bourgeois interests almost like the way the BJP does because it is also a bourgeois party, it must politically differentiate itself from the BJP. If secularism is not the basis – or not the sole basis – for differentiation, then what (else) might it be? The answer is: to the extent that regional parties seek to represent peasants and small-scale property owners ('small masters' in Lenin's words), the BJP's neoliberal policies – like such policies of the Congress – are adversely affecting these strata, creating, among other things, agrarian crisis and farmers' suicide. The BJP's major weakness is this: it can satisfy the need for a religion and for a sense of belonging to a Hindu rastra, but it cannot feed people with Hinduism, temple-building and mosque-destroying. Even to go to a temple, one needs to have eaten or one needs to eat soon after the visit! One needs shelter, education, healthcare, affordable transportation, leisure, a good environment, and freedom from fear of being killed or hurt for one's religious and other view. With its blatantly free market pro-business policies, the BJP cannot

---

63   Note that in spite of all the talk about neoliberalism, it is the case that being in the government and being able to use governmental power is a source of immense amount of income and wealth, earned by helping the business class make money at the expense of the masses and indeed the nation as a whole.

FORWARD MARCH OF THE RIGHT AND THE RELATIVE WEAKNESS 505

satisfy these needs. The BJP's policies are, and will be, depriving ordinary people of what they need to live. And it is the conflict between what the BJP is and what people need, and therefore, the conflict between the BJP and other parties that are reasonably secular and that may seek to somewhat address people's issues in part to distinguish themselves from the BJP, that can be, and should be made use of, by the Left.[64] One should also consider the fact that there is some potential conflict within the big bourgeoisie in relation to the fascistic threat. Through fascistic forces such as the BJP, the ruling class keeps the masses *divided* against its class rule. The BJP's right-wing economic policies help the big business. But the ruling class's support for the BJP beyond a point can potentially backfire. The BJP's majoritarian communalism can lead to minority communalism of Sikhs, Muslims, etc. This can then undermine the territorial unity of the nation (e.g. a large national market, etc.) and thus go against the economic interest of the ruling class.[65] Besides, communal-fascistic violence can lead to an enormous loss of property, including capitalist property. A proper business environment requires a politically calm situation. So potential adverse implications of the BJP's communalism, in a situation where there is not yet a fascistic state that can completely destroy any protest against fascistic tendencies, can lead to some support from the ruling class, for its traditional party (the Congress). Growing disenchantment against communal strife and attack on living standards caused by the fascistic tendencies led and aided by the BJP is also causing a part of the 'molecular' anger of the masses to be channelized towards the Congress already (as seen in the by-elections in 2018 and in

---

64   Support from the Left may include: not contesting against the non-BJP secular parties in areas of Left's electoral weakness, and outside support in the parliament to keep the BJP outs. Yet, the Left parties must tell the workers and peasants that such support is highly conditional and that all parties, BJP or not, are their targets, when it comes to the livelihood issues, because all these parties, more or less, pursue (neoliberal-)capitalist policies and that even with respect to democratic rights and secularism, the so-called non-BJP parties are vacillating allies.

65   'The ruling class...realises that to keep India, with its enormous size and diversity, united, such a communal agenda would not serve the purpose. The geographical unity of India needs to be maintained for the ruling classes in order to consolidate and strengthen its class rule. A communal divide like what the BJP is mounting today, also justifies the ideological foundations of separatist movements like Khalisthan etc. This can only act contrary to the interests of the leadership of the Indian ruling classes in their effort to maintain the geographical unity of the country.... Thus, we find representatives of the big business-like Tatas coming out openly against such communal violence'. It is also the case that 'the ruling classes exercise their class rule through agents, which are political parties. When an avowedly communal party makes a concerted bid for state power sections of the bourgeoisie themselves will vacillate and some will extend support to it' (Yechuri, 1993: 14–15).

the Gujarat elections in late 2017), sharpening its conflict with the BJP. In other words, a certain amount of conflict within the ruling class and within the sphere of bourgeois politics where its interests are represented, can create a limited potential for a *temporary* and *conditional* Left compromise with bourgeois forces, in order to fight fascistic tendencies and remove a major obstacle to the Left movement. But whether that potential will be realized by the Left and in what form depends. I will repeat that the Left's main approach to the fight against the fascistic tendencies cannot be the electoral approach, including making temporary electoral compromises with non-BJP bourgeois parties.

Note that the secular-bourgeois forces' aim is less to protect capitalism against the proletarian struggle at this juncture, and more to preserve a democratic form of the state of the capitalist class, thus there is a contradiction between the fascistic sections of the bourgeois political formation and the bourgeois political parties that are a little more democratic and secular, a contradiction that can be exploited by the Left. It is true that the smaller bourgeois parties, and the big bourgeois parties (the Congress) and the BJP are not united now but they will be united when there is a revolutionary situation (and in fact, they were all – including the BJP – united when it came to supporting the legislation to approve of India's subordination to imperialism). But that does not mean that they always and under all conditions share the same ideas and engage in same practices. They are all similar (because they are all bourgeois) and there are differences among them because they are different in terms of how to implement the bourgeois economic-political and cultural agenda. The situation resonates, to some extent, with the one Trotsky describes:

> Just now their interests [political parties'] diverge. At the *given* moment the question that is posed before the [democratic parties] ... is not so much one of defending the foundations of capitalist society against proletarian revolution as of defending the semi-parliamentarian bourgeois, system against Fascism [or fascistic tendencies]. The refusal to make use of this antagonism would be an act of gross stupidity.
>
> TROTSKY, 1932i; parentheses added

But how exactly to make use of that antagonism is a different matter.

5   Conclusion

The fascistic-nationalist movement is not only profoundly pro-capitalist but also is it shamelessly subordinating the interests of toiling masses to imperialism. This is the real treachery, and this is the real treason, as far as the toiling majority are concerned. The common people who really love their country as a part of the family of nations and who are mistakenly listening to their communal-fascistic misleaders must reflect on this cruel fact. As the most consistent supporters of principles of democracy and secularism and with its unique commitment to the welfare of the toiling masses, the Left must mobilize the basic classes (workers, and small-scale, non-exploiting, producers) to (a) fight for democratic rights and against fascistic tendencies, (b) fight for significant improvements in conditions of living, on the basis of immediate and transitional demands, *as a part of* – and *within the overall framework* of – the fight for a socialist society.[66]

The rise of the BJP represents the crisis not only of bourgeois economics but also of bourgeois politics: the bourgeois political-economic system, and therefore, the bourgeois ruling class, has, simply, failed to secure not only social rights but also democratic rights, including rights of religious minorities. So the blame for the current situation must be at the door not only of the BJP and these forces, but also the bourgeoisie itself, or the bourgeois system as a whole. That is why the fascistic threat is a class project, and not merely a political-cultural project. The threat exists in the following context: while the ruling class is losing its right to be the ruling class, the masses are not yet ready to say 'we cannot take it anymore', although some stirring in their consciousness is apparent. This contradiction is causing the BJP itself to be contradictory. The BJP's major contradictions are structural in that they are inter-related and are parts of the capitalist class system in India.

First, there is a contradiction between its promises (which are secular lies) and what it can deliver to the people, given its blatantly right-wing character. Politics of dividing and deceiving the masses is the DNA of class society.[67] And, fascism – or fascistic tendency – as the most extreme form of this politics – is

---

66   This framework is opposed to the framework within which the fight for a socialist society is postponed indefinitely, a framework that contradicts the idea that the humanity's fundamental problems are caused by capitalist *class relations* and cannot be significantly resolved as long as these relations exist.

67   Class society is a society that is defined by this: 'Wherever a part of society possesses the monopoly of the means of production' and therefore 'the worker, free or not free, must add to the labour-time necessary for his [her] own maintenance an extra quantity of labour-time in order to produce the means of subsistence for the owners of the means of production' (Marx, 1977: 344), and (partly) as a result of this, the needs of the majority remain unmet, which is why one social group (Hindus) mistakenly blames another social group (Muslims) for its miseries.

in the DNA of capitalism as a class society.[68] To hide its right-wing character, the BJP has to make promises which objectively contradict what it can deliver. Common people should critically reflect on the false promises of the party-in-power supported by fascistic forces, and on the dismal record of its government on development, democracy and governance. This failure is not coincidental. It is a *necessary* product given the right-wing, pro-business, pro-market, government which has been implanted on the poisonous soil of putrid communalism. Both the soil and the plant are bad for the nation and for the world at large.

Second, given rising economic inequality, and given the failure of all forms of the government to meet people's needs, the contradiction between political equality among all citizens, and economic inequality, is becoming more and more stark, a contradiction that is signified by the BJP embodying the fascistic movement. The contradiction is being sought to be resolved not by reducing economic inequality but by undermining the nominal political equality (i.e. by not treating citizens from different religious and other backgrounds as equal).

The nature of the BJP's fascistic tendencies highlights the vulnerability of bourgeois democracy. India's democratic character can no longer be taken for granted. Therefore, the rise of the BJP can potentially create fertile ground for more radical struggle against the bourgeois system itself: there is not only a contradiction between the BJP and the masses but also between the system as a whole and the masses. The genuine and long-term resolution of these contradictions requires the removal of the system. The situation points to the need to fight not only against the fascistic and anti-secular character of bourgeois politics in India and elsewhere. It also points to the following fact: on the basis of the fight against the right-wing politics/political economy, a fight has to be launched against the very logics of capitalist society, which are behind such right-wing politics and political economy. This is as true for India as it is for all the countries where fascistic forces are rising.

Democratic politics and fascistic politics in societies dominated by bourgeois mode of production and exchange are both forms of bourgeois class rule. If ultra-right politics, like its more-democratic variant, is the political intervention of the ruling class to cope with its own crisis, then arriving at a different politics requires the political intervention of the masses of workers and petty producers, and their organic intellectuals. It is only their struggle, launched on

---

68   If politics of division and deception of the masses is the DNA of the capitalist class society, then fascism is the nucleotides, the molecules that constitute the DNA.

the basis of sound theory and with the assistance of democratically-organized, multi-scalar, anti-capitalist, socialist, revolutionary organizations, that can ensure that every country will meet the basic needs of every man, woman and child of all religions, castes, races and locations, where a culture of democracy and of mutual love and compassion among the ordinary toiling people prevails.

Controlled by a Right-wing party, the BJP government, whether now or in the future, is not, and will not be, in sync with the political culture of a country, where the vast majority of its men and women of different religions and castes do not have the means to satisfy their basic needs and where there is a deeply-felt desire for democracy and secularism. The majority of Indians are religious. But they do not necessarily favor the political-sectarian use of religion to make one group hate another. They do not necessarily favor politicians who spread religious hatred for political gain. However contradictory and utopian religious ideas are, all religions propagate 'spiritually' uplifting ideas, even if it is the case that many religious ideas do contribute to the reproduction of unjust social arrangements. Religious ideas express, among other things, people's desire to be much better than what they normally are and what they can be. Religious ideas teach people to be 'spiritual', generous, loving and kind-hearted, so even if people are religious, they can oppose the misuse of religion for narrow, divisive political gains undermining the secular-democratic character of the country.[69] Arguably, this is why there is a high level of resentment against the BJP among a large proportion of Hindu voters. This suggests that there is opposition to the Hindu nationalist party's attempt to *unite* all Hindus to garner their votes on the basis of religion and on the basis of the utterly false notion that Hindus are under threat from Muslims.

Common people must ask, and the Left and progressive forces must encourage them to ask: who is it that fears the citizens united to fight for their rights against the economic elite? Is it not the case that what is under attack is

---

69   Calling for secularization the social sphere is important but it is limited. As long as there are reasons to be religious, people will be religious and when that happens, political use of religion is few steps away. 'The abolition of religion as the *illusory* happiness of the people is the demand for their *real* happiness. To call on them to give up their illusions about their condition is to call on them to *give up a condition that requires illusions*. The criticism of religion is, therefore, *in embryo, the criticism of that vale of tears* of which religion is the *halo*. ...Religion is only the illusory Sun which revolves around man as long as he does not revolve around himself' (Marx, 1843).

neither Hinduism from Islam, nor India as a nation from neighboring coun-tries, but 'the nation of ordinary people' who work for a living as wage-earners and/or as petty-producers, and whose most basic needs are not met? Are those elements attacking this nation of common people not the economic elite, which controls society's resources using them for their own profit, and which is supported by the BJP's politicians and the pliant officers, and by their propa-gandists in academia and the media? Is there not more common ground among them (wage-earners and among small-scale producers of different reli-gions and castes) than there are differences among them?

People must ask: whose interests are the politicians who spread religious hatred serving? How will religious hatred solve the country's major problems? How does religious hatred or a feeling of hyper-nationalism based on Hindu identity, help a society address problems of unemployment, poverty, inequali-ty, caste- and gender-based oppression, environmental pollution, natural resources depletion, the country's subjugation to powerful foreign powers, localised semi-feudal oppression, agrarian distress, lack of affordable health-care, housing and education? How can these problems be caused by the fact that some people are Hindus and others are not? Is it or is it not the case that: when political leaders and big business fail to solve people's major problems, they seek to divert people's attention *from* such failure *towards* non-issues by using religion, myths, false nationalism and so on, to divide the people? Is it not true that weakening the unity of common people diverts them from their fight against the business elite and the government such as the one led by BJP? Why is it that the right-wing government feels threatened by any attempt to forge a unity of secular political forces, prompting it to use undemocratic mea-sures against opposition forces? Those in the business world cannot also be allowed to maintain their 'silence': they must be asked by the masses this ques-tion: do they or do they not support the forces which are communal and which spread sectarian hatred and which repress any force of dissent?

Not only must one ask questions, and ordinary people *are* already asking questions, such as the ones posed above. They must also *fight* to deepen and defend their democratic rights, including the right to practice any religion, to eat any food, to engage in any occupation or to love anyone. They must also fight for economic security. And in fighting for their democratic rights and eco-nomic security, they must be conscious of what *binds* them: what binds them, irrespective of their different religions, is the fact that their democratic rights (*including* secularism) and their right to a decent livelihood, *are* under attack by this government, while the rich elite in control of big business and their right-wing lackeys (hangers-on) in academia and media are having *achhe din* (good times). The BJP and its authoritarian government, and all the reactionary forces on the ground supporting them, must continue to face the collective and democratic might of the toiling masses and progressive intellectuals. There is, and there can be, no force that is more powerful than the united force of the organized and class-conscious workers and small-scale producers. If they withdraw their labor from the farms, factories, offices, laboratories, schools and universities, or if they do not bring the products of their labor to the market, or if the unemployed, demanding decent jobs, start a non-cooperation movement by not only boycotting elections but also stopping the movement of commodities on roads and railway lines, then the system is in big trouble. It is time that the masses of India (and of South Asia) begin to ask fundamental questions about what kind of society they are living in, what kind of society they wish to live in, and how to get there. If the Hindutva-nationalistic forces are pitting the Hindu-dominated India against the Muslim-dominated Pakistan and treat Indian Muslims as de facto Pakistanis and consider Muslim immigrants from other countries as second-class citizens, then the workers and peasants of India and Pakistan and Bangladesh must fight together against the fascistic forces and against their ruling classes and not allow themselves to be divided along the lines of religion and nation.

In struggling against the regime and in the *current conjuncture*, what is clearly needed, and what needs to be demanded by common people, *as a minimum*, therefore, is a government that (a) respects the rights of religious minorities, low castes, women, and children, and that respects the general democratic rights of the ordinary citizen, both in words, speeches, and in actual practice, and (b) *simultaneously* prioritizes meeting the basic needs of the bottom 60–80% in a sustainable and long-term manner *over* ensuring achhe din for the class (the business class) which already has *achhe din*. But the current right-wing government is *not* the government that can do what the masses need. It cannot do what the nation – the nation of workers and peasants and small-scale entrepreneurs – needs. The type of the government that there is can give neither political democracy and social peace nor can it ensure that people have *daal* (lentils) and *chawal* (rice), and health-care and education and housing, etc. It must face the widest possible united opposition from political parties and people's movements that value principles of reason, democracy, secularism and welfare.

A struggle of the masses can start spontaneously. But to have some success, it needs political guidance. This is what the party of workers provides. In the fight against fascistic tendencies, which represent the extreme form of capitalist tyranny, the Left must play a leading role. It must dominantly focus on non-electoral activities aimed at class-based mobilization of workers and small-scale producers, much more than electoral activities, against fascistic forces. The Left should have its own mobilizational work: apart from mobilizing people against fascism, the Left must mobilize people (a) against curtailment of democratic rights more generally, and (b) against the on-going attack on living standards. Keeping its organizational independence, the Left must engage in these two forms of struggle, on the basis of concrete immediate and transitional demands, *as a part of* and *within the framework of*, the fight for socialism, a fight that is local, regional, national and global.[70] By being involved in struggles inside and outside the workplaces (farms, factories, offices), in the struggles that are economic, political and ecological, in the struggles for economic concessions and that are against social oppression of religious and caste minorities and women, the Left can truly be the tribune of the people in the Lenin sense. Such Left action is necessary to alleviate the suffering of the oppressed groups and to unite those members of its basic classes who are social oppressed (e.g. Dalits) with those who traditionally are not. In the process of such struggles, the lower classes can aspire for the ideological-political hegemony, and ultimately, for the status of 'the new ruling class'. One can imagine the economic and political struggles of workers and small-scale producers as three concentric circles, beginning, first, with the struggle around immediate economic and political demands, and then struggle around transitional economic and political demands, and finally, moving on to the struggle for a workers' and small-scale producers' government.

Within the extra-electoral struggles in all these different spheres, the Left must support the various progressive movements led by non-party Marxists and by non-Marxist radicals such as people's science movements, movements against obscurantism, and ecological movements.[71] The Left must also support the mass movements against social oppression and for economic concessions (e.g. higher wages) that are led by non-party Marxists and by non-Marxist radicals, including those involved in the literacy campaigns, temple entry movements on behalf of Dalits, right to information campaign, and so on. Within the extra-electoral struggles in all these different spheres, the Left, keeping its organizational independence, must build, and must not shy away from, principled *alliances* with non-communists (e.g. non communist progressive scientists and

---

70   'We have known for a long time that only a revolutionary tactic engenders, as a by-product, "reforms" or concessions from the government' (Trotsky, 1934).

71   It is important that the Left be involved in the science movement (to popularize science) and ecological movement because communal-fascistic forces are trying to communalize both science and ecological movements on the basis of their espousal of 'vedic science' and 'dharmic ecology', respectively (see Nanda, 2005).

FORWARD MARCH OF THE RIGHT AND THE RELATIVE WEAKNESS

artists), on the ground of liquidationism, or on any other ground. The Left in India (and elsewhere) must pay serious attention to Lenin's advice on the need for alliance between communists and non-communists and to the idea that revolution cannot be made by revolutionaries alone.

> One of the biggest and most dangerous mistakes made by Communists (as generally by revolutionaries who have successfully accomplished the beginning of a great revolution) is the idea that a revolution can be made by revolutionaries alone. On the contrary, to be successful, all serious revolutionary work requires that the idea that revolutionaries are capable of playing the part only of the vanguard of the truly virile and advanced class must be understood and translated into action. A vanguard performs its task as vanguard only when it is able to avoid being isolated from the mass of the people it leads and is able really to lead the whole mass forward. Without an alliance with non-Communists in the most diverse spheres of activity there can be no question of any successful communist construction.
>
> LENIN, 1922

As far as the fight against the fascistic movement is concerned, the Left must make sure that: workers, self-employed non-capitalist producers, their political parties/movements, class-conscious trade union members, their progressive organic intellectuals and independent activists participating in class-based social movements, come together, at local, regional and national levels, starting from a city-neighborhood and a village. These elements must form multi-religion, multi-caste working class, and anti-fascism/anti-communalism action committees (or defense guards), with the aim of struggling against the attack on democratic and social rights of these basic classes and class-fractions, in the first instance. What is needed, in India (as elsewhere in similar contexts), is a *class*-based extra-electoral 'coalition' (i.e. a 'united front') of proletarian political forces that are organizationally independent of the big-business parties, in order to struggle for secularism and democracy (and more). Such extra-electoral struggle should be a vehicle for the development of democratic consciousness[72] and win the masses to the cause of a large-scale political project

---

72 Prejudice against religious minorities and Dalits *is* widespread among ordinary people, thanks to their own alienated living and working conditions requiring scapegoating and externalizing the source of their problems, and thanks to the ideological intervention of bourgeois-fascistic forces. The Left must fight this prejudice.

of defending and deepening democratic rights and to the cause of socialism/ communism. Apart from the extra-electoral struggle, the Left must fight the fascistic tendencies within the electoral arena, on the basis of the idea that the former struggle is to subordinate it to the electoral struggle.

It is to be stressed that the defeat of fascistic tendencies should not be equated to the electoral defeat of the BJP: the BJP may be defeated and yet fascistic tendencies will be involved in their usual ground- work, covertly and overtly, although without formal access to state power through the BJP they will lose some of their force. So the fight against fascistic tendencies must be a much greater fight than the electoral fight to defeat the BJP. And no other po-litical movement can engage in that fight more strongly than the Left can. It is also clear that when fascistic tendencies are weakened/eliminated and when the focus of Left's attention is more on class struggle against capital as such than on fascistic movements, the so-called secular parties which are compet-ing with one another are most likely to be united with those which are not, in order to fight the Left. That is all the more reason why the fight against fascistic tendencies must be seen as a part of the fight for establishing a socialist government.

The struggle against fascism or fascistic tendencies must ultimately be to cut its roots in capitalism. In the process of mobilizing the masses for conces-sions (including economic concessions within capitalism), the Left must de-velop their class consciousness and gradually prepare them to demand a work-ers' state, supported mainly by non-exploiting small-scale producers. The fight against fascistic tendencies, initially a *defensive* fight, should be seen positively as opening a door towards socialist struggle.

Any temporary and tactical agreement with non-fascistic bourgeois forces that might be made objectively necessary because of the relative weakness of the Left can, once again, be justified only if the genuine aim of the Left is to prepare the masses to fight for socialism, and not to just fight for a capitalism that is more democratic, more egalitarian and less neoliberal. The masses and the leaders and the Left intellectuals must breathe, live, and fall in love with, the very idea of a more humane society that is democratic in every possible manner, a society which goes by this name: socialism. Any temporary compro-mise on the socialist principle in order to fight fascistic tendencies is not worth it, if it is not consciously *seen as a part of* the project to advance the socialist cause, the masses' struggle for socialism:

> If communalism is not just an ideological, superstructural, epiphenom-enal force and if the totality of the communal forces are structurally root-ed in this predatory capitalism, then it necessarily follows that the

FORWARD MARCH OF THE RIGHT AND THE RELATIVE WEAKNESS   515

struggle against communalism is not only a matter of an ideological struggle on behalf of secularism but part of a struggle against capitalism itself. That is, ... the real, enduring alternative to communalism is communism as such. [In] India, secularism is no longer a bourgeois virtue, as it once was for the Enlightenment bourgeoisie in Europe and among many during our anti-colonial struggle.

AHMAD, 2013: 22

The threat from the fascistic movement and the massive crisis of livelihood of the masses are reason enough for a thorough rethinking of what kind of Left is needed. This rethinking involves rethinking the stage of revolution itself: must the Left not fight to abolish capitalism rather than to fight for a better form of capitalism? Is it really the case that capitalism is not ripe, for a struggle to begin to overthrow it? As we have seen in Chapter 3, India is dominantly a capitalist society: the most general form of capitalism does exist as the dominant form of class relation in India, and the transition to a more developed form of capitalism is blocked by capitalism itself, operating in a world of imperialism. Let the Indian Left read and reflect on Lenin's *April Theses*. And let leaders of the communist movement, advanced workers and Marxist intellectuals reflect honestly and seriously in a way that is non-sectarian, the following lines from Vladimir Lenin's most trusted comrade and his co-architect of 1917:

All talk to the effect that historical conditions have not yet "ripened" for socialism is the product of ignorance or conscious deception. The objective prerequisites for the proletarian revolution have not only "ripened"; they have begun to get somewhat rotten. Without a socialist revolution, in the next historical period at that, a catastrophe threatens the whole culture of mankind. The turn is now to the proletariat, i.e., chiefly to its revolutionary vanguard. The historical crisis of mankind is reduced to the crisis of the revolutionary leadership.

TROTSKY, 1938

Indeed, 'Without a socialist revolution, ... a catastrophe threatens the whole culture of mankind', and fascism *is* a part of that catastrophe.

Philosophically speaking, capitalism exists at the level of fundamental class *relation*, which has three aspects (relation of exchange, relation of property, and relation of value and surplus value) (Das, 2017a: Chapter 7), and at the level of mechanisms and the *effects* of the *mechanisms* of capitalist accumulation on the masses. And, capitalist society can be (more/less) fascistic and (more/less) democratic. It is important for the Left to fight against the adverse effects of capitalist accumulation for short-term progressive policies and against fascistic tendencies, on the basis of immediate and transitional demands. Now, given the danger that fascistic tendencies pose to them, the secular-democratic bourgeois and petty bourgeois forces may at best want to confine their political activity to the creation of a polity that merely weakens such tendencies making the society more democratic, leaving intact the capitalist class relation. And that political aim, however limited from the Left vantage-point, does overlap with the Left's aim to undermine – to revolt against– fascistic tendencies. But such a revolt has to be also a revolt against fascists' pro-business policies and against the attack on workers and small-scale producers' living standards. And there is still more to do: fighting for democracy and against fascistic tendencies, and for some economic concessions is not enough. These fights must grow over into the fight for socialism.

The question is: does the Indian Left agree with this perspective?

CHAPTER 14

Conclusions and Reflections

In this concluding chapter, I will summarize the main points made in each chapter and draw out their implications for political practice. A major challenge in social analysis of a country is to arrive at a general perspective. This perspective, I have argued, must be the class perspective.

Class analysis must stress the relation of exploitation between classes on the basis of control over the productive resources on the part of the minority class (the exploiters). And in terms of capitalism as a class relation, it must see capitalism as a series of inter-connected relations: of exchange, property, production, value and surplus value. Class relations promote and fetter the development of productive forces, which impact class relations, which have ultimate primacy over productive forces. So, class defines the character of its economy, which in turn sets limits within which the state generally functions.[1] The state is fundamentally a class state. It is the class character of economy and of the state that must be the crucial explanation of forms of economic development, technological change, dynamics of poverty, and the political activity in which the exploiting and exploited classes and their agents engage in.

To be dialectical, class analysis must take seriously that which is not class: it must take seriously mechanisms of *non-class* oppression (or relations and practices of social-cultural *difference*). In India, caste and gender have been emphasized, and rightly so. In addition to women (and children) and low castes (especially, Dalits), it is very important to stress the oppression of religious minorities, and especially, Muslims, in contemporary India. Oppression of religious minorities is deeply connected to class exploitation, and both are aspects of what I call the fascistic tendency in India.

Class absolutely matters. One can agree with Herring (2013: 139) when he says that: 'economic class determines not only who gets what, but how: what must be done, can be done, to alter life chances?' And because that is the case, 'some obfuscation of class universally serves political interests' (p. 131), i.e. the interests of those who benefit from the class system. Such an obfuscation might be intellectually justified by saying that the Marxist notion of class is a Western notion, and that it cannot be applied to India because Indian society is too complex, because caste is the backbone of Indian society and that

---

1 Over a long period of time, class relations generally influence politics (see Moore, 1993), which, in turn, have a certain influence on class relations.

© KONINKLIJKE BRILL NV, LEIDEN, 2020 | DOI:10.1163/9789004415560_015

India has many other social divisions, and so on. To quote, once again, Andre Beteille, who is not a Marxist and who is one of foremost Indian thinkers, again: 'Marxism occupies a central place among the intellectual resources of the modern world, and we can neglect or reject it only at our own cost' (Beteille, 2000: 46–47). And in more recent times, Jal (2014: 77) has said this from a Marxist perspective: 'Give up the essence of Marxism, give up the masses, humanism and internationalism; and the spectres of fascism, neo-conservatism and Stalinism will strike back'.

In this book, apart from outlining what a class analysis should look like at a general level (Chapter 2), I use the class perspective to examine a variety of issues that concern contemporary India, including: the Maoist movement considered to be the largest threat to the state's security, and the fascistic tendencies as a threat not only to democracy and secularism but also to the economic rights and political organizations of workers and peasants.

1   Class Character of Indian Economy/Society

In thinking about the class character of Indian society/economy, one has to bear in mind a set of key points. These include the following. Class is a relation/ process which is objectively expressed in the form of large groups of people in terms of their relation to social economy, in both rural and urban areas. This relationship is produced by the fact that a minority class controls the means of production, production process, and the surplus product, while the majority class does not. Class exists at multiple levels: history of class society, capitalism, capitalism at a specific stage of development, capitalism, and neoliberal capitalism, in India, etc. Capitalism is to be seen, above all, as a class relation (more below), and as such capitalism in India has similarities to, and differences from, the capitalism from advanced countries. In examining Indian class society, one may begin with the two class model. But one has to bear in mind the fact that class polarization including proletarianization, occurs through certain mechanisms which can be countered, to some extent, by other mechanisms, which is why one finds intermediate classes between capitalists and workers. Indian capitalist society is characterized by a system of class relations of: accumulation by class differentiation, accumulation by dispossession, and accumulation by exploitation (which in turn comes in two forms of subsumption of labor, as explained below). Classes and class-fractions (intra-class divisions) have common and different interests. Classes undergo changes over time, and conditions of class can vary over space, especially, in a large country such as India. At a concrete level, there are non-class relations within class relations, such that we have not only a worker as a category but also a Dalit

CONCLUSIONS AND REFLECTIONS

worker. It is very important to understand how class relations of exploitation feed into and are supported by non-class relations of oppression/domination/ exclusion such as those based in not only caste and gender but also, and increasingly, religion. Ideas about class and objective conditions of existence of class inter-connect, while the objective conditions have a degree of primacy over ideas. Similarly, class politics and objective conditions of existence of class set limits within which class politics – and indeed non-class politics – are played out, with a degree of autonomy. Just as class polarization is subjected to mechanisms and counter-mechanisms, similarly, class politics, especially, lower-class struggle, which comes in different forms (e.g. trade union struggle, political struggles by the Indian communist movement), is subjected to pro-cesses that are conducive to, and those that impede, the lower-class struggle. The lower-class struggle exists along with what I call class struggle from above (i.e. what urban capitalists and rural large-scale landowners do against the lower classes). Actions of the property-owning class and its state, including the fascistic attack on lower classes and their organic intellectuals, can be seen as class struggle from above.

2 Capitalism as Class Relations of Subsumption of Labor

Like everything, class as an objective reality comes in many forms. Capitalism is a form of class. How to conceptually think about capitalism in India, and not just class in India, is a big intellectual challenge. By deploying Marx's notion of subsumption of labor, I have critiqued a restrictive concept of capitalism that many Indian Marxist political economists subscribe to. This is a concept in which the development of capitalist class relations is conflated with the devel-opment of productive forces *under* such relations. In the restrictive concept, capitalism as such is equated with advanced capitalism, rather than the latter being seen as a higher *form* of capitalism. Therefore, in this restrictive concept, where there is a lower level of economic development, it is assumed that capi-talism does not exist or that it exists only partially.

In advancing a subsumption of labor perspective, I claim that formal sub-sumption of labor is the most abstract – general – form of capitalism. For Marx, real subsumption of labor entails the formal subsumption, but the converse is not necessarily true (Marx, 1977: 1019). Contrary to what Marx might (some-times) have believed (perhaps, this was one of Marx's Eurocentric moments), the transition to real subsumption – the transition to a form of capitalism associated with system-wide productivity-raising technological change – is not automatic. I accept that there *is* a long-term tendency towards the real subsumption of labor, associated with a rise in the ratio of constant to variable capital, that follows formal subsumption in which lots of workers are hired to work for long hours on an enormous amount of raw materials with little labor-shedding technological change used. This long-term tendency, under certain conditions, is countered by the possibilities for a prolonged process of formal subsumption. The transition to real subsumption is mediated by the balance of power between capital and labor, including more overt struggle against formal subsumption of labor, within a context where the national economy is shaped by imperialism and the world market.

In India, there *are* the necessary conditions for capitalist relations (e.g. a class of legally 'free' laborers; commodity production; investment of money in production and exchange to make more money). Therefore, as capitalists elsewhere, property owners hiring these nominally free laborers possess the same sorts of causal powers (e.g. they can earn profits) and suffer from the same sorts of causal liabilities (e.g. they can lose their means of production if they do not produce commodities efficiently, i.e. at the value). They are capitalists whether or not they use, for example, the Green Revolution type technology or biotechnology or any other form of technology. In some areas, property owners may be formally subsuming labor, and in other areas there may exist real subsumption. The ways in which capitalists' powers and liabilities are expressed in actual patterns of investment, and the effects of the exercise of these powers and liabilities on the development of productive forces (i.e. whether the transition from formal to real subsumption of labor under capital happens), other things constant, depend on the balance of power, or struggle, between property owners and workers. The forms and outcomes of the struggle – which are affected by the overall capitalist development and developmental activities of the capitalist state at the national and provincial scales – condition the extent to which competing capitalists cut costs of production through the use of technology aimed at increasing labor productivity per hour or through, for example, the formal subsumption of labor. The formal subsumption may benefit specific capitals in specific places but opportunities for formal subsumption, along with imperialist exploitation, may counter the long-term and system-wide tendency towards the development of productive forces that Marx associates with real subsumption of labor. Real subsumption does happen but there are serious limits to it. From the perspective of many participants in the celebrated Indian Mode of Production debate, it is the social relations of usury or rental extraction from direct producers that fetter the development of productive forces under capitalism. While this may be true in specific cases, a larger nation-wide obstacle is formal subsumption of labor itself: being able to appropriate surplus value in its absolute form on the basis of formal subsumption alleviates the pressure to have to resort to real

CONCLUSIONS AND REFLECTIONS

subsumption in a systemic way. In other words, a nation-wide obstacle to the development of productive forces is capitalism itself, in its most general form (i.e. formal subsumption of labor).

This conclusion has a general theoretical implication, i.e. an implication for the debate on fettering, for example.[2] The idea is that existing class relations block possible *further* development of productive forces (leading to a slow or slower growth rate, for example), a situation I will call 'development-fettering'. Use-fettering means that the rational use of *existing* resources is blocked by the current set of class relations. That is, productive capacities that have already been *developed* are at present un-*used* or under-*used* due to existing class relations. The discrepancy between capacity and use is not to be seen in an absolute sense, however. As Cohen (2000) says, the question is not under-deployment (or use) of resources, but 'grotesque over-deployment in some directions and injurious under-deployment in others', indicating an irrational deployment of resources.[3]

The mode of production in India is decidedly and near-exclusively capitalist. This is capitalist at least in the sense of formal subsumption of labor under capital. And it is decidedly not semi-feudal. Of course, the semi-feudal thesis continues to be subscribed to by many (see Kar, 2018; Sugden, 2017).

The view of capitalism and capitalist (uneven) development offered here is different from that of many Indian Marxists. For them, to the extent that the development of productive forces has taken place, it has taken place due to capitalist reinvestment of surplus in specific areas. Patnaik, like Bhaduri, thinks that only when technological change happens is there capitalism. What follows from this is that, for her, uneven *development of productive forces* is a function of the spatially limited amount of *development of capitalist social relations*. This is a mistaken view. The development of capitalist relations in India, including in rural areas, is much more widespread than the theory advanced by these scholars would allow for. As I have said before, this is in the sense that (and to the extent that) property owners (including landowners), as bearers of the capitalist social structure, are subject to the same sorts of profit-making opportunities as well as constraints in capitalist societies as elsewhere. But in

---

2 That social relations fetter the development productive forces is a common Marxist argument. For a discussion on the topic, see Sitton, 1996; also Das, 2001c on the importance of the 'fettering argument' in the less developed country context.

3 One can also examine what I will call use-fettering. Use-fettering is the *irrational* use of existing resources located, caused by class relations domestically and internationally. Consider the fact that while millions are starving, vast amount of resources are being used to produce high value luxury goods such as shrimps for the world market, within an international division of labor created by imperialism.

what ways they do so (for example, whether they use labor-saving technology) is a different matter. Like most large countries, India is highly diverse, both ecologically and in terms of other factors (e.g. the degree of concentration of means of production, etc.). There is geographical variation in the factors that shape the potential/actual balance of power between capital and labor. So one will expect that in some areas or sub-sectors of economic activity, property owners, including those who must cut costs under the pressure of the world market, are unable to rely mainly on the use of labor that works for low wages and for long hours, and are therefore economically compelled to use productivity-raising technological change, thus manifesting capitalism's long-term tendency towards real subsumption. This mechanism causes productive forces to be developed in some areas or sub-sectors to a greater extent and more systematically than in other areas, causing uneven development *under* capitalism. In other words, a more *general* tendency under the capitalist mode of production (i.e. the pressure on competing capitalists to make a profit, the pressure coming from the capitalist class relations) interacts with *locally* existing contingent conditions (e.g. balance of power between the basic classes) to produce geographically uneven development (Das, 2017c), the concrete forms of which must be subjected to empirical analysis at the local scale.[4]

All political economists agree that there is uneven development in India. Most of them think that uneven development exists because of the existence of 'non-capitalist' relation (e.g. pre-capitalist type relations) in some areas, associated with low level of economic development, and capitalist relations in other areas, associated with higher level of development. My argument, however, is that, uneven development is mainly taking place because of, and in the framework of, social relations that are predominantly *capitalist* in terms of *class relations*. At the level of mechanisms (and not surface 'appearances'), uneven development is partly a product of uneven transition to the real subsumption of labor under capital. Uneven development is a *capitalist* matter.

Further, there is a relatively ignored fact that uneven development is happening within the framework of varied class relations in a backward country (backward in terms of the lower level of labor productivity per hour), one where technological change is partly happening under the influence of the world market, and where, therefore, uneven development is *uneven and combined* development. But what is the *combined* character of uneven development? This concept refers to 'a peculiar combination of different stages' in the

---

4 Note that this does not mean that the local scale is autonomous of the functioning of the capitalist class relation. Uneven development at time T_1 creates different areas with their specificities, which, in turn, interact with the general dynamics of capitalist class relation at T_2 to produce another round of uneven development, and so on.

CONCLUSIONS AND REFLECTIONS

history of economic development of less-developed countries. It means that, for example, in a less developed country, technologically backward 'peasant land-cultivation' can co-exist with an industry which 'in its technique and capitalist structure' is 'at the level of the advanced countries', and in certain respects it can even surpass industry in advanced countries (Trotsky, 2008: 8)., In India, robots, tractors, threshers coexist with technologically-backward production processes, mass scientific ignorance, massive functional illiteracy, and superstitious beliefs.

It is not just that capitalist development is *uneven* but also that capitalist relations are *combined* with pre-capitalist relations (e.g. serfdom). This is an advance over the perspective (for example, that of Harvey, Myrdal, etc.) that focusses only on the unevenness of capitalist development. Trotsky's perspective, like that of Harvey (1982), however, does not distinguish between different forms of capitalist class relation itself. It thus abstracts from the ways in which the balance of power between capital and labor intervenes in the transition from one form of capitalist class relation (formal subsumption) to another form (real subsumption) and thus limits the extent to which and the pace at which a higher level of capitalist development (indicated by higher per hour labor productivity) can happen, whether in farming or industry, and irrespective of what the state policies are. It thus abstracts from the obstacles to the transition *within* capitalism, and therefore obstacles to economic development. His perspective of uneven and combined development needs to be broadened a little in the light of the class theory of capitalism around subsumption of labor, as presented here. In India and similar other backward countries, it is not just that capitalism is combined with pre-capitalist relations existing in specific areas. The matter is more complex than that.

Firstly, what is happening is that class relations of formal subsumption of labor, hybrid subsumption, and localized pre-capitalist relations, including relations of commons, as in aboriginal areas, co-exist with class relations of real subsumption, the latter being, in part, driven by an external influence (i.e. imperialism as indicated by the operation of the capitalist world market backed by militarily powerful states of advanced countries). Secondly, there are not straightforward ways in which India (and other similar countries), operating under the impact of the world market, can move to the stage of real subsumption of labor quickly, and exhibit a systemic tendency towards a rise in productivity of labor per hour. The introduction of advanced techniques could strengthen not only the use of unfreedom and extra-economic relations, but also relations of formal subsumption of labor. We may recall that: formal subsumption of labor can exist 'alongside the *specifically capitalist* mode of production in its developed form' i.e. the real subsumption (Marx, 1977: 1019). In other words, enterprises using advanced technology can – and do – resort to a regime of long hours and low wages, just as they can use unfree labor.[5] Besides, while the imperialist world market can contribute to economic development based on a degree of technological change (through such processes as the relocation of enterprises to take advantage of cheap skilled and unskilled labor; the need to sell new technologies as commodities), imperialism can also inhibit long-term systemic economic development, given its exploitative character causing, for example, transfer of surplus to advanced countries in various forms. As long as there is the class relation of capitalism, there will be imperialism, which is a relation of exploitation of direct producers of India and other poorer countries by the big business of advanced countries. And as long as there is imperialism, its main tendential effect is to limit development in the periphery rather than to promote it, a tendency that reflects the mechanisms of uneven development at the global scale. The long-term tendency for the average rate of profit to fall in imperialist countries, thus causing periodic economic crises there, also impacts India and other low-income countries, in part by reducing their exports and by increasing the need to raise the rate of exploitation of labor in, and to acquire cheaper natural resources from, these countries. Besides, India itself is experiencing its 'own' profitability crisis, as Michael Roberts suggests, and this crisis further limits India's development prospects, including in the industrial sector. Given all these traits of global capitalism and of capitalism in India (and other low-income countries), good or bad state policies and stronger or weaker state capacities can make only marginal difference and only for a short time period. Quite simply, capitalism has become a barrier to the development of productive forces – a barrier to economic development – under the rule of capitalist class relations.

The second major implication of my discussion of the class character of capitalism in India is this: associated with the uneven and combined development of capitalism is the topic of capital switch. Once we assume that there is a class with money (property owners, more generally) intending to make money by investing it in production and exchange, the concept of switching capital comes to be an important one. There are three forms of capital-switch. (1) When the rate of profit is low in the production sphere, capital switches to financial, etc. services (Smith, 2010). (2) And, according to Harvey, when there is overaccumulation in the sector that produces commodities that are produced and consumed within a given time period (primary circuit),

---

5   Note that unfree labor is definitely not a necessary indicator of non-capitalist relation (e.g. semi-feudalism) (Brass, 2012) and that it can be made use of by capitalists who resort to both formal and real subsumption of labor, although the possibility of relative surplus value can, to some extent, reduce the pressure to resort to formal subsumption (see Das, 2013c).

CONCLUSIONS AND REFLECTIONS

capital is switched to the sectors that specialize in the built environment for production and for consumption (e.g. durables) and into science and education as well as social welfare and repressive and consent-generating activities (Harvey, 1978). (3) Within economically less developed capitalist social formations, capital switch takes different forms. (3a) One form is one that Utsa Patnaik (1986) and others have dealt with: when property owners can make more money by investing it in production, they will switch capital from rental and usurious activities to production. Patnaik says: the person renting out her land to peasants will switch to what she calls *capitalist* production if she can make more profit in production than by leasing out land (i.e. the rental income) and by lending money-capital at a higher rate of interest (usury). But a rate of profit that can prompt switching capital to production is very high (because rental income and usurious interest are very high), and is difficult to obtain, unless there is a quantum jump in productivity caused by technological change. In other words, the obstacle to the switch to capitalist production comes from *outside* of capitalist production. (3b) Further, there is the switch of capital from formal subsumption (or indeed from hybrid subsumption) to real subsumption of labor in capitalist production, as I have discussed. This switch is not yet complete. This leads us to the topic of the specificity of capitalism in India, and this is the third implication of my discussion of the class character of capitalism in India.

How different is Indian capitalism from the capitalism of the European core? For Subir Sinha (2017: 540), capitalism, or what he calls mature capitalism, exists with 'capitalists and workers responding to "the dull compulsion of economic force"'. It is characterized by 'generalized commodity production, in which the imperative of accumulation drives capitalists' behaviour, and where labour [sic] becomes a commodity'. India does not have capitalism in this sense, for Sinha. The incomplete transition to generalized commodity production 'is the central point of difference between capitalism in India and in the original trajectories of the European core' (Sinha, 2017: 540). And, this incompleteness is signified by the fact that non-capitalist ways of life 'are kept alive by development interventions [of the state] to benefit those who are excluded from capitalist relations but have some political power in the form of laws and justice and solidarity discourses that ... put limits to the violence of the universalization process on extra-economic grounds' (p. 541). Interestingly, according to 'more traditional' political economists of the 1970s mode of production debate genre, it is the non-capitalist, or pre-capitalist, relations that act as a fetter on the development of capitalist class relations (as in the work of Patnaik and others), while according to such recent writers as Sinha (and Sanyal, 2013), influenced by the cultural turn and post-modernism, 'non-capitalist forms of subjectivity … put limits' on the universalization of capitalism. So, what limits capitalism is not an agent within capitalism (i.e. the working class) but an agent that is outside of capitalism ('non-capitalist forms of subjectivity'). While the recent writers wish to distinguish their thinking from that of the more traditional political economists, they end up in the camp of the latter. As well, politically, it is easy to see how close their thinking is to some of the discourse that informs class struggle in India (e.g. Naxalism, discussed in Chapters 8–9).

It is true that wage-labor co-exists with other forms of labor, although this does not license resorting to the descriptive concept of 'classes of labor' of Henry Bernstein (2007), that many others make use of. This concept is problematic not least because it conflates class-fractions with class. But to the extent that wage-labor co-exists with other forms of labor, India's capitalism cannot be credited with any uniqueness relative to advanced countries. In all capitalist countries, wage-labor exists along with other forms of labor, to varying degrees, with wage-labor as the dominant form of labor. But that does not mean that the imperative of *capitalist* accumulation does not exist where wage-labor as the dominant form of labor coexists with other forms of labor, as in India. Capitalism does not require that *all* labor power become a commodity. As long as a sufficient amount of labor power is in the commodity-form, capitalism's fundamental mechanisms (e.g. competition, appropriation of surplus value, etc.) can be set in motion. In fact, the existence of a semi-commodified labor power is no barrier to capital's pursuit of surplus. Capital can benefit at the expense of petty producers in multiple ways, including by getting raw materials at below-market price from these producers and benefit from their wage-labor when offered for sale. The *main* difference between India and the European core is *not* what the likes of Sinha and Sanyal say. The main difference is that India is characterized by the dominance of formal subsumption of wage-labor under capital (i.e. capitalism in its more general form), which co-exists with real subsumption of labor (as well as relations of hybrid subsumption and remnants of pre-capitalist exploitation based on extra-economic coercion and natural economy), in a context of the operation of the world market and imperialist subjugation. There *is* an incompleteness, but one that is indicative of combined development in capitalist society. But this is not in the sense of the incomplete transition to capitalism, for India is decidedly a capitalist country already. Much rather, the incompleteness exists in the sense that there is an incomplete – ongoing – transition to real subsumption of labor, within the landscape of uneven and combined development of *capitalist* social formation.

To view that Indian or any other social formation is decidedly capitalist has a different political implication than the contrary view which has a much less progressive implication. This contrary view is that (a) the social formation is

CONCLUSIONS AND REFLECTIONS

not dominantly capitalist or is capitalist in limited ways, and (b) obstacles to capitalist development are in pre- or non-capitalist relations. There are two implications of this view. One is that capitalist class relation is everywhere and all times associated with higher level of development of productive forces, and therefore, capitalism must be promoted/protected always and everywhere. Another is that: the obstacles to capitalist development are not in capitalism as such and can be removed by forces other than those that seek to abolish capitalism. That is, a democratic government still operating within the logic of capitalist relations can remove these barriers and promote a nicer form of capitalism, a capitalism without non-capitalist barriers.

If a country such as India is dominantly semi-feudal or not capitalist enough, then the political energy is to be directed against semi-feudal landlords or at the creation of advanced capitalism somehow. This is a strategy that licenses a long and indefinite wait for the fight for socialism (= abolition of class relations) to start and requires collaboration with some good (progressive) capitalists. In reality, the time for that strategy never comes, in part because the political work that happens now has little connection to the socialist project. But if what is present is already capitalism, albeit one that is not very progressive, and one that is not going to be very progressive for a long period of time because of all the constraints on the transition to real subsumption of labor within the contemporary imperialist world market, then the nature of class politics must be seen in an entirely different manner: this means that revolution as the highest point of class struggle against capitalism must be on the agenda right now. The core of this agenda must be the anti-capitalist struggle of the working class which is the object of capitalist exploitation including in its most general form (i.e. formal subsumption of labor). This class must be politically allied with small-scale producers which are adversely impacted, in so many ways, by the capitalist class (and by its class partner, i.e. rent-receiving landlords). The combined and common goal of these two toiling classes must be a socialist state, a state of workers and self-employed small-scale producers who constitute the majority of the population. By driving all propertied classes (precapitalist or capitalist) from their ruling positions, such a state can create conditions for a higher level of development of productive forces and for a society without exploitation and oppression.

3 Capitalist Class Relation in a Neoliberal Form

Like everything, capitalism comes in many forms. It comes in the forms of formal and real subsumption of labor, from one vantage point. It also comes in the form of, for example, social-democratic or state-interventionist and neoliberal forms, from another vantage point. Neoliberalism *is* a specific form of capitalism, whether in advanced countries or in countries such as India, although the critical analysis of capitalism has been replaced by that of neoliberalism as such. Neoliberalism is not to be seen primarily as a set of government policies which can be replaced by another. Much rather it is to be seen as 'a predictable and inevitable strategic response on the part of capital and the state to a deepening crisis of the capitalist profit system' (Smith, 2018: 21). It is mistaken to belive that neoliberalism, and not capitalism, is facing a crisis (Chibber, 2017). Neoliberalism is a form of crisis-ridden capitalism. Capitalism and neoliberal capitalism are both crisis-ridden.

The neoliberal state experiences internal contradictions, like the capitalist form of the state as such. There is clearly a contradiction between the declared public aims of neoliberalism (the well-being of all) and its actual effect, which is rising income and wealth inequality between the big business (top 1% or so) and the rest. As I am completing this chapter, Oxfam has just reported that in India, top 10% of the population owns 77.4% of the national wealth, and top 1% holds 51.53% of the national wealth, while bottom 60% owns merely 4.8% of the national wealth (Samuel, 2019). Additionally, there are more specific contradictions that Harvey (2005) has so well described which apply to India as well: between the need for the state to let markets function freely and the need to intervene in order to deliberately create a business climate; the need to enforce market rules in an authoritarian way and the ideas of individual freedom; the integrity of the financial system and its volatile character; between competition and monopolistic tendencies; and between individual market freedom and loss of solidarity, and so on. As a new stage in the development of capitalism emerging in the wake of the post-war boom, neoliberalism has several general traits (deregulation, privatization, liberalization, financialization, etc.) that are affecting all spheres of life, including culture, the state and everyday life.

Like all the different forms of capitalism, neoliberalism operates differently in different national contexts. A dialectical conceptualization of neoliberalism in India (where it goes by the name of New Economic Policy, or NEP) must be rooted in a general theory of neoliberalism, and it must be sensitive to the differences and similarities between the pre-1991 and post-1991 regimes in India, and to both the economic and the non-economic character of the NEP. Such a conceptualization must also see the governmental or policy aspect of the NEP as rooted in the class character of Indian society.

As in many other countries, so in India, neoliberal capitalism has meant a series of *reduction* in: corporate contributions to society/state (= reduction in taxes); the power of unions; state control over pricing of services and over

CONCLUSIONS AND REFLECTIONS

business activities; state's restrictions on trade; state's support for the less-well off (e.g. farmers); the scope of state ownership of productive enterprises and of facilities (schools, etc.) and commons, and so on. As a result, there has been the opposite of this reduction: an *expansion* of the *effect* of class power of ruling class and expansion of the misery for the masses.

In any fundamental sense, there was not a time before or since independence when the Indian capitalist class did not have its power to exploit labor and dispossess small-scale producers. So neoliberalism, strictly speaking, is not the restoration of class power, as some scholars think (e.g. Harvey, Dumenil, etc.). Yet, to the extent that there was *some* restriction on its power within the political sphere (e.g. what it could produce and what it could not), neoliberalism is an *effect* of changing balance of political power between the capitalist class and the masses in the 'post-Soviet' world. On the basis of its growing economic strength, supported in many ways by the state, between the 1950s and the mid-1980s, and with support from imperialist capital and its institutions, Indian capitalist class has now been able to impose its economic will in a much more strident manner than before. NEP is a political expression of the capitalist class's 'desire' and need to bridge the gap between its economic power (in terms of its control over property) and its political power. NEP *is* a policy, but it is more than that. It is the political articulation of the interests of the Indian capitalist class in the context of a globalizing capitalism. Neoliberalism is 'capitalism without Leftist illusions' (e.g. illusions that there can be such a thing as humane capitalism on a long-term basis). India's NEP is a policy *on behalf* of capital. It is therefore a policy *of* capital, mediated and implemented by the state, at central and provincial scales. India's NEP is more than a governmental policy. It is a programme of the bourgeoisie that promotes economic growth and bestows benefits to certain relatively privileged sections of the population (e.g. IT engineers), but has devastating impacts on the toiling masses.

Neoliberalism in rural areas (or agrarian neoliberalism) in a country where 70% of the population are villagers and where almost half of the workforce depends on agriculture, is particularly ruthless in its impacts. Neoliberalism has also produced enormous spatial unevenness. Neoliberalism in India, like in the periphery as such, is also a part of the imperialist project, being implemented via burgeoning 'new compradore' elements both in the bourgeois class and outside. Given the adverse impacts of neoliberalism, it has inspired massive resistance from below, which has been countered by the state via a combination of: heavy repression; meagre concession; and mind-numbing deception (i.e. the false idea that neoliberal growth is good for all). Interestingly, if the Left has struggled for power at the regional level to alleviate sufferings of the masses, the Left has ended up, in practice, becoming, more or less, a conduit through which neoliberalism has been delivered to the detriment of the interests of the masses. Of course, this is not to say that Gujarat and Kerala are the same. They clearly are not.

If we see neoliberalism as a form of capitalism, this view has also specific political implications. India, along with other less developed countries, are often seen as countries that have less income and more absolute poverty. Instead, I argue that India (like the other less developed countries) must be fundamentally seen in class terms: as one that has suffered from aborted – or incomplete – revolutions against the propertied class. They have suffered from: aborted democratic revolution, including agrarian revolution against feudal(-type) relations, aborted national (or anti-imperialist) revolution, and untried anti-capitalist revolution. A dialectical view of neoliberalism and the NEP connects them both to the democratic and agrarian questions, the national question, and the question of socialism itself.

Consider the democratic question. There has been massive resistance to the NEP, as mentioned earlier, to which the state is responding in a most undemocratic (= repressive) manner. The state is also promoting *venal* capitalism; massive corruption in the public offices has been endemic since the 1990s, a time during which markets have been less regulated, thus refuting the argument that de-regulation reduces corruption. Corruption implies undemocratic use of public offices for private gains ('private' meaning the nexus of the business world and the state managers). The neoliberal state itself is managed by people who are increasingly and openly allied with the moneybags and money-making, while being on the payroll of the state, which is supposed to work for everyone.

Given that all the parties – including the Left parties – are forced to follow neoliberalism, the room for democratic dissent is shrunk, and this is more so now, with the election of a government in 2014 led by a Hindu-fundamentalist party with fascistic tendencies. This has a more specific implication: by making all political parties/groups equal as far as their adherence to neoliberalism is concerned, the NEP has created a situation where casteism and religious fundamentalism are used to divide the poor electorate and to garner votes. This creates conditions for the perpetuation of undemocratic relations based on religious and caste identity. This also creates a condition where capitalists can subject workers – those who belong to specific vulnerable social groups – to super-exploitation and weaken any potential resistance by dividing the masses along the lines of religion, caste, gender, etc. Given that various petty-bourgeois or regionalist parties (some of which call themselves, bizarrely, socialist) thrive by playing identity politics, it is not unusual for a party or a coalition of parties in power to buy their support for neoliberal policies by giving some material concession to identity politics (e.g. reservation in promotion for scheduled castes). Identity politics becomes a vehicle of capitalist and landlord class politics, that is to say, politics in the service of neoliberalism.

The NEP is also creating new aspects of the agrarian question, the question about peasants' property and about their miseries caused by national and international agribusiness (*not* feudal or semi-feudal landlords) and by the neoliberal state acting on behalf of agribusiness. So the democratic question broadly understood – including democratic governance, equal rights of citizens irrespective of their castes or religious backgrounds, and the agrarian question – becomes important in new ways in neoliberal times. Neoliberalism has created the need for a heightened battle for democracy.

Consider the national question. This question is no longer about fighting formal colonialism. The new national question has many elements. It is about fighting 'new imperialism', which is predominantly practiced through economic mechanisms and ultimately backed up by the threat of force. It is the imperialism of the powerful governments of the developed world, of MNCs, and of international institutions (IMF, the World Bank, MNCs, major creditors, and 'aid' agencies). This is an imperialism that is justified and sold to ordinary people through the discourse of development (as growth). It is also sold using chauvinistic ideas about India's 'superpower status', which is only as a regional subordinate of the supreme guardian of global capitalism, the USA. The postcolonial neoliberal state itself, managed by people with the neoliberal mentality ('neoliberality'), has become a new mechanism of imperialism. So, neoliberalism has heightened the need for anti-imperialist struggle and for the sovereignty of oppressed nations. As well, an important aspect of space-economy is the phenomenon of SEZs where the usual laws of the land, including labor laws do not operate. These can be compared to the princely states of colonial times, and do not contribute to national unity, and must be gotten rid of. The national question and the democratic question (i.e. the questions of the new imperialist subordination, the state and society becoming more undemocratic, and of peasants losing land) are rooted in the fact that the NEP represents capitalism in its most naked and ruthless form.

If the above assessment is broadly correct, it indicates a very different sort of solution to the national and democratic question and to the specific problems, such as mass impoverishment, spatially uneven development and agrarian crisis, that neoliberalism is creating, than what the traditional Left has been offering. The intellectual and political fight against the NEP cannot be merely about changing the dirty clothes of the state (meaning changing its policy and making it regulate the affairs of capitalism, as in 'olden times'). It cannot be about interrupting, deconstructing, and destabilizing things and narratives about neoliberalism and wider society a bit here and a bit there, although the struggle for the regulation of business is not entirely unnecessary. The idea that there is such a thing as neoliberalism (or capitalism) with a human face is, once again, based on the lie, the deception, that the basic interests of capital are fundamentally compatible with the basic interests of the toiling masses in a sustainable, contradiction-free, manner. Unregulated growth, control of society's resources by big business, the exploitation of labor, income inequality, and ecological devastation cannot be compatible with socially coordinated wealth creation, equality, solidarity, popular democracy, and satisfaction of human needs. If this critique is right, then the intellectual and political project must have the larger goal of theoretically and practically transcending the very conditions that produce the neoliberalism model itself and going beyond the content of whose form neoliberalism is.

Indicative of the hegemony of neoliberalism, in India (as elsewhere), is the fact that scholars talk about neoliberalism more than about capitalism. So a major discursive, or ideological, success of neoliberalism is that it has hidden capitalism under its *choli* (a short-sleeved blouse worn by many Indian women). Scholars often explain society's economic, social and ecological problems in terms of neoliberalism, and not capitalism. That is, when critical ideas about economy are produced, they are often against neoliberalism as such and not against capitalism per se. Form is prioritized over content.

What is problematic about neoliberalism, including neoliberal policy, is not *this or that* aspect of it (e.g. the idea that it increases poverty and inequality or the idea that restriction on short-term capital flows or shrinking government intervention is the problem). Rather, the *whole* 'thing' is the problem. So it requires a totalizing (dialectical) critique, one that situates its limited benefits in relation to its enormous costs and sees it from multiple vantage points.

There is nothing wrong with critiquing neoliberalism, and there is nothing wrong with raising anti-neoliberalism demands. The demands must be made. But the scope of this anti-neoliberalism is narrow. It remains merely a partial demand aimed at fighting for a better capitalism. The political action that is merely anti-neoliberalism fails to convert the fight against neoliberalism into a transitional demand. Anti-neoliberalism must be a transitional demand which must be made to connect the existing (lower) level of consciousness to the level of consciousness that is needed for a fundamental challenge to class relations in India.

To reiterate the point just made: much critical discourse and much progressive politics, in India (and outside India), are stuck with a critique of neoliberalism as such, in the hope for a world that is less neoliberal, rather than a world that is not capitalist. Just as a restrictive concept of capitalism discussed in Chapter 3, a concept in which capitalism exists only when there is economically advanced capitalism, has justified a capitalist politics of the Left that aims to produce a better (= more democratic) and more advanced capitalism, similarly, similarly, a critique of capitalism that, more or less, equates capitalism to

CONCLUSIONS AND REFLECTIONS 533

neoliberalism, is bound to encourage a bourgeois politics of the masses, one that aims for a capitalism that is a little more state-directed than it is now.

4 Capitalist Class Relation, Technological Change, and Labor

We have seen that capitalism can be seen in terms of its multiple forms (e.g. forms of subsumption; neoliberalism, etc.), and we have also seen that formal subsumption can, in certain ways, be an obstacle to technological change. There is another way in which one can examine capitalism: this is to examine the ways in which technological change under capitalism does happen with potential redistributive effects on the worker. Given the importance of agriculture in a less developed country such as India, the topic of technological change in that sector is of special interest. A major form of technological-change has been the Green Revolution (GR), which has similarities with the on-going 'gene revolution' (biotechnology revolution). While the GR seems to be somewhat associated with the ratio of the rural population below the poverty line *at a point in time,* there seems to be no association between the GR and the important issue of poverty *reduction*. This is the case whether or not the population factor is held constant. The GR technology and the population factor, the twin neo-Malthusian mechanisms in which Lipton and others invest so much causal power, seem to have no statistical relation with poverty reduction (at the State level in India). Poverty reduction has taken place both with and without technological advancement. And persistence of poverty characterizes both technological advancement and the lack of it.

The real test of the relation between the GR and poverty lies in its impact on what happens to the poverty process over time (not just at a point in time) and in different States (not just in some particular places). Poverty has been, and arguably, can be, reduced without the GR (or for that matter, without any other technology or an increase in the economic output as such). And, in some cases, GR can have some favourable impact on the poor (through its impact on non-farm employment and by other means). But it is not necessary that that will be the case generally. Given the GR, poverty reduction is possible but not necessary. More generally, technology is neither a necessary nor a sufficient condition for reduction in absolute poverty. If the lack of technology was a necessary cause of poverty, one in seven people in the United States of America would not have to live below the line of absolute poverty. While the GR technology does not have any necessary poverty reduction impact, it cannot also be said that it has any necessary poverty-increasing impact, *independently* of social relations within which technology operates. There is simply no necessary relation between technology and poverty reduction, positive or negative. Much of what I have said about technology in its Green Revolution form applies to technology in its biotechnology form. A transition seems to be occurring from the Green Revolution to the gene revolution (biotechnology). The latter is linked to neoliberal capitalism. Biotechnology companies are pushing for the use of GM (genetically modified) seeds to be used on the ground that with these seeds, cultivators will increase their yields and therefore their income. The arguments in favour of the use of GM seeds are almost identical to those for the Green Revolution (HYV seeds) and therefore can be critically assessed in the way that this chapter does for the Green Revolution. Like the Green Revolution, the gene revolution is controversial, and for similar reasons (Bownas, 2016; Herring and Paarlberg, 2016). GMO seeds are extremely expensive to buy (Plahe et al., 2017; Shiva et al., 2002). These seeds have to be bought every year (a cultivator cannot save the seeds from the current year for use in the next year). The use of the seeds requires other chemicals have led to some of the farmers going into debt, and some of them are committing suicide. The effects of GMO seeds, like those of HYV seeds, will depend on the overall political-economic, or class context, in which these seeds are accessed and used (Carroll, 2017). If in India's Maharashtra State, the districts using GM cotton seeds are the districts where numerous indebted farmers have committed suicide, this points to the need to examine the GM technology in relation to the context of class relations within which it works.

The analysis of the GR–poverty relation sheds light on the relation between technology and society, or to use the terminology of Marxist political economy, the relation between social relations and productive forces (especially, technology) (Cohen, 2000; Liodakis, 1997; *Science & Society*, 2006). The analysis supports the general theoretical idea about the class character of technology, that technological change and its social consequences for people are shaped by capitalist social relations of production (Smith, 2010). Technology, as a 'thing' exists and operates, in the context of certain social relations, which shape how it produces its effects. So technology is not only a thing but is also a relationship. Technology itself cannot solve humanity's problems such as poverty, as its effects are mediated by capitalist class relations.

It is in fact no longer sufficient to define technology solely as use-values, as the equipment, techniques, etc. That definition is not false. But it fails to capture the historically specific nature of technology under *capitalist class relations*. This means that whether a technology is used and when used what its effects on common people will be, depend on whether it can remove certain natural barriers to production and exchange and increase the quantity of use-values produced. It also depends on whether the technology can generate profits (especially, in the form of extra surplus value caused by a rise in productivity of labor). Under capitalism, the fundamental aim of technological change

CONCLUSIONS AND REFLECTIONS

is not to satisfy human needs. This view is contrary to technology fetishism. In the latter view, technology (whether it is mechanical, biological, electronic, etc.) holds the key to the resolution of society's problems. Harary (2018) calls such a view 'technological utopia'.

Because technology works in the context of social relations, technology, understood non-deterministically and dialectically, can be a window on to the understanding the structure of social relations itself. It is worth repeating Marx's point from *Capital* volume 1:

> Technology reveals the active relation of [human beings] to nature, the direct process of production of [their] life, and thereby it also lays bare the process of the production of the social relations of [their] life, and of the mental conceptions that flow from those relations.
> MARX, 1977: 493

While it is true that technology reveals the character of social relations of production, what is more true is that the entire 'regime' of production process – including what kind of use-values are produced and whether they are produced for the world market and how (and with what kind of techniques) – reveals the nature of social relations of production. It is useful therefore to examine the regime of production for the world market under neoliberal capitalism.

5   Export-Oriented Neoliberal Capitalism, Social Oppression, and Dual Metabolic Rift

In an interesting way, in policy circles, the emphasis on agricultural production and that on the neoliberal approach to development have come together in recent times. In the late 2000s, the World Bank suggested that agriculture – commercial agriculture, that is – could deliver economic development and poverty reduction in the Global South. And, internationally, neoliberal approach to development is promoted by the World Bank and other similar institutions. Neoliberalism (which is the main topic of Chapter 4), which is often known as NEP (New Economic Policy) in India, includes at least two inter-connected things. One is the state's relative withdrawal from welfare provision (which has implications for the social wage and the balance of power between capital and labor over wages, etc.). Another is the promotion of a regime of relatively de-regulated production which is enabled by trade liberalization and which is based on a politically vulnerable non-unionized (mobile) working class to produce cheap commodities for export. These two approaches – stress on agriculture and a neoliberal approach – are combined when export-oriented, de-regulated production of nontraditional agricultural goods from poorer countries such as India (to richer countries but not just to richer countries) is encouraged. Shrimp aquaculture is a very important aspect of this process. Shrimp production is a specific instance of a larger system of production. It is a form of 'New Agricultural Production' (NAP): the production of luxury (or high-value) non-traditional agri-commodities for export (Watts, 1996). NAP fits in with, and is a part of, a larger process: neoliberalism, or, agrarian neoliberalism. In India, NAP is a part of NEP.

Production of shrimp – like the production of all things – requires labor. In most cases, this labor takes the form of *wage*-labor. All wage-laborers *are the same* at one level in that they all have a specific relation with capital in terms of relations of exchange, property and production of surplus value. At another level (at a more concrete level), wage-labor *is differentiated* along lines of social relations of gender, age, location and ethnicity, so we deal with not wage-labor as such but, for example, indigenous wage-labor, child wage-labor, etc. The exploitation and domination of aqua-laborers happens in ways in which capitalist relations are mediated by place-specific relations of difference. The exploitation and domination of aqua-laborers are also shaped by the specificities of nature-dependent production (e.g. the biophysical character of labor process). Just as forces of nature such as land and water are 'exploited' in shrimp-culture, meaning that the shrimp-production process extracts a lot more out of nature than it returns to it, laborers on shrimp-farms are similarly exploited: the wage they receive to produce a 'cheap' commodity for export are less than the net value embodied in the shrimps that they produce. Akin to the metabolic rift, this is a social rift. The two rifts are parts of the same process: relation between capital and the immediate producer.

Shrimp culture is justified by the 'rhetoric of poverty alleviation'. This kind of development discourse is contradicted by the materiality of the real situation: those who produce shrimps, like millions of people performing other kinds of work, do not receive a decent wage, and are forced to experience all the three forms of LMR (Labor Metabolic Rift). The inadequacy of wages takes many forms. The 'gross wages' are low. Their *net* wages are also low because of the various hidden 'costs of work' (e.g. deductions from wages; costs of illness that is caused by work). Real wages are low in relation to laborers' basic needs. Relative wages – wages relative to the profit – earned by entrepreneurs are also low (workers are aware of this 'class inequality' in part from the lavish life style of the aqua-entrepreneurs). To Kautsky's words (1988: 385), they work 'like beasts of burden by day [and are] housed worse than beasts of burden by night'. The conditions of aqua-laborers, including the ways in which their lives in the workplace and labor market are controlled, are similar those of the

CONCLUSIONS AND REFLECTIONS

workers subjected to sweatshop conditions more generally (Mezzadri, 2016, 2018; Pattenden, 2016).

The regime of low wages and poor working conditions in shrimp areas is caused and reproduced by multiple concrete mechanisms. Increasingly divorced from the means of production such as land and access to water bodies, and without savings or secure long-term employment, workers, including women and child workers, rely on this or that capitalist for their social reproduction. Each owner presumes that the workers whom they employ only for 4–5 months will somehow survive for the rest of the year from family production, meager crumbs thrown at their families in their own villages from the government (whose welfare commitment is dwindling anyway), or from the employment by other owners. If employers have to employ certain workers on a more permanent basis, they might have *some* interest in their long-term social reproduction. This is not the case. The other concrete mechanisms behind the regime of low wages and poor working conditions include: deliberate delay in, and withholding of, the payment of wages; strict labor control regimes including use of chemicals maximizing work effort; and capital's power to impose and define the 'piece' and the 'wage' in the piece-wage system, even in the face of occasional protests. Interestingly, these are some of the processes that Marx talks about in *Capital* volume 1.

There are also several subjective processes that reproduce low-wage capitalism. These include the specific form of working class consciousness that suggests a form of empathy for the 'suffering' employers. This is a form of consciousness – a bourgeois consciousness of workers – that overlies an incipient 'anti-capital' consciousness, or consciousness in its 'embryonic form' (Lenin 1977b: 113). Underlying workers' empathy for employers who pay low wages and commit what Marx would call 'fraudulent tricks' is the mistaken idea that wages are paid to a laborer out of the sale of products of her labor. According to this idea, the magnitude of wages depends on the actual price at which the employer is able to sell the shrimps, so if shrimps sell for less, wages will be less. Shared by both employers and laborers, this idea, this illusion, contributes to the reproduction of capitalist relations. It is useful to quote Marx here again:

> Wages are not a share of the worker in the commodities produced by him. Wages are that part of already existing commodities with which the capitalist buys a certain amount of productive labor-power.
>
> MARX, 1976: 36

The temporality of wage-form of labor – the *fact* that wages are paid *after* the product of labor is sold contributes to an *illusion* in the minds of workers.

Workers' spontaneous consciousness is generally contradictory. While there is evidence of illusion as just mentioned, there is also evidence that workers are conscious of the fact their situation is objectionable. While many workers are conscious of the need to be organized against these conditions, some show more passive resistance. The latter is indicated when some say that 'No one should work in shrimp-culture in his or her life'. What if a large number of workers believe in this? What if local branches of Left parties suddenly have their veil over their eyes removed? Unfortunately, the reality is that the locally-based Left parties have failed to do anything to mobilize workers and raise the workers' consciousness.

One can see that the processes underlying the low-wage regime discussed above are connected to the politics of wage-labor relations, i.e. to the issue of the balance of power between capital and labor. Even such economic factors as unemployment causing low wages are not just economic factors: unemployment makes political resistance against low wages difficult to launch. But employers know that workers *can* resist. That is why they take pre-emptive steps to stop any possible unity among workers.

The relations between capital and labor are being mediated by specific social relations (and cultural constructions) of gender, age, and ethnicity (one of whose local forms is aboriginality). These are utilized by employers to create a vulnerable workforce, which makes it possible to super-exploit without much political trouble. Importantly, relations between capital and labor are also mediated by the geographical character of labor. Generally, a social wage (e.g. government welfare) and local 'social capital' can tip the balance of power between the employer and the employee slightly, in favour of the employee. Migrant workers, however, are denied this advantage. At one level, capital's laborers do not have to be migrants, or indeed, women or children. But in actual practice, in a specific places and times, social difference makes a difference to capital's attempt to pocket the economic difference between (a) the value that the oppressed worker produces and the value of the wage that the worker is lucky to receive, and (b) between the value of labor power (what wages should be) and what they actually receive.

It is also important to notice how the relation between capital and labor operates through the biophysical nature of the labor process. This happens in many ways. The shrimp production process is nature-dependent: it can be affected by unpredictable rains and floods. Shrimps can catch diseases. We need to, however, connect the nature of the nature-dependent production to its social (capitalist) nature. Consider how the unpredictability of the biophysical process as well as the fact that the production process has to be continuous (i.e. shrimps have to be watched for 24 hours) contribute to a form of consent to the regime of long hours and difficult (night) work in the mind of laborers:

CONCLUSIONS AND REFLECTIONS

they (including child laborers) are made to believe that shrimps are like children, can become sick, and need to be constantly looked after through long hours of work. The biophysicality of the labor process acts as a mask to hide its capitalist character. It also acts as a form of labor control: if shrimps have not been fed well throughout the night at proper intervals, the employer will know this from a specific form of the physical movement of shrimps. Aqua-labor is controlled in other ways as well. For example, women laborers' work intensity is sought to be enhanced through the use of chemical technology when, for example, chemicals are mixed with shrimps to help the laborers de-head them faster. Ensuring the safety/health of the biological product (shrimp) is paramount; this leads the employers to hire nonlocals who are easier to discipline and who have limited ability to inflict Luddite class revenge (e.g. by harming the shrimps in the event of a labor dispute). The biophysical process also affects laborers' health, producing what Fracchia (2008) would call the 'body in pain'. The men, women and children, who produce a popular delicacy for the national and global markets, cannot even eat with their own hands the simple food (rice, etc., and not shrimp) that they can buy with their meager wages. Their hands have blisters due to the use of chemicals at the production and beheading sites. It is as if each shrimp, a commodity, records in its body the annals of low wages, unending night shifts, and long hours of work as well as the unfulfilled desire of the poor laborers to enjoy a socially acceptable level of living. The aqua-labor process signifies the production of a use-value as well as the capitalist character of that production.

Workers' conditions are of little concern to owners, however. If a worker is crippled, another can be hired. There is plenty of labor power available, whose production has no/little direct cost to individual employers. But if one shrimp is below the expected size or if it dies, what is lost is value (labor power already spent) and surplus value (profit), which have no substitute. When a use-value (e.g. edible shrimps) produced by the worker is lost, the value is also lost, and with that, any surplus value in it is also lost. So shrimps' health is of great interest to owners. If shrimps are not healthy, owners cannot sell them in the global market for an expected profit on their investment. It is human labor that produces shrimps, but shrimps become more 'valuable' than human beings and their labor.

Like many other export commodities from the countries of the periphery, shrimps are being produced dominantly under social relations of global capitalism. This is capitalism based on the formal subsumption of labor (which is the topic in Chapter 3), a mode of capitalist production based on long working days and the payment of low wages (i.e. wages that do not even cover subsistence needs). Formal subsumption of labor comprises what I called LMR 2 and LMR 3 (as well as LMR 1) in Chapter 6. Wages and the working day are touching their physical minimum and physical maximum respectively. In the context of global demands for reduced state intervention in national economies, Third World comparative advantage supposedly lies in 'cheap' environmental and labor resources. 'Cheap', however, only signifies the relationship between commodities exchanged; hidden are the material realities of production. It is also unlikely that the low-wage regime described here is specific to the spatial context under study (India). It is likely to be common to most shrimp-exporting poorer countries.

Relevant here is Marx's (1977: 164) notion of commodity fetishism where relations between commodities produced in different places replace relations between people producing these, both in reality and in our consciousness. In commodity fetishism, it appears as if being bought and sold for a profit is in the very DNA of a thing (a use-value) such as shrimp. That a dollar in the USA or Canada can buy – or that a certain amount of a product can be exchanged for – several counts of cheap foreign shrimps, this relation of exchange, is not written in the body of the commodity-shrimp, how-much-ever we may twist and turn and pinch these edible (non-human) creatures. Much rather, this relation of exchange is based on specific social relations under which the laboring human creatures producing this commodity live, work and suffer. These are the social relations of capitalist property and of production, of the class relations. And these class relations are defended by the state.

6   Class, Capitalism, and the Capitalist State

Yet, to do a class analysis of the state often prompts a charge of analytical bias (because the state is often assumed to work as a neutral agent), as well as the charge of economism and 'classism'. The latter charge implies that a class analysis of the state reduces the state to class relations and to its economic imperatives, and thus ignores non-class social relations such as caste and gender, etc. Those who make these charges – including those who put their faith in the state's ability to solve the fundamental problems of the majority-class, which must sell its labor power and/or small amount of products of their labor (as small-scale producers) – must answer the following: if the capitalism that India has is not particularly conductive to a sustained and systemic increase in labor productivity per hour per person and to an economic regime which is not based on making people work long hours for barely 400 Rupees a day, if whatever limited welfare benefits were provided to the lower classes are being cut or in constant danger of being cut, if technological change that has happened

CONCLUSIONS AND REFLECTIONS

does not benefit the lower classes much, if export-oriented production does not help those who produce things for export, if the desperate masses have to struggle against their dispossession and against extreme forms of exploitation and oppression, and if a fascistic movement, including fascistic politicians, are curtailing democratic rights of ordinary people and are deepening the neoliberal assault on the toiling masses, what explains all this and why does the state not do anything?

It is a truism, albeit a crucial one that is defended in this book, that class relations and the attendant material conditions, constitute the most important context for all forms of intervention by the state and for the very form (territorial and political form) of the state itself. Of course, within this class context other social relations – i.e. those of caste, religion, ethnicity, region and nation – operate and influence the state and its class character. And within the limits set by class relations, state officials and politicians exercise power relations over the masses, in a way that cannot be reduced to capitalism and that benefits the officials and politicians: in India, bureaucrats and politicians-in-power behave as kings and queens with respect to the masses.

Because capitalism is the dominant mode of production in India, the state is a capitalist state, and thus an 'agent' of capitalist development, *both* in pre-neoliberal and neoliberal times, and *both* in rural and urban areas. The relation of partnership between the two arms of capital relation – the state and the capitalist class – has been justified in terms of two major ideologies: one is the ideology of state control and socialism, and another is one of free market. Ideology does not mean total lies. Ideology refers to ideas that are partly true and partly false and that contribute to the reproduction of an in-egalitarian and exploitative order (Eagleton, 1991). The ideology of state control over the business world in India in the early years of the post-1947 period was not entirely a lie. There *was* a degree of state control. There was a degree of state intervention on behalf of the masses. Even the ruling class understood from the very beginning (since the 1940s) that a small degree of state control and a small degree of pro-poor re-distribution is a remedy to potential social upheaval in the aftermath of 1917. In the neoliberal times, the other ideology, the ideology of free market has justified interventions by the state that are more blatantly in the interest of capital than before. In other words, the state has always worked, more or less, in the interest of the capitalist class. Its policies (as well its form – federal-liberal-democratic form) have been accordingly influenced by the interests and actions of the dominant classes. Of course, state policies have also been, to some extent, shaped by the lower-class struggles, actual or potential. What I say about the capitalism – state relation in India is supported by comments on the topic from Ronald Herring, a long-time critical commentator on Indian political economy: the structural power of capital is evident in the imperative facing every governmental regime of whatever nominal ideology to maintain 'business confidence', or spur investment, increase growth rates and employment, improve foreign exchange positions, or improve geopolitical security' (Herring, 2013: 131). Herring adds: 'no explicit mobilization is necessary for these outcomes; if capital is not pleased with such policies, it will move away or stop investing' (ibid.). Much discussion of class politics curiously ignores this 'most materially significant element of class power' (p. 131). Parties and governments are forced to serve capital in the national interests – and this is what Miliband (1983) refers to when he talks about the 'partnership' between capital and an 'autonomous' state elite. But these same parties and governments are not forced to serve the subordinate classes in the same national interest (Herring, 2013: 139). From the standpoint of capital and its state, these classes, the majority, are obviously not the nation, and their interest in a decent standard of living and in a democratic polity and culture, is not the national interest.

Like any capitalist state, the state in India must sustain the myth that capitalist accumulation (which goes by the name of 'growth' or 'Vikas', etc.) benefits not just the already-better-off entrepreneurs, and that the poor also gain some significant advantages from it. The myth needed is that the exploiters (misnamed as employers and wealth-creators) and the exploited, benefit from the same process. This myth legitimizes the state. As well, the legitimacy of the post-1947 state derived in no small measure from two assumptions: that, unlike colonial government which served 'foreign' interests, it would serve domestic ones; and that, to this end, it would promote economic development from which the nation as a whole would benefit. Increasingly, however, the distinction between the pre-1947 and post-1947 development projects is being eroded, as the neoliberal state not only facilitates the dispossession and exploitation of the poor by international and domestic capital, but also encourages the latter to undertake export-oriented cultivation. Farm crops are once again being seen to be produced mainly for an elite (= 'foreign') market, much as they were during the colonial era. This can contribute to the broader process of delegitimizing the state, a situation which in turn can intensify class struggle 'from below This can prompt the repressive 'from above' response by the neoliberal state protecting the interests of the capitalist class in India.

Because of a continuing failure on the part of the state to promote development in the interest of workers and small-scale producers and because of its current neoliberal policies supportive of domestic and foreign capital, this apparatus may indeed face a legitimation crisis, especially in rural areas and in urban slums. The extent to which such a legitimation crisis will be, in fact, realized depends on how the lower classes and their organizations respond to the

CONCLUSIONS AND REFLECTIONS   543

situation theoretically and politically. And to the degree that a crisis does take shape, much will also depend on how the state responds, in particular the use of coercive power at its disposal, and how in turn lower classes respond to this. Indeed, the topic of how the lower classes fight for their rights and how the state responds, is an important one.

7   Lower-Class Struggles and the State Response

Relations of class (as well as caste- and gender-based social oppression that exploited classes are subjected to) have created extremely difficult conditions of living for workers and peasants, which the post-colonial capitalist state has, more or less, failed to significantly mitigate. The conjunctural combination of unjust conditions of living and state failure has created a situation ripe for *class* struggle, one instance of which is the Naxalite movement, a part of the world-wide Maoist movement.

The Naxalite movement is rooted in material conditions of existence, which are social-cultural as well as economic. It has fruitfully combined class politics (albeit in a rather limited manner) as well as those of cultural oppression. Many people within the state agencies, and many middle class people, do not fully understand Naxalites' pro-poor ideological significance. They homogenize the movement associating it exclusively with violence. They often mistakenly treat Naxalites merely/mainly as armed thugs, without any political and socio-economic program of development for the poor. However, the Naxalite movement does suffer from serious problems. This emanate from its inadequate class-based understanding and inadequate class-based practice. The material conditions of deprivation are produced dominantly by the specific ways in which capitalism works in the concrete conditions of India, which include remnants of feudalism, and liberal democracy (however distorted), within the system of global capitalism. The Naxalites have not fully and consistently understood the following: that the most important reason for rural distress, and indeed the distress of the majority of the country's population, is the *capitalist* character of the system, which is also mainly responsible for state's failure to mitigate some of the adverse effects of the system on the poor. In part because of the Naxalites' inadequate understanding of the system's dynamics, their dominant focus has been mistakenly on the rural/agrarian issue (in backward regions) and on its so-called 'semi-feudal' shell. This has meant that the movement has, more or less, been disconnected socially from the working class and spatially from urban areas, the main theatres of accumulation and exploitation by both domestic and imperialist bourgeoisie.

The *ideological* framing or representation of the Naxalite movement as terrorist, as a menace, as a security threat, as ultra-left extremism, along with state's own *political* shell (liberal-democratic form), give some legitimacy to the state to repress. In the Naxalite case, this is the fact that they are a communist movement and that a communist movement is automatically seen as a threat to the security of the capitalist state (Subramanian, 2004). This ethos, supported by many middle class people, legitimizes state repression. Further, the state has access to its own expanding *mobilizing structures:* network of police and paramilitary agencies, police informers, anti-Naxalite civilian militias that the state supports, all of which, of course, complement the private coercive means available to the propertied classes. Here it is important to mention how state-supported research calls for more state violence against Naxalism. Most importantly, the political-economic-ideological threat from Naxalites offers the *political opportunity* for repression.

There is no doubt that Naxalites use violent methods. One should also remind oneself that: landlords and some business houses use daily violence against ordinary people; government officials and politicians behave in the most rude manner with the masses, sometimes not shying away from using coercive measures; Hindu mobs burn Christians' houses, destroy mosques and massacre Muslims, with the covert/overt support of politicians; Islamic terrorists kill innocent Hindus; and higher castes also kill lower castes. Yet, Naxalite violence is seen as *the greatest* threat to the state and to the class order that the state must protect. This is *because* their violence is against: actions of specific sections of the property-owning class (e.g. landlords, traders, mining companies), the excesses of the capitalist class system, and functioning of state personnel and laws that *support* the exploitative property owners. In the case of the Naxalite movement, its violence is prompted by state violence (and by violence from the sections of the property-owning class itself). If this is the case, then the idea that the state is violent towards Naxalites just because they are violent is inadequate, if not entirely untrue. State violence is rooted in its own class *content* and in the class content (character) of the Naxalites. It does not primarily come from their *mode* of fighting. The physical threat from Naxalites is not the only reason for state violence. The state uses, and will use, violence against the Naxalite movement because the state must defend the interests of sections of the propertied class that the movement is fighting against.

Apart from challenging certain aspects of the class system, the Naxalite movement also seeks to build alternative modes of living *within* capitalism. And that is a threat to the state. In terms of its actual practice, the alternative development landscape that the Naxalites seek to produce somehow resonates with the post-Marxist (e.g. Gibson-Graham, 2006) idea of production of post-capitalist spaces within capitalism (see also Holloway, 2005). The lower classes that the movement seeks to mobilize are not just an agency of *resistance* (backed by *force* where necessary). The movement also plays a positive, albeit limited, developmental role. In a sense the Maoists are mimicking state practices of governmentality (Sundar, 2014a), or rather, what one might call 'state's developmentality'. The latter can be seen as developmental governmentality, which signifies the deployment of developmental activities and development discourse to discipline people and shape their consciousness that in turn legitimizes the capitalist state. Naxalites promote an alternative developmentality which produces consent of common people to Naxalism, and thus potentially enhances their politicization, posing a serious threat to the state. State violence is partly directed at *destroying* this consent. As Spacek (2017) says: 'force and development have become conceptually blended and hybridised in practice, leading to a colonisation of statecraft by policing and violence' (p. 176). Further: 'The police have become the developmental agents in the [Naxal] region, responsible for carrying out infrastructural and social service delivery. They are the primary agents of the state', a state that is operating on the basis of 'architectures of force and spaces of violence' (p. 176). So, in so far as carrying out developmental activities is about producing consent to the legitimacy of the state and to the class rule that the state defends, and in so far as the coercive organs are the agents of developmental activities, the boundary between coercive and consent-making state activities begins to be blurred.

The state generally functions as one arm of the structure of private – property relations, and intervenes on behalf of the propertied classes (Das, 2017a: Chapter 8). Whatever else the state is, it is, above all, an armed body of people, separate from ordinary toiling masses who are the majority (workers and poor peasants). The state is basically an institution of class violence, functioning on behalf of the ruling classes, and against the ordinary people. The state uses violence against ordinary citizens if they fight against: (a) this *structure of private property relations*, (b) the *mechanisms* through which this structure works (e.g. competitive drive for profit, rent and interest; dispossessing people of their land in order to ensure access of the business world to people's resources), (c) and the *concrete effects* of these mechanisms (e.g. extreme poverty; ecological destruction). The state uses violence against ordinary citizens if they fight against the powerful *agents* of the state (e.g. parties; officers; police) who support these relations/mechanisms. The form of political movement of the masses does not matter much. Its content – its class content – does. That is: whether ordinary people are engaged in peaceful mobilization or whether they use a degree of violence (in self-defense), is generally beside the point. And when inequality level rises, the mask of democracy that a state wears is increasingly difficult to wear. State violence against ordinary people and against those who politically mobilize them *is* an intervention on behalf of the ruling classes and their political spokespersons and managers, whether or not the mobilization of ordinary people is violent. In the internal wars against Naxalism (and other acts of resistance) the state is deploying common people against themselves: most of the people who join the security apparatuses are from working class and peasant backgrounds, desperate to earn a living, and these people, are used by the elite to kill people like themselves (i.e. people from working class and peasant backgrounds who resist exploitation and oppression and undemocratic acts of the state).[6]

The state impersonates guerilla tactics of a section of the Naxalite movement to fight it (Sundar, 2014a). By doing so, it is turning what I would call the 'homo sufferer' (working masses) into Agamben's 'homo sacer': those people who the organs of the state could kill without being guilty of committing murder. In India's so-called red corridor, there is an important contradiction: the red corridor's monetary value is multiple times the nation's annual income, and yet it contains the world's most impoverished people (especially among low castes and aboriginal communities). To 'resolve' this kind of exceptionally intense contradiction which signifies the contradiction between a small elite and the majority of the population, the state creating a (quasi-) 'state of exception', 'a legal civil war that allows for the physical elimination not only of political adversaries but of entire categories of citizens who for some reasons cannot be integrated into the political system' (Agamben, 2005: 2). This civil war is the class struggle from above against the masses, i.e. the lower classes (workers and poor peasants, including those who are from the adivasi and Dalit backgrounds).

The state is able to engage in violence against Naxalites by producing an epistemological exaggeration: a political-geographic overestimation of the threat to the state, a knowledge-claim, a ruling class ideology, which would justify the increased level of violence by the state. By saying that the Naxalite threat can be anywhere anytime, the state of exception can potentially be produced anywhere anytime within the nation. The border moves inside, so the military can be engaged, if needed. That this feeds into, and is supported by, right-wing, hyper-nationalist groups and individuals, is not surprising. The state's approach to lower classes is, more or less, the same, whether its affairs are managed by the BJP or the Congress or indeed by regional parties.

---

6   It is interesting that: in a speech in June 1975, Jayaprakash Narayan called on the police and the army to disobey what he described as illegal orders (Smith, 1979).

CONCLUSIONS AND REFLECTIONS

The post-colonial state labelling the Naxalite movement as a menace, as criminal, as unpatriotic, etc. is symbolic violence, as is its tendency to see any social justice movement as Naxalite and therefore violent. In this sense, the post-colonial state's approach to militant movements for social justice is similar to the colonial state's attitude to militant freedom fighters. In September 2018, the state arrested five well-known social justice activists, labelling them 'urban Naxals' for their alleged connection to the Naxalite movement (Hindu, 2018). The deployment of the construct of 'Urban Naxal' is a means of expanding state's battle against the Naxalite movement to the cities. This urbanization of state's fight against Naxalism which is a rural phenomenon, is also a form of an all-out war against *any form* of dissent that the state cannot cope with or tolerate. Someone who is seen as an enemy of *the state* is equated to an enemy *of the people* in order to justify penal interventions. This seeing does not see that the state works on behalf of the fundamental interests of a tiny minority of the population, propertied classes, and that it even works at the behest of certain individuals or fractions belonging to the propertied classes. The state must create its enemy, its other, to justify its own existence and to deflect attention from state's real enemy (nation of workers and peasants, the majority of the population), whose interests are antagonistic to the ruling class-minority which the state must protect. The state cannot *overtly* declare the majority of the nation as its enemy but its actions treat the majority as the enemy or as if it is the enemy: *anyone* who resists the class rule and its effects is labelled a Naxalite and can be harmed, whether or not they have anything to do with Naxalism. So the state has *de facto* launched a war against the enemy within, against the majority of the people, via its war against the localized Naxalites. Just as the state is generally a false protector of common people's interests, the enemy it constructs is also generally false, or not as true as portrayed by the state.

Symbolic violence can create a condition for 'subjective violence', which is the violence performed by 'a clearly identifiable agent' (Zizek, 2008: 1, 10). This agent can be the agent of the ruling classes (their security agents or hired hoodlums) or of the state apparatus. State's subjective violence is reinforced by, and complements, the subjective violence by the ruling class, and to which Naxalite movement responds by its own subjective violence.

Systemic violence refers to the 'catastrophic consequences of the smooth functioning of our economic and political systems' (Zizek, 2008: 2). This is the violence that prompts the other two forms of violence (symbolic and subjective forms). Class rule is behind systemic violence and the state supports the class rule. The state is launching a violent war on people because they are fighting against systemic violence (i.e. they are fighting against a war on their livelihood and on their democratic right to protest injustice). State violence against Naxalites is an instance of a general form of violence, a violence that is necessary to thwart all forms of actual/potential opposition to systemic violence (i.e. to class rule). The government claims that its coercive forces are there to counter the Naxalites, but in actuality its aim is to intimidate into silence the democratic movements such as people resisting land grabs or fighting police repression. Where are these coercive forces of the state when the propertied classes and their goons inflict violence against ordinary people and when Hindu mobs lynch innocent Muslims? By creating drastic panic among people and curtailing people's freedom, the state makes it possible for corporations to be free to 'suck out the minerals and forest resources' (Dias, in Ismi, 2013). One form of freedom comes at the expense of another. Between two equal freedoms, it is the freedom that can be backed by greater violence that wins. The money buried in the mines is much more important than the respect for democratic rights of the exploited and oppressed (in the indigenous communities).

What state violence – the *de facto* 'everywhere-endless-war' against its people fighting for justice – means is this: while a 'society' will not tolerate violence against the state, it will very easily tolerate violence against the body and soul of its common citizens, including little children who are malnourished, who have to work as bonded labor abused by labor contractors and employers (Das, 2019), and who are assaulted by security people, in Naxalite areas. Why do the counts of security personnel killed while fighting against some segments of the Naxalite movement more important than the counts of the little children dying premature death and of women dying while giving birth, because of the failure of the state to provide for better conditions of life?[7]

Someone can argue that all states, when challenged by non-state forces, will behave the same way as the Indian state is doing in response to the Naxalite challenge. He/she might ask: would a socialist state (a state that comes to exist just after a revolutionary overthrow of capitalism) allow people to challenge it in the way that the Naxalite movement does? The answer is no. But there is a difference. It is a class difference. In class divided societies, the ruling class constitute the minority, and the majority are the exploited classes. All states of class societies, including capitalism, are states of, and for, a minority (the class

---

7　'3,000 children die every day from poor diet-related illness' (Qazi, 2018). Five women die every hour during childbirth in India, according to World Health Organization (Times of India, 2016).

CONCLUSIONS AND REFLECTIONS

that controls society's productive resources) and against the majority. These states use violence to suppress the majority. That is very undemocratic. A socialist state, is different, however: it would be the first state that is the state of the majority (workers and peasants) who need the state to stop overthrown classes from returning to power and to construct a society that is democratic in economic, political and cultural spheres. Therefore, any challenge from the overthrown propertied classes, who constitute a tiny minority, will need to be crushed by the state on behalf of the people. That response of the state is not comparable to the fact that a capitalist state violently crushes an opposition to it from the masses, the majority. The question is not: how does the state respond when it faces a challenge? The question is: what is the main purpose of the state with respect to the basic classes? The class character of the state and the class character of the challenge are important to keep in mind. State violence to preserve the privilege of a minority is not the same violence that may be necessary to preserve the economic and political power of the vast majority.

One must be critical of state violence, the scope of which has been *expanding*. There is another aspect of the reality which cannot be denied. This is that the Naxalite theory and strategy are self-*limiting* (Das, 2010, 2015). This is for various reasons. Firstly, there is the fact that the Naxalite movement is *not* fundamentally against the totality of capitalist class relations. The Naxalite movement is also problematic in that, whether or not it uses violence, it mistakenly treats the peasantry (or, the rural poor) as the main revolutionary agent rather than an ally of the urban working class. The deployment of anarchic and secretive violence by certain segments of the movement is against the principle that the masses can only self-emancipate themselves and that they will do this on the basis of their political organization and organized action, and not on the basis of secretive violence. But if the state can inflict violence on a movement which is not particularly anti-capitalistic and if it does not mobilize urban workers, then one can imagine how violent the state will be in relation to a movement that is fundamentally anti-capitalistic, mobilizing the main revolutionary agent (the working class) to fight for a socialist society characterized by popular democracy in every sphere of life, and not for a better – more democratic – form of capitalism.

We have seen that state repression is particularly likely when lower-class struggles target property relations that cause ordinary citizens to suffer. Whether these movements are violent, and whether the state is a liberal-democracy is a contingent matter. The liberals' argument that democracy pacifies the state collapses when one considers how repressive the liberal-democratic Indian state is towards a movement such as the Naxalite movement, even if this movement is not seeking to go beyond capitalism. The response of the state to the Naxalite movement is symptomatic of a wider tendency across countries, including India: states are turning to authoritarian methods to suppress ideological and political dissent. This is because with rising inequalities and given the crisis-tendencies of capitalism, states are increasingly unable to buy legitimacy by granting benefits, however limited, for the benefit of the majority. The states are increasingly unable to respond to the fact that there is a fundamental contradiction between big business's interests in profit and interest, and working masses' interest in obtaining access to food, shelter, health-care, education, culture and sustainable environment. The pacifying effect of democracy that some social movement theorists stress will work if the ordinary people remain pacified and do not exercise their (class-) agency in the face of exploitation and oppression and wait indefinitely for some benefits from above (e.g. state; NGOs, etc.). Lower-class struggles show limit to liberal democracy. Liberal democracy is not pacifist but it expects lower classes to remain pacified even when they are under attack by the state. Similarly, the state itself fails to obey its own laws while killing lower class members who fight for justice and yet the state expects them to obey the rules of law in their fight for justice.

The Indian state sees the Naxalite movement, especially, the activity of the more militant section of it (CPI-Maoist), as the greatest threat to itself and to democracy, and this perception is in part because the Naxalite movement does use physical force against oppressive elements where necessary and possible. But is the Naxalite movement really the main danger to democracy? It is not. The main anti-democratic force is not the Naxalite movement (sometimes called the Far Left) but it is the Far Right.

8   Economic Development and Democracy under the Right-Wing Government

There has been a resurgence of the Far Right in India since the early 1990s. This tendency is represented by the Modi government installed since 2014. Under the Modi government, the overall record of development has been an epic of dismal failure. This is the case, especially if we consider the issues that affect the lives of the masses such as: unemployment and under-employment; low wages; increasing concentration of wealth and income; agrarian crisis; increasing attack on democracy and secularism and attendant communalization of society and polity, and so on. The ultra-rich has had *achhe din*. But the vast majority of people of different castes and religions live and work under economic and political conditions which, generally speaking, have not been improving.

According to the Prime Minister (or his erudite speech writer), *development* has become a vibrant *mass movement*. Development as a mass movement is a beautiful idea. Development *should* become a mass movement. It *will* become a mass movement when *masses*, democratically self-organized, *move* to take control over their lives. Development will become a mass movement when the masses (toiling workers and small-scale producers) control how nation's resources are used – i.e. when *they* are able to decide and say that nation's resources and their *own* labor are used to satisfy *their* own needs, and *not* the needs of the business class for profit, not the needs of the political class for accumulating election funding and power, and not the needs of the top and pliant bureaucratic and intellectual layers for their financial and other privileges.

Controlled by a right-wing party, the government is brazenly pro-big business and panders to a narrow, upper-middle class urban segment of highly educated technical personnel, who, in turn, churn out pro-BJP and communal propaganda meant to dupe the masses, including by using social media. The overall economic orientation of the government is indicated by 'Modinomics' (India's version of 'Reaganomics'). Modinomics is, fundamentally, an anti-people package of pro-market, pro-business policies. Its aim is to create the conditions for enabling profits for the corporates through a combination of: super-exploitation of the masses on the basis of flexible labor policies; extreme austerity; reducing corporate tax liability; and surrendering society's natural and financial resources and state-owned enterprises to private business-owners. Modinomics is a vision of the most extreme form of neo-liberal capitalism that Indian embarked on, with Manmohanomics of Dr. Manmohan Singh who served India as the Finance Minister and then as the Prime Minister. The multiple failures of the post-2014 government can be tied to its blatantly Right-wing nature. The government is right-wing for a reason: it is right for the business class, a class which is on the wrong side of history. It is right-wing because its fundamental aim is to serve the business class. It therefore cannot be expected to do much that is right for wage-earners, farmers, the poor and small-scale entrepreneurs, in any systematic, logical and long-term manner, *even if* some in government may have good intentions and even if some crumbs may fall and do fall to the people in exchange for political support.

To judge a government's policy requires one to consider, for example, the extent to which the things (or use-values) it provides its common citizens have a commodified or decommodified character (see Polanyi, 1944/2001; also Block and Polanyi, 2003). The more de-commodified the things are, the better it is for the majority, simply because the majority do not have a lot of money in their hands. One must ask: is water or education or healthcare of good quality provided to citizens in adequate amount by the government as a free use-value or, at least, at a minimal price, relative to the income of the people? From the standpoint of the majority, the purpose of a government is to provide an *antidote* to the ravages of the market, at least as far as the consumption of basic necessaries is concerned. However, true to its right-wing economic policies, what the BJP government calls 'development' is a commodity. The so-called developmental benefits are market-mediated and even corporate-mediated and constitute the mechanisms for the creation or expansion of the market for commodities. This is exactly what the neo-liberal-capitalist state does (Harvey, 2005: 2). What use are electricity wires or LPG connections if people have no money to pay for electricity and LPG? What use are roads if these roads siphon off natural resources and the surplus of an area to other places, especially, big cities, or if the roads take one to the places where there is neither decent wage-work nor free or subsidized government-provided services, or if roads allow the coercive forces to crush common people's movement for justice? A road or electricity is a 'very trivial thing' because everyone knows that it is needed by everyone but it tends to attain 'metaphysical subtleties' (Marx, 1977: 163), when it is seen in the context of the commodity-driven society that this right-wing government is intent on extending and deepening.

The impact of the existing BJP government can be seen as the sum of (a) the impact of its right-wing economic policy, (b) its communal policy of authoritarian-communalism-hyper-Hindu-nationalism, and (c) the interaction between the two. Common people are directly hurt by BJP's development policy and economic thinking, buttressed by right-wing economists, including some from the US, who had previously been marginalized. The communal-authoritarian policy that divides people and that crushes the right to dissent also directly affects the masses, in part by undermining their potential for resistance against the economic and the political elite. And given that BJP's economic policy is implemented in a context of communal-authoritarianism supported by vigilantism and mob violence, the adverse impact of the economic policy is magnified: its adverse impact is greater than what it would be if BJP was not *both* communal and economically right-wing. The Hindu-fascistic movement thrives on what I would call 'communal fetishism': just as in commodity fetishism, people are forced to live their lives as if to be bought and sold (for a profit) is a natural trait of the things they need, similarly, in communal fetishism, a Hindu with a communal consciousness lives as if a non-Hindu inherently possesses traits that are against the interests of Hindus and therefore deserves to be hated.

CONCLUSIONS AND REFLECTIONS   553

If you are a Dalit or from a religious minority or indeed a woman who wants to live like an ordinary citizen with all the rights that men enjoy, then your life is one of fear. Or, if you speak against the regime of unreason, religious obscurantism, and on-going attacks on secular ideals, then your life is one of fear as well. The world's largest democracy is reduced to this. The question is why? Why is this turn to the extreme right-wing thinking and practices, which are characteristic of a fascistic movement?

9   Capitalist Political Economy and Turn to Fascistic Tendencies

In understanding the rise of fascistic forces, one has to keep in mind Marx's theory of politics in class society. It is in 'the direct relationship of the owners of the conditions of production to the immediate producers', in which we find the hidden basis of 'the political form of the relationship of sovereignty and dependence' (Marx, 1991: 927). He also says that: 'all struggles within the state' – for example, struggles over democracy, etc. – the forms in which the struggles of the different classes are fought out (Marx and Engels, 1978: 54). Avoiding economic reductionism, Marx asserts that while politics is based on economic matters, politics also reacts back on economic matters.

The rise of the BJP is a national-scale manifestation of a global phenomenon which is the fact that the big business facing an economic and social crisis is resorting to social reaction, the politics of hatred, and authoritarianism (both authoritarianism from above – the state; and authoritarianism from below – rightwing forces on the ground). The increasing strength of right-wing forces, including the rise of the BJP as the political head of these forces in India, has been engendered by three political-economic mechanisms:

a.   The first is the crisis of global capitalism that is manifested in India. Associated with this is the crisis of post-colonial national capitalism, and the attendant crisis of the livelihood of common people. The bourgeois system of the world and India's backward capitalism operating within the influence of imperialism and imperialist institutions, have been simply incapable of meeting the basic needs of the toiling classes. Masses have been subjected to exploitation (and indeed, super-exploitation), dispossession, and immiserization in its absolute and relative forms.

b.   The combination of the mechanisms of exploitation, dispossession, and immiserization requires legitimization/ justification in the minds of the masses. To the extent that these mechanisms are not accepted by the masses, they engage in potential/actual opposition, which in turns prompts a ruling class response in the form of authoritarianism. The latter also requires justification. There is thus a need for double justification (consent from the masses): the system of exploitation/dispossession/immiserization needs justification, and the coercive response to the lower-class struggle against the system also requires justification. There is a need for actively weakening of the lower-class opposition too. The ideology of religion and associated Hindu-nationalism, apart from the use of caste-based politics, provides such justification (consider all the calls for making sacrifices – accepting austerity and low wages, etc. – in the name of the nation). It also divides the masses along the lines of religion and fake view of nationalism that considers vast sections of the population as anti-national. Deployment of religion and religion-based politics is supplemented with lies and false promises, to obtain consent to the system, and this, in a liberal-democracy, includes obtaining votes for fascistic political outfits. All in all, a structural space is created for increasing strength of fascistic forces, which have been existing in India since the 1920s.

c. Capitalism produces a class-agency for the fascistic project. It produces a reserve army of labor and pauperized small-scale producers (who are on their way to becoming completely propertyless), the elements of which, in a poor economy without social benefits (or with very limited benefits) from the government, are vulnerable to lumpenization and criminality. Having been 'spiritually destroyed and morally disoriented by the cruelties they suffer in their everyday life', these victims of (neoliberal) capitalism, not surprisingly, form the bulk of the fascist storm troopers (Ahmad, 2013: 3). There are vast sections of the population whose needs are not met by capital or the state, and they blame their situation on, for example, minorities.

10   Bourgeois Political System, and the Fascistic Movement

Just because capitalism creates a need for fascistic forces and just because capitalism creates lumpen elements that can be used by the fascistic project, that does not necessarily mean there will be fascistic forces in *active operation*. One has to understand the politics of the fascistic tendencies and not just their necessary political-economic conditions. There are indeed bourgeois-*political* dynamics of the rise of fascistic tendencies.

The failure of bourgeois politics as well as Left politics to defend democracy and secularism is a crucial (intermediate) process contributing to the rise of the BJP. The Congress and the BJP are two faces of Indian bourgeois politics, both promoting neoliberal capitalism, and the BJP using the religious divide to distinguish itself in the election market in a much more aggressive, unabashed

CONCLUSIONS AND REFLECTIONS

and overt manner than the Congress. There has indeed been a decline of the relatively secular bourgeois national party (Congress) and attendant 'capital flight' from the Congress to the BJP. One might say that: as Nehruvianism (semi-statist developmental model with very muted elements of social democracy), in part influenced by the Bombay plan, saved the Indian bourgeoisie from any communist threat, potential and actual during the post-1917 period, the fascistic threat came in its turn to liberate the bourgeoisie from Nehruvianism, in a conjuncture where a strong Left movement is not present to counter the fascistic movement.

The Left defines the current stage of Indian revolution as a democratic revolution, a stage at which an important task of the Left is to protect the democratic rights of minorities. Yet, what we see is the fiercest attack on democratic rights from communal-fascistic forces. The fascistic forces have come to constitute a very powerful obstacle to the Left movement, including in the traditional bastions of Left influence. These forces are a clear threat to the communist movement on the ground, as we have been seeing in Tripura and Kerala (and also in West Bengal), where communists and their offices are being physically attacked.

The BJP's goal is to see an India that is not only 'Congress-free' ('Congress-mukt') (because Congress has generally tried to defend secular values) but also 'Left-free' ('Left-mukt') or indeed 'Communist-mukt'. This shows that the right-wing forces are much more than mere religious-sectarian forces. Their threat is much more than the threat to secularism and bourgeois democracy. They are fundamentally capitalist, anti-proletarian, anti-communist forces whose fascistic aim is to destroy not only the democratic-secular ethos of the nation but also the organizations of the class-conscious masses, of workers and peasants of India. The BJP makes use of whatever elements of the democratic system it can use, to subvert the values of the democratic system itself in the service of a communal-bourgeois agenda and to establish a system where political power is always in the hands of the majority-religion.

A part of the blame for this tragic situation must indeed be on the Left itself: its failure to develop socialist consciousness and strong democratically-functioning socialist organizations. Indeed, much of what we see in India and elsewhere in terms of fascistic tendencies can be captured by these lines except that we are not talking about fascism but fascistic tendencies: 'Fascism is a product of ... a sharp social crisis' and 'the revolutionary weakness of the ... proletariat' (Trotsky, 1931a). The proletarian movement is in part weak due to bourgeois-reformist organizations and by the traditional communist parties which have failed 'to unite the workers under the banner of the revolution' as well as by the far left tendencies to do much to organize the workers. 'Through the fascist agency, capitalism sets in motion the masses of the crazed petty bourgeoisie, and bands of the declassed and demoralized lumpenproletariat' all of whom capitalism itself 'has brought to desperation and frenzy' (Trotsky, 1944). But during a transitional stage, when traits of fascism and liberal-capitalism are combined, such extreme measures are not yet necessary. Normal resources play the dominant role, supplemented by fascistic forces. The latter forces play not only a coercive role but also a consent-generating role: deploying myths about the past, and lies, and brainwashing people about what a nation means, about the superiority of a religion (Hindutva), and so on, in order to make people believe in the fascistic vision. The petty bourgeois fascist forces also seek to undermine ideas about labor and proletarian movement. The significance of assistance that capital mobilizes from normal resources (e.g. police personnel) relative to the assistance from fascistic forces on the ground can also change depending on the severity of the crisis and the strength of the anti-capitalist proletarian forces.

The increasing strength of right-wing forces represents a most extreme form of the latent tendency towards an attack on democracy, the tendency that exists in capitalist societies when there is massive inequality in wealth and income, under conditions of capitalist economic crisis. Fundamental to the worldview of the fascistic forces are the idolization of *free market economics* in the interest of the business class, and the deployment of *authoritarian politics*. Authoritarian politics is necessary to implement free market economics to help the property-owning classes. This is especially so in a society like India where millions of people are not only subjected to economic miseries caused by capitalist class relation and lower level of economic development under the rule of capital, but are also fighting against their miseries, and who therefore have to be suppressed/managed through authoritarian means, if the business class has to be kept happy. The ideology and practices of free market economics and authoritarian politics are dressed up by right-wing demagogic leaders. These two catchwords – development and good governance (or similar terms) – resonate with common people who are economically poor and who have also been subjected to apathy on the part of politicians and bureaucrats. These catchwords are used, along with hyper-nationalism based in the idea of the supremacy of a religion (e.g. Hinduism), to help produce/spark a *mass movement*. In short: blatant free market economic ideas and policies, rabid religious nationalism, and authoritarian intolerance towards rational dissent: all these come together, support each other, and produce a grassroots movement.

The BJP is definitely not an ordinary political party. Yet, the *perception* that it is an ordinary party has been slowly produced, over decades, by the corporate media, and sections of the middle class and of the business world. It is extra-ordinary that the BJP has in fact become an ordinary political party

CONCLUSIONS AND REFLECTIONS

which one could choose from a set of parties on the ballot box. It is also an extra-ordinary fact that the views of this party and of its fascistic supporters including RSS ideologues on a given topic have become a part of polite, civilized and public discussions on television channels, and in classrooms, conferences and teas-shops, and at dinner tables. This shows how far to the right public life has moved in India.

It is less true to say that the BJP is a communal party that just happens to support the business class. It is more true to say that BJP is fundamentally a bourgeois party that makes use of communal hatred to attain political influence and in the process serves bourgeois interests (as well as some reactionary interests of a bigoted section of the citizenry). Communalism (religious-sectarian hatred), or antagonism based in religious difference, may have a degree of autonomy with respect to capitalism, if not with respect to class as such. But once it exists, capitalism makes full use of it and feeds into it.

When all parties more or less aspire to satisfy the demands of the business class, then in the competitive market for votes, it helps a party if it can make use of gimmicks such as religious pride and hyper-nationalism to package itself as a unique commodity in the electoral market. The BJP is a national party that is not only pro-business but also communally divisive, a party that crushes not only economic rights but also democratic rights of toiling masses. While the BJP government defends the interests of the top 1–10% by not restricting the greedy pursuit of profit, it hurts the economic interests of the masses *and* undermines their power to fight back. The fascistic-nationalist movement is not only profoundly pro-capitalist but also is it shamelessly subordinating the interests of toiling masses living in India to imperialism. It makes use of religion, hyper-nationalism and historical distortions in order to divide the masses. It resorts to authoritarianism to weaken those who oppose it and its policies, bypassing parliament and harassing critics. It now seems a common BJP strategy to engineer a communal riot, polarize voters and win elections based on hatred and fear. And once this communal party is in power, there are further communal attacks as the perpetrators know that they will be directly or indirectly protected by the BJP. Communal riots often give a sense of satisfaction to the economically desperate lumpen elements created by capitalism, making them believe that they can achieve something in life. But they are, generally, unaware of being mere pawns in the larger communal-corporate 'game'. They are unaware of the fact that the fascistic politics they are engaging in are the politics by the masses but against the masses, i.e. that that politics is against their own interests. When the common people are divided on the basis of sectarian hatred and distracted from real issues because of hyper-nationalist hysteria, the ruling class and its politicians benefit. If the consciousness that prompts people to politically intervene in line with their class interests that are irreconcilable with ruling class interests, is class consciousness, then fascistic consciousness that the BJP feeds into and relies on is the polar opposite of class consciousness.

The rise of the BJP represents the crisis not only of bourgeois economics but also of bourgeois politics: the bourgeois political-economic system, and therefore, the bourgeois ruling class, has, simply, failed to secure not only social rights but also democratic rights, including rights of religious minorities. So the blame for the current situation must be at the door not only of the BJP and these forces, but also the bourgeoisie itself, or the bourgeois system as a whole, and this is indicative of what can be called a great Indian consensus: mechanisms of systematic attack on democratic rights, including the rights of religious minorities, have been slowly and steadily put in place, a process which has quickened when India 'fell for' the Washington consensus (i.e. neoliberal capitalism). That is why the fascistic threat is a class project, and not merely a political-cultural project. The threat exists in the following context: while the ruling class is losing its right to be the ruling class, the masses are not yet ready to say 'we cannot take it anymore', although some stirring in their consciousness is apparent.

Controlled by a Right-wing party, the BJP government, whether now or in the future, is not, and will not be, in sync with the political culture of a country, where the vast majority of its men and women of different religions and castes do not have the means to satisfy their basic needs, and where there is a deeply-felt desire for democracy and secularism. The majority of Indians are religious. But they do not necessarily favor the political-sectarian use of religion to make one group hate another. They do not necessarily favor politicians who spread religious hatred for political gain. However contradictory and utopian religious ideas are, all religions propagate 'spiritually' uplifting ideas, even if it is the case that many religious ideas also contribute to the reproduction of unjust social arrangements, which, in turn, necessitate religious beliefs. Religious ideas express, among other things, people's desire to be much better than what they normally are and what they can be. Many religious ideas teach people to be 'spiritual', generous, loving and kind-hearted, so even if people are religious, they can oppose the misuse of religion for narrow, divisive political gains undermining the secular-democratic character of the country. Partly because of this, and partly because of the correct perception that peoples' economic needs cannot be met by religious politics, the majority of of citizens, including, Hindus, generally speaking, have not supported the Hindu nationalist party's attempt to *unite* all Hindus to garner their votes on the basis of religion and on the basis of the utterly false notion that Hindus are under threat from Muslims or from the Muslim-majority of Pakistan.

CONCLUSIONS AND REFLECTIONS 559

11 What Is to Be Done?

The nature of the BJP's fascistic tendencies highlights the vulnerability of bourgeois democracy, of the entire bourgeois system.[8] India's democratic character can no longer be taken for granted. The bourgeois class and its political arms (parties, etc.) have failed to defend bourgeois democracy, including secularism. The 'defense' of democracy and secularism has now fallen on the shoulders of proletariat, more clearly than before. Therefore, the rise of the BJP can potentially create a fertile ground for more radical struggle against the bourgeois system itself.

Democratic politics and fascistic politics in societies dominated by bourgeois mode of production and exchange are both forms of bourgeois class rule. If ultra-right politics, like its more-democratic variant, is the political intervention of the ruling class to cope with its own crisis, then arriving at a different politics requires the political intervention of the masses of workers and petty producers, and their organic intellectuals. As Bannerji (1995: 35) puts it so eloquently: 'Misery does not automatically produce communism, and the desire for change born of suffering does not spontaneously know "what is to be done" to end oppression'. It is only their struggle, launched on the basis of sound theory (which has to be Marxist theory) and with the assistance of democratically-organized, multi-scalar, anti-capitalist, socialist, revolutionary organizations, that can ensure that every country meets the basic needs of every man, woman and child of all religions, castes, races and locations, where a culture of democracy among the ordinary toiling people prevails, and, where to quote Tagore, the Nobel Laureate:

> Where the mind is without fear and the head is held high
> Where knowledge is free
> Where the world has not been broken up into fragments by narrow domestic walls [of religion or caste, etc.] ...
> Where the clear stream of reason has not lost its way into the dreary desert sands of dead habit...
>
> TAGORE, 1913: 31; parenthesis and ellipses added

Common people must ask, and the Left and progressive forces must encourage them to ask: who is it that fears the citizens united to fight for their rights

---

8 The re-election of the BJP in 2019 with an enhanced mandate has confirmed this fear. The 2019 election happened after the completion of this book, so I do not talk about this. See Das (2019b) on this, which effectively functions as an epilogue to the book.

against the economic elite? Is it not the case that what is under attack is neither Hinduism from Islam, nor India from Pakistan or from Muslim immigrants, but 'the nation of ordinary people' (who work as wage-earners and/or as petty-producers, and whose most basic needs are not met, from the ruling class and its state)? Is it not true that: those who are attacking this nation of common people are the economic elite, which controls society's resources using them for their own profit, and which is supported by the BJP's politicians and the pliant officers who apparently constitute the steel frame and by their subservient propagandists in academia and the media? Is there not more common ground among them (wage-earners and among small-scale producers of different religions and castes, within India and across South Asia and the world) than there are differences among them, including those based in religion?

People must ask: whose interests are the politicians who spread religious hatred serving? How do the oppression/domination of religious minorities and an emotional feeling of hyper-nationalism based on Hindu identity, help a society address problems of: unemployment, poverty, inequality, caste- and gender-based oppression, environmental pollution, natural resources depletion, the country's subjugation to powerful imperialist powers, localized semi-feudal oppression, agrarian distress, and the lack of affordable health-care, housing and education? How can these problems be caused by the fact that some people are Hindus and others are not? Is it, or is it not, the case that: when political leaders and big business fail to solve people's major problems, they seek to divert people's attention *from* such failure *towards* non-issues by using religion, myths, false nationalism and so on, to divide the people? Why is it that the right-wing government feels threatened by any attempt to forge a unity of secular political forces, prompting it to use undemocratic measures against opposition forces? Those in the business world cannot also be allowed to maintain their 'silence': they must be asked by the masses this question: do they support or oppose the forces which are communal and which spread sectarian hatred and which repress any force of dissent?

Not only must one ask questions such as the ones posed above, but also must they fight to deepen and defend their democratic rights, including the right to practice any religion, to eat any food, to engage in any occupation or to love anyone. And in doing this, they must be conscious of what *binds* them: what binds them, irrespective of their different religions, is the fact that their democratic rights (*including* secularism) and their right to a decent livelihood, *are* under attack by this government, while the owners of big business and their right-wing lackeys (hangers-on) in academia and media are having *achhe din* (good times). The BJP and its authoritarian government, and all the reactionary forces on the ground supporting them, must continue to face the collective and democratic might of the toiling masses and progressive intellectuals. There is, and there can be, no force that is more powerful than the united

CONCLUSIONS AND REFLECTIONS

force of the organized and class-conscious workers and small-scale producers. If they withdraw their labor from the farms, factories, offices, laboratories,
schools and universities, or if they do not bring the products of their labor to
the market (as small-scale producers), or if the unemployed, demanding decent jobs, join the currently employed people and/or start a non-cooperation
movement by not only boycotting elections but also stopping the movement
of commodities on roads and railway lines, then the system is in big trouble. It
is time that the masses of India (and of South Asia) begin to ask fundamental
questions about what kind of society they are living in, what kind of society
they wish to live in, and how to get there. In fact, the combination of Hindutva and nationalism keeps alive permanently the threat of a war between a
Muslim-dominated Pakistan and an increasingly Hinduized India, which, as
a potential and/or a reality is a vote-catcher for the Hindu-nationalist party.
Then there is a strong and urgent need for the common people of India and
other countries to mobilize themselves on the basis of their common class and
democratic interests, against the bourgeois system, including its right-wing
movements, and not allow them to be divided on the basis of nationality or
religion.

A struggle of the masses can start spontaneously. But to have some success,
it needs theoretical and political guidance. This is what the party of workers
and its allied organizations and organic intellectuals of the workers and peasants inside and outside the party, provide. In the fight against fascistic tendencies, which represent the extreme form of capitalist tyranny, the Left must play
a leading role. To fight against fascistic forces, it must dominantly focus on
non-electoral activities (including battles on the streets and inside the trade
unions, peasants' and women's organizations and the organizations to defend
secularism) aimed at class-based mobilization of workers and small-scale producers, much more than electoral activities. The Left should have its own mobilizational work: apart from mobilizing people against fascistic forces, the
Left must mobilize exploited men and women (a) against curtailment of democratic rights of all citizens and specific democratic rights of religious minorities, low castes, women, aboriginal peoples and other oppressed groups, and
(b) against the on-going attack on living standards. Keeping its organizational
independence vis-à-vis bourgeois-landlord forces, the Left must engage in
these two forms of struggle, on the basis of immediate and transitional demands, *as a part of* and *within the framework of*, the fight for socialism, a fight
that is local, regional, national and global. By being involved in various forms
of struggle – struggles inside and outside the workplaces (farms, factories,
mines, offices), struggles that are economic, political and ecological, the struggles for economic concessions and struggles are against social oppression of
religious and caste minorities and women and against ecological damage – the
Left can truly be the tribune of the people in the Lenin sense, fighting both

tyranny wherever it is manifested and exploitation of workers and peasants. Such Left action might produce concessions to alleviate the suffering of the oppressed and exploited people and will unite those members of its basic classes who are socially oppressed (e.g. *Dalits*) with those who traditionally are not; struggles produce – or contribute to – unity because to succeed, struggles *require* unity. The Left political intervention will also allow common people to be aware of the power of united struggle and of the limits to what is possible to accomplish in the form of improvement in their conditions, under capitalism. The truth that capitalist class relation and the capitalist state, whether in India or elsewhere, will not guarantee democratic rights and decent standard of living has to be proven in practice, one that requires prior theoretical and political preparation. The fight against the social oppression of workers and small-scale producers from Dalit and aboriginal background and the fight against oppression of female workers and female small-scale producers must be a top priority. In the process of all these different types of struggle, the working class, allied with small-scale producers, can aspire to the ideological-political hegemony, and ultimately, for the status of 'the new ruling class'. Keeping in mind the importance of 'stadiality' (Laibman, 2005) within an overall framework of uninterrupted class struggle ending in the abolition of all forms of class rule, one can imagine, not in any absolute sense though, the economic and political struggles of workers and small-scale producers as three concentric circles (or better, perhaps as a spiral or a helix), beginning, first, with the struggle around immediate economic and political demands, and 'then' struggle around transitional economic and political demands, and finally, moving on to the struggle for a workers' and small-scale producers' government. The Left's intervention cannot be shaped by and merely reflect, the present level of class consciousness (which is low), nor can it engage in ultra-leftism which assumes as if a socialist revolution around the corner right now, obviating the need for patient time-consuming political and ideological work aimed at raising the level of class consciousness.

Within the extra-electoral struggles in all these different spheres, and being fully aware of the importance of united front activities, the Left must provide tactical and critical support to the various progressive movements led by non-party Marxists and by non-Marxist radicals such as people's science movements, progressive artists and literary movements, movements against obscurantism, and ecological movements. The Left must also provide tactical and critical support to the mass movements against social oppression and for economic concessions (e.g. higher wages) that are led by non-party Marxists and by non-Marxist radicals, including those involved in temple entry movements on behalf of Dalits and the protection of democratic rights. Within the extra-electoral struggles in all these different spheres, the Left, keeping its

CONCLUSIONS AND REFLECTIONS

organizational independence, must build principled *alliances* with non-communists, including progressive scientists. The Left in India (and elsewhere) must pay heed to Lenin's advice on the need for alliance between communists and non-communists and to the idea that revolution cannot be made by revolutionaries alone.

In so far as the Left parties, much more than other parties, consistently fight against communalism and call for progressive policies at the national scale, and as far as the fight against the fascistic movement is concerned, they must make sure that: workers, self-employed non-capitalist producers, class-conscious trade union members, their progressive organic intellectuals and independent activists participating in class-based social movements, come together, at local, regional and national levels, starting from a city-neighborhood and a village. These elements must form multi-religion, multi-caste, working class, anti-fascism/anti-communalism action committees (or defense guards), with the aim of struggling against the attack on democratic and social rights of these basic classes and class-fractions, in the first instance. What is needed, in India (as elsewhere in similar contexts), is a *class*-based extra-electoral 'coalition' (i.e. a 'united front' on a tactical basis) of political forces that are organizationally independent of the big-business parties, in order to struggle for secularism and democracy (and more). Such extra-electoral struggle should be a vehicle for the development of democratic consciousness and win the masses to the cause of a large-scale political project of defending and deepening democratic rights and to the cause of socialism/communism. From such struggles, will organically emerge politically advanced workers, and from them, a stratum that will show proletarian leadership ability and revolutionary intention. Of course, a top priority must be given to the development of a cadre that learns the history of communist struggles in India, South Asia and the world, and that is steeped in the Marxism of the MELLT (Marx, Engels, Lenin, Luxemburg, Trotsky), (Das, 2017a), the theory that shapes the socialist program which in turn shapes struggles and theoretical reflections on the struggles.

Apart from extra-electoral struggle, the Left must fight the fascistic tendencies within the electoral arena, on the basis of the idea that the extra-electoral struggle is to subordinate the electoral struggle and that the main reason for electoral politics is not to try to capture power through elections and establish socialism (this is an impossibility) but to use the parliament and provincial assemblies as the political spaces where the Left can raise awareness not only about common people's problems and the failure of the capitalist system to address these, but also about its own alternative solutions and to measure the degree of support it has from the masses. Within the electoral sphere, the Left cannot practice neutrality ('political indifferentism', in Marx's words) with respect to whether there is a secular bourgeois democratic government or a communal-fascistic bourgeois government that kills dissent in every pore of society, just as it cannot be neutral to whether a bourgeois government spends money on workers' primary education and one that does not (see Marx, 2010).

The Left itself *should not be* a part of the bourgeois-secular front against the fascistic tendencies. That would be multi-class bloc. Keeping its organizational independence, the Left should be outside of the front and exercise its autonomy to criticize and to mobilize the masses against the front on economic and other policies that may affect the masses adversely. The ultimate aim of the Left is not a liberal-democratic secular bourgeois government but a proletarian-democratic secular socialist government of workers and peasants.

It is to be stressed that the defeat of fascistic tendencies should not be equated to the electoral defeat of the BJP: the BJP may be defeated (as in provincial elections in late 2018) and yet fascistic forces will be involved in their usual ground-work, covertly and overtly, although without formal access to state power through the BJP, these forces will lose some of their force. So the fight against fascistic tendencies must be a much greater fight than the electoral fight to defeat the BJP. And no other political movement can engage in that fight more strongly than the Marxist Left can. It is also clear that when fascistic tendencies are weakened/eliminated and when the focus of Left's attention is more on class struggle against capital as such than on fascistic movements, the so-called secular parties (i.e. the Congress and its allies) are most likely to be united with those which are not (i.e. the BJP and its allies), in order to fight the Left. That is all the more reason why the fight against fascistic tendencies must be seen as a part of the fight for establishing a socialist government and why the Left must maintain its organizational independence vis-à-vis bourgeois forces, secular or not.

Mainly on the basis of the revolutionary struggle against capitalism and its state, the struggle that aims to establish a workers' state, the Left must seek to stop fascistic forces from controlling governmental power and being a great threat to class-based mobilization. The ruling class attack on secularism and growing strength of fascistic tendencies is indicative not only of the low level of consciousness and lack of unity among members of basic classes but also of the fact that the struggle against the attack on secularism is an inherent part of class struggle itself. As Yechuri (1993) says, 'The struggle against the communal forces today is, at the same time, the struggle for maintaining the unity of these classes and to that extent, is an integral aspect of the class struggle' (p. 15). In fact, the struggle against fascism must ultimately be to cut its roots in capitalism. In the process of mobilizing the masses for concessions (including economic concessions within capitalism) both during the rule of communal fascistic forces and when a secular government is in power, the Left must develop their class consciousness and gradually prepare them to demand a workers'

CONCLUSIONS AND REFLECTIONS

state, supported mainly by non-exploiting small-scale producers. The fight against fascistic tendencies, initially a *defensive* fight, should be seen positively as opening a door towards socialist struggle.

Any temporary and tactical agreement with bourgeois forces that might be objectively necessary because of the relative weakness of the Left can, once again, be justified only if the genuine aim of the Left is to prepare the masses to fight for socialism, and not to just fight for a capitalism that is more democratic, more egalitarian and less neoliberal. Any temporary compromise with bourgeois secular forces, outside of the strategy for socialist revolution, would not only not contribute to the socialist movement but also would it not significantly defeat the fascistic forces. Ahmad (2013: 22) writes: 'in the context of the extremely wide dissemination of communal consciousness in the country at large, secularism has emerged as a specifically communist virtue'. The fight against communalism is to be a part of the fight for communism. The fight for communism must be taken out of the documents of communist parties/groups as a long-term goal divorced from current struggles, and be given a material expression through agitation, education and organization of masses *now*. 'A revolutionary victory can become possible only as a result of long political agitation, a lengthy period of education and organization of the masses' (Trotsky, 1934). Revolution and socialism must be parts of popular common sense: these must be *talked about* in the everyday life of the masses and of communist leaders – i.e. at the picket lines, in party meetings, on the street, in the eating places, in the Marxist and progressive reading group meetings and in the corridors of university departments where communists work, in schools, in books on comics and stories, in films, in the theatres, in the editorial board meetings of online and in-print Marxist journals. Revolution and socialism must be discussed during protests against militarism, fascistic attacks on minorities, encounter-killings, violence against women and children, police brutality against striking workers and peasants, corruption scandals involving both the business class and state officials/politicians, and cuts to funding for welfare, and indeed in *every* place where masses live their daily lives. The masses and the Left leaders and the Left intellectuals must eat, breathe, live, and fall in love with, the very idea of a more humane society, one that is democratic in every possible manner, a society which goes by this name: socialism or communism.

I have used the term Left (or Marxist Left) to denote both the existing Left and the Left that the masses need for their fight for socialism. Are these two views of the Left the same or at least similar? In fact, the actually-existing Left falls short by miles from the 'imagined' Left, even if there is much common ground between the two. The threat from the fascistic movement and the massive crisis of livelihood of the masses are reason enough for a thorough rethinking of what kind of Left is needed. In India, there is a crisis of revolutionary leadership, a crisis of the Left. This crisis is not only one of larger more-or-less reformist communist parties/groups and their trade unions and mass organizations, but also of the smaller Far Left groups. What is definitely needed is a 'new' Left, one that is to be much to the left of the existing mainstream Left (electoralist or not) and that is much less sectarian and much more united than the small Far Left groups, whether they are based in India or not. This rethinking involves rethinking the ways in which the small Far left groups operate, which exhibit sectarian tendencies, which remain permanently fragmented and/or are fragmenting, and which are engaged in excessive negativism in relation to other Marxist Left groups. After all, not only are theory and political programs political but also how an organization conducts itself is political. As well, there is a serious need to rethink the theory and strategy of revolution that is subscribed to by the larger communist parties that are currently operating as a political force on the ground as the actually-existing Left. Must this Left not fight to abolish capitalism rather than to fight for a better form of capitalism, and must it not take seriously the idea that reforms are more or less by-products of revolutionary struggle? Is it really the case that capitalism is not ripe, for a struggle to begin to overthrow it? As we have seen in Chapter 3, India is dominantly a capitalist society: the most general form of capitalism (i.e. the formal subsumption of labor) does exist as the dominant form of class relation in India, and the transition to a more developed form of capitalism is blocked by capitalism itself, operating in a world of imperialism. Let the Indian Left read and reflect on Lenin's *April Theses*. And the leaders of the communist movement, advanced workers and Marxist intellectuals might want to reflect in a non-sectarian way on these lines from Vladimir Lenin's most trusted comrade and the co-architect of 1917:

> All talk to the effect that historical conditions have not yet "ripened" for socialism is the product of ignorance or conscious deception. The objective prerequisites for the proletarian revolution have not only "ripened"; they have begun to get somewhat rotten. Without a socialist revolution, in the next historical period at that, a catastrophe threatens the whole culture of mankind. The turn is now to the proletariat, i.e., chiefly to its revolutionary vanguard. The historical crisis of mankind is reduced to the crisis of the revolutionary leadership.
>
> TROTSKY, 1938

Indeed, 'Without a socialist revolution, … a catastrophe threatens the whole culture of mankind', and fascism *is* a part of that catastrophe. This is as true about the West as about the less developed capitalist countries such as India.

CONCLUSIONS AND REFLECTIONS

Capitalism exists at the level of fundamental class *relation*, which has three aspects (relation of exchange, relation of property, and relation of value and surplus value) (Das, 2017a: Chapter 7). Capitalism exists at the level of *mechanisms* that these relations set up, and at the level of the *effects* of the *mechanisms* on the masses. And, capitalist society can be (more/less) fascistic and (more/less) democratic. It is important for the Left to fight against the adverse effects of capitalist class relation for short-term progressive policies and against fascistic tendencies, on the basis of immediate and transitional demands, both in the workplaces and more widely. There is a need for civil polite polemical struggles among various Left groups with the aim of clarification of principles with respect to the theory and strategy of revolution. And, there is a need for united front type struggles on the part of independent individual communist groups and parties against the effects of capitalism on people's lives, with the aim of getting beyond the class relation of capitalism. It is from such polemical struggles and struggles against the current society that a future Left will gradually emerge. There is currently *no* Left party/group that can successfully fight against the effects of capitalism, against fascistic tendencies and against wage-slavery. Now, given the danger that fascistic tendencies pose, the secular-democratic bourgeois and petty bourgeois forces will at best want to confine their political activity to the creation of a polity that merely weakens such tendencies making the society more democratic,[9] leaving intact the capitalist class relation. Yet, that political aim, however inadequate from the Left vantage-point, does have some common ground with the Left's aim to eliminate fascistic tendencies. But there is a difference, from the Left standpoint: that fight has to be also a fight against fascists' pro-business policies and against the attack on workers and small-scale producers' living standards. And there is still more to do: fighting for democracy and for some economic concessions is not enough. It is worth repeating Marx and Engels's point on this. As socialists:

> it is our interest and our task to make the revolution permanent until all the more or less propertied classes have been driven from their ruling positions, until the proletariat has conquered state power and until the

---

9 They would do so because of the pressure of genuine secular-democratic forces on the ground whom these non-Left parties represent and because access to state power is a means of access to power and resources for the secular-democratic parties who are in a competitive relation with the BJP and its allies. From a class standpoint, the non-BJP parties' commitment to secularism and democracy will always remain wooly and vacillating, given the existence of the pressure coming from bourgeois political economy for fascistic politics.

> association of the proletarians has progressed sufficiently far – not only in one country but in all the leading countries of the world – that competition between the proletarians of these countries ceases and at least the decisive forces of production are concentrated in the hands of the workers. Our concern cannot simply be to modify private property, but to abolish it, not to hush up class antagonisms but to abolish classes, not to improve the existing society but to found a new one.
>
> MARX and ENGELS, 1850

If we apply these principles to the current context, where there is a low level of economic development along with massive poverty, and where fascistic forces are gaining strength, it will be possible to say something, in a general way, as to 'what is to be done'.

The most important thing that needs to be done is this: the political mobilization of the 400-million-plus Indian working class, *allied with* petty producers, *independent* of all bourgeois forces *as part of a South Asian and an* international working class offensive against capitalism. Such an independent socialist mobilization of the exploited and oppressed masses in India will be advanced by, and will contribute to, a similar movement in countries such as the UK and the US (where Hindutva-based fascistic tendencies are already raising their ugly head). But who will do it?

The independent mobilization of the masses on the basis of a socialist program requires that efforts be made towards a reforging and regroupment of revolutionary socialist individuals and groups to form a democratically-organized party of class conscious workers. Informed by principles of *non-sectarian* class politics and the avoidance of a left version of the personality cult and petty-bourgeois ego clashes, this reforging must bring together *all* socialists, strategically and/or tactically, who are against not only the fascistic politics of the BJP's Hindu majoritarianism but also against caste-based identity politics, the liberal democratic politics of so-called secular parties such as Congress and its regional offshoots. It must also include those who are critical of the mainstream communist parties' electoralist, reformist, stage-ist politics. The leadership of existing communist parties, given their history, theory and program shaped by Stalinism, are *incapable* of mobilizing the masses for a socialist movement. However, it is conceivable that there are rank-and-file individuals and factions within the current communist parties who can join the new socialist movement; instant hatred against everyone associated with the existing communist parties is inadequate and is a potential sign of sectarianism.

This revolutionary socialist movement requires a revolutionary theory and that can only come from what I have referred to as the Marxism of the MELLT.

CONCLUSIONS AND REFLECTIONS

The movement must encompass three inter-connected fights, as mentioned before. One is the fight for a secular-democratic society, a society without the BJP/RSS agenda and a society where the democratic questions (i.e. issues concerning social oppression, landlordism, and new forms of imperialism) are resolved. In particular, the RSS/BJP agenda must be ideologically and politically countered, as militantly as possible, by workers and semi-proletarians mobilized in *every locality*, and nationally and overseas (among the diaspora). The fight for a democratic-secular society, the fight to resolve the democratic questions, must include the support for oppressed nationalities (e.g. Kashmiris) to exercise their *right* to independence from Pakistan and India. Another is the fight for economic concessions, including those based on transitional demands. These two inter-connected fights must be fought under the leadership of the working class, *as a part of* the struggle for a socialist society in India, in South Asia and globally, a society that is democratic in every sphere of life (economic, political, cultural and at the level of the family), that is ecologically sustainable and that practises solidarity with the oppressed and the exploited in every country of the world.

The question is: to what extent do the politically advanced workers, the leaders of the Left movement from different theoretical and political traditions, and Left intellectuals in India (and elsewhere) agree with such a perspective, the perspective of Marx and Engels as well as those Marxists who have followed them critically and closely?

APPENDIX 1

Processes Influencing the Balance of Power between Capital and Labor

The first process is the *availability* – and economic affordability – of a given productivity-raising technology (which can be mechanical, chemical, bio-technical, etc.). Secondly, and in the context of nature-dependent production, favorable ecological conditions are particularly important.[1] These do not exist everywhere. Thirdly, for accumulation and struggle against employers to happen in any significant manner, there must be a substantial amount of concentration of property in the hands of a few owners. Unless there are a few property owners with a sufficient amount of means of production under their control, and even if wage-labor relations dominate, accumulation by private owners, and especially, via technological change, will be inhibited, and class struggle against the employers over wages and working conditions may not be particularly intense because of the absence of strong economic-cultural differences between laborers and property owners who are operating as relatively small-scale capitalists. Fourthly, there is the issue of inter-sectoral relations in terms of production of consumer demand: for example, the development of non-agricultural economic activities in rural areas and associated increase in the total amount of investment, expands the market for farm goods and may increase the demand for (farm-) labor. The latter can enhance labor's bargaining power resulting in higher wages, to which capital can respond by introducing technology, with the real subsumption of labor as the result. Finally, there is the issue of capitalist state interventions. Government assistance including subsidized food and employment generation on public projects – which partly reflects struggle of direct producers – leads to the tightening of the labor market and covers a part of the reproduction of labor power, including sections of the reserve army. All this enhances the bargaining power of labor. From the standpoint of capital itself, state interventions also matter. The state intervention on behalf of the working class and poor peasantry creates an internal market for capital. And by manipulating relative prices, the state can make the terms of trade between two sectors (e.g. agriculture and industry) favorable for one. This can increase the amount of capital in the hands of property owners in the favored sector and therefore may make technology

---

1 Money invested cannot be got back before a certain time period (e.g. until a crop matures), which is determined by nature's time rather than capital's time. This means that capitalists can be slow to sink money in farming, making the development of agrarian capitalism over time a slow process (Mann and Dickinson, 1978).

© KONINKLIJKE BRILL NV, LEIDEN, 2020 | DOI:10.1163/9789004415560_016

affordable by it. It should be noted that all these contextual factors (including the ways in which ecological conditions are made use of) are connected to the overall *capitalist* development of the country, directly or indirectly, and this overall *capitalist* nature of development indirectly defines the context within which capital-labor confrontation takes places and which affects the possibility of the transition from formal subsumption. This transition as a spatially uneven process contributes to uneven (and combined) development.

APPENDIX 2

A Suggested Research Program on Agrarian Neoliberalism

1. Why does neoliberalism impact labor and environmental resources in rural areas?
    1.1. How do production processes, wages, and employment differ amongst different types of subsistence and commercial farms, and between places, and why?
    1.2. Does neoliberalism promote change from formal subsumption of labor (deployment of labor on the basis of low wages and long hours) to real subsumption of labor (deployment of labor on the basis labor-saving technology), and how?
    1.3. Is there greater interaction between agriculture and industry and between rural and urban areas, under neoliberalism, and with what consequences for the different classes in rural areas? How do economic development processes and state interventions within a given 'city-region' (a large city and its surrounding rural areas) impact the possibilities for a political alliance between urban workers and rural non-exploiting petty-producers to demand radical concessions and to challenge capitalist relations?
    1.4. How do agricultural production relations transform local ecologies and lead to (adverse) consequences for the environment and laboring bodies?
2. How does neoliberalism lead to new patterns of deployment of labor and land in rural areas specifically in the form of what is called 'new agriculture'?
    2.1. With respect to 'new agriculture', which refers to the conversion of land-use to production and export of luxury crops, how do production/labor processes differ across different types of farms, and between places, and why?
    2.2. How closely is 'new agriculture' related to food availability, employment, wages, and poverty over time and across regions?
    2.3. How do new agricultural production relations transform local ecologies and lead to (adverse) consequences for the environment and laboring bodies?
3. Why does neoliberalism, promising to promote fast economic growth and benefit the masses, turn out to be a contradiction-prone and problematic development project?

3.1. How is the state's selective 'withdrawal' from the economy under neoliberalism related to rural economic development, food security and poverty?

3.2. How does neoliberalism create and intensify conflicts (e.g. between workers and employers; and between different users of natural resources)?

3.3. By spatially concentrating investment and laborers, might new agriculture enable political organization of the masses over social and ecological issues?

3.4. How do state and agribusinesses respond to various conflicts? What material and discursive strategies are employed to promote social norms supportive of agrarian neoliberalism?

3.5. How are conflicts expressed within state institutions, and between the state and civil society at large? How does the democratic state justify support for agribusiness whilst reducing subsidies for poor populations, as under WTO rubric? Is a legitimacy crisis emergent in rural areas for a state no longer appearing as guarantor of welfare in the everyday lives of the poor? What connection might there be between agrarian neoliberalism and growing influence of fascistic tendencies among certain classes and groups in rural areas?

Bibliography

Adduci, M. 2017. "Neoliberalism, mining and labour in the Indian state of Odisha: Outlining a political economy analysis." *Journal of Contemporary Asia* 47, no. 4: 596–614.

Agamben, G. 2005. *The state of exception.* Chicago: University of Chicago Press.

Agarwala, R. 2006. "From work to welfare: A new class movement in India." *Critical Asian Studies* 38, no. 4: 419–444.

Agarwala, R. 2013. *Informal labor, formal politics and dignified discontent in India.* Cambridge: Cambridge University Press.

Agarwala, R. 2019. "Using legal empowerment for labour rights in India." *Journal of Development Studies* 55, no. 3: 401–419.

Aguiar, L., and Herod, A., eds. 2006. *The dirty work of neoliberalism: Cleaners in the global economy.* Oxford: Blackwell.

Ahluwalia, M.S. 1978. "Rural poverty and agricultural performance in India." *Journal of Development Studies* 14, no. 3: 298–323.

Ahluwalia, M.S. 2002. "Economic reforms in India since 1991: Has Gradualism worked?" *Journal of Economic Perspectives* 16, no. 7: 67–88.

Ahmad, A. 2013. "Communalisms: Changing forms and fortunes." *The Marxist* XXIX, no. 2.

Alauddin, M., and Tisdell, C. 1991. *The Green Revolution and economic development: The process and its impacts in Bangladesh.* Basingstoke: Macmillan.

Alauddin, M., and Tisdell, C. 1995. "Labour absorption and agricultural development Bangladesh experience and predicament." *World Development* 23, no. 2: 281–295.

Alavi, H. 1965. "Peasant and Revolution." In *The Socialist Register 1965*, eds. R. Miliband and J. Saville, 241–277. London: The Merlin Press.

Alavi, H. 1972. "The State in Post-colonial Societies: Pakistan and Bangladesh." *New Left Review*, no. 74: 59–81.

Albright, M. 2018. "Will we stop Trump before it's too late?" *New York Times.* https://www.nytimes.com/2018/04/06/opinion/sunday/trump-fascism-madeleine-albright.html.

Ali, A. 2006. "Rice to shrimp: Land use land cover changes and soil degradation in Southwestern Bangladesh." *Land Use Policy* 23, no. 4: 421–435.

Allinson, J., and Anievas, A. 2009. "The uses and misuses of uneven and combined development: an anatomy of a concept." *Cambridge Review of International Affairs* 22, no. 1: 47–67.

Ambani, M. 2018. "Building a global-scale corporation in India." In *India Transformed,* ed. R. Mohan, 554–566. Washington D.C.: Brookings Institution Press.

Amin, S. 2005. "India: A great power?" *Monthly Review* 6, no. 9: 1–13.

Amsden, A. 1998. *Asia's next giant: South Korea and late industrialization*. Oxford: Oxford University Press.

Anandan, S. 2018. "4 years of Modi: Dalits are being stripped of their dignity." *National Herald*. https://www.nationalheraldindia.com/opinion/4-years-of-modi-dalits-are-being-stripped-of-their-dignity.

Anandhi, S., and Kapadia, K. 2017. *Dalit women: Vanguard of an alternative politics in India*. Abingdon, Oxon: Routledge.

Anderson, L., and Seligson, M.A. 1994. "Reformism and radicalism among peasants." *American Journal of Political Science* 38, no. 4: 944–972.

Anderson, P. 1980. *Arguments within English Marxism*. London: Verso.

Anievas, A., Saull, R., Davidson, N., and Fabry, A. 2014. *The longue durée of the far right: An international historical sociology*. London: Routledge.

Ansari, A. 2011. *Communalisation of Indian society*. Delhi: Aakar.

Arun, M. 2017. "Demonetisation shook the economy. Did it break it, or leave it healthier?" *India Today*. https://www.indiatoday.in/magazine/msn-it/story/20171113-dem onitisation-note-ban-bjp-modi-economy-arun-jaitley-gdp-1077353-2017-11-04.

Ashman, A. 2009. "Capitalism, Uneven and Combined Development and the Transhistoric." *Cambridge Review of International Affairs* 22, no. 1: 29–46.

Aston, T., and Philpin, C. 1985. *The Brenner Debate: Agrarian class structure and economic development in pre-industrial Europe*. Cambridge: Cambridge University Press.

Auvinen, J. 1997. "Political conflict in less developed countries 1981–89." *Journal of Peace Research* 34, no. 2: 177–195.

Avakian, B. 2008. *Away with gods*. Chicago: Insight Press.

Azam, J., and Bhatia, K. 2017. "Provoking insurgency in a federal state: Theory and application to India." *Public choice* 170, no. 3–4: 183–210.

Bagchi, S. 2017. "Naxalbari at 50." *The Hindu*. https://www.thehindu.com/society/naxal bari-at-50/article18514656.ece.

Bahl, V. 1995. *The making of the Indian working class: A case of the Tata Iron and Steel Company, 1880–1946*. New Delhi: Sage.

Baker, D. 2006. "The political economy of fascism: Myth or reality, or myth and reality?" *New Political Economy* 11, no. 2: 227–250.

Baker, K., and Jewitt, S. 2007. "Evaluating 35 years of the green revolution technology in villages of Bulandshahr district, western UP, north India." *Journal of Development Studies* 43, no. 2: 312–339.

Balagopal, K. 2006. "Chattisgarh: The physiognomy of violence." *Economic and Political Weekly* 41, no. 21: 2183–2186.

Banaji, J. 2003. "The fictions of free labor: Contract, coercion, and the so-called unfree labor." *Historical Materialism* 11, no. 3: 69–95.

Banaji, J. 2010. "The ironies of Indian Maoism." *International Socialism*, issue 128. http://isj.org.uk/the-ironies-of-indian-maoism/.

Banaji, J., ed. 2016a. *Fascism: essays on Europe and India,* Gurgaon: Three Essays Collective.

Banaji, J., ed. 2016b. "Preface." In *Fascism: Essays on Europe and India,* ed. J. Banaji. Gurgaon: Three Essays Collective.

Banaji, J., ed. 2016c. "Postscript." In *Fascism: Essays on Europe and India,* ed. J. Banaji. Gurgaon: Three Essays Collective.

Banaji, J., ed. 2016d. "Trajectories of fascism: Extreme-right movements in India and elsewhere." In *Fascism: Essays on Europe and India,* ed. J. Banaji. Gurgaon: Three Essays Collective.

Bandyopadhyay, D. 1994. "Reflections on Land Reforms in India since Independence." In *Industry and Agriculture in India since Independence,* ed. T. Sathyamurthy. New Delhi: Oxford University Press.

Banerjee, S. 1980. *In the wake of Naxalbari: A history of the Naxalite Movement in India.* Calcutta: Subarnarekha.

Banerjee, S. 1984. India's simmering revolution: The Naxalite uprising. London: Zed.

Banerjee, S. 1986. "Rural scene." In *Agrarian Struggles after Independence,* ed. A.R. Desai. New Delhi: Oxford University Press.

Banerjee, S. 1999. "Strategy and forms of political participation among left parties." In *Class formation and political transformation in post-colonial India,* ed. T. Sathyamurthy, 202–237. Delhi: Oxford University Press.

Banerjee, S. 2002. "Naxalbari: between past and future." *Economic and Political Weekly* 37, no. 22: 2115–2116.

Banerjee, S. 2006. "Beyond Naxalbari." *Economic and Political Weekly* 41, no. 29: 3159–3163.

Banerjee, S. 2008a. "On the Naxalite movement: a report with a difference." *Economic and Political Weekly* 43, no. 21: 10–12.

Banerjee, S. 2008b. "A Political cul-de-sac: CPI(M)'s tragic denouement." *Economic and Political Weekly* 43, no. 42: 12–15.

Banerjee, S. 2012. *Marxism and the Indian left: From 'interpreting' India to 'changing' it.* Kolkata: Purbalok.

Banerjee, S. 2017. "Half-a-century of Maoist journey in India from Naxalbari to Chhatisgarh." *Economic and Political Weekly* 52, no. 21.

Bannerji, S. 2000. "Organized business and politics in India." In *Politics in India,* ed. R. Chatterji. Kolkata: Levanta Books.

Banerjee-Guha, S. 2009. "Neoliberalising the 'urban': New geographies of power and injustice in Indian cities." *Economic and Political Weekly* 44, no. 22: 95–107.

Bannerji, H. 1995. *Thinking through: Essays on feminism, Marxism, and anti-racism.* Toronto: Women's press.

Bannerji, H. 2006. "Making India Hindu and male – cultural nationalism and the emergence of the ethnic citizen in contemporary India." *Ethnicities* 6, no. 3: 362–390.

Bansil, P. 1992. *Agricultural statistics compendium,* vols. 1–2. Technical and Economic Research Institute, New Delhi.

Barbier, E., and Suthawan, S. 2004. *Shrimp farming and mangrove loss in Thailand.* Cheltenham: Edward Elgar.

Bardhan, P. 1984. *Land, labour and rural poverty: Essays in development economics.* Oxford University Press, Delhi.

Bardhan, P. 1990. *Political Economy of Development in India.* Delhi: Oxford University Press.

Bardhan, P. 1998. *The political economy of India's development.* New Delhi: Oxford University Press.

Bardhan, P. 2005. "Nature of opposition to economic reforms in India." *Economic and Political Weekly* 40, no. 48: 4995–4998.

Barker, C. 2006. "Capital and revolutionary practice." *Historical Materialism* 14, no. 2: 55–82.

Barraclough, S., and Finger-Stich, A. 1996. *Some ecological and social implications of commercial shrimp farming in Asia.* UN Research Institute for Social Development #74, Geneva.

Basile, E. 2013. *Capitalist development in India's informal economy.* New York: Routledge.

Basole, A. 2016. "The agrarian question in India." *In contemporary readings in Marxism: A critical introduction,* ed. R. Kumar. Delhi: Aakar Books.

Basu, A. 2013. "The changing fortunes of the Bharatiya Janata Party." In *Routledge handbook of Indian politics,* eds. A. Kohli and P. Singh, 81–90. London: Routledge.

Basu, D. 2009. "Analysis of classes in India: A preliminary note on the industrial bourgeoisie and Middle class." *Sanhati* http://sanhati.com/excerpted/1919/.

Basu, P. 2002. *Towards Naxalbari.* Calcutta: Progressive Publishers.

Basu, S. 2004. *Does class matter? Colonial capital and workers' resistance in Bengal (1980–1937).* Delhi: Oxford University Press.

Basu, D., and Das, D. 2013. "The Maoist Movement in India: Some political economy considerations." *Journal of Agrarian Change* 13, no. 3: 365–381.

Basu, T., Datta, P., Sarkar, S., and Sen, S. 1993. *Khaki shorts and saffron flags.* Hyderabad: Orient Longman.

Baviskar, A., 2003. "Between violence and desire: Space, power, and identity in the making of metropolitan Delhi." *International Social Science Journal* 55, no. 175: 89–98.

Bear, L. 2017. "'Alternatives' to austerity: A critique of financialized infrastructure in India and beyond." *Anthropology today* 33, no. 5: 3–7.

Beck, T. 1995. "The green revolution and poverty in India: A case study of West Bengal." *Applied Geography* 15, no. 2: 161–181.

Beeson, M. 2009. "Developmental states in East Asia: A comparison of the Japanese and Chinese experiences." *Asian Perspective* 33, no. 2: 5–39.

Behera, C. 2002. "India: Prospects for Conflict and Peace." *Swisspeace and Swiss Agency for Development and Cooperation.* www.isn.ethz.ch/researchpub/publihouse/fast/crp/2000/crp_india_2000.htm.

Belton, B., and Little D. 2008. "The development of aquaculture in Central Thailand: Domestic demand versus export-led production." *Journal of Agrarian Change* 8, no. 1: 123–143.

Belton, B., Haque, M., and Little D. 2012. "Does size matter? Reassessing the relationship between aquaculture and poverty in Bangladesh." *Journal of Development Studies* 48, no. 7: 904–922.

Belton, B., Padiyar, A., Ravibabu G., and Rao, G. 2017. "Boom and bust in Andhra Pradesh: Development and transformation in India's domestic aquaculture value chain." *Aquaculture* 470: 196–206.

Bentall, J., and Corbridge, S. 1996. "Urban rural relations, demand politics and the new agrarianism in North West India: the Bharatiya Kisan union." *Transactions of the Institute of British Geographers* 21, no. 1: 27–48.

Bernstein, H. 1996. "Agrarian questions then and now." *Journal of Peasant Studies* 24: 22–59.

Bernstein, H. 2007. *Capital and labor from centre to margins.* Keynote address at conference on Living on the Margins. Vulnerability, Exclusion and the State in the Informal Economy, Cape Town. http://pdf.steerweb.org/WFP%20ESSAY/Bernstein_dsi.pdf.

Beteille, A. 2000. *Chronicles of our time.* Delhi: Penguin Books.

Beteille, A. 2007. *Marxism and class analysis.* New Delhi: Oxford University Press.

Berti, D., Jaoul, N., and Kanungo, P. 2011. *Cultural entrenchment of Hindutva: Local meditations and forms of convergence.* New Delhi: Routledge.

Bhaduri, A. 1973. "A study in agricultural backwardness under semi-feudalism." *The Economic Journal* 83, no. 329: 120–137.

Bhaduri, A. 1983. *The economic structure of backward agriculture.* London: Academic Press.

Bhaduri, A., Rahman, H.Z., and Arn, A. 1986. "Persistence and polarization: A study in the dynamics of agrarian contradiction." *Journal of Peasant Studies* 13, no. 3: 82–89.

Bhagwati, J. 1998. "The design of Indian development." In *India's economic reforms and development: Essays for Manmohan Singh,* eds. I.J. Ahluwalia and I.M.D. Little, 23–39. New Delhi: Oxford University Press.

Bhagwati, J. 2001. "Growth, poverty and reforms." *Economic and Political Weekly* 36, no. 10: 843–846.

Bhalla, G.S. 2007. *Indian agriculture since Independence.* Delhi: National Book Trust.

Bhalla, S. 1995. "Development, poverty and policy: The Haryana experience." *Economic and Political Weekly* 30, no. 41–42: 2619–2621, 2623–2625, 2627–2631, 2633–2634.

Bhalla, S. 1999. "Liberalisation, rural labour markets and the mobilisation of farm workers: The Haryana story in an all-India context." *Journal of Peasant Studies* 26, no. 2–3: 25–70.

Bhandari, R. 2008. "The disguises of wage-labor: Juridical illusions, unfree conditions and novel extensions." *Historical Materialism* 16, no. 1: 71–99.

Bhardwaj, A. 2015. "RSS mouthpiece defends Dadri lynching: Vedas order killing of sinners who kill cows." *The Indian Express.* https://indianexpress.com/article/india/india-news-india/rss-mouthpiece-defends-dadri-vedas-order-killing-of-sinners-who-kill-cows/.

Bharadwaj. K. 1982. "Regional Differentiation in India." *Economic and Political Weekly* 17:14–16.

Bhat, M., and Bhatta, R. 2004. "Considering aquacultural externality in Coastal Land allocation decisions in India." *Environmental & Resource Economics* 29: 1–20.

Bhatia, B. 2006. "On armed resistance." *Economic and Political Weekly* 41, no. 29: 3179–3183.

Bhatia, R. 2017. "The Year of Love Jihad in India." *New Yorker.* https://www.newyorker.com/culture/2017-in-review/the-year-of-love-jihad-in-india.

Bhattacharya, D. 2017. "50 years of Naxalbari: With Sangh in power, a new political energy needed now." *Catch News.* http://www.catchnews.com/politics-news/50-years-of-naxalbari-with-sangh-in-power-a-new-political-energy-needed-now-60954.html.

Bhattacharyya, S. 2001. "Capitalist development, peasant differentiation and the State: Survey findings from West Bengal." *The Journal of Peasant Studies* 28, no. 4: 95–126.

Bhattacharyya, S. 2013. *Two decades of market reform in India: Some dissenting views.* New York: Anthem Press.

Bhattacharyya, A., and Basu, S. 2018. *Marginalities in India: Themes and perspectives.* Singapore: Springer Verlag.

Bhelari, K. 2003. "Partners in progress: Maoist Naxals are trying out all ways to win the hearts of people." *The Week*, 22 June.

Bhowmik, S. 2014. *The state of labour: The global financial crisis and its impact.* India: Routledge.

Bidwai, P. 2015. *The Phoenix moment: Challenges confronting the Indian left.* New Delhi: Harper Collins.

Block, F., and Polanyi, K. 2003. "Karl Polanyi and the Writing of 'The Great Transformation.'" *Theory and Society* 32, no. 3: 275–306.

Bobbio, N. 2005. *Liberalism and democracy.* London: Verso.

Boer, R. 2009. *Criticism of heaven.* Chicago: Haymarket.

Boer, R. 2011. *Criticism of religion.* Chicago: Haymarket.

Boer, R. 2012. *Criticism of theology.* Chicago: Haymarket.

BIBLIOGRAPHY

581

Boer, R. 2013. *Criticism of earth.* Chicago: Haymarket.

Boer, R. 2014. *In the vale of tears.* Chicago: Haymarket.

Bond, P. 2014. "BRICS and the tendency to sub-imperialism." *Pambazuka News.* https://www.pambazuka.org/governance/brics-and-tendency-sub-imperialism.

Bond, P., and Desai, A. 2006. *Explaining uneven and combined development in South Africa.* http://146.230.128.54/ccs/files/Bond%20Desai%20Uneven%20and%20Combined%20Development.pdf.

Bordoloi, Sudarshana, and Das, R. "Modernization Theory." In *International Encyclopedia of Geography: People, the Earth, Environment and Technology,* eds. Douglas Richardson, Noel Castree, Michael F. Goodchild, Audrey Kobayashi, Weidong Liu, and Richard A. Marston. Hoboken, NJ: John Wiley & Sons.

Borooah, V.K. 2008. "Deprivation, Violence, and Conflict: An Analysis of Naxalite Activity in the Districts of India." *International Journal of Conflict and Violence* 2, no. 2: 317–333.

Bownas, R. 2016. "Lost in transnationalism? GMOS in India and the eclipse of equitable development discourse." *Journal of South Asian Development* 11, no. 1: 67–87.

Boyd, W., Prudham, S., and Schurman, R. 2001. "Industrial dynamics and the problem of nature." *Society and natural resources* 14, no. 7: 555–570.

Brass, P.R. 1997. *Theft of an idol: Text and context in the representation of collective violence,* Princeton, NJ: Princeton University Press.

Brass, T. 1990. "Class struggle and the deproletarianization of agricultural labour in Haryana (India)." *Journal of Peasant Studies* 18, no. 1: 36–67.

Brass, T. 1994. "Some observations on unfree labor, capitalist restructuring, and de proletarianization." *International Review of Social History* 39, no. 2: 255–275.

Brass, T. 1995a. "Reply to Utsa Patnaik: If the Cap Fits..." *International Journal of Social History Review* 40, no. 1: 93–117.

Brass, T. 1995b. "The Politics of Gender, Nature and Nation in the Discourse of the New Farmers' Movements." In *New Farmers' Movements in India,* ed. T. Brass. London: Frank Cass Publishers.

Brass, T. 1999. *Towards a comparative political economy of unfree labour.* London and Portland: Frank Cass Publishers.

Brass, T. 2000. "Labour in post-colonial India: A response to Jan Breman." *The Journal of Peasant Studies* 28, no. 1: 126–146.

Brass, T. 2002. "Rural labour in agrarian transitions: The semi-feudal thesis revisited." *Journal of Contemporary Asia* 32, no. 4: 456–473.

Brass, T. 2003. "Why unfree labour is not "so-called": The fictions of Jairus Banaji." *The Journal of Peasant Studies* 31, no. 1: 101–136.

Brass, T. 2011. "Primitive accumulation, capitalist development and socialist transition: Still waiting for Godot?" *Journal of Contemporary Asia* 41, no. 1: 1–24.

Brass, T. 2012. *Labor regime change in the 21st century*. Leiden: Brill.

Brass, T. 2017a. "Class struggle and unfree labor: The (Marxist) road not taken." *Science & Society* 81, no. 2: 197–219.

Brass, T. 2017b. "Who these days is not a subaltern? The populist drift of global labor history." *Science & Society* 81, no. 1: 10–34.

Breman, J. 1985. *Of peasants, migrants and paupers: Rural labor circulation and capitalist production in West India.* Oxford: Oxford University Press.

Breman, J. 1989. "The disintegration of the Hali system." In *South Asia*, eds. H. Alavi and J. Harriss. New York: Monthly Review Press.

Breman, J. 1990. "Even dogs are better of the ongoing battle between capital and labor in the cane fields of Gujarat." *Journal of Peasant Studies* 17, no. 4: 546–608.

Breman, J. 1996. *Footloose labor: Working in India's informal economy.* Cambridge: Cambridge University Press.

Breman, J. 2003. *The labouring poor in India: Patterns of exploitation, subordination, and exclusion.* New Delhi: Oxford University Press.

Brenner, R. 1982. "The agrarian roots of European capitalism." *Past and Present* 97: 16–113.

Brenner, R. 1985. "Agrarian class structure and economic development in pre-industrial Europe." In *The Brenner Debate*, eds. T.H. Aston and C. Philipin, 10–63. Cambridge: Cambridge University Press.

Brenner, R. 1986. "The Social Basis of Economic Development." In *Analytical Marxism*, ed. J. Roemer, 23–53. Cambridge: Cambridge University Press.

Bridi, R. 2017. *The political-economy of science and (bio)technology: The emergence of agricultural biotechnology in the Canada.* (Ph.D. dissertation). York University, Toronto, Canada.

Brohman, J. 1996. "Postwar development in the Asian NICs: Does the neoliberal model fit reality?" *Economic Geography* 72, no. 2: 107–130.

Bukharin, N.I. 1933. "The theory of Capitalism." *Marxist.org.* https://www.marxists.org/archive/bukharin/works/1933/teaching/3.htm.

Burkett, P. 1996. "Value, capital and nature: some ecological implications of Marx's critique of political economy." *Science and Society* 60, no. 3: 332–359.

Burkett, P. 1999. *Marx and nature: A red and green perspective.* New York: St. Martin's Press.

Burkett, P., and Hart-Landberg, M. 2003. "A critique of 'catch-up' theories of development." *Journal of Contemporary Asia* 33, no. 2: 147–171.

Burkhart, R.E. 2002. "The capitalist political economy and human rights: Cross-national evidence." *Social Science Journal* 39, no. 2: 155–170.

Bush, S. 2008. "Contextualising fisheries policy in the Lower Mekong Basin." *Journal of Southeast Asian Studies* 39, no. 3: 329–353.

Byres, T. 1972. "The dialectic of India's Green Revolution." *South Asian Review* 5, no. 2: 99–116.

BIBLIOGRAPHY

Byres, T. 1981. "The new technology, class formation and class action in the Indian countryside." *Journal of Peasant Studies* 8, no. 4: 405–454.

Byres, T. 1983. *The Green Revolution in India.* Milton Keynes: The Open University Press.

Byres, T. 1989. "Agrarian structure, the new technology and class action in India." In *South Asia,* eds. H. Alavi and J. Harriss. New York: Monthly Review Press.

Byres, T. 1991. "Agrarian question and differing forms of capitalist agrarian transition: An essay with reference to Asia." In *Rural Transformation in Asia,* eds. J. Breman and S. Mundle. Delhi: Oxford University Press.

Byres, T. 1996. *Capitalism from above and capitalism from below.* London: Macmillan.

Byres, T., ed. 1997. *The state, development planning & liberalisation in India.* Delhi: Oxford University Press.

Byres, T. 2003. "Structural change, the agrarian question and the possible impact of globalization." In *Work and well-being in the age of finance,* eds. J. Ghosh and C. Chandrasekhar, 171–211. New Dehli: Tulika.

Byres, T. 2013. "Development planning and the interventionist state versus liberalization and the neoliberal state: India, 1989–1996." In *Two decades of market reform in India: Some dissenting views,* ed. S. Bhattacharayya, 27–54. New York: Anthem Press.

Callinicos, A. 1988. *Making history: Agency, structure and change in social theory.* Cornell: Cornell University Press.

Callinicos, A. 1993. *Race and class.* London: Bookmarks.

Callinicos, A. 2004. *Making history: Agency, structure in social theory.* Leiden: Brill.

Callinicos, A. 2010. "Editor's introduction." *International Socialism.* http://isj.org.uk/the-ironies-of-indian-maoism/.

Caparaso, J., and Levine, D. 1991. *Theories of political economy.* Cambridge: Cambridge University Press.

Carchedi, G. 2010. *Behind the crisis.* Leiden: Brill.

Carling, A., and Wetherly, P., eds. 2006. "Rethinking Marx and history (a special issue)." *Science & Society* 70, no. 2: 46–154.

Carroll, M. 2017. "The sticky materiality of neoliberal neonatures: GMOs and the agrarian question." *New Political economy* 22, no. 2: 203–218.

Carter, B. 1995. "A growing divide: Marxist class analysis and the labor process." *Capital & Class* 19, no. 1: 33–72.

Castell, M. 1983. *The city and the grassroots: A Cross-cultural theory of urban social movements.* Berkeley: University of California Press.

Castree, N. 2001. "Commodity fetishism, geographical imaginations and imaginative geographies." *Environment and Planning A* 33: 1519–1525.

Castree, N. and Braun, B. 2001. *Social Nature: Theory, Practice and Politics.* Oxford: Blackwell.

Center for Monitoring Indian Economy (CMIE). 1987. *Basic statistics relating to the Indian economy,* vol. 2. Bombay.

Chacko, P. 2018. *Marketizing Hindutva: The state, society, and markets in Hindu nationalism.* Cambridge: Cambridge University Press.

Chadha, G. 1984. "The landless and the poor in green revolution regions of India." *Agricultural Situation in India* 39, no. 5.

Chadha, G. 1994. *Employment, earnings and poverty.* New Delhi: Sage.

Chakrabarti, A. 2012. "The Indian communist movement at a crossroads: A Marxian assessment." *Rethinking Marxism* 24, no. 3: 458–474.

Chakrabarti, A., and Cullenberg, S. 2003. *Transition and development in India.* New York: Routledge.

Chakrabarti, A., Chaudhury, A., and Cullenberg, S. 2009. "Global order and the new economic policy in India: The (post)colonial formation of the small-scale sector." *Cambridge Journal of Economics* 33, no. 6: 1169–1186.

Chakrabarti, S. 2009. *Red sun: Travels in Naxalite country.* New Delhi: Penguin Books.

Chakrabarty, B. 2008. *Indian politics and society since independence: Events, processes and ideology.* London: Routledge.

Chakrabarty, B. 2014. *Communism in India: Events, processes and ideologies.* New York: Oxford University press.

Chakrabarty, B. 2015. *Left radicalism in India.* Abington: Routledge.

Chakravarti, A. 2001. *Social power and everyday class relations: Agrarian transformation in North Bihar.* New Delhi: Sage.

Chakravarti, A. 2018. *Is this Azaadi? Everyday lives of Dalit agricultural laborers in a Bihar village.* Delhi: Tulka.

Chakravarty, M. 2016. "The richest 1% of Indians now own 58.4% of wealth." *Livemint.* https://www.livemint.com/Money/MML9OZRwaACyEhLzUNImnO/The-richest-1-of-Indians-now-own-584-of-wealth.html.

Chakravorty, S. 2016. "Land acquisition in India: The political-economy of changing the law." *Area Development and Policy* 1, no. 1: 48–62.

Chancel, L., and Piketty, T. 2017. "Indian income inequality, 1922–2015: From British Raj to billionaire Raj?" *World Inequality Database.* https://wid.world/document/chancelpiketty2017widworld/.

Chandan, A. 1979. "Victims of green revolution." *Economic and Political Weekly* 14, no. 25.

Chandavarkar, R. 2009. *Origins of industrial capitalism in India.* Cambridge, GBR: Cambridge University Press.

Chandra, B. 1989. *India's struggle for independence.* New Delhi: Penguin.

Chandra, B. 1992. "The Indian capitalist class and imperialism before 1947." In *Class, state and development in India,* B. Berberoglu. New Delhi: Sage.

Chandra, B. 2008. *Communalism: A primer.* Delhi: National Book Trust.

Chandra, N. 1974. "Farm efficiency under semi-feudalism – a critique of marginalist theories and some Marxist formulations." *Economic and Political Weekly* 9, no. 32–33–34.

BIBLIOGRAPHY

Chandra, U., and Taghioff, D. 2016. *Staking claims: The politics of social movements in contemporary rural India.* New Delhi: Oxford University Press.

Chandramohan, C. 1998. "Political economy of agrarian conflicts in India." *Economic and Political Weekly* 33, no. 41: 2647–2653.

Chandrasekhar, C. 2018. "Neoliberal anti-populism." *Frontline* https://www.frontline.in/columns/C_P_Chandrasekhar/neoliberal antipopulism/article6279859.ece.

Chandrasekhar, C., and Ghosh, J. 2006. *The market that failed: A decade of neoliberal economic reforms in India.* New Delhi: Leftword Books.

Chandrasekhar, C., Patnaik, P., and Sen, A. 1999. "The proliferation of the bourgeoisie and economic policy." In *Class formation and political transformation in post-colonial India*, ed. T. Sathymurthy. Delhi: Oxford University Press.

Chang, D. 2003. *Demystifying the developmental state: A critique of the theories and practices of the state in the development of capital relations in Korea.* (Ph.D. thesis). University of Warwick, England.

Chang, D. 2013. "Labour and 'developmental state': A critique of the developmental state through of labour." In *Beyond the development state: Industrial policy into the twenty-first century,* eds. B. Fine, D. Tavasci, and J. Saraswati, 85–109. London: Pluto.

Chari, S. 2004. *Fraternal capital: Peasant-workers, self-made men, and globalization in provincial India.* Stanford: Stanford University Press.

Chatterjee, I. 2012. "Feminism, the false consciousness of neoliberal capitalism? Informalization, fundamentalism, and women in an Indian city." *Gender, Place and Culture* 19, no. 6: 790–809.

Chatterjee, P. 2000. "Development planning and the Indian state." In *Politics and the State in India*, ed. Z. Hasan. New Delhi: Sage.

Chatterjee, P. 2004. *The politics of the governed: Reflections on popular politics in most of the world.* New York: Columbia University Press.

Chatterjee, P. 2005. "Making autonomous geographies: Argentina's popular uprising and the unemployed workers movement." *Geoforum* 36, no. 5: 545–561.

Chatterjee, P. 2017. "Gramsci in India: Capitalist hegemony and subaltern politics." *Studi Storici* 58, no. 4: 963–986.

Chattopadhyay, B., Sharma, S.C., and Ray, A.K. 1987. "Rural/Urban terms of Trade, Primary Accumulation and the Increasing Strength of the Indian Farm Lobby." In *Food Systems and Society in Eastern India,* eds. B. Chattopadhyay and P. Spitz. Geneva: UNRISD.

Chattopadhyay, P. 1990a. "On the question of the mode of production in Indian agriculture: A preliminary note." In *Agrarian relations and accumulation: The mode of production debate in India,* ed. U. Patnaik. Delhi: Oxford University Press.

Chattopadhyay, P. 1990b. "An anti-kritik." In *Agrarian relations and accumulation: The mode of production debate in India,* ed. U. Patnaik. Delhi: Oxford University Press.

Chattopadhyaya, D. 2013. *Religion and society.* Delhi: Aakar.

Chauhan, B.R. 2003. "Village community." *The Oxford Companion to Sociology and Social Anthropology Volume 1*, ed. V. Das, 409–457. Delhi: Oxford University Press.

Chaudhuri, K. 2001. "A Naxalite Offensive in Orissa." *Frontline* 18, no. 18. https://www.frontline.in/static/html/fl1818/18180400.htm.

Chhibber, P. 2010. *Democracy without associations transformation of the party system and social cleavages in India.* Ann Arbor: University of Michigan Press.

Chhibber, P., and Nooruddin, I. 2004. "Do party systems count? The number of parties and government performance in the Indian States." *Comparative Political Studies* 37, no. 2: 152–187.

Chibber, V. 2003. *Locked in place: State building and late industrialization in India.* Princeton: Princeton University Press.

Chibber, V. 2006. "On the decline of class analysis in South Asian studies." *Critical Asian Studies* 38, no. 4: 356–387.

Chibber, V. 2017. "Our road to power." *Jacobin.* https://www.jacobinmag.com/2017/12/our-road-to-power.

Chibber, V., and Usmani, A. 2013. "The state and the capitalist class in India." In *Routledge handbook of Indian politics,* eds. A. Kohli and P. Singh, 204–210. London: Routledge.

Chossudovsky, M. 1999. *The globalization of poverty: Impacts of IMF and World Bank Reforms.* London: Zed Books.

Clarke, K. 2017. "Social forces and regime change beyond class analysis." *World Politics.* 69, no. 3: 569–602.

Clarke, S. 1991. *The state debate.* New York: St. Martin's Press.

Cleaver, H. 1972. "The contradictions of the Green Revolution." *American Economic Review* 62, no, 2: 177–186.

Cohen, D. 2014. "Is India about to elect its Reagan?" *The Hindu.* https://www.thehindu.com/opinion/op-ed/Is-India-about-to-elect-its-Reagan/article11640720.ece.

Cohen, G. 2000 (1978). *Karl Marx's theory of history: A defence.* Princeton: Princeton University Press.

Communist Party of India (Marxist-Leninist-Liberation). 2008. "CAG audit interim report: NREGA being mocked in spirit?" *Communist Party of India (Marxist-Leninist Liberation).* http://www.cpiml.net/liberation/2008/02/cag-audit-interim-report-nrega-being-mocked-spirit.

Cook, N. 1996. "Population and poverty in classical theory: testing a structural model for India." *Population Studies A Journal of Demography* 50, no. 2: 173–185.

Corbridge, S. 1993. "Marxisms, modernities, and moralities: Development praxis and the claims of distant strangers." *Environment and Planning D* 11, no. 4: 450–471.

Corbridge, S., and Harriss, J. 2000. *Reinventing India: Liberalization, Hindu nationalism and popular democracy.* New Delhi: Oxford University Press.

Corbridge, S., Williams, G., Srivastava, M., and Veron, R. 2004. *Seeing the State: Governance and Governmentality in Rural India*. Cambridge: Cambridge University Press.

Cox, K. 1990. "Territorial structures of the state: Some conceptual issues." *Tijdschrift voor economische en sociale geografie* 81, no. 4: 251–266.

Cowan, T. 2018. "The urban village, agrarian transformation, and rentier capitalism in Gurgaon, India." *Antipode* 50, no. 5: 1244–1266.

Cowen, M., and R. Shenton. 1996. *Doctrines of development*. London: Routledge.

CPI(M). 2017. 'Thinking together'; People's Democracy. http://peoplesdemocracy. in/2017/0402_pd/thinking-together.

CPI(M). 2018. "Press Communique. March 30." Party Central Office, New Delhi.

CPI-ML (Liberation). 2008. "CAG audit interim report: NREGA being mocked in spirit?" http://www.cpiml.net/liberation/2008/02/cag-audit-interim-report-nrega-being -mocked-spirit.

CPI(Maoist). 2014. Strategy and tactics of Indian revolution. http://www.banned thought.net/India/CPI-Maoist-Docs/Founding/StrategyTactics-pamphlet.pdf.

CPI-ML. 2011. "POSCO Project: No to corporate corruption and loot!" *Communist Party of India (Marxist-Leninist) Liberation*. http://www.cpiml.net/liberation/2011/06/ posco-project-no-corporate-corruption-and-loot.

CPI(ML). 2018. General Programme of CPI(ML); http://cpiml.net/documents/10th-party-congress/general-programme-of-cpiml.

Crowley, T. 2014. "The Many Faces of the Indian Left." *Jacobin*. https://www.jacobin mag.com/2014/05/the-many-faces-of-the-indian-left/.

D'Costa, A. 2005. *The long march to capitalism: Embourgeoisment, international and industrial transformation in India*. New York: Palgrave MacMillian.

D'Costa, A. 2011. "Geography, uneven development and distributive justice; The political economy of IT growth in India." *Cambridge Journal of Regions Economy and Society* 4, no. 2: 237–251.

D'Costa, A. 2013. "Globalization, the middle class and the transformation of the Indian state in the new economy." In *Two decades of market reform in India: Some dissenting views*, ed. S. Bhattacharyya, 125–142. New York: Anthem Press.

D'Costa, A. 2017. *The land question in India: State, dispossession, and capitalist transition*. Oxford: Oxford University Press.

D'Mello, B. 2018. *India after Naxalbari: Unfinished history*. New York: Monthly Review Press.

Da Corta, L., and Venkateshwarlu, D. 1999. "Unfree relations and the feminisation of agricultural labour in Andhra Pradesh, 1970–95." *Journal of Peasant Studies* 26, no. 2–3: 71–139.

Dale, G. 2010. Karl Polanyi: The limits of the market. Cambridge: Polity Press.

Damas, M. 1991. *Approaching Naxalbari*. Calcutta: Radical Impression.

Damodaran, H. 2018. "Labour markets: The 'puzzle' of rural wages." *Indian Express.* https://indianexpress.com/article/india/labour-markets-the-puzzle-of-rural-wages -5019670/.

Dantawala, M. 1987. "Growth and equity in agriculture." *Indian Journal of Agricultural Economics* 42, no. 2.

Das, A.N. 1982. *Agrarian movements in India: Studies on 20th century Bihar.* London: Frank Cass.

Das, A.N. 1997. *Swami and Friends: Sahajananda Saraswati and Those who Refuse to Let the Past of Bihar's Peasant Movements Become History.* Paper for the Peasant Symposium, University of Virginia, May 1997. Charlottesville, Virginia.

Das, G. 2012. *India grows at night: A liberal case for a strong state.* New Delhi: Penguin.

Das, K. 2000. "Informal Sector." In *Alternative Economic Survey.* Delhi: Rainbow Publishers.

Das, R. [Raju]. 1995. "Poverty and agrarian social structure: A case-study in rural India." *Dialectical Anthropology* 20, no. 2: 169–192.

Das, R. [Raju]. 1996. "State theories: A critical analysis." *Science and Society* 60, no. 1: 27–57.

Das, R. [Raju]. 1998a. "The green revolution, agrarian productivity and labour." *International Journal of Urban and Regional Research* 22, no. 1: 122–135.

Das, R. [Raju]. 1998b. "The social and spatial character of the Indian state." *Political Geography* 17, no. 7: 787–808.

Das, R. [Raju]. 1999a. "Politicism and idealism in state theory." *Science and Society* 63, no. 1: 97–104.

Das, R. [Raju]. 1999b. "Geographical unevenness of India's green revolution." *Journal Contemporary Asia* 29, no. 2: 167–186.

Das, R. [Raju]. 1999c. "The spatiality of class and state power: The case of India's land reforms." *Environment and Planning A* 31, no. 12: 2103–2216.

Das, R. [Raju]. 2000. "The state society relations: The case of an anti-poverty policy." *Environment and Planning C* 18, no. 6: 631–650.

Das, R. [Raju]. 2001a. "The political economy of India." *New Political Economy* 6, no. 1: 103–117.

Das, R. [Raju]. 2001b. "The spatiality of social relations: An Indian case-study." *The Journal of Rural Studies* 17, no. 3: 347–362.

Das, R. [Raju]. 2001c. "Class, capitalism and agrarian transition: A review and critique of some recent arguments." *Journal of Peasant Studies* 29, no. 1: 155–174.

Das, R. [Raju]. 2002. "The Green Revolution and poverty: A theoretical and empirical examination of the relation between technology and society." *Geoforum* 33, no. 1: 55–72.

Das, R. [Raju]. 2004. "Social capital and poverty of wage labourers: Problems with the social capital theory." *Transactions Institute of British Geographers* 29, no. 1: 27–45.

BIBLIOGRAPHY

Das, R. [Raju]. 2005. "Rural society, the state and social capital in Eastern India: A critical investigation." *Journal of Peasant Studies* 32, no. 11: 48–87.

Das, R. [Raju]. 2006. "Marxist theories of the state." In *Alternative theories of the state*, ed. S. Pressman, 64–90. New York: Palgrave Macmillan.

Das, R. [Raju]. 2007. *"Looking, but not seeing: State* and/as class in rural India." *Journal of Peasant Studies* 34, no. 3–4 (Special issue on Peasant, State and Class): 408–440.

Das, R. [Raju]. 2009. "What's the Left to do in India." *A Socialist Project Review*, no. 26: 58–61.

Das, R. [Raju]. 2010. "Radical peasant movements and rural distress in India: A Study of the Naxalite Movement." In *India's New Economic Policy*, eds. W. Ahmad, A. Kundu, and R. Peet, 281–306. New York: Routledge.

Das, R. [Raju]. 2012a. "From labor geography to class geography: Reasserting the Marxist theory of class." *Human Geography: A New Radical Journal* 5, no. 1: 19–35.

Das, R. [Raju]. 2012b. "Academia as a site of class struggle." *Radical Notes.* http://radical notes.com/journal.

Das, R. [Raju]. 2012c. "Reconceptualizing capitalism: Forms of *subsumption of* labor, class struggle, and uneven development." *Review of Radical Political Economics* 44, no. 2: 178–200.

Das, R. [Raju]. 2012d. "The dirty picture of neoliberalism." *Links: International Journal of Socialist Renewal.* http://links.org.au/node/2818.

Das, R. [Raju]. 2013a. "The relevance of Marxist academics." *Class, Race and Corporate Power* 1, no. 1.

Das, R. [Raju]. 2013b. "Capitalism and regime change in the (globalizing) world of labour." *Journal of Contemporary Asia* 43, no. 4: 709–723.

Das, R. [Raju]. 2013c. "The market for education, civil servants and the India state." *Sanhati.* http://sanhati.com/excerpted/8813/.

Das, R. [Raju]. 2015. "Critical observations on neoliberalism and India's New Economic Policy." *Journal of Contemporary Asia* 45, no. 4: 715–726.

Das, R. [Raju]. 2016. "The attack on democracy and secularism in India." *Bullet: Socialist Project E-Bulletin, No. 1252.* http://www.socialistproject.ca/bullet/1252.php.

Das, R. [Raju]. 2017a. *Marxist class theory for a sceptical world.* Leiden/Boston: Brill.

Das, R. [Raju]. 2017b. "David Harvey's Theory of Accumulation by Dispossession: A Marxist Critique." *World Review of Political Economy* 8, no. 4: 590–616.

Das, R. [Raju]. 2017c. "David Harvey's theory of uneven geographical development: A Marxist critique." *Capital and Class* 41, no. 3: 511–536.

Das, R. [Raju]. 2018a. "Contradictions of India's Right-wing Government, and Growing Disenchantment." *Journal of Contemporary Asia* 49, no. 2: 313–328.

Das, R. [Raju]. 2018b. "A Marxist perspective on sustainability: Brief reflections on ecological sustainability and social inequality." *Links: International Journal of Socialist Renewal.* http://links.org.au/marxism-ecological-sustainability-social-inequality.

Das, R. [Raju]. 2019. "Politics of Marx as non-sectarian revolutionary class politics: An interpretation in the context of the 20th and 21st centuries." *Class, Race and Corporate Power*, March issue.

Das, R.J. and Chen, A. 2019. "Towards a Theoretical Framework for Understanding Capitalist Violence Against Child Labour." *World Review of Political Economy* 10, no. 2: 191–219.

Das, R. [Raju], and Mishra, D. 2019. "Industrialization and Geographically Uneven Development." Unpublished manuscript.

Das, R. [Ritanjan]. 2018. Neoliberalism and the transforming left in India: A contradictory manifesto. London: Routledge.

Das, T. 2018. "Changing colours of government-business relations." In *India Transformed,* ed. R. Mohan, 224–236. Washington, DC: Brookings Institution Press.

Das, R. [Ritanjan], and Mahmood, Z. 2015. "Contradictions, Negotiations and Reform: The Story of Left Policy Transition in West Bengal." *Journal of South Asian Development* 10, no. 2: 199–229.

Das Gupta, C. 2016. *State and capital in independent India: Institutions and accumulations.* Cambridge: Cambridge University Press.

Das Gupta, M., Grandvoinnet, H., and Romani, M. 2004. "State-community synergies in community-driven development." *Journal of Development Studies* 40, no. 3: 27–58.

Dasgupta, A. 2012. "Reverse pessimistic climate and boost investor sentiment." *The Hindu.* https://www.thehindu.com/business/Economy/reverse-pessimistic-climate -and-boost-investor-sentiment-pm/article3577372.ece.

Dasgupta, A. 2018. "Technological change and political turnover: The democratizing effects of the Green Revolution in India." *American Political Science Review* 112, no. 4: 918–938.

Dasgupta, B. [Biblab]. 1977. *Agrarian change and the new technology in India united nations research institute for social development.* Geneva: United Nations Research Institute for Small Development.

Dasgupta, B. [Biblab]. 1998. *Structural adjustment, global trade and the new political economy of development.* New Delhi: Vistaar.

Dasgupta, B. [Byasdeb]. 2017. "Flexible labour and capital accumulation in a post-colonial country." In *Accumulation in post-colonial capitalism,* eds. I.K. Mitra, R. Samaddar, and S. Sen, 27–57. Singapore: Springer.

Dasgupta, A., Gawande, K., and Kapur, D. 2017. "(When) do antipoverty programs reduce violence? India's rural employment guarantee and Maoist conflict." *International organization* 71, no. 3: 605–632.

Datt, G., and Ravallion, M. 2010. "Shining for the poor too." *Economic and Political Weekly* XLV, no. 7: 55–60.

Datta, A., 1998. *Land and labour relations in Southwest Bangladesh*. London: Macmillan.

Davenport, C. 2004. "The promise of democratic pacification: An empirical assessment." *International Studies Quarterly* 48, no. 3: 539–560.

BIBLIOGRAPHY

Davey, B. 1974. *The economic development of India.* Nottingham: Spokesman Books.

Davidson, R. 2012. *The emotional life of your brain.* New York: Hudson Street Press.

Davidson, R. 2016. "The Four Keys to Well-Being." *Greater Good Magazine.* https://greatergood.berkeley.edu/article/item/the_four_keys_to_well_being.

De, S., and Saha, P. 2002. "BJP's politics of expediency: permeating Hindutva and legislating neo-liberal reforms." In *Class, ideology, and political parties in India,* ed. A. Jana and B. Sarmah. New Delhi: South Asian Publishers.

De Angelis, M. 2004. "Separating the doing and the deed: capital and the continuous character of enclosures." *Historical Materialism* 12, no. 2: 57–87.

De Zwart, F. 2000. "The logic of affirmative action: Caste, class and quotas in India." *Acta Sociologica* 43, no. 3: 235–249.

Demeritt, D. 2002. "What is the 'social construction of nature'? A typology and sympathetic critique", *Progress in Human Geography* 26, no. 6: 767–790.

Della Porta, D. 1995. *Social movements, political violence, and the state: A comparative analysis of Italy and Germany.* New York: Cambridge University Press.

Della Porta, D. 2014. "On violence and repression: A relational approach." *Government and Opposition* 49, no. 2: 159–187.

Desai, A.R. 1975. *State and Society in India.* Bombay: Popular Prakashan.

Desai, A.R., ed. 1986. *Agrarian struggles in India since Independence.* Delhi: Oxford University Press.

Desai, A.R. 1989. "Rural development and human rights in Independent India." *Economic and Political Weekly* 12, no. 31: 1291–1296.

Desai, M. 2003. "From movement to Party to Government: Why social policies in Kerala and West Bengal are so different." In *States, Parties and Social Movements,* ed. J. Goldstone, 170–196. Cambridge: Cambridge University Press.

Desai, R. 2002. *Slouching towards Ayodhya.* Gurgaon: Three Essays Collective.

Desai, R. 2011. "Gujarat's Hindutva of capitalist development." *South Asia: Journal of South Asian Studies* 34, no. 3: 354–381.

Deshmane, A. 2017. "Selling spirituality." *Frontline.* https://frontline.thehindu.com/the-nation/selling-spirituality/article9870620.ece?homepage=true.

Dev, S.M. 2000. "Economic reforms, poverty, income distribution and employment." *Economic and Political Weekly* 35, no. 10: 823–835.

Dhanagare, D.N. 1991. *Peasant movements in India, 1920–1950.* Delhi: Oxford University Press.

Dhar, A. 2007. "The approach to planning should change." *The Hindu.* https://www.thehindu.com/todays-paper/tp-opinion/ldquoThe-approach-to-planning-should-changerdquo/article14829064.ece.

Dhar, A. 2009. "Atrocities on SCs/STs disturbing." *The Hindu.* https://www.thehindu.com/todays-paper/tp-national/Atrocities-on-SCsSTs-disturbing-Manmohan/article16510646.ece.

Dhawale, A. 2000. "The Shiv Sena: Semi-fascism in action." *The Marxist* 16, no. 2. https://www.cpim.org/marxist/200002_marxist_sena_dhawle.htm.

Ding, X., and Ying, X. 2015. "The uneven and crisis-prone development of capitalism: A review of the tenth forum of world association for political economy." *World Review of Political Economy* 6, no. 4: 583–601.

Dias, W. 2005. "One-day general strike in India exposes need for socialist-internationalist strategy." *World Socialist Web Site.* http://www.wsws.org/en/articles/2005/09/indi-s29.html.

Dirlik, A. 2014. "Mao Zedong thought and the Third World/Global South." *Interventions-International Journal of Postcolonial Studies* 16, no. 2: 233–256.

Djurfeldt, G., and Sircar, S. 2017. *Structural transformation and agrarian change in India.* London: Taylor & Francis Group.

Dixon, C., 1990. *Rural Development in the Third World.* London: Routledge.

Dobkowski, M., and Walliman, I., eds. 2003. *Radical perspectives on the rise of fascism in German.* Kharagpur (India): Cornerstone (Original work published in 1989, by New York: MR Press).

Dollar, D., and Kraay, A. 2000. "Growth is good for the poor." *World Bank.* http://www.worldbank.org/research/growth/absddolakray.htm.

Donnelly, J. 1989. "Repression and development: The political contingency of human rights tradeoffs." In *Human Rights and Development: International Views,* ed. D.P. Forsythe, 305–328. New York: St. Martin's Press.

Doshi, S., and Ranganathan, M. 2017. "Contesting the unethical city: Land dispossession and corruption narratives in urban India." *Annals of the American Associations of Geographers* 107, no. 1: 183–199.

Draper, H. 1977. *Karl Marx's theory of revolution: State and bureaucracy.* New York: Monthly Review Press.

Dreze, J., Sen, A. 1995. *India: Economic development and social opportunity.* Delhi: Oxford University Press.

Dreze, J., Sen, A. 2002. *India: Development and participation.* Delhi: Oxford University Press.

Dryzek, J.S. 1996. "Political inclusion and the dynamics of democratization." *American Political Science Review* 90, no. 3: 475–487.

Dudley, R., and Miller, R.A. 1998. "Group Rebellion in the 1980s." *Journal of Conflict Resolution* 42, no. 1: 77–96.

Duménil, G., and Lévy, D. 2005. "The neoliberal (counter-)revolution." In *Neoliberalism: A critical reader,* eds. A. Saad-Filho and D. Johnston, 9–19. London: Pluto Press.

Dutta, A. 2018. "BJP Is trying hard to undercut Congress's soft Hindutva in Madhya Pradesh." *The Wire.* https://thewire.in/politics/bjp-is-trying-hard-to-undercut-congresss-soft-hindutva-in-madhya-pradesh.

Dutta, M. 2018. "Against All Odds: Tracing the Struggles of Workers to Form a Union Inside a Special Economic Zone in Tamil Nadu, India." In *Workers' movements and strikes in the twenty-first century: A global perspective,* eds. J. Nowak, M. Dutta, and P. Birke, 97–114. London: Rowman and Littlefield International.

Dyer, G. 1997. "Output per acre and size of holding: The logic of peasant agriculture under semi feudalism." *Journal of Peasant Studies* 24, no. 1–2: 103–131.

Eagleton, T. 1999. *Ideology.* London: Verso.

Earl, J. 2003. "Tanks, tear gas, and taxes: Toward a theory of movement repression." *Sociological Theory* 21, no. 1: 43–68.

Earl, J., Soule, S.A., and McCarthy, J.D. 2003. "Protest under fire? Explaining the policing of protest." *American Sociological Review* 68, no. 4: 581–606.

Earl, J., Martin, A., McCarthy, J., and Soile. S. 2004. "The use of newspaper data in the study of collective action." *Annual Review of Sociology* 30: 65–80.

Echeverri-Gent, J. 1995. *The state and the poor: Public policy and political development in India and the United States.* New Delhi: Vistaar Publications.

Eicher, C.K. 1995. "Zimbabwe maize based green revolution preconditions for replication." *World Development* 23, no. 5: 805–818.

Engels, F. 1883. "Frederick Engels' Speech at the Grave of Karl Marx." *Marxists.org.* https://www.marxists.org/archive/marx/works/1883/death/burial.htm.

Engels, F. 1848. "Principles of communism." In *Communist Manifesto*, K. Marx and F. Engels. https://www.marxists.org/archive/marx/works/download/pdf/Manifesto.pdf.

Engels, F. 1890. "Letter to J. Bloch." *Marxists.org.* https://www.marxists.org/archive/marx/works/1890/letters/90_09_21.htm.

Engels, F. 1894/1951. "The Peasant Question in France and Germany." In *Selected Works,* vol. 2, K. Marx and F. Engels. Moscow: Foreign Languages Publishing House.

Escobar, A. 1992. "Imagining a post-development era? Critical thought, development and social movements." *Social Text,* no. 31/32: 20–56.

Farid, H. 2005. "Indonesia's original sin: Mass killings and capitalist expansion, 1965–66." *Inter-Asia Cultural Studies* 6, no. 1: 3–16.

Ferguson, J. 1994. *The anti-politics machine: 'Development', depoliticisation and bureaucratic power in Lesotho.* Cambridge: Cambridge University Press.

Fernandes, L. 1994. "Contesting class- gender, community, and the politics of labor in a Calcutta jute mill." *Bulletin of Concerned Asian Scholars* 26, no. 4: 29–43.

Fernandes, L. 2014. *Routledge handbook of gender in South Asia.* Routledge: Milton Park.

Fernandes, L. 2016. "India's middle classes in contemporary India." In *Routledge handbook of contemporary India,* ed. K.A. Jacobsen, 232–242. London: Routledge.

Fernandez, B. 2018. "Dispossession and the depletion of social reproduction." *Antipode* 50, no. 1: 142–163.

Fields, G. 1995. "Income distribution in developing economies: conceptual, data and policy issues in broad based growth." In *Critical issues in Asian development: Theories, experience and policies*, ed. M.G. Quibria. New York: Oxford University Press.

Financial Express. 2018a. "Modi's minister makes bizarre claim; PM never said demonetisation was about black money, says MoS Shukla." *Financial Express*. https://www.financialexpress.com/economy/modis-minister-makes-bizarre-claim-pm-never-said-demonetisation-was-about-black-money-says-mos-shukla/1297529/.

Financial Express. 2018b. "Ease of doing business ranking 2019: know what worked for India and what didn't in its 23 notch leap to 77th slot." *Financial Express*. https://www.financialexpress.com/economy/ease-of-doing-business-ranking-2019-know-what-worked-for-india-and-what-didnt-in-23-notch-leap-to-77th-slot/1368596/.

Findlay, A. 1995. "Population crises: The Malthusian spectre." In *Geographies of global change,* eds. R. Johnston, P. Taylor, and M. Watts. Oxford: Blackwell.

Fine, B. 2001. *Social capital versus social theory: Political economy and social science at the turn of the millennium.* London: Routledge.

Fine, B., and Saad-Filho, A. 2017. "Thirteen things you need to know about neoliberalism." *Critical Sociology* 43, no. 4–5: 685–706.

Flaherty, M., and Karnjanakesorn, C. 1995. "Marine shrimp aquaculture and natural resource degradation in Thailand." *Environmental Management* 19, no. 1: 27–37.

Flaherty, M., Vandergeest, P., and Miller, P. 1999. "Rice paddy or shrimp pond: Tough decisions in rural Thailand." *World Development* 27, no. 12: 2045–2060.

Foley, B. 2018. "Intersectionality: A Marxist Critique." *Science & Society* 82, no. 2: 269–275.

Fominaya, C.F., and Wood, L., eds. 2011. "Repression and Social Movements." *Interface: A Journal for and About Social Movements* 3, no. 1: 1–11.

Foucault, M. 1979. *Discipline and punish: The birth of the prison.* New York: Vintage Books. Translated from the French by Alan Sheridan.

Fracchia, J. 2008. "The capitalist labour-process and the body in pain: The corporeal depths of Marx's concept of immiseration." *Historical Materialism* 16, no. 4: 35–66.

Franke, R., and Chasin, B. 1991. "Kerala state, India: Radical reform as development." *Monthly Review* 42, no. 8: 1–23.

Frankel, F. 1971. *India's Green Revolution: Economic gains and political costs.* Princeton: Princeton University Press.

Frankel, F. 1990. "Caste, land and dominance in Bihar: Breakdown of the Brahminical order." In *Dominance and state power,* vol. 1, eds. F. Frankel and M. Rao, 46–132. Delhi: Oxford University Press.

Frankel, F. 1994. *Dominance and state power in modern India: Decline of a social order,* volume 1. Delhi: Oxford University Press.

BIBLIOGRAPHY

Frankel, F. 2005. *India's political economy, 1947–2004 The gradual revolution*. New Delhi: Oxford India.

Freebairn, D. 1995. "Did the green revolution concentrate incomes? A quantitative study of research reports." *World Development* 23, no. 2: 265–279.

Friedmann, H. 1993. "The political economy of food: A global crisis." *New Left Review* 197: 29–56.

Frontier. (n.d.). www.frontierindia.scriptmania.com/V15PAGE5.htm.

Fuller, C., and Véronique, B., eds. 2001. *The everyday state and society in Modern India*. London: Hurst.

Gabriel, M. *Love and capital*. New York: Back Bay Books.

Ghertner, D.A. 2014. "India's urban revolution: Geographies of displacement beyond gentrification." *Environment and Planning A* 46, no. 7: 1554–1571.

Ghose, D. 2018. "Rahul Gandhi tests 'soft Hindutva' in poll-bound Madhya Pradesh as Congress borrows heavily from BJP's electoral strategy." *Firstpost*. https://www.first post.com/politics/rahul-gandhi-tests-soft-hindutva-in-poll-bound-madhya-pradesh-as-congress-borrows-heavily-from-bjps-electoral-strategy-5283511.html.

Ghosh, J. 1998. "Liberalization Debates." In *The Indian economy since independence*, ed. T. Byres. New Delhi: Oxford University Press.

Gibson-Graham, J.K. 2006. *A post-capitalist politics*. Minneapolis: Minnesota University Press.

Giddens, A. 1981. *A contemporary critique of historical materialism*. London: Macmillan.

Gidwani, V. 2008. *Capital, interrupted: Agrarian development and the politics of work in India*. Minneapolis: University of Minneapolis Press.

Gill, S. 1988. "Contradictions of Punjab model of growth and search for an alternative." *Economic and Political Weekly* 23, no. 42: 2167–2173.

Gill, S. 1994. "The farmers movement and agrarian change in the green revolution belt of North West India." *Journal of Peasant Studies* 21, no. 3–4: 195–211.

Gimenez, M. 2005. "Capitalism and the oppression of women: Marx revisited." *Science & Society* 69, no. 1: 11–32.

Gimenez, M. 2017. "Intersectionality." *Science & Society* 81, no. 2: 261–269; no. 3: 450–452.

Gimenez, M. 2018. Intersectionality: Marxist critical observations. *Science & Society* 82, no. 2: 261–269.

Goldman, A., and Smith, J. 1995. "Nature of green revolutions." *World Development* 23, no. 2.

Gomes, J. 2015. "The political economy of the Maoist conflict in India: An empirical analysis." *World Development* 68: 96–123.

Gonzalez, O., Beltran, L., Caceres-Martinez, C., Ramirez, H., Hernandez-Vazquez, S., Troyo-Dieguez, E., and Ortega-Rubio, A. 2003. "Sustainability Development Analysis of Semi-Intensive Shrimp Farms in Sonora, Mexico." *Sustainable Development* 11, no. 4: 213–222.

Goss, J., Burch, D., and Rickson, R. 2000. "Agri-food restructuring and Third World transnationals: Thailand, the CP Group and the Global Shrimp Industry." *World Development* 28, no. 3: 513–530.

Goss, J., Skladany, M., and Middendorf, G. 2001. "Dialogue: Shrimp aquaculture in Thailand: A response to Vandergeest, Flaherty, and Miller." *Rural Sociology* 66, no. 3: 451–460.

Goodman, D., and Watts, M., eds. 1997. *Globalising food: Agrarian questions and global restructuring.* London: Routledge.

Government of India. 1969. "Home ministry, research and policy division, 1969." In *The Causes and Nature of Current Agrarian Tensions,* ed. A. Desai. New Delhi.

Government of India. 1986. "The Causes and Nature of Current Agrarian Tension." In *Agrarian struggles in India since Independence,* ed. A.R. Desai. Delhi: Oxford University Press.

Government of India. 1998. *Rural Development Statistics, 1998.* Hyderabad: National Institute of Rural Development.

Government of India. 1998. Union Home Minister Shri L.K. Advani's Speech. The High Level Meeting of Chief Ministers and Police Chiefs on Naxalism, Hyderabad, June 15, 2009.

Government of India. 2003. India: *Rural Development Statistics, 2002–2003.* Hyderabad: National Institute of Rural Development.

Government of India. 2005. *India: Rural Development Report.* Hyderabad: National Institute of Rural Development.

Government of India. 2007. *Rural Development Statistics: 2005–2006.* Hyderabad: National Institute of Rural Development.

Government of India. 2008. *Rural Development Statistics: 2007.* Hyderabad: National Institute of Rural Development.

Government of India. 2015. "Ministry of labour and employment. Annual Report." *Government of India.* https://labour.gov.in/sites/default/files/Chapter%20-%204.pdf.

Grabowski, R. 2005. "Agricultural revolution, political development, and long-run economic growth." *Canadian Journal of Development Studies* 26, no. 3: 393–408.

Griffin, K. 1974. *The political economy of agrarian change: An essay on the Green Revolution.* London: Macmillan.

Griffin, K. 1989. *Alternative strategies for economic development.* New York: St. Martin's Press.

Grossman, H. 1929. *Law of the accumulation and breakdown.* https://www.marxists.org/archive/grossman/1929/breakdown/

Gudavarthy, A. 2005. "Dalit and Naxalite Movements in AP: Solidarity or Hegemony?" *Economic and Political Weekly* 40, no. 51: 5410–5418.

Guha, R. 1983. *Elementary aspects of peasant insurgency in colonial India.* Delhi: Oxford University Press.

Guha, R. 2002. "Chipko: Social history of an 'environmental' movement." In *Social movements and the state,* ed. G. Shah. Delhi: Sage.

Guha, R. 2006. "The guru of hate." *The Hindu.* https://www.thehindu.com/todays-paper/tp-features/tp-sundaymagazine/the-guru-of-hate/article3232784.ece.

Guha, R. 2007. "Adivasis, Naxalites and democracy." *Economic and Political Weekly* 42, no. 32: 3305–3312.

Guha, R. 2012. *Patriots and partisans.* New Delhi: Penguin Books.

Gupta, A. 2000. "Blurred boundaries: The discourse of corruption, the culture of politics and the imagined state." In *Politics and the State in India,* ed. Z. Hasan. New Delhi: Sage.

Gupta, A., and A. Sharma, 2006. "Globalization and Postcolonial States." *Current Anthropology* 47, no. 2.

Gupta, A. and Sivaramakrishnan, K. 2011. "Introduction: The state in India after liberalization." In *The State in India after Liberalization: Interdisciplinary Perspectives,* eds. A. Gupta, and K. Sivaramakrishnan, 1–28. New York: Routledge.

Gupta, D., and Sriram, K. 2018. "Impact of security expenditures in military alliances on violence from non-state actors: evidence from India." *World Development* 107: 338–357.

Gupta, T.D. 2003. "Recent developments in the Naxalite movement – Communists in India." *Monthly Review* 45, no. 4: 8–24.

Gupta, T.D. 2006. "Maoism in India." *Economic and Political Weekly* 41, no. 29: 3172–3176.

Gurr, T. 1986. "Persisting Patterns of Repression and Rebellion: Foundations for a General Theory of Political Coercion." In *Persistent Patterns and Emergent Structures in a Waning Century,* ed. M. Karns, 149–170. New York: Praeger.

Gurr, T. 1988. "War, revolution, and the growth of the coercive state." *Comparative Political Studies* 21, no. 1: 45–65.

Habib, I. 2014. "Major historical problems in the light of Marxism." In *Marx, Gandhi and Modernity,* ed. A. Bilgrami. Delhi: Tulika Books.

Habib, I. 2015. *Religion in Indian history.* Delhi: Tulika Books.

Habib, I. 2017. "Seventy years on, India cannot allow the divisive forces to triumph again." *The Wire.* https://thewire.in/history/bjps-fascist-character-grave-danger-democracy-civil-rights-india.

Hale, A., and Opondo, M. 2005. "Humanizing the cut flower chain: Confronting the realities of flower production for workers in Kenya." *Antipode* 37, no. 2: 301–323.

Hansda, R. 2017. "Small-scale farming and gender-friendly agricultural technologies: the interplay between gender, labour, caste, policy and practice." *Gender, Technology, and Development* 21, no. 3: 189–205.

Haragopal, G. 2017. "Maoist Movement: Context and Concerns." *Economic & Political Weekly* 52, no. 21.

Hardin, C. 2014. "Finding the 'neo' in neoliberalism." *Cultural Studies* 28, no. 2: 199–221.

Harris, R., and Seid, M., eds. 2000. *Critical perspectives on globalization and neoliberalism in the developing countries.* Leiden: Brill.

Harriss, J. 1988. "A review of South Asian studies." *Modern Asian Studies* 22, no. 1: 43–56.

Harriss, J. 1991. "The green revolution in North Arcot: Economic trends, household mobility, and the politics of an awkward class." In *The Green Revolution Reconsidered,* eds. P.B. Hazell and C. Ramaswamy. Baltimore: The John Hopkins University Press.

Harriss, J. 1992. "Does the 'Depressor' Still Work? Agrarian Structure and Development in India: A Review of Evidence and Argument." *Journal of Peasant Studies* 19, no. 2: 189–227.

Harriss, J. 2011a. "What is Going on in India's 'Red Corridor'? Questions about India's Maoist Insurgency-Literature Review." *Pacific Affairs* 84, no. 2: 309–327.

Harriss, J. 2011b. "How far have India's economic reforms been 'guided by compassion and justice'? Social policy in the neoliberal era." In *Understanding India's New Political Economy: A Great Transformation?*, eds. S. Ruparelia, S. Reddy, J. Harriss, and S. Corbridge, 127–140. New York: Routledge.

Harriss, J. 2011c. "'New politics' and the governmentality of the post-liberalization state in India: an ethnographic perspective." In *The state in India after liberalization: Interdisciplinary perspectives,* eds. A. Gupta and L. Sivaramakrishnan, 91–108. London: Routledge.

Harriss, J. 2013. "Politics and redistribution in India." In *Routledge handbook of Indian politics*, eds. A. Kohli and P. Singh. London: Routledge.

Harriss White, B., and Janakarajan, S. 1997. "From green revolution to rural industrialization in South India." *Economic and Political Weekly* 32, no. 25: 1469–1477.

Harriss-White, B., and Janakarajan, S. 2004. *Rural India facing the twenty-first century: Essays on long-term village change and recent development policy.* London: Anthem Press.

Harvey, D. 1974. "Population, resources, and the ideology of science." *Economic Geography* 50, no. 3: 256–277.

Harvey, D. 1978. "The urban process under capitalism." *International Journal of Urban and Regional Research* 2, no. 1–4: 101–131.

Harvey, D. 1982. *Limits to capital.* Chicago: Chicago University Press.

Harvey, D. 1990. "Between space and time: Reflections on the geographical imagination." *Annals of the Association of American Geographers* 80, no. 3: 418–434.

Harvey, D. 1996. "Justice, nature and the geography of difference." Oxford: Blackwell.

Harvey, D. 1998. "The body as an accumulation strategy." *Environment and Planning D: Society and Space* 16, no. 4: 401–421.

Harvey, D. 2000. *Spaces of hope*. Edinburgh: Edinburgh University Press.

Harvey, D. 2003. *The New Imperialism*. Oxford: Oxford University Press.

Harvey, D. 2005. *A brief history of neoliberalism*. New York: Oxford University Press.

Harvey, D. 2006. *Spaces of global capitalism*. London: Verso.

Harvey, D. 2016. "Neoliberalism is a political project (an interview)." *Jacobin*. https://www.jacobinmag.com/2016/07/david-harvey-neoliberalism-capitalism-labor-crisis-resistance/.

Harwood, J. 2013. "Development policy and history: Lessons from the green revolution." *History and Policy*. http://www.historyandpolicy.org/policy-papers/papers/development-policy-and-history-lessons-from-the-green-revolution.

Heble, A. 1979. "The green revolution: its social and economic consequences." *How*.

Heller, P. 1995. "From class struggle to class compromise: redistribution and growth in a South Indian state." *Journal of Development Studies* 31, no. 5: 645–672.

Heller, P. 1999. *The labor of development: Workers and the trans formation of capitalism in Kerala, India*. Ithaca & London: Cornell University Press.

Heller, P., and Fernandes, L. 2006. "Hegemonic aspirations: New middle class politics and India's democracy in comparative perspective." *Critical Asian Studies* 38, no. 4: 495–522.

Heller, P., and Fernandes, L. 1996. "Social capital as a product of class mobilization and state intervention: Industrial workers in Kerala, India." *World Development* 24, no. 6: 1055–1071.

Heller, P., and Fernandes, L. 1999. *The labour of development: Workers and the transformation of capitalism in Kerala, India*. Ithaca: Cornell University Press.

Henderson, C.W. 1991. "Conditions affecting the use of political repression." *Journal of conflict resolution* 35, no. 1: 120–142.

Herath, G., and Jayasuriya, S. 1996. "Adoption of HYV technology in Asian countries." *Asian Survey* 36, no. 12: 1184–1200.

Herod, A. 1994. "On workers' theoretical (in)visibility in the writing of critical urban geography: A comradely critique." *Urban Geography* 15, no. 7: 681–693.

Herod, A. 1999. "Reflections on interviewing foreign elites: Praxis, positionality, validity, and the cult of the insider." *Geoforum* 30, no. 4: 313–327.

Herring, R. 1999. "Embedded Particularism: India's failed developmental state." In *The developmental state*, ed. M. Woo-Cumings. Ithaca, NY: Cornell University Press.

Herring, R. 2006. "Why did "operation cremate Monsanto" fail? Science and class in India's great terminator-technology hoax." *Critical Asian Studies* 38, no. 4: 467–493.

Herring, R. 2013. "Class politics in India: Euphemization, identity, and power." In *Routledge handbook of Indian politics*, eds. A. Kohli and P. Singh. London: Routledge.

Herring, R.J., and Agarwala, R. 2006. "Introduction – Restoring to class: Puzzles from the subcontinent." *Critical Asian Studies* 38, no. 4: 323–356.

Herring, R., and Paarlberg, R. 2016. "The political economy of biotechnology." *Annual Review of Resource Economics* 8: 397–341.

Hess, D., and Martin, B. 2006. "Repression, backfire, and the theory of transformative events." *Mobilization* 11, no. 2: 249–267.

Hilton, R., ed. 1978. *The transition from feudalism to capitalism.* London: Verso.

Hindustan Times. PTI. 2002. "Major Naxalite Outfits." *Hindustan Times.* https://www.hindustantimes.com/india/major-naxalite-outfits/story-oveBIOPZoV4HdB5La2w7dM.html.

Holloway, J. 2005. "No." *Historical Materialism* 13, no. 4: 265–284.

Houston, I., and Pulido, L. 2000. "The work of performativity." *Environment and Planning D: Society and Space* 20, no. 4: 401–424.

Houtzager, P. 2000. "Social movements amidst democratic transitions: Lessons from the Brazilian countryside." *Journal of Development Studies* 36, no. 5: 59–88.

Hristov, J. 2005. "Indigenous Struggles for land and culture in Cauca, Colombia." *Journal of Peasant Studies* 32, no. 1: 88–117.

Huang, Y. 2015. "Can capitalist farms defeat family farms? The dynamics of capitalist accumulation in shrimp aquaculture in South China." *Journal of Agrarian Change* 15, no. 3: 392–412.

Huitric, M., Folke, C., and Kautsky, N. 2002. "Development and government policies of the shrimp farming industry in Thailand in relation to mangrove ecosystems." *Ecological Economics* 40, no. 3: 441–455.

Human Rights Watch. 1999a. *Broken People: Caste violence against India's 'untouchables'.* New York: Human Rights Watch.

Human Rights Watch. 1999b. "The pattern of abuse: Rural violence in Bihar and the state's response." *Human Rights Watch.* http://www.hrw.org/reports/1999/india/India994-06.htm.

Ilaiah, K. 2000. "Caste, or class or caste-class: a study in Dalitbahujan consciousness and struggles in Andhra Pradesh in 1980s." In *Class, caste, and gender*, ed. M. Mohanty, 227–255. Delhi: Sage.

India Together. 2007. "NREGA battling cancerous corruption in Orissa." *India Together.* http://www.india together.org/2007/oct/gov-nregs.htm.

Indian Aquaculture Authority (IAA). 2001. "Shrimp Aquaculture and the Environment." http://aquaculture.tn.nic.in/pdf/farming.pdf.

Indian Express. 2017. "BJP-RSS new enemies of Naxalite movement, say leaders." *The Indian Press.* https://indianexpress.com/article/india/bjp-rss-new-enemies-of-naxalite-movement-say-leaders-4678690/.

Indian National Congress. 2017. "Modi govt. diluting MNREGA." *Indian National Congress.* https://www.inc.in/en/in-focus/the-systematic-strangulation-of-mgnrega-under-modi-s-watch.

BIBLIOGRAPHY

International Communist League. 2014. "India: Hindu far right sweeps elections: For a socialist federation of South Asia!" *International Communist League.* https://www.icl-fi.org/english/wh/227/india.html.

Islam, M. 2008. "In search of "white gold": Environmental and agrarian changes in rural Bangladesh." *Society and Natural Resources* 22, no. 1: 66–78.

Ismi, A. 2013. "Maoist Insurgency Spreads to Over 40% of India. Mass Poverty and Delhi's Embrace of Corporate Neoliberalism Fuels Social Uprising." *Global Research.* http://www.globalresearch.ca.

Jacob, S. 2015. "Towards a comparative subnational perspective on India." *Studies in Indian Politics* 3, no. 2: 229–246.

Jaffrelot, C. 2011. *Religion, caste, and politics in India.* New York: Columbia University Press.

Jaffrelot, C. 2013. "Caste and political parties in India." In *Routledge handbook of Indian politics*, eds. A. Kohli and P. Singh. London: Routledge.

Jain, H.K. 2010. *Green revolution: history, impact and future.* Houston: Studium Press.

Jairath, V. 2014. "Studying communal riots in India: Some methodological issues." In *Political sociology of India,* ed. A. Kumar. Delhi: Sage.

Jal, M. 2014. *The new militants.* Delhi: Aakar.

Jalal, A. 1995. *Democracy and authoritarianism in South Asia.* Cambridge: Cambridge University Press.

Jamieson, M. 2002. "Ownership of sea-shrimp production and perceptions of economic opportunity in a Nicaraguan Miskitu Village." *Ethnography* 41, no. 3: 281–298.

Jamil, G. 2017. *Accumulation by segregation: Muslims localities in Delhi.* Delhi: Oxford University Press.

Jannuzi, F. 1996. *India's persistent dilemma: The political economy of agrarian reform.* London: Orient Longman.

Jawed, S. 2017. "Fact check: Are rural roads constructed in 2016–17 at an all-time high as claimed by BJP?" *Altnews.* https://www.altnews.in/fact-check-rural-roads-constructed-2016-17-time-high-claimed-bjp/.

Jeffrey, C. 1997. "Richer farmers and agrarian change in Meerut District, Uttar Pradesh, India." *Environment and Planning A* 29, no. 12: 2113–2127.

Jeffrey, C., Jeffery, P., and Jeffery, R. 2005. "Reproducing difference? Schooling, jobs, and empowerment in Uttar Pradesh, India." *World Development* 33, no. 12: 2085–2101.

Jeffrey, C., and Lerche, J. 2000. "Stating the difference: State, discourse and class reproduction in Uttar Pradesh, India." *Development and Change* 31, no. 4: 857–878.

Jenkins, S. 2011. "The politics of India's special economic zones." In *Understanding India's new political economy*, eds. S. Ruparelia, S. Reddy, J. Harriss, and S. Corbridge. London: Routledge.

Jessop, B. 2002. *The future of the capitalist state.* Cambridge: Polity Press.

Jha, A., Gupta, S., and Ramaswamy, S. 2017. "India risk survey 2017." *Pinkerton/FICCI.* http://www.ficci.in/Sedocument/20416/India-Risk-Survey-2017-Report.pdf.

Jha, S.K. 2003. "Jharkhand: Anti-naxal strategy and use of POTA." *Institute for Conflict Management,* no. 1021, 2003. http://www.ipcs.org/article/naxalite-violence/jharkh and-anti-naxal-strategy-and-use-of-pota-1021.html.

Jodhka, S., Rehbein, B., and Souza, J. 2017. *Inequality in capitalist societies.* London: Routledge.

Jones, H. 1990. *Population geography.* London: Paul Chapman.

Jones, K. 2018. "Indian court dismisses Maruti Suzuki workers' bail application." *World Socialist Website.* https://www.wsws.org/en/articles/2018/10/23/mswu-023.html.

Jones, S. 2014. "US corporate profits soar as productivity rises and wages stagnate." https://www.wsws.org/en/articles/2014/12/04/wage-d04.html.

Jose, A. 1988. "Agricultural wages in India." *Economic and Political Weekly* 23.

Josh, B. 2011. *A history of the Indian communists: from united front to left front.* New Delhi: Sage.

Judge, P., ed. 2014. *Towards sociology of Dalits.* Delhi: Sage.

Kallis, A. 2003. *The fascism reader.* London: Routledge.

Kannan, K. 1999. "Rural labour relations and development dilemmas in Kerala: Reflections on the dilemmas of a socially transforming labour force in a slowly growing economy." *Journal of Peasant Studies* 26, no. 2–3: 140–181.

Kapadia, K. 1997. "Mediating the meaning of market opportunities – Gender, caste and class in rural South India." *Economic and Political Weekly* 32, no. 52: 3329–3235.

Kapadia, K. 2002. *The violence of development: The politics of identity, gender and social inequalities in India.* London: Zed.

Kar, G. 2018. "The enduring prevalence of semi-feudal agrarian relations in India." *Journal of Labour and Society* 21, no. 2: 193–213.

Karat, P. 1992. "BJP: A reactionary response." *The Marxist* X, no. 3.

Karat, P. 2000. "CPI(M) programme: Basic strategy reiterated." *The Marxist* 16, no. 3. http://www.cpim.org/marxist/200003_marxist_progrm_pk.htm.

Karat, P. 2004. "Implications of BJP rule: The election battle ahead." *The Marxist* 20, no. 1.

Karat, P. 2014. "The rise of Narendra Modi: A joint enterprise of Hindutva and big business." *The Marxist* XXX, no. 1.

Kautsky, K. 1988. *The Agrarian Question.* Winchester, Massachusetts: Zwan Publications.

Kaviraj, S. 1988. "A critique of the passive revolution." *Economic and Political Weekly* 23, no. 45/47: 2429–2433, 2436–2441, 2443–2444.

Kaviraj, S. 1991. "On state, society and discourse in India." In *Rethinking Third World Politics,* ed. J. Manor, 72–99. Harlow: Longman.

Kaviraj, S. 2011. "On the enchantment of the state: Indian thought on the role of the state in the narrative of modernity." In *The state in India after liberalization: Interdis-*

BIBLIOGRAPHY

ciplinary perspectives, eds. A. Gupta and L. Sivaramakrishnan, 31–48. London: Routledge.

Kennedy, J., and Purushotham. S. 2012. "Beyond Naxalbari: A comparative analysis of Maoist insurgency and counterinsurgency in Independent India." *Comparative Studies in Society and History* 54, no. 4: 832–862.

Kerswell, T., and Pratap, S. 2019. *Worker Cooperative in India.* Singapore: Springer Singapore.

Khanna, G., and Zimmerman, L. 2017. "Guns and butter? Fighting violence with the promise of development." *Journal of Development Economics* 124: 120–141.

Khatkhate, D. 2006. "Indian economic reform, a philosopher's stone." *Economic and Political Weekly* 41, no. 22: 2203–2205.

Khera, R. 2008. "Empowerment guarantee act." *Economic and Political Weekly* 43, no. 35: 8–10.

Khilnani, S. 2017. *The idea of India.* New York: Farrar, Straus and Girour.

Kishor, C.S. 1998. "Poverty alleviation after post liberalisation: Study of a tribal block in Orissa." *Economic and Political Weekly* 33, no. 28: 1846–1851.

Klak, T., and Myers, G. 1997. "The discursive tactics of neoliberal development in small third world countries." *Geoforum* 28, no. 2: 133–149.

Kodras, J.E. 1997. "The changing map of American poverty in an era of economic restructuring and political realignment." *Economic Geography* 73, no. 1: 67–93.

Kohli, A. 1987. *The state and poverty in India: The politics of reform.* Cambridge: Cambridge University Press.

Kohli, A. 2012. *Poverty amid plenty in the new India.* Delhi: Cambridge University Press.

Kosambi, D. 1957. *Exasperating essays: Exercises in the dialectical method.* Poona: Bhagawat.

Kotovsky, G. 1964. *Agrarian Reforms in India.* New Delhi: People's Publishing House.

Krishna, A. 2002. "Enhancing Political Participation in Democracies – What is the Role of Social Capital?" *Comparative Political Studies* 35, no. 4: 437–460.

Krishna, C. 2003. *Fascism in India: Faces, fangs, and facts.* New Delhi: Manak Publications.

Krishna, S. 2015. "Number fetish: Middle-class India's obsession with the GDP." *Globalizations* 12, no. 6: 859–871.

Krishnan, S. 2017. "The engineering India's middle-class politics." *Contemporary South Asia* 25, no. 4: 364–379.

Kruks-Wisner, G. 2018. "The pursuit of social welfare: citizens claim making in rural India." *World Politics* 70, no. 1: 122–163.

Kujur, R. 2006. "Under development and Naxal movement." *Economic and Political Weekly* 41, no. 7: 557–559.

Kumar, A. 1999. "Massacres by landlord militia rock India's second most populous state." *World Socialist Website.* http://www.wsws.org/articles/1999/feb1999/ind2-f24.shtml.

Kumar, A. 2008. "Dissonance between economic reforms and democracy." *Economic and Political Weekly* 43, no. 1: 54–60.

Kumar, C. 2018. "India lost 11.73 lakh man days to strikes in 2017." *Times of India.* https://timesofindia.indiatimes.com/india/india-lost-11-73-lakh-man-days-to-strikes-in-2017/articleshow/62539692.cms.

Kumar, S. 2017. "After silent revolution: Most marginalized Dalits and local democracy in Uttar Pradesh, North India." *Studies in India Politics* 5, no. 1: 18–31.

Kumar, V. 2002. "Dalits." *Alternative economic survey.* New Delhi: Rainbow Publishers.

Kumara, K. 2017. "Indian economy in a downward spiral." *World Socialist Website.* https://www.wsws.org/en/articles/2017/10/11/inec-o11.html.

Kumara, K. 2018a. "India: Modi government accelerates anti-worker privatization drive." *World Socialist Website.* https://www.wsws.org/en/articles/2018/04/09/modi-a09.html.

Kumara, K. 2018b. "Indian Prime Minister Modi to tout pro-business record at World Economic Forum." *World Socialist Website.* https://www.wsws.org/en/articles/2018/01/23/modi-j23.html.

Kumara, K. and Kumar, A. 2016. "Indian government's demonetisation causes mass hardship and economic chaos." *World Socialist Website.* https://www.wsws.org/en/articles/2016/11/21/inde-n21.html.

Kumbamu, A. 2019. "The Naxalite movement, the oppressive state, and the revolutionary struggle in India." In *The Palgrave handbook of social movements, revolution, and social transformation,* ed. B. Berberoglu, 233–247. Cham: Palgrave.

Kundu, S. 2018. "RBI Working Paper Series No. 03 Rural Wage Dynamics in India: What Role does Inflation Play?" *Reserve Bank of Canada.* https://www.rbi.org.in/Scripts/PublicationsView.aspx?id=18117#C7.

Kunnath, G. 2006. "Becoming a Naxalite in rural Bihar: Class struggle and its contradictions." *Journal of Peasant Studies* 33, no. 1: 89–123.

Kunnath, G. 2013. "Anthropology's ethical dilemmas reflections from the Maoist fields of India." *Current Anthropology* 54, no. 6: 740–752.

Lebowitz, M. 2003. *Beyond Capital: Marx's political economy of the working class.* New York: Palgrave Macmillan.

Lebowitz, M. 2005. "The politics of assumption and the assumption of politics." *Historical Materialism* 14, no. 2: 29–487.

Leftwich, A. 2000. *States of development: On the primacy of politics in development.* Cambridge: Polity.

Lenin, V. 1899. The *development of capitalism in Russia, volume of collected works.* Moscow: Progress Publishers.

Lenin, V. 1901. "What is to be done?" *Marxists.org.* https://www.marxists.org/archive/lenin/works/1901/witbd/iii.htm.

Lenin, V. 1908. "Marxism and revisionism." *Marxists.org.* https://www.marxists.org/archive/lenin/works/1908/apr/03.htm.

Lenin, V. 1913. "The three sources and three component parts of Marxism." *Marxists. org.* https://www.marxists.org/archive/lenin/works/1913/mar/x01.htm.

Lenin, V. 1914a. "Tactics of the class struggle of the proletariat." https://www.marxists .org/archive/lenin/works/1914/granat/ch05.htm.

Lenin, V. 1914b. "Summary of dialectics." *Marxists.org.* https://www.marxists.org/ar chive/lenin/works/1914/cons-logic/summary.htm.

Lenin, V. 1917. "On compromises." *Marxists.org.* https://www.marxists.org/archive/len in/works/1917/sep/03.htm.

Lenin, V. 1918. "The proletarian revolution and the renegade Kautsky." Marxists.org. https://www.marxists.org/archive/lenin/works/1918/prrk/democracy.htm

Lenin, V. 1919a. "A great beginning." *Marxists.org.* https://www.marxists.org/archive/ lenin/works/1919/jun/19.htm.

Lenin, V. 1919b. "The state." *Marxists.org.* https://www.marxists.org/archive/lenin/ works/1919/jul/11.htm.

Lenin, V. 1920. ""Left-wing" communism: An infantile disorder: No compromises." *Marxists.org.* https://www.marxists.org/archive/lenin/works/1920/lwc/ch08.htm.

Lenin, V. 1921. "Once again on the trade unions: The current situation and the mistakes of Trotsky and Buhkarin." *Marxists.org.* https://www.marxists.org/archive/lenin/ works/1921/jan/25.htm.

Lenin, V. 1922. "On the Significance of Militant Materialism." *Marxists.org.* https:// www.marxists.org/archive/lenin/works/1922/mar/12.htm.

Lenin, V. 1977a. *Selected Works*, vol. 1. Moscow: Progress Publishers.

Lenin, V. 1977b. *The state and revolution.* Moscow: Progress Publishers.

Lenin, V. 1977c. *Selected works*, vol. 3. Moscow: Progress Publishers.

Lenin, V. 1978. *Revolutionary adventurism.* Moscow: Progress Publishers.

Lerche, J. 1999. "Politics of the poor: Agricultural labourers and political transformations in Uttar Pradesh." *Journal of Peasant Studies* 26, no. 2–3: 182–241.

Lerche, J., Shah, A., and Harriss-White, B. 2013. "Introduction: Agrarian questions and left politics in India." *Journal of Agrarian Change* 13, no. 3: 337–350.

Levien, M. 2011. "Special economic zones and accumulation by dispossession in India." *Journal of Agrarian Change* 11, no 4: 454–483.

Levien, M. 2012. "The land question: Special economic zones and the political economy of dispossession in India." *Journal of Peasant Studies* 39, no. 3–4: 933–969.

Levien, M. 2013. "Regimes of dispossession: From steel towns to special economic zones." *Development and Change* 44, no. 2: 381–407.

Levien, M. 2017. "Gender and land dispossession: A comparative analysis." *Journal of Peasant Studies* 44, no. 6: 1111–1134.

Levien, M. 2018. *Dispossession without development: Land grabs in neoliberal India.* Oxford: Oxford University Press.

Liberation. 2003. "Women agricultural labour struggles: Key issues." http://www.cpiml .org/liberation/year_2003/february/aadhi%20zameen%202.htm.

Liodakis, G. 1997. "Technological change in agriculture: A Marxist critique." *Sociologia Ruralis* 37, no. 1: 61–78.

Lipton, M. 1989. *New seeds and poor people.* London: Unwin Hyman.

Lockwood, D. 2014. The *Indian bourgeoisie: A political history of the Indian capitalist class in the early twentieth century.* London: I.B. Tauris.

Lofgren, H. 2016. "The Communist Party of India (Marxist) and the Left government in West Bengal, 1977–2011: Strains of governance and socialist imagination." *Studies in Indian Politics* 4, no. 1: 102–115.

Lokniti. 2018. "Lokniti-CSDS-ABP News Mood of The Nation Survey-3." http://www.lokniti.org/pdf/Lokniti-ABP-News-Mood-of-the-Nation-Survey-Round-3-May-2018.pdf.

Louis, P. 2000. "Shankarbigha revisited." *Economic and Political Weekly* 35, no. 7: 507–509.

Louis, P. 2005. "Jehanabad II: Viewing Bihar." *Economic and Political Weekly* 40, no. 51: 5371–5372.

Lowy, M. 2010. *The politics of combined and uneven development.* Chicago, IL: Haymarket Books.

Luxemburg, R. 2009. *The Rosa Luxemburg Reader*, eds. P. Hudis and K. Anderson. New York: MR Press.

MacCulloch, R. 2005. "Income Inequality and the Taste for Revolution." *Journal of Law & Economics* 48, no. 1: 93–123.

Mackel, K.A. 2010. "Fascism: A political ideology of the past." *Inquiries Journal* 2, no. 11. http://www.inquiriesjournal.com/articles/317/fascism-a-political-ideology-of-the-past.

Maitra, K. 2012. *Marxism in India: From decline to debacle.* New Delhi: Lotus Collection.

Maitra, P. 1997. "Globalization of capitalism, agriculture and the negation of nation states." *International Journal of Social Economics* 24: 237–254.

Mallick, C. 2018. "Public-private discord in the land acquisition law: Insights from Rajarhat in India." *Singapore Journal of Tropical Geography* 39, no. 3: 401–420.

Mallick, R. 1994. *Indian communism: Opposition, collaboration, and institutionalization.* Oxford: Oxford University Press.

Malreddy, P.K. 2014. "Domesticating the 'New Terrorism': The case of the Maoist insurgency in India." *European Legacy-Toward New Paradigms* 19, no. 5: 590–605.

Mandel, E. 1969. "Marxist theory of the state." *Marxists.org.* https://www.marxists.org/archive/mandel/1969/xx/state.htm.

Mandel, E. 2002. "Anticipation and hope as categories of historical materialism." *Historical* Materialism 10, no. 4: 245–259.

Mander, H. 2016. "The poor have been forgotten more and more." *Governance Now.* https://www.governancenow.com/views/columns/the-poor-have-been-gotten-more-more-harsh-mander-economic-reforms.

BIBLIOGRAPHY

Mann, M. 2004. *Fascists.* Cambridge: Cambridge University Press.

Mann, S.A., and Dickinson, J.M. 1978. "Obstacles to the development of a capitalist agriculture." *Journal of Peasant Studies* 5, no. 4: 466–481.

Mannathukkaren, N. 2011. "Redistribution and recognition: Land reforms in Kerala and the limits of culturalism." *The Journal of Peasant Studies* 38, no. 2: 379–411.

Mao T. 1926. "Analysis of classes in Chinese society." *Marxists.org.* https://www.marxists.org/reference/archive/mao/selected-works/volume-1/mswv1_1.htm.

Mao T. 1961. "Selected Works." *Marxists.org.* https://www.marxists.org/reference/archive/mao/selected-works/index.htm.

Martinez-Alier, J. 2001. "Ecological conflicts and valuation: Mangroves versus shrimps in the late 1990s." *Environment and Planning C: Government and Policy* 19, no. 5: 713–728.

Marx, K. 1843. "A contribution to the critique of Hegel's philosophy of right: Introduction." *Marxists.org.* https://www.marxists.org/archive/marx/works/1843/critique-hpr/intro.htm.

Marx, K. 1845. "Theses on Feuerbach." *Marxists.org.* https://www.marxists.org/archive/marx/works/1845/theses/theses.htm.

Marx, K. 1873. "Political Indifferentism." *Marxists.org.* https://www.marxists.org/archive/marx/works/1873/01/indifferentism.htm.

Marx, K. 1967. *The eighteenth Brumaire of Louis Napoleon.* Moscow: Progress.

Marx, K. 1976. *Wage-labour and capital.* New York: International Publishers.

Marx, K. 1977. *Capital,* vol. 1. New York: Vintage.

Marx, K. 1991. *Capital,* vol. 3. London: Penguin Books.

Marx, K. 2000. *Selected Writings,* ed. by D. McLellan. New York: Oxford University Press.

Marx, K. 2010. *The first international and after.* London: Verso.

Marx, K., and Engels, F. 1845. "Theses on Feuerbach." *Marxists.org.* https://www.marxists.org/archive/marx/works/1845/theses/theses.htm.

Marx, K., and Engels, F. 1848. "The Communist Manifesto." *Marxists.org.* https://www.marxists.org/archive/marx/works/download/pdf/Manifesto.pdf.

Marx, K., and Engels, F. 1850. "Address of the central committee to the Communist League." *Marxists.org.* https://www.marxists.org/archive/marx/works/1847/communist-league/1850-ad1.htm.

Marx, K., and Engels, F. 1964. *On religion,* ed. R. Niebuhr. Atlanta: Scholars Press.

Marx, K., and Engels, F. 1976. *Collected works,* vol. 6. New York: International Publishers.

Marx, K., and Engels, F. 1977. *Selected works.* Moscow: Progress Publishers.

Marx, K., and Engels, F. 1978. *The German Ideology,* ed. C. Arthur. New York: International Publishers.

Marx, K., and Engels, F. 1982. *Selected correspondence.* Moscow: Progress Publishers.

Mason, T. 1995. *Nazism, Fascism and the working class.* Cambridge: Cambridge University.

Mazumdar, S. 2016. "Theorizing the capitalist state." In *Contemporary readings in Marxism*, ed. R. Kumar. Delhi: Aakar.

Mazzadri, A. 2017. *The sweatshop regime: Labouring bodies, exploitation, and garments made in India.* Cambridge: Cambridge University Press.

McAdam, D., McCarthy, J.D., and Zald, M.N., eds. 1996. *Comparative perspectives on social movements: Political opportunities, mobilizing structures, and cultural framings.* New York: Cambridge University Press.

McCartney, M. 2013. "Going, going, but not yet quite gone: the political economy of the Indian intermediate classes during the era of liberalization." In *Two decades of market reform in India: Some dissenting views,* ed. S. Bhattacharyya. New York: Anthem Press.

McDowell, L. 2001. "Father and Ford revisited: gender, class and employment change in the new millennium." *Transactions of the Institute of British Geographers* 26, no. 4: 448–464.

McDowell, L. 2008. "Thinking through class and gender in the context of working class Studies." *Antipode* 40, no. 1: 20–24.

McMichael, P. 2000. "A global interpretation of the rise of the East Asian food import complex." *World Development* 28, no. 3: 409–424.

Mehta, J. 2002. "Give poverty a face, please." *Alternative Economic Survey: 2000–2001,* 29–34. Delhi: Rainbow Publishers.

Menon. N., ed. 1999a. *Gender and politics in India.* Delhi: Oxford University Press.

Menon, N., ed. 1999b. "Introduction." In *Gender and politics in India,* ed. N. Menon. Delhi: Oxford University Press.

Meyer, R. 2016. "Precarious workers' movements and the neoliberal state." *Working USA – The Journal of Labor and Society* 19, no. 1: 37–55.

Mezzadri, A. 2016. "Class, gender and the sweatshop: On the nexus between labour commodification and exploitation." *Third World Quarterly* 37, no. 10: 1877–1900.

Mezzadri, A. 2017. *The sweatshop regime: Labouring bodies exploitation, and garments made in India.* Cambridge: Cambridge University Press.

Mezzadri, A., and Fan, L. 2018. "'Classes of labour' at the margins of global commodity chains in India and China." *Development and Change* 49, no. 4: 1034–1063.

Mies, M. 2012. *The lace makers of Narsapur: Indian housewives produce for the world market.* Victoria, Australia: Spinifex Press.

Miliband, R. 1983. "State power and class interests." *New Left Review* 1/138, March–April.

Miller, B.A. 2000. *Geography and Social Movements.* Minneapolis: University of Minnesota Press.

Misra, A. 1994. "Bihar changing peasant struggle." *Economic & Political Weekly* 29, no. 19.

Misra, V., and Hazell, P. 1996. "Terms of trade, rural poverty, technology and investment: the Indian experience, 1952–53 to 1990–91." *Economic and Political Weekly* 31, no. 13: A2-A13.

Mitra, S. 2011. *Politics in India: Structure, process and policy.* London: Routledge.

Mittal, S. 2018. "Rise of the new entrepreneurial classes and the emergence of a high-growth economy." In *India Transformed*, ed. R Mohan, 567–574. Washington, DC: Brookings Institution Press.

Miyamura, S. 2010. "Diverse trajectories of industrial restructuring and labor organising in India." *Third World Quarterly* 37, no. 10: 1921–1941.

Moberg, L. 2015. "The political economy of special economic zones." *Journal of Institutional Economics* 11, no. 1: 167–190.

Mohammad, N. 2018. "How Many jobs are really being created by the Modi govt's Mudra Scheme?" *The Wire.* https://thewire.in/labour/modi-mudra-loan-scheme-job-creation-reality.

Mohanty, M. 1977. *Revolutionary violence: A Study of the Maoist Movement in India.* New Delhi: Allied.

Mohanty, M. 2004. "Introduction: Dimensions of power and social transformation." In *Class, caste, and gender,* ed. M. Mohanty. Delhi: Sage.

Mohanty, M. 2006. "Challenges of revolutionary violence." *Economic and Political Weekly* 41, no. 29: 3163–3168.

Mohanty, M. 2017. "Adivasi Swaraj is the answer to violence." *Economic and Political Weekly* 52, no. 21.

Moore, B. 1993. *Social origins of dictatorship and democracy: Lord and peasant in the making of the modern world.* Boston: Beacon Press.

Morris, A. 2000. "Charting futures for sociology: Reflections on social movement theory." *Contemporary Sociology – A Journal of Reviews* 29, no. 3: 445–454.

Mosse, D. 2018. "Caste and development: Contemporary perspectives on a structure of discrimination and advantage." *World Development* 110: 422–436.

Mukherjee, A. 2015. "Imperialism, nationalism and the making of the Indian capitalist class, 1920–1947." In *SAGE series in modern Indian history,* eds. B. Chandra, M. Mukherjee, and A. Mukherjee. Los Angeles: Sage.

Mukherjee, M. 2004. *Peasants in India's non-violent revolution: Practice and theory.* New Delhi: Sage.

Mukherji, N. 2012. *The Maoists in India: Tribal under siege.* London: Pluto.

Mukherji, P. 1984/2000. "Naxalbari movement and the peasant Revolt in North Bengal." In *Social movements in India*, ed. M.S.A. Rao, 17–90. Delhi: Manohar.

Mukherji, P. 2014. "The Indian state in crisis? Nationalism and nation-building." In *Sociology of India*, ed. A. Kumar. Delhi: Sage.

Mukherji, R. 2008. "The political economy of India's economic reforms." *Asian Economic Policy Review* 3, no. 2: 315–331.

Mukherji, R. 2017. "Governance reform in a weak state: Thirty years of Indian experience." *Governance – An International Journal of Policy Administration and Institutions* 30, no. 1: 53–58.

Mullings, B. 1999. "Insider or outsider, both or neither: Some dilemmas of interviewing in a cross-cultural setting." *Geoforum* 30, no. 4: 337–350.

Murali, K. 2002. "Andhra Pradesh: Continuing militancy in Telengana." *Economic and Political Weekly* 37, no. 8: 692–695.

Murali, K. 2017. *Caste, class, and capital: The social and political origins of economic policy in India.* Cambridge: Cambridge University Press.

Murphy, J. 2011. "Indian call centre workers: Vanguard of a global middle class?" *Work Employment and Society* 25, no. 3: 417–433.

Murphy, J., and Jammaulamadaka, N. 2017. *Governance, resistance and the post-colonial state: Management and state building social movements.* New York: Routledge.

Murthy, N. 2018. "The impact of the 1991 economic reforms on Indian businesses." In *India Transformed,* ed. R. Mohan, 609–618. Washington, DC: Brookings Institution Press.

Nadkarni, M. 1976. "Tenants from the dominant class: A developing contradiction in land reforms." *Economic and Political Weekly* 11, no. 52: A137, A139–A146.

Nadkarni, M. 1991. "Review: The mode of production debate: A review article." *Indian Economic Review* New Series 26, no. 1: 99–104.

Nag, P.K., and Nag, A. 2004. "Drudgery, accidents and injuries in Indian agriculture." *Industrial Health* 42, no. 2: 149–162.

Naher, F. 1997. "Green revolution in Bangladesh production stability and food self- sufficiency." *Economic and Political Weekly* 32, no. 26: A84–A89.

Nair, S. 2018. "Farmers badly hit by demonetisation, admits Agriculture Ministry." *The Hindu.* https://www.thehindu.com/news/national/farmers-badly-hit-by-demoneti sation-admits-agriculture-ministry/article25550924.ece?homepage=true.

Nanda, M. 1995. "Transnationalization of third world state and undoing of Green Revolution." *Economic and Political Weekly* 30, no. 4: PE 20–30.

Nanda, M. 2005. *The wrongs of the religious Right.* Gurgaon: Three Essays Collective.

Nanda, M. 2007. *Postmodernism and religious fundamentalism.* Pondicherry: Navayana.

Nanda, P. 2015. "Industrial strikes and lockouts see steep decline in India." *Livemint.* https://www.livemint.com/Politics/tjP4DiG7Uro95iNCiebrAO/Industrial-strikes-and-lockouts-see-steep-decline-in-India.html.

Nandy, A. 2003. *The romance of the state and the fate of dissent in the tropics.* New Delhi: Oxford University Press.

Naruzzaman, M. 2005. "Economic liberalization and poverty in the developing countries." *Journal of Contemporary Asia* 35, no. 1: 109–127.

Naseemullah, A. 2016. "The contested capacity of the Indian state." *Indian Review* 16, no. 4: 407–432.

Nathan, D. 1999. "Agricultural labour and poor peasant movement in India." In *Class Formation and Political Transformation in Post-colonial India*, ed. T. Sathyamurthy. New Delhi: Oxford University Press.

Navlakha, G. 2006. "Maoists in India." *Economic and Political Weekly* 41, no. 22: 2186–2189.

Nayar, B. 2001. *Globalization and nationalism: The changing balance in India's economic policy 1950–2000.* New Delhi: Sage Publications.

Nayyar, R. 1996. "New initiatives for poverty alleviation in rural India." In *Economic reforms and poverty alleviation in India,* eds. C. Rao and H. Linnemann. New Delhi: Sage.

NCRB. 2016. "Crime in India." *National Crime Records Bureau.* http://ncrb.gov.in/Stat Publications/CII/CII2016/pdfs/NEWPDFs/Crime%20in%20India%20-%202016% 20Complete%20PDF%2029117.pdf.

Neiberg, M. 2018. *Fascism.* London: Routledge.

Neiland, A., Soley, N., and Varley, J. 2001. "Shrimp aquaculture: economic perspectives for policy development." *Marine Policy* 25, no. 4: 265–279.

Nelson, L. 2003. "Decentering the movement: Collective action, place, and the 'sedimentation' of radical political discourses." *Environment and Planning D-Society and Space* 21, no. 5: 559–581.

Niclas- Tölle, B. 2015. *The socialist opposition in Nehruvian India, 1947–1964.* Frankfurt am Main: Peter Land Edition.

Nielsen, K.B. 2016. "The everyday politics of India's "land wars" in rural eastern India." *Focaal-Journal of Global and Historical Anthropology* no. 75: 105–118.

Nielsen, K.B., and Nilsen, A.G. 2016. *Social movements and the state in India: Deepening democracy?* London: Palgrave Macmillan.

Nigam, A. 2006. *The insurrection of little selves: The crisis of secular-nationalism in India.* Delhi: Oxford University Press.

Nilsen, A.G. 2008. "Political economy, social movements and state power: A Marxian perspective on two decades of resistance to the Narmada dam projects." *Journal of Historical Sociology* 21, no. 2–3: 303–330.

Nilsen, A.G. 2010. *Dispossession and resistance in India: The river and the rage.* London: Routledge.

Nilsen, A.G., and Roy, S. 2015. *New subaltern politics: Reconceptualizing hegemony and resistance in contemporary India.* New Delhi: Oxford University Press.

O'Connor, J. 2017. "Marxism and the three movements of neoliberalism." *Critical Sociology* 36, no. 5: 691–715.

Oberoi, R. 2018. "4 years of Modi govt: 8 charts that show why the euphoria is gone & next big positive missing." *Economic Times.* https://economictimes.indiatimes.com/ markets/stocks/news/4-years-of-modi-8-charts-that-show-why-the-euphoria-is-gone-next-big-positive-missing/articleshow/64314349.cms.

O'Brien, P. 2007. "Global economic history as the accumulation of capital through a process of combined and uneven development: an appreciation and critique of Ernest Mandel." *Historical Materialism* 15, no. 1: 75–108.

Odisha Government. 2004. *Odisha human development report*. Bhubaneswar: Odisha Government: Planning and Coordination Department.

Odisha Government. 2005. *District statistical handbook: Puri*. Bhubaneswar: Odisha Government: Directorate of Economics and Statistics.

Ollman, B. 1993. *Dialectical Investigations*. New York: Routledge.

Ollman, B. 2003. *Dance of the dialectic*. Urbana: University of Illinois Press.

Omvedt, G. 1993. *Reinventing revolution: New social movements and the socialist tradition in India*. Armonk, NY: M.E. Sharpe.

Ondetti, G.A. 2006. "Repression, opportunity, and protest: Explaining the take-off of Brazil's landless movement." *Latin American Politics and Society* 48, no. 2: 61–94.

Oommen, T.K. 1971. "Green revolution and Agrarian conflict." *Economic and Political Weekly* 6, no. 26: A99, A101–A103.

Oseland, E., Håvard Haarstad, H., and Fløysand, A. 2012. "Labor agency and the importance of the national scale: Emergent aquaculture unionism in Chile." *Political Geography* 31, no. 2: 94–103.

Oslender, U. 2004. "Fleshing out the geographies of social movements: Colombia's Pacific Coast black communities and the 'aquatic space.'" *Political Geography* 23, no. 8: 957–985.

Ostry, J., Loungani, P., and Furceri, D. 2016. "Neoliberalism: Oversold?" IMF: *Finance and Development*. https://www.imf.org/external/pubs/ft/fandd/2016/06/pdf/ostry.pdf.

Otsuka, K., Gascon, F., and Asano, S. 1994. "Green revolution and labour demand in rice farming the case of Central Luzon, 1966–1990." *Journal of Development Studies* 31, no. 1: 82–109.

Oxfam. 2018. "Richest 1 percent bagged 73 percent of wealth created last year." OXFAM *India*. https://www.oxfamindia.org/pressrelease/2093.

Oya, C. 2005. "Agrarian neoliberalism." In *Neoliberalism: A critical Reader*, ed. A. Saad-Filho. London: Pluto.

Page, B. 1993. *Marxism and spirituality: An international anthology*. Westport, Connecticut, and London: Bergin and Garvey.

Paige, J.M. 1975. *Agrarian revolution*. New York: Free Press.

Palmer-Jones, R. 1993. "Agricultural wages in Bangladesh what the figures really show." *Journal of Development Studies* 29, no. 2: 277–300.

Palshikar, S., Kumar, S., and Lodha, S. 2017. *Electoral politics in Indi: The resurgence of the Bharatiya Janata Party*. London: Routledge, Taylor and Francis.

Panitch, L., and Albo, G., eds. 2016. *Socialist Register 2016: The politics of the right*. London: Merlin Press.

BIBLIOGRAPHY

Parker, J. 2012. "Unravelling the neoliberal paradox with Marx." *Journal of Australian Political Economy* 70, no. 70: 193–213.

Parthasarathy, D. 2015. "The poverty of (Marxist) theory: peasant classes, provincial capital, and the critique of globalization in India." *Journal of Social History* 48, no. 4: 816–841.

Parthasarathy, G. 1987. "Changes in the incidence of rural poverty." *Indian Journal of Agricultural Economics* 42, no. 1.

Parthasarathy, G. 1995. "Public intervention and rural poverty: case of non-sustainable reduction in Andhra Pradesh." *Economic and Political Weekly* 30, no. 41/42: 2573–2575, 2577–2581, 2583–2586.

Parsai, G. 2007. "Manmohan to head land reforms council." *The Hindu.* https://www.thehindu.com/todays-paper/Manmohan-to-head-land-reforms-council/article14866257.ece.

Patel, R., and McMichael, P. 2008. "Third worldism and the lineages of global fascism: The regrouping of the global South in the neoliberal era." *Third World Quarterly* 25, no. 1: 231–254.

Pathy, J. 1998. "Contemporary struggles of the tribal peoples of India." *Indian Journal of Social Work* 59, no. 1.

Patnaik, P. 1995. *Whatever happened to Imperialism.* New Delhi: Tulika.

Patnaik, P. 2010. "The state under neo-liberalism." *MRZine.* http://mrzine.monthlyreview.org/2010/patnaik100810.html.

Patnaik, P. 2011. "Future of Marxism." In *Another millennium?,* ed. R. Thapar. New Delhi: Penguin.

Patnaik, P. 2016. "Nationalism, Hindutva and the assault on thought." *Communist Party of India: Marxist,* XXXII *1.* http://www.cpim.org/content/nationalism-hindutva-and-assault-thought.

Patnaik, P. 2017a. "Neoliberalism and inequality are inseparable." *News Click.* https://newsclick.in/neoliberalism-and-inequality-are-inseparable.

Patnaik, P. 2017b. "Why India needs the Left." *The Wire.* https://thewire.in/196923/india-left-future-economy-social-policy/.

Patnaik, P. 2018a. "The dramatic rise in wealth inequality." *People's Democracy.* http://peoplesdemocracy.in/2018/0128_pd/dramatic-rise-wealth-inequality.

Patnaik, P. 2018b. "The state under neoliberalism." http://citeseerx.ist.psu.edu/viewdoc/download?doi=10.1.1.527.9907&rep=rep1&type=pdf.

Patnaik, U. 1972. "Development of capitalism in agriculture – I." *Social Scientist* 1, no. 2: 15–31.

Patnaik, U. 1983. "Classical theory of rent and its application to India: Some preliminary thoughts on sharecropping." *Journal of Peasant Studies* 10, no. 2–3: 71–87.

Patnaik, U. 1986. "The agrarian question and development of capitalism in India." *Economic and Political Weekly* 21, no. 18: 781–793.

Patnaik, U. 1990a. *Agrarian relations and accumulation: The mode of production debate in India.* Delhi: Oxford University Press.

Patnaik, U. 1990b. "Capitalist development in agriculture: Note." In *Agrarian relations and accumulation: The mode of production debate in India*, ed. U. Patnaik. Delhi: Oxford University Press.

Patnaik, U. 1990c. "Capitalist development in agriculture: Further comment." In *Agrarian relations and accumulation: The mode of production debate in India*, ed. U. Patnaik. Delhi: Oxford University Press.

Patnaik, U. 1990d. "On the mode of production in Indian agriculture: Reply." In *Agrarian relations and accumulation: The mode of production debate in India*, ed. U. Patnaik. Delhi: Oxford University Press.

Patnaik, U. 1990e. "Some economic and political consequences of the green revolution in India." In *The Food Question: Profits versus people,* eds. H. Bernstein, B. Crow, M. McKintosh, and C. Martin. New York: Monthly Review Press.

Patnaik, U. 1991. "Food availability and famine: a longer view." *The Journal of Peasant Studies* 19, no. 1: 1–25.

Patnaik, U. 1995. "On capitalism and agrestic unfreedom." *International Review of Social History* 40, no. 1: 77–92.

Patnaik, U. 1999. *The long transition: Essays on political Economy.* New Delhi: Tulika.

Patnaik, U. 2002. "Deflation and Deja vu: India's Agriculture in the World Economy." In *Agrarian studies: Essays on agrarian relations in less developed countries*, eds. V. Ramachandran and M. Swaminathan. New Delhi: Tulika.

Patnaik, U. 2003. "On the inverse relation between primary exports and food absorption in developing countries under liberalized trading regimes." In *Work and well-being in the age of finance,* eds. J. Ghosh and C. Chandrasekhar, 256–287. New Delhi: Tulika.

Patnaik, U. 2007. *The republic of hunger.* Gurgaon: Three Essays Collective.

Patnaik, U. 2013. "Theorizing food security and poverty in the era of economic reforms." In *Two decades of market reform in India: Some dissenting views*, ed. S. Bhattacharyya, 93–124. New York: Anthem Press.

Patnaik, U. 2016. "Growing inequalities in the South in the Present Era of primitive capitalist accumulation." *Studies in Peoples History* 3, no. 1: 59–70.

Patnaik, P., Chandrasekhar, C.P., and Ghosh, J. 2004. "The political economy of the economic reform strategy: The role of the Indian capitalist class." In *Class, caste, and gender*, ed. M. Mohanty. Delhi: Sage.

Pattenden, J. 2011. "Gatekeeping as accumulation and domination: Decentralization and class relations in rural south India." *Journal of Agrarian Change* 11, no. 2: 164–194.

Pattenden, J. 2016. "Working at the margins of global production networks: local labour control regimes and rural-based labourers in South India." *Third World Quarterly* 37, no. 10: 1809–1833.

Pattenden, J. 2018. "The politics of classes of labour: Fragmentation, reproduction zones and collective action in Karnataka, India." *Journal of Peasant Studies* 45, no. 5–6: 1039–1059.

Paul, S. 1990. "Green revolution and poverty among farm families in Haryana, 1969/70–1982/83." *Economic and Political Weekly* 25, no. 39: 1809–1833.

Paul, S, and Sarma, V. 2017. "Industrialization-led displacement and long term-welfare: Evidence from West Bengal." *Oxford Development Studies* 45, no. 3: 240–259.

Paulini, T. 1979. *Agrarian movements and reforms in India: The case of Kerala.* Breitenbach: Verlag Stuttgart.

Paxton, R. 2004. *The anatomy of Fascism.* New York: Vintage.

Pearse, A. 1980. *Seeds of plenty, seeds of want: Social and economic implications of the Green Revolution.* London: Clarendon Press.

Peck, J., and Theodore, N. 2001. "Contingent Chicago: Restructuring the spaces of temporary labor." *International Journal of Urban and Regional Research* 25, no. 3: 471–496.

Peck, J., and Tickell, A. 2002. "Neoliberalizing space." *Antipode* 34, no. 3: 380–404.

Pedersen, J.D. 1992. "State, bureaucracy and change in India." *Journal of Development Studies* 28, no. 4: 616–639.

Peet, R. 1983. "Relations of production and the relocation of United States manufacturing industry since 1960." *Economic Geography* 59, no. 2: 112–143.

People's Democracy. 2017. "Thinking together." *People's Democracy.* https://peoplesde mocracy.in/2015/0712_pd/thinking-together.

Pereira, A. 2016. "BJP tops list of reelected MPs in terms of assets and criminal cases." *Firstpost.* https://www.firstpost.com/politics/bjp-tops-list-of-reelected-mps-in-terms-of-assets-and-criminal-cases-1557703.html.

Petras, J. 1997. "Imperialism and NGOs in Latin America." *Monthly Review* 49, no. 7.

Petras, J., and Veltemeyer, H. 2007. "The 'development state' in Latin America: Whose development, whose state?" *Journal of Peasant Studies* 34, no. 3–4: 371–407.

Phyne, P. 2010. "A comparative political economy of rural capitalism salmon aquaculture in Norway, Chile and Ireland." *Acta Sociologica* 53, no. 2: 160–180.

Pillai, P. 2003. *Left Movement and Agrarian Relations, 1920–1995.* New Delhi: South Asian Publishers.

Plahe, J., Wright, S., and Marmbo, M. 2017. "Livelihood crises in Vidarbha, India: Food sovereignty through traditional farming systems as a possible solution." *South Asia: Journal of South Asian Studies* 40, no. 3: 600–618.

Plekhanov, G. 1971. *Fundamental problems of Marxism.* New York: International Publishers.

Poe, S.C., and Tate, C.N. 1994. "Repression of human rights to personal integrity in the 1980s." *American Political Science Review* 88, no. 4: 853–872.

Pokrant, B., and Reeves, P. 2007. "Work and labor in the Bangladesh brackish-water shrimp export sector." *South Asia: Journal of South Asian Studies* 26, no. 3: 359–389.

Polanyi, K. 1944/2001. *The great transformation: The political and economic origins of our time*, 2nd ed. Boston: Beacon Press.

Post, C. 1999. "Ernest Mandel and the Marxist theory of bureaucracy." In *The Legacy of Ernest Mandel,* ed. G. Achcar. London: Verso.

Poulantzas, N. 1968. *Political Power and Social Classes.* London: New Left Books (cited from the English Translation, NLB, London, 1973).

Pradhan, D., and Flaherty, M. 2008. "National initiatives, local effects: Trade liberalization, shrimp aquaculture, and coastal communities in Odisha, India." *Society & Natural Resources* 21, no. 1: 63–76.

Pramanik, S., and Nandi, N. 2001. Women fishworkers and their role in the inshore fishing areas of Sundarban. *Man in India* 81, no. 1: 169–177.

Prasad, P. 1989. *Lopsided growth: Political economy of Indian development.* Delhi: Oxford University Press.

Prasad, P. 1990. "Reactionary role of usurer's capital in Rural India." In *The mode of production debate in India,* ed. U. Patnaik. Delhi: Oxford University Press.

Prasad-Aleyamma, M. 2018. "Cards and carriers: migration, identification and surveillance in Kerala, South India." *Contemporary South Asia* 26, no. 2: 191–205.

Prashad, V. 2015. *No free left: The futures of Indian communism.* New Delhi: Leftword.

Pratt, G. 2004. *Working Feminism.* Edinburgh: Edinburgh University Press.

Pred, A. 1984. "Place as historically contingent process: Structuration and the time-geography of becoming places." *Annals of the American Association of Geographers* 74, no. 2: 279–297.

Premchand, A. 2017. *Contemporary India: Society and its governance.* Milton: Taylor and Francis.

Pressman, S., ed. 2006. *Alternative theories of the State.* New York: Palgrave.

Pushpendra. 2000. "Liberalization and Agrarian reforms: some recent controversies." In *Land reforms in India: Volume 5*, eds. B.N. Sinha, and Pushpendra, 45–63. New Delhi: Sage.

Qazi, M. 2018. "Malnutrition ravages India's children." *The Asian Age.* http://www.asianage.com/india/all-india/030118/malnutrition-ravages-indias-children.html.

Radice, H. 2008. "The developmental state under global neoliberalism." *Third World Quarterly* 29, no. 6: 1153–1174.

Rahul, N. 1995. "Green revolution and subsistence agriculture you reap as you sow." *Economic and Political Weekly* 32, no. 18: 930–932.

Rai, P. 2007. "NREGA battling cancerous corruption." *India Together.* http://www.indiatogether.org/nregs-government--2.

Rao, C. 1994. *Agricultural growth, Rural poverty and environmental degradation in India.* Delhi: Oxford University Press.

Rao, J.M. 1998. "Agricultural development under state planning." In *The State, Development Planning and Liberalisation in India,* ed. T. Byres. Delhi: Oxford University Press.

BIBLIOGRAPHY

Rao, J.M. 1999. "Agrarian power and unfree labour." *Journal of Peasant Studies* 26, no. 2–3: 242–262.

Rao, S. 2018. "Gender and class relations in rural India." *Journal of Peasant Studies* 45, no. 5–6: 950–968.

Ram, N. 1972. "Development of Capitalism in Agriculture." *Social Scientist,* vol. 1, no. 5: 51–57.

Ramakrishnan, V. 1999. "A history of massacres." *Frontline* 16, no. 5. https://www.front line.in/static/html/fl1605/16050300.htm.

Ranganathan, S. 2018. *Hinduism: A contemporary philosophical investigation.* New York: Routledge.

Ray, R. 2002. *The Naxalites and their ideology.* Delhi: Oxford University Press.

Rediff. 2006. "Naxalism single biggest internal security challenge: PM." *Rediff India Abroad.* http://www.rediff.com/news/2006/apr/13naxal.htm.

Renton, D. 2007. *Fascism: Theory and practice.* Delhi: Aakar (originally published by Pluto).

Rieman, R. 2018. *To fight against this age: Fascism and humanism.* New York: W.W. Norton & Company.

Rigg, J. 1989. "The green revolution and equity: Who adopts the new rice varieties and why?" *Geography* 74, no. 2: 144–150.

Roberts, D. 2011. "Reconsidering Gramsci's interpretation of Fascism." *Journal of Modern Italian Studies* 16, no. 2: 239–255.

Roberts, M. 2016. *The long depression.* Chicago: Haymarket.

Roberts, M. 2017. "Modi rules, Harvard doesn't." *Michael Roberts Blog.* https://thenext recession.wordpress.com/2017/03/14/modi-rules-harvard-doesnt/.

Roberts, M. 2018. "China workshop: Challenging the misconceptions." *Michael Roberts Blog.* https://thenextrecession.wordpress.com/2018/06/07/china-workshop -challenging-the-misconceptions/.

Robinson, W., and Barrera, M. 2012. "Global capitalism and twenty-first century fascism: a US case-study." *Race and Class* 53, no. 3: 4–29.

Ronnback, P., Troell, M., Zetterstrom, T., and Babu, D. 2003. "Mangrove dependence and socio-economic concerns in shrimp hatcheries of Andhra Pradesh, India." *Environmental Conservation* 30, no. 4: 344–352.

Routledge, P. 1997. "Space, mobility, and collective action: India's Naxalite movement." *Environment and Planning A* 29, no. 12: 2165–2189.

Roy, A. 2011. *Broken republic.* New Delhi: Penguin Books.

Roy, A. 2009. "The heart of India is under attack." *The Guardian.* https://www.theguard ian.com/commentisfree/2009/oct/30/mining-india-maoists-green-hunt.

Roy, B. 2002. "Naxalite violence: Legacy of another era." *Times of India.* https://timeso findia.indiatimes.com/edit-page/Naxalite-Violence-Legacy-of-Another-Era/article show/15602206.cms.

Roy, I. 2018. *Politics of the poor: Negotiating democracy in contemporary India.* Cambridge: Cambridge University Press.

Roy, M.S. 2011. *Gender and radical politics in India: Magic moments of Naxalbari (1967–1975).* New York: Routledge.

Roy, T. 2005. *Rethinking economic change in India: Labour and livelihood.* London: Routledge.

Roy Chowdhury, S. 2015. "Bring class back in: Informality in Bangalore." *Socialist Register* 51: 73–92.

Rubin, I. 1973. *Essays on Marx's theory of value.* Montreal: Black Rose Books.

Rudolph, L.I., and Rudolph S.H. 1987. *In pursuit of Lakshmi: The political economy of the Indian State.* Chicago: Chicago University Press.

Rudra, A. 1983. "Mode of production in Indian agriculture." *Economic and Political Weekly* 18, no. 12: 421.

Rudra, A. 1988. "Emerging class structure in rural India." In *Rural poverty in South Asia,* eds. T. Srinivasan and P. Bardhan. New York: Columbia University Press.

Rudra, A., Majid, A., and Talib, B. 1990 (1969–70). "Big farmers of Punjab." In *Agrarian Relations and Accumulation: The mode of production debate in India,* ed. U. Patnaik. Delhi: Oxford University Press.

Rukmini, S. 2017. "On religious hostilities, India ranked just slightly better than Syria: Pew study." *Huffpost.* https://www.huffingtonpost.in/2017/04/13/on-religious-hosti lities-india-ranked-just-slightly-better-than_a_22037994/.

Rummel, R.J. 1984. "Libertarianism, violence within states, and the polarity principle." *Comparative Politics* 16, no. 4: 443–462.

Ruparelia, S., Reddy, S., Harriss, J. and Corbridge, S., eds. 2011. *Understanding India's new political economy,* London: Routledge.

Rutherford, T. 2010. "De/Re-centering work and class?: A review and critique of labor geography." *Geography Compass* 4, no 7: 768–777.

Rutherford, T., and Gertler, M. 2002. "Labor in lean times: geography, scale and national trajectory of work place change." *Transactions of the Institute of British Geographers* 27, no. 2: 195–212.

Sackley, N. 2015. "The road from serfdom: economic storytelling and narratives in the rise of neoliberalism." *History and Technology* 31, no. 4: 397–419.

Sagar. 2006. "The spring and its thunder." *Economic and Political Weekly* 41, no. 29: 3176–3178.

Sahay, S. 2006. *The Indian working class movement during freedom struggle.* Patna: Janaki Prakashan.

SAHRDC (South Asia Human Rights Documentation Centre). 2002. "Emerging state of insecurity: India's war against Itself." *SAHRDC.* www.hrdc.net/sahrdc/hrfeatures/HRF51.htm.

Sainaith, P. 2001. "Age of inequality." In *India: Another millennium?*, R. Thapar, 152–168. New York: Penguin.

Sainaith, P. 2009. "Neo-liberal terrorism in India: The largest wave of suicides in history." *Counterpunch.* http://www.counterpunch.org/sainath02122009.html.

Sainaith, P. 2013. "Farmers' suicide rates soar above the rest." *The Hindu.* https://www.thehindu.com/opinion/columns/sainath/farmers-suicide-rates-soar-above-the-rest/article4725101.ece.

Samal, K. 2003. "Fishing communities on Chilika Lake." *Economic and Political Weekly* 38, no. 31: 3319–3325.

Samanta, A. 1984. *Left extremist movement in West Bengal.* Calcutta: Firma KLM Private Ltd.

Samuel, V. 2019. "What is inequality?" *Oxfam India.* https://www.oxfamindia.org/blog/what-inequality.

Sanchez, A., and Strumpell, C. 2014. "Anthropological and historical perspectives on India's working classes." *Modern Asian Studies* 48, no. 5: 1233–1241.

Sanyal, K. 2013. *Rethinking capitalist development: Primitive accumulation, governmentality and post-colonial capitalism.* London: Routledge.

Sarangi, A. 2017. "State formation and political economy of India: The Rudolphian paradigm." *Indian Review* 16, no. 3: 344–356.

Sarkar, R., and Sarkar, A. 2016. "The rebel's resource curse: A theory of insurgent-civilian dynamics." *Studies in Conflict and Terrorism* 40, no. 10: 870–898.

Sarkar, S. 1983. *Modern India: 1885–1947.* Delhi: Macmillan.

Sarkar, S. 2016. "The fascism of the Sangh Parivar." In *Fascism: Essays on Europe and India,* ed. J. Banaji. Gurgaon: Three Essays Collective.

Sarmah, B., and Baurua, J., eds. 2014. *Neoliberal state and its challenges.* Delhi: Aakar.

Sass, R. 2000. "Agricultural 'killing fields': The poisoning of Costa Rican Banana Workers." *International Journal of Health Services* 30, no. 3: 491–514.

Sathyamurthy, T. 1996. "State and society in a changing political perspective." In *Class formation and political transformation in post-colonial India,* ed. T.V. Sathyamurthy. Delhi: Oxford University Press.

Saul, J. 1974. "The State in postcolonial societies: Tanzania." In *The Socialist Register 1974,* eds. R. Miliband and J. Saville. London: The Merlin Press.

Saull, R. 2015. "Capitalist development and the rise and 'Fall' of the far-right." *Critical Sociology* 41, no. 4–5: 619–639.

Saxton, A. 2007. *Religion and the human impact.* Delhi: Aakar.

Sayer, A. 1992. *Method in social science: A realist approach.* London: Routledge.

Sayer, A. 2000. *Realism and social science.* London: Sage.

Schatzman, C. 2005. "Political challenge in Latin America: Rebellion and collective protest in an era of democratization." *Journal of Peace Research* 42, no. 3: 291–310.

Schiller, B. 1998. *The economics of poverty and discrimination*. Eaglewood Cliffs: Prentice Hall.

Schultz, K. 2018. "Indian children's book lists Hitler as leader 'who will inspire you.'" *The New York Times.* https://www.nytimes.com/2018/03/17/world/asia/india-hitler-childrens-book.html.

Science & Society. 2018. "Intersectionality: A symposium." *Science & Society* 82, no. 2: 248–291.

Sen, A. [Amartya]. 1999. *Development as Freedom*. New Delhi: Oxford University Press.

Sen, A. [Amartya]. 2005. *The argumentative India: Writings on Indian history, culture and identity.* London: Allen Lane.

Sen, A. [Anupam]. 2017. *The state, industrialization and class formations in India: A Neo-Marxist perspective on colonialism, underdevelopment and development.* London: Routledge.

Sen, A. [Arindam]. 2017. "The movement-party dialectics: Tebhaga-Telangana to Naxalbari-CPI(ML)." *Economic and Political Weekly* 52, no. 21.

Sen, S., Debabrata, P., and Lahiri, A. 1978. *Naxalbari and after: A frontier anthology.* Calcutta: Kathashilpa.

Sengupta, M. 2008. "How the state changed its mind: Power, politics & the origins of India's market reforms." *Economic & Political Weekly* 43, no. 21: 35–42.

Shah, A. 2006. "Markets of protection – The terrorist Maoist Movement and the state in Jharkhand, India." *Critique of Anthropology* 26, no. 3: 297–314.

Shah, A. 2013. "The agrarian question in a Maoist guerrilla zone: Land, labour and capital in the forests and hills of Jharkhand, India." *Journal of Agrarian Change* 13, no. 3: 424–450.

Shah, A. 2017. "Humaneness and Contradictions: India's Maoist-inspired Naxalites." *Economic and Political Weekly* 52, no. 21.

Shah, A., and Jain, D. 2017. "Naxalbari at its golden jubilee: Fifty recent books on the Maoist movement in India." *Modern Asian Studies* 51, no. 4: 1165–1219.

Shah, G. 1988. "Grass-roots mobilization in Indian politics." In *India's democracy*, ed. A. Kohli, 262–304. Hyderabad: Orient Longman.

Shah, G. 2004. *Social movements in India.* New Delhi: Sage.

Shah, G., Mander, H., Thorat, S., Deshpande, S., and Beviskar, A. 2006. *Untouchability in rural India.* Delhi: Sage.

Shakir, M. 1986. *State and politics in contemporary India.* New Delhi: Ajanta Publications.

Shantha, S. 2018. "In Dantewada's Naxal area, 'political participation' looks completely different." *The Wire.* https://thewire.in/politics/chhattisgarh-elections-dantewada-naxals.

Shariff, A. 1999. *India: Human development report.* New Delhi: Oxford University Press.

BIBLIOGRAPHY

Sharma, D. 2017. "Farm output may have increased in three years, but farmers welfare has not." *The Wire*. https://thewire.in/agriculture/modi-three-years-farmers-agriculture.

Sharma, H.R. 1992. "Agrarian relations in India since independence." *Journal of Indian School of Political Economy* 4, no. 2: 201–262.

Sharma, T. 1992. *Technical change, income distribution and rural poverty*. New Delhi: Shirpa Publications.

Sharma, U. 2002. *Caste*. Delhi: Viva Books.

Sharma, R., and Poleman, T. 1993. *The new economics of India's Green Revolution: Income and employment diffusion in Uttar Pradesh*. Ithaca: Cornell University Press.

Sheth, N. 2014. "Trade unions in India: A sociological approach." In *Political sociology of India*, ed. A. Kumar. Delhi: Sage.

Shiva, V. 1991. *The violence of the green revolution: Third world agriculture, ecology and politics*. London: Zed Books Ltd.

Shiva, V. 2000. *Stolen harvest: The hijacking of the global food supply*. Cambridge: South End Press.

Shiva, V., Jafri, A., Emani, A., and Pande, M. 2002. *Seeds of suicide: The ecological and human costs of globalisation of agriculture*. New Delhi: Navdanya.

Shrestha, N., and Patterson, J., 1990. "Population and poverty in dependent states Latin America considered." *Antipode* 22, no. 2: 121–155.

Shrimali, R. Forthcoming. *Corporate hijack of agriculture: Case of contract farming in India*. Singapore: Palgrave.

Simeon, D. 1986. "Communalism in modern India: a theoretical examination." *Mainstream*. http://www.sacw.net/article2760.html.

Simeon, D. 2016. "The law of killing: A brief history of Indian fascism." In *Fascism: essays on Europe and India*, ed. J. Banaji. Gurgaon: Three Essays Collective.

Singer, W. 2012. *Independent India, 1947–2000*. London: Pearson.

Singh, H. 2014. *Recasting Caste: From the sacred to the profane*. New Delhi: Sage.

Singh, I. 1990. *The great ascent: The rural poor in South Asia*. Baltimore: The John Hopkins University Press.

Singh, P. 1995. *The Naxalite Movement in India*. Delhi: Rupa Publication.

Singh, R. 2010. *On nationalism and communalism in India*. Delhi: Aakar.

Singh, S. 2002. "Agricultural labourers." In *Alternative economic survey*. New Delhi: Rainbow Publishers.

Singh, S. [Supriya]. 2017. *Commercialization of Hinterland and dynamics of class, caste and gender in rural India*. Newcastle: Cambridge Scholars Publishing.

Singhal, S., and Nilakantan, R. 2016. "The economic effects of a counterinsurgency policy in India: a synthetic control analysis." *European Journal of Political Economy* 45: 1–17.

Singharoy, D. 2004. *Peasant movements in post-colonial India*. New Delhi: Sage.

Sinha, A. 2011. "An institutional perspective on the liberalization state in India." In *The state in India after liberalization: Interdisciplinary perspectives*, eds. A. Gupta and K. Sivaramakrishnan, 49–68. London: Routledge.

Sinha, A. 2016. "A distinctive Indian political economy: New concepts and a synthesizing framework." *Studies in Indian Politics* 4, no. 2: 266–273.

Sinha, S. 2009. "Workers and working classes in contemporary India." In *Beyond Marx: Theorizing the global relations of the 21st century,* eds. M. van der Linden and K. Roth. Leiden: Brill.

Sinha, S. 2017. "Histories of power, the 'Universalization of Capital' and India's Modi government: Between and beyond Marxism and post-colonial theory." *Critical Sociology* 43: 4–5.

Sitton, J. 1996. *Recent Marxian theory.* Albany: State University of New York Press.

Skocpol, T. 1982. "What makes peasants revolutionary?" *Comparative Politics* 14, no. 3: 351–375.

Smith, J. 2016. *Imperialism in the twenty-first century: Globalization, super-exploitation, and capitalism's final crisis.* New York: Monthly Review Press.

Smith, J. 1979. "Jayprakash Narayan dies." *Washington Post.* https://www.washington post.com/archive/local/1979/10/09/jayaprakash-narayan-dies/5a363a02-4138-49e2-8a4e-d977f8304104/?utm_term=.caefi3d50dbe.

Smith, M. 2018. *Invisible leviathan: Marx's law of value in the twilight of capitalism.* Leiden: Brill.

Smith, N. 2007. "Nature as an accumulation strategy." In *The Socialist Register 2007*, eds. C. Leys and L. Panitch. London: The Merlin Press.

Smith, T. 2010. "Technological change in capitalism: Some Marxian themes." *Cambridge Journal of Economics* 34, no. 1: 203–212.

So, A. 2007. "Peasant conflict and the local predatory state in the Chinese countryside." *Journal of Peasant Studies* 34, no. 3–4: 560–581.

Song, H. 2013. "Marxist critiques of the developmental state and the fetishism of national development." *Antipode* 45, no. 5: 1254–1276.

Spacek, M. 2017. "Internal borderlands: Architectures of force and state expansion in India's central 'frontier'." *Conflict Security and Development* 17, no. 2: 163–182.

Spivak, G. 2000. "Discussion: An afterword on the new subaltern." In *Subaltern Studies 11,* eds. P. Chatterjee and P. Jeganathan, 305–334. New Delhi: Permanent black.

Sreeraj, A.P., and Vakulabharanam, V. 2015. "High growth and rising inequality in Kerala since the 1980s." *Oxford Development Studies* 44, no. 4: 367–383.

Srinivas, N. 1998. "Explaining small scale organization forms in Kerala fisheries." In *Entrepreneurship and Innovation: Models of Development,* ed. R. Kanungo. Delhi: Sage.

Srinivas, M.N. 2012. "Sociology in India and its future." In *Indian sociology: Issues and Challenges,* ed. L. Bhai. Delhi: Sage.

Srivastava, A. 1997. "Bihar to check leak of government funds to Naxals." *Indian Express.*

Srivastava, R. 1999. "Rural labour in Uttar Pradesh: Emerging features of subsistence, contradiction and resistance." *Journal of Peasant Studies* 26, no. 2–3: 263–315.

Srujana, B. 2017. "British Raj to billionaire Raj—India's journey into neoliberalism." *Newsclick.* https://newsclick.in/british-raj-billionaire-raj-indias-journey-neoliberalism.

Stanley, D. 2003. "The economic impact of mariculture on a small regional economy." *World Development* 31, no. 1: 191–210.

Steger, M., and Roy. 2010. *Neoliberalism: A very short introduction.* Oxford: Oxford University Press.

Stern, R. 2000. *Democracy and dictatorship in South Asia: Dominant classes an political outcomes in India, Pakistan, and Bangladesh.* Santa Barbara: ABC-CLIO.

Stern, R. 2011. *Changing India: Bourgeois revolution on the subcontinent.* Cambridge: Cambridge University Press.

Steur, L. 2014. "An 'expanded' class perspective: Bringing capitalism down to earth in the changing political lives of Adivasi workers in Kerala." *Modern Asian Studies* 48, no. 5: 1334–1357.

Stonich, S. 1995. "The environmental-quality and social-justice implications of shrimp mariculture development in Honduras." *Human Ecology* 23: 143–168.

Stonich, S., Bort, J., and Ovares, L. 1997. "Globalization of shrimp mariculture: The impact on social justice and environmental quality in Central America." *Society & Natural Resources* 10, no. 2: 161–179.

Storper, M. and Walker, R. 1989. *The capitalist imperative.* New York: Blackwell.

Subadevan, S., and Naqvi, I. 2017. "Contesting urban citizenship: the urban poor's strategies of state engagement in Chennai, India." *International development planning review* 39, no. 1: 77–95.

Subramanian, A., ed. 2008. *India's turn: Understanding the economic transformation.* New Delhi: Oxford University Press.

Subramanian, D. 2015. "No room for class struggle in these undertakings: Providing social welfare for Indian state sector industrial workers (circa 1950–2000)." *Modern Asian Studies* 49, no. 5: 1526–1579.

Subramanian, K. 2004. "The Naxalite Movement and government response: A critical assessment." *Mainstream* XLII, no. 52.

Subramanian, S. 1998. "Combating Naxalite violence." http://www.aapssindia.org/articles/art2/naxalite.html.

Subramanian, S. 2008. "Control and access: The everyday dimensions of property." *Contributions to Indian Sociology* 42, no. 1: 93–122.

Sud, N. 2014. "The state in the era of India's sub-national regions: liberalisation and land in Gujarat." *Geoforum* 51: 233–242.

Sugden, F. 2017. "A mode of production flux: the transformation and reproduction of rural class relations in lowland Nepal and North Bihar." *Dialectical Anthropology* 41, no. 2: 129–161.

Sugden, F., and Punch, S. 2014. "Capitalist expansion and the decline of common property ecosystems in China, Vietnam and India." *Development and Change* 45, no. 4: 656–684.

Sundar, N. 2006. "Bastar, Maoism and Salwa Judum." *Economic and Political Weekly* 41, no. 29: 3187–3192.

Sundar, N. 2011. "The rule of law and the rule of property: law-struggles and the neoliberal state in India." In *The state in India after liberalization: Interdisciplinary perspectives,* eds. A. Gupta and L. Sivaramakrishnan, 175–194. London: Routledge.

Sundar, N. 2014a. "Mimetic sovereignties, precarious citizenship: state effects in a looking-glass world." *Journal of peasant Studies* 41, no. 4: 469–490.

Sundar, N. 2014b. "No surprises here: Modi's Naxalite policy." http://nandinisundar .blogspot.ca/2014/09/no-surprises-here-modis-naxalite-policy.html.

Sunilraj, B., and Heath, O. 2017. "The historical legacy of party system stability in Kerala." *Studies in Indian Politics* 5, no. 2: 193–204.

Surjeet, H.S. 1986. *What the AIKS Stands For.* New Delhi: All India Kisan Sabha.

Surjeet, H.S. 1992. *Land reforms in India.* New Delhi: National Book Centre.

Swaminathan, M. 2000. "Consumer food subsidies in India: Proposals for reform." *The Journal of Peasant Studies* 27, no. 3: 92–114.

Sweezy, P.M. 1986. "Feudalism-to-Capitalism revisited." *Science & Society* 50, no. 1: 81–84.

Tagore, R. 1913. *Gitanjali.* http://www.spiritualbee.com/media/gitanjali-by-tagore.pdf.

Teitelbaum, E. 2006. "Was the Indian labor movement ever co-opted? Evaluating standard accounts." *Critical Asian Studies* 38, no. 4: 389–417.

Teitelbaum, E. 2013. "Labour regulation, trade unions and unemployment." In *Routledge handbook of Indian politics*, eds. A. Kohli and P. Singh. London: Routledge.

Teltumbde, A. 2010. *The persistence of caste.* Delhi: Navayana.

Teltumbde, A. 2016. *Dalits: Past, present and future.* Abingdon, Oxon: Taylor and Francis.

Tendulkar, S., and Bhavani, T. 2007. *Understanding reforms.* New Delhi: Oxford University Press.

Tendulkar, S., and Jain, L. 1995. "Economic reforms and poverty." *Economic and Political Weekly* 30, no. 23: 1373–1375, 1377.

Teubal, M. 2000. "Structural adjustment and social disarticulation: The case of Argentina." *Science and Society* 64, no. 4: 460–489.

Thapar, R. 2016. *Indian society and the secular.* Gurgaon: Three essays collective.

Thara, K. 2016. "Protecting caste livelihoods on the western coast of India: An intersectional analysis of Udupi's fisherwomen." *Environment and Urbanization* 28, no. 2: 423–436.

The Economic Times. 2008. "Jyoti Basu supports Buddhadeb's view on capitalism." *The Economic Times.* https://economictimes.indiatimes.com/jyoti-basu-supports-bud dhadebs-view-on-capitalism/articleshow/2676957.cms?from=mdr.

BIBLIOGRAPHY

The Hindu. 2017. "'Unforgiveable': The Hindu's editorial on December 7, 1992 on Babri Masjid demolition." *The Hindu.* https://www.thehindu.com/news/national/unfor givable-editorial-on-the-babri-masjid-demolition-published-by-the-hindu-on-de cember-7-1992/article21272508.ece.

The Hindu. 2018a. "Who is an urban Naxal, asks Romila Thapar." *The Hindu.* https:// www.thehindu.com/news/national/who-is-an-urban-naxal-asks-romila-thapar/ar ticle25088465.ece.

The Hindu. 2018b. "Need for an employment policy to solve jobless growth." *The Hindu.* https://www.thehindu.com/news/national/need-for-an-employment-policy-to-solve-jobless-growth/article25041745.ece.

The Indian Express. 2018. "Why a new report agrees with Piketty on inequality, blames policy." *The Indian Express.* https://indianexpress.com/article/explained/pay-gap -income-inequality-policy-sc-st-religion-bias-5074635/.

Thompson, E.P. 1966. *The making of the English working class.* New York: Vintage Books.

Thorner, A. 1982. "Semi-feudalism or capitalism: Contemporary debate on classes and modes of production in India." *Economic and Political Weekly* 17, no. 51: 2061–2066.

Thorner, D. 1969. "Maliks and money-lenders – Their role." In *Rural Sociology in India,* ed. A.K. Desai. Bombay: Popular Prakashan.

Thorner, D. 1973. *Agrarian prospect in India.* Delhi: Allied Publishers.

Tilly, C. 2005. "Repression, mobilization and explanation." In *Repression and mobiliza- tion,* eds. C. Davenport, H. Johnston, and C. Muller, 211–226. Minneapolis: University of Minnesota Press.

Times of India. 2016. "Five women die every hour during childbirth, according to World Health Organization." *Times of India.* https://timesofindia.indiatimes.com/india/5-women-die-every-hour-during-childbirth-in-India-WHO/articleshow/52781552. cms.

Times of India. 2018. "Shashi Tharoor warns of 'Hindu Pakistan' under BJP rule, Sambit Patra hits back." *Times of India.* https://timesofindia.indiatimes.com/india/if-bjp-wins-2019-ls-polls-it-will-pave-the-way-for-creation-of-hindu-pakistan-shashi-thar oor/articleshow/64951115.cms.

Tisdell, C., Maitra, P., eds. 2018. *Technological change, development, and the environ- ment: Socio-economic perspectives.* Milton: Routledge.

Tiwana, B., and Singh, P. 2015. "Nation state, marketization of social services and uncer- tainty of livelihood in India." *World Review of Political Economy* 6, no. 1: 33–57.

Toye, J., and Jackson, C. 1996. "Public expenditure policy and poverty reduction: Has the world bank got it right?" *Institute of Development Studies Bulletin* 27, no. 1: 56–66.

Trotsky, L. 1928. "The Third International after Lenin: 11. Strategy and tactics in the imperialist epoch (Part 3)." *Marxists.org.* https://www.marxists.org/archive/trotsky/ 1928/3rd/ti06.htm#p2-08.

Trotsky, L. 1929. "Leon Trotsky's Writings on Britain: The Anglo-Russian Committee: Trotsky on the struggle in Britain in retrospect." *Marxists.org*. https://www.marxists.org/archive/trotsky/britain/v2/ch02g.htm.

Trotsky, L. 1930. "The Turn in the Communist International and the Situation in Germany." *Marxists.org*. https://www.marxists.org/archive/trotsky/germany/1930/300926.htm.

Trotsky, L. 1931a. "Germany, the key to the international situation." *Marxists.org*. https://www.marxists.org/archive/trotsky/germany/1931/311126.htm.

Trotsky, L. 1931b. "Permanent Revolution." *Marxists.org*. https://www.marxists.org/archive/trotsky/1931/tpr/prge.htm.

Trotsky, L. 1932a. "Bourgeoisie, petty bourgeoisie and proletariat." *Marxists.org*. https://www.marxists.org/archive/trotsky/1932/08/onlyroad2.htm.

Trotsky, L. 1932b. "Bureaucratic ultimatism." *Marxists.org*. https://www.marxists.org/archive/trotsky/1932/01/whatnext5.htm.

Trotsky, L. 1932c. "Centrism 'in general' and the centrism of the Stalinist bureaucracy." *Marxists.org*. https://www.marxists.org/archive/trotsky/1932/01/whatnext9.htm.

Trotsky, L. 1932d. "Democracy and fascism I." *Marxists.org*. https://www.marxists.org/archive/trotsky/1932/01/whatnext2.htm.

Trotsky, L. 1932e. "Democracy and fascism II." *Marxists.org*. https://www.marxists.org/archive/trotsky/1932/01/whatnext3.htm.

Trotsky, L. 1932f. "Germany: The Only Road (Part 1)." *Marxists.org*. https://www.marxists.org/archive/trotsky/germany/1932/onlyroad1.htm.

Trotsky, L. 1932g. "Germany: The Only Road (Part 2)." *Marxists.org*. https://www.marxists.org/archive/trotsky/germany/1932/onlyroad2.htm#s9.

Trotsky, L. 1932h. "Strike strategy." *Marxists.org*. https://www.marxists.org/archive/trotsky/1932/01/whatnext11.htm.

Trotsky, L. 1932i. "What next? Vital questions for the German proletariat. Part I." *Marxists.org*. https://www.marxists.org/archive/trotsky/germany/1932-ger/next01.htm.

Trotsky, L. 1932j. "What next? Vital questions for the German proletariat. Part II." *Marxists.org*. https://www.marxists.org/archive/trotsky/germany/1932-ger/next02.htm.

Trotsky, L. 1932k. "What next? Vital questions for the German proletariat. Part III." *Marxists.org*. https://www.marxists.org/archive/trotsky/germany/1932-ger/next03.htm.

Trotsky, L. 1932l. "What they say in Prague about the united front." *Marxists.org*. https://www.marxists.org/archive/trotsky/1932/09/onlyroad7.htm.

Trotsky, L. 1933a. "The German Catastrophe: The Responsibility of the Leadership." *Marxists.org*. https://www.marxists.org/archive/trotsky/germany/1933/330528.htm.

Trotsky, L. 1933b. "What is national socialism?" *Marxists.org*. https://www.marxists.org/archive/trotsky/germany/1933/330610.htm.

Trotsky, L. 1934a. "Bonapartism and fascism." *Marxists.org.* https://www.marxists.org/archive/trotsky/germany/1934/340715.htm.

Trotsky, L. 1934b. "Whither France." *Marxists.org.* https://www.marxists.org/archive/trotsky/1936/whitherfrance/ch00.htm.

Trotsky, L. 1938. "Transitional program." *Marxists.org.* https://www.marxists.org/archive/trotsky/1938/tp/transprogram.pdf.

Trotsky, L. 1939. "Three conceptions of the Russian Revolution." *Marxists.org.* https://www.marxists.org/archive/trotsky/1939/xx/3concepts.htm.

Trotsky, L. 1940. "Bonapartism, fascism and war." *Marxists.org.* https://www.marxists.org/archive/trotsky/1940/08/last-article.htm.

Trotsky, L. 1944. "Fascism what it is and how to fight it." *Marxists.org.* https://www.marxists.org/archive/trotsky/works/1944/1944-fas.htm.

Trotsky, L. 1974. *Writings of Leon Trotsky*: 1938–1939. New York: Pathfinder.

Ullrich, O. 1992. "Technology." In *Development Dictionary*, ed. E. Sachs. London: Orient Longman.

Upadhya, C. 1997. "Social and cultural strategies of class formation in coastal Andhra Pradesh." *Contributions to Indian Sociology* 31, no. 2: 169–193.

Upadhyay, S. 2018. "Workers and the right wing: The situation in India." *International Labor and Working-class History* 93: 79–90.

Vaddiraju, A.K. 1999. "Emergence of backward castes in South Telengana agrarian change and grass roots politics." *Economic Political Weekly* 34, no. 7: 425–430.

Vaidyanathan, A. 1986. "Labour use in rural India: A study of spatial and temporal variations." *Economic and Political Weekly* 21, no. 52: A130–A146.

Vakulabharanam, V., and Motiram, S. 2011. "Political economy of agrarian distress in India since the 1990s." In *Understanding India's new political economy*, ed. S. Ruparelia, S. Reddy, and S. Corbridge. London: Routledge.

Vakulabhranam, V., Zhong, W. and X. Jinjun. 2009. "Patterns of Wealth Disparities in India during the Era of Liberalization." Working Paper, Graduate Economics Research Center, Nagoya University.

Vanaik, A. 1990. *The painful transition: Bourgeois democracy in India.* London: Verso.

Vanaik, A. 2011. "Subcontinental strategies." *New Left Review*, no. 70.

Vanaik, A. 2017. *The rise of Hindu authoritarianism: Secular claims, communal realities.* London: Verso.

Vanaik, A. 2018. "India's two hegemonies." *New Left Review*, 112. https://newleftreview.org/II/112/achin-vanaik-india-s-two-hegemonies.

Vanden, E. 2018. "Targets of violence: evidence from India's Naxalite conflict." *Economic Journal* 128, no. 609: 887–916.

van der Linden, M. 2007. "The 'law' of uneven and combined development: some underdeveloped thoughts." *Historical Materialism* 15, no. 1: 145–165.

Vandergeest, P., Flaherty, M., and Miller, P. 1999. "A political ecology of shrimp aquaculture in Thailand." *Rural Sociology* 64, no. 4: 573–596.

Varadarajan, S. 2009. "Modi's 'action-reaction' quote." *Reality, one bite at a time: India, Asia and the World.* http://svaradarajan.blogspot.com/2009/10/modis-action-reaction-quote.html.

Varma, S. 2018a. "Indian millionaires up 20%, while 670 million Indians' income rises 1%." *News Click.* https://newsclick.in/indian-millionaires-20-while-670-million-indians-income-rises-1.

Varma, S. 2018b. "Glimpses of four years of Modi's Achche Din." *News Click.* https://newsclick.in/glimpses-four-years-modis-achche-din.

Varma, S. 2019. "Agri workers' wages grew just 3% per year during Modi rule." *News Click.* https://www.newsclick.in/agri-workers-wages-grew-just-3-year-under-modi-rule.

Varshney, A. 1993. "Self-limited empowerment: Democracy, economic development and rural India." *Journal of Development Studies* 29, no.4: 177–215.

Varshney, A. 1994/1998. *Democracy, development and the countryside: Urban rural struggles in India.* Cambridge: Cambridge University Press.

Vasudevan, R. 2008. "Accumulation by dispossession in India." *Econmomic and Political Weekly* 43, no. 11: 41–43.

Velaskar, P. 2016. "Theorising the interaction of caste, class and gender: A feminist sociological approach." *Contributions to Indian Sociology* 50, no. 3: 389–414.

Veltmeyer, H. 1997. "New social movements in Latin America." *Journal of Peasant Studies* 25, no. 1: 139–169.

Veltmeyer, H., Petras, J., and Vieux, S. 1997. *Neoliberalism and class conflict in Latin America: A comparative perspective on the political economy of structural adjustment.* New York: St. Martin's Press.

Verma, H.S. 2005. *The OBCs and the ruling classes in India.* Jaipur: Rawat Publications.

Veron, R., Williams, G., Corbridge, S., and Srivastava, M. 2006. "Decentralized Corruption or Corrupt Decentralization? Community Monitoring of Poverty-alleviation Schemes in Eastern India." *World Development* 34, no. 11: 1922–1941.

Vicol, M. 2019. "Potatoes, Petty Commodity Producers and Livelihoods: Contract farming and agrarian change in Maharashtra, India." *Journal of Agrarian Change* 19, no. 1: 135–161.

Vidyasagar, K. 2005. *Communist politics in India: Struggle for survival.* Delhi: Academic Excellence.

Vidyasagar, R. 1999. "New agrarianism and the challenges of the left." In *Class formation and political transformation in post-colonial India,* ed. T. Sathyamurthy, 202–237. Delhi: Oxford University Press.

Vijayabaskar, M., and Menon, A. 2018. "Dispossession by neglect: Agricultural land sales in southern India." *Journal of Agrarian Change* 18, no. 3: 571–587.

Vogel, L. 2014. *Marxism and social oppression.* Leiden/Boston: Brill.

BIBLIOGRAPHY

Volodin, A. 2018. "The logic of directed development in postcolonial India." *Herald of the Russian Academy of Sciences* 88, no. 1: 96–103.

Vyas, V.S., and Bhargava, P. 1995. "Public intervention for poverty alleviation." *Economic and Political Weekly* 30, no. 41/42: 559–2561, 2563–2565, 2567–2569, 2571–2572.

Walker, K. 2008. "Neoliberalism on the ground in rural India: predatory growth, agrarian crisis, internal colonization, and the intensification of class struggle." *Journal of Peasant Studies* 35, no. 4: 557–620.

Wallace, H.S. 2017. "American Fascism, in 1944 and Today." *The New York Times.* https://www.nytimes.com/2017/05/12/opinion/american-fascism-trump.html.

Watts, M. 1996. "Development III: The global agrofood system and late twentieth-century development, (or Kautsky redux)." *Progress in Human Geography*, 20, no. 2: 230–245.

Webster, N. 1990. "Agrarian relations in Burdwan District, West Bengal: From the economics of Green Revolution to the politics of Panchayat Raj." *Journal of Contemporary Asia* 20, no. 2: 177–211.

Weeks, J. 1981. *Capital and exploitation.* Princeton: Princeton University Press.

Weeks, P. 1992. "Fish and people: Aquaculture and the social sciences." *Society & Natural Resources* 5, no. 4: 345–357.

Whitehead, J. 2007. "Hegemony and the decline of the Narmada Bachao Andolan in Gujarat, 1998–2001." *Critical Asian Studies* 39, no. 3: 399–421.

Whitehead, J. 2010. *Development and dispossession in the Narmada Valley.* Delhi: Pearson.

Wickremasinghe, N., and Jones, K. 2004. "India: Stalinists to promote Congress power bid." *World Socialist Web Site.* http://www.wsws.org/en/articles/2004/05/ind-m13.html.

Williams, G. 2004. "Evaluating participatory development: Tyranny, power and (re-) politicisation." *Third World Quarterly* 25, no. 3: 557–578.

Williams, M. 2009. *The roots of participatory democracy: Democratic communists in South Africa and Kerala, India.* New York: Palgrave Macmillan.

Wilson, K. 1999. "Patterns of accumulation and struggles of rural labour: Some aspects of agrarian change in central Bihar." *Journal of Peasant Studies* 26, no. 2–3: 316–354.

Witsoe, J. 2011. "Corruption as power: Caste and the political imagination of the postcolonial state." American Ethnologist 38, no. 11: 73–85.

Wood, E. 1995. *Democracy against capitalism.* New York: Cambridge University Press.

Wood, E. 1997. "The non-history of capitalism." *Historical Materialism* 1, no. 1: 5–21.

Wood, E. 2003. *The empire of capital.* Delhi: Leftword.

Wood, E. 2007. "A reply to critics." *Historical Materialism* 15: 143–170.

World Bank. 1997. *India: Achievements and challenges in reducing poverty.* The World Bank, Washington.

World Bank. 2007. *World development report: Agriculture for development.* The International Bank for Reconstruction and Development/The World Bank, Washington.

World Economic Forum. 2018. "The inclusive development index." *World Economic Forum.* http://www3.weforum.org/docs/WEF_Forum_IncGrwth_2018.pdf.

Wright, E. 1995. "The class analysis of poverty." *International Journal of Health Services* 25, no. 1: 85–100.

Wright, E. 2015. *Understanding class.* London: Verso.

Yapa, L.S. 1979. "Ecopolitical economy of the green revolution." *Professional Geographer* 31, no. 4: 371–376.

Yapa, L.S. 1993. "What are improved seeds: An epistemology of improved seeds." *Economic Geography* 69, no. 3: 254–273.

Yapa, L.S. 1996. "What causes poverty? A postmodern view." *Annals of the Association of American Geographers* 86, no. 4: 707–728.

Yechury, S. 1993. "Communalism, religion and Marxism." *The Marxist* 10, no. 4; 11, no. 1.

Yuval, N.H. 2018. *21 lessons for the 21st century.* London: Jonathan Cape.

Zizek, S. 2008. *Violence.* New York: Picador.

Index

Keywords below include concepts that reflect social processes at a more general level and in the Indian context.

aboriginal 89, 146, 153, 158, 222–24, 305, 324, 326, 328–29, 333, 340, 364, 368, 487, 546

absolute surplus value 6, 77, 79, 81–82, 107, 115, 117 *see also* Surplus value

abstraction 4, 18, 27, 36, 46–48, 50, 199, 256, 408, 468 *see also* Dialectics

achhe din (good days) 13, 347, 350, 365, 368, 371–72, 510–11, 550, 560

advanced capitalism 78, 98, 105, 107, 110, 114, 127, 167, 410, 519, 527, 532 *see also* Capitalism

advanced countries 7–8, 14, 65, 96, 107–109, 112, 149–50, 159, 161–63, 168–69, 174, 206, 208, 236, 246, 265, 276, 376, 377, 380, 381, 398–99, 410, 469, 477, 512, 518, 523–24, 526, 528, 530, 533, 566 *see also* Imperialism

advanced workers. *See* Class consciousness

Agamben, G. 340, 546

Agarwala, R. 2–3, 22, 25, 28–31, 38, 41–42, 58, 258

Agitation. *See* Political movement

agrarian class differentiation. *See* Class differentiation, Polarization

agrarian crisis 15, 165, 289, 359, 371, 398, 404, 489, 492, 504, 531, 550

agrarian question 33, 48, 75, 80, 83, 85, 117, 138, 163–65, 169, 173, 177, 257, 236, 247, 272, 286, 289, 291–92, 326, 530–31, 571

agribusiness 136, 164, 211, 230, 256, 261, 264–265, 296, 430, 531, 574

agriculture 7–9, 17, 38, 44, 50–52, 65, 67, 70–72, 75, 80–83, 86–94, 97, 103–4, 136–38, 165, 168–69, 172–75, 177–79, 182, 185–86, 192, 194, 202–7, 213–15, 220–24, 236, 246–47, 249, 255, 265, 271, 277, 289, 297, 301–2, 305, 360, 367, 535–36 *see also* Aquaculture, Farmers, Agrarian question, New agriculture

Ahmad, A. 381, 388–89, 408, 414–15, 419, 432, 435, 439–40, 447, 450, 456

alienation 60, 276, 407–8, 417, 444, 501

Aligarh Muslim University 367

alliance 130, 148, 150, 164, 329, 332, 345, 380, 386, 388, 390–92, 462, 465, 469, 472, 483, 486, 493, 497–500, 513, 549, 564, 567, 573

allies. *See* Alliance, Temporary revolutionary compromise

Ambani 49, 135, 353, 427

Ambedkar, B. 443, 364

ancient India 407, 411, 429, 433, 464

Andhra Pradesh 82, 85–86, 89–90, 195–98, 211, 298, 300–1, 303, 326, 328–29, 336, 425–26, 488

antagonism 5, 14, 33, 114, 120, 123, 266, 323, 335, 339, 411, 458, 506, 557 *see also* Contradiction

anti-capitalism 116, 155, 244, 308–9, 345, 427, 453, 489, 499, 509, 527, 530, 549, 559

anti-colonial struggle 149, 235, 243–44, 388–89, 450, 515

cross-class 284

anti-communism 387, 425, 455, 555–56

anti-fascism/communalism 513, 563

anti-imperialism 117, 155, 163, 165, 244, 283, 450, 530–31

anti-terror laws. *See* Repression by the state

April Theses 475, 515, 566

aquaculture 9, 18, 32, 34, 138, 175, 203–6, 209–31, 536–38, 540 *see also* Shrimp culture

aqua-labor. *See* Labor

Argumentative Indian 27

Aristotle 307–8

Asia-Pacific region 435

Assam 82, 193, 195, 198, 303, 426, 488

assets *see also* Wealth, Inputs, Property 29–31, 38, 50, 52, 119, 142, 144, 197–98, 290, 293, 321, 328–29, 342, 355

Association for Democratic Reforms 355

austerity 137–38, 167, 465 *see also* Neoliberalism

INDEX

authoritarianism   15, 160, 164, 276, 378–81, 384, 386, 412, 418, 439, 445, 451, 458, 511, 553, 557, 560
   Bonapartist   379, 384, 439
Ayodhya   368, 390, 442–43

Babri Masjid   390, 440, 442–43, 446 *see also* Communalism
Backward Classes   257, 314, 367, 396 *see also* Caste
Banaji, J.   68–69, 72–73, 78, 97–104, 376, 388, 436, 447, 488
Banerjee, S.   156, 284, 289, 301–5, 309–10, 322, 326, 333, 471
banks   47, 141, 147, 214, 217, 289, 350–51, 356–57, 434 *see also* Financial
Bannerji, H.   35, 231, 446, 559
Bardhan, P.   9, 34, 74, 126, 134, 234, 248, 251–52, 268
belief   7, 124, 161, 222, 244, 252–53, 266, 275, 410–11, 416, 432–33 *see also* Consciousness
Bengal Peasant Conference   301
Bernstein, H.   3, 23, 25, 34
Beteille, A.   2, 22, 24–27, 32, 38, 59, 241, 518
Bhaduri, A.   24, 33, 68–73, 75, 105, 242, 521
Bharti group (of companies)   427
Bhattacharya, D.   492
Bidwai, P.   66, 471
big business. *See* Bourgeoisie, Monopolies, Business houses
Bigul Kishan   302
Bihar   193, 195–96, 198, 290, 300–1, 303, 328–29, 332, 334–35, 425–26, 456, 484, 488
biological aspects of production. *See* Biophysical aspects of production
biophysical aspects of production   9, 32, 34, 138, 175, 183, 210–15, 219, 221–25, 228–29, 535–39 *See also* Workplace, Nature-dependent production
biotechnology. *See* Technology
BJD (Biju Janata Dal)   484, 486
BJP (Bharatiya Janata Party)   13–14, 349, 358, 361–62, 366–68, 370–71, 375–76, 386–95, 420–34, 436–44, 446–52, 455–56, 458, 460, 483–84, 486–89, 491, 493–94, 503–11, 514, 552–60, 564 *see also* Communalism, Fascistic tendencies

demagogy of   160, 421, 430–32, 448, 455–56
contradictions of   450–52
BJP government   19, 145, 348, 350, 353–54, 357–60, 364–69, 372–75, 391, 436, 552, 557–58
   record of   348, 360, 367, 373–75, 436, 552
   pro-business character of   353, 355, 437, 449, 470
black money   13, 347, 354, 356, 431, 434 *see also* Corruption
Bolshevik Leninist Party of India   475
Bolshevik Party   497
Bombay Plan   236, 243–45, 388, 452, 555
Bose, S.   443
bourgeois economics   160, 270, 451, 460, 507, 558
bourgeoisie *see also* Capitalist class, Business houses, Ruling class
   big,   114, 126, 133, 136, 146–49, 236–37, 243, 246, 278, 299, 327, 350–51, 386, 388, 399, 400, 410, 412, 427, 453, 485, 493, 505, 510, 524, 560
   national   149, 155, 306, 309
   post-colonial   420, 442
   progressive   265, 403
   urban   34, 165, 178, 181, 243, 246, 248–51, 254–56, 294, 332, 519
bourgeois system/society   15, 281, 305, 346, 377, 379, 408, 418, 420, 424, 451–52, 476–77, 480, 507–8, 553, 558–59, 561
Brahmin   34, 46, 53, 55, 56, 57 *see also* Caste
Brass, T.   24, 39, 53, 61, 72–73, 92, 177, 189, 256, 261, 265
Brenner debate   66 *see also* Capitalism
BSP (Bahujan Samaj Party)   484, 486
Buddhism   406, 417, 464
built environment   96, 111, 145–47, 524 *see also* Geographical space
bureaucracy   237, 248, 253–54, 279, 293 *see also* State elite
business class. *See* Bourgeoisie
business climate   60, 123, 161, 223, 350, 357, 391, 405, 420, 427, 505, 528
businesses   44, 74, 95, 97, 110, 114, 117, 121–22, 131–36, 145–51, 162–63, 200, 216, 222, 243–46, 250, 252, 264, 280, 292, 321, 330, 332, 339, 350–354, 357–61, 364, 371–74, 380, 399–401, 429, 432, 455, 478, 485, 510, 523–24, 529, 534, 541, 545, 551,

INDEX

633

556, 560 *see also* Capitalism, Bourgeoisie
regulation of. *See* State control over economy
small 56, 91, 93, 124, 137, 187, 192, 199, 214, 292, 358, 360 *see also* Petty bourgeoisie
business houses. *See* Bourgeoisie
Byres, T. 3, 24, 126, 169, 176–78, 205, 242

capital 9–11, 25, 29, 73–74, 76–90, 96–106, 110–14, 118–21, 125–28, 131–33, 136, 139, 143, 147–53, 162, 186, 201, 206–10, 226, 242–43, 251, 257–58, 263–65, 281, 288, 292, 295–97, 307, 380, 401, 428–31, 453, 469, 520–26, 529, 537, 542, 556, 571 *see also* Global capital
  foreign 123, 128, 131–33, 136, 148–49, 250, 276, 281, 296–97, 380, 542 *see also* Global capital
  imperialist. *See* Imperialism
  mercantile form of. *See* Mercantile capital
  movement of 88, 123, 137, 166, 452, 532, 555
  provincial 487 *see also* Scale
  regional 504, 270, 485, 493
  relation of labor to. *See* Capitalism, Labor, Class
  rural, or ruralization of 48, 242, 249, 25
  switching of 71, 110–11, 114, 211, 524–25
  urban, or urbanization of 11, 48, 138, 242, 249, 375
capital accumulation 1, 28, 39, 46, 52–53, 67–68, 74–75, 79, 93, 96–99, 104–5, 118–21, 129, 133, 136–37, 143–46, 149, 152, 158, 186–87, 189, 191, 206–8, 210, 245–46, 250, 254, 266–68, 271, 281, 320–21, 379, 469–70, 515–16, 518, 521, 526, 571 *see also* Investment
capitalism 1, 2–10, 13–14, 17–19, 26, 35–40, 45–48, 50–55, 59, 61–69, 71–80, 83–84, 88, 99–118, 120–23, 129–30, 134–35, 139, 154–58, 165–67, 182–87, 206, 223–24, 230, 236, 240, 243–47, 251–53, 264–65, 292–93, 298, 305–11, 317, 319, 338, 344, 353, 377, 380–83, 396–404, 413–18, 423–24, 431, 450–55, 458, 467–70, 478–79, 500–2, 506–8, 511, 514–34, 531, 544, 553, 561, 564–68, 572 *see also* Global capitalism
  agrarian. *See* Agrarian question

  backward/peripheral 17, 66, 80, 85, 128, 297, 356, 388, 297, 399, 418, 423, 424, 452, 522–23, 553
  globalizing. *See* Global, International
  historical development of 39, 69–70, 80, 110–11, 119, 122, 161, 380, 469, 515, 525, 528, 530 *see also* Transition to real subsumption
  humane form of 114, 162, 527–29
  low-wage 217, 227, 231, 537
  restrictive concept of 105, 167, 519, 532
capitalism as subsumption of wage labor. *See* Subsumption of wage labor
capitalists' associations/institutions 12, 15, 60, 152–53, 402–3, 428
capitalist class 5–6, 9–12, 15–16, 29, 33–36, 39–49, 50–57, 60–69, 72–73, 76–82, 91–92, 95, 98–101, 104–22, 124, 127, 130–35, 142, 144–58, 160–65, 173, 186, 191, 200–1, 205, 209, 225–29, 234–37, 242–56, 266, 270, 276–81, 284, 292–95, 303–12, 315, 325, 338, 344–45, 348–51, 353–57, 373–74, 378, 381–84, 389, 391, 401, 405, 420–31, 434, 438, 441, 449–58, 466–67, 470, 474, 478, 489–90, 495–98, 503–10, 515, 520–29, 533–37, 541–42, 550–51, 555–59, 567, 571 *see also* Ruling class, Business houses
  basic interests of the 50, 152, 166, 280, 479, 482, 532, 541
capitalist class relations. *See* Capitalist class
capitalist crisis 5, 14, 25, 58, 63, 82, 107, 111, 119, 121, 127, 146, 208, 264, 345, 383, 395, 402, 412, 418, 452, 461, 483, 524, 528, 550, 553 *see also* Capitalist accumulation
capitalist development 7, 72–75, 104–6, 109, 113–15, 122–24, 159, 170, 230, 252, 278, 280, 327–28, 422–24, 431, 520, 523, 527 *see also* Industrialization, Development
  belated 36, 500
  state-assisted/dirigiste 127–28, 130–34, 155, 157, 243, 262, 278, 389–90, 461
capitalist economy, global. *See* Capitalism
capitalist exploitation. *See* Exploitation
capitalist production 8, 67–69, 71, 76–77, 81, 97, 102, 105–6, 111, 114, 397, 508, 525, 559
capitalist profit. *See* Exploitation, Profit
Capital volume 1 17, 65, 76, 78, 100, 121, 209, 298, 307, 535, 537 *see also* Marx

INDEX

caste 2, 11, 27–29, 35–36, 39, 42, 47–48, 55–57, 59, 62, 90, 164–65, 205, 218, 238–41, 261–62, 268–70, 286, 289–91, 312–15, 322, 327–29, 333, 339, 362–64, 367–68, 405, 410, 440, 464, 468, 492, 509–13, 530–31, 558–63
   capitalism/class and 47, 57, 239, 367, 439
   gender and 47, 55–56, 61, 250, 280, 290–91, 304, 313, 436, 517, 519, 540
   higher/upper 13, 36, 53, 55, 57, 270, 290, 313, 314, 325, 329, 332, 338, 362, 367–68, 371, 376, 432, 439, 544
   low/lower 35, 36, 55, 58, 205, 253, 257, 268, 270, 274, 289–91, 304, 313, 328, 329, 332, 338, 340, 436–37, 511, 517, 544–46
   middle 94–95, 236, 270, 335, 396
   scheduled 164, 286, 313, 363, 436, 472–74, 531
Catholicism 396 *see also* Marxist theory, Religion
Central Bureau of Investigation in India 451
central government 128, 148, 237, 252, 264, 267, 276, 302, 342, 354, 369 *see also* State form
Chakrabarti, A. 2, 26, 28–29, 34, 42, 69, 241, 335, 471, 492
Chandra, B. 3, 25, 67, 236, 243–44, 389, 394
Chandrasekhar, C. 126, 134, 143, 255, 492
Charu M. 301, 326, 346
Chatterjee, P. 10, 28, 239, 275–76, 398
Chattopadhyay, P. 68, 74–75, 255
Chibber, V. 10, 24, 41, 234–36, 245, 268, 380, 421, 528
child labor/worker 92, 206, 213–14, 219, 226, 231, 287, 462, 537, 539
children 42, 45, 55, 58, 213, 219–22, 224–26, 228–29, 290–91, 343–44, 360, 362, 466–67, 538–39, 548 *see also* Child labor
Chilika lake in Odisha 205, 211–12, 218, 261
China 26, 97, 104, 127, 129, 146, 157, 230, 276, 301, 307, 429, 435, 462
Christians 329, 338, 371, 396, 434, 406, 440, 449, 460, 544
cities 28, 37–38, 51, 54, 60, 120, 138, 142, 146–48, 216, 218, 231, 272, 303, 307–8, 341–42 *see also* Urban
   big 145–47, 362, 375, 447, 487, 552, 573
   global 120

citizens 56, 237–39, 316, 318, 331, 385, 387–89, 451, 508–9, 511, 552, 559, 561
city-region 148, 573 *see also* Urban, Rural
civil society 25, 30–31, 32–34, 138, 223, 239, 274, 308, 346, 395, 439, 574 *see also* NGO
civil society activism 154, 159, 324, 361, 491 *see also* Political movement, NGO
class analysis 2–5, 10–11, 17–63, 108, 112, 144, 146, 159, 163–165, 186–87, 190, 200, 217, 225, 233–36, 239–40, 243, 250–52, 265, 268–69, 273, 276, 280, 284, 299, 304–5, 309, 314–15, 321, 329, 338, 340, 416, 446, 517–18, 523, 530, 534, 540–41, 544–45, 567
class antagonisms/contradiction/conflict 4, 33, 42, 136, 242, 249, 265, 273, 495, 548, 568
class coalition 243, 247, 249, 251–54, 301, 327, 367, 380, 393, 513, 530, 563 *see also* Alliance
class consciousness 3, 24, 26, 33, 58–59, 206, 227, 258, 309, 311–13, 333–34, 414, 423, 455, 465, 473–74, 477–78, 483, 493, 499, 501–2, 537, 555, 558, 562, 565 *see also* Consciousness, Trade union consciousness
   bourgeois 41, 156, 223, 227, 252, 279, 405, 537
   workers' 223, 464, 474, 483, 491, 511, 515, 561, 563, 566, 568, 569
class differentiation 37, 39–41, 49–53, 58, 63, 72, 84, 90, 107–9, 115, 170, 183, 187, 251, 260, 305, 504, 518 *see also* Polarization, TCPH
class(es) 1–6, 9–11, 15, 19–64, 122, 130, 137–38, 150, 154–55, 160, 202–4, 209, 234–43, 247–51, 254–57, 262, 267–71, 274, 278, 282–84, 289, 291–95, 314–15, 319–20, 325–27, 331, 344–45, 373–74, 377–80, 385–87, 415–16, 419, 423, 465, 498–502, 513, 517–20, 554, 561
   basic 16, 85, 398, 460, 465, 480, 483, 507, 512–13, 522, 562–64
classes, exploited. *See* Classes, working
classes, exploiting/dominant. *See* Classes, propertied
classes, propertied 2, 5, 9, 12, 18, 25, 29, 33–34, 43–44, 49–53, 57–68, 71–74, 79–80, 85–86, 90–92, 94–95, 99–107, 110–11,

INDEX

121–22, 134, 152–53, 164, 177–78, 185–88,
190–91, 213–15, 217–23, 226–29, 233–36,
242–51, 254–70, 273, 275, 281, 283–84,
288, 292, 295, 312, 319–21, 326, 330–40,
342–45, 353, 357, 377–78, 389–91,
398–99, 401–05, 408–10, 412, 416–18, 421,
427–28, 446, 449, 451–52, 456, 469–70,
480–81, 498, 505–08, 512, 520–30,
537–39, 544–48, 547–49, 553, 558–64, 571
classes, working   2–3, 5, 10–13, 25–26, 33, 37,
44–45, 48, 52–53, 57–60, 63, 114–16, 122,
141, 151, 155–58, 210, 215, 224–25, 228,
242, 250, 257, 270, 274, 282–83, 290, 296,
306, 308–13, 320, 345–47, 353, 357,
380–81, 399–400, 412–18, 453–54, 456,
494–95, 498–99, 500–3, 527, 538–43,
546–49, 553, 562–63 *see also* Exploited,
Worker, Labor, Lower classes
class exploitation. *See* Exploitation,
Inequality, Private property
class formation   25, 42, 58–59, 231, 273
class-fractions (or class strata)   4–5, 45, 53,
59, 61–62, 258, 319, 413, 430, 439, 469,
498, 500, 513, 518, 563
class interests   2, 11, 26, 30–31, 34, 41–43, 94,
160, 240, 242, 243, 251, 256, 264, 267,
294–95, 330, 332, 421, 405, 445, 456, 458,
470, 498, 505
classism   280, 299, 540
class-less. *See* Socialism
class polarization   3, 24, 32, 36–38, 50, 61, 518–19
see also Class differentiation, TCPH
class politics   9, 23, 25, 27, 37, 42–43, 52,
58–60, 62, 115, 164, 206, 234, 257, 269,
273, 286, 314–15, 396, 405, 456, 479, 90,
491, 519, 527, 531, 543, 568
class power   121, 127, 162, 186, 189, 191, 319,
529, 542
class processes. *See* Class relations,
Exploitation
class project   14, 60, 122, 129, 138–39, 397, 451,
507, 558
class relations   4–6, 8–11, 29–31, 35–39,
43–45, 48–63, 74–75, 108, 113–14, 183,
206, 223, 231–33, 236–41, 245, 253–55,
263, 279–81, 288–91, 294, 315, 396–97,
445, 454, 515–23, 540–41, 566–67 *see
also* Class mechanisms, Production
relations

class rule. *See* Class society
class society   4, 12–13, 19, 34, 36, 38, 41, 46, 48,
54–55, 58, 62, 63, 266, 282, 290, 310, 314,
319–20, 341, 343–44, 377–78, 396, 399,
408, 410, 411, 454, 477, 505, 517, 507–8,
544–48 *see also* Capitalism
class state. *See* State
class structure. *See* Class relations
class struggle   1–3, 5–6, 11–13, 17–18, 23, 25,
35, 41–43, 58–62, 65, 79–80, 82–90,
93–95, 106–7, 129, 137, 149–52, 155, 183,
187, 191, 208–10, 224, 228, 241–44,
255–75, 281–85, 289–91, 300–3, 309–17,
322, 346, 347, 374, 381, 387, 390, 396,
401–5, 410, 418, 453, 463, 467–68, 476,
479–80, 487, 496–97, 502, 506, 512–13,
516, 519–23, 535, 538, 541–543, 549–50,
554–56, 562–64, 567, 571 *see also* Labor,
Left movement, Naxalite movement,
Peasant movement, Violence
class theory. *See* Class analysis, Primacy of
class over non-class relations, Primacy
of class over productive forces
coercion   34, 39, 73, 91, 244–45, 266–67, 317,
320–21, 354, 401, 426, 429
extra-economic   72–73, 77, 104, 113, 250,
267, 307, 317, 327, 332, 399, 526
colonialism   8, 81, 128, 202, 240, 243, 246,
274–78, 281, 283, 294, 416, 426, 440, 450,
492, 542, 547
combined development. *See* Uneven
development
commodities   36–37, 50, 57, 100–4, 111–12,
118–19, 120, 133, 185–86, 203, 224–25,
229–31, 251, 263–64, 277, 296–97, 307,
332, 374, 417, 458, 524–26, 535–36,
539–40, 552, 557
high-value/luxury   8, 137–38, 202, 277
production of   50, 54, 67, 69, 74, 102–3,
109, 111, 120, 520, 525
commoditization   144, 170, 314
commodity fetishism   231, 267, 499, 540, 552
common people   13–15, 50, 124–25, 142–43,
153, 253, 267, 316, 318, 334, 336, 338–40,
345–48, 362, 375–76, 385–86, 397–98,
400–2, 410, 418, 446–48, 455–56,
480–83, 487, 489, 491, 507–11, 544–49,
552–53, 556–62 *see also* Masses, Lower
classes

636 INDEX

commons   49, 52, 96, 109, 138, 162, 261, 264, 316–17, 381, 481, 523, 529 *see also* Property, Dispossession, Primitive accumulation

communal(ism)   14, 108, 153, 159–60, 280, 346–47, 364, 367, 371, 375, 381, 385–96, 405, 408, 411, 415, 418, 423, 426–50, 453, 456–61, 475–790, 505–15, 550–65 *see also* BJP

religious minorities'   426, 505

Hindu   155, 164, 329, 363, 381, 389, 395, 398, 418, 421, 422, 433–36, 440, 444, 458, 484, 530, 552, 561

Hindu-diaspora's   252, 447

communal distortions of history   458, 510, 560, 557

communal-fascism   387, 429, 448, 456, 482, 507, 555, 563–64 *see also* BJP

communal-fascistic forces. *See* Fascistic forces

communal riots/violence/incidents. *See* Violence

communism   14, 16, 129, 234, 244, 308–9, 382, 387, 453, 457, 406, 426–27, 435–40, 455, 466, 459–60, 469, 471, 473, 478, 480, 501–2, 513–15, 555, 559, 565–67 *see also* Left

communist-free India   503

Communist Manifesto   5, 31, 64, 120, 282–83, 324

communist movement. *See* Left movement

communist parties. *See* Left parties

Communist Party of India   88, 114–15, 223, 257, 284, 301, 303, 313, 322, 327, 469–70, 479

Communist party of India (Marxist-Leninist) (Liberation)   114, 261, 291, 293, 303, 326–27, 329, 346, 435, 471

Communist Party of India (Marxist)   115, 156, 223, 257, 267, 301, 303, 392, 469, 471, 479, 491

communists. *See* Communism

community   21, 28, 30, 40, 238, 274, 412, 414–15, 431, 436, 440

Community Development Blocks   212, 272

companies. *See* Businesses

competition   77, 79, 110, 112, 119, 123, 125, 148–49, 155, 161, 268–70, 526, 528

compradore   150, 303 *see also* Class, Imperialism

concept   1, 3, 22–23, 26, 28, 38, 58, 62, 75–76, 102, 104–5, 168, 185, 198, 123, 237–38, 323, 384, 388, 407, 449, 519, 522, 524, 526

conceptualization   12, 17, 19, 29, 40, 72, 74, 98, 117, 161–62, 180, 238, 260, 312, 316, 377, 381, 396, 528

concessions   4, 30, 36, 121, 132, 143, 149, 156–58, 163–64, 221, 249, 258, 263–67, 312–13, 330, 334, 388, 403–5, 416, 436–37, 461–62, 465, 467, 481–82, 512, 514, 529–30, 562, 573 *see also* Reforms

Confederation of Indian Industry   135, 246, 428 *see also* Capitalist associations

conflicts   23, 42, 50, 236, 261, 265, 314, 319, 321, 406, 410, 497–98, 500, 504–6, 574 *see also* Class conflict, Contradiction

Congress   12, 15, 126, 155–56, 266, 284, 353, 358, 367, 387–92, 398, 420–27, 430–32, 436, 441–42, 446, 448, 452, 473, 484–86, 488–89, 493, 504–6, 554–55

Congress-mukt/Congress-free   455, 555

Congress party. *See* Congress

Congress party's similarity with the BJP   420, 452, 554

consciousness   12, 42, 54, 159, 206, 210, 227–28, 231, 311–12, 316, 391, 406, 416, 463, 465, 473, 479, 498–99, 501, 532, 537–40, 558 *see also* Class consciousness, Ideology

communal   394, 396, 428, 552, 565

democratic/democratic-secular   473–74, 483, 486, 513, 563

false   26, 263

trade union   19, 54, 227, 348, 538, 473–74, 483, 538 *see also* Trade union struggle

consent production   322, 324, 333–35, 341, 391, 401–5, 418, 426, 431, 435–36, 538, 545, 554 *see also* Ideology

constitution   153, 247, 322–23, 389, 392, 422

consumption   34, 77, 111, 145, 204, 207–8, 255, 288, 296, 374, 524, 552

contradictions in society   5, 58, 62, 114–15, 126, 130, 136, 161, 182, 233, 273, 278, 340, 345, 399–400, 403, 450–52, 493, 506–8, 528, 546, 550, 573 *see also* Antagonism

Corbridge, S.   170, 237, 296, 332, 389, 396

corporates   279, 354, 361, 374, 551, 416 *see also* Businesses, Capitalist class

INDEX

corruption 139, 143, 147, 151, 163–64, 246, 262, 309, 323, 329, 356, 361, 367, 530 *see also* Black money

courts 41, 133, 146–47, 154, 162, 310, 325, 442–43 *see also* Laws

cows 14, 288, 309, 364, 390, 411, 422, 435 *see also* Hindutva, Communalism

credit 92, 115, 118–19, 128, 176, 214, 288–89, 351 *see also* Loan

crimes 323, 328–30, 335, 342, 362–64, 414–15, 419, 452, 462, 554 *see also* Atrocities against minorities, Violence

crisis 63, 80, 114, 119, 161, 208, 276–81, 380, 383, 386–87, 390, 400, 404, 411, 418, 450–54, 467, 470, 507–8, 528, 553, 556, 558–59, 566 *see also* Agrarian crisis, Capitalist crisis

critique 18, 21, 23, 26, 31, 35, 38–39, 42, 65–66, 72, 74, 154–55, 158, 167, 172–73, 176, 225, 236, 238, 532

Cullenberg, S. 2, 26, 29, 42, 69

cultural turn 10, 237, 525

culture/cultural 2, 14, 19, 22, 29, 63, 96, 109–10, 123–24, 148, 159–61, 206, 237, 248–49, 311, 313, 325, 337–39, 377, 345, 394–96, 411, 415, 427–29, 432–33, 447, 464, 466, 473, 492, 509, 515, 544, 549, 559, 566 *see also* Belief, Consciousness, Discourse

curve of capitalist politics 382–83 *see also* Fascism

Dalits 13–14, 35–36, 46, 53–57, 261, 214, 287, 289–91, 300, 313, 329–31, 334–35, 340, 362–64, 367–70, 375–76, 436, 512–13, 517–18, 546, 562 *see also* Caste, Social oppression

debts 8, 50, 177, 200, 289, 296, 328, 412, 481, 534 *see also* Loan, Interest

Delhi 55, 147, 258, 264, 272, 332, 421, 443, 485

demagogy. *See* BJP

democracy 11, 13, 14–18, 41, 86, 127–28, 136–37, 138, 151, 166, 233, 241, 246, 254, 262, 265–70, 275, 281, 308–12, 315–22, 337–42, 346, 355, 361, 375–91, 397–99, 403–4, 411, 416–17, 422–26, 438, 451–55, 446, 450, 452, 456–57, 461, 465–71, 478, 481, 491–92, 496, 498, 506, 508, 511, 527, 541, 542–45, 550, 555, 559, 563, 567–68, 580

pacifying effect of 318, 345, 549–50

popular 132, 166, 345, 379, 387, 439, 532, 549

reformist 15, 382, 420, 431

democratic question 117, 163–65, 530–31, 569 *see also* Semi-feudalism, Agrarian question

Democracy Index 360, 362

democratic upsurge, second 236

democratic rights 53, 56, 60, 164, 318, 377, 378, 380, 405, 415–16, 423, 451, 458–59, 461, 463–65, 467, 479–80, 482–83, 504–5, 507, 510, 511, 530, 541, 550, 557–58, 560–63 *see also* Oppression, Communalism, Fascism, Minorities

curtailment of 56, 463–64, 483, 512, 561

minorities' 378, 429, 436, 459, 555

threat to 63, 323, 333, 346, 380, 465, 478

democratic values 394, 398–99, 432, 447, 483

demolition of Babri Masjid 390, 421, 442–43 *see also* Violence

demonetization 254, 355–57, 360

deprivation 11, 27–28, 266, 283, 291, 315, 543 *see also* Poverty

deproletarianization 53, 93, 189, 265 *see also* Agrarian question

developed countries. *See* Advanced countries

development, economic 5, 8, 10, 12–14, 19, 47, 49, 61–67, 71, 78, 89, 96–97, 105–8, 114–17, 124, 147–51, 168–70, 175, 202, 224, 235–36, 243–46, 251–52, 264, 268–69, 273–75, 299–301, 329–30, 333–36, 339–41, 347–49, 359, 367–68, 373–74, 408, 415–16, 454–56, 465–66, 489, 492, 517–18, 521–24, 527, 550–52, 571–74 *see also* Industrial development, State

barriers to 46, 52, 64, 66–67, 69–71, 75–76, 82, 106, 112, 114, 134, 183, 198, 200, 223, 247, 250, 273, 490, 517, 520, 521, 524–27

developmental governmentality 339, 545

developmentalist 6, 117, 170, 236

developmentality 252, 339, 545

Development of Capitalism in Russia 51

development of productive forces 62, 64, 66, 69–71, 74–76, 103, 105–6, 113, 116, 294–95, 517, 519–21, 524, 527 *See* Development

development proper vs development on
paper 334
DFID 150
dialectics 9, 11, 35, 54, 134, 161, 256, 283, 292,
383, 395, 450, 477, 480, 517, 528, 530,
532, 535
difference. *See* Social oppression, Caste,
Gender, Women, Children, Aboriginal
direct producers 4–5, 52, 63, 66, 71–73,
75–76, 79, 91, 94–95, 99, 101, 106–7,
249–50, 263–64
discourse 122–25, 159, 165, 252, 321, 323, 406,
432, 440, 446, 526, 531 *see also* Culture,
Ideology
development discourse 225, 239, 252,
339, 432, 536, 545
discrimination 35–36, 265, 289, 309, 327,
333, 339, 408, 464, 482, 486 *see also*
Social oppression
dispossession 3, 28, 34–35, 38–40, 48–52,
56–63, 107–09, 115–16, 121, 127, 137,
152–53, 162, 165, 177, 209, 246, 260, 263,
277–78, 296–98, 339, 398–404, 418, 466,
470, 481, 493, 529, 531, 541–42, 545,
553–54 *see also* Primitive accumulation
accumulation by 39, 52, 262, 518
class analysis and 34, 40
districts 87, 200, 212, 270, 272, 284, 298, 314,
324, 332, 534 *see also* Scale
DMK (Dravida Munnetra Kazhagam) 484
dollar billionaires 144, 354, 356, 489–90
dollar millionaires 141, 257
domination 57, 71, 105, 225, 240, 247, 335,
382, 384, 396, 536, 560
dowry 54, 92, 329, 413 *see also* Gender,
Women
Dreze, J. 173, 269, 290
Dumari village in Bihar's Naxalite
region 334–35

East Asia 273
ecological. *See* environmental issues, Natural
resources, Nature-dependent
production, Political ecology
economic concessions. *See* Reforms
economic growth. *See* Growth
economic inequality. *See* Inequality
economic policies 60, 93, 375, 422–23,
426–28, 431, 483, 486, 489, 552 *see also*
Government Policies

progressive 141, 432, 487, 491
economic reforms. *See* Neoliberalism
economics 9, 22, 233, 251, 299
economy 5, 10, 40, 45, 87, 119, 121, 135, 142,
144, 187–88, 230, 434, 437, 463, 465,
517–18, 520, 522, 540, 571
education 42, 92, 125, 134, 142–43, 159, 217,
238, 248, 251–53, 269–70, 328, 341, 345,
349, 426, 476, 479–82, 510–11, 550, 552,
560, 564–65
institutions of 266, 299, 429, 441
election 13, 20, 92, 127–28, 130, 137, 143, 152,
155–57, 266–69, 272, 347, 358, 360, 362,
365–67, 370–71, 391–94, 421, 425–31,
437, 440–41, 447, 458, 464, 472–74,
479–93, 497, 500, 501, 505, 511, 514, 551,
563, 557, 559, 561–64
first-past-the-post 491
election commission 421, 472, 485 *see also*
State agencies
election funding, secretive 60, 349, 354, 361
see also Election, Corruption
election market 432, 452, 455, 458, 554, 557
electoral. *See* electoral
electricity 136, 312, 349, 374–75, 403, 411, 55
elites 144, 148, 154, 237, 239, 254, 246–48,
251–52, 281, 317, 319, 338, 362, 396, 446,
542, 546 *see also* State elites
economic 293, 321, 340, 378, 500, 509–10,
560
political 291, 319, 375, 404, 430, 500, 503,
552
emergency
1970s 390, 423
nutritional 145
undeclared 13, 360, 376
employees. *See* Working classes
employers. *See* Propertied class
employment (opportunities) 67, 72, 85–88,
124, 126, 128, 146, 148, 167, 170–71,
174–80, 184, 186–87, 198, 204–5, 217–18,
221, 226, 256–58, 264, 296–97, 358–59,
399, 413–16, 481, 489, 537, 573
insecure 15, 398
non-farm 87, 175, 199, 288, 297, 533, 571
security of 53, 258, 357, 466
employment generation 85, 133, 203, 293,
321, 351, 358, 399–400, 424, 571
Engels, F. 64, 120, 282, 284, 396–97, 406, 409,
466, 476–77, 563, 568–69

INDEX 639

England 79, 95, 97, 260 *see also* United Kingdom

enterprises. *See* Businesses

environmental issues 9, 84, 94, 139, 200, 203–6, 209, 215, 219, 225, 229, 277, 328, 330, 343, 451, 465, 512, 534, 539, 548, 561, 571–73 *see also* Lagoon, Forests, Flood, Land

equality 41, 156, 166, 204, 243, 244, 268, 286, 307, 314, 333, 378, 392, 403–5, 469, 473, 514, 532, 565

capitalism and 130, 156, 473

equal rights 146, 153, 164, 321, 378, 400, 531

ethnicity 11, 23, 28, 63, 220, 225, 228, 241, 261, 280, 289, 297, 386, 408, 416, 455, 536, 538, 541

Euro-centric 208

Europe 66, 80, 111, 113, 208, 211, 380, 408, 515, 525–26

class analytics in 31

colonial-capitalists of 426

fascism in 376

secularism as defined in 389

(transition to) capitalism in 72, 79, 515

everyday life 32, 43, 45, 159, 161, 237, 415, 419, 435, 528, 554, 565–66, 574

exchange 33, 38, 40, 48, 58, 67, 90, 98, 103, 120, 231, 515, 517, 520, 524, 534, 536, 540

exchange-value 110, 120–21

exclusion 23, 28, 314, 398, 519 *see also* Discrimination, Social oppression

Expert group on poverty 193

exploitation 4, 10–12, 15, 29, 39–42, 47, 52–59, 66–70, 76–81, 89, 97–104, 107, 113–14, 137–38, 144–46, 185, 189, 206–10, 215, 225, 234, 240–44, 247–49, 256–57, 268, 271, 289, 294, 297, 305, 308–16, 332, 396, 398, 404, 418, 466–67, 477, 517–19, 524, 541–43, 553–54

capitalist 1, 6, 33, 49, 97, 102, 104, 106, 117, 145, 161, 166, 189, 207, 216, 231, 246, 309, 398, 423, 463, 467, 527–28, 532

index of 32

super- 56, 127, 133, 164, 208, 210, 221, 294, 320, 325, 354, 551, 553 *see also* Fraudulent tricks by capital, Labor

export 1–2, 8, 131, 137–38, 146, 202–5, 207, 210–11, 218, 219, 224–25, 229–30, 235, 255, 261, 277, 297, 535–36, 539, 541 *see also* Globalization, Agribusiness

extra-electoral 16, 156, 269, 303, 460, 479–80, 490, 512–14, 562–63

factories 3, 24, 77, 132, 216, 298, 309, 321, 344, 400, 443, 511–12, 561 *see also* Workplace

families 33, 42, 51, 87, 89, 91, 93, 214–15, 217, 221, 226, 231, 246, 286, 295, 335, 358, 423–24

family labor 32–34, 39, 49, 56, 69–70, 81, 97, 99, 104–5, 116, 120, 141, 173, 176, 184, 216, 286–89, 293, 358, 361

famine 203, 264, 277, 463

Far Left 346, 476, 503, 550, 566 *see also* Left

farm 74, 87, 90, 181, 211–15, 242, 286, 289, 293, 295, 298, 511–12, 561, 571, 573

farmers 17, 70, 81, 87–88, 92–93, 129, 131, 133, 136–37, 151, 177–79, 189, 200, 211–12, 220, 223, 289, 324, 351, 359–60, 366–70, 374, 534 *see also* Agriculture

bullock capitalists as 33

capitalist/commercial 33, 44, 68, 86–87, 136, 170, 175–79, 182, 247, 261, 265, 270, 286, 289, 292, 295

indebted 200, 534

small 174–77, 179–82, 182, 183, 203, 205

Farmers Liberation March 368

farmers' suicide 145, 200, 289, 298, 360, 504, 534 *see also* Debt, Poverty, Agrarian crisis

farming. *See* Agriculture

contract 136, 255

farm inputs. *See* Technology

farm-land. *See* Land

Far Right 346, 394, 439, 550 *see also* Right-wing

fascism 19, 376–88, 392, 395–96, 400, 405, 411–17, 431, 435, 438–39, 444–47, 450, 453–57, 460, 464–65, 469, 471, 477–78, 500–2, 506–8, 512, 514–16, 555–57 *see also* Right-wing, Capitalism, Curve of capitalist politics, Fascistic tendencies

class agency of 380, 419, 453, 554, 555

Marxism and 438, 439, 444, 460

fascism in the Global South 376, 380–81, 395–96

fascistic consciousness/ideology 386, 416, 426, 434–35, 444, 453, 483, 558

fascistic forces/foot-soldiers 1, 13–16, 19, 57, 60, 146, 160, 272, 277, 288, 310, 329, 338, 342, 346–48, 361, 364, 374–78, 384,

640 INDEX

fascistic forces/foot-soldiers (cont.)
386–89, 390, 392, 394, 395, 397, 401,
402–4, 407, 412–16, 418–20, 423, 425–30,
433–37, 438–50, 455–57, 460–61, 464,
467–71, 482–83, 487–88, 489–92, 504–5,
507, 508, 509, 511–15, 541, 544, 546,
548–59, 561, 563–68
fascistic mass-movement. *See* Fascistic forces,
Political techniques of fascistic
movement
fascistic organizations 386–387, 388, 415,
432, 436, 455, 499
fascistic tendencies 2, 13–16, 19–20, 348,
376–77, 380–88, 391–97, 409–21, 427,
429–31, 433–35, 437–39, 447–48,
451–62, 465, 467, 478–80, 484, 500–3,
505–8, 513–19, 553–58, 563–65, 567
communalism and 360, 368, 387, 425,
435–36, 459, 467, 512, 514, 555, 564
capitalist/bourgeois reaction as 43,
178, 311, 381, 387–88, 409, 425, 427,
429–30, 440–41, 447, 483, 489, 494, 511,
560
fatalities of Maoists. *See* Repression by the
state
Fernandes, G. 23, 27–28, 34, 387
fertilizers 93, 136, 168, 174–76, 178, 263, 360
see also Agriculture
feudal 67–69, 78, 104, 163–64, 265, 294, 303,
305, 311, 326, 465, 530–31 *see also*
Semi-feudal
FICCI (Federation of Indian Chambers of
Commerce and Industry) 152–53,
402–3
fight against fascistic tendencies 371, 479,
490, 493, 503, 506, 514, 564
fight against oppression and injustice 42,
62, 156, 165–67, 257–58, 283–84, 291,
303–6, 309–10, 315, 336–40, 342–44, 356,
404, 458–63, 465, 467–69, 473–74,
477–83, 489–90, 493–94, 497, 501–4,
506–16, 531–32, 544–46, 547–50,
559–67, 569 *see also* Political
movement
Financial 119, 129, 133–36, 147, 149, 161, 263,
350, 374, 380, 398, 453, 528, 551 *see also*
Banks
Flaherty, M. 203–5
floods 137, 228, 538 *see also* environment

food 4, 7, 70, 138, 168–69, 173, 175, 178–79,
181–82, 184–85, 205, 207–8, 214–15,
287–88, 292, 294, 298, 334–35, 429 *see
also* Poverty
availability of 179–80, 183–84, 203, 277,
298, 573
government-subsidized 138, 203, 264,
287, 299, 571
Green revolution and 175, 182, 192, 194
prices of 70, 171, 174–75, 178, 183, 287
production of 9, 78, 137, 169, 171, 175, 178,
179, 183, 203, 298
self-sufficiency of 8, 169, 175, 202
food security 137, 198, 481, 574
forced commerce 70, 73 *see also* mercantile
capital
formal subsumption of wage labor. *See*
Subsumption of wage labor
Forward Bloc 471
Foucauldian 252 *see also* Governmentality
freedom 72–73, 89, 131, 166, 256, 266, 320,
343, 360–63, 406–8, 449, 490, 501, 504,
528, 548
free market economics 128, 152, 246, 373,
454–57, 479, 487, 556 *see also*
Neoliberalism
front 84, 197, 311, 431, 483, 489–91, 564
bourgeois-democratic 490

Gandhi, M. (Mohandas) 235, 389, 392,
444
Gandhi, R. 421
Gandhians 310
Gandhian socialism 426
gender 21, 23, 27–29, 35–36, 42, 47, 55–57,
61–62, 89, 92, 104, 175, 212–16, 220–21,
225, 241, 250, 261, 266, 287, 289, 290–91,
313–15, 464, 466, 492, 511, 517, 536, 543
see also Women
generosity/kindness 166, 417 *see also*
Buddhism
geographical space 54, 57–58, 89, 120, 143,
145–47, 149, 238, 268, 270, 273, 282, 284,
297–98, 304, 311, 313–14, 324, 338, 341,
419, 430, 531, 554
geography of capitalist development. *See*
Uneven development
geography of Naxalism. *See* Naxalite areas,
Naxalbari region

INDEX

geography of society and state 1, 24, 51, 68, 84, 87, 96, 104, 111, 124, 129–31, 145–49, 170, 202–23, 228, 230, 241, 252, 256, 257, 270, 282–85, 292, 296–97, 307, 309, 314, 324, 341, 408–9, 414, 422, 447–48, 457, 464, 487, 505, 524, 531, 535, 538, 540, 546 *see also* Rural, Villages

Germany 65, 400, 431, 427, 444, 469–70, 492, 503

Gidwani, V. 3, 23

global 116–17, 120252, 264, 270, 447, 450 *see also* International, Foreign

global capitalism 1, 9, 80, 83–84, 105, 109, 112, 130, 149–53, 160, 162, 165, 203–4, 210, 229, 231, 236, 244, 255, 276, 327, 296–97, 315, 327, 424, 428–30, 487, 493, 523–25, 529, 531, 539, 543

Global Hunger Index 360

globalization 39, 51, 96, 123, 127, 135, 145, 149, 151–52, 166, 229–30, 383, 391 *see also* Global capital, Global capitalism, Export

Global South. *See* Less developed countries, BRICS

GM technology. *See* Technology

God 159, 407–8 *see also* Religion

God of the market. *See* Market fetishism

Godaan 309

Godhra 441 *see also* Communalism

Golwalkar 434 *see also* RSS

goodwill 434, 437 *see also* Generosity

governance 154, 159, 164, 239, 431–32, 448, 455, 508, 531, 556

government 13, 19, 114–16, 134–35, 141, 143–44, 152–54, 156–57, 237, 276–77, 287–89, 321, 347–51, 353–62, 365–66, 368–69, 371, 373–74, 384, 394, 467–68, 479–82, 493, 508, 510–12, 551–52

governmentality 239, 339, 545

Government of India (GOI) 64, 91, 259–61, 267, 286, 289, 298–301, 323

government policies 9, 24, 49, 51, 54, 58, 85, 106–8, 114, 118, 129–32, 136–39, 151, 154, 155, 161–63, 166–67, 175, 202, 218, 228, 242, 247–48, 262–65, 267–72, 275, 277, 291–93, 296, 321, 335, 337, 339, 350, 353–55, 358, 361, 374, 398, 427, 440, 451, 479, 481–82, 493, 501–5, 528–29, 532, 538, 541–42, 551, 556–57 *see also* State, Government, Pro-poor policies

GR (Green Revolution) 7–8, 18, 81–84, 90–92, 103, 169–84, 188–200, 192–97, 202, 264, 291–92, 295, 520, 533–34

Greece 307

Green Revolution. *See* GR

Green Revolution technology. *See* Technology

ground rent 113, 246, 249–50 *see also* Rent, Usury

growth, economic 7, 34, 119, 122–24, 126–28, 135, 137, 139–41, 150–51, 158–60, 163–65, 167–69, 184, 187–89, 197–98, 236, 285, 288, 304, 342, 344, 347, 348, 358–59, 411, 424, 431, 450, 453, 489, 521, 542 *see also* Development

jobless 358, 399

Gujarat 82, 89, 193, 195, 421, 425–27, 436, 440–41, 447, 480, 482, 488, 506

Gupta, A. 10, 131, 137, 237, 239, 261, 281, 315, 320, 331, 337

Gurr, T. 317–18, 337

Habib, I. 56, 406, 438, 447

Haragopal, G. 311, 335

Harriss, J. 3, 23–24, 29, 71, 198–99, 236, 274, 326, 332, 389, 396

Harvey, D. 38, 103, 108, 111, 118–21, 123–25, 127, 145–47, 161–62, 206, 209, 260, 282–83, 523–25, 528–29

Haryana 82, 90, 93–94, 192–96, 198, 426, 488

health 63, 126, 128, 142, 175, 199, 203, 214–16, 229–30, 269–70, 329, 349, 354, 539

hegemony 325, 408, 479, 512, 562 *see also* Consent, Ideology

Heller, P. 28, 41, 87, 195, 257, 268, 271, 387, 471, 503

Herod, A. 206

Herring, R. 2–3, 22, 25, 29–31, 38, 41–42, 58–61, 159, 200, 246, 258, 471, 480, 534, 542

Himachal Pradesh 193, 195–96, 198, 425–26, 488

Hindi-Hindu-Hindustan agenda 346

Hindu communal(ism). *See* Communalism

Hinduism 238–39, 360, 371, 387–89, 394, 406–9, 426, 429, 432–36, 439–41, 443, 446, 448, 455, 504, 510–11, 556, 560 *see also* God, Religion, *Upanishad*

Hindu Mahasabha 450 *see also* RSS

Hindu nation 14, 160, 360–62, 381, 386–88, 376, 387, 396–97, 418, 429, 432, 433, 436, 440, 441, 448–49, 554

Hindu nationalism/nationalist. *See* Hindu nation

Hindu-nationalist government 323, 371, 381, 386

Hindu nationalist party 323, 367, 509, 558, 561 *see also* BJP

Hindu Pakistan 392

Hindu *Rastra* or Hindu state 13, 376, 392, 426, 434, 504

Hindus 55–56, 126, 153, 338, 371, 388–91, 395, 397, 399–400, 410, 421–22, 432–35, 440, 442, 447–49, 456, 509–10, 544, 552, 558

Hindu-spiritual market 429 *see also* Alienation

Hindutva (Hindu supremacy). *See* Communalism

soft 277, 412, 421, 429 *see also* Congress

historical materialism 10, 27, 32, 115, 240, 282, 289

history 12, 39, 46, 55–56, 66, 73, 76, 79, 100, 105, 108–9, 111, 117, 119, 124, 130–31, 168, 171–72, 207, 209, 212, 268, 275, 282–84, 301, 306, 313–16, 322, 333, 339, 381–84, 386, 388, 390–391, 392, 394, 397–98, 409, 423, 433, 438, 421, 441–42, 475–77, 479, 492, 499, 515, 524, 566, 571 *see also* Communal distortion of history

Hitler, A. 388, 427, 439, 444–45, 460, 492

Holloway, J. 338, 544

households. *See* Family

hunger 28, 41, 277, 323, 360, 451, 490 *see also* Poverty, Food

hybrid subsumption 17, 78, 85, 89–91, 95, 100, 107–13, 523, 525–26 *see also* Pre-capitalist, Subsumption of wage labor

ideas about society 1, 5, 57–59, 72, 106, 122, 124–25, 161, 250, 252–53, 280, 282–83, 306–8, 329, 394, 402, 409–10, 435–36, 475, 519, 528 *see also* Ideology, Theory

identity 22–23, 27, 31, 55, 206, 222, 268, 276, 404–5, 408–10, 416, 438, 447, 487 *see also* Religion, Difference

identity politics 164, 263, 268, 289, 391, 403–5, 408–9, 416, 438–39, 530–31, 568

ideological. *See* Ideology

ideology 11, 14, 57, 133, 149, 154, 156, 158, 166, 241, 243, 269, 278, 280, 290, 306, 311, 323, 326, 330, 333, 335–37, 376, 379, 386–87, 389, 394, 395–96, 403, 416, 421, 429–31, 438, 445, 465, 470, 473, 474, 482, 483, 541, 544

illusions 4, 57, 162, 227, 266, 365, 373, 410–11, 444, 446, 509, 529, 537–38 *see also* False consciousness

illusory. *See* illusion

IMF 150, 165, 168, 531 *see also* Capitalists' institutions

immiserization 15, 165, 177, 398, 401, 418, 452, 531, 553–554 *see also* Inequality

imperialism 17, 95–96, 109, 113–15, 128–29, 131, 145, 149–50, 162–65, 215, 230, 235–36, 269, 277, 286, 294–97, 300, 303, 306, 315, 380, 388, 390–92, 418, 424, 428, 446, 448, 450, 456, 462, 487, 479, 506–7, 510, 520–21, 523–27, 529, 531, 543, 553, 560 *see also* International, Global capitalism

imperialist capital. *See* Imperialism

imperialist world-market. *See* Imperialism

Inclusive Development Index 359 *see also* Development

income 1–2, 44, 49, 52, 64–65, 70–71, 111, 114, 120–29, 133–34, 136–43, 148, 159, 172–77, 183, 187–90, 197, 204–5, 224, 243, 247–48, 273, 286–88, 296, 340, 348–49, 359, 371, 399–400, 405, 424–25, 431, 525, 528–30, 546 *see also* Development, Growth

India Aquaculture Authority 211

India Kisan Sangharsh Coordination Committee 368

Indian Administrative Service 159, 252, 287

Indian Express 139, 346, 358

Indian Kisan Sabha 257

Indian mode of production debate 7, 17, 29, 64–69, 71–72, 79, 92, 97, 106, 110, 170, 247, 256, 520, 525

criticisms of 72–76

Indian Penal Code 291, 331

India's Reagan 131, 373, 551

India Trinamool Congress 485

INDEX 643

indigenous   35, 55, 47, 217, 299, 287, 313, 331, 344, 327, 356, 368 *see also* Aboriginal, Social Oppression

Industrial Dispute Act   153 *see also* Trade union struggle

industrialists   54, 131, 141, 156, 449, 465–66 *see also* Bourgeoisie, Industry, Capitalists

industrialization   17, 44, 47, 51, 65, 69, 88, 95, 128, 135, 137, 156, 169, 182, 203, 243, 273, 296, 399, 430, 473 *see also* Capitalist accumulation, Subsumption of wage labor

  export-oriented   229–30

  import-substituting   10, 234

industry   3, 7, 9, 67, 88, 95, 97, 104, 109, 119, 122, 135, 141, 152, 156–58, 186, 191, 203–6, 231, 243, 245, 246, 248, 251, 254, 357, 412, 428, 523, 571, 573

inequality   7, 14–15, 27–30, 40, 50, 60–63, 119, 125–28, 134, 138–42, 148, 150, 154, 160, 166–70, 176, 179–81, 243, 265, 268–69, 279, 320, 340, 354–56, 359, 398, 401, 411, 425, 451, 454, 465, 489, 508, 528, 532, 545, 556

  class and   27, 41, 226, 261, 492, 536

  political   128, 265, 320, 451, 508

inequality in income. *See* Inequality

inequality in wealth. *See* Inequality

informal sector   25, 30, 53–54

infrastructure   34, 141, 144–48, 157, 175, 243, 341, 349 *see also* Built environment

injustice   12, 27–28, 40, 62, 160, 263, 282, 313, 316, 335–36

inputs. *See* Technology, Productive forces

institutions   9, 125, 128, 145, 150, 162, 165, 172, 237, 252, 263, 266, 270, 275, 299, 318, 320, 332, 361, 390, 418, 424, 429, 436, 441, 474, 529, 535, 553, 574 *see also* Imperialist, International institutions, Education, State agencies

Integrated Rural Development Policy (IRDP)   292–93 *see also* Poverty

intellectuals   2–3, 21–28, 31, 37, 40, 59, 65–66, 69, 97, 108, 128, 168, 177, 204, 237, 240, 242, 252, 254, 264, 266, 267, 293, 324, 394–95, 409, 422, 491–92, 512, 518, 525–26, 532, 562 *See* Theory

Left/progressive   14, 376, 447, 471, 482, 491–92, 511, 514, 560, 565, 569

international   9, 66, 75, 124, 130–31, 137, 149, 152–53, 202, 210, 243–44, 407, 428, 438, 468, 475, 518, 521 *See* Global

international capitalist institutions   19, 122, 125, 129, 149, 150, 165, 348, 531

International Socialism   129

intersectionality   3, 27, 28, 29, 35, 291

investment   67–68, 70–71, 74, 81, 92, 94, 110, 122, 128, 147–49, 167, 169, 175, 177, 200, 248, 571, 574 *see also* Capitalist accumulation

Iran   435

Ireland   65

Islamic State   367

Italy   492

IT-related industries   119, 122, 387, 412–13, 447, 529 *see also* Industry, NEP

Jammu and Kashmir   195–96, 198, 426, 442, 440, 488

Japan   65, 210–11, 234, 435, 462

Jharkhand   324, 329

Jharkhand Mukti Morcha (JMM)   484

Jinnah   367

justice   12, 238, 280, 282, 299–300, 304, 310, 312, 316, 318, 325, 328, 333, 315, 336, 548, 550, 552

Karat, P.   421, 426–27, 436–37, 444, 446, 493

Karnataka   82, 195, 198, 425–26, 458, 488

Kautsky, K.   162, 226, 536

Kaviraj, S.   237, 247–48, 252, 279

Kerala   86–88, 186, 193, 195, 198, 262, 269, 271, 480, 482, 488

Keynesianism   6, 117, 130

Khalistani movement   422

Kohli, A.   150, 252, 272, 471

knowledge   26, 136, 150, 170, 190, 253, 463, 559 *see also* Intellectuals, Theory

labor or laborer   5–6, 9, 14–16, 22–25, 28, 30–63, 67–117, 120–21, 132–39, 142, 146–48, 150–58, 169–171, 174–91, 199, 200–232, 244, 256–59, 268, 273, 276, 277, 286–88, 290–97, 305–11, 315, 320, 332, 344–45, 357–60, 373–74, 380–81, 385–87, 398, 401–04, 410, 413–415, 427,

labor or laborer (cont.)
434, 456, 460, 462, 465–68, 471–75, 507, 510–14, 518–29, 533–40, 549, 551, 560–65, 571, 573 *see also* Class, Child labor, Class struggle, Women labor

agricultural/rural   25–26, 37, 67, 81, 87, 103, 133, 175, 189, 218, 251, 256, 273, 287–88, 290–91, 302, 330, 358, 471–72

aqua-   9, 18, 203–4, 220, 225–29, 231–32, 536, 539

balance of power between capital and. *See* Class struggle

capital's relation to   6, 8–9, 79–80, 106–7, 120, 205, 208, 228, 234, 236, 520, 522–23, 535, 538

cheap. *See* Wages

'classes of'   3, 25, 34, 526

Class-conscious. *See* Class consciousness

exploitation of. *See* Exploitation

fraudulent tricks by capital against   215, 220, 226–27, 537

free labor (or double freedom of)   68, 72–73, 99, 113, 307–8

landless. *See* Landless

migrant/footloose. *See* Migrant

technology's relation to   186, 187, 191

unfree   39, 53, 73, 84, 85, 89–91, 93, 98, 100, 110, 226, 247, 257, 265, 268, 287, 297, 305–7, 328, 329, 333, 343, 465, 523, 524, 548, 465

unskilled   129, 131, 139, 208, 524

vulnerable   63, 104, 164, 220, 222, 224, 228, 530, 538 *see also* Social oppression

labor contract   53, 73, 85, 91, 94, 101, 132, 136, 145, 151, 213, 215, 246, 258, 357, 466

short-term   54, 94, 132, 151, 213, 357

labor contractors   206, 256, 343, 357, 548

labor control in the workplace   90, 95, 118, 206, 219, 226, 228, 231, 537, 539

managers/supervisors and   44, 100, 213–16, 220–23, 248, 441, 546

micro-geography and   223

labor geography (labor studies)   206

laboring bodies   149, 208, 210, 217, 225, 573

labor laws   60, 160, 350, 354, 357, 374, 531, 551
see also Reforms, Laws

labor market   73, 79, 87–88, 90, 101, 132, 174, 178, 209, 222, 226, 247, 272, 293, 320, 327, 417, 536

labor metabolic rift (LMR)   207–10, 225–26, 230, 536, 539 *see also* Nature-dependent production

labor power   6, 23, 34, 44, 48–51, 54, 73, 98–104, 112, 117–20, 178, 186, 189, 207–10, 215, 218, 221–22, 227, 229, 242, 244, 251, 256, 267, 287–88, 307, 344, 413, 500, 526, 537, 539–40

reproduction of   186, 207, 571

sale of   74, 98, 120, 258, 291

value of   49, 54, 56, 76, 133, 186, 222, 230, 247, 256, 399

labor process   23, 69, 75–76, 78, 82, 90–95, 98–101, 188–90, 206, 210–11, 214, 219, 228, 257, 265, 539 *see also* Biophysical conditions

labor productivity   1, 6, 64–65, 70–71, 75, 77, 80, 87, 89, 92, 97, 104, 111, 114, 128, 139, 142, 169–70, 186–90, 208–9, 292, 294, 298, 380, 399, 519–23

labor struggles. *See* Trade union struggle, Class struggle

labor surplus. *See* Reserve army of labor

labor unions. *See* Trade unions

Labour Bureau   259–61

lagoon   211, 214, 216–17, 223, 261 *see also* Environmental issues

land   33–34, 52, 66, 70–71, 84–87, 90–94, 115, 133, 136–37, 146, 156, 177, 180, 183, 190–98, 203–4, 242–43, 246, 249–50, 255–56, 277, 286–97, 302, 309, 326–31, 339–41, 431, 434, 465–66, 460 *see also* Environment

land concentration   72, 75, 91, 93, 177, 181, 267, 286–87, 297, 314, 319, 328

land grab. *See* Primitive accumulation, Dispossession

land-hunger   71, 181

landless   25, 33, 44, 67, 71, 90, 180, 183, 264, 286, 289, 295, 297, 309, 326, 332–33, 335, 339

landlord armies   291, 310, 326 *see also* Violence

landlordism. *See* landowners

landlords. *See* Landowners

landowners   29–30, 32–34, 38, 53, 55, 67–72, 87–95, 98, 104, 114–16, 164, 175, 177, 189, 243, 246, 248–51, 256, 265, 269–72, 287, 289, 291–96, 302–5, 321–22, 324–26, 328,

INDEX

330–35, 337–38, 421, 441, 464–65, 469, 470, 485, 490, 494, 519, 527, 531, 544 *see also* Propertied class

capitalist 33, 198, 247, 249, 251, 292, 295, 409, 439, 468, 479

higher caste 57, 93–94, 290–91, 367, 439

semi-feudal 114, 164, 265, 270, 303, 527, 531

land ownership 33, 69, 71, 286, 296

land reforms 30, 54, 85, 115, 137, 188, 195, 198, 243, 247, 251, 264, 268–71, 286, 291–97, 328, 330–31 *see also* Government policies

land-speculation 137

language 28, 124, 128, 304, 313, 337, 394, 473

laws 68–69, 84, 98–99, 109, 112, 128, 151, 154, 168, 268, 324–25, 331, 333, 337–38, 361, 427–30, 441–43, 550

Left 5, 14–16, 19–21, 26, 59, 63, 113–14, 154–58, 163, 167, 223, 262, 271–74, 305, 308, 311, 313, 323, 337, 367–68, 377, 390, 392, 394, 407, 420–21, 423–25, 438, 442, 446, 451–53, 459–64, 467–83, 485–86, 488–94, 496, 498, 500–3, 504–7, 511–16, 519, 544, 554–55, 561–67, 569 *see also* Far Left

electoralism of 474, 566, 568

electoral struggle of 480–83

Marxist criticisms of 304–15, 345, 423, 459, 468–78, 555, 565–69

need for unity within the 311, 477, 479, 497, 501–4, 513, 562–63, 567–68

relative electoral weakness of 461

Left and progressive forces 424, 461, 478, 492, 504, 509, 559

Left culture 162, 477, 529 *see also* Culture

Left Front 88, 156–57, 267, 271, 471–73, 482, 485 *see also* Front

Left intellectuals. *See* Intellectuals

Left-led government 156, 195, 271, 296, 301, 302, 471

Left movement. *See* Left

Left-mukt (left-free) 455, 503, 555

Left organizations 59, 88–89, 272, 301, 377, 509, 559, 555

Left parties 14–15, 26, 42, 59, 86, 88, 114–15, 129, 156, 223, 227, 257, 261, 267–70, 272, 284, 291, 293, 301–3, 305, 308, 313, 322, 326–29, 346, 386, 392, 422, 424, 435, 461,

463, 465, 467, 469–71, 473–75, 477, 479, 480, 484, 489, 491, 493–94, 499–504, 538, 555, 565–68

Left politics. *See* Left movement, Class politics

Left's relative popularity quotient 472–74, 486

Leftwich, A. 254

Left-wing communism 494

Left-wing extremism 323, 330 *see also* Naxalite movement

legislation 42, 151, 235, 294–95, 506 *see also* State, Government policies

legitimacy 151, 267, 271, 274–81, 318, 321–23, 334, 337, 341, 345, 542, 544–45, 550

crisis of 12, 19, 275, 277, 280, 574

legitimacy threat. *See* Legitimacy

Lenin, V. 22, 38, 45, 50–52, 72, 75, 112, 156, 177, 227, 305–6, 311–12, 377–78, 392, 444, 461, 463, 485–86, 492–97, 499–504, 512–15, 562–63, 566

Lerche, J. 3, 25, 28, 72, 85, 90–91, 113

less developed countries 9, 14, 23, 65, 79, 83, 85, 95–96, 108–9, 113–15, 133, 135, 149–53, 159, 169, 162–63, 165, 168, 175, 178, 224, 229–30, 233–36, 245, 250–251, 294, 296, 306, 339, 376, 377, 380–81, 388, 410, 424, 470, 454, 472, 485, 522–24, 529, 535, 536, 539, 540 *see also* Peripheral countries, Global South, BRICS

class character of 163–65 *see also* Imperialism

liberalization 127, 129, 130–31, 133, 135, 137, 151–52, 161, 167, 195, 234, 251, 255, 297, 396, 455, 528 *see also* NEP, Neoliberalism

license-control raj 131

life expectancy 173, 298, 359

Lipton, M. 7–8, 18, 169–89, 192, 196–98, 533

livelihood 15, 101, 112, 137–38, 154, 204–5, 343–44, 396, 398, 479, 548, 553

loans 72, 90, 99, 132, 149–50, 242, 245, 247, 249, 289, 292, 350–51, 358 *see also* Credit, Bank, Financial

write-off of 351–52

local aspects of state and society 8, 12, 16, 30, 32, 43–44, 75, 85, 88–93, 158, 181, 202–3, 216, 218, 220–23, 238, 248–49, 257, 263, 267, 268–70, 272, 276, 287, 296–97, 303, 306, 317, 322–23, 330,

local aspects of state and society (cont.)
332–34, 326, 343, 405, 410, 460, 522, 523, 547, 560, 573 *See* Community Development Blocks, Districts, Geography of society and state

Lokniti   358–59, 367–72

Lok Sabha election   368

loot of society's resources by capitalists   336, 353–54, 415, 353 *see also* Commons

lower classes   2, 4, 11, 41, 163–64, 233, 247–48, 255–56, 262–76, 279, 396–97, 402, 404, 412, 519, 540–44, 546, 550 *see also* Labor, Peasant, Small-scale producer, Classes

lynching. *See* Violence

Luddite movement   87, 229, 539 *see also* Class struggle

lumpenproletarian. *See* Lumpenproletariat

lumpenproletariat   15, 409, 412–13, 415–17, 440, 453, 556 *see also* Fascistic forces

Luxemburg, R.   260, 475, 502, 563

Machinery   79–82, 88, 91–96, 110, 178 *see also* Technology

machines. *See* Machinery

Madhya Pradesh   82, 195, 198, 300–1, 421, 425–26, 433, 488

Maharashtra   200, 534

Make in India. See Industrialization

Malthusianism   7, 18, 173, 180, 182–84, 197, 533 *see also* Population

Mandel, E.   266

Mander, H.   159–60, 279

manufacturing. *See* Industrialization

Maoism. *See* Mao

Maoist movement. *See* Mao, Naxalite movement

Mao, Z.   32, 150, 242, 307

market   14, 38, 40, 49, 67–72, 74, 84, 86, 93, 96, 103, 105, 117–21, 125, 128, 130, 133–34, 136, 139, 144, 149, 159, 161, 167, 174–75, 187–88, 246, 251, 270, 280, 289, 316, 318, 374, 410, 487, 541, 458, 552, 528, 557, 571
    domestic   48, 117, 128, 130, 243, 245, 294–95, 505, 571
    foreign/global   117, 130, 133, 137, 151, 229, 264, 539

market fetishism/idolatry   145, 159

marriages, inter-caste   329

Maruti workers   153, 158

Marx's *Capital*   377

Marx and Engels   64, 120, 282, 284, 312, 396, 406, 409, 418, 476, 553, 569

Marxism   2–3, 7, 10, 16, 19–26, 29–32, 38, 59, 66, 104–5, 108, 181–83, 200, 203, 234–36, 287–89, 300–7, 312, 380, 396–97, 406, 438–39, 460–61, 469, 471, 475–77, 482–84, 494, 503–4, 512, 515, 517–19, 521, 534, 559, 562–69 *see also* Dialectics, Historical materialist, Marxist class analysis
    analytical   10, 134, 234
    post-Marxism   2, 29, 42, 69, 75, 154, 208, 338, 544
    post-modernist. *See* Post-Marxism
    revolutionary   475, 502 *see also* MELLT Marxism
    three streams of   238, 471–78, 503–4

Marxism-Leninism-Maoism   303

Marxist intellectuals. *See* Marxism, Intellectuals

Marxist Left. *See* Marxism

Marxist parties. *See* Left parties

Marxist streams. *See* Marxism

Marxists. *See* Marxism

Marx, K.   22, 42, 58, 65, 72–73, 76–80, 97, 99–107, 110, 201, 207–10, 222, 227, 255, 267, 282–83, 306–7, 312, 320–21, 383, 396–97, 416–18, 454, 461–63, 476–78, 499, 519–20, 535, 537, 553, 563, 568–69

masses   12–15, 41, 49, 57, 59, 114–15, 121–24, 144, 150–53, 163, 166, 210, 248–51, 254, 286, 288–89, 295, 297, 300, 305–6, 311–16, 332, 349–40, 342–45, 373–75, 377–80, 408–9, 432, 437–38, 448–55, 465–70, 480–83, 490–92, 500–15, 529–32, 541, 545–546, 549–68 *see also* Lower classes, Labor, Peasant, Common people, Exploited classes

mass movement   15, 303, 312, 317, 326, 329, 347, 371, 373, 385, 386, 439, 448, 455–56, 487, 502, 551, 556, 562 *see also* Movement

material conditions of life   18, 35, 56–58, 62, 76, 283, 285–87, 294, 300, 304, 307, 311, 314–15, 394, 396, 406–7, 416, 445, 491, 495–96, 504, 519, 543

material interests   30, 53, 57, 122, 231, 266, 439

materialist conception 10, 397, 206–7, 225, 239, 536 *see also* Marxism

mechanization. *See* Technological change

media 19, 125, 131, 252, 348, 438, 441, 444, 446, 510, 560 *see also* Culture, Ideas, Ideology, Discourse, Television

communalizing 349

corporate 444, 455, 556

MELLT Marxism 568, 569

mercantile capital 29, 33, 44, 49, 54, 78, 90, 92, 98–99, 102, 136, 182, 291 *see also* Capital, Capitalism

merchants. *See* Mercantile capital

metabolic rift 5, 9, 63, 203, 207–9, 225, 536 *see also* Environment

middle ages 78, 396

middle class 34, 37, 44–45, 122, 131, 137, 148, 154, 159–60, 304, 314, 337, 381, 385, 387, 389, 412, 427, 431–32, 444, 447, 491, 500, 543–44 *see also* Classes, Professionals, Elites

Mies, M. 92, 231

migrants 104, 202–22, 214, 217, 218, 221–22, 228, 256, 297, 307, 414, 422, 457, 538 *see also* Remittance

military forces 41, 279, 310, 320, 324–25, 332, 335, 412, 414, 440, 442–43, 497 *see also* Repression by the state

minerals 131, 327, 330, 340, 343, 546, 548 *see also* Red corridor, Environmental issues

capitalist extraction of, 47, 309322, 325, 332

minimum wages 30, 258, 287, 293, 310, 320, 330–31, 328, 333, 354, 357 *see also* Wages

Ministry of Agriculture 360

minorities 28, 60, 120, 122, 124, 144, 331–32, 342, 344, 378, 386, 392, 394, 419, 421–22, 426, 428, 436, 438–39, 446, 448, 460–61, 505, 547–49 *see also* Violence, Democratic rights

atrocities against 35, 290–91, 363, 368, 371, 428 *see also* Violence

MNCs 95, 136, 156, 159, 165, 380, 531 *see also* Globalization, Imperialism

mobilization, political 12, 16, 59, 88, 115, 311, 316, 320, 324, 326, 328–29, 331, 340, 345, 368, 439, 441, 456, 458, 460–61, 464–68,

475, 481, 490, 501, 507, 512, 514, 545–46, 549, 561, 564, 568 *see also* Opposition, Class Struggle, Fight, Resistance

mobs. *See* Right-wing mobs

mode of production, dominant 6, 11, 64, 67, 72, 75–78, 82, 92, 97–98, 107, 110, 241, 280, 508, 522–23, 541, 559 *see also* Capitalism

Modi government 353, 354, 355, 358, 359, 363, 365, 367–69, 371, 385, 435, 444, 550

Modi, N. (Narendra) 126, 131, 150, 158, 346–48, 350, 367–68, 372–73, 386, 388, 427–28, 435, 441, 444–47, 455 *see also* BJP

authoritarian personality of 445

Modinomics 373–74, 551 *see also* India's Reagan, Reaganomics

Mohanty, M. 55, 241, 312–13, 338

money 13, 71, 74, 96–97, 100–3, 110–11, 118, 123, 131, 134, 139, 142–44, 146–47, 151, 176, 190, 201, 214–15, 219–20, 245, 292, 293, 347, 353–58, 373, 399, 429–31, 434, 480–81, 487, 520, 524–25 *see also* Black money

moneybags 229, 332, 427, 530 *see also* Capitalists, Bourgeoisie

money lenders/lending 29, 33, 44, 74, 98–99, 110–11, 272, 288, 289, 302, 309, 328, 525 *see also* Usury

monopolies 49, 106, 114, 117–18, 230, 250, 306, 317, 326, 334, 383, 385, 431, 507 *see also* Bourgeoisie

Muslim-dominated Pakistan 433, 511, 561

Muslim immigrants 511, 560

Muslims 35, 56–57, 153, 257, 364, 388, 389, 421–22, 427–28, 431–38, 440–42, 444–45, 447, 449–50, 456, 485–86, 505, 507, 511, 548 *see also* Riots, Right-wing mobs

Left support for. *See* Left

massacre of 338, 541, 544

places of worship of 338, 390, 421, 442–43, 458, 544

myths or mythology 125, 245, 248, 253, 281, 403, 406, 410, 433, 441, 510, 542, 560

NAC (New Agricultural Countries) 8, 202 *see also* New agriculture, NAP

Nagaland 440

NAP (New Agricultural Production) 138, 224, 536

Nathan, D. 257, 273, 290

nation 123–24, 129, 153, 238, 244, 275–77, 280–81, 323–24, 331, 340–42, 354, 385–86, 409, 427, 432–35, 438–39, 441, 448–50, 455–56, 464, 487, 504–5, 510–11, 541–42, 546–47, 554–56 see also Imperialism

oppressed 165, 510, 531, 560

national 16, 34, 43, 75, 106, 117, 135, 152, 157, 181, 203–4, 230, 261, 270, 272, 276, 292, 322, 324, 331, 391, 490, 505, 520, 540, 542, 553 see also Scale

National Commission for Enterprises 264

nationalism 123–25, 262–63, 276, 279, 350, 354, 360, 366, 385, 381, 388, 395, 416, 418, 421, 429, 433, 435, 438, 449, 450, 456, 510, 554, 560, 561

anti-imperialist 435, 450

fascistic 434–35, 450

hyper-, 13, 342, 366, 373, 376, 429, 435, 439, 455, 457, 458, 462, 479, 480, 510, 546, 556–57, 560

imperialist 435

religious 367, 381, 450, 455, 556

secular Arab 435

nationality 11, 241, 313, 403, 561

National Land Reforms Council 264

National Land Reforms Policy 264

National Planning Commission 236

national question 117, 163, 165, 530–31 see also Nationalism, Imperialism

National Rural Employment Guarantee Scheme 137, 264, 293

National Stock Exchange 350

nation of toiling masses 277, 342, 510, 547, 560

natural resources 18, 129, 131, 144, 146, 149, 197, 230, 241, 314, 327, 330, 336, 342, 357, 374, 429, 465–66, 486, 510, 552, 560, 574 see also Environmental issues, Commons

nature-dependent production 84, 202, 207, 209, 219, 225, 228, 536, 538, 571 see also Environmental issues, LMR, Political ecology, Production

depletion of 204, 261, 510, 560

Naxalbari region 12, 284, 301–3, 313, 334, 346

Naxalism 284–85, 298–300, 303, 305, 307, 309–11, 322–24, 335, 337, 339, 342–44, 346, 544–47, 549

Naxalite movement 12, 18–19, 43, 129, 153, 157–58, 269, 284–85, 289–91, 299–316, 319, 321–39, 333–46, 471, 474–75, 518, 543–50 see also Maoist movement

geography of 299, 308, 312, 323, 329, 333, 336, 340, 344, 546, 548 see also Naxalbari region

groups/splits within 299, 304, 306, 308, 311, 312, 319, 326–29

Marxist critique of 304–315, 543

Naxalite development activities as a part of 19, 147, 304, 326–38, 544

Nehru, J.

ideas of 95, 130, 134, 252, 388, 389, 395, 396, 452–53, 555

neoliberal capitalism. See Capitalism, Neoliberalism

neoliberal ideas 125, 131, 143, 150, 152, 159, 236, 373, 431, 508, 551 see also Neoliberality

neoliberalism 1–2, 5–6, 8–9, 15–18, 34, 49–50, 53, 117–19, 121–39, 141–67, 160–64, 166, 211, 217–18, 224, 236, 237, 248, 251, 252, 255, 259, 268, 274–79, 281, 296–97, 305, 374, 391, 398, 420–24, 427, 456, 459, 474, 478, 490, 493, 504, 527–36, 542, 551–52, 573–74

agrarian/rural 8, 18, 135–36, 138, 163, 224, 529, 536, 573–74

deregulated production under 9, 202, 224, 535–36

proponents of 125–26

struggle against 153, 167, 459, 478, 532

neoliberality 165, 531

neoliberalization 127, 148, 150, 154, 157, 277, 328

neoliberal political parties 155, 156, 160

neoliberal socialism 157

neoliberal state. See Neoliberalism

NEP (New Economic Policy) 125–26, 130–32, 134–35, 138–39, 144–45, 147, 149, 151, 154–56, 158, 160–66, 528–31, 535–36 see also Neoliberalism

New Agricultural Countries (NACs). See New agriculture

new agriculture 8, 137–39, 202–3, 224, 255, 277, 297, 536, 573–74

INDEX

new international division of labor   9, 202
NGO   267, 274, 293, 327, 346, 550 *see also*
   Civil society
NICs (Newly Industrialized Countries)   8, 202
Nifty   350
Nilsen, A.   256, 260, 262–63
NIRD   193–96, 198
non-capitalist   49, 63, 69, 75, 108–9, 112–14,
   198, 240, 242, 247, 250, 265, 466, 522,
   524–27
non-class relations   4, 11, 27–28, 35–36, 55,
   59, 61–62, 280, 291, 313, 477, 517–19, 540
   see also Social oppression
non-violence   311, 318, 321, 325 *see also*
   Generosity
North-East India   392
North India   86, 367

objective conditions in society. *See* Material
   conditions
Odisha/Orissa   82–85, 193, 195, 198, 205,
   211–12, 216, 218, 261, 270, 276, 300–3, 327,
   330, 426, 484, 488
officials. *See* State elites
Omvedt, G.   3, 25, 261–62
Oommen, T.   87–88, 170
opposition. *See* Resistance, Class struggle,
   Mobilization
organizations, political   59, 66, 88, 152–53,
   272, 274, 301, 329, 331, 345, 378–79,
   384–87, 453, 493–94, 497, 499, 501, 518,
   549, 555, 561, 565, 574
OXFAM   139, 354, 528

paramilitary forces   60, 146, 324, 336, 338, 451
   see also Repression by the state
parliament   13, 42, 164, 348, 357, 428, 436,
   438, 480, 488, 501, 505
Parthasarathy, G.   175–76
Patel (Sardar Patel)   392, 443
Patnaik, P.   130, 141–44, 218, 255, 278–79, 386,
   388, 449, 492
Patnaik, U.   25, 32–34, 52, 67, 68, 70–74,
   80–81, 92, 93, 105, 111–12, 114, 137, 145,
   169, 170, 173, 179, 198, 203, 215, 224, 273,
   277, 296, 298, 492, 521, 525
peasant/peasantry   3, 23, 38, 53–54, 61, 67,
   70–71, 73, 94, 101, 109, 114–15, 136–38,
   141–42, 150, 158, 177, 198, 236, 245, 260,

286–97, 301–14, 328, 331, 333, 345, 381,
   399–401, 412, 456, 475–76, 479, 486–87,
   500–5, 511, 523, 546, 555, 561–65 *see also*
   Primitive accumulation, Agrarian class
   differentiation, Landowners
   middle   33, 44, 112, 165, 308, 500
   poor   33, 93–94, 155–56, 160, 165, 256–57,
      287–91, 294, 297, 302, 305, 330, 339–40,
      463, 468, 545–46, 571
   rich   33, 256, 265, 270, 295
peasant movement. *See* Class struggle
People's War Group   326 *see also* Naxalite
peripheral capitalism   17, 66, 80, 128, 297,
   388 *see also* Capitalism, Subsumption
   of wage labor
peripheral countries. *See* Less developed
   countries
perspective   14, 17, 38–39, 41, 46, 93, 97, 106,
   109, 136, 149, 155, 158, 192, 195, 197, 236,
   238, 256, 383, 430, 516–17, 520, 523, 569
   see also Theory
petty bourgeois(ie)   15, 44, 58, 78, 112, 128,
   142, 164, 170, 278, 288, 289, 293, 304, 306,
   362, 380–82, 390, 400, 405, 409, 412, 413,
   424, 431, 438–39, 445, 453, 465, 467, 481,
   508, 530, 556, 559, 556, 568 *see also*
   Small-scale producers, Elites, Peasant,
   Middle Class
petty commodity producers   34, 78, 112, 128,
   142, 170, 289, 362, 465, 467, 481, 508, 559,
   568
philosophy   168, 207, 394, 407 *see also*
   Dialectics
Piketty, T.   139–40
Polanyi, K.   374, 551
polarization   3, 24–25, 36–38, 52, 177 *see also*
   Inequality, TCPH
police   267, 270–71, 284, 291, 301–2, 319–21,
   324–25, 329, 330, 332–33, 335–37,
   340–41, 344–45, 379, 428, 436, 442–43,
   453, 463, 544–46, 556, 565 *see also*
   Repression by the state
political culture   310, 360, 471, 509, 558 *see*
   also Culture
political demands   128, 130–32, 138, 178–79,
   186, 255, 258, 286–87, 312–13,
   318, 329–31, 333, 405, 411–14, 465,
   481–82, 494, 497, 512, 562 *see also*
   Mobilization, Class struggle

political demands (cont.)
  difficult/radical   312, 333
  partial   167, 465, 532
  revolutionary/socialist   244, 502
  transitional   465, 481–82, 507, 512, 516, 532, 561, 567, 569
political ecology   205, 225 *see also* Environmental issues
political economists   32, 88, 105, 108, 205, 519, 522, 525–26 *see also* Intellectuals
political economy   11–13, 19–21, 28, 39–41, 51, 118, 169, 182, 200, 208, 225, 239–40, 254–55, 262, 347–48, 376–77, 394–97, 424, 508, 534, 542, 553, 567 *see also* Capitalism, Capitalist accumulation, State
political forces   2, 26, 36, 56, 129, 331, 391, 478, 510, 513, 560, 563, 566
  progressive   83, 424, 451, 454, 492, 509, 559
political indifferentism   42, 476, 563 *see also* Sectarianism
political movement   12, 18, 25, 54, 60–62, 86–87, 123, 132, 165–67, 191, 221–23, 227, 236, 257–58, 262, 268, 274, 282, 300–2, 309, 312–20, 331–32, 336–37, 340–42, 345–47, 379–80, 401, 406, 408, 412, 416, 438, 463, 470, 476–78, 481–82, 477, 494–96, 501, 511–12, 514, 519, 531–32, 545, 547, 552, 562, 564–65 *see also* Fight against oppression, Class struggle, Mobilization
  anti-caste   512, 554, 562, 568
  anti-colonial   420, 443, 444, 450
  anti-fascist   376
  ecological   261, 512, 562
  grassroots   274, 386, 455, 491, 556
  farmers'   39, 368, 476
  people's science   512, 562
political parties   1, 15, 139, 146, 154–56, 159–60, 163–64, 248, 266–69, 272–75, 279, 303, 310–11, 318–19, 361, 366–67, 378, 384–85, 387, 391, 401, 421–26, 429–30, 436, 446–48, 452–55, 458, 461, 471–72, 475, 477, 483, 484–87, 489–91, 493–96, 498, 500–6, 508, 511, 513, 530, 555–57, 563, 567
  bourgeois   60, 129, 155–56, 263, 266–70, 301, 331, 378, 424–25, 446, 458, 480, 493, 498, 502–4, 557

non-BJP   426, 446, 488, 493, 504–5, 567
Left. *See* Left parties
Non-Left parties   387, 391, 446, 491, 493, 501, 567
political power. *See* Power
political practices/relations   5, 14–15, 19, 26, 40, 66, 111, 113, 154, 235, 242, 263, 274, 283, 289, 300, 311, 318, 332, 374, 380, 382, 390, 396, 408, 415, 420, 423, 446, 457, 460, 468, 471, 473, 483, 494, 500, 517, 527, 551, 566 *see also* Politics
political project   166, 380, 426, 444–45, 491, 501, 513, 532, 563
political relations. *See* Political practices
political struggles. *See* Political movement
political system   12, 16, 59, 318, 340, 343, 347, 388, 443, 452, 546–47
political techniques of the fascistic movement   430–49
politicians   92, 143, 147, 326, 151, 244, 246, 250, 253, 262, 292–93, 296, 328–30, 332, 354–55, 361, 428, 440, 509–10, 541, 544, 556, 558, 560
politicism   10, 235, 479
politicization of the masses   268, 331–32, 339, 545
politics   14–16, 21–23, 28, 56, 60–62, 153–54, 262–63, 274, 275, 277, 279, 303, 313, 347–48, 394–97, 477, 404–5, 408–9, 415–18, 422, 432, 438, 471, 496, 507–8, 517, 519, 553–54, 557
  bourgeois   1, 14, 59, 114–15, 155–56, 160, 167, 343, 377, 381–84, 386, 396–98, 408, 420, 427, 451–53, 460–64, 479–80, 482–83, 489–90, 493, 500, 506–8, 532, 533, 554, 564–65, 568
  crisis of   14, 377, 382, 451–52, 454, 475, 506 *see also* Communalism, Fascism
poor people   12, 40, 67, 71, 72, 138, 149, 171, 172, 174–77, 182–84, 187–89, 200, 211, 229, 238, 252, 257, 284–85, 289–93, 298–99, 301, 310, 312, 316, 326–30, 332, 334, 340, 359, 410, 431, 471–74, 546, 539, 574 *see also* Poverty
popular front, national   490
population   36–37, 137–41, 179–80, 183–85, 187–88, 191–92, 196–97, 297–98, 300, 305, 340, 342, 359–60, 363, 398, 411, 413,

417–19, 455–56, 491, 527–29, 533, 546–47, 554 *see also* Malthusianism

population growth 84, 180, 183–84, 186, 191, 196

post-colonial capitalist state 1, 18, 165, 239, 243–46, 275, 277–78, 284–86, 293, 314, 334, 531, 543, 547 *see also* State

post-colonial conditions 36, 128, 130, 139, 172, 208, 238–39, 244, 294, 381, 418, 553

post-modernists 26, 42

POTA (Prevention of Terrorism Act) 324 *see also* Repression

poverty 1, 7, 18, 54, 126, 128–29, 132, 134, 143, 163, 168–76, 179–85, 187–88, 190–200, 215, 245, 274–76, 282–83, 285–89, 291–93, 297–301, 309, 315–16, 339, 359, 360, 454, 510, 530, 532–34, 543, 545, 568, 573–74 *see also* Deprivation, Poor people

poverty reduction 8, 129, 134, 172, 176, 180, 183, 184, 187, 188, 198, 194–99, 224–25, 533, 535

power 10, 28, 60, 79–80, 85–88, 94–96, 103–4, 112, 114, 120–21, 155–57, 162–64, 179–82, 217, 236–39, 247–49, 252–54, 266–73, 279, 318, 331–34, 338, 360, 392–94, 423–24, 430–33, 466, 478–80, 489, 491–93, 504, 520, 525, 528–30, 541–43, 549, 555, 564

power tillers 94–95 *see also* Technology

Prashad, P. 205, 243–44, 246, 471

pre-capitalist relations 56, 67–68, 76, 78, 83, 100, 108–9, 112–13, 240, 257, 294, 295, 410, 522–23, 526 *see also* Hybrid subsumption

pre-formal subsumption of wage labor. *See* Subsumption of wage labor

prices 70, 90, 93, 136–38, 141, 175, 179, 182, 186, 246, 288, 328, 332, 367–69, 526 *see also* Commodities, Market

primacy of class relations over non-class relations 2, 22, 29, 35–36, 55, 61, 474, 517

primacy of class relations over productive forces 62, 74, 185

Prime Minister 126, 323, 350, 371, 442, 444, 551

primitive accumulation 28, 52, 81, 84, 89, 103, 109, 115, 133, 142, 244, 246, 248, 260, 266, 297, 327, 398 *see also* Dispossession

private property 32–33, 44, 49–50, 73, 128, 177, 215, 243–45, 250–51, 254, 286–87, 308–9, 318, 321, 339, 374, 399, 407, 466, 490, 498, 545, 551 *see also* Class exploitation

privatization 34, 127, 129, 132–33, 142, 150–52, 160–61, 258, 260, 269, 399–400 *see also* Dispossession, Primitive accumulation

pro-business policies 13, 118–19, 132, 143, 156, 159, 347, 351, 353, 357, 373, 426, 431–32, 448–49, 458, 479, 504, 508, 516, 551, 557, 567 *see also* Government policies

producers 78, 99, 101–2, 169, 225, 231, 241, 267, 409, 417, 513, 526, 563

small-scale 49, 51, 98–99, 263

production 1–11, 32–34, 42–45, 51, 56–59, 63–64, 66–82, 94–107, 110–11, 117–20, 145–47, 177, 181, 185–86, 188–91, 201–4, 206–11, 224–26, 229–31, 283, 290, 294, 298, 396–97, 407, 409, 417, 466, 524–25, 534–37, 539–41, 573 *see also* Mode of production, Nature-dependent production

family-based 116, 226, 287, 297, 537 *see also* Small-scale production

mode of production. *See* Indian mode of production debate, capitalism, Subsumption of labor

production process 77, 100–1, 105, 133, 136, 148, 149, 155, 219, 228, 297, 466, 523, 535, 538 *see also* Labor process

production relations. *See* Class relations, Social relations of production

productive forces 11, 46–47, 62, 64, 66, 69–71, 74–76, 80–82, 93, 97, 103, 105–7, 113, 115, 116, 136, 173, 176–78, 185–86, 189–90, 197, 230, 264, 283, 292–95, 450, 466–67, 519–22, 527 *see also* Uneven development

productivity. *See* Labor productivity

professionals 44, 412–13, 447 *see also* Middle class

profit 70–71, 74, 96, 121, 123, 129–30, 133–34, 143–45, 148, 182, 186, 191, 215, 217–18, 229, 231, 246, 250–51, 276, 289, 292, 294, 306, 373–74, 398–99, 427–29, 465–66, 470, 481, 512, 524–25, 539–40, 550–52 profit (cont.)

rate of 51, 71, 74, 107, 111, 114, 119, 383, 524–25

proletarianization 3, 24, 36–38, 52, 61, 177, 182–83, 205, 270, 381, 518 *see also* Class differentiation, TCPH

proletarians/proletariat 23–25, 38, 49, 51–52, 54, 57–58, 73, 88, 90, 112, 116, 145, 155, 163, 309, 311, 319–20, 374, 378–79, 382, 409, 412–19, 453–54, 465, 468–70, 495, 497–500, 554, 566–68

conservatism of 416–17

leadership of the 466, 563

proletarian struggle. *See* Class struggle

property 2, 22, 32–33, 39, 41, 42, 48–52, 54, 56, 58, 84, 120, 142, 144, 152, 162, 164, 173, 187, 190, 243, 245, 277, 399–401, 407, 505, 515, 567, 571 *see also* private property

collectively-owned 50, 104, 142, 260, 320, 399–400, 481

property owners. *See* Capitalist class, Landowners, Propertied classes

large-scale 45, 48, 250

small-scale 39, 52, 142, 187, 190, 277, 308, 399, 481, 504

property-owning classes. *See* Property owners

property relations 1, 27, 42, 48, 52, 54, 58, 60, 69, 118, 154, 173, 186, 188–91, 242, 245, 251, 295, 309, 318, 320–21, 339, 345, 545, 549 *see also* Exploitation

pro-poor policies 134, 137, 155, 175, 194–96, 206, 224, 258, 263–64, 269, 271, 275, 279, 293, 296, 321, 403, 426, 481–83, 488, 490, 493, 563, 567

protests. *See* Political movement

provincial/sub-national 75, 81–82, 85, 104, 108, 131, 134, 156–57, 162, 211, 237 *see also* Scale

249, 261, 270–72, 284, 296, 302, 323–24, 333, 342, 480, 485, 487, 493, 520, 529

provincial level of government. *See* State government

Punjab 68, 81–82, 84, 93, 192–96, 198–99, 303, 422, 426, 488

race 27–28, 35, 208, 210, 289, 313, 385–86, 405, 408–10, 430, 464

Rajasthan 82, 193, 195, 198, 425–26

Raju Bhai (a landless peasant supporter of Naxalism) 309, 335

Ramdev 429

Rashtriya Janata Dal (RJD) 446, 484

raw materials 7, 95, 102, 105, 118, 169, 179, 181, 294, 520, 526 *see also* Inputs

Reaganomics 373, 551 *see also* Modinomics

real subsumption of wage labor. *See* Subsumption of wage labor

red corridor. *See* Naxalite areas

reformed democracy 19, 405

reformism 59, 104, 252, 262, 268, 383, 462, 465, 474, 503, 568

reforms 12, 126, 135, 141, 146, 148, 150–52, 154, 159, 161, 167, 243–44, 271, 316, 320, 331, 405, 419, 452, 461, 463, 467, 474, 482, 490, 502, 512, 514, 516, 532, 554, 561–62, 564, 567 *see also* Concessions

struggle for 130, 462–63, 471, 482–83, 569

regime of low wages. *See* Wages

regional aspects of society 21, 25, 28, 43–44, 59, 66, 147–48, 217, 237, 246, 270, 273, 280, 284, 289, 294–95, 322, 330, 335–36, 341, 381, 423, 468, 476, 487, 529, 541, 545 *see also* Scale

regional disparities. *See* Uneven development

regionalism 241, 405

regional political parties 423, 483–88, 493, 504, 546

federation of 486–87, 489

regions. *See* regional aspects of society

relative surplus value 69, 78, 82, 83, 107, 524

Reliance Industries Limited 135

religion 14–16, 35–36, 56–57, 165, 266, 277, 364, 381, 388–90, 403–12, 415–18, 432–33, 439–40, 447–49, 458, 464, 486, 490, 503–4, 509–11, 513, 531, 554, 556–61, 563 *see also* Nationalism, Communalism, Identity

class and religion 405–10

identity based in 164, 367, 391, 405, 408, 411, 416, 432–33, 457

majority 13, 376, 433–34, 449, 456, 464, 486, 555

politics of. *See* Communalism

spiritually uplifting ideas and 509, 558

religion-related terrorist groups 364

religious belief 14, 153, 375, 388–89, 396, 406–11, 416–18, 421, 429, 440–41, 464, 509, 553–54

INDEX

religious fundamentalism 164, 381, 390, 530
  see also Communalism
religious groups 364, 407, 410, 433, 436, 449,
  451, 463–64
religious harmony 367, 369
religious minorities 13–15, 58, 153, 266, 323,
  347, 366, 375–76, 394–95, 433–37,
  440, 443, 451, 456, 464, 478, 486,
  487, 489, 511, 513, 517, 552, 558,
  560–61
remittance 24, 51, 87 see also Migrants
rent 44, 67, 70–71, 73–75, 88, 91, 94, 111, 114,
  177, 198, 242, 247–49, 251, 271, 287, 291,
  330–31, 525 see also Ground rent
  capitalist rent 70, 467
rent barrier to capitalist development 70–71
re-peasantization 93
repression by the state 15, 18–19, 152–54,
  265–68, 303, 316–19, 322–25, 331,
  336–38, 340, 343–44, 400, 402, 404, 454,
  546, 552
reproduction 12, 55, 58, 92, 104, 207, 223, 225,
  227, 240, 242, 244–45, 247, 250, 265,
  279–80, 283, 289–90, 322, 396–97
reserve army of labor 15, 16, 46, 63, 67, 79,
  85, 87, 113, 124, 132, 138, 142–45, 178, 183,
  18687, 191, 196, 208, 210, 218, 228, 246,
  256, 270, 297, 306, 368, 371, 387,
  398–99, 404, 411–14, 417, 419, 424, 432,
  439, 452, 460, 467, 538, 550, 554,
  560
Reserve Bank of India 358
resistance 29, 56, 79, 86, 151, 153–54, 228,
  250, 268–69, 274, 317–19, 322, 339, 343,
  375, 390, 396, 400, 403–5, 410, 412, 418,
  424, 431, 450–51, 463, 470, 480, 487, 510,
  538, 545–48, 552, 560 see also Class
  struggle
  anti-dispossession 343, 548
revolution 114–16, 155, 158, 163, 169, 183, 275,
  284, 306–9, 453–54, 462, 465, 466, 468,
  476–78, 495, 497, 500, 502–3, 506, 513,
  515, 527, 530, 563–67
  agent of 115, 306–9, 345, 454, 499, 515,
    549, 566
  agrarian 114, 163, 530
  democratic 114, 155, 157, 303, 305–6,
    308–11, 410, 459, 477, 530, 555
  overthrow of capitalism by 264, 308,
    344, 502, 548

permanent/uninterrupted nature
  of 466, 468, 477–78, 515–16, 523, 527,
    562, 567, 568
  Russian (October) 244, 502
  Socialist 115, 163, 305–6, 308, 311, 454, 477,
    514, 515, 562, 565–66
  strategy/tactics of 381, 512, 566–67
  stop overthrown classes from
    returning 344, 549
  two-stage theory of 114–16, 305, 306,
    311, 459, 477, 515, 527, 555,
    568
revolutionaries 158, 169, 307, 309, 313, 383,
  466, 494, 499, 502, 513, 563
revolutionary adventurism 311, 477
revolutionary classes 475, 496, 499
revolutionary compromise, temporary 205,
  294, 461–62, 474, 480, 492, 494–97,
  499–506, 514, 565 see also Lenin,
  Revolution
revolutionary intention 495, 501–2, 563
revolutionary leadership, crisis of 311, 515,
  566 see also Sectarianism
revolutionary organizations 509, 559
revolutionary party 3, 26, 158, 454, 471,
  496–97, 502, 568
Revolutionary Socialist Party 471
right-wing government 13, 19, 284, 323,
  347–48, 350, 353, 355, 375–76, 390, 427,
  449, 510–11, 550, 552, 560 see also
  Fascistic tendencies, RSS
right-wing Hindu-nationalist government. See
  Right-wing government
  economic policies of 19, 374–75, 552
right-wing mobs. See Fascistic forces
right-wing movement. See Fascistic forces,
  BJP, RSS
right-wing party 13, 373, 428, 451, 509, 551,
  558 see also BJP
risk 59, 124, 136, 146, 310, 403, 428, 441
Roads 124, 146, 298, 308, 336, 341, 349,
  374–75, 454, 552, 561 See Infrastructure,
  Built environment, Geographical space
Roy, A. 309, 324, 328, 330, 332
RSS (Rashtriya Swayamsevak Sangh) 129,
  214–15, 260, 292, 328, 346, 352, 386–88,
  390–92, 421, 425–26, 429, 431–32,
  434–36, 440, 444–46, 448, 450 see also
  Communal, Fascistic tendencies,
  Sangh Parivar

RSS (cont.)
class character of 387–90, 394, 425, 446, 470
Rudolph and Rudolph 9, 33, 233–34
Rudra, A. 33, 68–69, 71, 74, 178
ruling class. *See* Classes, Capitalist class
rural areas 5, 9–11, 33–36, 63, 64, 67, 69–71, 85, 89, 103, 107, 126–28, 136–39, 147–48, 170–73, 175, 181, 192–98, 202, 205, 215, 224, 231, 240, 247, 249, 250–58, 265, 272–75, 284–86, 289–90, 294–301, 308–9, 316, 330, 332, 359–60, 487, 519, 533, 573–74 *see also* Villages
rural economic crisis 15, 398, 284 *see also* Agrarian crisis, Neoliberalism
Russia 51, 121, 244, 127, 387, 497, 502
Russian bourgeoisie 497
Russian communist movement 460
Russian Marxism 283

Saad-Filho, A. 117–19
sabka saath 354, 359, 364, 367
sabka vikas 354, 359, 367
sadak 349
Samajwadi Party (SP) 484
Sangh Parivar 323, 363, 386–87, 395, 429, 432–36, 439, 441, 446, 448, 456, 484, 490–92 *see also* Communalism, Fascistic tendencies, RSS
intellectual deficit in 492
Sanyal, K. 111–13, 525–26
Sarkar, S. 13, 244, 333, 335, 337, 339, 376, 492
scalar aspect of the state 322 *see also* Local aspects of state and society, State form, Scale
scale 43–44, 138, 145, 106, 166, 169, 177, 272, 274, 282, 313, 322, 346, 349, 360–61, 464–65, 474 *see also* International, Local, National, Provincial, Regional
Scheduled Castes (SCs) 164, 286, 300, 313, 363, 436, 472, 531
Scheduled Tribes (STs) 257, 286, 304 *see also* Indigenous, Aboriginal
Science & Society 66, 200, 291, 534
Science congresses 447
SCs. *See* Scheduled Castes
secular/secularism 14, 16, 19, 63, 376, 387, 388–92, 394, 398, 403–4, 407, 416,

420–27, 438, 442–43, 448, 450–52, 455–56, 461, 468–70, 479, 483–86, 488–93, 498, 504–11, 515, 518, 554–55, 558–61, 563–65
secular bourgeois 155, 398, 452, 490, 506, 555, 563, 564
secular-democratic 398, 470, 489–91, 564, 567, 569
secularists. *See* Secular
secular parties 488, 490, 505, 514, 564, 568
security personnel 324, 326, 344, 428, 548 *see also* Police, Repression by the state
seeds 136, 173, 184, 188, 200, 213, 287, 360, 468, 534 *see also* Agriculture
GMO 200, 534
HYV 200, 534
self-employment 25, 32–33, 93, 204, 292, 358
self-exploitation 24, 37, 51 *see also* Exploitation
semi-feudal 68–69, 75, 104, 114–15, 242, 249, 294, 303, 305–8, 465, 510, 521, 524, 527, 560
semi-proletarians 51, 112, 116, 145, 163, 257, 292, 297, 311, 319, 465, 479, 500, 569 *see also* Peasant, Small-scale producers, Lower classes
Sen, A. 3, 27–28, 40–41, 173, 182, 269–70, 281, 290, 302, 309, 407
serf/serfs 67, 72, 100, 104, 282
sharecroppers 93, 98–99, 301–2
shelter 4, 15, 168–69, 173, 187, 345, 398, 416, 504, 550
Shimla 259–61
Shiva, V. 170, 172, 176, 199, 309, 534
Simeon, D. 395–96, 448
Singh, Bhagat 443, 446
Singh, M. (Manmohan) 12, 126, 131, 150, 551
Sinha, S. 2–3, 22–24, 26–27, 37, 111–13, 525–26
slaves 72, 100, 262, 282, 307
small-scale producers 3–5, 16, 33, 34, 38, 48–52, 59–61, 97–98, 105, 112, 115–16, 127, 174, 208, 271–72, 288, 398, 406, 419, 452, 456, 460, 466–67, 500, 504, 510–14, 527, 554, 560–62, 565

INDEX

655

small-scale production. *See* Small-scale producers

social capital   221, 228, 239, 248, 274, 276, 538 *see also* Migrants

social democracy   26, 382, 501, 502, 503

social formation   69, 75, 83, 104, 110–11, 113, 121, 158, 242, 249, 525–26 *see also* Capitalist mode of production

social movement. *See* Political movement, Naxalite movement

social oppression   4–5, 9, 11–15, 18, 27–28, 35–36, 47, 56–57, 59, 220, 222, 241, 253, 262, 285–86, 291, 313–14, 320, 398, 401, 463–64, 477, 492, 510, 512, 517–19, 543, 559–62

social relations   4–7, 9–12, 17–20, 28–30, 33, 35, 36, 43–50, 55, 58, 61–66, 69, 71, 77, 97–98, 100–1, 105–8, 114, 123, 148, 153, 188–89, 191–92, 198–201, 204–7, 230, 231, 233, 236, 239–43, 247–50, 253, 267, 280, 285–86, 303, 307, 331, 334, 384, 396, 399, 406, 409, 415, 417, 423, 429, 432, 450, 485, 487, 496, 517–19, 521–22, 532–36, 538, 540–41, 553, 567, 571 *see also* Class relations, Social relations of production, Non-class relations

social relations of production   6, 8, 39, 53, 69, 74, 80, 90, 106, 185, 202, 213, 234, 256, 450, 534–35

social reproduction   226, 258, 537

Social Revolutionaries   407, 497

social wage   87, 138, 221, 224, 228, 465, 535, 538

socialism   116, 155–56, 157, 163, 235, 243–44, 305–8, 344, 345, 346, 407, 408, 454, 461, 466–69, 471, 473, 478, 481–82, 493–94, 499, 507, 514–15, 527, 548–49, 563, 565–66, 568, 569

socialist government   116, 514, 564

socialist revolution. *See* Revolution, Socialism, Communism

socialists   51, 158, 164, 234, 236, 387, 390, 470, 476, 559, 567–68

socialist struggle   20, 114–15, 155, 305, 469, 473, 475, 478, 482–83, 491, 494, 512–16, 527, 561, 563, 565, 568 *see also* Class struggle

Socialist Unit Center of India   471

Socialist Worker   300

socially oppressed groups   56, 200, 222, 244, 286, 288, 300, 309, 401, 436, 438, 469, 471, 482, 487, 538, 569 *see also* Social oppression

sociologists   2, 21, 205–6, 224

South India   86, 145, 231

SP. *See* Samajwadi Party

Special Economic Zones (SEZs)   131, 296–97, 531

Spivak, G.   3, 24

Srinivas, M.   2, 21, 26–27, 186

Stalinism   115, 157, 476, 518, 568

standard of living   125–26, 429, 431, 461, 465, 467, 469, 478, 480, 493–94, 512, 516, 561

standpoint. *See* Perspective, Theory

state   9–13, 17, 36, 40–43, 50, 59–60, 119, 123–39, 146–52, 159, 161–67, 192, 194–96, 212, 232–45, 248–51, 254–57, 264–68, 272–76, 279–81, 285, 291–94, 295–97, 298, 312–14, 316–28, 330–47, 379, 388–90, 397–400, 423–25, 447, 463–66, 470, 473, 480, 505, 517, 527–31, 540–50, 564, 567, 571

autonomy of   131, 234, 246, 248

deception by   4, 151, 166, 402–5, 508, 532

nation-,   117, 273, 295, 322

state actors. *See* State elites

state agencies   5, 41, 45, 62, 88–89, 92, 150, 237, 248–49, 252, 262, 271, 276, 308, 314, 343, 402, 441, 543, 547

state apparatuses. *See* State agencies

state control over economy   119, 135, 147, 162, 166, 280, 350, 487, 528, 532, 541

state elites   5, 10, 41, 45, 62, 133–34, 143, 147, 150, 163–65, 212, 236–39, 240, 242, 248, 251–55, 261–63, 267, 276–79, 287–88, 293, 296, 309, 317, 328–30, 338–40, 361, 364, 399, 413, 463, 530, 541–45, 565

state form   263, 265, 267, 270, 317

liberal-democratic   11, 133, 166, 241, 265–70, 300, 306, 316–18, 324, 345, 382, 397, 468, 506, 549, 574 *see also* Democracy

territorial   233, 265, 270, 280–81, 541 *see also* Geography of society and state, Scale

State government   134, 237, 261, 270–72, 302, 342, 487 *see also* State form state interventions   10, 12, 18, 58, 76, 84, 130, 180–81, 230, 233–36, 243, 246–48, 250, 255, 263–64, 277, 280, 283, 292, 294, 317, 322, 407, 524, 528, 540–41, 571, 573 *see also* State policies

state managers. *See* State elite

state officials. *See* State elites

state of exception. *See* Repression

state-owned banks   245, 353, 398

state-owned companies   34, 62, 83, 130, 157, 160, 175, 245–46, 248, 254, 258, 269, 278, 279, 295, 353, 361, 374, 399, 413, 429, 434, 466, 481, 484, 551

state-owned natural resources   328, 330, 361, 399, 401, 479, 481

state power. *See* State

state's developmentality   252, 339, 545

state's developmental role   22, 41, 111, 136, 156, 234–35, 240, 245–46, 252, 262, 273–77, 281, 296, 312, 326, 339, 368, 525, 545 *see also* Development

state violence. *See* Violence, Repression by the state

stock market indices   350

STs (Scheduled Tribes)   257, 286, 304

subaltern studies   24

sub-contracting   114, 274

sub-imperialism   63, 150, 388

subjectivity, non-capitalist forms of   112, 525

subsistence   72, 76–78, 92, 99, 104, 182, 184, 186, 188, 222, 230, 264

subsumption of wage labor   6, 17, 53, 63–66, 76, 78, 80, 83–86, 88–90, 92, 95–113, 229–30, 399, 518–19, 523, 539, 571, 573 *see also* Hybrid subsumption, Labor, Transition to real subsumption

  workers' empathy for employers   222, 227, 537 *see also* Ideology, Labor

Sugden, F.   34, 104, 521

Sundar, N.   151, 237, 323, 333, 339–40, 545–46

surplus value   6–7, 29, 48–49, 52, 54, 60, 67, 68–69, 74–83, 99–102, 105–7, 111–21, 155, 185–86, 189, 207–10, 229, 249, 307–8, 398–99, 515, 524, 534, 539, 567 *see also* Exploitation

Swatantra Party   130

sweatshop conditions in aquaculture   206, 212–13, 216–17, 219–21, 226, 231, 311, 537

Tagore, R.   559

Tamil Nadu   82, 88, 193–98, 211, 291, 303, 425–26, 485, 488

taxes   132–34, 142–43, 162, 188, 330, 350–51, 365, 373, 398, 463, 467, 481

TCPH (Tendency for the class polarization to happen)   50–51 *see also* Class polarization

technological change   5–9, 17, 34, 41, 63–68, 71–75, 78, 82–91, 95–97, 102–10, 132, 145, 162, 167–69, 171–74, 176–92, 194, 196–201, 236, 239, 291–92, 298, 306, 318–20, 377–78, 399, 403, 408, 430, 448–49, 517, 520–25, 533–35, 571, 573

technology. *See* Technical change

  bio-chemical/bio-   7, 18, 103, 169, 172, 189, 200, 219, 299, 520, 533–34, 539

  information   34, 168, 412 *see also* IT industry

  productivity-raising   71, 74, 79, 85, 92, 107, 189, 258, 519–20, 522, 571

  pro-poor benefits from   18, 136, 140, 174, 287, 334, 498

  social (class) nature of   7, 168–69, 172, 182, 185, 200–1, 534

technology fetishism   535

Telangana   303, 425–26, 488

Television (TV)   49, 441, 446, 447

temple entry movements   512, 562 *see also* Political movement

tenants   30, 69–71, 74, 93–94, 98, 177, 271–72, 286–87, 329 *see also* Landowners, Peasants

tendency for the rate of profit to fall (TPRF)   51, 107 *see also* Capitalist crisis

Thailand   65, 205, 211

theory/theoretical   18–19, 40–43, 51, 72, 105–8, 111–13, 118, 155, 185–88, 201, 204–8, 235–38, 257, 307–8, 311, 314, 317, 397, 405, 409–10, 432, 438, 464, 474–75, 478, 494, 507, 521–22, 535, 561–563, 566–68 *see also* Perspective, Thinking

Thorner, D.   32, 70, 71

totality   46, 51, 54–55, 106, 114, 116, 120, 396, 398, 470, 477

tractors   78, 82, 86–88, 94–95, 173, 178, 191, 213, 258, 523 *see also* Technology

traders   12, 23, 44, 92, 138, 165, 289, 293, 316, 331–32, 338, 470, 480–81, 544 *see also* Usury, Money lending

INDEX

657

trade unions   60, 87, 96, 110, 129, 151–52, 157, 162, 223, 258, 274, 379, 405, 421, 476, 462–63, 491, 495, 497, 513, 528, 561, 563

trade union struggles/strikes   12, 43, 84–87, 89, 129, 152, 156–57, 221, 229, 258, 260–61, 265, 314, 332, 347, 401–2, 467, 476, 495–96, 519, 539 *see also* Consciousness

transfer of resources from poor to rich countries   96, 150, 167, 230, 276, 524 *see also* Imperialism

transition to real subsumption of labor   6, 84, 86, 89, 95, 113, 115, 526–27 *see also* Capitalism, Subsumption of wage labor, Uneven and combined development

transitional demands. *See* Political demands

Transparency International   361 *see also* Corruption

tribes   28, 287, 289, 299–300, 305, 313, 327, 436

Tripura   271, 392, 394, 455, 459, 482, 491, 492, 494, 555

Trotsky, L.   95–96, 108–9, 378–79, 382, 384, 400–1, 404–5, 410–13, 416–18, 438, 453–54, 462, 465, 468, 475, 497, 500–3, 506, 523, 555–56, 565–66

truth   127, 307, 361, 375, 385, 436, 499, 562

tyranny   463, 511, 561, 562

ultra-left extremism   337, 543 *see also* Naxalism

ultra-nationalism   450

ultra-leftism   562

under-employment/unemployment. *See* Reserve army of labor

uneven and combined development   63, 66, 95, 108–10, 113, 148, 410, 522–24, 526 *see also* Transition to real subsumption

uneven development   1, 18, 28, 43–44, 84, 85, 107–9, 113, 127, 145–49, 222, 230, 270, 273–74, 289, 306, 315, 331, 457, 467, 521–24, 531, 543, 572

Union Government's Labor Bureau   152

united front   301–2, 311, 477, 479, 502–4, 513, 563 *see also* Popular front, Left

United Kingdom   568, 150, 276

United Nations   324

United States   65, 82, 97, 127, 129, 141, 199, 208, 210–11, 375–76, 384–85, 387, 404, 435, 447, 456, 533

capitalism in   97, 235

imperialism of   234, 292, 434, 447

markets in   264

unorganized Left   154

Upanishad   407

unreason   375, 386, 434, 553 *see also* Fascistic tendencies, BJP

urban areas   34, 63, 126, 129, 141, 144–48, 181, 191, 250, 252, 255, 256, 263, 268, 271–73, 280, 299, 304–5, 309, 345, 439, 360, 475, 541, 543, 549, 573

urban bourgeoisie   34, 165, 178, 181, 243, 246, 248–51, 254–56, 294, 332, 519 *see also* Bourgeoisie

urban capitalists. *See* Urban bourgeoisie

urban Naxal   153, 324, 342, 547 *see also* Naxalite movement

urban petty bourgeoisie   145, 306, 439, 453

urban working class   145, 250, 268, 273, 307–8, 311, 345, 360, 414, 475, 549, 573

usury   67, 69–71, 75, 78, 92, 94, 97–99, 104, 106, 111, 114, 170, 198, 246–49, 291, 520, 525 *see also* money lender

Uttarakhand   425–26, 488

Uttar Pradesh   82, 85–86, 90, 193, 195–96, 198, 270, 368, 422, 426, 484, 488

Vajpayee, A.   444

Vanaik, A.   14, 270, 345–46, 376, 380–81, 388, 395, 439, 442–43, 450, 471

Vandergeest, P.   204–5

vantage point   6, 17, 155, 411, 495–96, 527 *see also* Theory

Varshney, A.   33, 179, 247

vigilante groups   336, 402, 429, 435, 441 *see also* Right-wing mobs

vikas (Development)   13, 347, 354, 359, 360, 367, 449, 542

villagers   71, 237, 276, 287, 298–99, 336, 349, 529

villages   85–86, 90–91, 145–46, 148, 198, 214, 217, 220–21, 223, 262, 264, 266, 270–72, 290, 298–99, 302, 327, 330, 334, 336, 349, 414, 465, 481 *see also* Rural

clusters of   108, 212, 272

violence   12, 238–39, 287, 310–11, 315–18, 320–23, 325–26, 332, 334–46, 341–43, 362, 364, 378–79381, 389, 392, 394, 395, 408, 415, 430, 435–41, 453, 464, 543–49

violence (cont.)

certain Left-wing forces' 257, 323, 326, 327, 333–38, 544

capitalist state's 12, 19, 267, 316, 317, 319, 321, 324–26, 330–32, 335–46, 544–46, 548–49 *see also* Repression by the state, Police

proprietary classes' 291, 310, 325–26, 332, 402, 464

right-wing forces' 59, 159, 336–39, 364–66, 389–90, 402, 415, 417, 421, 427–29, 435–43, 447–48, 458, 503–5, 548, 557 *see also* Right-wing mobs

voters 262, 268, 358, 364, 367–69, 371–72, 446, 455, 471–72, 481, 485–86, 490–91

votes 59, 127, 263, 266, 268, 328–29, 361, 366, 391–92, 421–22, 425–26, 448, 458, 464, 471–72, 480–81, 486, 488, 490–91, 503, 557–58

wage-earners. *See* Labor

wage employment 25, 205, 249, 291, 293

wage labor. *See* Labor

wages 15, 49, 70, 76–77, 85–91, 93–95, 98–99, 104–05, 116, 122, 144–45, 169–71, 177–79, 185–91, 204–10, 214–30, 247, 256, 287–88, 293, 320–21, 357–58, 401, 413–16, 463, 535–39

daily 54, 77, 91, 93, 302, 360

delayed payment of 215, 220, 226–27

gross vs net 226, 536

higher 30, 85–86, 90–94, 175, 258, 290, 332, 449, 512, 562, 571

low 79, 89, 92–93, 95–97, 104, 107, 110, 132, 136, 205, 217–23, 225–31, 277, 294, 297, 354, 398–401, 404, 429, 522, 524, 537–40

money 174, 178, 183–84, 195

need for living 133, 226, 269, 292–93, 297, 312, 466, 481–82, 536

piece 93, 219, 227, 537

real 79, 84–85, 90, 93, 95, 121, 178, 183, 185–86, 226, 287, 358, 536

relative 226, 481, 536

wage work. *See* Labor

water 131, 137, 144, 174, 176, 178, 203, 207, 209, 213–14, 220, 225, 474, 528 *see also* Environmental issues

wealth 45, 46, 49, 52–53, 120–22, 141–46, 207–9, 242, 321, 353–55, 357, 359, 412, 528

creators of 134–35, 143, 281, 486, 542

capitalist 49, 52, 144

welfare 15, 37, 51, 88, 117, 122, 126, 132, 134, 140, 149, 167, 258, 288, 385, 405, 411, 486, 507, 511, 540, 565, 574 *see also* Reforms, Concessions

West Bengal 68, 82, 84, 156, 157, 193, 195, 198, 271, 300–1, 304, 322, 485, 488, 491

West Bengal Left Front 156

Western societies 21, 23, 231, 323, 429

Western Europe 67–68, 79, 113 *see also* Europe

What is to be done? 227

what is to be done, the question of 19, 113–16, 161, 163–66, 227, 394, 483, 460–67, 478–92, 511–16, 559–69 *see also* Class, struggle, Socialist struggle, Temporary revolutionary compromise

women 27, 35–36, 55, 57–58, 89, 166, 206–7, 212–17, 220–31, 250, 253–54, 262, 289–90, 313, 335–36, 362, 364, 429, 436, 465, 467, 511–12, 532, 537–39, 548, 561–62 *see also* Gender

aboriginal 213, 328

low caste 290–91, 304, 436

women labor/worker 36, 46–47, 58, 89, 213, 215, 217, 220, 229, 231, 320, 539, 562

work, long hours of 64–65, 77, 92–96, 104–7, 110, 210, 214–15, 218–20, 226, 228–29, 289, 291, 358, 360, 520, 481, 522–24, 538–40

worker organizations 258

workers. *See* Labor

working class. *See* Labor

workplaces 6, 42, 57, 117, 209, 215, 221, 226, 476, 561, 567 *see also* Biophysical conditions, Exploitation, Labor

World Bank 9, 122, 128, 150, 165, 194, 203, 205, 224, 531, 535

World Economic Forum 359

World Hindu Council 439

world market 5, 8, 63, 67, 107–9, 113, 123–24, 132, 202, 219, 230, 424, 520–23, 526, 535 *see also* Global, Imperialism

Wright, E. 31, 188

WTO 203, 297, 574

Yapa, L. 170, 172, 176

young people 87, 220–21

Zizek, S. 342–43, 547

Printed in the United States
By Bookmasters